THE HMONG OF CHINA

SINICA LEIDENSIA

EDITED BY

W. L. IDEMA

IN COOPERATION WITH

P.K. BOL • D.R. KNECHTGES • E.S. RAWSKI
E. ZÜRCHER • H.T. ZURNDORFER

VOLUME LI

TUTA SUB AEGIDE PALLAS
· 1 6 8 3 ·

THE HMONG
OF
CHINA

Context, Agency, and the Imaginary

BY

NICHOLAS TAPP

BRILL

LEIDEN · BOSTON · KÖLN

2001

This book is printed on acid-free paper.

On the cover : The Bridal feast

Library of Congress Cataloging-in-Publication Data

Tapp, Nicholas.
The Hmong of China : context, agency, and the imaginary / by Nicholas
Tapp.
p.   cm. — (Sinica Leidensia, ISSN 0169-9563 : v. 51)
Includes bibliographical references and index.
ISBN 9004121277 (alk. paper)
1. Hmong (Asian people)—History. 2. Hmong (Asian people)—Kinship.
3. Hmong (Asian people)—Social life and customs. I. Title II. Series.

DS731.M5 T36 2001
951'.00495942—dc21   01-025173
                                                                         CIP

Die Deutsche Bibliothek – CIP-Einheitsaufnahme

Tapp, Nicholas :
The Hmong of China : context, agency, and the imaginary / by Nicholas
Tapp. – Leiden ; Boston ; Köln : Brill, 2001
(Sinica Leidensia ; Vol. 51)
ISBN 90-04-12127-7

ISSN 0169-9563
ISBN 90 04 12127 7

PRINTED IN THE NETHERLANDS

For Jing

It is Cézanne's genius that when the over-all composition of the picture is seen globally, perspectival distortions are no longer visible in their own right but rather contribute, as they do in natural vision, to the impression of an emerging order, of an object in the act of appearing, organizing itself before our eyes.

Merleau-Ponty; 'Cézanne's Doubt', *Sense and Non-Sense*, 1964

CONTENTS

LIST OF DIAGRAMS, FIGURES, ILLUSTRATIONS
AND TABLES

Diagrams

Figures

Illustrations

Tables

ACKNOWLEDGEMENTS

My grateful thanks to the British Academy for a Larger Personal Award which enabled me to carry out post-doctoral research in Sichuan, Guizhou and Yunnan (1989-91), to Dr. Chiao Chien who as my Department Chair at the Chinese University of Hong Kong arranged practical matters so that I was able to take up the Award, and to Mr. Yang Qing Bai of the Minorities Affairs Commission in Chengdu who facilitated my research in Sichuan. Also to the Minority Nationalities College of Guiyang who hosted my research in Guizhou, and to the Academy of Social Science in Kunming who hosted my work in Yunnan in 1991. In the field I owe a great debt of thanks to my various and changing research assistants; Mr. Ren Hai of the Sichuan University Museum and Mr. Chen Qing Hua of the Minority Affairs Commission but above all to Mr. Peng Wen Bin of the Southwest Nationalities College who spent two months with me in Sichuan. My thanks also to Mr. Yu Xiao Gang of the Academy of Social Sciences who accompanied me on my Yunnan research with Mr. Yan En Quang, and to Mr. Huang Hai who came with us in Guizhou. Finally I should like to express a deep sense of gratitude to Mr. Yang Qing Bai's brother, Mr. Yang Wanli and his family who put up with eight of us during my research.

NOTE ON ORTHOGRAPHY

For Chinese, *hanyu pinyin* has been generally used, except when quoting from other authors. In Hmong, RPA (see Heimbach 1969) has been used. In this system, since Hmong has no final consonants, doubling of vowels indicates a final nasalisation (so 'Hmoo'= 'Hmong'), while any ending consonants indicates the tone value of the word (so 'Hmoo*b*'='Hmong', pronounced in the *high tone*). In the accepted RPA, taken from White Hmong in Laos and Thailand, an ending -b indicates a high tone, an ending -j indicates a high falling tone, an ending -v indicates a mid rising tone, no ending consonant indicates an intermediate tone, an ending -s indicates an ordinary low tone, an ending -m indicates a low tone glottally stopped at the end, and an ending -g indicates a a low guttural tone. In the standardised Chinese version of Hmong (Chuanqiandian dialect) taken from the Bijie area of Guizhou, this converts to -b, -x, -d, -t, -l or -k, -f, -s, with completely different tone values. The tones of the Sichuan Hmong in this area were very different from South East Asian Hmong, and I have tried to indicate this where possible by using RPA. Where I have used the equivalent Chinese romanised system, this is noted.[1]

---

[1]   The standardised Chinese version of Hmong (Chuanqiandian Miao branch) taken from the Bijie area of Guizhou converts from RPA to -b, -x, -d, -t, -l or -k, -f, -s, with completely different tonal values (high becomes high falling (43), high falling becomes mid falling (31), mid rising becomes high (55), the low a low falling (21) or mid (33), the unmarked a higher tone (44), the low guttural a low rising (13), the low stopped a low rising (24); closer to Green Hmong (Lyman 1970) than White Hmong (Downer 1967). The tones I recorded in Gongxian were quite similar to this, except for the mid rising which became a very high falling (51).

FOREWORD

This work is concerned with issues of interpretation which are commonly thought of as hermeneutic; problems to do with the anthropological interpretation, and understanding, of 'other cultures' and cultural forms, problems to do with the interpretation of texts and symbols. In it I have attempted to unite a consideration of theories of the sign and its relationship to 'context', with a consideration of the classic sociological problem of the relationship between 'agency' and the structure or discourse which informs it, in the form of how to account for resistance to a dominating rhetoric which apparently encapsulates and immobilizes agency.[1] In this way I have attempted to solve some real problems in the ethnography of Hmong culture which have arisen from a study of the 'same' cultural group in China by comparison with previous accounts of them in South East Asia.

The text of the first Part takes the form of a discussion of the historical and ethnographic construction of the identity of the Hmong as a tribal, segementary, mountain-dwelling people by conscious contrast with, and in opposition to, a majority 'Han Chinese' identity, which has expressed itself historically in repeated messianic uprisings of the Hmong against the Chinese state, mirrored in legends which reinforce and commemorate this opposition. As with the Ainu in relation to the Japanese (Friedman 1990), it is through defining themselves for significant others that the Hmong have established their own specificity. Yet the analysis of what has been defined as Hmong culture shows us that large parts of it at least are shared with the Chinese, and may be the results of historical processes of adoption or absorption, mimesis or emulation, or may refer to a prior historical condition in which the essentialising differentiation of a 'Hmong' from a 'Han' identity had not yet occurred. How then are we to understand this paradoxical ambivalence at the heart of Hmong culture, this denial of similarity and affirmation of difference despite the presence of resemblance—

---

[1] Such an enterprise should be particularly relevant to the study of ritual, which Bloch (1986) persuasively argued must be understood as standing somewhere between an action and a (propositional) statement.

which is an inversion of metaphor if metaphor is understood as the discovery of resemblances in differences? Is it possible to read the traces of a historical agency in these processes of affirmation and denial, this apparent disavowal of identification, or are we to understand the constitution of the Hmong as a historical subject to be irrevocably caught within the trappings of a more powerful, Chinese rhetoric which has framed and defined it?

The second Part comprises a village-based study of a Hmong village in the marginalised heartland of rural China, in Sichuan province, the first study in fact of *the Hmong* in China to be made.[2] The Hmong in China are one of four main cultural groups classed by the Chinese as 'Miao', and often their own identity becomes invisible threough the veils of official rhetoric. I found this part of Sichuan to be a culturally hybrid area, where Hmong could 'pass' as Han and yet remained, consciously and articulately, Hmong in their own views, as in their cultural performances and language. Particular attention is paid to relations between the Hmong and Han in the village. The Hmong rituals of shamanism, ancestral respect, and death are examined as much for what they tell us about this hybrid situation as for the essentialist conceptions of a purely, and unique, Hmong identity which they embody. Some of the narrative of Part II takes the form of an analysis of the patrilineal clans and their affinal relations in and beyond the village, since it is through a system of descent shared with the Han that local identifications, differences and alliances are defined and confirmed. Yet within and throughout this complex system of descent and affinity we find a constant crossing over of Hmong, Han and other identities, through mechanisms of incorporation, absorption, and adoption which enable the transformation of identities as well as their fixing and location.

Within the village the analysis of the dominant Yang clan shows how divisions of a national character between Taiwan and China were symbolically overcome through the reunion of separated Hmong brothers, and how the investment of Taiwanese capital in the district, in the context of Chinese economic reforms and a partial retreat of the state, had led to a re-signification of Hmong cultural

---

[2] Both Simon Cheung (1996) and Louisa Schein (1993) studied non-Hmong groups classified as 'Miao' in China; the Hmu and the Ge respectively of Southeast Guizhou.

practices which expressed itself in the reconstruction of the Yang genealogy in which I was myself involved, and in plans for a clan ancestral hall after a very 'Chinese' model. Part II also shows how clan loyalties and rivalries were epitomised through the account of two weddings joining villagers with the members of another village and the members of one clan with another in such a way as to affirm their differences. The wedding is revealed as a focus and encapsulation, a locus of the expresssion and tranformation of identities in a context of historical cultural hybridity and fluidity.

I locate the site of critical agency in the Chinese-Hmong rhetoric constitutive of Hmong identity in the Hmong attempt to establish their own difference and specificity, as revealed in a series of everyday legends about a culture hero who is an Orphan, and these tales form the heart of the narrative of the third Part of this book. The Orphan is shown to be the figure of a pre-social, pre-linguistic potentiality, logically prior to the differentiation into patrilineal clans (in the idiom of which Hmong/Han differences are also subsumed), and yet posited as prior in this way by the same rhetoric of identity and differentiation which he seems to precurse, since he is gendered as male. This speaks of a complete invisibility accorded to women in the cultural discourses considered. Yet the Orphan achieves identification, and a general transformation of identities, through contracting an ideal marriage with a supernatural maiden, and thereby achieves supreme material success in the form of power and sovereignty. This points to a transformation of identity which is already accomplished; the dumb Orphan speaking, as the wildcat becomes a woman, and poverty is transformed into wealth. The status of the interpretation of these kinds of cultural forms and their textual interpretations within a social context is examined, as well as the very different ethnographic contexts in which it has been possible to position a study of the Hmong, and the problems of choosing between them, or of deciding on the 'correct version' of a text, cultural form, or narrative, are considered. An elaboration of the notion of context may itself supply part of an answer to the problems of 'unlimited semiosis', or over-interpretation, discussed by Eco (1992).

Part One:
Contextualising the Hmong

Introduction

The Hmong of East and South East Asia have classically been depicted by outside researchers as an isolated, homogenous, tribal group of shifting cultivators; and indeed that is how they tend to present themselves to those who have visited them in South East Asia. Consider, for example, Savina's (1930) poetic rhapsody (well translated by Geddes);

> From time immemorial there has existed in China a race of men whose origin we do not know. Living continually on the heights, away from all other Asiatics, these men speak a particular language unknown by all those who surround them, and wear a special dress which is seen nowhere else.

Somewhat similarly, Lemoine (1978) remarks;

> Despite alternate attempts at their destruction or assimilation by the Han Chinese, their segmentary tribal organisation has allowed them to preserve their language and culture for over 2,000 years of history.

And Geddes himself remarked (1976) that:

> The preservation by the Miao of their ethnic identity despite their being split into many small groups surrounded by different alien peoples and scattered over a vast geographical area is an outstanding record paralleling in some ways that of the Jews but more remarkable because they lacked the unifying forces of literacy and a doctrinal religion and because the cultural features they preserved seem to be so numerous.

Well, full marks to the Hmong for this 'outstanding record' of having maintained their cultural autonomy over such a long period of time; this was certainly the question which had first concerned me when I originally went to China. Yet in China, working with Hmong who were mostly bilingual in (local) Chinese, many features of whose social organisation were not radically different from those of the local Han Chinese peasantry, who wore modern Chinese clothes and moreover had remained settled in the same villages cultivating the same fields for several centuries (and reflecting back on the archaically Chinese characteristics of Hmong society and culture in Thailand), I was forced to rethink the paradigms of cultural essentialism beloved by earlier writers; and also to question my own motives for originally wishing to learn about and live among the Hmong. Certainly the Hmong of North Thailand had always emphasised their own cultural distinctiveness to me, painting sharp contrasts between their own, White Hmong, society and that of the Han Chinese which had formed much of the substance of my original understanding. But how far had I, and other ethnographers, gone in reflecting and reinforcing the intrinsic relativisms of our own informants (Moerman 1965, 1968)? How far, in effect, had both colonial and post-colonial discourse gone in constructing an image of 'Hmong culture' as tribal and segmentary in antithesis to the 'despotic', hierarchically structured societies of Thailand, Vietnam and China which aroused the indignation of western individualistic values?

My first engagement with the Hmong minority peoples whose shifting cultivation villages spread across the mountains of south China, Vietnam, Laos and Northern Thailand arose from spending two years in southern Thailand working as a voluntary English teacher. In 1976 the Vietnam War had just ended, and fears of the spread of communism across the borders of Laos and Vietnam and into Thailand were widespread among the political establishment of the time. In the notorious incident of 6th. October 1976, the military dictatorship in Bangkok massacred a number of student protesters at Thammasat University. Some of my students were involved in these protests. The morning after the massacre took place, I was shown photographs, in one of the few newspapers which had not been confiscated, of the garotted and mutilated bodies of the university students in Bangkok. Looking for a way out of my affiliation to the Thai Ministry of Education, I accepted an off-hand (but kind) commission from the Minority Rights Group of London, to travel up to North Thailand and report on the situation of the 'hill tribes' there, of whom at that time I knew nothing. Looking for a way out of a personal predicament, I found the Hmong, and was immediately entranced by the apparent uniqueness, unfamiliarity, and 'otherness' of their culture and way of life. The Hmong appeared to me remote and mysterious, and I remember opium smoke wreathing the faces of men in the dark candlelit interiors of wooden Hmong houses as they discussed the rebel fighting in Burma, and the women swinging up the mountain path as they returned at evening from the fields, with babies in the field baskets on their backs.

I was gripped with a passion to know more about the Hmong, and it was this I thought I might be able to achieve when I learned that the ESRC would sponsor anthropological fieldwork among the Hmong in return for the production of a thesis.[1] So I returned to Thailand to live with the Hmong in 1981, in a small village in northern Thailand, for a year and a half, and through experiencing everyday life in a village that was thoroughly 'Hmong', felt I had achieved some understanding of what it felt, and what it meant, to be 'Hmong'. It was enough at any rate to write a thesis on the Hmong of Northern Thailand, completed in 1985.[2]

Through the 1980s, the Hmong began at times to grip the popular imagination in much the same way as they had gripped mine. Not only were most of the Hmong in Thailand up to the mid-80s producers of opium (always a newsworthy subject), but Hmong people from neighbouring Laos were among the refugees who had fled Indochina after the end of the Vietnam War. Some of these claimed to have been the victims of chemical warfare in Laos, which led to intense media interest in the Hmong for some time, and a series of apparently inexplicable nocturnal deaths among the Hmong refugees from Laos who had been resettled in the United States also attracted public attention. A knowledge of Hmong society and culture became a sometime asset, sought after by a number of agencies.

Ultimately, however, how could one claim to have a thorough knowledge of Hmong society and culture, merely on the grounds of having lived, as a suffered visitor, in one of their villages for a year and a half, participating in cultural events, conducting interviews, and assembling statistical data? I have discussed this question with Hmong many times, and it is rarely believed that any outsider can attain an adequate appreciation of Hmong culture on this basis. In Thailand I had tried to understand the intricacies of the wedding ceremonies and funeral rituals, and cut my wrists to ribbons harvesting corn. I had walked around the mountains and rivers with a geomancer, inspecting grave sites. I had sat through countless shamanic rituals, until the process was almost as much a part of my

---

[1] Economic and Social Research Council.

[2] Categories of Change and Continuity among the White Hmong (Hmoob Dawb) of Northern Thailand, University of London 1985.

own life as it was of the fathers and mothers whose children's souls constantly go missing, trapped by demons or errant among the rocks and boulders of the mountainside, and must be recalled by the shaman to the child's body in case his soul departs forever on the road to the Unknown. I had been seated with male elders at weddings once I had been initiated into a clan so that it was clear where I should sit, and learned to receive the humbled prostrations of the junior generation with dignity, as if it were my own right. I had interviewed and recorded, taken notes and cross-checked, translated narratives and photographed, counted pigs and chickens and taken language lessons. But ultimately, any researcher must remain forever an 'Other'. No outsider can ever fully 'understand' or adequately appreciate the sense of what it is to be brought up as a Hmong; the proverbs, lullabies, jokes, games—things to say and things to do; the courtesies, greetings, introductions, farewells—the routines, the duties, rights and responsibilities involved in forging a local identity, in a particular context, defined as 'Hmong' in relation to those not so defined.

These are all things which an external researcher, or any visitor for a short period, can only observe from some necessary distance and take note of, arbitrarily, without having the cumulative experience of these social practices which those who identify together as 'Hmong' must share as a local, largely unthought (because it does not need to be thought) reality. The distance between that kind of habitual (or embodied) and our more cognitive (theoretical) knowledge, between insider and outsider perceptions, remains broad. While 'insiders' certainly may attain a measure of 'decontextualised' (more abstract) knowledge of their own societies,[3] and outsiders too may obtain a measure of 'tacit' knowledge of societies other than those they are habituated to, the mixture of such understandings remains essentially different. Yet without some kind of interpretive understanding—empathy—of the felt realities of a

---

[3] As Geertz 1983 notes for the 'experience-distant' concepts of society a 'native' may acquire. Charles Taylor (1993) traces this kind of tacit understanding to Wittgenstein's notion of the unarticulated, and compares it to Bourdieu's habitus.

community, any analysis which seeks to be more explanatory must necessarily be incomplete and partial.[4]

It had to be this kind of marginal and incomplete, experientially based, knowledge of what I took to be the essential features of Hmong social organisation, which I took with me when I later went to research the Hmong in their motherland of China, from where they have migrated, over several centuries, to the countries of South East Asia. Yet achieving an understanding of the same cultural group in the very different context of China was an altogether different proposition.

The Hmong

The Hmong in Thailand, who have emigrated there through Laos, Vietnam and Burma from China over the past one hundred years, live in scattered mountain villages, and until recently have practised a pioneer form of shifting cultivation in which maize, upland rice, and the opium poppy, have formed an integrated annual cycle (Geddes 1976). Rice forms the staple diet, while the Hmong in Thailand are well enough off to feed most of the maize to their swine, unlike those in Vietnam or China. Opium has been cultivated largely in response to demands from Chinese middlemen traders, formerly supplying royal or colonial opium monopolies in the region. Yunnanese Chinese, often Muslim, still patrol the mountain villages of the northern uplands through Burma, Thailand, Laos and Vietnam, and the hill villages of ethnic minorities have been on these upland Chinese trading routes for centuries (Leach 1960; Forbes 1987). Many of the older Hmong men are fluent in Yunnanese Chinese, and frequently enough one comes across a Yunnanese Chinese trader who has settled in a Hmong village and married a

---

[4] It was Sperber who talked of the importance of 'tacit' knowledge, which he saw as either 'implicit' in the sense that it can be made explicit, or 'unconscious', in understanding cultural symbolism. He also distinguishes an 'encyclopaediac' knowledge (of the world) from the 'semantic' knowledge (of categories); symbolic knowledge is as he sees it something in-between, a kind of learning and remembering, both ritual and verbal, and not wholly expressible semantically; 1975:108. An interpretivist would deny that there can be 'encyclopaediac' knowledge of this positivist kind without the semantic knowledge which must structure it.

Hmong woman. There were two of these in the village I studied. As relatively recent immigrants from neighbouring countries, the Hmong have been classified by the Thai Government as one of the six main ethnic minorities of Northern Thailand, known as *chao khao* or 'hill people', and they have occupied a peripheral social position in the Thai state, unrecognised as citizens of Thailand and without any rights to the lands they form which traditionally formed a part of the royal monopoly on forested uplands and highlands.

Since 1959, when opium production was officially banned in Thailand although unofficially sponsored by many bureaucrats and businessmen, the Thai Government, together with foreign aid organisations, has made unremitting efforts to convert the Hmong economy of shifting cultivation to one of permanent, settled agriculture, accompanied by efforts to forcibly relocate them to lowland settlements, teach them the Thai language and convert them from their own unique blend of shamanism with pantheism to Thai Buddhism. Many Christian converts have also been made by missionaries of various persuasions. During the 1960s and early 1970s, alienated by these measures, many of the Hmong supported the underground Communist Party of Thailand, and engaged in a war of resistance from the forests against the Government. This has contributed to the popular perception of them as uncouth, subversive and illicit. Today shifting cultivation has been largely replaced in Thailand by permanent settlements, but new problems have arisen. While some Hmong have received Thai citizenship, many still have not, and many still have no title to their lands. The vegetables now grown by many Hmong villagers in response to government demands to end the production of opium have been seen as a cause of pollution in the valleys below, because of the chemical pesticides and fertilisers needed to ensure their fertility on barren mountainsides, and new moves have recently been made to forcibly relocate upland Hmong to lowland villagers. At the same time, heroin addiction and HIV/AIDS have spread at an alarming rate through the upland villages in Thailand. Heroin made out of the opium now produced by neighbouring countries has largely replaced opium in Thailand as it is easier to transport and less easy to detect.

The Thais, like the Lao and Vietnamese, derogatively refer to the Hmong as 'Meo', a term taken from the Chinese name for them and other related cultural; groups, 'Miao'. The Hmong speak a unique language related to three others in China in a family of 'Miao' languages with whom they some millenia ago may have had common historic and linguistic roots. Today, however, there is little in common between the Hmong and the three other main groups classified as 'Miao' in China (the Hmao, Hmu, and Gho Xiong); they have no knowledge of each other and they cannot understand each others' languages.[5] These Miao languages are more widely related to the languages of one neighbouring people, the Yao, who live in similar locations in China and in South East Asia. This 'Miao-Yao' language family, as it is called, is not for sure related to any other, although various attempts have been made to claim it as Sino-Tibetan, or Tai-Kadai (Downer 1967; Lemoine 1972; Benedict 1975).[6]

Whether the Hmong of today, as represented by those who call themselves and see themselves as Hmong in China and South East Asia, can be identified with Chinese historical records of non-Han southern people where the name 'Hmong' never appears, only 'Miao', is a moot historical point. Long ago Lehman (1967) made the point that no 'genetic-linguistic group' can necessarily be identified with its historical linguistic ethnonym, and it is certainly the case that while the Hmong in South East Asia today are generally referred to as 'Meo' or 'Miao' which they resent as a derogatory term, and while the Hmong in China are officially classed with other groups as 'Miao' (which as an official classification allowing them certain privileges as minorities is not necessarily resented by them), in the past—and to some extent today—the term 'Miao' has been used by the Han Chinese in an extremely vague and general way to refer to uncultured southwestern peoples. Ruey (1962), who also worked with Hmong people in Sichuan, has divided the periods in which 'Miao' are referred to in Chinese chronicles into a 'legendary' period (c.2300-200BC); and then a period in which 'Miao' was used to refer generally to southern barbarians ('Man') up to AD1200; and

---

[5] I prefer the spelling Gho Xiong. In Chinese transliterations it is usually spelt 'Ghao Xong', but the 'ao' is an elision from 'o' and it should be 'Xiong' in either *pinyin* or RPA. The 'Gh'is 'q'in IPA.

[6] I strongly disapprove of a current tendency to relabel the 'Miao-Yao' languages 'Hmong-Mien' on account of their most prominent ethnonyms. Only a minority of Miao speakers call themselves Hmong or recognise the term; similarly with the Mien among the Yao speakers.

a 'modern' period since then. Since 1200, we can be moderately certain that when the Chinese records refer to 'Miao', Hmong speakers were included, probably also with others. The contentious period is from the end of the end of the Han to the Song; 'Miao' was used extremely widely in this millenium, and may as well as have referred to Hmong as to other peoples then in southern China. Before that time, again, the use of the term 'Miao' was more specific, but we have no actual historical proof of precisely which genetic-linguistic group it was used to refer to. It is quite probable that it was Hmong-speakers who were referred to in this way and at this time, but the interesting point is that the Hmong in China today are classified by the use of the term 'Miao' which as we shall see has particular historical connotations.

In Thailand, particularly since the impact of tourism in the 1980s, being a 'Hmong' has now become, in spite of this history of oppression and marginalisation, a public, and proud, declaration of cultural identity, difference and uniqueness. When I first arrived in the Hmong village in Thailand in 1980, well primed with anthropological codes of conduct, I had tried to explain, honestly and from the start, that I had come to study the society of the Hmong, about which I intended to write. The only way I knew how to say this at the time, was that I had come to *learn* (i.e.study) the *customs* (*kevcai*, traditions, ways) of the Hmong (in fact, you can't say this directly in Hmong; it requires elaboration).The man who was to become my adoptive 'father' was deeply impressed by this statement; as he said, they had had many people coming there to try and *change* their customs, but I was the first who had come there with an interest in *learning* them. On that basis, of a shared understanding on the value of cultural heritage, an invitation to live with his family was issued, which I took up. The Thai state did not oversee this process, apart from issuing research permissions and attaching me to an official research institute which allowed me to choose my own location and manner of working. The relative openness and accessibility of the Hmong in Thailand, even at a time when a serious communist insurrection involving the Hmong was in process, contrasted strongly with my later experiences in China.

In Thailand the structures of the state seem at times barely to impinge on the Hmong, who continue to don their traditional costume, fail to learn Thai, practice shamanism much as previous generations have done, and often situate their villages away from roads expressly to avoid government interference.While the Thai state, through its army and border patrol police projects, and various agricultural and educational programmes, taxation and land use policy, has made unremitting efforts to influence the Hmong way of life in ways approved of by the state, most of these projects foundered among the apparent anomie of Thai society, with state agencies often openly pitted against others.[7] The Hmong in their Thai villages have in fact succeeded to a remarkable extent in living their own lives, without excessive state interference or government controls. The material improvements which have taken place are largely due to unaided Hmong efforts. An effective exclusion of the Hmong from full participation in the Thai state, particularly through the denial of citizenship and land tenure rights, has resulted in a high degree of cultural autonomy.

Cultural Problems

What most struck me about the Hmong in Thailand, was the extent to which the Hmong there still lived in a romantic 'world of their own'—a world seemingly far removed from the noise and turmoil of the modern towns of the Thai nation-state, and the enigmatic corruption of the Thai civil service.[8] Of course, they too inhabited that world, and moved in it, as did I, and yet when the Hmong shaman leaped backwards onto his bench with a great cry, scattering fire and water about him in the darkened room where women nursed their sick children, the ritual appeared to express the capacity for an infinite removal, an immediate detachment, from the realm of everyday practicality associated with the Thai state, in which trucks bearing the cabbages government had persuaded them to grow broke down on their way to the markets, and midnight conversations were

---

[7] Thai society was originally taken as the model of a 'loosely structured social system' by Embree (1950:191); Brummelhuis (1984) interprets this as pointing to 'a high degree of system integration with a low level of social integration', describing the Thai social system as one which is 'well integrated, but does not strictly "prescribe" its individual's social behaviour'. See Keyes (1977, 1989).

[8] Cf.Bloch (1986); 'Ideology is partly, as it were, in a world of its own and therefore it does not have a direct connection to the political'.

conducted with furtive Chinese strangers who had come to make opium purchases.

It was a markedly 'Hmong' world of experience which they, and I by proxy, entered at such ritually charged times—what seemed an essentially Hmong cultural world, constantly evoked and referred to by the plaintive love-chants of young girls who did not wish to be married, the endlessly intricate embroidery of the women by hurricane lamp and firelight, the sobbing laments at a funeral ritual for a 'younger brother' who had been killed in the far-away wars of Laos, or the songs of the funeral specialist as he guided the soul of the corpse gently back to the village of his mother and his father, his first ancestors, the ancestral Hmong village in China where he would find rest. This was a world where, to be defined as Hmong, was to be identified as neither Han, nor Yi, the two main cultural groups among whom the Hmong had lived in south China.[9]

In Hmong funeral rituals there are ordeals in which the departing soul of the deceased is instructed not to turn to the left, nor to the right, not to take the higher, nor the lower, road, for these are the roads of the Yi and the Han people, but to take the middle road, the unattractive, plain, mud-trampled road, for that is the way for those who are Hmong. In this archetypally Hmong world, symbolically recreated on so many occasions and through so many minute details and emphases of speech, gesture and action, to be Hmong means unequivocally neither to be Han, nor to be Yi. This strong feeling of *cultural contrast* with others was reinforced by the many legends and songs I was told in Thailand, of battles in the past between the Hmong and the Han Chinese, of Chinese trickery and deviousness, gain and victory, of Hmong defeat and loss.

This, it seemed, essentially 'Hmong' world of cultural representations was not merely a matter of ritual and ideology, a purely conceptual world divorced from the exigencies of everyday

---

[9] Mab was the Hmong term used to refer to the Yi, who are the Tibeto-Burman speaking people of Southwest China and Northern Indochina, including the Lisu and Lahu, Akha and Naxi. Suav was the term used, in an everyday context, to refer to the Han Chinese people who traded with the Hmong for opium, and sometimes settled in Hmong villages as shop-keepers—yet it meant 'foreign' as well, since Westerners could be referred to as 'White Suav'.

living and practical consciousness[10]—although certainly ritual and ceremony evoked and supported it. It was embedded and rooted in the simple routines of everyday life, in riddles and proverbs, in the courtesies and politenesses required for greeting a stranger (which entails extensive kinship knowledge), in the techniques of building a house (with its pillars and rafters representing various spirits) or felling a tree (with a ritual to propitiate the spirit of the earth). This was a culturally constituted realm of social practice. It may indeed have been this sense of a specifically 'Hmong' world, of which I imagined myself to be more and more a part, which first attracted me to live with the Hmong and learn more of them; yet what I found in Thailand was not the result of such initial impressions and imaginings, but a living reality the mystery and power of which I felt I was only able to catch brief glimpses.

It was some time before I recognised that this cultural world, which I—and to a large extent the Hmong—thought of as uniquely Hmong, was in fact, largely based on a *Chinese* model. Although there are components in the elaborate system of beliefs the Hmong claim today which a textual kind of analysis might isolate as 'indigenously Hmong' (such as the beliefs in an original, ancestral Mother and Father, in a feminine Sun and a masculine Moon, in an original evil deity who seeks to devour humans as fast as they are created), yet much of the Hmong Otherworld was pictured as a celestial or infernal hierarchy, presided over by Imperial Chinese officials (such as the 'Fourth Mandarin')[11] who controlled life and death, issuing permits for a given number of years of life on earth from behind huge writing-desks with mighty brush pens. Many other features of Hmong social organisation and daily etiquette proved not to be specifically Hmong, although they seemed unique in the isolated situation of the Hmong in northern Thailand, but to be shared with neighbouring peoples of southern China including the Han Chinese themselves, from the names of surnames to matters of daily routine like women stepping aside for men to pass on the path, from back-baskets to farewells. In a somewhat similar way,

---

[10] As Bloch (1977) argued for such 'cultural worlds'. See Hobart (1986) for trenchant criticism of the cultural model of 'Utilitarian Man' on which Bloch's own model was based.

[11] Lemoine (1972b).

researchers in South East Asia long failed to recognise the religious practices of the related highland Yao peoples to be an obscure school of Daoism but presented them as an isolated tribal religion (see Ch.2). It eventually became clear to me how much the Hmong in fact *shared* with the Han Chinese (from whom they were so concerned to differentiate themselves) their traditional beliefs and symbolic forms which, like those of the Han themselves, had in turn been largely modelled on the structure of one of the longest lasting bureaucracies the world has known—that of the Chinese Empire. And if one were to assume an intrinsic difference of a Hmong cultural essence from that of a Han one (as I argued one shouldn't), one could give many examples of apparently 'Chinese' influences upon the Hmong and neighbouring peoples—or the apparent permeation of Hmong culture by that of the Han Chinese.[12] For example, the practice of geomantic sitings for graves and houses, through a system well described for the Chinese by Freedman (1966, 1968) and Feuchtwang (1975)—or the Hmong language itself, which shows clear evidence of three main periods of loans from standard Chinese.[13]

The Hmong in Thailand were, as I came to realise, in effect still imaginary habitants of a ritual and political world their grandparents or great-grandparents had left decades previously; the realm of the 'great dynasties', as they persist in referring to their motherland of China, rather than those of the 'lesser dynasties', the lands outside China particularly in South East Asia. It seemed to me that it must have been their strong sense of still belonging to a far wider, Chinese community which explained their largely successful resistance to the assimilationist agendas of Thai development projects, the often deliberate remoteness of their village locations, the conceptual distance between the Hmong village I had lived in and the modern Thai city of Chiangmai, with its banks, hotels, shops and airports.

So the Hmong village of Nomya, where I had worked in Thailand, seemed to be a village whose conceptual remoteness from the Thai

---

[12] My original (1985) argument, in keeping with what was becoming the spirit of the times, was that all these clearly Chinese influences were just as much Hmong as they were 'Chinese', since they were not recognised as Chinese by the Hmong, and perhaps dated back to a 'pre-cultural fission' time in which Hmong and Han identitries were not so clearly differentiated. Although glamorous, I now see this as a specious and sophistical view.

[13] See Downer (1963, 1966).

state allowed its inhabitants to regard themselves as the outpost of a Chinese civilisation long since dead and vanished. The sense seemed to prevail among the Hmong of North Thailand of belonging to a much wider community, or 'great tradition', even though that community and tradition—of late imperial China—had long since disappeared. And their anachronistic membership of such a 'Chinese' civilization seemed to be reflected in the ritual universe they inhabited and activated whenever pain or misfortune struck, whenever they performatively cited the myths of birth and death.

Yet Hmong spokesmen and Hmong ritual performances in Thailand continued to define their ethnic and cultural identity in terms of a series of radical negative *oppositions* to that of the Han Chinese. A series of oft-told legends of the kind I was most interested in narrated how the Hmong, chased out of the lands of the 'great dynasties' to the lands of the lesser dynasties, by the wicked, powerful, persecuting, avenging Han Chinese, dropped their precious writings in the great river they had to cross—and to this day, *unlike the Chinese* (and this was largely the point of these stories), have had no form of writing of their own. Nor a land of their own, since the Hmong Emperor (*Huab Tais*) was geomantically tricked and murdered by the ancestor of the Emperors of China, so that until today they have remained shifting cultivators with no rights to the land they work, unlike people *like the Han* and Thai who have fertile rice-lands and do not have to move constantly to find fresh fields. Nor have they in general had power, wealth, or status, and in many legendary accounts the loss of these is traced directly to the superior Chinese mastery of the magic arts of geomancy (*fengshui* in Chinese; *loojmem* in Hmong) which are believed to assure worldly prosperity and success. Hmong social memories conspicuously tended, in legendary accounts and quite often in ordinary talk, to cite Hmong identity in terms of an original loss of 'power/knowledge', which they attributed directly to the Han Chinese.[14]

It became clear that if I was to be able to explicate this Hmong sense of belonging to a vanished civilisation, or arrive at any understanding of the relationship of the Hmong to Chinese society, I would need to research a Hmong village in China, since the Hmong

---

[14] Hutheesing (1990) describes a similar sense of the loss of 'elephant repute' among the neighbouring Lisu.

of Thailand confessed to only having only dim recollections of the actual details of their life in China. In this aim I was also importantly conforming to Hmong expectations, since the Hmong of Thailand and Laos—and even more so those who had emigrated overseas—so often told me that their own knowledge of their cultural heritage was faulty, but that it was surely better preserved in their original motherland of China. Indeed, most Hmong outside China still believe this; there is something like a theory of 'deteriorating knowledge' which is often used to explain the failures of shamanic cures. In this theory, which one often encounters in discussions with Hmong, it is assumed that each generation fails to pass on some of its own knowledge to the succeeding generation, so that over the course of time wisdom and capability inevitably become eroded. The simile often given is of an old father on his deathbed, still reluctant to pass on all his secrets to his sons for fear they may surpass him. Power, knowledge, capability, sovereignty, is always located in these accounts in the long-ago, and that agency is located in the lands of China where, it is almost always assumed, Hmong traditions and customs must have been better preserved than in their dispersal to the lands of the 'lesser dynasties'. Any Hmong with a concern for his past and culture (and there are many of these) will wish to visit China to see how Hmong culture should be 'properly' performed. China is the site of the past, and of social memories which show an abiding resentment for having been expelled out of their rightful home and lands in China. To revisit China is to go back in time, to go back to 'the village of the mother and father' where the soul of the deceased is led to be reborn, to revisit cousins who must be closer to the ways of the grand-parents than one has been able to be oneself. As Hmong cultural traditions were constantly excused to me as a degenerate version of their pristine condition in China, so too the cultural identity of Hmong was constantly phrased in terms of contrasts of a binary kind with that of the Han Chinese (the *suav*). At the same time it appeared that many Hmong cultural traditions were shared with the Han Chinese, or represented versions of Han Chinese cultural forms which had been lost by the Han. China formed an originary 'context' to which Hmong cultural traditions were constantly referred, and the nostalgic longing for the authentic, uncontestable version of a Hmong cultural identity displayed not only by many Hmong cultural forms but also by Hmong individuals, and often redoubled among the refugees from South East Asia now overseas, was picked up by the researcher working with them. It was very clear that I needed to go to China to resolve these issues.

Yet in China I was to find the Hmong there citizens of 'a state whose borders have never adequately been defined' (Pye 1990), and their own identity far more equivocal than it had seemed, or was presented, in Thailand.

China and the Chinese

China remained a closed country to most overseas researchers for many years after the Revolution of 1949. Even since the economic reforms and liberalisation which took place from 1979 onwards, it is still not easy to gain research permission, and it is even more difficult to be allowed to stay there for any length of time, living in villages, observing and taking part in everyday life, interviewing villagers and local leaders in the way that ethnographic fieldwork require. Access to research on those defined as members of the officially recognised 'national minorities' of China depends upon being able to work within Chinese society and, in a sense, being accepted within certain circles of Chinese society; in particular, by state officials who oversee research and contact with foreigners, and national minority affairs, and by official scholars and colleagues who have undertaken their own research in similar areas, and may or may not wish to help an untutored outsider.

The power of the Chinese state is extended into rural villages in China through the party apparatus which is represented in each village and through the mass people's organisations such as the Women's Federation, Youth League and Peasants' Association, as well as through the formal machinery of government bureaus and offices.

The authority of the communist party has only rarely been seriously challenged in its fifty years of hegemony. Personal networks based on relative age, locality, common experience and gender permeate a state bureaucracy whose power under Maoism has been argued to have penetrated every corner of private Chinese life. Bureaucratic state structures are penetrated however by this system of personal relationships known as *guanxi*. This flexible and complex elaboration of personal statuses, within a more formal, rigid system of administration, crosscutting the formal structures of administration, is important not so much because it is an instrumental system of personal patronage so much as because it is expressively fluid and dynamic. *Guanxi* has been analysed as an expression of civil society which nevertheless permeates the state (Yang 1994), and the 'blurry interpenetration' of state with society in China has been emphasised (Leonard and Flower 1996).

Specialists confidently speak of 'China' as a single entity, when they are really generalising from only a very limited experience of one part of it. More so than in many other societies, the 'conscious models' of the way things are, on which outsiders rely for their knowledge of 'things Chinese', are often designed to accomplish certain effects in the mind of the recipient rather than to truly convey the character of an event or institution, a form of conduct or particular attitude. Chinese anthropologists themselves have maintained since early in this century that it is impossible for any outsider to arrive at any real understanding of Chinese society; Leach (1982), with typical perversity, maintained that it might be even more difficult for a Chinese anthropologist to study his own society.

To some extent I would agree with the Chinese anthropologists, like Fei Xiaotong (1939); it is particularly difficult in China for an outsider to penetrate the underlying motivations and patterns of event in a society so infinitely stratified, so indefinitely extended in time and space, so complex in hierarchy and yet so fluid in the interpretation of such hierarchies. We may find better understandings of 'China' in the works of novelists and poets; and better accounts, too, in fictionalised accounts by Chinese anthropologists than in more theoretical works. It was explicitly for these reasons that Lin Yaohua, one of the earliest Chinese ethnologists, chose to present his material in the form of a novel (Lin 1948).

It is almost impossible to generalise about Chinese society, of which the Hmong in China form a part, and many analysts have tied themselves in knots trying to do so. This may be because, as Feuchtwang (1991) pointed out, China has paradoxically always held out two quite contrary images of itself to the West; one an image of enlightened rationality, the other of extreme bigotry and superstition. Given the complexity of the society and societies of China, quite contrary theoretical positions and viewpoints can be argued with relative ease.

The very different images of Chinese society which prevail, well illustrating what Baudrillard (1981) called 'the impossibility of a determined discursive position', relate to real contradictions within Chinese society itself. And the very depth of Chinese history makes it sometimes easier to remark its continuities rather than its ruptures and radical departures. The image of China as a place of superior enlightenment, of which Feuchtwang speaks, derives largely from early accounts of the scholarly meritocracy and the system of examinations which assured bureaucratic status. As early as the mid-seventh state officials were being selected through public civil examination (Shue 1988). The principles of hereditary succession which continued to dominate the administration of most other polities were challenged in China as early as the Han dynasty by the growth of a centralised system of standardised scholarly examinations, based on the study of classical texts. By the Song (960-1277) the basis of a meritocracy had been established which continued to order the affairs of state until the mid-twentieth century. Yet the elite was hardly unified, nor was the state monolithic. By late imperial times, the Chinese 'gentry' who acted as a crucial interface between central administration and the regional power of localities were composed of an upper stratum of higher degree holders and officials, those with lower degrees, and notable members of local elites such as lineages and guilds who were not necessarily degree holders.[15]

Towards the later nineteenth century, the emergence of capitalist forms of production in the towns and countryside increasingly strained this flexible alliance of the scholarly meritocracy with a property-owning class of rural gentry. . Yet an essentially unbroken bureaucratic tradition was followed, after 1949, by a rationalized modern bureaucracy regulated and supervised by the highly organised structures of the Chinese Communist Party.

As is well known, these traditions of meritocratic bureaucracy have succeeeded in maintaining order among the largest 'unified' population in the world over an extraordinarily long period of history. The unifying character of the Chinese writing system—the system of characters into which the sounds of different Chinese

---

[15] See Fei (1953); Wakeman (1975).

languages can be transcribed and their meanings conveyed, has often been pointed to by historians as crucial in Han unification of China. Indeed the supremacy of literacy in Chinese culture has been a long one, since it was on the acquisition of varying degrees of literacy that status in the imperial civil service depended, and according to which standards of 'civilisation' (*wenming*) were largely judged. The Chinese term for 'culture' itself, *wenhua*, includes the character for literacy, and is closely associated with literate abilities.

Those of non-Han Chinese ethnic origin within the borders of the territory claimed by the Empire or even beyond them, who wished to become acculturated to a prestige society or express their political loyalty to the civilising state which insisted on its moral superiority, often adopted patrilineal Han surnames and despatched their sons to schools where they would receive a proper training in Chinese. Uxorilocal in-marrying Han males contributed to this process (see Shepherd 1993). Adopting Chinese customs and dress, within a generation or two a family—or the branch of a family—would 'become Chinese', and this is a process which continues, in many different forms, today. Such processes of the acculturation of neighbouring groups have been instrumental in the formation of present-day Chinese identities, and it has been a pressing question therefore to determine to what extent the Hmong of China have managed to create and retain a sense of their cultural difference despite the historical strength of these great movements of popular transformation in which social identities have so many times been lost, transformed and found again.

Although acculturation did not necessarily result in assimilation (Shepherd 1993), these processes of acculturation and absorption into a wider Chinese 'civilisation' must have accounted in the past for the extinction of whole cultural groups. Schafer (1969) considered half the present-day 'Han Chinese' population of southern China to have resulted from the assimilation of originally non-Han peoples.[16] The apparent ease with which a 'Chinese' identity was adopted by members of non-Han groups was taken in the past as evidence of a particularly liberal and enlightened attitude on the part of the Han Chinese towards their neighbours of different

---

[16] See Fei Xiaotong (1991).

languages and diverging social practices. As Thierry (1989) puts it of the days before the Mongol Yuan dynasty (1277-1367), the 'basis of the relationship between the Hans and the Barbarians was not originally...of an ethnic nature, but rested on a relationship to Civilization.' In earlier times, it is argued, 'civilization' was equated with 'humanity'; the 'uncivilised' non-Han were seen as essentially 'non-human', who might nevertheless be 'humanised' by becoming Han. Dikotter (1992:x) similarly notes that early Han Chinese perceptions of minorities 'remained embedded in an ethnocentric framework that stressed socio-cultural differences' which could be transformed, rather than in primordial racial differentiations.

To some extent this sort of 'culturalist' attitude often remarked by earlier observers for Chinese attitudes towards foreigners and minorities represents a folk model of Chinese civilization presented by the Chinese elite themselves to outsiders, by claiming a privileged understanding of what they themselves defined as 'Chinese' culture. Ebrey (1996) has recently examined these Confucian culturalist concepts of inclusive identity, making the point that it coexisted with a patrilineal conception of ethnicity which defined a large 'we-group' labelled as Xia, Hua, or Han.[17] However, racism in the form we know it is certainly a modern construct, in China as elsewhere, and it is true that traditional elite attitudes towards 'outsiders' in China were probably more culturally oriented than racial. While the roots of a modern racialism, based on notions of common descent from the Yellow Emperor and physical characteristics such as jade-white skin and black hair, may have existed in China for a very long time, it is clear that they took their present, territorialised form only after the impact of western nationalism transformed traditional notions of cultural difference into a 'discourse on race' which emerged in the nineteenth century (Dikotter 1992). It is important to realise, however, that the notion of a Chinese 'civilisation' has never been entirely confined to the Han Chinese people, nor even to the limits of the Chinese empire, or modern nation-state.

The contrary image of China, as a place of superstition and bigotry (remarked by Feuchtwang), stems I believe in large part from the power and persistence of popular forms of religiosity, such as

---

[17] Like Ebrey (1996), I use the term 'Han identity' in its modem sense despite the complexity of earlier usages which included terms such as 'Hua' and 'Xia'.

those practised by the Hmong. In both modern and pre-modern China, religion has occupied a unique position in relation to the state. Modern China is at once highly urban-oriented, structurally complex, bureaucratic, and secular to a remarkable extent. Young people in cities grow up in an atmosphere from which almost all supernatural beliefs have been purged, apart from a vestigial but deep-rooted belief in the powers of fate and fortune (*ming*).[18] The modernising secular Chinese state disapproves strongly of religious activity, and only permits orthodox religious activity in organised form and under state supervision, outlawing both what it categorises as 'abnormal' religious activities and 'superstition'.

For this disapproval the socialist philosophy on which the state is founded may be seen to provide an adequate justification, since under the Leninist thesis adopted by the Chinese Communist Party, as socialist consciousness deepens, religious beliefs (like the beliefs in nationalism and ethnic identity with which the question of religion in China is so importantly connected), as the products of a bourgeois or feudal 'false consciousness', will slowly wither away and disappear altogether with the class exploitation which lead to such beliefs. Yet as Heberer (1989) notes, this official disapproval of unsanctioned religious and superstitious practices hardly represents a new attitude in China. Since the fourth century BC the educated elite had adopted an enlightened attitude of rational scepticism towards unorthodox beliefs and practices associated with the supernatural.

Religion in China has been characterised by a historical weakness of institutional organisation (Yang 1954), and its diffused nature lent itself to a close association with the secular institutions of society—through the worship of scholars and education, of the lineage and family, of the Emperor, of the patron deities of merchant guilds and local village associations. Yet since very early days religion has never been identified with the state; Feuchtwang (1991) remarks on the oddness of a state and polity which required no justifying mysteries. While the state did suborn and co-opt forms of worship and religious behaviour, popular forms of religiosity flourished among the lower orders of society well beyond the sanction of the state. A sceptical, 'enlightened' attitude towards heterodox religion

---

[18] For a similar survival of beliefs in Tyche, Fate, among the later Greeks, see Dodds (1928).

and 'irrational' beliefs in the supernatural, then, is of very long standing in China. At the same time, like 'culturalist' notions of identity, such attitudes have been confined to the educated literati, those who claimed *wenhua* or literate culture, the magistrates and other officials of the civil service, the scholars and intellectuals.

While the social institutions of pre-modern China were enmeshed with orthodox religious structures which permeated local associations and kinship structures, the secular modern state has insisted on a sharp separation from all forms of religiosity. The dangers of such a radical secularisation, in a society not formerly characterised by such a strict division between society and religion, are of course that religious beliefs are likely to become closely identified with emerging social forces in a way which may directly imperil the authority of the state. We can see this in the Buddhism of separatist Tibet, in the deification of Mao Zedong, in recent moves to repress the Falun Gong. In the late nineteenth and early twentieth centuries religion directly challenged the state through large-scale social movements associated with esoteric societies.

It is particularly in the countryside and in remote areas that the power of the folk, or popular, religion of China has been immense (Yang 1954; Potter & Potter 1990; Feuchtwang 1992). The domestic worship of ancestors, temple celebrations, processions and festivals, divination and fortune-telling and the matching of horoscopes for wedding couples, the geomantic resiting of ancestors' bones, the shamanic possessions of mediums and the elaborate rituals of Daoist priests, have flourished throughout most historical periods as if official urban scepticism was of no account. Popular religion is seen as a force which, like the force of ethnicity, may directly threaten the order of the state and national integrity. This is the reason for its official control and censorship, and why questions of religion and nationality have become so closely identified in regions where large-scale organised opposition to centralised authority has emerged.

Quite different conceptions of China are reflected in debates which have taken place about the nature of the reappearance of religious practices in China since 1978. For some observers, what seems to have happened recently, since a more liberal economic policy was introduced after the Cultural Revolution in 1978, is an astonishing revival of traditional forms of culture and religion which had been assumed to have largely disappeared or been eradicated in the thirty years of socialist control after the Revolution. Since 1980 temples have been rebuilt and ancestral worship permitted, major festivals have been reinstituted, mediums from Hong Kong have been officially invited to consecrate new temples (Liu 1995) and geomancy is studied by urban architects (Liu 1998), in what appears to have been a general revival of religion. These religious phenomena are often linked by state discourse with other features of the old society which it was thought had been left behind, such as the sale of women in marriage or for prostitution, the abandonment of baby daughters, the formation of clan and lineage associations, and the commissioning of written genealogies as the Hmong of Sichuan were doing. As Vivienne Shue pointed out, the extension of the socialist state's authority over the periphery after 1949 'may in some respects have preserved and strengthened the old peasant social formation.' Shue argued that state penetration of the village periphery was never as absolute as most models had suggested; rural communities were often in a position to bargain with central authorities, since the Chinese state was itself a complex entity, made up of varying interests (Shue 1988).

The Potters took this argument to an extreme in their claim that traditional rural social structures in south China had remained relatively unaffected by the momentous political and economic changes of the previous fifty years, and that in general there had been 'remarkable continuity in the deep structures of the old society' (Potters 1990:256); farmers had been able to evolve their own strategies of 'covert resistance' (Scott 1985) to avoid or avert most of the direct effects of official campaigns and policies. They (1990:336) referred to a general 'resurgence of...ritual life', and described how 'the symbolic structures which express the old social order have re-emerged'.

This view was itself a reaction against previous models of the radical changes thought to have been undergone by Maoist social structure, and has since been seriously disputed by others such as Siu (1990:300), who have argued that what has recurred bears only a superficial resemblance to certain features of traditional society, and that for example the practice of popular religion in contemporary China entails quite different perceptions of power and meaning for present-day practitioners from those of the past. Siu (1989) shows how the apparent 'resurgence' of ritual is in fact a 'recycling' of 'cultural fragments' in the context of new perceptions of power, linked with the enormous penetration of the state in modern China (and post-reform anxieties at its potential retreat). And it is undeniable that what has occurred over fifty years of socialist rule in China has been an immeasurable strengthening of state power over ordinary peoples' everyday lives; state power now intrudes into the most private recesses of family and personal life in the form, most obviously, of the number of children one is allowed to have and the methods of contraception one should use. Pye (1991) and other liberal political scientists concur with this general view of how the expanding power of the Chinese state has effectively limited the expansion of a dynamic civil society.[19]

There is some truth in both views of the recent extension of state power in China. Certainly both personal and communal strategies of deception and aversion are common at all levels of social and institutional life in China, as indeed generally in both peasant societies (Scott 1985) and bureaucratic systems (De Certeau 1984). And the continued practice of shamanism by Hmong and other groups in China, as we see in Part II, must be seen as some evidence of the success of efforts at covert resistance to anti-religion, anti-superstition campaigns. It is in some recognition of the effective power of local authorities and communities that central policies are often couched in terms which allow for a range of local applications in the light of varying 'local conditions'.[20] Yet Siu's argument that those features of traditional village life which scholars have assumed are revivals in fact 'differ substantially...from their counterparts in the past' (Siu 1989:292) is also often valid. State penetration has in fact been extreme and radical in China, as one can easily see through

---

[19] Recently Faure & Siu have proposed a potential compromise between these views, taking into account some of the arguments on the traditional 'culturalism' of China as described here, to the effect that while historically there had been a distancing of local communities and regions from the *political* power of the state, at the same time there was a ubiquity and pervasiveness of the *cultural* ideals associated with and which supported the central state. As they put it, the late imperial state presented itself 'less as an administrative machinery than as a cultural idea'; as the former, the state was remote, as the latter, it was penetrating in its power to shape awareness of viable options (Faure & Siu 1995:18).

[20] See Potter and Potter (1990:272) on the system of 'policy bargaining' characteristic of the Chinese bureaucratic hierarchy.

a comparison of the situation of the Hmong in China with that of the Hmong in Thailand.

Each village in China's recent history has had its production targets and quota, benefits and rates of taxation, annually set and monitored, its fertility and mortality rates controlled and recorded. In every village party members report to higher cadres and oversee the appointment of the village committee, with its head, accountant, and usually women's representative responsible for population policy. Each household has its members registered, and generally its farming or productive land now allocated according to the number of household members. In the days of the commune, labour and productivity controls were still more stringent. The power of the state has been direct, obvious and obtrusive, and overt expressions of cultural autonomy carefully controlled.

Party membership is not always known, and it is well known that it is not always known, so that private unguarded comments criticising local officials or policy, religious or illicit activities, may well be reported—and it is well known that they may be reported.[21] Villagers tend to be habitually guarded in their communications even with other villagers, and, particularly since the Cultural Revolution, quite often with members of their own families.

There is an exceptionally high appreciation of the public value of information, the power of a generalised knowledge, and its likely or possible effects and uses, throughout Chinese society, which must surprise anyone who has previously worked in a more simply organised society where the value of information is of course also recognised, but in a more local and private sense. One can attribute this, again, to the long history of bureaucratic management and literate surveillance which has maintained the political unity of China over such a length of historical time, and the progressive extent of state penetration of everyday life which there has been.

A general concern with surface and visibility, with presentation to the outside world, must have been immeasurably increased by the extraordinary modern extension of political state power into the remoter areas of China in Maoist days, into the least significant of village hamlets, into areas such as the Liangshan mountains where

---

[21] See Chapter 3, Part II.

formerly the members of ethnic minorities maintained considerable autonomy, and into the deepest recesses of personal and domestic life through population and reproductive controls, regulations on ritual and belief, the control of production and distribution, the mass campaigns against traditional culture and 'unhealthy' customs. The power of writing and reportage is strong and visible.

Information itself is a commodity of which one does not give freely, since it is always worth something to somebody, and those who seek free information are much like those who seek free bed and board. Since one's words and how these are reported may bear importantly on one's future, one guards them carefully, and takes care only to let those things which one wants to be known be known. Information is fully recognised as a function of representation, determining images of the self according to which evaluations of conduct will be made; words are guarded circumspectly, in order to convey the current or most appropriate impression. Throughout the uncertain nineties this has changed radically among the younger generation in the cities, where the authority of the party and of state ideology has become seriously eroded if not irrelevant. In the countryside, however, and in many work units where former class enemies work side by side, much of this suspicion still remains.

The Scope of Nationalism

The social position of the Hmong, and other ethnic minorities in China, can only be understood against a dominating historical ideology of nationalism, culture and civilisation, now attached to socialist modernisation, in which specific local identities are defined at the same time as they are constitutive of it. It is therefore important that the power of the Middle Kingdom, even as late as the encounter with western powers in the early Qing, was not traditionally conceived as territorially based or bounded. Since the first century China had attempted to construct a protective shield of subservient states around its borders to reinforce the centrality of its civilization and avoid direct relations with states seen as 'barbarian'. Like the tributary state system, which extended to Japan and Korea and large parts of South East Asia, the *tusi* or 'local chieftain' system, administered in southern China, depended on the co-optation of local elites through their adoption of Chinese culture and manners.

With its roots in the Han dynasty, the *tusi* system survived its late imperial reforms and Republican abolition, and something of its strength in neighbouring regions may be sensed in the tombstones of Shan chiefs in Burma who had adopted Han Chinese patronymics since the sixteenth century (while remaining Shan).[22] Here are cases of conformity to imperial authority which did not necessarily entail a loss of ethnic identity or outright acculturation (Shepherd 1993). Chinese attitudes towards national identity have only recently come to accord with modern international definitions, as was shown in the claims of Chinese nationality for overseas Chinese born in South East Asia which persisted through the 1950s. Pye (1991) has argued very strongly that China still has a 'relatively inchoate and incoherent form of nationalism', which unlike in other developing countries has been basically antagonistic to modernization. Pye insists on a political definition of nationalism, distinct from the primordial sentiments of ethnic or cultural identity, a separation which, as he sees it, has failed to take place in China. So that China has remained, as he puts it, what Europe might have been had the Holy Roman Empire never disintegrated and modern nation-states not appeared. It is this sense of a wider Chinese cultural world which I had found so compelling for the Hmong of northern Thailand, even though their families had emigrated from China several generations previously. The Hmong of China, however, are located within a very different modern political entity.

The modern state of China defines itself as a 'multi-national state' comprising fifty-six 'nationalities' (*minzu*), of whom the Hmong form part of one, and the vanguard of whom are the numerically and politically dominant Han Chinese. The concept of 'nationality' applied to ethnic minorities such as the Hmong is of particular interest for the light it sheds on state-minority relations, since after 1949 it was based on Stalin's (1913) definition of a 'nation' (*natsiya*, the stage seen as following that of the 'nationality' or 'pre-nation', *narodnost*) as a stable community, historically constituted, with a common language, territory, economic life, and intellectual spirit expressed in a common culture, which he (1929) had limited to the economic stage of capitalism. While 'clans' (*rod*) and 'tribes'

---

[22] Hill (1982) in Tapp (1985).

(*plemya*) were seen by Soviet theoreticians as corresponding to the stage of classless primitive communism, and the 'nation' as clearly a class formation, the stage of the 'nationality' was assimilated to the stages of slave and feudal society believed to have preceded the formation of capitalist societies.[23]

Stalin's original Trotskyite translator, Li Lisan, had found no difficulties in converting Stalin's 'clan' into Chinese *shizu*, his 'tribe' as *buluo*, and his 'nation' as *minzu*, but had to coin the uncomfortable term *buzu* for the problematic stage of 'nationality', covering the stages between the 'tribal' and the 'national'. Yet the Han people, on the criteria hitherto reserved for the 'nation', would surely have formed a 'nation' as early as the Qin and Han Dynasties, when the Great Wall enclosed a common territory, a unified system of weights and measures signified a common economic life, and a unified script for the language was introduced, as the historian Fan Wenlan pointed out (1954) in his argument that it would be inappropriate to refer to the Han as a *buzu*, and that they should be termed a *minzu*. Fan was much criticised for this apparent attempt to separate the Han from other peoples of China, and a consensus began to emerge that the Han could not have formed a 'nation' much before the advent of capitalism, which might be dated from the Opium Wars of the 19th. century, and might therefore have to be referred to as a *buzu* before that time (Wei Jingming 1956).

It was still generally assumed that the notion of 'nation' could only be applied to modern, capitalist forms of social organisation, in which case it followed that only the Han Chinese could properly be termed a 'nation' (whether from the Han dynasty or from the 19th. century), while the remaining millions of Chinese citizens would have to be classified as belonging to less advanced forms of social organisation such as the 'nationality', or even 'tribe' or 'clan'. However, the divisiveness, and practical unacceptability, of reserving the term *minzu* for the Han and perhaps some others was soon realised. An intensive linguistic study of the Marxist texts then revealed that the term for 'nation' had in fact been employed quite loosely prior to the time of Stalin; when Engels had talked of the transformation of 'tribes' into 'nations', it was clear that he had

---

[23] Thoraval (1990). See also Harrell (1995).

traditional nations, not modern capitalist formations, in mind. Stalin had merely employed the term 'nation' in a restricted sense, to refer to the modern capitalist nations. There was then no real reason to translate 'nationality' as *buzu*, with its derogatory overtones, since Stalin had simply understood 'nationality' to mean pre-capitalist 'nations'. So it was decided to 'unify' the translations, and use *minzu* to translate both *natsiya* (nation) and *narodnost* (nationality) and to use this term to refer to all ethnic groups within China.[24] Academic and political debates on the issue took place throughout the 1950s (cf. Fan Wenlan 1958), but once it was agreed that Stalin's definition of 'nation' could also be applied to pre-capitalist, stateless formations, the apparent dilemma of how to refer to the pre-modern, post-tribal, was resolved.

All officially recognised ethnic minority groups in China thus became defined as *minzu* ('nationalities'), but this has led to the two odd but highly indicative and functional ambiguities noted by Thoraval.[25] Firstly, since the time of Sun Yatsen the 'Chinese nation' has been officially defined as *Zhonghua Minzu*, which is understood to include a majority of the Han people (*Han minzu*) as well as other non-Han peoples described as 'border peoples' (*bianjiang minzu*) under the Kuomintang, and 'minority peoples' (*shaoshu minzu*) since then, so that as Thoraval says, China is seen as a great *minzu*, itself composed of 56 *minzu*, among which the Han are somehow a little more '*minzu*' than the others! Because of the absence in Chinese nouns of indications of the plural, the idea of *Zhonghua minzu*, although officially referring to a single entity (the Chinese *minzu*), also subsumes connotations of plurality; the *minzu* of China. But when one needs to specify this plurality, one has to insert an additional particle; *Zhonghua ge minzu* ('the nationalities *of* China').

The second main ambiguity Thoraval notes in the term *minzu*, is that the phrase *minzu wenti*, usually understood to mean 'the problems or issues of (minority) nationalities' (since almost always when 'nationalities' are discussed, it is in fact 'minority nationalities' or *shaoshu minzu* who are meant), may equally well be understood as 'the national question/problem'. This close identification of issues of

---

[24] 'Nationality' remains the official English translation.

[25] J.Thoraval (n.d.).

national identity with the questions of ethnic minorities, shown in the ambiguity of the phrase *minzu wenti*, demonstrates very clearly how integral the definition of (culturally classified) minorities is to the modern definition of the Chinese (political) state—that in other words, a *political* notion of modern ethnicity (Cohen 1974:97), of a kind many anthropologists might prefer to Pye's more 'culturalist' version of ethnicity, is accepted from the outset in official discussions and statements of policy concerning the minorities in China.[26] The imperative need for control of well-organised groups such as those of Tibet, Xinjiang and Inner Mongolia, as well as trans-border groups such as the Hmong, Dai and Hani in the southwest, to the safeguarding of China's modern territorial borders, is well recognised (and we should remember that in English it is the People's Republic, not the Peoples' Republic). Indeed, this assumed coincidence of people, nation, state, and government, may seem more a typical example of modern nationalist ideology (Hobsbawm 1990) than of Pye's 'inchoate' nationalism. Yet this modernist demand for social congruence is still rooted in a cultural notion of civilisation which is Teutonic in its appeal to a supra-national identity which is not necessarily territorially bounded.

The arbitrary nature of the Chinese classification of ethnic minority groups, launched in the early 1950s through an arduous process of research and investigation (see Lemoine 1989; Harrell 1995), groups together largely acculturated peoples such as the Islamic Chinese (Hui), many of them descendants of Han who converted to Islam, and the Manchu; highly organised societies with a history of their own states and religion such as the Dai and the Tibetans; smaller isolated indigenous groups such as the Maonam of Guangxi; and larger dispersed populations such as the Miao and Yi, who often crosscut national borders (Tapp 1995). It is important to 'rectify names', said Confucius, and it is indeed largely through the processes of naming, classifying, 'hailing' and thereby fixing of subjects, that state power has been exerted over the extent of China's cultural diversity. Through classifying diverse groups together as

---

[26] Cohen (1974) defined ethnicity as 'strife between ethnic groups' and that is the sense I follow here. Ethnic groups were seen as emerging in the course of competition for scarce resources.

minzu, it also becomes possible to formulate a broad common policy towards the minority nationalities.

Many anomalies of this classification remain, some noted by Fei (1981); there have been cases where opinions differed within a particular group as to whether they formed an autonomous cultural group or belonged to another or stronger one, or where fierce conflicts (such as between landlords and peasants) within a group led to their refusal to be identified as members of the same group; there have been isolated Han groups who have come to evolve into distinctive cultural entities, and descendants of originally non-Han minorities who have become so acculturated to Han society that they now regard themselves as Han Chinese and have been assimilated. There have been dispersals of original groups who continued to be classed as members of the same group despite having evolved radical differences from each other, or alternatively had become known under different terms and subsequently lost all recognition of their original affinity.[27] And there are many still smaller groups, such as the Khmu, Deng and Mangren noted by Heberer (1989:38), the 'Xifan' examined by Harrell (forthcoming) and the Ge studied by Cheung (1996) who are now actively campaigning for recognition as a 'national minority'.

China is proud of its policy of positive discrimination on behalf of those classified in this way as national minorities, which allows them in certain areas limited exemption from the restrictions of the population control policy, and lower pass marks for college and university admissions.[28] Rather than fulfilling earlier (1931) promises of total autonomy for minority regions, the CCP instituted a system of limited regional autonomy after 1949 under which regions, prefectures or counties are designated as minority ones, according to the percentage of minority peoples among their populations, and receive specific privileges such as representation in local and national government, educational and economic assistance, and the right to develop their own languages and scripts. These 'autonomous minority areas' have been very carefully defined, often to avoid the predominance of any one particular minority group, or to divide up a

---

[27] Fei (1981) in Tapp (1988).

[28] See Sautman (1990) on Chinese anti-radicalism.

much larger cultural group (like the Tibetans, and the speakers of Tai languages). Yet the privileges received in this way are real enough, and the overall success of China's nationalities policies is often pointed to in the frequency with which particular groups strive to be officially recognised as separate minorities, the children of mixed marriages prefer to retain their minority status, and in some areas (like Gongxian in Sichuan) Han settlers deliberately choose to immigrate into or settle in minority areas.[29] These officially marked and distinctive identities, such as Miao, Yi, or Hui, need however to be carefully distinguished from the ways in which local groups and communities actually define themselves. As we have seen, the term 'Miao' is in fact composed of four main cultural groups, each with a clear sense of their history, culture and language. The Hmong are only one of these groups.

The formation of such an explicit national minorities policy since 1949 has, I argued in 1988, had the unintended effect of freezing the dynamic historical processes of transformation so many have spoken of, under which local populations have slowly throughout history become 'Sinified' through the adoption of Chinese manners and practices, dress and language (whether or not this resulted in the loss of a separate sense of identity), at the time as individual Han became assimilated by native cultures, and new identities evolved through interaction with each other. The present policy provides concrete incentives to retain or revive minority status rather than assimilate, although it may marginally contribute to Han acculturation among the very small number of minority students who reach tertiary levels of education (Sautman 1998). Yet local prejudices against the 'non-Han', which in the past must have been instrumental in furthering processes of assimilation as individuals and whole groups strove to be recognised as 'Han', persist and are much in evidence at the village level (Tapp 1995). It is these ingrained chauvinisms which act against the declared attempt of the state to raise minorities to a more advanced and equal level and which contribute to the failure of a policy of enlightened discrimination as it appears on paper. Indeed at certain times in history the state may have had an interest in opposing Han acculturation and assimilation, while encouraging the

---

[29] For a Han view of this, see Jankowiak (1993:33-34).

political loyalty of certain minority groups to the state through propagating Confucian ideals of civilised conduct as Shepherd (1993) points out. Ebrey (1996) makes a similar point to this when she asks why those who had, historically, become acculturated were so reluctant to admit to non-Han ancestry in their genealogies, and suggests that the reason 'Chinese' (*sic*) did not feel 'entirely comfortable' with the idea that others could become 'Chinese' was because of the ideology of patrilineal descent which excluded those not descended from a supposed common ancestor. The point is surely (as I put it in 1995) that local racial prejudices and cultural antagonisms (chauvinism) have always acted against larger state projects of culturalist unity. I would emphasise the depth of these local and everyday prejudices in accounting for the general lack of resentment against policies of affirmative action on behalf of ethnic minorities which Sautman (1998) finds in China. During periods of leftist policy, such as the Great Leap Forward (1958-59) and the Cultural Revolution (1966-76), local prejudices against minorities surfaced as part of a general revulsion against traditional cultural forms and the divisions of class and nationality. The atrocities suffered by minorities during these periods are well known. The flights of national groups across borders, the armed insurrections and protests which have taken place, the repression of religion, and the enforced as well as spontaneous immigration of Han settlers into minority areas, are now very well documented (Moseley 1965; Dreyer 1968; Pye 1975; Heberer 1989; see also Gladney 1991; Mackerras 1995). While Sinologists may argue whether 'race' is or is not a 'Chinese' concept (Dikoter 1997; Stafford 1993), at the felt everyday level of practical engagements prejudices of a racial kind are commonplace. The ambiguity of the phrase *minzu wenti*, referring both to national and ethnic minorities issues, is well founded in concrete facts.

None of this looks much like Pye's (1990) 'inchoate' nationalism. However, to the extent that he is correct in maintaining that 'China remains a civilisation pretending to be a nation-state', then this must pose particular problems for the transnational identities of those who, like the Hmong, are only partly within 'China' as currently territorially defined. As we have seen, *modern* conceptions of the Chinese state depend vitally upon, are predicated on, how the Hmong as well as other national minorities are defined and define themselves in relation to the territorially bounded state. But it was the integrality of Hmong (and other non-Han) society to the original *historical* constitution of the Chinese state which had concerned me when first trying to understand the apparently 'Chinese' characteristics of the Hmong cultural world presented in Northern Thailand as though they were entirely and exclusively 'Hmong' property.

Another researcher on the Hmong in Thailand once confessed to me his inability to comprehend why a people of such a simple and apparently 'primitive' lifestyle, practising shifting cultivation and with no permanent political units of a higher order than the local lineage, should be possessed of so extraordinarily a rich and complex 'culture'. Hmong society, as he saw it, was top-heavy with excess cultural baggage. Similar questions have haunted the minds of many colonial administrators and modern developers working with peoples whose 'cultural' practices appear to them an irrational block to economic progress and social enlightenment. Even Bloch (1977) talked of certain societies having 'so much social structure that it is a positive embarrassment'. Yet if a 'Hmong' social system is in some way integral to the *historical* constitution of Chinese society and the Chinese state (as indeed from a Han Chinese standpoint it must be seen to be), then the complex elaborations of their wedding ceremonies and the punctilious detail of their funeral rituals might make a perfect sort of mimetic sense, as directly reflecting the complex nature of their insertion into one of the most complex societies in the world.

And it is important to avoid reducing the complexity of historical interactions between the Hmong and Han society to over-sharp distinctions of the type Lévi-Strauss (1976), for example, suggested when he distinguished between the 'cold', historically static societies of those without writing, and the 'hot', historically dynamic and changing societies with traditions of writing and literacy. It is true that an oral tradition has been vital to the transmission of Hmong culture and the maintenance of a Hmong identity. And it is true that the cultural distinctions between themselves and the Han Chinese are expressed in conscious Hmong contrasts between their loss (lack, deprival) of a writing-system and the highly literate civilisation of the Chinese. But the Hmong, like other people like them around the borderlands of the Chinese Empire, who demonstrate a conscious awareness of the importance of writing systems and the significance of their own lack of such systems, are better seen as *a-literate* than as either definitively with a writing system or definitively without a writing system.[30]

Since the mid-eighteenth century, Hmong have frequently engaged in large-scale messianic revolts against centralised authority, often linked with the revelation of a Hmong writing system to a prophet who announces the coming of a Hmong Emperor and the establishment of a Hmong kingdom. No very adequate analysis has yet been undertaken of the social dynamics of these movements, which have taken place in China as much as in South East Asia, and in recent as well as in colonial and pre-colonial history. These repeated attempts to gain political power, imbued with ideas of royalty and sovereignty, can also be taken to contradict any over-sharp distinction between the 'egalitarian' structures of Hmong society and the 'hierarchical' political structures of state-linked Tai or feudal Chinese society. And this relationship to centralised authority, among a dispersed group of shifting cultivators, is reminiscent of Leach's (1954) classic description of the Kachin, whose ranked Tai-style chiefdoms cyclically collapsed owing to intrinsic contradictions of the social system (or in combination with infrastructural factors as Friedman in 1972 argued). Leach too was working in these Chinese borderlands areas, and perhaps trying to account for a similarly complex articulation with the social systems of neighbouring peoples of divergent cultural orientations.

So, modern definitions of the Hmong as 'Miao' are, like those of other *minzu*, integral to the constitution of the present-day territorial Chinese state, as is shown in the definition of China itself as a 'multi-national state' and the political importance attached to work with the minority 'nationalities' (*minzu gongzuo*). But there is also a historical sense in which exclusionary Chinese definitions of the Hmong (as 'Miao') have long been seen as fundamental to the original establishment of a Chinese civilization which was not conceived as clearly territorially bounded. Earlier commentators (Savina 1930; Lemoine 1972; Geddes 1976) made much of dynastic legends which described the defeat of the ancient 'Miao' as taking place immediately before the Han Chinese state was first established

---

[30] Tapp (1989). See Goody (1987) on the interface of the oral with the literate.

by the Yellow Emperor. Some have argued that the 'Miao' may well have been the very first, aboriginal inhabitants of North China, displaced into their present locations by the ever expanding pressure of the ancestors of the Han (Weins 1954). In this historical sense, the Chinese state as a historical subject is seen to be predicated on the historic primordial defeat and expulsion of the 'Miao' under whom are still officially classed the 'Hmong' of today; a kind of *sine qua non* of Han Chinese identity. In local modern Chinese 'Miao-zi' remains today in common usage as a derogatory general term for uncivilised minorities and outsiders, a positing of the 'other' in ways which may be seen to be constitutive of a unitary Han identity by denying any autonomous agency to these 'others'. As Derrida has shown from a standpoint of general theory, it can be just what is overtly excluded as secondary or minor which is, in fact, essential and prior to a definition. The cultural category of 'Miao' under which the Hmong are grouped in present-day China cannot be seen as antithetical to that of the Han Chinese, as it so often has been, but rather should be seen as dangerously supplemental to that category. In the historical relations between the Hmong and Han, we are dealing with a subtle and complex accomodation, made up of rejection and resentment, envy and desire, exclusion and re-admission, exploitation and violence, domination and resistance, the celebration and the disavowal of difference. Moreover, imaged as 'Miao', these historical and continuing inter-cultural relations have become wrought into the fabric of the modern territorial Chinese state, in such a way that the Hmong of China rarely appear visible, except in the guise of 'Miao' adornments to an enveloping Chinese habit.

Ladders and Mosaics

The analysis of the sort of questions of inter-cultural influence I am concerned with has been haunted by evolutionary and diffusionist paradigms inherited from the nineteenth century. Classic Marxian theory was able to account for the transmission of the specifically European ideas and technologies associated with capitalism through theories of imperialism and monopoly capital, and shared with the modernization theorists of the 1950s the evolutionist assumption that the adoption of such culturally specific characteristics would

accompany an inevitable transition towards more modern and
'developed' forms of socio-economic organisation.[31] The
dependency theorists of the 1960s, and more recent theorists of the
'world system', argued for a vision of the international community as
interlocked through a series of centripetal and centifugal forces
emanating from unequal concentrations of capital and power in the
metropoles, which is diffusionist in inspiration.

While anthropology, in its sustained attempt to emulate the
universalistic science of linguists, threw out diffusionist theories of
cultural change together with evolutionist paradigms of social change
early in the present century,[32] these two great paradigms of progress,
the evolutionist and diffusionist, have continued to dominate many
studies of development. If the Leninist thesis on imperialism
furthered earlier evolutionary paradigms of progress, which were
later also adopted by modernization theorists in a modified form,
theories of dependency and globalization have reflected a paradigm
which is at once older and more long-lived than the evolutionary
Social Darwinism of the nineteenth century; diffusionism.

Nor were diffusionist ideas expelled so thoroughly from the
mainstream of western anthropological theory as evolutionism was.
In religious studies this can be seen particularly clearly. Catherine
Bell (1989) has described how the first stage of modern studies in the
history of religion was dominated by Redfield's view of the schism
between the 'Great Tradition' of religious knowledge, maintained by
literate urban elites, and the 'Little Tradition' of the rural peasantry.
We might see such bald dichotomies between elite and folk culture
as a late reflection of the *diffusionist* vision of the spread and
expansion of 'high' cultures and their absorption of local traditions.
Whether such paradigms of general hegemonic processes concern the
Sanskritisation or Sinicisation of local traditions,[33] or are used to
describe the medieval absorption of superstition by the Church

---

[31] Of course this kind of progressivism was a general sociological assumption
shared by Weber and Durkheim besides Marx; see Roxborough (1979), and Giddens
(1971, 1991) on the problems of 'secularization' theory.

[32] See Stocking (1987).

[33] Great/Little Tradition dichotomies were reflected for India by Srinivas' (1952)
distinctions between All-India and Local Hinduism, also in Marriott's (1955)
description of processes of 'universalization' and 'parochialization'.

(Thomas 1971), they are alike predicated on a common diffusionist outlook related to the basic theorem that as culture expands, earlier 'relic' forms may be found surviving in outlying patches, remote or isolated geographical areas, as was argued particularly in the case of linguistic innovations (e.g. Sapir 1913).[34] Dichotomies of this type have seemed perhaps peculiarly appropriate to the Chinese context, where the rupture of cities from the surrounding countryside is of such obvious political significance.[35]

In Bell's 'first-stage' position, we can see the continuing importance, throughout the 1950s, of diffusionist theories and hypotheses, even in an anthropology supposedly purged of such influences. The influence of Redfield has really been quite considerable, informing the attitudes of generations of American scholars of religion and culture to the present day, and particularly those of Chinese religious and cultural specialists. 'Chinese folk religion' or the 'popular religion of China' has become a widely accepted academic construct, despite serious doubts about the validity of any over-arching category of 'Chinese religion' (Feuchtwang 1991) which Hmong religious practices in China, as we shall see, illustrate.

The revival of Elias' work on civilisation, heralded by Bourdieu's (1984) analysis of class and consumption, formed another striking illustration of the continuing power and attraction of diffusionist hypotheses to a renewed concern with global intercultural influences and the materiality of cultural expressions. Bourdieu himself, in a

---

[34] Bell brilliantly describes how this 'first-stage' position in the analysis of religious cultures gave way to a 'second-stage' position concerned with underlying structural similarities and correspondences between the variant forms of a single tradition. Bell's 'second-stage' position is essentially structuralist, to which Dumont's vision of Hinduism can be assimilated besides the works she cites, of Tambiah on Buddhism and Freedman on Chinese religion. And Bell points to a current, 'third-stage position' marked by an interest in the emergence of order itself, characterised by a ('post-modern') fragmentation of formerly coherent images, and expressed in a more detailed emphasis on the particular forms of ritual activity in which social order is constructed or expressed, such as pilgrimage, carnival, and possession.

[35] As Tanaka (1991) remarks, Dumont elevated the structural coherence and homogeneity assumed by an earlier generation of functionalists, from the realm of social structure where they had falsely assumed it to lie, onto an ideal plane of metaphorical construction where it could no longer be falsified.

deconstruction of Arnold's (1869) thesis that culture entails the 'pursuit of perfection', has analysed the cultural discriminations of 'taste' in which social differentiation is expressed in France, demonstrating how appropriations of material culture may express social identity. On a grander scale the processes of perfectibility and emulation he describes are reflected by Elias' magisterial work on the adoption of courtly etiquette by the French bourgeoisie, in a way which forced an ever more frenetic revision and adoption of new forms of etiquette, speech and costume by members of the elite in order to 'distinguish' themselves from these apeing commoners, an account which seems to provide an explanation (albeit an elite-focused one) of fashion itself. In both Bourdieu and Elias we find visions of the adoption and accomodation of superior forms of culture by inferior orders which echo diffusionist models of cultural radiation without fully subscribing to them.

And it would surely be tempting to depict the shaven forehead and queue of the Manchu dynasty retained to this day by some Hmong men, the archaic Chinese forms of Hmong greetings and prostrations, the clumsy recitation of traditional Chinese forms of verse at Hmong weddings, the Confucian idioms of propriety and of correct women's conduct, of the behaviour appropriate to guests and visitors, which survive today among Hmong both in Thailand and in China, in some such terms as these; as evidence of the long slow march southwards of the dominant, conquering Chinese civilization (emphasised by scholars of the old school),[36] and its inexorable devouring of neighbouring, indigenous traditions; some doomed rat-race attempt, on the part of a marginalised minority, to catch up with the manners and customs of a people envied for their power and splendour, grandeur and might—doomed because, by the time the periphery successfully adopts the distinguishing characteristics of the metropolitans, the centre has inevitably already changed out of all recognition, forcing renewed distinctions and marginality on the hordes hammering at the gates of privilege. And indeed this is partly what an analysis of Hmong society and culture in terms purely of a dominating model of 'Sinicisation' such as Skinner's[37] would lead

---

[36] Fitzgerald (1935); Weins (1954); Moseley (1973); also Harrell (1995).

[37] Stevan Harrell (personal observation, 10 August 1999).

one to; the Hmong as people who throughout history have vainly sought to emulate (what they saw as the) the cultural characteristics of the Han Chinese civilization, but who have always been defeated by the passage of time, ethnic prejudice, and above all the dominant economic forms which have marginalised their way of life and social customs. An unadulterated model of sheer cultural domination would emerge, and of consumer complicity in that domination and passivity in the acceptance of its superiority.

Historians, economists, political scientists, anthropologists and sociologists from China itself do not assent to such an overtly diffusionist form of logic, although diffusionist ideas sometimes colour their explanations of social change. Usually basing themselves on classic evolutionary typologies of technology and social organisation, derived out of Morgan through Engels, they tend to assume that social systems such as that of the Hmong must simply be cases of arrested historical development; that in the long ladder of inevitable individual progress towards monogamous forms of partnership, the nuclear family, permananent cultivation, and a class society, the Hmong somehow simply got stuck at some earlier stage, characterised by shifting agriculture and a 'tribal' form of social organisation. This is explanation enough (as such evolutionists see it), of the survival among the Hmong of other 'quaint' forms of early Chinese social organisation and custom, such as the love-duets sung by courting couples, or the right of a man's younger brother to marry his widow. Indeed Granet (1930) wrote of such antiphonal love-songs, still common among the Hmong, as among the earliest customs reported in China, and many Sinological commentators have couched their descriptions of Hmong society in terms of how the Hmong still retain archaic vestiges of ancient Chinese social custom and have found their main interest in them for this reason. Of course, despite their historic differences, 'evolutionism' and 'diffusionism' were in fact complementary philosophies; diffusionism does in space what evolutionism does in time. 'Survivals' in evolutionary theory are 'relic forms' for diffusionism. The 'mosaic' of diffusion depends on the 'ladder' of evolution (Friedman 1995); only the historical sequence of the rungs has been denied by diffusionism. In this 'evolutionistic' view, the Hmong and the Han started from the same stage of social development; only the Han progressed, while the Hmong and others in present-day China did not.

A variant, but more optimistic, form of the diffusionist approach in general, has been constituted by the work of those concerned with the analysis of sub-culture.[38] Pioneers of cultural studies originally argued that the styles of subcultures might represent a structuralist-like attempt to resolve 'contradictions' in the parent culture, or an imperfect ('symbolic') appropriation of dominant rhetoric through the reversal or ironic exaggeration of cultural signs, as in the 'Back to Africa' theme of the Rastafarians, the aggressive proletarianism of the skinhead.[39] Subcultures have been taken to express a kind of subversion, through parody, of dominant meanings and intentions, a mockery and appropriation of conventionally authenticated symbols for purposes quite other than those they were intended for, and meanings quite other than those they were supposed to represent, like the mod adoption of suits; a 'trans-coding' or re-signification ('Black is beautiful', 'Queer Theory') of meanings which is only made possible by the infinite extensibility of meaning, its lack of any final fixity or closure, stemming as Hall (1997) sees it from the arbitrary Saussaurian nature of the sign.

And these generally positive views of the power of symbolic resistance by 'subaltern' groups have been insisted on by anthropologists rightly uncomfortable with the passive roles attributed to cultural actors by theorists of economic and cultural globalisation and its supposedly 'homogenising' effects. In the field of material culture, Miller (1987) gave many examples of successful active appropriations, such as the Italian development of the motor scooter as the 'feminine equivalent of the more macho motor bike'. Yet such forms of symbolic resistance (if that is what they are) often remain merely 'symbolic', in the sense of ineffectual, in relation to a dominant or hegemonic rhetoric, and may as easily be read as evidence of the expansion of a dominating culture as of the successful appropriation or 'sublation' of a part of that culture by a less powerful group.[40] Irony is a powerful weapon, but it does not

---

[38] For example, Stuart Hall (1976).

[39] See Hebdige (1979:37).

[40] The Hegelian notion of sublation refers to the reappropriation of the externalised other. In Miller's (1987) formulation, society as subject attempts to reappropriate its externalised mass cultural expressions as object from which it has become alienated.

crumble the walls of the Tower unaided; and creative recontextualisations do not necessarily amount to positive resistance, as Miller (1987) wisely remarked. It is elsewhere we must look for real agency, in concrete assertions and choices of specific identities differentiated from those of others who are exploitative, dominating and masterful.

In this more 'positive' reading of the diffusionist spread of culture, the adoption of forms of culture seen as 'superior', by those who occupy inferior social positions, is interpreted as an act of agency by the members of a subordinate group, rather than as an act of domination by a superior group.

It might for example be tempting to interpret the Hmong use of a form of geomantic divination which has always been seen as uniquely Chinese[41] as some such attempt as this—an attempt actively to appropriate, or to subvert, elements of a dominant Chinese idiom. Such geomantic symbols and motifs (of the dragon, of imperial authority, in particular) have also often been used in the actual messianic uprisings of the Hmong against the state. This Hmong use of 'Chinese' geomancy, it could be argued, is similar to the claims which the local Tai leaders of messianic rebellions in Thailand, Laos and Burma laid to the very Hindu-Buddhist cosmo-mythological symbolic systems which legitimised the reigning monarchs they sought to overturn.[42] And this ability to adopt and reinterpret the symbols of a dominating culture might then be taken to show that the apparently antiquated 'Chinese' features of 'Hmong' social organisation and culture in fact demonstrated some historic attempt at *resistance* to, or ironic subversion of, the centralised moral authority associated with the Chinese state. Then these apparently Chinese features of Hmong social organisation and culture would exemplify a *counter*-hegemonic tendency (rather than an example of the successful domination of Hmong culture by the Chinese, and a Hmong attempt to emulate Chinese manners), of the kind which

---

[41] Aijmer (1968); Freedman (1966, 1968); Feuchtwang (1975).

[42] See Turton and Tanabe (1984); Keyes (1977).

ethnographers of China have liked to emphasise in their analyses of local responses to state power.[43]

But there are serious theoretical problems with the sort of optimistic and positive approaches which have been adopted, towards forms of what might be interpreted as symbolic resistance, by analysts uncomfortable with the notion of the inevitable domination of a world culture, and particularly where they have been adopted through a lens of historical retrospection. Were the cargo cults really a sign of native vitality and resistance to European domination, as Worsley (1968) interpreted them; 'an early effort to grasp the bases of the colonial production of value, and to redirect it to the well-being of the dominated' (Comaroff and Comaroff 1992:261)? Or should the classic cargo cults be seen as a tragic example of the irrresistibility of even the symbols of a global European domination, which have continued to inexorably absorb and assimilate, incorporate and devour all forms of local knowledge and culture? Did the indigenous Indians under Spanish colonization *really*, as De Certeau (1984) claims, subvert the laws, rituals and representations imposed on them 'not by rejecting or altering them, but by using them with respect to ends and references foreign to the system they had no choice but to accept'? Or did the South American appropriation of the figure of the devil (Taussig 1980) merely reflect the success of an otherwise inadequate Catholic critique of capitalist accumulation? Were the Tswana 'style wars' in South Africa, in which 'fantastic fashions...flourished on the frontiers', *really* an attempt at 'redeploying the very signs that the colonizers imprinted on the supple surfaces of their lives', as the Comaroffs (1992:43) fashionably present it? Or were they more a sign of the power of those signs? Does the Congolese *sapeur* consuming Western designer clothes really represent a 'challenge to the political order' (Friedman 1992), or a symbolic acquiescence in a process of cultural imposition?

The generality of this theoretical problem is shown by Judith Butler's (1993) consideration of the film Paris Is Burning, where in the black drag performances we witness 'a subject who repeats and

---

[43]   See, for example, Anagnost (1985) on the emergence of a modern-day imperial pretender in Hunan, or the legends of imperial violence and terror of the state recorded among the Cantonese by Watson (1991).

mimes the legitimating norms by which it itself has been degraded'. How are we to account for this ambivalent appropriation and subversion, she asks—it is not *first* an appropriation and *then* a subversion; 'Sometimes it is both at once; sometimes it remains caught in an irresolvable tension, and sometimes a fatally unsubversive appropriation takes place'. Her argument is, though, that this is not an appropriation of dominant culture in order to remain subordinated by its terms, but an appropriation that seeks to 'make over the terms of that domination, a making over which is itself a kind of agency'.

It would be extremely problematic—and illegitimate—to depict the Hmong incorporation of Chinese deities (such as that of the 'Fourth Mandarin' in Hmong mortuary rituals) as evidence of some deep-rooted ironic Hmong resistance to, or subversion of, the emblems of a dominating culture. This would in fact be an *optimistic* reinterpretation of a *diffusionist* view of the universalising spread of culture. It would be equally problematic to depict this incorporation of Chinese symbols as some unadulterated example of successful Han cultural hegemony. This would be a *pessimistic*, classically *diffusionist* view, echoed in much 'world systems' theory, denying any agency to the Hmong in this historical process of interaction and exchange. And it can hardly be acceptable, nowadays, to discuss such intercultural borrowings purely in the light of the *survival* among the Hmong, their retention, of some archaic form of social organisation and associated forms of culture which the ancestors of the Hmong may have shared with the ancestors of the Han, and which may have predated their division from other Chinese peoples and their separation into ethnically distinct peoples. This would be an *evolutionistic* view.

Neither theories of evolutionistic survivals from a common origin, nor of ironic subversions expressive of resistance, nor of an unquestioned cultural dominance and hegemony, can adequately account for those cultural forms which the Hmong share with the Han despite explicit attempts, by Hmong individuals and in ritual texts, to distinguish (and therefore construct) a Hmong cultural identity in terms of, and by contrast with, a cultural identity defined as, and assumed to be, Han—which has historically opposed them, and is well understood to have done so. Yet these diffusionist and evolutionist paradigms of social change, the 'mosaic' and the 'ladder' views as Friedman (1995) has called them, must play an important part in our examination of the intricate relationship of Hmong society with the Chinese state, since these paradigms of cultural exchange and appropriation, dominance and adoption, continue to haunt so much of current anthropological and developmental theory, and have thereby largely determined current understandings of the Hmong, and others. Friedman's argument is that the evolutionist 'ladder' and the cultural relativist 'mosaic' have tended to be replaced by a rather uncomfortable vision of 'leaky mosaics', of not wholly bounded cultures interacting with each other in various ways. This clearly is not a satisfactory situation; I hope that by examining some of the particular contexts in which such structural processes of cultural appropriation and resistant autonomy have taken place, we may achieve a better understanding of the management of identity in a situation where particular forms of culture are marked as 'superior'.

Appropriating Rhetoric

Returning to the question of the transmission and diffusion, acceptance/rejections, of dominant Han ideas and culturalist models of correct, 'civilised' conduct, in China and throughout Chinese society, which has posed as many problems for historians of Chinese society concerned with the communication of literate neo-Confucian models of conduct across local cultural and linguistic barriers[44] as it has for those working with non-Han ethnic minorities in China—we can see that the near-impossibility of baldly evaluating any 'cultural influence' as *either* a form of imposition, *or* a form of appropriation by a subaltern group, is the most pressing of all questions in the general understanding of cultural discourse. To what extent is it possible to resist a dominating rhetoric in a society of which one is a part, or in which one is assumed to be a part? What *are* the possibilities of resistance to a hegemonic set of beliefs and practices, and the limits to the power and extent of such an ideology? At what point can we say, this is *not* the imposition of a dominating rhetoric; this *is* the successful appropriation and subversion of parts of that

---

[44] See for example Johnson (1985).

rhetoric by a disadvantaged group? And yet, no answers of this kind may be possible; it may be precisely in the sort of inter-ethnic spaces examined in this book, and in their creative re-workings and refashionings, that the sites of critical agency are to be located, as Judith Butler (1993) finds for gender relations. The task of looking for these answers however is imperative indeed if she is right in claiming that agency may be found precisely in the 'constrained appropriation of regulatory law', that it is immanent to power rather than a 'relation of external opposition' to it..

Culler (1988) noted that regulation may 'mask itself by producing discourse which is apparently opposed to it but sustains the network of power'.[45] In this sense the historical painting of the Miao and others by Chinese texts as rebellious subjects has contributed to their emergence as solidary identities in the multi-national modern nation-state of China (Litzinger 1995), and to the constitution of an 'unmarked' Han identity defined in terms of striking contrasts of this kind.[46] Yet not all this is rhetoric; there were constant 'Miao' rebellions in Chinese history, and there is a keen sense of culturally 'Hmong' identity among a part of those marked as 'Miao' today. In Culler's remark the notion of 'discourse' is seminal, specifically in Foucault's sense which transcended the dichotomy of science from ideology, or as Bloch (1991) would have put it, between revealing and concealing types of knowledge ('cognition' and 'ideology'). The Gramscian sense of hegemony similarly transcended the limitations of ideology to a particular class, group or sector.[47] The central issue here, of the limitations and extent of a dominant cultural discourse— and what could have been more all-encompassing or inescapable than the Neo-Confucian rhetoric of late imperial China, or the rhetoric of socialist modernisation similarly implicating the state, with its emphasis on respect for conventional authority and propriety of conduct?[48]—was most literally translated into anthropologese by

---

[45] Cf. A.P. Cohen (1982) on how marginalised cultures elaborate their culture as a bulwark against central domination.

[46] Blum (1994) in Harrell (forthcoming).

[47] So that 'ideology' is now generally used to refer to more implicit, less 'contestable', assumptions.

[48] So much so that Borges' example of a totally arbitrary classification system had to be 'Chinese'. See Harrell (1995) on the Chinese 'civilizing project'.

Bloch (1977), in an early and much recited article on relative notions of time, where he discussed the common Durkheimian assumption that knowledge is socially determined, that forms of knowledge must vary between societies and cultures.

Bloch raised the question of the extent to which it was—at all - possible to stand back, to stand aside for a moment from the constrictions of one's own language, and question its basic assumptions in (what Bloch supposed to be) a 'scientific' manner; in a manner which would reveal the genuine workings of the world as empirically experienced through practice, in such a way that one might change society. There must, therefore, be two kinds of consciousness; an enlightened, scientific, pragmatic one, and another one befuddled by cultural and social conventions. For Foucault this stepping outside one's cultural idiom was not a real possibility; ultimately it appeared impossible to avoid the infinite dispersals of a 'discourse', and Culler found problems, therefore, with understanding why this essentially pessimistic view should ever have been heralded as a revolutionary statement.[49] But in Bloch's argument, it was almost impossible to understand why any social change could occur unless one assumed that some questioning of or resistance to a dominating consciousness was possible.[50] I am not concerned here so much with how Hmong may themselves be able to 'step outside' a cultural discourse defined as 'Hmong' and evaluate it critically, but with the role of Hmong social agency itself in the context of a larger and more powerful rhetoric of civility associated with the Chinese state.

Bloch's early critique of cultural relativism posed the same question Giddens defined as the main sociological problem of the century; the problem of agency and structure, which Bloch, Bourdieu, Sahlins and others can all be seen as attempting to resolve

---

[49] As Hall and many others have noted, for Foucault the subject cannot be located outside discourse (meaningfully, that is).

[50] Indeed Derrida turned the tables on Foucault in his critique of Foucault's (1967) attempt to analyse madness in the very language of western reason which had constituted the notion of madness in the first place ('*Nothing* within this language, and *no one* among those who speak it, can escape...' Derrida 1978:34).

in various (sometimes very similar) ways.[51] All these theoretical attempts point in the same direction, mediating between strategy and rule, or ideology and practice, through notions of the habitus or structuration, yet none has been wholly satisfactory. A general denial of agency has haunted almost all the major theories of action and socialization, the deterministic 'meta-narratives' of the past, which form our own recent cultural baggage.[52] Without wishing either to go into a history of theories of the person and self, or at this point to examine in more detail those 'local structure of desire and identity' in which selfhood may be produced (Friedman 1990), my point here is that although these dominant grand paradigms of the ultimate causes of human action (the Freudian, the Marxian, the Darwinian, for example) are essentially incompatible, they have had the similar effect of absolving actors of ultimate responsibility for their actions. Hence the concern to resuscitate 'agency'. Determinist theories can only be considered to be compatible in a very weak sense; that there are a number of constraints of different kinds and natures on the unconditional freedom of human action, all of which working together may decide its final course. The general dominance of theories of action which have sought to explain action in terms of inevitable constraints has led to an overwhelming over-determination of human action, so that it may only be in choices of a utilitarian kind between different kinds of constraint that any genuine liberty is allowed for. And here the role of 'individual' decision, motivation or moral responsibility is very minimal indeed.

Of course there have also been rebellions against the yoke of determinism[53] in the name of voluntarism. It is because of its claim to a virtual monopoly on theories of agency that empiricist utilitarian

---

[51] Appiah (1991), insisting on a separability of the discourses of structure and agency, also remarks this agon of structure and agency as 'perhaps' the central issue in this century's humanist criticism.

[52] Perhaps only the phenomenological tradition of philosophy, and the symbolic interactionists in social theory, have attempted anything like an adequate theorisation of agency.

[53] See Sallnow on how social theories stressing the 'collectivity' as opposed to those stressing the 'individual' reflect Durkheim's vision of *homo duplex*, caught between (utilitarian) self-interest and (idealist) moral values of society; a duality we can find also of course in the Freudian distinction of the unconscious from the conscious and super-ego, and in much older formulations of the angelic and bestial sides of the personality, the Cartesian opposition of reason to the physical senses.

rationalism has become the main dogma of modern science, and the notion of the utilitarian actor, rationally maximising his perceived advantages, proved so central to the voluntarist tendency of the social sciences.[54] Here agency is commonly assumed to reside in simple choices between alternatives, rather than in the 'constrained appropriation' of norms Butler speaks of.

Philosophical utilitarianism has been criticised on the grounds of its consequentialism (analysing the nature of actions solely in terms of their results) and lack of consideration of values such as social justice and integrity, as well as on various other grounds (see Strawson and Williams 1973). The utilitarian model of economic man has also been well criticised within anthropology, mostly on the (Durkheimian) grounds of its neglect of the wider social and cultural context in which individual decision-making is thought to take place, and the specificity of the utilitarian model to the western liberal tradition which produced it. The notion of a utilitarian actor, deciding whether to conform to a genetic or a psychological imperative, is clearly absurd. This 'ego-centred' notion of a calculating actor, gifted with a perfect knowledge of the probable outcomes of his actions, and detached from any socio-cultural anchorage, has always sat somewhat uncomfortably within more general, Durkheimian, sociological assumptions of a 'false consciousness' among actors on which the rationale for social science has classically been based. How is it possible for an actor to behave rationally, to take decisions which entail choices between alternative courses of action in terms of their probable returns, if he is at once mystified about the deeper causes and consequences of his own actions? How easy is it for an agent to simply choose between a Hmong, Yi, or Han identity, as much of the earlier work on 'optative' ethnicity suggested?

It is not really necessary to have recourse to theories of dual consciousness as Bloch did, a realistic consciousness contrasting with a more culturally determined one, to resolve this sort of question about how 'rational action' fits with 'mystification'. The sensible sociological answer must be that it is perfectly possible to have a good idea of the immediate results of a given course of action,

---

[54] Iris Murdoch (1992:47) rightly remarks that some form of utilitarianism 'is probably now the most widely and instinctively accepted philosophy of the western world'.

while remaining unaware of its wider implications or more long-term consequences. That is, that there are inevitable limits to our knowledge of the causes and effects of our actions, whch social science might ideally help to remove. Merton's concept of the 'latent' functions of social action has been elaborated in sociology through the doctrine of the 'unintended consequences' of action which contribute to the forward course of historical change, in such a way as to seemingly bridge the divide between the voluntaristic notion of an omniscient utilitarian actor and the more deterministic notion of a mystified victim of false consciousness and 'ideology'.

In this kind of still largely functionalist framework, typically taking effects to be causes, one might say that it is precisely these unintended consequences of social action, escaping individual consciousness, which go to constitute that part of society which is forever external to the individual, the 'social facts', the moral forces of society which constrain, determine, or act as limiting conditions on, the freedom of individual actions. Of course, any social action may have effects which are of a wide variety of consequences besides social ones, and all these effects can be seen as potentially contributing to further constraints on individual decision. The individual, then, can (in this functionalist view) calculate rationally what action to take only up to a limited extent, for he is perpetually constrained by the wider ('moral') constraints of culture and society, which have themselves been historically formed out of both the intended and the unintended consequences of individual actions. Yet individual action too can impinge on and alter these wider social constraints, again either intentionally or unintentionally. So we have a functionalist circle, characteristic of some theories of socialization, in which cultural values become embedded in the individual through socialization, and within this magic circle of values and enactment, constraining code and creative performance, both the rational utilitarian actor and the mystified victim of false consciousness can sit, if not very comfortably.[55] Essentially, Hmong agents continue to be reproduced as Hmong, Han as Han, in a way which we already

---

[55] Surely we have been right to be careful not to confuse interpretive understandings (*verstehen*) with causal explanation, (manifest) intention with (latent) effect, but we may need also to go back to older physical distinctions of final from efficient, material and formal causes (to say nothing of first causes).

know does not always happen at the level of individual agency, and which is also belied by the hybrid nature of much of the Hmong cultural heritage.

Interpretation and Authority

What should particularly concern us in any ethnographic attempt to demonstrate the production of cultural differences, is the extent to which this, after all, somewhat rough-and-ready, post-hoc, thesis about the consequences of actions which succeed in escaping the intentions or motivations of their protagonists, can be compatible with more general theories of meaning, such as those ushered in by 'reception theory' and 'reader-response criticism',[56] in which the unintended meanings of a text have been analysed in a somewhat equivalent way. Can it be said that the meanings of a text, of a cultural form, a cultural product, escape the intentions of their authors (and eventually receivers) in a similar way to those consequences of social action which in general evade the intentions of their performers? Could the Hmong employment of a distinctively 'Chinese' form of geomantic practice in such a way as to express their differences from the Han, and their assertion of a prior right to the lands of China, be seen in terms of a kind of historical drift, in which the cultural actions of Han Chinese somehow come adrift from their original moorings, giving rise to unforeseen consequences which then rebound with new meanings on their originators?

This kind of conflation of meanings with consequences is more or less what Ricoeur first suggested in 1971, where textualisation was seen as liberating the text from the intentions of its author much as actions become dissociated from their agents and develop new consequences, especially actions like cultural works, which through this 'distanciation', can transcend the social conditions of their production and like texts develop new referents, to constitute 'new worlds'.[57] Meanings, like effects, are never 'fixed', and are always

---

[56] Eagleton; Tompkins (1980).

[57] However, it should be recognised that this is itself a metaphor, since meanings may be effects, but they are not the only ones, while effects may gather their own multiple meanings. If significances are intentions, these require interpretations, and a social act may be variously interpreted as well as having its own results.

subject to future resignifications. Miller (1987) employs this conflation when he suggests that just as a text is not reducible to the intentions of its author, so the emergence of a material object from a world of capitalist or state capitalist production does not mean that it necessarily represents the interests of capital.

The great problem here is, that while postmodern and interpretivist aesthetic theories of the free-floating meanings of signifiers which have followed from this are tied up with linguistic theories of ambiguity, and notions of endlessly different creative interpretations by future readers and receivers, who in a sense re-author the texts which are given them (which is an *affirmation* of the power of individual agency), as Hmong might be said to 're-author' Chinese or indeed their own cultural texts, the sociological theory of unintended consequences is on the contrary bound up with notions of moral and social constraints on both the actions and understandings of these future individual actors, who are thereby largely condemned forever to reproduce cultural and social forms whose significance they cannot fully understand (a *denial* of the validity of agency).

We do need to distinguish the original meanings, whether of individual texts or of conventional cultural symbols, whether consciously intended and as such amenable to what Ricoeur called a classical hermeneutics of recovery, or implicit and unrecognised and therefore appropriate for a critical rather than persuasive 'hermeneutics of suspicion' (Gadamer 1984), from meanings as they are understood and received. It is only in the case of an originally intended and conscious meaning (although this too may be subject to and depend on variable interpretations), that the meaning is by definition 'rational' in that the ends-means relationship is intrinisic to the text or cultural form in which it has been expressed, and in that sense exclusive of other intentions, capable of formulating an authorised or orthodox version, an originary 'context' of the type a hermeneutics of recovery might indeed reveal. It is often this originary context which ethnologists have been in search of, an authoritative version for example of 'the Hmong village' located in a particular setting, of the type which it was for a long time assumed that Margaret Mead and Malinowski had provided. It is this notion of ethnographic authority which has recently been so signally challenged, and this problem which a comparative study of Hmong society in the very different contexts of China and South East Asia poses. This, we should be clear, derives from the notion of an *originary* context, associated with that romanticism Susan Stewart (1993) saw as pointing towards a 'lost point of origin', an imaginary point before the splitting of the signifier and signified.

But from the point of view of the 'first author' of a text, or an innovatory social actor, it would seem that the problem must be one of how to gain some extent of control and limit the theoretically infinite future interpretations of the meaning of a *text*, or the unlimited ramificatory consequences of one's *actions* (and their interpretations!).[58] For after all, we are speaking about the same thing in one respect; the creation of a cultural *text* is a *social* act, and it is the *interpretation* of social action which is at issue when we discuss either its manifest or latent functions. And in considering this problem we begin to move towards the imagination of a genuine *theory of effects*; towards an economy of meaning which may be at the same time a rhetoric of power. We arrive, then, at the realm of how it is possible for the authorial self to *control* meanings and limit their possible range of interpretations, how we ensure that our actions do not have consequences which we do not desire, which is a question of power.[59] To give a concrete example taken from the narrative of nation-states, to what extent might socialist rhetoric be seen as representing a challenge to the authority of the state in China, rather than reinforcing the authority of its enunciating subject as is always supposed?

From an *authoral* point of view,[60] poor Shakespeare could not ensure that his dramas would not be interpreted in a Freudian way, or in the light of postcolonial theory; I cannot be sure that the words I speak will not be taken 'out of context'.[61] And then, given this lack of control over future revisions of our meanings and consequences of our acts, what becomes of authorial creativity, of our Chomskyian performative capacity to endlessly innovate and create new

---

[58] The fear here is the fear of the 'anarchic self' of which Michaels (1980) accused the American pragmatists, and Peirce; see below.

[59] Compare Bloch (1975) on political rhetoric, Bernstein (1975) on restricted codes.

[60] By 'authoral' I am returning to the root of the word which fuses the notion of 'author' with that of 'authority'.

[61] See Pease's (1992) discussion of readings of the Prospero-Caliban bond.

utterances, novel works of art, or original forms of social action, if all action and intention is subject to such future revision or even censorship, such unpredictable horizons of expectation?

The fear expressed here is a fear of what Eco (1992) calls 'unlimited semiosis', a terror of the 'anarchic self' (Michaels 1980) infinitely re-authoring texts, a fear of utter subjectivity and complete indeterminacy of meaning. Texts, it seems, *must* have some determinate meanings, or else anything could be inferred! But Michaels imputes this generalised fear of the indeterminacy of meanings to the assumption of a mentalist, 'Cartesian model' of a completely autonomous self, reacting to a completely autonomous text (rather than for example the more 'dialogic' encounter of text with reader preferred by Bakhtin). It is this model of the self, as he argues, that we must get away from, and which Peirce's own argument that the self is *inferred*, is itself a sign, leads away from. The self (which must be deciphered) is itself a text, also embedded in a system of signs; it is never radically free to impose its own meanings on any and all texts (Michaels 1980).[62] This book may in a sense be said to be concerned with deciphering a Hmong self, or a Hmong sense of self, but we need to realise that this is a work which individual Hmong agents may also be engaged in. We need also to be acutely aware of the differences between an identity defined as 'Hmong', and an identity defined as 'Miao'. Since Miao identity, if we may be so bold, is itself a text embedded in a larger system of signs associated with the Chinese state enterprise, it may seem reasonable, as Michaels argued, that we should try not to represent historical Miao identity as some kind of totally autonomous Consciousness interpreting and playing on a separable 'Chinese' text with complete freedom. Indeed, it would seem to make more sense to look at how constructions of a 'Miao' identity are immanent in a rhetoric of Chinese powerfulness, rather than forming the kind of 'relation of external opposition' painted by both previous ethnographers and Chinese historical texts.

---

[62] Drawing attention to the sociological attack on the author by Foucault and Barthes, Miller (1987) too pointed out how the rejection of the individualistic, autonomous liberal subject tended to become a denial of agency.

Beyond Mentalism

Certainly we would not want to be accused of Cartesian mentalism in our approaches to this problem.We can trace the modernist privileging of Reason most clearly in early psychoanalytic theory (the reasonable Conscious against the irrational, but motivating, Unconscious) and in the general triumph of utilitarianism, predicated on assumptions of clear, rational goals and purposes, in the natural and social sciences. In the repressive model of the self we find in Freud, the 'play' of the unconscious must be controlled, as free expression must be limited in the repressive model of the state. These repressive models, privileging the rational and sovereign, are utterly different from the model of the creative, responsible self we may find for example in Bakhtin. The kind of cultural phenomenology which has explicitly opposed this privileging of reason represents a deliberate attempt to move beyond the 'mentalism' of past approaches to its embeddedness in social action (Csordas 1994).

As Charles Taylor (1993) put it, to move away from the notion of the 'mentalist Individual' we must see the agent as *engaged in practices, not just* the subject of representations. Hence the reintroduction of 'the body and the other' as against the presumption of a 'monological Consciousness', and hence the recognition of the inarticulacy of much understanding, that rules are not necessarily the thoughts of actors (Taylor 1993). It does follow from this, though, that agency cannot be entirely located in the realm of practical engagement with which such tacit and inarticulate understandings are associated; there is also a realm of imaginative counter-factuality which has not been fully considered, but which I give examples of in Part III of this book.

Eco (1992) somewhat plaintively appeals for more attention to the 'intention of the text', as opposed either to the 'original intention of the author' or the 'intention of the interpreter' which he himself had previously advocated. Yet how to arrive at this *intention operis*, this 'threshold situation where Mr. Wordsworth was no longer an empirical person and not yet a mere text', without some sort of appeal to *total context* (which is necessarily open-ended, and not limited to the 'originary')? Eco's own answer to the problem of finding criteria to *limit* interpretation, or rather what he calls *over-interpretation*, the 'unlimited semiosis' he traces to Peirce's notion of the endless transformation of interpretant into sign or representamen, is in fact largely contextual; he appeals to the *consensus of the community* which Peirce had invoked, and similarly to Gadamer's notion of an *'interpretive tradition'* (Eco 1992) Ethnographers need to take such claims very seriously, for as they have appealed to theories of the text, so textual specialists have largely appealed back to the social 'contexts' in which ethnographers are supposed to have specialised.

Michaels was surely right to advise us not to fear the endless creativity of interpretations, the ultimate lack of control by an authoral self taken to be a kind of disembodied Consciousness. But Michaels still assumed a merely individual self, engaged with a particular text, whose capacity to create entirely novel contexts must by definition be limited, and here the role of an intersubjective imagination which may be fundamentally non-intellectual is not considered. If however we free Consciousness from 'the individual' altogether—by locating it for example in a playful realm of cultural production—we can imagine that *future* contexts might indeed be boundless and without closure, without that terror which goes with the assumption of an isolated consciousness losing control over its products, and that 'Chineseness' might indeed be reinterpreted in radically different and novel ways through such means.

Representation and Agency

Responsibility and human agency cannot be not be so easily dismissed as deterministic theory would have had it; both the post-modern concern with questions of 'voice' and the concern with 'empowerment' in development discourse have reflected an awareness of this. It is now a commonplace to note how authoritative written ethnographies, validated by reference to the authenticity of fieldwork experience (their originary 'contexts'), have tended to conceal the collaborative way in which academic narratives are arrived at, their 'polyphonic' production and plural authorship (Clifford 1988). As Spencer (1997) notes, Marx's 'They cannot represent themselves, they must be represented', despite its use in Said's 1978 *Orientalism*, was not actually about writing books. But writing books is still, of course, part of an authoritative historical rhetoric which has denied agency to those defined as 'other', politically and textually.[63] An ethnography of this sort, therefore, concerned with portraying peoples who have both represented themselves in particular ways and been represented by the authoritative political rhetoric of modern Chinese historiography, runs a double danger of downplaying the *capabilities* of Hmong agents which can only be resolved by attempting to incorporate as much of the original voices of Hmong and Han villagers as is possible.[64]

The 'crisis of representation' discussed at the end of the 1980s was originally seen to arise from an uncertainty about 'adequate means of decribing social reality', in the light of the collapse of past paradigms and grand meta-narratives (Marcus and Fisher 1986; (Lyotard 1979). Even in the idea that there could be a 'crisis' of representation, however, representation was still generally assumed to evoke a referential context, a 'presence' rooted in the kind of empirically experienced reality (there ARE people out there we speak of or for, this statue is a representation OF a man) which theories of language and meaning have consistently questioned (cf. Rorty 1991; Taylor 1995). The main concern in critiques of interpretivism (Spencer 1997) continued to be a *realist* one, of whether a given representation (say, Mead's or Malinowski's) is an 'accurate' one or a distancing, 'distorting' one. And the only solution to such questions (besides linguistic convention) has to be a direct comparison between the representation and the object it purpots (we assume) to represent, so that the 'object' represented (the concept, the Idea, the landscape) thereby gains a spurious authenticity in relation to its various 'representations' (the landscape painting), rather as interpretations may be thought to infinitely recede from their original contexts. This, then, has to be an interpretation of the facts to be judged as any other, since those facts are only available to us through interpretation, but we do need to privilege the voices and

---

[63] The ambiguity noted for our concept of 'representation' (that is, its political or symbolic sense; see Hughes-Freeland 1991 on Javanese dance) may be more of an ironic tension than an ambiguity; the tension between speaking *about* someone (who thereby has no voice) and speaking flit them (or directly communicating their views and opinions; cf. Spencer (1997).

[64] Giddens (1984) helpfully analysed action in terms of both the 'knowledgeability' and 'capability' of agents, remarking that 'capability' should *not* be identified with the decision-making capacities of agents.

presentations of villagers in this account since it is with contextualisations of the Hmong that we are concerned. Yet the longing for an originary context is not limited to romantic ethnographers, as we shall see, but is also very crucially an aspect of the way Hmong tend to phrase their own historical past; their social memory.

Bloch's hypothesis[65] that a 'practical' knowledge, cross-culturally shared, might reveal the workings of an empirically verifiable world (besides reflecting older contrasts between 'science' and 'ideology') showed a similar faith in an uncontentious, invariable external reality to that reflected in Sperber's more careful arguments about semi-propositional 'representational beliefs', like convictions or culturally bound assumptions, which might be only half-understood and therefore not of a verifiable, 'propositional' type (Sperber 1985:54-6). Who can say whether it is more important that interpretations are socially situated, as Sperberians and many others would stress, or that all social experience is mediated through interpretive understandings, which would be more my own tendency?[66] The interpretations-as-situated views are actually variants of a correspondence theory of truth, itself based on a positivist understanding of empirical reality which supplies an originary context, such as a particular Hmong village in Sichuan, for all possible future meanings.[67]

We should surely now accept the need for a phenomenological *epoche*, a kind of temporary 'bracketing', of what is assumed to be the contextual reality towards which language points, and the general inadequacies of 'mimetic' theories of representation.[68] It must by now be recognised that understandings can at best be only partial, that any observer is necessarily immersed, like Merleau-Ponty's Cézanne, in the world that appears to be his spectacle. If different views of Hmong society are presented from a Thai context and a Chinese context, or by previous and future ethnographers, or by

---

[65] Repeated in Bloch 1986:188.

[66] Sperber's (1985) distinction of descriptive (propositional) representations from non-descriptive ones which may be either interpretive or reproductions, is an elaboration of the distinction between mathematical and metaphorical models.

[67] Despite Sokal!

[68] Hughes-Freeland (1991).

different groups of Hmong themselves and those who control powerful representations of them, we should not necessarily leap to radical constructivist views of cultural identity, since this runs the danger of ignoring the very facticity and materiality of cultural and ethnic identity which has so often been expressed in violent genocide. We do need to recognise that context is formed by a variety of interpretations, and as Hobart (1986) put it 'the potentially infinite range of relevant contexts'.

Creating Contexts

It was Saussure who is said to have originally dislodged the subject as author of meaning, and released meaning for infinite recessive interpretations through his emphasis on the conventional rather than natural character of the sign. Yet attempts to resurrect an individual, authoral agency within a general theory of meaning have often been caught in an isolating Crusoe-esque notion of the individual arising from the misleading opposition between 'society' and the 'individual', even where it is recognised that an individual agency is separable from a subject position.[69] Chinese political rhetoric, and it must be said the rhetoric typified here of western academic discourse, makes it all too easy to lose sight of what agency Hmnong villagers in China may actually have. What we need, perhaps, is an account in which individual agency is understood as reaching out, through a kind of inter-subjectivity and *communitas*, towards a humanism which is not reducible to individual whim or 'emotion', but in which the creative capacity to control destiny and determine fate, through the imaginative posing of alternatives to a current or assumed situation which may transform it, is recognised as ultimately *un-conditional*, and essentially *un-determined*.[70] Agency needs to be associated with code and structure besides performativity and competence.

---

[69] Appiah (1991).

[70] The real enemy of utilitarian rationalism is not, then, the grand deterministic theories of human action and causation we have noted, but rather idealist phenomenological interpretivism, well mirrored in the classic tensions between Anglo-American and 'Continental' philosophies.

We know, or seem to know, that it cannot be the case that human agency is limited to choices between equally all-determining constraints. It is not the case that Hmong are cyphers, hieroglyphs to be deciphered simply in a language of Han Chinese dominance. Nor is it the case that Hmong villagers in Sichuan are free rational actors, choosing happily whether to adopt one or another kind of given identity. I would suspect that there is an important sense in which the creativity of human actions and decision-making processes, like that of speech itself in the original Chomskian formulation of (implicit) linguistic competence,[71] is boundless and without closure, and not simply in the sense that they may lead to quite unexpected outcomes. How can one be certain that such a claim is not one which merely expresses the individualist values of a particular type of market-oriented society, which are then attributed to little-understood societies such as that of the Hmong? Indeed in terms of current social theory one cannot be, and this is a problem which should concern us. Yet, the ultimate proof of the capacity for a genuine self-determination which is not dependent on any particular historical or social conjuncture must lie in the possibility of self-destruction, as Nietzsche (1887) saw when he spoke of man's ultimate 'will to nothingness' (and Mishima too, who perfected his life through death, making of it a conscious, wilful work of art). We know that acculturation does not necessarily result in a loss of identity (Keyes 1978), and that ethnicide is not genocide. Yet if we are to understand anything of the workings of a creative agency within a dominating rhetoric of power, we do need to examine wider inter-cultural relations in their historical and imaginative settings, where we may glimpse, perhaps, something of the ultimately unconditional nature of human creativity.

And this unconditional creativity is perhaps similar to what Sartre had in mind when he spoke of freedom and absurdity, yet it need not necessarily follow that the 'senselessness' of things is, as he saw it, necessarily absurd or productive of despair. It is surely at least equally conceivable that it should rather be eloquent of the As-Yet unspoken meanings with which existence will, eventually, be

---

[71] This competence was, as he saw it, one element in a theory which would be able to 'accomodate the characteristic creative aspect of language use' (Chomsky 1966:45).

endowed, the Not-Yet immanent in the present and the past. And it is therefore partly in the realm of historical legend that we find, in the remainder of this book, some of those meanings and potentialities played out.

Part Two:
Walnut Village

PREAMBLE

As Yangshen wrote of the county of Gongxian in southern Sichuan province, where I lived and worked in 1989, 'gorges and mountains surround the earth and sky, waterfalls and passages touch the River'.[1]

Sichuan, with an area of 570,000 sq.km. and a population then in excess of 100 million, 87% of whom lived in rural areas, was before the 1997 separation of Chongqing from the province roughly the same size as France. It is described as one of China's three main forestry areas and one of its five main pastoral areas. Well irrigated since at least the third century BC, Sichuan's fertile plains supply a significant proportion of China's rice, while much of mountainous western Sichuan incorporates parts of what are properly Tibet. The province is also the source of the three great rivers of the Salween, Mekong and Yangtse, which run through southern China and much of mainland South East Asia. Sichuan's water zones account for a fifth of China's total water resources, and the controversial 'Three Gorges' dam now being built there bears witness to a particularly mammoth model of future development..

Ninety-two percent of Sichuan's forested, or otherwise undeveloped, areas are estimated to be in ethnic minority regions, which should not be not particularly surprising in the light of official figures showing that that ethnic minorities occupy more than half the total area of the province, and which are well in accordance with general statistical data often cited on the national minorities in China which show them as accounting for only approximately 8.14% of the total population of China, but occupying an alarming 62% of the land. And as many as a third of China's minority nationalities, numbering altogether over 80 million, are estimated to live in the three southern provinces of Yunnan, Guizhou and Sichuan, which I was fortunate to be able to visit from 1985 onwards. About a quarter of the 24.7 million people of these 30 indigenous nationalities were estimated to live below the official poverty line.[2] In 1978 the average

---

[1] Gongxian County Annals.

[2] Then reckoned at ¥200 per capita annual income plus 200kg. grain consumption. ¥12 are currently about £1, so that the increased per capita income (in which non-capital goods are included) in 1988 would have been about £38.58.

per capita income of the ethnic minorities in Sichuan was only ¥90. With the economic reforms initiated since then this had risen to ¥463 by 1988, the year before my research. Most villages in the county of Gongxian where I was were nevertheless without basic health or educational amenities, sanitation or electricity.

It was probably as a direct result of fears that all foreign contacts might shortly be curtailed in the immediate aftermath of the Beijing massacre, as a well as a more immediate need to remove any officially invited foreign researchers as quickly as possible from urban centres, that research permissions which had been difficult to obtain suddenly became available and I and my family were able to leave for the southwestern Sichuan county of Gongxian, where I was due to research the kinship system of the Hmong minority people, within a few days of June the fourth. We had visited the county and the village twice before, but now were able to stay with a Hmong family in a rice-farming village. Upcountry Hmong farmers knew little of events in Beijing, or even in Chengdu, only that there had been a clash between the students and the government. While some sympathised with the student demands for more democracy and less corruption, most feared a repetition of the Cultural Revolution and that general lawlessness might return again. Recent as well as distant history in this part of China has been a long succession of strife and conflict, with rare intervals of peace and prosperity. The fragile peace of today, the relative rule of law and order, is still extremely precious to those generations who remember the period before the 1980s.[3]

Some accounts place the arrival of the Hmong peoples (or their Miao ancestors), whose culture I had first studied in Thailand, in the region at a very early date.[4] The ancient general Xuan Yuan, who is supposed to have defeated the legendary Miao chieftain Chiyou in the first millenium BC, is described as driving the Miao ancestors of the Hmong from the north to the south of China, forcing them to migrate down to the southern provinces of Guizhou, Yunnan and Sichuan. According to the official histories, centralised control was first exerted over this region when the Emperor Guangwu of the

---

[3] But see Endicott (1988). I think the fears expressed at that time of the return of lawlessness were real.

[4] Miao is the official term under which the Hmong are grouped in China.

eastern Han dynasty (AD 23-220) despatched General Tang Meng to attack the county of Bodao, and captured the county of Yelang. An administrative district by the name of Nanguang Xian, under the wider administrative control of Jianwei Jun, was then established in the area by the emperor of the Shu Han Kingdom (220-265), which was based in Sichuan during the period of the 'Warring States'. Nanguang Xian was larger than the present-day Hmong county of Gongxian, and had its county seat in the southwest of Gongxian. After 584 the name of Nanguang Xian was changed to Xie Zhou (a prefecture rather than a county), as the central government of the Sui dynasty (589-618) succeeded in temporarily subduing the entire region. In 677, under a further extension of centralised administration, the area was retitled Gongzhou (Gong here meaning 'hard' or 'solid'),[5] and its borders partially redefined. During the Mongol dynasty of the Yuan (1280-1368) which finally conquered southwest China on a permanent basis, the meaning of Gong was changed to its present spelling, said to derive from the 'black jade' found in the county.

The Yuan dynasty developed an administrative system of appointing 'native officials' to rule over non-Han ethnic groups, in areas under tenuous central government control or those recently acquired. Under the Yuan a native chieftain (*tusi*) was first appointed to Gongzhou, and minor local officials (*tuli*) were stationed at Shangluo and Xialuo. The *tusi* system was based on much earlier strategies of 'using barbarians to rule barbarians' (*yiyi zhiyi*) and was to become fully established in the southwest under the Ming dynasty (1368-1644) which succeeded the Yuan.

We know therefore that a local tribesman named Luzhao, belonging to the Yi minority, was appointed as *tusi* of Yongning prefecture (which now covers the Hmong county of Gongxian) in the 17th. year of the founding Emperor of the Ming Dynasty, Hongwu (1385). Those referred to in the Chinese records as Yi were probably the speakers of Tibeto-Burman languages such as the Nosu and Lisu of other parts of Sichuan and Yunnan.[6] In general throughout these parts of southwestern China, the Miao groups fell under the control of local elites who were often the members of Tibeto-Burman

---

[5] Zhou refers to a prefectural division.

[6] See Harrell (forthcoming).

groups, just as across Vietnam and Laos they were subjugated to Tai feudal rulers, and those referred to as Yi in this area may well have been the remnants of the earlier Bo peoples. Even under the Ming, however, these *tusi* administered areas often proved intractable and difficult to integrate properly into the administrative structures of the centralised state. Local *tusi* tended to represent the interests of their own constituencies in direct opposition to the concerns of central government. The first great revolt of the Miao, in these provincial borderlands, is reported to have taken place in 1513, and was explicitly directed against the Ming rulers. So it is clear that there must have been people known as 'Miao' in this region since at least 1500. Under Jiajing (1522-66), some Miao were appointed to local administrative positions as *tusi*.

The most widely quoted official account of this period we have, tells how in the Wanli Era (1572-1620) of the Ming dynasty, a native of the place called He En inherited the *tusi* title. And he led a whole army of the 'Miao' to capture Jianwu (then known as Jiusi), as well as the 'Ha' Kings of the Bo (named Ahda and Maojiaogan), who were then resisting centralised control. For this he was rewarded with an order of merit 'of the third degree' and a personal fortune. Stories about this great local campaign, and of the tragic local resistance it suppressed, in which more than 300 Bo captives were taken, are still told today in Gongxian by Miao and Han farmers, Miao and Han bureaucrats,

A survey by local county officials in Gongxian showed that the main nine Hmong surnames represented in the county had arrived in Gongxian or the neighbouring counties of Xingwen and Junlian either in 1573-74, or in a later wave, in 1723-37. All of these surnames (except the Wang) said they had traversed Yunnan province before their arrival in Sichuan. Two lineages (the Liu and the Ma) claimed that they had had ultimate 'northern origins'. But the term they used for their northerly place of origin, 'Huguang', is in fact the old term for a Ming dynasty province including Hubei, Hunan and parts of Guizhou, although Huguang was usually assumed, by the local Hmong and Chinese I met, to refer to the four provinces of Hunan, Hubei, Guangdong and Guangxi.[7] The Yang and Ma surnames said that their families had migrated to Yunnan

---

[7] Lombard-Salmon (1972); Jenks (1994).

straight from Guizhou, and it seems likely, therefore, that the Hmong of this part of Sichuan had migrated back up into Sichuan from Yunnan, after first being expelled out of Guizhou into Yunnan. The majority of Hmong lineages had actual records (either written, or in sung legend) of having immigrated into Sichuan directly from the neighbouring Yunnanese county of Weixin (formerly known as Zaxi), while the remainder appeared to have migrated back up to Sichuan all the way from Wenshan in the far south of Yunnan, near the Vietnam border.[8] The earliest dates of arrival were given as 1573-4, the second and third years of the reign of the Ming dynasty Emperor Wanli, when the campaign against Jianwu took place.

Most probably the Hmong in the area had first arrived in the sixteenth century from Yunnan, after leaving Guizhou as result of their own suppression by imperial troops, as part of an imperial effort to suppress a local rebellion or resistance by another local group. For the rebels of 1573 were not actually Hmong (nor Miao, in which other groups are sometimes included), although they may well have been supported as well as opposed by various local Miao, Yi, and other groups. The 1573 rebels belonged to a vanished people known as the Bo, whose strange 'hanging coffins' are still suspended from the karst mountain formations which mark the area. The desolate fate of the Bo people, who tried to resist Chinese domination, is remembered to this day by all the Hmong, and local Han people, of Gongxian I was able to meet. Although other more famous counties in the neighbouring provinces of Yunnan and Guizhou also display these 'hanging coffins', the local Gongxian government hope that the county may become a tourist area for this reason.

> Whose coffins are those hanging on the cliffs?
> The kind-hearted sisters are immensely missed
> The mountains are mourned by sleeting snow and coriander
> The wind sends the fir and pine crying in grief
> The flowers bloom in sunshine in sacrificial worship
> Stars overlook the mourning stall throughout the night.[9]

The spirits of these vanquished inhabitants of the past continue to haunt the memories of those in the present, and are commemorated

---

[8] Wenshan was formerly officially known as Menzi, and known to the Hmong as Kaihuafu.

[9] Cliff poem found at Makuangba, near Gongxian.

in the names of local features of the landscape, as well as in narratives which define present-day identities..

Towards the later years of the Ming, local unrest increased. From 1622 (in the reign of Tianqi), the local chieftain She Chongming, who had succeeded to the title of *tusi* of Yongning, staged a major revolt against the declining authority of the Ming emperors which lasted as long as a decade, capturing the major market centre of Chongqing and moving north to besiege Chengdu, the provincial capital of Sichuan. The Miao of Gongxian and the surrounding areas supported this revolt of the 'Yi', and are said to have referred to She Chongming as their 'King'.

Other accounts of 'Miao' settlement in the Southest Sichuan region, which may well refer to a later wave of Miao migration, claim that Miao were first forced to settle in Sichuan at around this time in the 1630s, in the confused period between the Ming and Qing dynasties. In these accounts the settlement of the Miao in Sichuan came about as a direct result of the famous rebel general Zhang Xianzhong's strategy of encouraging the emigration of ethnic minority peoples out of the provinces of 'Huguang' towards Sichuan where he was to establish his base in Chengdu. In the early Qing dynasty (1644-1912), efforts to replace the local *tusi* chieftains by centrally appointed officials, and to subordinate them to Chinese officials, particularly during the Kangxi (1661-1722) and Yongzheng (1723-1735) reigns, led to further insurrections of both the Miao and Yi minority peoples against the Han Chinese who were progressively settling in and colonising the southwest, establishing military garrisons, occupying Miao agricultural lands and stealing Miao cattle, or mining for copper, gold, silver, cinnabar, iron and lead. The commerce in cotton and silk, salt and timber was also dominated by Han traders and middlemen. In 1735 a major imperial pacification of the Miao regions in Guizhou was mounted,[10] which must have involved those across the borders in Sichuan and led to further population upheavals and migrations out of the Guizhou region. In 1793 a second major revolt which began in eastern Guizhou and Hunan and soon engulfed the three provinces of Yunnan, Guizhou and Sichuan and also involved the Gongxian area took place, in which local Miao and Han united with other local groups such as the

---

[10] Lombard-Salmon (1972;237).

Zhongjia. This is indicative in pointing to a certain unity, or coalition, of local interests which was able to surpass cultural distinctions, but which was united in its opposition to the imposition of centralised governmental controls and growing state encroachment and economic exploitation. This uprising was succeeded by the widespread popular insurrection which began in Guizhou two years later and lasted in west Hunan until 1806, and was to be followed by savage reprisals with Miao villages burned to the ground and whole populations scattered.[11] Local uprisings and rebellions persisted throughout the nineteenth century in the Guizhou region, often marked by excessive tax demands or other impositions. The widespread 'Miao' rebellion of 1854-73 sparked by iniquitous local taxation has been well examined by Jenks (1994). The memories of these rebellions and subsequent repressions are built into present-day stories and songs, and inscribed in the very contours of the landscape of Gongxian, where heroic deeds of the past, the resistances and triumphs, are commemorated in the names of rivers, mountains and passes.

By 1916 Protestant missionaries had penetrated this part of Sichuan, and their influence was to continue until the 1930s and beyond. In 1932 the American missionary Graham visited the Hmong village of Wangwuzhai in Gongxian and recorded songs and customs for the Museum of West Sichuan. During the provincial banditry of the 1920s, and the more organised civil wars of the 1930s which persisted until Liberation was declared in 1949, there was considerable turmoil and population movement in the area.

After the eighteenth-century Chinese campaigns to force the Hmong to wear Chinese dress and to speak Chinese, to be educated in Chinese schools and to adopt Chinese surnames, the Protestant Christian misionaries had tried in their own way to reform local Hmong cultural practices. Samuel Pollard, a Cornish Methodist who worked in Yunnnan around the turn of the century, introduced football games and gymnastics to replace the autumnal love duets and New Year games of catch between courting couples. Pollard had concentrated on another Miao group, the A Hmao, but he had some Hmong converts and the area was repeatedly visited by missionaries. It seemed to me that the Hmong kinship system and their weddings

---

[11] Lombard-Salmon (1972;239).

would best express what sense of cultural identity they might have after these various efforts to suppress or destroy them, which must have been violently renewed during the Cultural Revolution, and that a study of their kinship system might also allow me to look at other aspects of their society. I went to Gongxian, therefore, officially entitled to study the 'Hmong kinship system', and was able with the aid of a British Academy award to spend six months of 1989 in Sichuan undertaking most of the research on which this study is based.[12] I first visited Hmong areas of Yunnan in 1985, and made repeated visits to Hmong and Yao areas in China from 1986 to 1992, including areas in Hunan, Guangdong and Guangxi provinces. Further formal research visits to Hmong areas in Guizhou and Yunnan were made in 1990 and 1991, and this together with my period in Gongxian has led to the general concentration on the borderlands of the three provinces of Yunnan, Guizhou and Sichuan reflected in these pages.

---

[12] This award was for eight months of research; I was unable to spend all of this in Sichuan, but completed two further months with related Hmong groups in the neighbouring parts of Yunnan and Guizhou in 1990 and 1991.

CHAPTER ONE

THE VILLAGE

The Hmong minority village of Wutong, in Yuhe township, Gongxian county, in the Yibin prefecture of Sichuan, is situated about 1800 feet above sea level in the lower foothills of the mountains which stretch into Guizhou and Yunnan provinces, spread across the flanks of two hills with panoramic views across the county. The timber houses of villagers are located at great distances away from each other and it is impossible to see the village from any one point. Narrow footpaths wind up the steep slopes between small fields of rice or corn. The village is approximately one hour from the county capital of Gongxian, a small market town composed of muddy lanes and blocks of government buildings, where the railway line from Chengdu ends. The monsoon weather tends to be cool, at around 14 degrees, and there are often mists swirling around the housetops in the mornings and light frosts at night. A dirt road leads from Didong, the nearest market town, to the foot of the mountains across which the village is spread, but not to the village itself (Diagram 1).

This was a relatively wealthy village, which had supplied more than its due quota of school teachers and local officials, and received a proportionate amount of local government assistance in recognition of this, particularly in the form of the electrification which none of the other Hmong villages in the county had. Bulbs were strung up in the dark interiors of most houses to read by, and there were three TVs in the village. Most villagers were bilingual in Hmong and Sichuanese Chinese, and it had become customary to wear traditional clothing only on festive and ritual occasions. Twenty-eight out of the 103 households were Han Chinese families, but the village was dominated by the Hmong Yang clan, with forty households. The village had one primary school, housed in a low white-washed building, which only opened in the mornings.

The nearest productive enterprise of any note was the coal mine at Didong, and there was more coal mining around Gongxian itself, the county seat, where some villagers found work in the winter. Parties

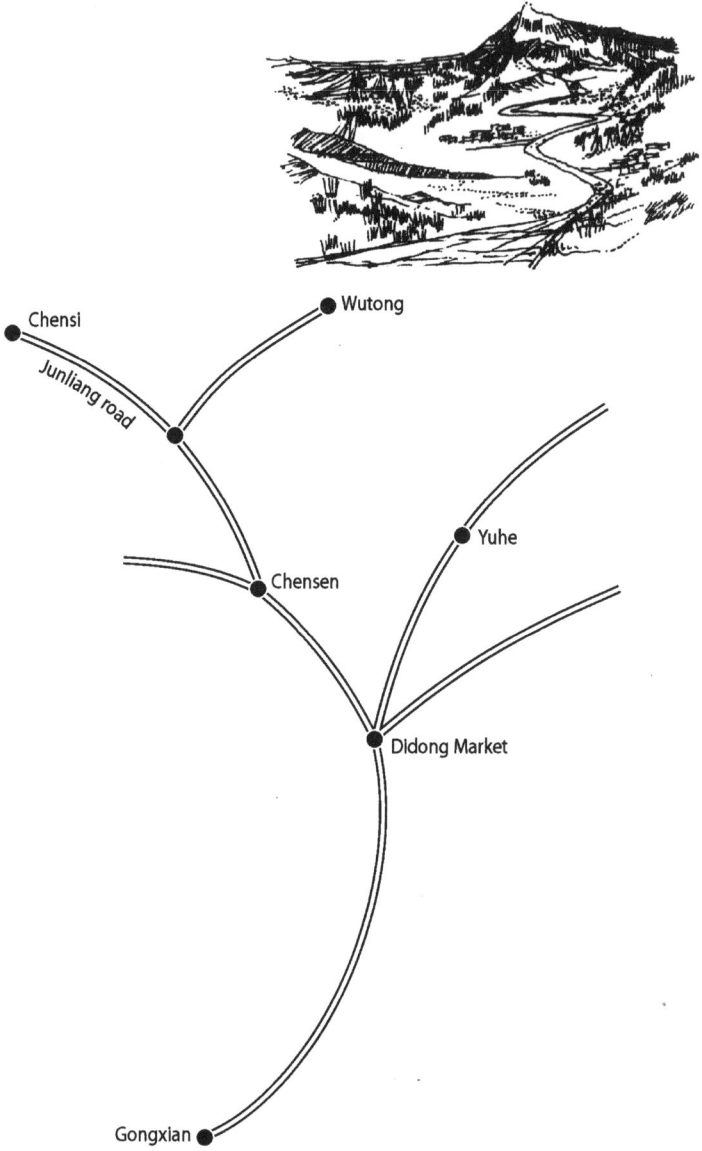

Diagram 1: Didong area

of four men from the village would carry sacks of coal from the Didong mine on shoulder-poles up the hill for their households every week. Most families had a member or two who went to market once every 10-15 days; there was a three-day rotating market, starting in Didong on the first of each month, in Xianglo on the second day and Gongxian on the third before returning to Didong on the fourth and so on, all through the month except for rest days on the tenth, twentieth and thirtieth; a nine-day cycle between three points, starting again on the first, eleventh and twenty-first of each month.[1] The traditional (30-day month) Chinese farmers' calendar is used for these market days, and also consulted on a good many other occasions, for example when planting the maize, to see if the ground is 'hot' or 'cold' (*yin* or *yang*, even or odd days). What they brought to sell in these markets was mostly eggs and chickens, a little tobacco, and pigs—as well as homemade baskets, and bamboo shoots at ¥1.20 a cluster.

Nobody made wine in the village, so this had to be purchased from outside, and this was a major luxury expense for most villagers, together with clothes, for which cash from corn sold to the state was mostly used, since the rice was not sold. The villagers would progress in small groups early in the morning on the way to the market, with great baskets of maize on their backs. One household in the village, however, had invested in a mechanical corn and rice thresher; otherwise the threshing was still all manual. It cost 80 *fen*[2] to husk 100 *jin* of rice, and Y1.20 to grind 100 *jin* of corn into meal; only 60 *fen* for 100 *jin* of potatoes, but Y3 for 100kg. of rice powder. Plantations of tobacco which had been communally farmed stretched up the mountains, with some tea although this was only informally grown; the commonest vegetables were the *dong gua* or white gourd, cabbage and Chinese cabbage, sweet potato, potato and taro, white mulberry (*sangshu*), radishes and *datucai* or rutabaya.

The main forest was composed of mixed evergreens with broadleaf varieties, including gingko and sour jujube, *qishu*, the lacquer tree, fast-growing *qingmu* for timber and firewood, camphor, the ubiquitous China fir (*Cunninghamia lanceolata*) which has been

---

[1] See Skinner (1964-5).

[2] 10 *fen* are 1 *mao*, 10 *mao* are 1 *yuan*; one cent.

planted throughout southern China through state and collective
projects, and many types of bamboo, like *mianzhu*, which was said to
be pest-prone, and the quick-growing *zizhu*. Many of the houses were
surrounded by small orchards of plums and crooked pear, oranges
and tangerines, walnuts, peaches and apples.Game still included wild
boar and deer and monkeys, foxes, rabbits and hares, and a type of
hill porcupine. The village used to be surrounded with much more
natural forest, but most of it was first destroyed in the Anti-Japanese
war and then again in 1958-59. Fairly indiscriminate felling had
taken place before the economic reforms following 1979, particularly
because of the increasing population through the days of the Cultural
Revolution and the increased need for firewood and fencing. China
Fir trees with 20-year rotations had been planted since then in
monoculture at Fenghuang.

Housing

Houses were of the picturesque half-timbered and whitewashed type
Graham describes for the area in the 1930's, based (in the Han style)
on a tripartitite division of the main house around a central hall, and
often with a spacious front courtyard fronting the mountainside,
enclosed or part-enclosed by extensions and out-houses. The slope
was steep and rainwater filled the gulleys which ran past the houses.

There was no sign, in Sichuan, of the traditional Hmong house
structure to be observed throughout South East Asia, and well
described by Lemoine (1972a) for Laos; an all-wooden structure,
with named ancestral house-posts and rafters associated with
particular spirits, and fixed locations for the relationships between
hearth, altar, and main door. Yet although clearly very Sinitic, these
were not really Han houses either; the Hmong of this part of Sichuan
had evolved their own unique type of housing, some thatched and
some tiled, best compared to the long extended wooden structures,
with spaces for dining and sleeping and reception of guests,evolved
by some of the wealthier Hmong in the mountains of North Vietnam.
And similarly to these, they were mostly situated at considerable
distances from each other, widely scattered in groups of two to three
over the foothills and mostly not within sight of each other, separated
by fields; the house I stayed in was over 30 metres in length, which
was not unusual in the village, and the total width of the village,

from Li Peishu's house at the top of Group Two, to Wang You Cai's house at the end of Group One, was about 1,000 by 500 metres across. The distances between houses varied from 50 to 100 metres.

Traditionally Hmong houses in this region had also been on a basically tripartite pattern, commonly known as 'three-post houses' by the three lateral posts which divided internal sections, though there could also be larger houses made with 5,7 or 9 posts. The hearth was to the left of the central room and the sleeping area to its right, and they were mostly constructed of bamboo with some wood.

Diagram 2 conveys some idea of the household composition within these houses, which were either long elongated structures divided into several partitions but extending into semi- and full courtyard designs, or smaller simpler structures on a tripartite model.

It was from 1987 that for the first time since 1949, restrictions on local building in China were relaxed, and in the countryside farmers were to be observed rebuilding their houses in a frenzy of activity resulting in a boom of local brick and tile industries and a crisis of local forest resources. It was also around this time that the owner of this house had begun to take over sole general management of the local construction enterprise. But, as the diagram shows, his house—like those of many others in the village—was already quite capacious enough even before that time. For originally this had been the house of the present owner's father, which three older brothers had all now left. The basic (typically southern Chinese) tripartite division of the house around a central ancestral hall was still observable in the front portion of the older part of the house, but since they had been able to run the bedrooms along in a sort of long corridor *behind* where an ancestral altar would traditionally have been (they did not have one), the entire front portion of the house could be converted into a reception, storage and dining area, where local officials and members of labour exchange groups could be wined and dined, and sacks of grain and fertilizer stored. Outhouses including pigstyes and toilets (progressively separated into male and female), were to the right of this, and the cooking area and kitchens to the left near the hearth.

In effect after 1984 a new house had been added on to the left by extending the row of bedrooms into five new rooms with wallpaper and lightbulbs, where the entire family then moved, and extending the old cookery area into a new kitchen and attached dining space after the model of many local guest-houses in China.

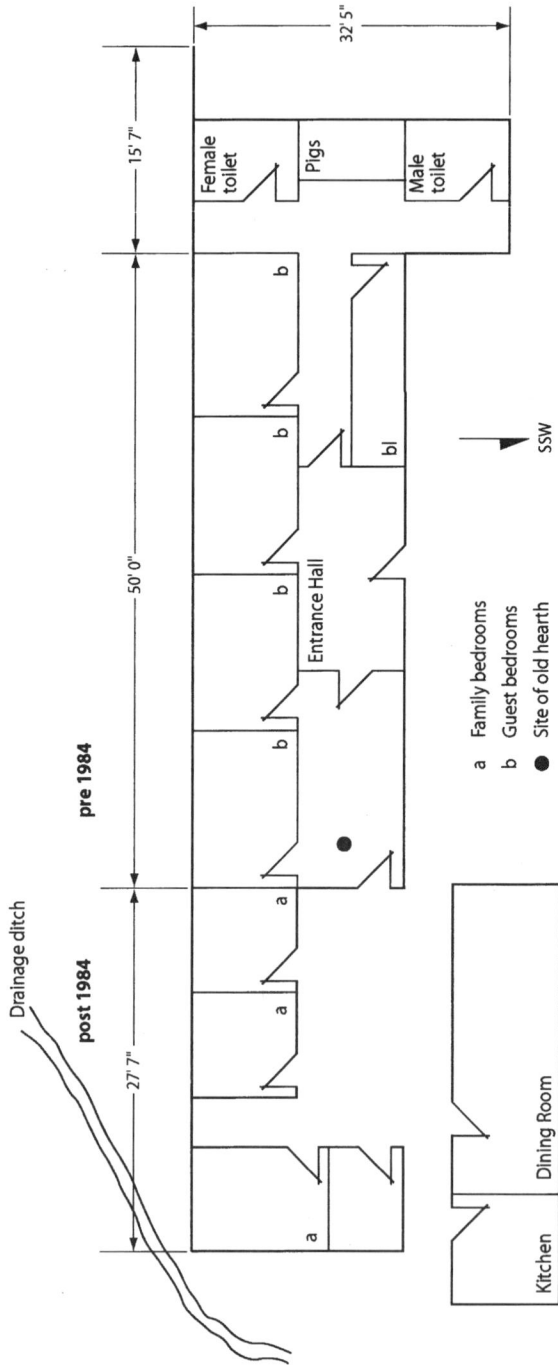

Diagram 2: Household composition

Demography

The village was dominated by members of the Yang clan, and known locally as 'the Yang village' for that reason. I was able to record the demographic composition of 82 families in all, some of which were further sub-divided into two families, and altogether they illustrate the household composition of the village well (Appendix X).

The village was composed of 99 registered households and a total population of 498 in 1989.[3] These were still divided into old production teams which corresponded to their geographical locations, with populations of 98 in the first, 202 in the second (with 44 households), and 198 (with thirty-eight households) in the third 'teams' (or hamlets) and with differential access to land (wet rice land was lacking in group three, across a gulley in the slope of the two hills).

Including absentees and those who had not officially been recorded as resident, but were in fact resident in the village, there was a total population of 368 in Groups Two and Three which formed the main part of the village, in 82 households; apart from the Han Chinese (surnamed) Xie with 6 households and (surnamed) Li with 12, there were 2 Han households surnamed Huang, and 2 Han households surnamed Sun. There were 2 Hmong households surnamed Ma and one surnamed Gu. The remaining three clans were also Hmong; 3 Zeng households, 8 Wang, and 46 Yang households (counting widows in with their husband's surname groups). The 22 Han Chinese households totalled 106 members (9 surnamed Huang, 11 Sun, 35 Xie and 51 Li), leaving a Hmong population of 262 greatly in the majority in Groups Two and Three. Apart from the Gu (with 7 members) and Ma (with 9 members), the smallest of the other three Hmong clans was the Zeng, with 18 members, followed by the 39 Wang and all far outnumbered by the 189 members of the Yang.[4]

---

[3] For economic purposes, membership of households was reckoned slightly differently, and often young children were not included in these.

[4] The data is based on the village household records, and were gone through with the village accountant and my research assistant and other village members who intervened to correct, modify or add to them, and were later again checked through household interviews. Nevertheless they reflect and are based directly upon

No less than 133 out of a total population of 363[5] were aged 16 or under, that is, over a third, while very few were aged 60 or over (only 22 in all). From a total population of 366,[6] the male population was 185 and that of females 181; an unusually balanced figure for villages in China but possibly reflecting the greater preference among the Hmong for girl children and the relative affluence of the village.

The great majority of the households were officially classified as two-generational, mostly nuclear type, ones; only 6 single generation households were recorded (including household number 37 who actually lived with household number 41, and 17 three generational ones besides two of four generations. This had much to do with how households are officially recorded and is in fact plain misleading. The same may be said for household size, with household size (on these figures) ranging from 1 to 9, averaging 4.48. In fact many of the households officially divided still worked together as economic units or formed effective large extended families living under one roof.

The data, inasmuch as it is generalisable, shows the much younger ages of many wives than their husbands, although this is not invariable and some wives are slightly older than their husbands; an apparent tendency to the formation of nuclear families; the near equality of the sex ratio; several cases of female-headed households; and a tendency to form late families (in many cases, reproduction has taken place over a very lengthy period, and there were households composed of relatively elderly parents with very young children, often those where much older siblings have already left to form their own families). In many of these cases, tragedies of the Cultural Revolution, or of the famine during the Great Leap Forward, had either delayed marriages or ruined families so that new families had been started later.

And certainly the dynamic process of social life was very clear; husbands were about to leave to join their wives in more affluent

---

the official order of households and division of households and calculations of membership in households.

[5] Subtracting five members of absentee household 9 whose ages were not recorded.

[6] Since the sex of two absentee children in household 75 was not determined.

locations, elder sons had broken away to begin their own families, in-marrying women had preferred to leave their household registrations in their original homes, husbands had deserted their wives or wives left their husbands, children were leaving the village to study or for work, widows and widowers had moved in or remained with one of their children or had preferred not to do so.

Particularly close relations had been established between the Chinese Xie and Li clans in the village, while the small but significant Hmong Zeng minority had intermarried with members of both the dominant Yang and Wang clans, and I describe the genealogical patterning of this in some of the following chapters.

The poverty and mixed composition of Group One separated it markedly from the Groups Two and Three which comprised the main village of Wutong, and this was clearly expressed in the spatial distancing of the Group One settlement from Groups One and Two. The agriculture practised in Group One and the economic status of the Group was also markedly different from the rest of the village.

Group One comprised only 19 households, 9 of them Han Chinese and 10 Hmong. Again the Yang households were in the majority among the Hmong section of Group One, accounting for seven of the ten Hmong households. Four of these, all brothers (two pairs of half-brothers, sons of Yang Wanshu), at households O,P,Q and R, formed an integral part of the main Yang clan (lineage Y3b) settled in Groups Two and Three, while three (two brothers and their first paternal cousin) represented close members of a more distant branch.[7]

Another Hmong household in Group One was that of a widow of one of the leading members of the main Yang group in the main part of the village (lineage Y2a); this was generally still seen as a Yang household. There was also a Xiong household affinally connected to the Y3b Yang, and one Wang household who had followed other Wang families in settling matrilocally in the area with their Yang fathers-in-law or brothers-in-law.

Of the 9 Chinese households in this Group, one belonged to an absentee named Jiang who had left the village to find work in Chengdu, and another was occupied by a Xie (Xie Shaoping) who

---

[7] For lineage branches, see diagrams in Chapter 7.

was an offshoot of the other Xie in Groups Two and Three. The remaining seven Han families were surnamed Hu and had little to do with the rest of the village. They were extremely impoverished; one (Hu Guoyuan, at household G) had never married because he said of the unwillingness of girls to move into the area. The Hu had been settled in the area for over a hundred years, and it was said that the Hmong Yang had originally come to their help against 'bandits', who subsequently revenged themselves on the Hmong Yang. The Hu were considered as indebted to the Hmong. The household map shows clearly the clustering there was between the Hmong and the Han in this Group, and between the various Yang branches of the Hmong. And we can see that even here the Hmong retained a slight majority over the Han, as they did to a much greater extent in the main part of the village (Groups Two and Three), while among the Hmong surnames, the Yang again very clearly predominated.

The Calendar

Ploughing began in the third lunar month, after the New Year celebrations and the slack winter season, when cattle were lent from group top group and some six people together could work 6 *mu* of land. Cattle were freely lent when asked for, even if the owner would have preferred to use them first himself; just as neighbours must be invited when pigs are killed at festivals—nearly half the villagers had no cattle. Planting of seeds took place in the fourth month, both on the irrigated and dry fields, of corn and taro or sweet potatoes. In the fifth month the rice was transplanted through labour exchange groups based on family relationship and the proximity of fields, one in Group Two for instance was composed of ten families. And the corn had to be hoed, and the wheat harvested, and hemp was cut to sell to the state (they remembered making cloth a long time ago in the village, but had no tradition of batik like the Green Hmong or the Hua Miao), so this was the busiest time of the agricultural year.

In the sixth month the corn was hoed again, and tobacco and potatoes or sweet potato planted, the potatoes often in the corn fields, often by themselves. Manure was manually spread on the seedlings and chemical fertilisers on the irrigated as well as the maize fields, which cost on average either ¥33 or ¥22 (depending on quality) per 40kg. sack, and the use of it approximated 25kg. per person—they used their own cash to buy it, but at the state prices. The seventh month was freer, when the tobacco had to be tended and the house cleared to make space for drying tobacco. The eighth month was when the tobacco was dried and the sweet potatoes harvested from the corn fields. In the ninth month it usually took a family about ten days to harvest all its corn and rice, with everyone helping together; everyone must help if they can. Coal and materials for repairing houses are also often collected at this time, with the neighbours asked to help.

In the tenth month some sweet potatoes were harvested and the land prepared for wheat, which is planted either on the land which has just been cleared of corn, or on land which is to be turned over to potatoes in the following year, since the harvesting time for wheat and planting time for sweet potatoes just coincide. This was not too busy a time.

The eleventh and twelfth months are thought of as a time for *a si* ('playing') and making money, but the wheat was planted and sweet potatoes or taro harvested in the eleventh month. The first month is seen in the same way, when it is said 'the Han can make money', but certainly some Hmong here also do find work opportunities outside the village at this time (coal mining, forestry, and road construction were the commonest kinds of off-season labour). Coal or iron mining in Xingwen, where few went, paid ¥8 or ¥9 per day. But this was also a time for repairing the home, for weddings, for *a pleg* (the post-mortuary ritual known as *ua vaj* in Thailand), and a time to buy wood, to sell maize and buy wine.

Apart from the wet rice fields, there were fields where corn was rotated with wheat, and fields where wheat alternates with potato. Now that it has become possible to plant a mixture of corn and wheat, wheat can be followed by corn and then by sweet potato on the same dry fields, before the cycle starts again. According to one of the leading farmers, when the wheat is high, but not yet ready to be harvested, corn should be interplanted with it, and then the wheat cut and sweet potatoes (or taro) planted; but this should only be done once, and it was best to change to another crop in the following year. Corn can always be grown on the same land, but as the yield declines, it is best to change the type of seed used.

Economic Composition

The total area available to the village in 1988 was 3,302 *mu*,[8] of which 140 were wet rice fields and 533 dry land for corn and wheat, most of the rest being forest or bare mountainland. Three categories of cropland were used; poor, medium, and rich. There were wide differences of land-holding between different households which are correlated with household size and composition under the Household Responsibility System initiated after 1982. The average income per capita was estimated at ¥400 in 1989—a high figure in comparison with the figures for Gongxian as a whole, which were ¥260, and one which denoted a relatively prosperous farming community. The total yield of grain in 1988 was more than 180,000 kg. The people ate corn mixed with rice if possible (*pobkwm fan*), as well as sweet potatoes and wheat, sorghum, potato and soybean, with lettuce, cucumbers and various types of green leafy vegetables besides the ubiquitous peppers, beans and peas. The main productive crops were corn, wet rice, sweet potato, wheat, sorghum, potato and soya bean; the main vegetables were Chinese cabbage, lettuce, hot pepper, cucumber, 'four-season' bean and cowpea. The other main item of cultivation was a cash crop, tobacco, partly collectively cultivated under village leadership, of which the villagers produced 21,000 kg. in 1987, while the figures for corn, rice, sweet potato and wheat were 100,000, 40,000, 25,000 and 7,500 respectively.[9]

It transpired that many of the households had given up reckoning exact yields since the household reforms. However, we can see from the Tables below that arable land was minimal, that corn production greatly outweighed that of rice, and that consequently other means of obtaining income for the purchase of rice (such as the local tobacco industry which remained partly under collective management, or participating in the village construction business or local forestry work) were essential.

In fact the official figures were arrived at by a rather odd sampling process, which the Village Accountant explained. First households had been arbitrarily allotted, according to local knowledge, to three wealth grades; upper (self-sufficient), middle (semi self-sufficient),

---

[8] 1 *mu* = 0.0667 hectares.

[9] These are figures compiled for the Gongxian Agricultural Bureau.

and lower (poor); then 5-6 households had been randomly selected from each grade on the basis of which total production figures were arrived at, which were then further adjusted by the *xiang* office which considered them too low.

While again showing the scarcity of irrigated land as a whole, the Table below shows how the ratio of wet to dry fields increases from Group One to Group Three, making Group Three the most prosperous in terms of irrigated land. Group One is generally lower in these figures because of its lower population.[10]

To put this in more general context, it must be said that the majority of Hmong villages in south China, and all those around Wutong, have practically no irrigated rice lands; this is a luxury, and corn is the normal staple diet.

The total agricultural tax (*shangjiaonongshui*) varied not much between the Groups; . Altogether taxes calculated in cash, of which the largest proportion was accounted for by the agricultural tax, included 'deductions' for general expenses incurred by local officials, about which there is often controversy, fees for 'education' which were again much less for Group One and which are also fixed by local officials, and the 'Labour Levy' (*mingong jianqing*) since this could be remitted in cash if labour was not supplied on local projects such as building the new road. Labour levies were calculated at ¥1.30 for one day, ¥6.50 for 5 days. From the villager point of view, who mostly supplied this in labour, such labour relieved them of the necessity to pay a cash tax.

On rice no grain tax was demanded from Group One because, as we shall see, they had hardly any rice, but the amounts respectively expected from Groups Two and Three again make clear the relative prosperity of Group Three. Grain tax was also levied on sticky rice, planted in patches on 'dry' fields. And on corn Group One paid a due amount, besides the ubiquitous, but never discounted by peasants, 'vegetable oil tax',

---

[10] In Table 1, one additional household since 1988 had meant the addition of 3 *mu* of wet rice land. 'Dry land' covers corn and wheat.

Table 1: General survey (*gaikuang*) of Wutong population (1989)

	Group 1	Group 2	Group 3	Total	
Population	88	200	177	465	
Household	20	43	40	103	
Hmong	11	31	33	75	
Han	9	12	7	28	
Wet rice	26	53	64	143	(*mu*)
Dry land	240	185	180	605	
Total area	266	238	244	748	
Agric. tax	1580.04	1666.14	1689.24	4935.42	(*yuan*)
Deductions	288	561	516	1365	
Education	192	374	344	910	
Labour	201.5	474.5	390	1066	
Total paid	2261.54	3075.64	2939.24	8276.42	
Grain tax					
Wheat	2885	3302	2996	9183	(kg)
Rice	--	948	1303	2251	
Glut. rice	--	52.5	60.5	113	
Corn	400	468	500	1368	
Soya	496	628	591	1715	
Total	3781	5398.5	5450.5	14630	
Veg. oil	150	295	276	721	

While the agricultural tax and other charges calculated in cash were statutory levies determined according to the arable acreage allotted to each household (which in turn depended on the number of household members when the land had been distributed to households in 1983), but were paid in grain, the grain tax on productivity was compensated for by cash.[11]

The irony of this is that peasant perceptions are entirely different from official representations of the process. While peasants are in theory supposed to pay a certain amount of cash in agricultural tax to the government for the 'rental' use of what still are state-owned agricultural lands, they are 'allowed' to pay this in grain (so this is a real tax, although it can be waived in poor areas; either cash or grain must be surrendered in return for apparently nothing); and while they are supposed to render up a certain proportion of their harvest (prior to fulfilling grain quotas) in payment of the 'grain tax' which is a kind of tax on productivity, in fact the government *buys* this from them and gives them cash in hand for it. Of course the cash they get is nothing like the cash they could have got for it on the open market, and it is on a similar basis that the whole household responsibility system, with regard to the amount of produce which *must* be sold to the state before any surplus can be disposed of, was working in the southern areas. The grain tax in 1989 was about the same as that in 1988 and 1987, and was lessened for tree planters.

From the peasant point of view (and this is *only* where a surplus is produced) over and above the grain tax which is only exempted or compensated for in cash in poor areas, a certain proportion of their harvest has to be surrendered free (agricultural tax), a further proportion they must sell to the government at cheap rates (in this area, comprising the grain tax)—and some of this cash they may be able to use to pay the agricultural tax or other levies—but to make any profit for themselves, they have to produce beyond the limits set by the local agricultural and grain taxes, beyond the proportion of the harvest due to the state and the proportion which must be sold to the state.The government does however still provide side benefits in poor or minority areas, such as 3.5 *jin* of seed per annum per capita in Wutong.

To give just two representative examples of this, in Yang Xiangchao's household (no.28), comprising two adult labourers, they were allotted 2.59 *mu* of land, 0.4 irrigated and 2.19 unirrigated; vegetable oil tax was set at 3kg., agricultural tax at ¥15.96,

---

[11] Some adjustments to land allocations had been made in the case of death and marriage since then, but not very systematically.

management fees at ¥6. The education fee was ¥4 and 5 labour days were due in the year. Grain target was 702kg. and the grain tax was 62.5kg. (11.5 of rice, 41 of wheat, 4 of corn and 6 of soya). In Yang Wankun's household (number 11) comprising 7 labourers with 8.1 *mu* of land (1 *mu* irrigated), the grain target was 2,198kg. and grain tax set at 194.5 kg. (29.5 rice, 133 wheat, 14 corn and 18 soya). Vegetable oil tax was 9kg., agricultural tax was set at ¥43.40 and management fees at ¥16.50. The education fee was ¥11 and 5 days labour were due.

The villagers in Group One, which was basically unirrigated, were able to grow very little rice, which was why no tax was demanded for it, and they depended on corn which they mostly ate. When they could they bought rice to eat mixed with corn in a meal very common in southwest China and known as *pobkwm fan* or 'corn rice', a kind of sustaining porridge in a bowl. Villagers reckoned an average family of 3 adults and 2 children might eat one and a half *jin* (2 *jin*=1kg.) of grain per day, or 3 in 2 days, or 45 per month, which is about 540 *jin* or 270 kg. in a year.

In interviews people did not usually talk about *mu* but rather *zang* of which there are 6 in a *mu*. The Xiong household (C) in Group One reckoned for example they had produced some 500 *jin* of grainstuff in the year, and had had to buy about 300 more (rice), making a consumption of 800 *jin* per year for the whole family. Xiong Dingchao estimated their irrigated lands at about 5 *zang* per person, or about half a *mu* if there were 6 in the family (government figures gave this family 0.54 *mu* of irrigated land and 10 *mu* of dry).[12]

Although in theory it should have been possible to exchange corn for rice, or sell corn to buy rice, in practice this was hardly ever done since owing to the general availability of corn the exchange rates would have made this absurd; in theory, in terms of government and market rices, one and a half *jin* or 2 *jin* of corn should have been equivalent to 1 *jin* of rice, but in practice one might have parted with as much as eleven and a half *jin* of corn in order to receive a single

[12] The Group One village leader Wang Youcai's estimate tallied with this, of roughly 5.5 *zang* of irrigated land per person, giving 27.5 or nearly half a *mu*, for a household of five, and indeed government figure gave his family a little more than this (0.63 *mu* irrigated land), which is approximately right for his family of 7 members. They had produced some 600 *jin* of grain (mostly corn) and had had to buy a further 2-300 *jin* of rice, but still had lived mostly on corn.

jin of good rice. Some corn could however be sold to the state or in Gongxian town.

Considerable discussion in fact took place about relative exchange rates: 1 *jin* of corn was reckoned to sell for about 4 *mao* (¥0.4) while a *jin* of polished rice would have been 8 *mao* (¥0.8), but in fact as I have said nobody could exchange 2 *jin* of corn for 1 of rice. What was done was to sell soya beans, reckoned at about 8 *mao* per *jin*, and it was typically from such sales of soya beans that what cash there was available to buy rice came from. In fact the price of soya had risen in 1988 so that it had been possible to buy more rice than usual.

Not everyone however was able to do even this. Hu Guoyun, who lived in Group III with his son Hu Zhengtang, said their family of 6 (including his wife) had only made 200 *jin* , and actually (including his other son Hu Zhengzi who lived with his mother) had bought 300kg. in the last year, but that if they had been able to they would have bought 750kg.[13]

The productivity of the land varies markedly between different areas and different families, and local authorities try to allot a fair mixture of the worst, middling, and best arable land to each household according to its population, but this is often not possible, particularly when fields are cultivated near households in a generally infertile and unirrigated area like Group One (where 80% of the land was slope of 70% or above, contrasting with Groups Two and Three where 70% of the arable land averaged a 60% slope). Members of Group One had been allocated a little land over on the side of Groups Two and Three—most of their irrigated land, in fact—while on the other hand Yang Zhijun, in the main village, had been allotted all his land in the Group One area because the households around his own were clustered together too tightly.

Clearly this is a situation where households with very few members and consequently very little officially allocated land are unable to produce even the amounts required to sell in order to be able to obtain a little rice to eat, and in this context it makes good sense for lineage members to cluster together, as we will see them

---

[13] These extracts from interviews with Group One householders are designed only to indicate the kind of economic situation villagers may face.

do, so that labour/land richer households can come to the assistance of those less well off.

An annual cycle of corn to wheat to sweet potato was practised on most of the more hilly dry fields as we have noted.

The total grain yield for 1988 of the three Groups was reported as follows:

Table 2: Final grain yield calculations (1988)

	Group 1	Group 2	Group 3	Total
AREA (*mu*)				
Wheat	*30*	*50*	*50*	*130*
Rice	25	52	63	140
Corn	160	123	120	403
Sweet potato	35	40	40	115
Soy	20	20	15	55
'Small spring' (peas, broadbeans)	45	57	57	159
Total (not incl. wheat)	285	292	295	872
YIELD (*jin*)				
Wheat	*3800*	*6000*	*7700*	*17500*
Rice	12100	35000	43700	90800
Corn	67700	66100	61600	195400
Sweet potato	15600	13700	13700	43000
Soy	10300	10600	10600	31500
Sorghum	100	200	200	500
'Small spring'	4800	8300	9700	22800
Total (not incl. wheat)	110600	133900	139500	38400

Even taking into account the population differences between the Groups, the relative underproduction of rice by Group One is very apparent, as is the predominant production of corn. While Group One ate the sweet potatoes, Groups Two and Three generally fed their pigs with them in a mush of eggshells, and corncobs.

The figures for the production targets set for 1988 are particularly revealing, since these were based on actual reported production for the previous year, with (according to the Village Accountant) an overall 5% increase. Although these were not broken down by household, the figures do very clearly reveal what actual production was like, and the relation between that and what was expected. Since farmers typically under- estimated their yields, while productivity target figures slightly increase those of the previous year, productivity target figures are (in the absence of extensively sampled annual weighing and measuring) in fact a reasonably accurate index to current production figures (Table 3).

Comparing this with Table 2, we see that less 'small spring' crops had been planted than planned, with a corresponding decrease in productivity; more corn and less rice than planned had been produced, as was the case in most years; more sweet potato had been planted, with disappointing results; soya however had done better than expected, on less land than was targeted.

To give some idea of the householder effects of this, one of the better-off Group Two farming households, with five working adults, who expected to exceed the production target for the year, estimated they would be able to produce (of taxable crops) 8-900 *jin* of rice, more than 2,000 *jin* of corn, about 200 *jin* of wheat and 250 *jin* of soya, besides some 3,000 *jin* of sweet potatoes.

In general however people were expected to achieve only about 85% of the village targets, although this varied wildly between households. The household I stayed in had excellent fertile irrigated land by comparison to the very poor and barely irrigated, steep land allotted to most of Group One and some other villagers, and strategies varied greatly too, with some households planting as much as a third of their fields with wheat.In Group One almost all the households (more than three quarters of them) produced only sufficient rice for about 2 months consumption, and ate *pobkwm* all the year round as a result; not everyone could afford to buy additional rice, and when they did it was not sufficient to eat unadulterated with corn all the year round. Apart from the quality of fields and number of available workers in the family, factors such as good management and use of fertiliser made a considerable

Table 3: Rural economic plan (1988)

Item	Quantity		Output		
'Small spring' crops	175	(*mu*)	35700	*jin*	
'Big spring' crops	713		355000	comprising	
Rice	140		104000		
Corn	403		180000		
Sweet potato	90		46000		
Soya bean	80		25000		
Total grain	888		390700		
Vegetable oil seed	13		1300		
Peanut	30		6000		
Tobacco	190		400	paniers	
Hemp	150		4.5	tonnes	
Fruit	--		0.4	tonnes	
Plantation forest	25		--		
Saplings	20		--		
Bamboo	15		--		
Medicines	10		--		
Irrigation improvement	5		--		
Mulberry saplings	20				
	80000	(trees)	20	paniers	(cocoons)
Cattle	60	(head)			
Swine at end year	330				
Large swine	260		16	tonnes	(pork)
			215000	*jin*	(total meat)
Poultry	--		1	tonne	(eggs)
Total rural output value			¥210,000		
Total rural income			¥310,000		

difference between households. An example of effective management was considered to be intercropping corn with soya on a dry field in the first year, followed by winter wheat, and then irrigating it in the second year, again subsequently planting wheat. Group One planted approximately equal amounts of wheat and sweet potato, minimal rice, and much more corn and soya.

By comparison, the family fields of Yang lineage Y3c had long been well irrigated, and they claimed to have been the first in the village to use bamboo troughs to convey water to the rice fields. Their most productive riceland had always been a smooth flat area which in the past had depended on natural rainfall for irrigation. After a drought in the spring of 1940, under the direction of the present householder's uncle they had used bamboo tubes to channel water down the mountainside from a spring behind the house, and later had tried to dig channels since it was expensive to maintain and repair the water system.

In theory it should be possible to relate the acreages given for different types of crop to the number of 'mouths' and full workers in the household, since it is this number which acreages are supposed to be allotted on, and then to final productivity output figures expected. In practice, however, this would be a futile endeavour, since the last adjustment of fields according to labour capacity available had occurred five years previously; there had been considerable movement in and out of households since then, and household membership was often undeclared, uncertain or changing. Moreover, in the complex and involuted labour relations which had emerged since the economic reforms, very often one son would be helping his father while another tended his own fields or employed the member of another household to do it. It was not the purpose of the work to undertake a full economic analysis, although some sample measurements and weights were taken; the figures we have are indicative of rough correlations between household size, acreage and production of various types, and serve not only to demonstrate some of the difficulties of isolating households as discrete units, but also to illustrate the economic profile of the village in general terms.

Administrative Position of the Village

Power at the level of the village is the result of a complex accomodation of interests in which older political structures interact with the extraordinary changes which have taken place in China's rural economy since the economic reforms of the early 1980s. The now dual structure of party and government organs is based at the county (*xian*) level and extends in a widening bureaucratic pyramid to the regional (*diqu*), provincial (*sheng*) and national (*zhongyan*) levels . It would be unrealistic to depict this structure as based in the village (*cunzhai*) though it is reflected in the village through the village committee and the posts of village secretary and accountant which are reserved for members of the party. It is also reflected at the district (*qu*) and commune (*xiang*) levels where administrative offices are maintained. The 'districts' such as Didong or communes form the social focal points since they tend to be where the local markets are established and are often visited by villagers . But real administrative power resides at the county (*xian*) level, where most mid-level decisions regarding appointments and allocation of resources are taken. As we try to show in Chapter 8, this formal structure of administration is knitted together or cross-cut (as the case may be) by the network of *guanxi* or 'personal connections' which defines individual status and is based on a largely utilitarian ideology of reciprocity, although it also has expressive connotations of warmth and close friendship . This network of *guanxi*, in which some have glimpsed the emergence of civil society, meshed with and cross-cutting the official structures of government and party, has been mobilised to support the enterprise economy officially introduced in 1978 . Forms of private enterprise had of course existed before then, although often without authorisation or legitimacy, and it was largely through the networks of personal *guanxi* that ordinary people were able to short-circuit the workings of a complex bureaucracy and obtain goods and services which were otherwise unobtainable . Now that forms of private enterprise have become instituted within the wider 'context' of a socialist economy, personal relations of *guanxi*, whether based on kinship and affinity, locality, classmateship or acquaintance, are employed at every level in the unsystematic and personalised exchange of goods and services that provides the base of China's rural economy. In these respects the village of an agrarian ethnic minority does not function any differently from other Han peasant villages.

However, the Minority Affairs Bureau, which is represented at national, provincial, regional and county levels, does still occupy a pivotal role among other government and party institutions at the county level where ethnic minorities are significantly represented, and a dominant role in autonomous minority counties since they control the allocation of government funds in the latter. Gongxian, which had a Han population of 298,444 and a minority population of 12,984 (all Hmong except for 68 Hui Muslim Chinese, ten Yi, four Buyi, one Tibetan and one Zhuang), does not qualify as an autonomous county,[14] and while increasingly challenged by powerful forms of local enterprise with external contact networks, yet the role of the Bureau is significant there, since special funds had in the past been allocated to improve minority education and develop minority areas and were still available.

There has always been a route for able minority cadres directly from the county to the higher levels of administrative policy-making in China, and indeed significant top-down pressure for the members of ethnic minorities to be appointed to certain key influential positions . Despite the extraordinarily low levels of literacy in minority areas and a continued local emphasis of political training over other kinds of education in the face of a growing dissatisfaction with such education and desire for other types of mobility, it is still educational standards and literacy in Chinese as well as personal contacts which form the prerequisites to promotion in the party bureaucracy. The main institution of education for national minorities in Sichuan is the Southwest College of Nationalities in Chengdu (which in 1989 numbered five Miao teachers among its staff). The Southwest College of Nationalities was one of only four Nationalities Colleges at provincial level, falling directly under the authority (and funding) of the State Nationalities Commission in Beijing, and thus on the same level of authority as the provincial Minority Affairs Bureau in Chengdu. It was a kind of local boys' dream, at village or county level, and in the absence of other work

---

[14]   Figures are those compiled for the 1982 census. A county qualifies for minority status on a quota basis, which varies from 25% to 30% minority population by province.

oppportunities, to go there to study, and those who do, having attended the local primary school, being sent away to Didong or Gongxian town for secondary education, and perhaps receiving a scholarship from the Minority Affairs Bureau for further studies in Chengdu, have either continued their careers as schoolteachers or officials in Chengdu or returned to the county to take up local posts Bonds of friendship and loyalty have tended to be strong between classmates at secondary level and at this College, and the more prestigious of the local county officials had all graduated from this College and were literate and fluent in standard Chinese.

In this way there has been a small but significantly Hmong channel of administrative and economic influence within the regional bureaucracy, reaching directly from the village through the county and regional levels to Chengdu, which we may see as taking three main aspects; through the party, through the government, and through local enterprises of the type considered in Chapter 8. As we shall see there, the party vice-secretary of the county was a Hmong from the village who had followed the first of these routes, graduating from the Southwest College of Nationalities before returning to his home county in Gongxian. He saw himself as a patron of his fellow villagers and had been a fervent ideologue when younger. As we see in Chapter 3, he had adopted a poor Han villager's son as his protégé and was planning to sponsor his education. He had been able in the past to redirect significant county funding towards the village for electrification and the building of a road. The nearby villages had neither. Another Hmong from the village, whose family we consider in detail in Chapter 8, had reached the very top of the Minority Affairs Bureau hierarchy, with a central position in Beijing before he had returned to their Chengdu office, where he lived with his Han wife and children . He was the only Hmong at this level, in the Minority Affairs Bureau office in Chengdu, but had been able to sponsor other Hmong to rise in the hierarchy, so that two younger Hmong were now working in their office in Yibin, the regional centre, as a direct result of his influence, and two more at the local Bureau offices in Gongxian.

These Hmong cadres were all bilingual in (Mandarin) Chinese and Hmong and would revert to Hmong only when discussing sensitive or important matters in private. Another girl from a poor family in Wutong village had recently received a scholarship from the Bureau to complete her secondary school education in Chengdu.[15] It was, then, the party and the Minority Affairs Bureau which still provided the main routes of upward social mobility for these members of a national minority . However, another route had recently become available through the private enterprise system, which has been widened through increasing migration to other towns and cities since the time of my fieldwork. In the days of the commune and brigade villagers had established their own cooperative construction company which mainly worked in the local town of Didong, and employed village as well as town labour. With the establishment of economic reforms in 1978 this enterprise had attained a measure of autonomy from the local government and village leadership; it had become a local enterprise led by the man who had initiated it, who was in fact a younger brother of the Minwei (Minority Affairs Bureau) cadre in Chengdu. This enterprise had been particularly successful in 1981-82, winning local contracts in Didong where it accounted for most of the new construction, and bringing in sizeable profits for its managers and the labourers .

But it should not be thought that the existence of Hmong in positions of authority throughout various levels of the party and government amounted to an interest group of a particularistic nature (although in other areas and minority contexts the bureaucratic structure may indeed have allowed the emergence of such interest groupings). The party vice-secretary was of a different surname to that of the enterprise manager and his elder brother in Chengdu; the Hmong who were working in the Minority Affairs Bureau offices at Yibin came from an altogether different area, and the Hmong in the Bureau offices at Gongxian were from a variety of different villages and patriclans. In fact the family of the vice-secretary and the Bureau official in Chengdu were traditional enemies, as I show below, the former coming from a poor peasant background, the latter from a middle peasant background which had led to the vice-secretary leading the attack on the family of the cadre in the village during the Cultural Revolution. Surname cleavages and family loyalties still continued to dominate local identifications and perceived interests, as some of the following chapters may help to demonstrate, and

---

[15] I do not mention here other secondary school children housed in Didong, Gongxien or Yibin, at their parents' own expense .

tended to prevent the formation of strong blocs of Hmong interest
within either party or government structures. But at the same time a
sense of affinity existed between these Hmong cadres, based on their
cultural identification as 'Hmong' and their official positioning as
'Miao', which led to the perception of some common interests and
objectives shared with Hmong villagers in contradiction to their
solidarity with other cadres.

As a farming village like many others in southern China, inserted
fairly securely into the still dominant administrative structures of the
Chinese polity, this village where Hmong men wore modern clothing
and usually spoke Chinese outside their homes, could be analysed as
representative of other agrarian villages in China in their
relationships to the emerging free market and the state. Yet as I hope
to show, while most villagers took pains to be able to 'pass' as Han
Chinese, nevertheless a unique sense of identity was affirmed in
many social and cultural instances.

In the following chapters, I detail some of the social context in
which such identities are expressed, through a consideration of the
lineage structure of the village, the practices of shamanism, death
and ancestral worship which demarcated a specifically local identity
by contrast to the kind of 'national minority' identity demanded by
the state, and the wider ties of patrilineal kinship which reach out to
other villages and are denied and rearticulated in wedding ritual. We
shall examine the kind of social identifications which may take place
in a largely hybrid cultural situation, and the extent to which a sense
of intersubjective agency may be expressed through wider cultural
forms.

CHAPTER TWO

SOME IDENTITY PROBLEMS

The Disappearance of the White Hmong in China?

When I started work with the Hmong in China, in 1985, I was
naturally concerned to find members of the same 'White Hmong'
(*Hmoob Dawb*) group I had worked with in Thailand, particularly for
practicality of communication and comparison. In Thailand, in fact
throughout most of South East Asia, the Hmong fall into two easily
recognisable 'cultural divisions' which cross-cut particular patrilineal
clans and which nobody has been able to explain very clearly;
Cooper (1984:28) takes this to show how 'the same people, pursuing
the same economic activity within the same environment, can
maintain cultural distinctions wihout any apparent reason for doing
so'. These divisions are known as the Green (*Ntsuab*) Hmong and
the White (*Dawb*) Hmong.[1]

Womens' costumes in these cultural divisions are strikingly
different, intermarriage between the two groups is still rare, and they
have tended to settle in different villages. Domestic architecture, and
some features of ritual and ceremonial, are also systematically
divergent. The Green Hmong use batik; the White Hmong women do
not, traditionally wearing plain undyed white dresses, which have
now been replaced by dark pantaloons with aprons.Quite different
dialects are spoken by the two groups, with consistent variations
between them (for example, open final vowels in White Hmong are
always nasalised in Green Hmong; the consonant d in White Hmong
always becomes gl/dl in Green Hmong, and there are consistent
patterns of tone change between the two).

On arrival in China, therefore, I was at once confused to meet
Hmong from Sichuan, Guizhou, and Yunnan, who all claimed to be
'White Hmong' and yet pronounced the term for 'White' in entirely
different ways (*dli*, *dlais*, or *gle*)—but all using that distinctive
consonant 'gl/dl' which in Thailand only a Green Hmong could have

---

[1] *Ntsuab* in Hmong refers to the same colour range as *qing* in Chinese; that is,
'green' to 'blue', but since 'blue' can be referred to separately, 'green' is more
correct.

used, since it is specifically confined to their dialect and in fact distinguishes it. In China I met speakers of at least three sub-dialects of Hmong, none of which were the 'White Hmong' dialect well recorded in Thailand, Laos and Vietnam and which I was familiar with, who all claimed both to be 'White Hmong' and to be speaking it.

I toyed at first with the idea that there might be a number of different 'White Hmong' cultural groupings in China, all distinguished by different sub-dialects, but the situation was clearly more complex than this. It began to be clear that the sort of *isomorphism* of cultural division with dialect, which existed so clearly in South East Asia, was simply not applicable in most of China, where a much greater range of cultural and linguistic variation seemed to have existed in the past.

The complex situation regarding forms of Hmong identification in Sichuan well illustrates this. In Gongxian and Xingwen counties of Sichuan, cadres and local leaders (as opposed to local villagers) all maintained despite their dislike of the term that they were, or had been 'White Hmong', yet they continued to use what I recognised as a distinctively Green Hmong term for this (*dli*, and their dialect was certainly not the White Hmong dialect of Thailand and Laos, having very different tones, and the nasalised final endings characteristic of Green Hmong). Ling and Ruey (1947) had however declared that there were both 'Pe Miao' (White Hmong) and 'Hua Miao' in Gaoxian, Gongxian, Xingwen, Changning and Yunlian counties of southern Sichuan, and that because the White Hmong predominated, the entire area was known as the 'Pe Miao' area. And as we see below, Graham's work (1937, 1954) in the same region in the 1930s consistently referred to the people living there as 'White Hmong'. Yet these 'White Hmong' did not appear to speak White Hmong, did not wear the traditional dress I associated with the White Hmong, and their architecture was not recognisable as traditionally 'Hmong'. Moreover, at the village level, householders frequently assured me that they were just 'Hmong' plain and simple, the same as other 'Hmong' in Guizhou and Yunnan; they did not appear to recognise the colour terms vital in South East Asia at all.

I was given an official explanation of why certain local cultural distinctions such as 'White' or 'Green' Hmong might now have disappeared in this region, which I heard often enough from cadres and senior leaders in China, and owes something to previous work on other Miao groups in China.[2] According to these officials, all the traditional local distinctions of the 'Miao' by colour or costume or other means (such as Magpie Hmong, Dog Ear Miao, Basket Head Miao, Black Miao, Red Miao, Western Miao, River Miao etc.) were local feudal-era Han Chinese terms, mostly derogatory, for the Hmong in particular districts which originally had not been recognised by the Hmong at all. But over the course of history they had gradually been adopted by the Hmong themselves—an example of the processes of cultural diffusion we have discussed, or some ironic attempt at subversion of the dominant modes of reference and address? Now, it was explained, all such terms were taboo, since the Hmong had become officially classified as 'Miao' and recognised as all forming one people (*minzu*), under the new state nationalities policy initiated after Liberation.

While on the face of it this seemed a feasible enough explanation for why there might have been a reluctance by local villagers to be recognised as 'White Hmong' at all, and a general dislike of such terms by officials, nevertheless this explanation fell far short of accounting adequately for the depth and strength of these cultural divisions marked by colour terms as found beyond and around the borders of China where, as I have said, different dialects, and even different forms of architecture and costume, continue to mark these distinctions. Could it have been, I wondered, that the Hmong of South East Asia, isolated from the heartland and origin of their ancestry, had somehow managed to preserve much earlier, more archaic forms of social organisation, tribal or even totemic in origin (as Savina, 1924, had believed), which had entirely disappeared in China—as a diffusionist might have argued?

A Confusion of Past Styles

An enlightening conversation took place in the village in Sichuan between a man from Wangwuzhai who said he had thought he was a Green Hmong for years because he had been to college in the provincial capital, Chengdu, with a Green Hmong from Yunnan province who spoke exactly the same way as he did, and another

---

[2] See Shi (1986); Yang (1947); Liang (1950); Cheung (1996).

from Wutong who maintained that all of them in the area were White Hmong because *he* had gone to college with a White Hmong from Guizhou province who spoke in exactly the same way as *he* did! It was I who had to intervene (after only a few days in the village) to ask why they themselves seemed to be pronouncing the same Hmong words somewhat differently. At first it seemed that they were not wholly conscious of this, or did not like to notice it, but then they agreed that, yes, there *were* some small differences of speech between the two villages (Wutong and Wangwu) they came from, although these were both in the same county (Gongxian).

In time I learned that in Gongxian county alone, there had been at least three distinctive Hmong 'styles' (they used the Chinese term *daban* for these, which usually refers to differences of dress), marked by slight differences of dialect, women's costume and ancestry; these were generally reckoned to be those of Wangwu itself, of Guandou, and of Chenshi.

Let us look at some of the detailed differences noted for these Gongxian 'styles'. The *daban* where women used to wear white turbans (now often towels) was known as (1) the Wangwu style, which also covered Xinguangcun in Luobiao *xiang*; Gaofengcun and Lapingcun in Luohai *xiang*; Wutong itself in Yuhe *xiang*; and Xincun, in Caoying *xiang*.

The *daban* traditionally associated with black turbans (although the younger generation were now adopting white or coloured ones) was known as (2) the Guandou style, after the *xiang* of that name near Weixin; and this style was also to be found in Sanxi *xiang* and Shibei *xiang*.

And then there was (3) the Chenshi village style, where turbans were made of hair pinned up elaborately around a circular basketware cone over which cloth could be draped; a style also found in Guoshicun, and Datiancun of Chensheng *xiang* (as well as Weixin village near Wuxiu). Cloth was draped over the cone in Chenshi itself, and in Datian, but sometimes the hair was left unadorned.

Together with other differences in the placing of embroidery and appliqué, these then appeared to be the *daban* which had been recognised or become instituted over the past 50 years. But it was clear that there had already been considerable changes in this, with young women since Liberation and even more since the Cultural Revolution using brightly coloured commercial cloths for their Han peasant style tunics, borrowing Hmong skirts for festive occasions from girls of other districts, and wrapping modern towels of all colours around their heads as turbans when they went to market.

And it did appear rather probable that still earlier cultural distinctions may have already become submerged among these three main noted differences of tradition, since there were still obvious differences between the Wutong and Wangwu areas, although they were both supposedly of the same '*daban*'. To recap briefly at this point, the Hmong of both Wutong and Wangwu had ben referred to in the past quite clearly as 'White Hmong' by Graham and others; local officials (and some village elders) still maintained that they were, although they spoke a dialect which I recognised as nearer to Green than to White Hmong. There were also some differences between the dialects in the two places which led me to suspect that differences even between Wutong and Wangwu may have been greater in the past than now appeared. My suspicion of this was confirmed when I was told that in the past the Wutong women had traditionally worn trousers with aprons very like those which the White Hmong of Thailand wear today (I saw old photographs of these), while in Wangwu (which used batik, confined outside China to the Green Hmong), traditional dress comprised pink leggings and a very dark skirt with red-and-blue hems under an elaborately embroidered apron; much more like the dress which is a distinctive characteristic of the Green Hmong in South East Asia. It seemed possible, then, that there had been differences in the past between White and Green Hmong in the area which had now disappeared and might be reflected in the very small differences still remaining between the Hmong of Wutong and Wangwu.

Graham on the White Hmong and 'Hmong Ntsü'

As Graham put it, writing in 1937, 'It is possible that the Ch'uan (Sichuan) Miao (Hmong Sua or Chinese Miao) are a mixture of several smaller Miao groups who have been or are being absorbed into one cultural group in one cultural area'. If Graham was right, a process of 'uniformisation', or cultural levelling, among the Hmong of this area of Sichuan may have been continuing for most of this century.[3]

Graham recorded that the 'Ch'uan Miao' referred to themselves as 'Hmong Bo' meaning 'Old Hmong', and he also says that they were often called 'Hmong Sua' by others, meaning 'Chinese Miao' because of their adoption of Han practices. But he also says very clearly in a number of places that they were also called Hmong Gleh or 'White Hmong' because of the women's former or present practice of *wearing plain undyed skirts* 'in some localities' (Graham 1954). This is very significant, as the complete absence of batik is the most distinctive marker of 'White Hmong' identity (apart from their dialect) outside China. Elsewhere Graham also remarks that in the old days most of the clothing of the Ch'uan Miao was completely undyed, although he refers to their current adoption of batiking from neighbouring Miao groups, and he records his doubt as to whether they were really of the same group as the clearly distinguished White Hmong 'of southern Guizhou'. It seems clear enough from all this that there were certainly 'White Hmong' in the region in the past, whose women wore plain dresses with no batik exactly as traditional White Hmong groups have done elsewhere. It is also clear that they did not and do not speak the White Hmong dialect recognised in South East Asia, and that they may now have been absorbed by or merged with other Hmong groups.

Graham also distinguished three main styles or traditions among the Hmong of the region, although these do not exactly coincide with the three I was told about. The first group he distinguished were known as 'White Hmong', or familiarly in Chinese as Hoshan Miao ('Buddhist Monk Miao') because of the plainness of their dress; no batik again. These lived near *Chen Hsiung* in North Yunnan, and were differentiated from the *Lo Piao* Hmong near Wangwu, who were known in Chinese as the 'Basket' (Tau Tau) Miao because of their women's hairstyles. These Hmong of Lo Piao must correspond to what I have described as the Chengshi (Basket) style in Gongxian today, in which case Graham's first, *Chen Hsiung*, tradition may correspond either to that known as the Wangwu style today, or possibly to today's 'Guandou' tradition. He adds that a third group,

---

[3] Graham almost always means the Hmong when he refers to the 'Ch'uan' Miao, although he occasionally includes in this group the Xiao Hua Miao of North Yunnan whom he thought were being absorbed by the Hmong.

near Laowatan, were known as the 'Ch'ing Chi' Miao because their clothing resembled the plumage of a pheasant; and again this may correspond to either one of the contemporary Wangwu or Guandou styles.

There was in fact some disagreement about the three main contemporary styles I have described above, which in some cases meant considerable efforts of recollection for informants. Although everybody agreed there were three main traditions in the area, one informant saw Wutong and Wangwu as quite different by contrast with Chenshi (leaving out Guandou altogether), and another again disagreed with the placing of Wutong under Wangwu and claimed it was a part of the Chenshi tradition. Moreover, villagers native to both Wutong and Xincun, supposedly belonging to the Wangwu tradition, also claimed to know how to make the basket hair frames characteristic of the Chenshi style 'really properly'. All this would go to support the claim that there were in the past significant differences even between the Wutong and Wangwu areas, although they are practically indistinguishable today. In general then a number of smaller Hmong groups do appear to have been assimilated into a more general Hmong identity, and some villages, such as Wutong, may be the result of the blending and mixture of a number of different cultural traditions.

Confirming the generality of this sort of process, Graham describes the 'Ya Ch'iao Miao' or 'Magpie Miao' in 'the northern part of Kweichow' as 'a small group that had almost been absorbed'. Here we are on partcularly firm grounds, because Ruey Yih Fu (1958, 1960) studied these Hmong Yachio or 'Magpie Hmong' (who were also referred to locally as 'Han Miao') in detail, and we know exactly where they lived; along the headwaters of the Yungning River in southern Sichuan. These 'Hmong Yachio' referred to themselves as 'Hmong Ntsü'—which sounds very like the term the Green Hmong use for themselves ('Hmoob Ntsuab')—they did use batik, just like the Green Hmong, and their kinship terms, well recorded by Ruey and commented on by Kroeber, appear extremely close to those of the Green Hmong of South East Asia, far closer than those I recorded among the Hmong of Wutong (Appendix VII). This close-to-Green Hmong sort of identity does indeed now appear to have become completely lost in the more generalised kind of Hmong identity I encountered among the Hmong of this part of

Sichuan, although some of the costume and dialect of these 'Hmong Ntsü' may again have survived in the form of the slight differences apparent today between villages supposedly part of the same tradition, such as those of Wutong and Wangwu.

A Levelling Process

The remarkable extent of this kind of *submerged local cultural variation* was also common in other Hmong areas I visited; for example, in Weixin county of Yunnan, six distinct local cultural traditions were recognised (those of the Hmong Daus, Hmong Xi, Hmong Leng, Hmong Pa, Hmong *taus dli* (a derogatory term), and the Hmong just referred to dismissively as 'those Hmong from Guizhou'). In Xingyi county of Southeast Guizhou, differences were most marked between the Hmong Pw and Hmong Leng. I could extend this list with reference to Laos and Vietnam, where differentiations are commonly made between the Hmoob Xi, Hmoob Leeg and Hmoob Ntsuab, and where the Hmoob Daus or Hmoob Pua are also an easily identified group, with a dialect close to that of Wutong. Indeed *it becomes very evident that the clearcut division in Thailand between two distinct cultural groups of Hmong is somewhat unusual in the context of a wider consideration of the Hmong.*

In what is probably the area of the greatest Hmong cultural variety outside Guizhou, Wenshan of Yunnan (near the Vietnamese border), besides the Hmoob Dawb (White Hmong) and Hmoob Ntsuab (Green Hmong) of South East Asia, there are still today the Hmoob Sib (who are very close to the Hmoob Ntsuab), Hmoob Peg, Hmoob Pua, and Hmoob Xauv, and also the 'Hmoob Sua' ('Chinese Hmong') of Burma who wear extremely dark clothing. Graham was probably wrong to suggest that it was other groups of Hmong who called the Sichuan Hmong 'Hmong Sua'; it is more likely that this is one of the cases where the official Chinese view is correct, that it was first suggested to them (in Chinese) that they might be 'Han Miao' ('Sinicised Hmong'), and that they then reproduced the term (in Hmong) as a self-appellation for the benefit of outside investigators.

While 'Hmong Sua' is probably not a reliable indicator of traditional identity in the Sichuan area, 'Hmong Gleh' or White

Hmong almost certainly is, and it seems to have referred most clearly to the Hmong of Chen Hsiung who Graham describes as wearing exactly the kind of undyed plain clothes which have characterised other groups of White Hmong (including those of Thailand, Panzihua in Sichuan, and Wenshan of Yunnan) in the past.

The fact that the women of Wutong also wore exactly the kind of trousers which have generally replaced the undyed skirt for White Hmong women elsewhere, further reinforces the view that in the distant past there was a distinctive 'White Hmong' tradition in Sichuan, as Ruey and Ling (1947) also confirm. Whether or not this general tradition was associated particularly with Chen Hsiung, it must have been radically different from the 'Basket style' of Graham's Lo Piao, now referred to as the Chenshi style. However, it is also clear that this distinctive 'White Hmong' tradition has slowly been uniformised and absorbed, both to conform more with the traditions of other local Hmong groups, and presumably aided by the general loss of specific cultural features among the Hmong of this part of China as a result of Han acculturation, during the course of the present century. The Wangwu Hmong, meanwhile, who could also have originally been White Hmong, may have absorbed more influences from either the vanished Yochio Miao (Hmong Ntsü) or those described by Graham as the colourfully dressed ('pheasant-like') Ch'ing Chi Miao of Laowatan, as evidenced in the prevalence of batik in Wangwu and in their slight differences of dialect from that of Wutong.

Given the much greater extent of local cultural variations among Hmong-speakers which appear to have existed in China's past by comparison with Thailand, what may well have happened in China is that, with the enormous and unprecedented social changes and upheavals since Liberation, *a kind of 'levelling' process has taken place, between originally quite culturally divergent groups of Hmong*. Even in the 1930s, after all, Graham (1954) describes the beginning of this process of the blending and mixing of different Hmong groups, when the 'White Hmong' were already beginning to wear coloured clothes, small Hmong groups were merging and commonly adopting Han dress and language. It would seem that CCP policy since 1949 has contributed to and accelerated this general twentieth-century process of the loss of individual cultural characteristics in larger identities.

Ruey and Ling (1947) in very similar terms described the difficulty of distinguishing between the dress of originally distinct groups such as the Hua (Flowery) and Qing (Green) Miao who lived together with the Pe (White) Miao in Mengzu in Yunnan; 'several groups inhabiting the same area are likely to intermarry, so that after a considerable length of time has passed, it is difficult to identify them'. This well-recorded process of fusion must have been greatly reinforced by the relocations and population shifts which took place before and after Liberation, during the Land Reforms of the early 1950s and the Cultural Revolution of the mid-1960s.

The Archaism of Cadet Branches?

And it is interesting that (unlike modern Chinese ethnographers) Ling and Ruey seem to take it for granted that cultural divisions like 'White' and 'Green' among the Miao did represent real historical forms of identification by the people themselves, which emerged within an originally homogenous cultural and linguistic group as they adopted different migratory pathways towards the south. The model adopted here is one of unilineal kinship reckoning, in which branches spontaneously emerge from a common root; a genealogical view of variety emerging from unity. While the current Chinese view that such terms were feudal Han derogatories which came eventually to be accepted by local non-Han peoples may be applicable to some of the later terms for small groups (such as the 'Magpie' and 'Long-Horn' Miao), these far broader cultural divisions probably did represent earlier forms of differentiation which have been preserved in virtually pristine form in Thailand, at the furthest limit of the Hmong expansion—and in other, peripheral or inaccessible areas, such as along the Vietnam-China border. Yet should we for this reason take these 'archaic' forms of culture as somehow more representative of some 'authentic' form of Hmong culture, or should we see more orthodox forms of an originary Hmong culture in the recent breakdown into a more undifferentiated form of Hmong identity?

The official classification in China of all Hmong groups (together with some non-Hmong groups) since 1949 as members of the 'Miao', and the overt disapproval and discouragement of local forms of cultural variation, must have contributed to and facilitated what a genealogical model of ethnogenesis would see as a kind of *reversion* to an earlier, more inclusive form of ethnic identification, as (unspecified) 'Hmong', prior to the taking of different migration paths by an original northern group. Such a *generalised* form of Hmong identification would have been prior even to the historical emergence of major cultural divisions among the Hmong such as those of the 'White' or 'Green' Hmong which are either still well represented, or have become far more marked, in South East Asia.

China's nationalities policy, by according official recognition to only fifty-six of the more than four hundred names which had been submitted by 1953 (three-quarters of which came from Yunnan), has besides politicising ethnicity and contributing to ethnic separatism, also increased the tendency towards 'greater-group formation' and the fusion, rather than fission, of smaller ethnic and cultural groups (Tapp 1988; Harrell 1989). The Yi are a good example of this process, a broad general classification under which many smaller groups such as the Samei (Hsieh 1986), Sani and Nosu have been subsumed; so too are the 'Miao', a classification which groups together people who call themselves Hmu, Hmong, Mong, Gho Xiong, Ge/Gelao and A Hmo. Although they cannot talk each others' languages, there is now a renewed consciousness among many of these of belonging to a much wider national group, owing to their official classification as 'Miao'.

The broad cultural divisions exemplified by the White and Green Hmong of Thailand, at the limits of the historical expansion of the Hmong out of China, might be taken therefore to represent a much more 'primitive' state of affairs than that represented by the extraordinary processes of transformation and fusion which appear to have taken place in the context of much greater historical cultural variation among the Hmong of China. That is, compared with the situation in South East Asia, there appears to have been both much greater cultural variation within Hmong groups in China, and a greater loss of these distinctions; besides 'cousinly' relations with non-Hmong groups classified as Miao with whom certain characteristics may have been shared by certain Hmong groups of a type which did not exist outside the borders of China.

It is quite possible then to view the Hmong as historically having formed part of a much more widespread peasant farming population, some of whom were broken off by the inexorable expansion of the

Han Chinese population and their historical domination of natural resources in Southwestern China, and who subsequently dispersed into inaccessible locations at high altitudes (such as those of South East Asia), where their society then took on novel characteristics of segmentary solidarity and isolation—together perhaps with their enforced adoption of techniques of shifting cultivation. Others, who remained in the valleys and plains, evolved more complex forms of accomodation towards the Han people and the traditional Chinese state.

It is not so surprising that an earlier generation of cultural relativists working in Northern Thailand and Laos should have viewed the Hmong as an entirely separate and unique group, since a very similar research process took place with the people most closely related to the Hmong/Miao, the Yao/Mien people of South East Asia, who have likewise migrated out of and also remain in China. For many years otherwise competent researchers had remarked on the peculiarities of their tribal, animistic religion (Kandre 1967; Miles 1976; Chob 1972), and it was not until Lemoine (1972c, 1978, 1982, 1983) identified this religion as an archaic form of Daoism that it was recognised to what an extent the Yao too participated in the wider, 'Great Tradition' of 'Chinese' civilization.[4] As Eric Wolf put it, 'the concept of a fixed, unitary, and bounded culture must give way to a sense of the fluidity and permeability of cultural sets' (Wolf 1982:387). This is the difficulty we face here; to account for felt differences between the Hmomg and others without essentialising them.

This view, of the cultural divisions among the Hmong of Thailand as representing a more archaic state of affairs than that represented in present-day China, is an attractive one, which makes some sense of why it is that the clear isomorphism of dialect with culture group characteristic of the Hmong in much of South East Asia appears so problematic in the more dynamic social context of China.

The opposing view would argue that there is good historical evidence that shifting cultivation has always been the preferred traditional mode of subsistence for Hmong, that a cultural homogeneity of the type remarked by Geddes (1976) and others

---

[4] Lemoine (1982) expresses his debt to Strickman (1979, 1980) for successfully identifying the particular school of Daoism adopted by the Yao.

would have been maintained through the mobility of pioneer shifting cultivation coupled with strict rules of clan outmarriage which redistributed patterns of dialect, embroidery and custom across wide geographical distances; and that since the Sichuan Hmong only adopted permanent cultivation and setttlements since about 1573, more instituted forms of cultural differentiation which might otherwise have occurred under conditions of permanent settlement simply had insufficient time to develop fully before a conscious 'nationalities policy' after 1949 froze processes of ethnic change (such as Han acculturation) at the same time as tending to subsume small local cultural groups into larger overall classifications.

But talking of the 'traditional' is notoriously tricky in the long dynastic historical context of China. We have many historical examples of Hmong practising permanent wet-rice field agriculture whenever they have been able to, and no *a priori* reason, apart from historical chronicles which have always associated the 'Miao' with 'cultivation by the fire and sword', to paint their history with the single brush-stroke of shifting cultivation. The view that Hmong have only adopted shifting cultivation where they had to, and conform more to images of peasant farmers than of tribal segmentarists, has much to recommend it.

From this more 'polyfocal' point of view on Hmong history across the whole region, it almost seems as if the Hmong of South East Asia with whom I had worked inhabited a sort of cultural 'relic area' of the kind postulated by diffusionist theoreticians, where some sort of cultural 'ossification' had taken place, furthered perhaps by the mountainous terrain they inhabited and, more recently, by the need to satisfy the demands of an increasingly important tourist industry through the provision of appropiate images of traditionally dressed tribal Hmong cultivating opium through slash-and-burn agriculture on the mountain tops.

To summarise, the outlines of the process which, on this view, must have taken place are clear enough. Certain broad cultural distinctions, which may have corresponded to a particular stage of development of the Hmong as a whole, appear to have been retained in Thailand unaltered, so that the Hmong of South East Asia have generally presented the appearance of isolated tribes with distinctive dialects, as they have been usually considered (see for example Hinton 1969; Kunstadter 1983). However, this tribal, isolationist view of the Hmong may itself have emerged simply from the lack of a wider historical and geographical 'context'[5] among researchers who in the past were largely confined for practical reasons to South East Asia. In terms of the much wider historical and ecological *context* provided by work in China, it may well seem more appropriate (as I have suggested), to view the Hmong as historically having formed a widespread peasant farming society, a small proportion of whom have become isolated and peripheralised in the mountainous valleys of South East Asia (which as many commenters have noted prevent ease of communication between neighbouring groups), and consequently 'tribalised', both in their own views, and in the views of those researching them.

Diffusionist Parallels

By contrast with the 'frozen', static image which the culture of the Hmong in South East Asia now begins to present, seeming to confirm the most extreme diffusionist hypotheses, what seems to have occurred among the Hmong of China has been an extraordinary and lengthy process of diversification and re-unification, immeasurably accelerated by the rapid and momentous social changes of the past fifty years; perhaps a kind of cultural 'erosion' in the more 'open' context of China, marked by a mixture and a blending of a far wider range of different cultural traditions and influences. Not only have these processes of cultural unification actually occurred in modern China, through the blending and borrowing of local dialects, customs and costumes, and the loss of traditional cultural features through the attacks on culture in the Cultural Revolution, but there has been an intensified and explicit modern demand by Miao cadres that they should do so.

For example, at the first Miao Studies Association meeting organised in Guizhou in November 1988, where Chinese had to be the official language partly so that the members of the different groups classified as 'Miao' could understand one another, the merits of adopting a common costume for all the 'Miao' groups were seriously mooted and discussed (see Schein 1993:234, 261-3). There have also been repeated calls by the 'Miao' in China since the 1950s

---

[5] Tapp (1990).

for a unified 'Miao writing' to represent all the languages grouped as 'Miao' within China and even beyond it; overseas Hmong visitors from the US and France in 1988 greatly polemicised these demands by calling (officially) for an international unification of Miao scripts (see Cheung 1996), at the same time as (unofficially) for an international Miao-Hmong nationalist movement, which led to great concern and restrictions on further international exchanges by the Chinese authorities (subsequent Miao research meetings were more carefully monitored). Within the Chinese political context, these demands are exceptionally clear examples of the kind of 'greater-group' formation which has been one of the unintended results of China's official nationalities policy (Tapp 1986), now leading among some 'Miao' cadres to a kind of transnational identity production which may challenge state-bound versions of nationalism and displace 'disempowering localisms', as Schein (1998) sees it.

Developments since 1949, then, would have overthrown the kind of regional cultural variations and social stratifications which may have been expected to occur under conditions of permanant agricultural settlement since 1573, and even the far longer-term processes of linguistic and cultural variation between larger cultural divisions of the Hmong such as those represented by the 'White' and 'Green' Hmong of South East Asia which have been associated with different migratory pathways (which as we have seen were already beginning to disappear in the 1920s and 1930s; Graham gave batik 20 more years in 1937), and facilitated a reversion to an earlier, more inclusive and homogenous form of identification as 'Hmong' which historically clan exogamy and shifting cultivation may have maintained.

There has been considerable discussion among linguists about the difficulties of defining 'dialects', and one linguistic school, in an attempt to revive Schmidt's diffusionist 'Wave Theory', denied the existence of any isolable dialects, preferring to see variation as a stage in a constant, dynamic process of language change radiating out from a central point (Bailey 1973 in Petyt 1980). Exactly as with this 'dynamic' school of historical linguistics, we may be able to see both cultural and linguistic variations among the Hmong as corresponding to a particular phase in a process of historical development, which has in Thailand, the periphery of Hmong expansion, become isolated and ossified. What Baileys' theory suggests is that the most conservative forms of a language will tend to be found at the perimeter of its geographical extent, since the 'earlier and least general changes have time to spread furthest' (Petyt 1980). Bartoli and the Italian Neolinguists also hypothesised that where a language form was found in a more isolated, inaccessible, or peripheral area or was more generally distributed than another, then that form was probably the earlier one (see Bartoli 1925). While these sorts of linguistic theories may have been discredited as absolute laws, they are still taken to have 'considerable validity' as guidelines.[6]

Sapir's original (1913) formulation of this linguistic principle was that the greater the differentiation within a language 'stock', the greater the time which must be assumed for the differentiation to have taken place in, as with the greater geographical extent occupied by a particular language. Murdock (1964) echoes this, claiming that the ancestral homeland of any group of languages is to be found around the area showing the greatest extent of diversity, as does Lehman (1979). It does appear that the range of dialectal variation in Hmong has been much wider around Sichuan and Guizhou than it is beyond the frontiers of China, which would fit with generally accepted historical findings that the Hmong have dispersed and radiated outwards from a southern-central Chinese homeland. It also appears as if certain more archaic cultural divisions have been preserved among the Hmong of South East Asia in a way which has been lost, or is rapidly being lost, in Sichuan and Guizhou, and that these peripheral areas of Hmong expansion may therefore indeed represent more 'conservative' forms of cultural production. If cultural variation can be seen in anything like the same terms as linguistic variation, then the strong and marked cultural differentiations which persist among the Hmong in the peripheral areas of South East Asia would appear to represent earlier, more conservative cultural forms which have been largely lost around the heartland of the Hmong's original point of expansion in China. A diffusionist argument!

The possibilities considered here are all based on what I have called a genealogical model of ethnogenesis; that branches of variety spring from a unitary root. This is the model of patrilineal kinship,

---

[6] Chambers and Trudgill (1980); cf. Antilla (1972).

the nineteenth-century model of Indo-European languages and of evolutionary descent, and is often applied to cultural development by ethnologists and their informants. In the Chinese context, we may see how possible it was for an (inclusive) doctrine of Confucian culturalism to have coexisted with an (exclusive) ideology of patrilinel descent as Ebrey (1996) suggested, but there was nothing very odd in evolutionary models of patrilineal descent being applied to ethnic groups becoming Han through the 'diffusion' of Han culture in this way since notions of culture and of kinship descent were both based on a common 'genealogical' model which specified variety as emerging out of an original, orthodox unity (and the model is inclusive as well as exclusive; it is just that an inclusive unity is posited as prior to the later exclusive differentiation of branches and varieties). There is an obvious alternative to the genealogical model, where difference and variety are posited as an original condition, on which is then mentally imposed a social or cultural unity; we might call this the existentialist and to some extent post-structuralist model. It is to this latter model, with its emphasis on original differences and variation, order imposed on an underlying chaos, that Steiner's (1975) notion of language as being about lying and concealing the truth, rather than communicating, is applicable; here survival depends precisely on the ability to deceive others and the capacity to imagine alternatives to a current dilemma, which in turn depends on the fictive and counter-factual powers of language. The multiplicity of languages, and of cultural differences, is here seen as part of a strategy of keeping things to oneself and not allowing access to outsiders; a language (like a particular kind of culture) is a kind of code invented to confuse the opposition.

As we move in subsequent chapters through various considerations of a patrilineal ideology and the notions of cultural identity and difference which are revealed through it, I hope we may begin to envisage a way in which some of the classic incompatabilities between the genealogical model and the alternative model of original variety may be overcome through seeing both unity (identity) and difference (variety) as mutually constituting.

CHAPTER THREE

HAN ENDOGAMY

I have mentioned that most of the Hmong in Wutong were bilingual
in Hmong and Chinese and reserved the wearing of a standardised
form of their traditional costume for special occasions, and that there
were a number of Han Chinese households living in the village. Yet
the genealogies I collected (which covered all households) showed
considerable intermarriage between the Han families (surnames Pei,
Xie, Sun and Huang) and very few between the Hmong and the Han
despite the fact that the Han families had lived together with the
Hmong for over 5 generations. Most Hmong and Chinese informants
claimed that intermarriages between them never occurred, and there
were various explanations given for this, the most frequent being that
'our customs are different'. Although, as we shall see, this was not at
all strictly true, since individual marriages of Hmong with Han had
in fact occurred, yet certainly Hmong and Han endogamy had been
largely maintained. On the surface, relations between Hmong and
Han were presented as, and certainly seemed to be, perfectly
amicable at the village level. Indeed, many of the Han villagers could
speak Hmong, or if they could not speak it, could at least understand
(everyday) Hmong (which was explained as the result of their having
played together as children), and some of the Han villagers, as we
see in Ch.4, had even taken to consulting Hmong shamans when they
were ill. There was a certain hybridisation, a coalescence of Hmong
and Han cultural identities as they were presented at the local level,
with the Hmong adopting certain 'emblems' of Han identity, such as
speech and clothes, while the Han villagers for their part seemed to
respect the fact that they were living in a minority village (and
thereby gained special exemptions from taxes and educational
access).

But at the same time the separateness, and differences, of Hmong
and Han Chinese identity, were carefully and persistently insisted on,
and this was reflected in the rarity of the Hmong-Han marriages
which had taken place. In order to understand the strength of the
attachments between the Chinese families in the village, and
something of their cohesiveness as a community which was able

nevertheless to coexist with that of the Hmong, we must look in some detail at the exact details of their residential patterns and the ties which they had formed with themselves through the means of kinship.

The Li

At the North end of the village, downslope to the other side of the main track there was a cluster of Han Chinese houses at the very extremity of the village; those of Li Guoquan, Li Guoliang, and Li Peilong, separated from the double homestead of Li Peishu and Li Guohua (Li Peixiang), with Gu Yingshen's and Yang Xiangying's houses a little further away.

Over the near brow of the hill on the other side of the path, past the houses of Wang Zhailing and Wang Yingchen , there was a further cluster of Chinese Li houses; first that of Li Peibing, with those of Li Guoqian and Li Peixin to either side, and past Li Peixin's further up the mountain slope the house of Li Guicheng, and then at some distance away, past a cluster of Hmong Yang households and the three closely related (Hmong) Zeng households of Zeng Wanlu, Zeng Wanshou and Zeng Wanpei,[1] the house of Li Guojin (Diagram 3).

The Li families had moved into the village shortly before Liberation to rent land from the Hmong, and represented an extremely poor strata of dispossesssed rural peasantry at that time. The 'Pei' suffix signified the older generation and the 'Guo' suffix the present, mostly middle-aged, one. *Li Peishu* (at household no. 42) and *Li Peilong* (at household no.39) were brothers. Another brother (Li Peixiang) had died, leaving his son *Li Guohua* (at household no. 38) sharing the house with his father's brother.

Li Peixin (HH no.33) was their father's elder brother's son, their first cousin, while *Li Guoqian* (HH no.35), Li Guicheng (HH no.34) and Li Guojin (HH no.36) were his sons. *Li Peibing* (HH no.31) was his brother. *Li Guoquan* (HH no.41) and *Li Guoliang* (HH no.43) were sons of Li Peishu.

---

[1] The Tao household.

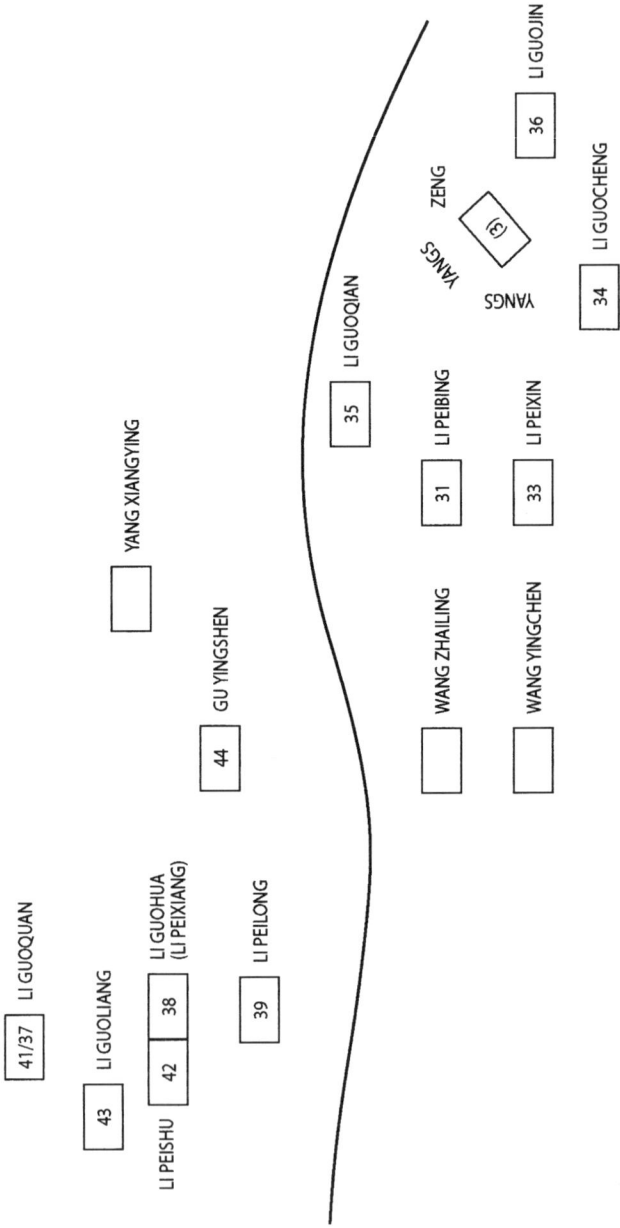

Diagram 3: Li households

Households shown:

- 41/37 LI GUOQUAN
- 43 LI GUOLIANG
- LI PEISHU
- 42 LI GUOHUA (LI PEIXIANG)
- 38
- 39 LI PEILONG
- 44 GU YINGSHEN
- YANG XIANGYING
- 35 LI GUOQIAN
- 31 WANG ZHAILING
- LI PEIBING
- 33 WANG YINGCHEN
- LI PEIXIN
- YANGS
- ZENG
- (3) YANGS
- 34 LI GUOCHENG
- 36 LI GUOJIN

A simplified form of this shown in Diagram 4 (or in map form, see Diagram 5).

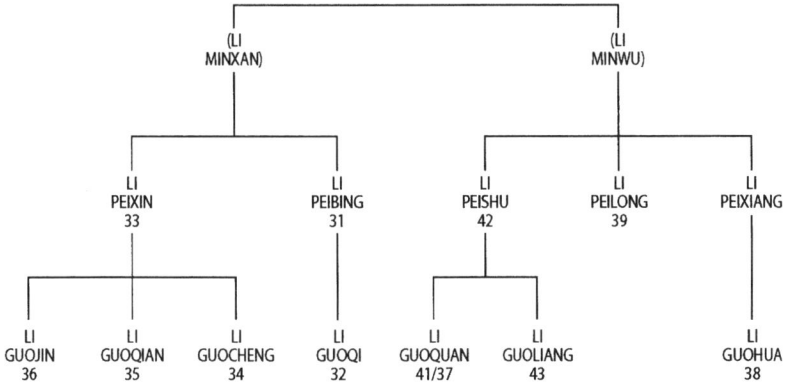

Diagram 4: Li family relations

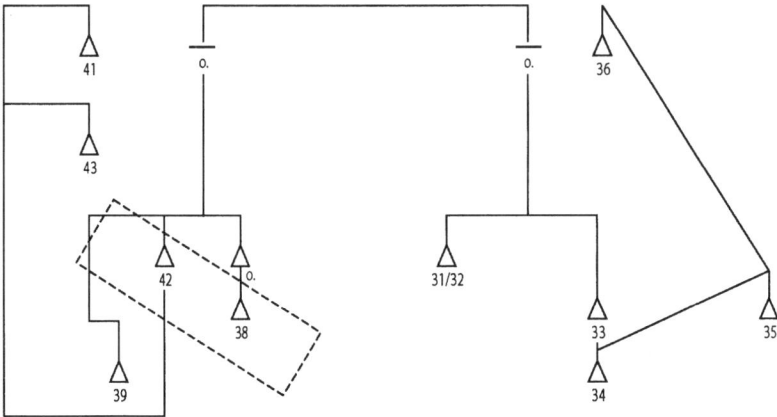

Diagram 5: Li household relations

These two clusters of patrilineal first cousins were clearly separated from each other in terms of their housing, while still occupying the same end of the village. In the one cluster, two brothers maintained separate households, while the three sons of one of these brothers had branched off to establish their separate households. In the other cluster, again two brothers were maintaining households separately from each other, and while the two sons of one of these brothers had similarly branched off to form separate households, the son of a deceased third brother remained with their father in whose house the deceased younger brother had originally lived.

Li Peilong, who was aged 59, the separated brother at the furthest extent of the village, had in fact had six daughters, five of whom had married out while the other had died. He had also had a son who had two boys and a girl of his own—and this was one of many cases where the image of nuclear households presented by village records had to be seriously modified, as one notes there were formerly six sisters inhabiting this house, while Li Shuping's (the son's) young daughter had been left out of the census records altogether.

Li Peishu, aged 56, in household number 42, who lived with his nephew while two of his sons had separated off, had actually had four sons himself, of whom only one was unmarried, besides two daughters who had married out. Two of his sons remained living with him, one with a wife and son of his own. If one were to add his deceased brother's son Li Guohua (HH no. 38) with the latter's wife and two sons, these two 'official' recorded households of 6 and 4 members each are transformed into a single household with a large extended family of 10 members, looking like Diagram 6.

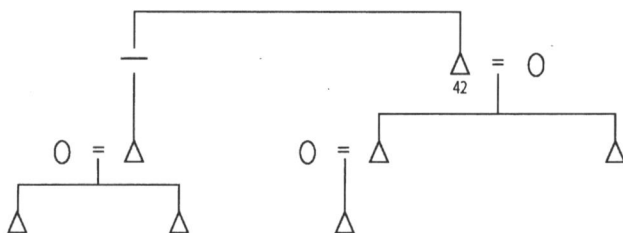

Diagram 6: Li Guohua's household

His two eldest sons had already established their own, separate, households; Li Guoliang at household no. 43, with a wife and two sons, and Li Guoquan at household no. 41 with a wife and son. Li Guoquan was said to have nearly 'died twice', after a beam had fallen on him the year before while building a house; since then he had become progressively weaker, but still had to look after his father's father's younger brother, Li Minfan, aged 78 and with no children of his own (at household no.37). So that Li Guoquan's household (no.41) could look like Diagram 7.[2]

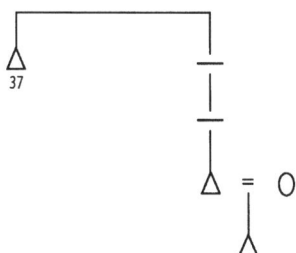

Diagram 7: Li Guoquan's household

Turning to the two brothers in the other cluster, households number 31 and 33 (Li Peibing and Li Peixin), the latter of whose three sons lived at households 34,35 and 36 respectively; the widower Li Peibing had had three sons and a daughter, of whom only the oldest son (Li Guoqi at household 32) had married and had a daughter. In fact as we have seen all his children still lived with him, transforming the two households at 32 and 31 of 3 and 4 members respectively into one household with 7 members, looking like Diagram 8.

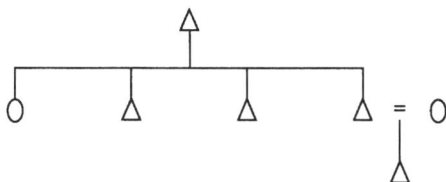

Diagram 8: Li Peibing's household

---

[2] And this would reduce the proper number of households in the village by one.

Li Peixin (at household no.33) had had a son and two daughters in addition to his three oldest sons who had all married and moved out; a daughter was not recorded in household registrations. His son at household 36, who as we have seen lived with his wife's three sisters and mother, also had an additional unrecorded daughter. His other son, Li Guocheng, lived at household 34 with his own wife, son and daughter, while his middle son, Li Guoqian (at HH no.35), lived separately, with a wife and three sons of his own.

In this family of a father (Li Peixin) living quite close to his brother's family, with three of his children remaining with him while three older sons had all moved out to start their own families but still remained in close proximity, we can see very clearly the processes of domestic fission which lead to the formation of new households, and some of the influences which may delay or counteract the process. For in fact the six children of Li Peixin and his Xie wife, three still with them although village records showed only two, were all who were left out of their original thirteen children, no less than seven of whom had died in infancy or early childhood.

What is of most interest about the genealogy, however, is the close intermarriages it shows with members of the Xie clan, also settled in the village.

For example, Li Guoqian (HH no.35) had married his actual mother's brother's daughter, who was a Xie; his father (Li Peixin at HH no.33) had married the sister of Xie Shaoju, whose daughter married his son. Li Peixin's brother at household 31, Li Peibing, had also married a Xie (Xie Huotsui), as had their first cousin at household 42, Li Peishu (marrying Xie Peijiang's elder sister Xie Peizhen), whose remaining son Li Guozhun had married a Xie Huachuen whose father was first cousin to his mother! Two daughters of Li Peishu's brother Li Peilong (at household 39) had married out to Xie men; Li Guomin had married Xie Yunzhang, and Li Guofen had married Xie Yuentsai.

And Li Peijuan, the brother of Li Peibing and Li Peixin, who lived in Yibin where he was a government clerk, had also married a Xie (Diagram 9).

Not only has there been a straight case of 'MBD' (mother's brother's daughter) marriage with Li Guoqian's wife, but also a very traditional customary arrangement of 'parallel marriage' where two Li *sisters* had married Xie first paternal cousins (conceptually

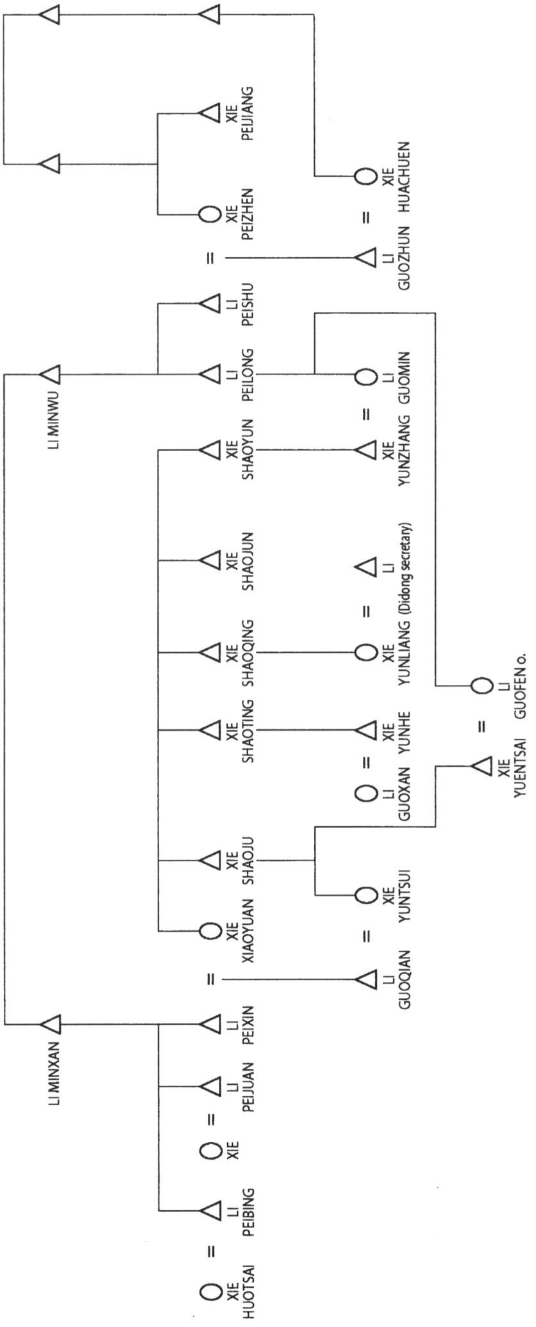

Diagram 9: Li and Xie relations

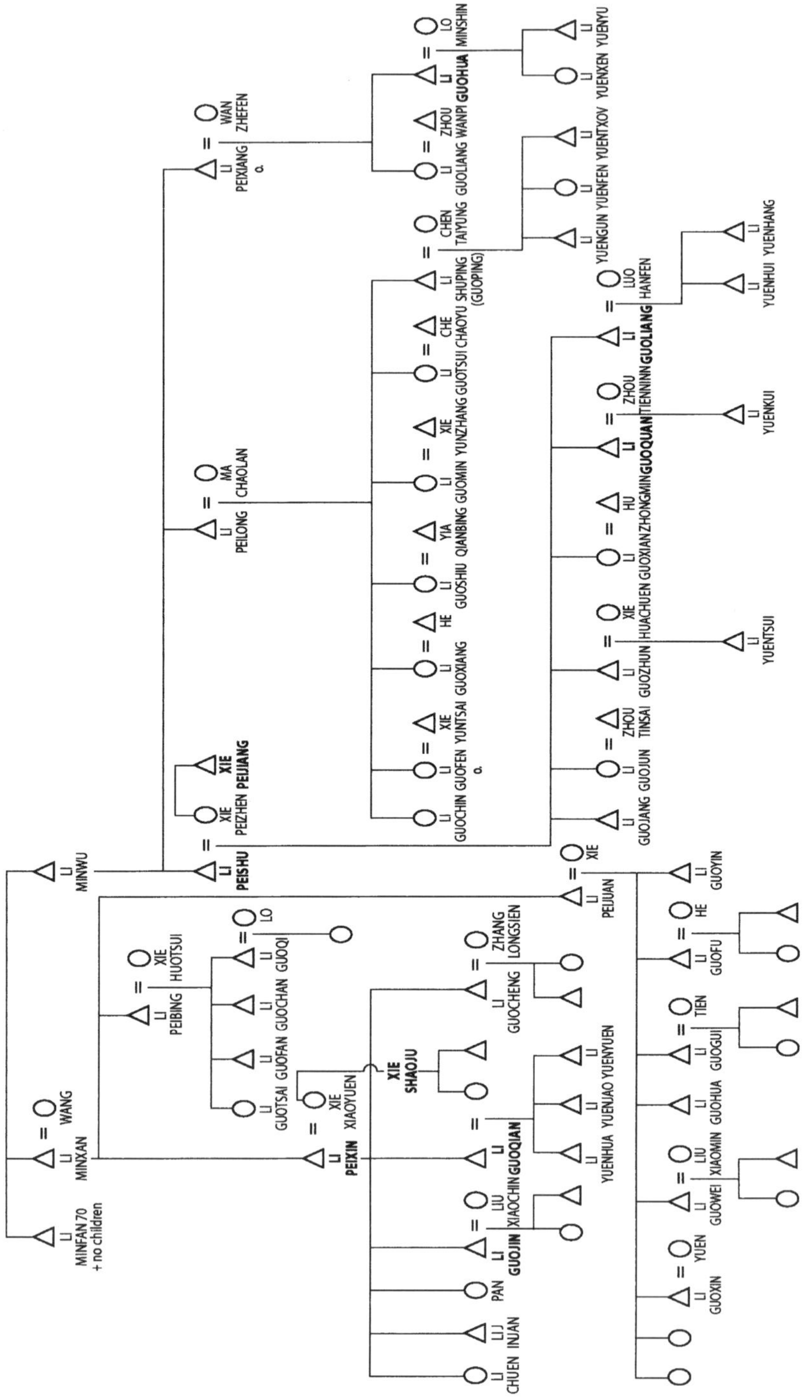

Diagram 10: Li genealogy

'brothers').[3] And there was a preponderance of other Li and Xie marriages (the diagram is based on abstracting all cases of these from the two family genealogies), where relations were either more distant, or may have been equally close (since there are regulations against first cousin marriages in China, people are often reluctant to specify these relations). Rather than illustrating the instability of any particular kind of alliance system, however, such liaisons reflect how carefully these two Han Chinese lineages had linked themselves with each other in a number and variety of different ways.

Another 'MBD' marriage at one remove had taken place in the case of Li Peishu's son (see Diagram 10, Li genealogy).

The Xie

The Li were closely related to the Xie through marriage, and village geography demonstrated many of these relationships in a way I found remarkable for a village which had been through Land Reform and the commune system, the Cultural Revolution and economic reform.

For the Xie lived mostly across the border between the northern and southern parts of the village, near the school, as we can see from the map, where the households of Xie Peijiang and Xie Shaojun are shown close together on the further side of the path, downhill, while Xie Shaoting's house was further south on the other side of the path, upslope, above that of Xie Shaoju and below that of Huang Shuling. Practically at the end of the village and a long way from the other homes was the female-headed house of Liao Hefen (formerly that of Xie Yunshu). Xie Xiaoping lived well away in Group One.

Xie Peijiang, whose sister had married Li Peishu, occupied household number 4; Xie Shaoting, whose sister had married Li Peixin (and whose daughter had married his son), was at house number 47; Xie Shaoju at 51 was his brother; so was Xie Shaojun at number 52.

Xie Yunshu at the very end of the village was the older son of Xie Shaoting and accounted for household number 48 except that he had

---

[3] Although addressed by specific kinship terms, there is a sense in which male members of a lineage segment of the same generation are thought of as fraternal relatives. For the importance of 'siblinghood', see Kelly (1974).

deserted his family who still lived there (he was working in the Didong *gongxiaoshe* or small trading post); another son of Xie Shaoting, Xie Yunhe, accounted for household 49 although he actually still lived with his father at number 47.

So the Xie households may be imaged as in Diagram 11.

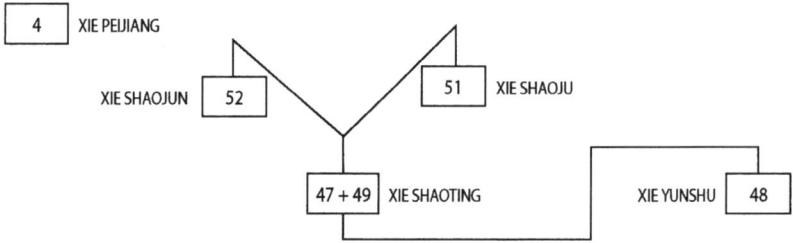

Diagram 11: Xie households

Although Xie Peijiang was of a different lineage to the other Xie, a very similar clustering of patrilineally related kinsfolk to that of the Li had occurred with the Xie; conceptual 'cousins' (HH nos. 4 & 47) were located in relative proximity, while two of the brothers of household number 47 had branched off to form separate households, and one son had branched off to some distance away.[4]

And one can see that, although not from the same lineage (*fang*), Xie Peijiang (HH no.4) and Xie Shaoting (HH no.47) had nevertheless not only located themselves fairly closely together, but were both connected to the Li surname through sister marriages.

Imaging the relations between these different households, we would have the situation shown in Diagram 12.

Thus, the Li and the Xie! *Two* distantly related Xie descent groups, located together in the same village, had formed 'alliances' with the same Li family through very similar means; MBD type

---

[4] And again, including households 47 and 49 together transforms two 'official' households with respectively six, and four members, to a single household of ten; . This reduces the number of households in the village by a further one.

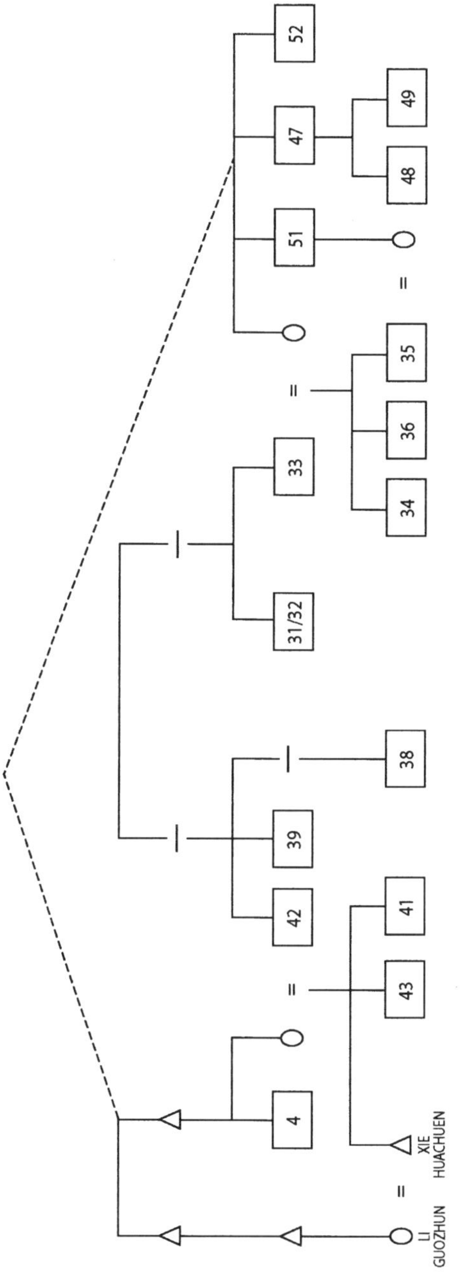

Diagram 12: The Li and the Xie

marriages in which the Li, as it really is seen locally, have been 'wife takers'.[5]

The two Xie descent groups had even established an odd sort of affinal ('brother-in-law') relationship between *themselves* through these connections with different branches of the Li, since the Li men they married were patrilineal first cousins, and therefore thought of (and referred to) as like 'brothers'. They are something similar to Kelly's (1974) 'matrilateral siblings'. Thus (Diagram 13).

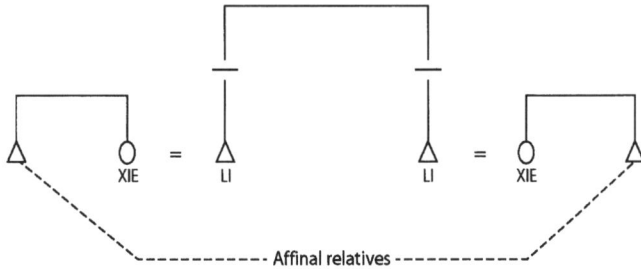

Diagram 13: Li and Xie affines

Xie Shaoting's family had moved into the village forty years before from Jinan to rent farmland from the local He landlord. While the Li family told me they didn't intermarry with the Hmong because this was such a traditional area and they didn't want to get a bad reputation, Xie Shaoting's family initially hotly denied having any relations with the Hmong at all. The younger members of Xie Peijiang's family, however, said they had no objections to such relations themselves; it was the older folk who were against it. As we have seen, the three Xie brothers, Xie Shaojun (52), Xie Shaoju (51) and Xie Shaoting (47), maintained separate households, while Xie Shaoting's son Xie Yunshu (48) had also moved out, and another son Xie Yunhe (49) still lived with him.

Xie Shaoting's father's brother's son was *Xie Shaoping*, a householder in Group One, the much poorer part of the village which

---

[5] I have retained the terms 'wife-giver' and 'wife-taker' throughout despite feminist objections to this kind of lineage theory, since they seem to me to very adequately express the real position of women in these male-dominated societies.

as we have seen was located at some distance away from the main body of the village in Groups One and Two.

Xie Peijiang (HH no.4) was of course of a different lineage (also shown by his birth order suffix, Pei). Besides a daughter and two sons recorded as living with Xie Shaojun at household 52 (one of whom was about to leave home to join his new wife), they had had one other daughter who had married out.

Xie Shaoju (HH no.51) lived with his wife and a son (Xie Yunkan) who had been dumb from birth, as well as another son (Xie Yuntsai), whose own wife had died in childbirth leaving him with a son. This wife was Li Guofen, the daughter of Li Peilong at household 39, and they had married another daughter, Xie Yuntsui, to Li Guoqian at household 35—whose father, Li Peixin, had married Xie Shaoju's sister (Diagram 14).

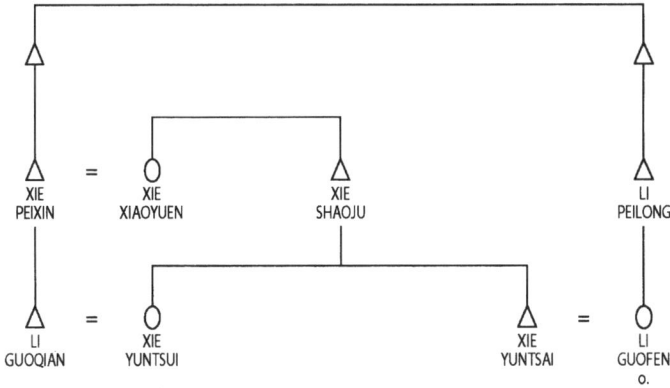

Diagram 14: Li Peixin's Xie affines

The third brother, Xie Shaoting (HH no.47), lived with his youngest son Xie Yunhua, his wife and two daughters, and also with another son Xie Yunhe (HH no.49), as shown in Diagram 15.

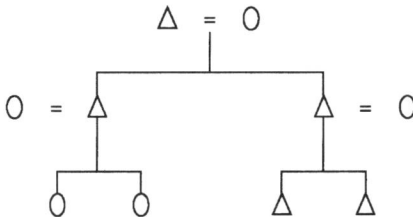

Diagram 15: Xie Shaoting's family

Xie Yunhe (49) who still lived with his father (47), had also as we noted married a Li girl, Li Guoxan, and had two daughters.

47's oldest son Xie Yunshu (48) was living in the Didong district shop while his wife 41-year old Liao Hefei and four children lived in their house at the top of the village. He had effectively left her with his three sons of 16,19 and 21 and daughter of 18, and this household was usually referred to as Liao Hefei's.

Now the three brothers Xie Shaojun (HH no.52), Xie Shaoju (HH no.51) and Xie Shaoting (HH no.47), besides the sister who had married Li Peixin, had also had two other brothers and another sister; these other brothers were Xie Shaoqing (who'd married a Fang surname girl and had five daughters and two sons, one of these daughters having married a Li who was the Didong party secretary), and Xie Shaoyun, whose son Xie Yunzhang had married Li Guomin the daughter of Li Peilong at 39 (out of a total of five sons and one daughter).

They had been wife-givers in another real 'MBD' type marriage with a Wu lineage; the daughter of Xie Shaoyun had married the son of Wu Songwun who had married Xie Shaoyun's sister Xie Shaojen (Diagram 16).

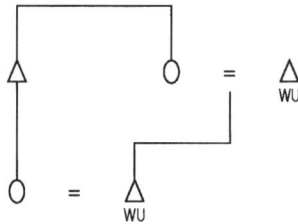

Diagram 16: Xie Shaoyun's family

From other genealogies as well, it did appears that MBD marriage of a fairly classic type, but over a two generation span only, has been quite a popular strategy of cementing relations between Han Chinese—despite the general disapproval of it which was often voiced.

Moving to the other branch of the Xie family, Xie Peijiang at household 4 (whose sister as we have noted married Li Peishu, and whose son Li Guozhun had married Xie Huachuen, daughter of the son of the brother of Xie Peijiang's old father), lived with his old father and mother and four teenage children—a boy and three girls (Diagram 17).

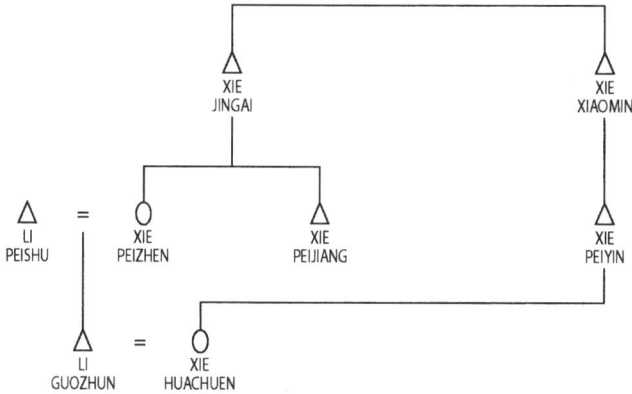

MDB marriage at one remove; MFBZD

Diagram 17: Xie Peijiang's family

The old father (Xie Jingai) had moved into 'Yangjiacun' ('the Yang village', as Wutong was locally known) during Land Reform as they were poor and needed land; prior to 1949 they had been landless agricultural labourers and mercenaries, moving around at least twice every year in search of seasonal employment in different places.

Xie Peijiang, aged 43, was one of the new village elite, as he was the main village teacher. He taught partly in Hmong which he had grown up speaking from the age of four or five; speaking Hmong, and maintaining a large ancestral altar, he was one of the most popular men in the village and received a lot of informal help from the Hmong, since they regarded him as a genuine teacher (see Ch.4). One of the oddest phenomena I found in the village was that his son did not actually live with him, but in the Hmong household of the county party secretary Zeng Minggao, who fed and housed the boy and generally treated him as if he were an adopted son. This was seventeen-year old Xie Huaping who was at Gongxian Middle School. His father hoped he would be able to go on to college, although he was very afraid that he would not be able to afford the expenses which would be necessary (more than ¥1,000 p.a.). I will return to this in considering the particular position of the three Zeng families in the village. One of his daughters, Xie Huayong, was also studying, at Didong Junior Middle School, and his sister had married a Liu trader in Didong, where his daughter stayed while she attended school.

From all of this one may be able to see something of the way in which very strong alliances and forms of cooperation, not only marital, had been formed in the village between the main representatives of the Han Chinese minority, the Li and the Xie. While the Li had moved in shortly before Liberation as tenant farmers and been benefited by the restructuring of local power relations which followed Liberation, the two Xie segments who had come later, with a history of migrant landlessness behind one of them, seemed to have taken care to ally themselves with the Li through strategic marriages of a particularly close nature—and in this process had confirmed their own perhaps quite distant lineage bonds.

In the patronage of the Xie schoolteacher's son by the Hmong party secretary, though, we see something else entirely (which also reflects on the numerically very weak position of the Zeng as a Hmong family in the village by comparison with either the Wang or Yang). The Zeng, as we shall see, had not only intermarried with the more numerically dominant Hmong lineages in quite a similar fashion to the relations the Li and Xie had formed with themselves, but they had also taken care to foster relations with the Han minority in the village through a number of means, of which their adoption of this Han boy was just one. These kind of relations, which crosscut divisions between the Hmong and Han Chinese which were phrased in genealogical as much as cultural terms, were in part due to conventional relationships of support and mutual dependency often expected in villages between cadres such as the party secretary and members of the village committee, the accountant and schoolteacher and sometimes (though not in Wutong) a medical officer or population representative. But they ran deeper than this, as I hope to show in the next chapter.

In Diagram 18 we can see all the connected Li and Xie households (a schematic version of this is given in Diagram 19).

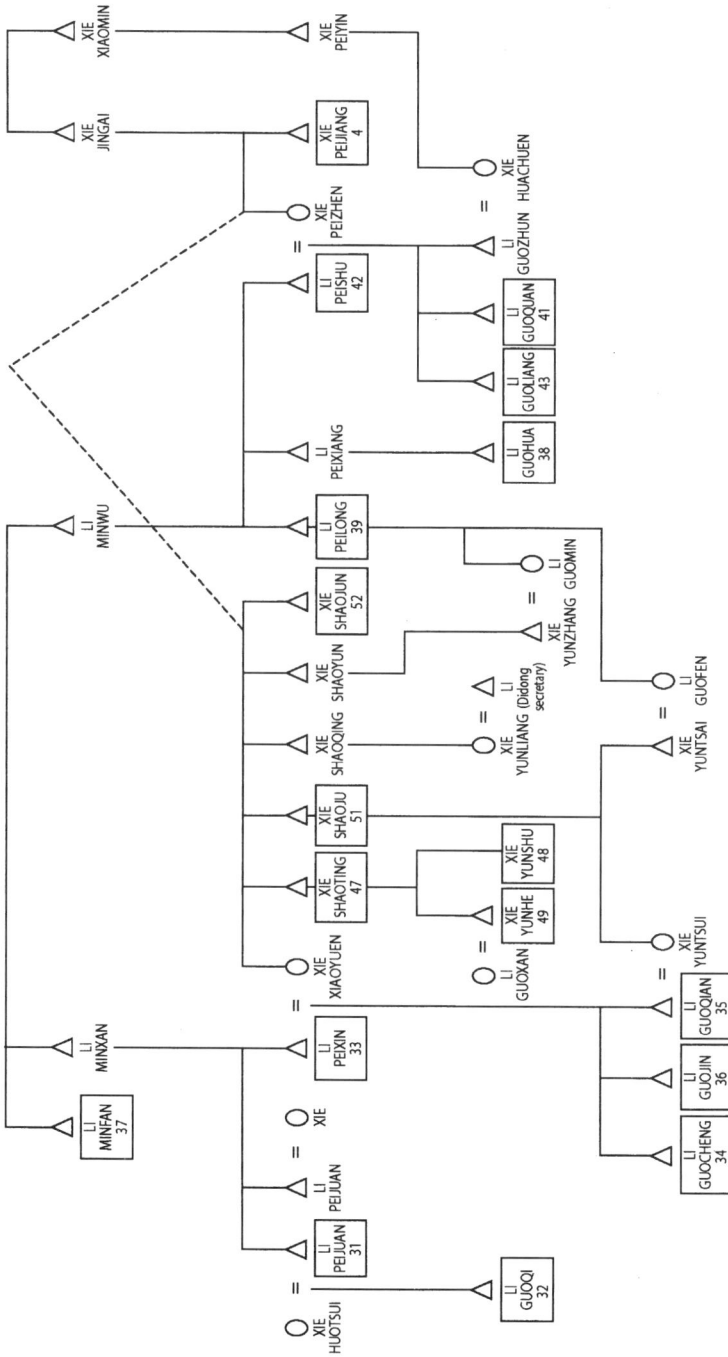

Diagram 18: All connected Li and Xie

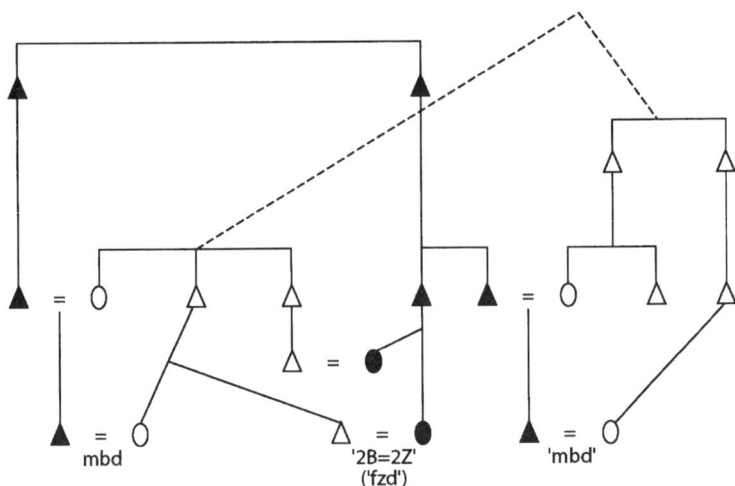

Diagram 19: Schematic version of connected Li and Xie

Of course members of the same surname in China by no means
necessarily descend from a common ancestor with the same surname,
although it is often thought that they may do so and in particular
regions where two groups named for example Chen might live
together a common ancestor might be invented to assert a fictitious
identity. The two Xie descent groups considered here had no real
known relationship, but they seem to have asserted something of this
kind through forming real 'MBD' relationships of exactly the same
kind with first cousins ('proto segments') in the same Li family.
Simply put, this is as in Diagram 20.[6]

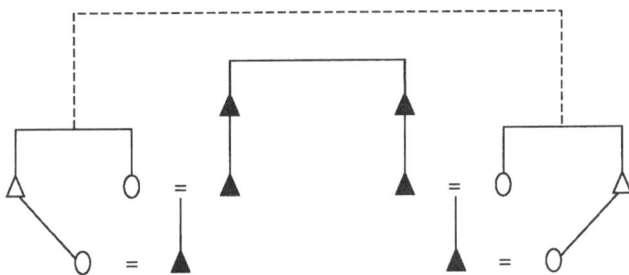

Diagram 20: Xie relations through the Li

---

[6] Here the Li are in black.

What if anything might be the significance of this? These relations are important I think when one remembers that these are post-Liberation, and technically illicit, marriages. If wives' families are inherently inferior to their husbands' as a classical analysis of Chinese kinship would have had it, should we then assume that the Li might have been attempting to establish some sort of social superiority over the Xie through these kinds of marriages? This seems rather improbable, and nothing that the Li or Xie said about these marriages appeared to confirm this kind of an analysis. I think it was most likely the establishment of a relationship of any sort which was aimed at, and that more important than the status ranking of the groups so joined was the oddly ambivalent relationship of affinity *and* descent unity which the two Xie groups established with each other through these means.[7] The Li of the village were certainly seen as 'one family', but so were both groups of the Xie, and the reasons given for this were that Xie women had married Li men who were 'like brothers', and all the local Xie men were therefore just like brothers-in-law to the Li men in the senior generation, and then logically like their Mother's Brothers in the next generation (and they were generally addressed affectionately in this way). As 'Mothers' Brothers' to the Li, then, Xie males of both groups were perceived as if they were in an identical sort of relationship; the two groups of the Xie who were formerly quite distant have set themselves up 'transitively' as a single group in relation to the Li family.

It is possible to look at this in two ways, though. If we consider the Li as *two* 'families', that is as two 'apical proto-lineages' (*fang*) represented by the two Li first cousins (and it is often thought of in this way), then the two Xie groups can be seen to have mimicked their cousinly relationship, and reaffirmed the *difference* between the two Xie groups as, in effect, two separate lineages. For they have *not* married actual Li brothers, but into two, prototypically divergent, Li lineages, and in that sense they have reminded us that the two Xie groups respect the difference of lineages, the 'fission' of siblings; exactly like the Li, these relationships may be saying (although this

---

[7]   On similarly ambivalent relationships, see Kelly (1974) on 'transitive' relationships, where the relation between two entities is defined and mediated by their relations to a third.

may in fact be quite untrue); they come from a common paternal stock but have diverged.

So the 'messages' given out by these sort of marriages are ambivalent; the two Xie groups are like each other, but different. But we are right to look for messages here, for these liaisons and marriages are very consciously arranged and undertaken, and still tend to be family affairs rather than matters of individual choice.

We can see how, through these forms of kinship, the in-moving Xie were able in the past not only to establish close affinal, and respectful, relations between themselves and the better established Li family which was already settled in the village; but they were also able to form bonds, bonds of unity and of difference, of equivalence and separation, between their own two quite separate descent groups. In one sense all Xie could be seen as much the same since their women had married Li men in similar ways; in another sense the fission of Xie lineages which is a process generally presumed and recognised as occurring has been reflected by their selection of Li *cousins* rather than brothers to marry; different Xie lineages marrying different Li lineages. In this way the patrilineal kinship idiom, as we can also see in some of the Hmong lineages, constantly implies identity and resemblance even as it works to establish difference and otherness. This is of course why it is such an exemplary idiom for expressing more general cultural identities and alterities.

In the relation between Li Peixin and the three Xie brothers, something quite different from the classic structuralist notion of pure MBD type marriages which, if repeated, were supposed to lead to a constant passage of Xie women into the hands of Li men, is happening; Li women are being returned, in what is nearly a kind of FZD (father's sister's husband) marriage! (Diagram 21).[8]

Lévi-Strauss originally talked of a system of direct sister exchange, which he saw as at the roots of much more complicated systems of exchange (Diagram 22).

Put into local terms, Li 'brothers' can be seen as marrying Xie 'sisters'; and Xie brothers as marrying Li sisters of the brothers who have married their sisters. Hence we find Diagram 23.

---

[8] In fact the two Xie men who married Li women have accomplished a FZ(HFBS)D marriage, but this is seen as 'FZD' at just one cousinly remove.

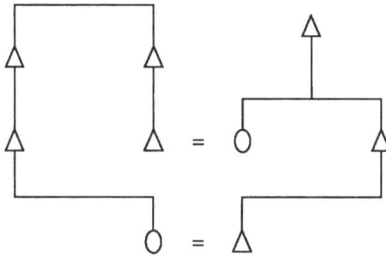

Diagram 21: Fathers' sisters' daughters

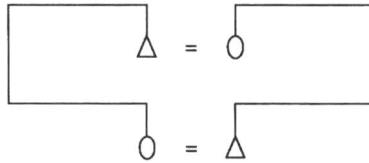

Diagram 22: Simplified father's sister's daughter marriage

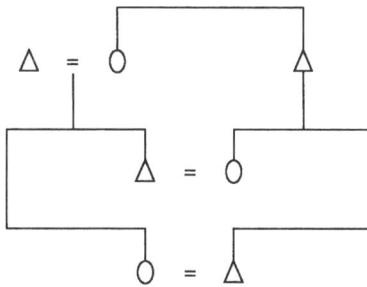

Diagram 23: Sister exchange

This was in fact the most basic form of marital exchange Levi-Strauss talked about, where two men exchange their sisters, which he saw as leading, of course, to more complicated systems in which MBDs become FZDs and two (patrilineal) lines could in theory (or at least in the eyes of local informants) be united closely together forever on the same basis, Li men marrying Xie women and Xie men marrying Li women to the exclusion of all other lines. At all events, it can be seen as a particularly close form of establishing attachments between local families.

It may be of interest that only one of the Xie descent groups had done this; the other had confined itself to the MBD type attachment. But these marriage patterns had only begun to form, since the settlement of both Xie and Li was quite recent, and moreover there had been a number of other Li and Xie marriages which it was not always possible to identify, but which may in some cases have been fairly close. Even in terms of this data, however, we can very see clearly the importance of the patterning of relations formed between the Li and Xie, and between both Xie families; the shaping of a separate Han identification around idioms of patrilineality which almost entirely excluded Hmong members.

The Sun

There were also two Han households of the Sun surname in the village. These were the household of Sun Huaixiang (HH no.53), the old Village Treasurer, aged 59, with the widow of his brother who had been executed for supporting the Guomindang, his own (surname He) wife, two sons and two daughters; and that of Sun Xiyuan (HH no.54), another son of the latter, who was 35 years old, together with his Chen surname wife and two young sons.

The Sun had moved down from Fenghuang ('Phoenix') village up over the slope of the mountain which was another majority Hmong settlement with a preponderance of the Yang clan, in 1948, just before the Liberation, and before that they had spent ten years moving as landless migrant labourers between the borders of Yunnan and Sichuan.

Sun Huaixiang, whose sister Sun Huailiang had married Xie Heyi, a daughter of Xie Shaoping in Group One (first cousin to Xie Shaoju in the main part of the village), and therefore was affinally most closely connected to the Xie, had for many years been the village party secretary, and had then acted as accountant. His disgraced brother's wife was also a Xie.

Sun Huaixiang had had eight children altogether, including his second son who was at household number 54. The oldest son had (like his father) married a He and had a small daughter of ten years old. He had moved out of the village and found work in the Gongxian market bureau. Two of his daughters had also married (into a Fu and a Zhang household respectively) and moved out of the village. Another son was married (to a Wang Xuyong), while one son and two daughters remained unmarried.

There were seven people in all officially living in his house, with four more at number 54; besides himself and his wife and his brother's widow, his two unmarried daughters and two of the sons, one married, still lived with him; his third son's Wang wife, who also lived with them, was not included in village records, perhaps because of having only recently married.

Besides the sister who had married the daughter of Xie Shaoping, another sister had married a Xie of a different line, another had married a Chen (like his own father's father, and his second son), and of his own two brothers, one had also married a Xie (the other a Wang). The children of these two brothers had married into a whole multitude of surnames; Yue and two Li, Ying and Liu and Wang and Zao and Zang, and Gu.

However, the father of Hu Zhengtang and Hu Zhengzhi in Group One (Hu Guoyun) had first married a Sun Huaizheng who had died, and she was nearly related to Sun Huaixiang, as a first cousin. So the Sun had some affinal links with the Xie in the village and with the Hu of Group One, although these were not close or extensive.

As the family told me, it was 'not their custom' to marry with the Hmong, and they could only speak a little Hmong. They told me, however, that their lack of marital relations with the Hmong in the village caused absolutely no problems for them, and boasted of the close working relations they had established with the Hmong, particularly with the Hmong who lived in the same house with them.

For reasons dating back to the days of the commune, Sun Huaixiang and his son's family at 54 (really a household of 11 members rather than two of 7 and 4, or 12 including the new Wang wife) shared the same large compound (near the primary school, which acted as a sort of centre of bureaucratic influence) with both Xie Peijiang (HH no. 4), the Chinese schoolteacher, and with the Hmong farmer Yang Wanwen (HH no.50), who had particularly close relations with the Han in the village since his own sister had married a Chinese, Huang Shulin at household number 45. In the 1960s, as villagers were divided into labour teams and groups, several of these housing arrangements between different families, and between Han and Hmong, had been made. Almost all of them had subsequently broken up, but this one had survived owing, it was said, to a particularly close working relationship established between the families. As the Sun stressed to me, although they themselves, as Han, formed the 'minority' here, they still maintained good relations with the Hmong.

The Huang

Despite a general absence of Hmong Han intermarriages, there was, however, one Han Chinese who spoke hardly any Hmong, who had unusually married into a Hmong clan and settled in to live in Wutong uxorilocally with the relatives of his Hmong wife. This was Huang Shulin (at household number 45) together with his son Huang Xijun (at household number 46). Huang Shulin had married the sister of Yang Wanwen (HH no.50), of the (Hmong) Yang Y2b lineage. Huang Shulin had quite recently moved in from Gongxian on his retirement as a coal miner, and lived in Wutong with his wife and four children, besides his older son Huang Xijun with his own (Liu) wife and baby son.[9] This was an unusual marriage, formed in the early 1960s when Huang Shulin had been a worker in Gongxian at a time of general famine and destitution. Yang Wanwen's sister had met him at the Didong market place and had gone to live with him in Gongxian.

As we shall see (Chapter 7) the Y2b lineage of the Yang, like their lineages X1 and particularly Y3b, were all supported by or supporting, poorer 'son-in-law' households who were also Hmong.[10] But here was one simple case where the ethnic contrast of Hmong with Han coincided with an affinal relation of contrast; Hmong and Han as brothers-in-law, where a relationship had been contracted between a Hmong woman and a poor Han worker. The Huangs were looked down upon and seen as subservient to the Hmong family they were attached to, even though Yang Wanwen's sister had originally deserted the village to be supported by her (Han) husband in

---

[9] Making these two households of six and three members in fact a single one.

[10] I have used this phrase because this is how these relations were phrased locally. In fact they are 'brother-in-law' relatives, descendants of which are referred to as 'sons-in-law' to signify their junior inferior position to the dominant lineages they are attached to.

Gongxian. Yang Wanwen often asked the Huang to help him in various ways, and it seemed that this was expected.

The Gu

Another uxorilocally settled poor son-in-law was Gu Yinshen (o household 44). He had himself married a young sister of Huan; Shulin, the Han considered above, and so could have been thought o as an attachment to the Han Chinese of the village (or to the Y2l lineage of the Hmong Yang to whom Huang Shulin was attached). But as if to confound such neat dichotomies, he was also in a kind of 'son-in-law' (or junior brother-in-law, since his father had been a real brother-in-law) relationship to two Hmong families of the Yang surname; those of Yang Wanyi (at household no.55) and Yang Wanfang (at household no.58). Yang Wanyi and Yang Wanfang belonged to different lineage segments of the Hmong Yang; Yang Wanyi to lineage Y1, and Yang Wanfang to lineage Y3b. As if to mark the ambivalent position of this family, his house ocupied a particularly peripheral position in the village, where he lived with his wife and five children.

The Gu had only moved into the village fifty years before. Most of the Gu family's nearest relatives were in Chengshen, and there were many Gu in Dingshin *xiang* of Xingwen county in Yunnan. Gu Yinshen's own father, who had started life working in a paper mill at Didong, had formed a connection with the father of Yang Wanyi and this had been their introduction to the village where they settled. Yang Wanyi's Y1 lineage (like the Y3b but not the same extent) had acted as rural employers or petty landlords under the local Han landlord (surnamed He), who had been driven out during Land Reform. In Chapter 7 we see how these lineages had sponsored a number of other poorer affinal relatives to move in and work for them. The Gu had been labourers for the He family, as well as carrying wood and polishing rice and building watch towers for the Hmong Yang during the civil wars.

The affinal connection with the Yang was firstly, that Gu Yinshen's father's sister, after the death of her first (Xiong) husband) had married a Yang and by him had had a son who was in fact Yang Wanyi. A young son by her first marriage, who had as it is said 'followed his mother' into her second marriage, had taken his

stepfather's surname to become Yang Wanjin. So there was a strong
connection to the Yang of lineage of lineage Y1, through Yang
Wanyi's Gu mother.

But besides this, Gu Yinshen's brother (Gu Yingui) had also
married a Yang girl; Yang Wanliang, who was the eldest sister of
Yang Wanfang, of the Y3b lineage. After Gu Yingui's death, his
wife had remarried to a Xiong (Xiong Kaiming), taking with her her
young daughter by her first marriage (who eventually married a
Wang). There almost seemed to be a subdued and muted structuralist
pattern, shown here and in some other cases, of returning 'stepsons'
through widow remarriage. While 'Aunty Gu' (Gu Yinshen's
father's sister) had in a sense presented the Yang with a Xiong baby
(who became Yang Wanjin) from her first marriage, in the next
generation a Yang girl (Yang Wanliang) had been able to give the
Xiong surname back a Gu baby from her first marriage (to Gu
Yingui).

So Gu Yinshen was in a dependent affinal relationship (which I
have called a 'son-in-law relationship'), through both his paternal
aunt and uncle, simultaneously to the Y1 lineage of Yang Wanyi and
the Y3b lineage of Yang Wanfang which, as we will see, had formed
a number of similar links with the Hmong clans of the Wang and the
Xiong. And there was a kind of reciprocity at work here, since the
original marriage of his aunt to the Yang which had cemented the
dependent working relationships the Gu family developed with that
of Yang Wanyi had been followed by his uncle's marriage to a Yang
girl. And there had been other, more distant, unions between the Gu
and the Yang.

The most remarkable feature of the Gu, and one of the reasons
why their home was situated far on the outskirts of the village near
the Han clan of the Li, and perhaps also why they had contracted
marriages both with Hmong and Han, was that they were neither
wholly Han nor Hmong. The local Hmong referred to them as
Hmong Ntsuab (Green Hmong), but this had nothing to do with the
Green Hmong of South East Asia. Instead it referred to a people very
widely distributed all through Northwest Yunnan, Sichan, Guizhou,
as well as parts of North Vietnam and Laos, who are called 'Hua
Miao' or 'Dahua Miao' in Chinese, and refer to themselves as

'Hmao' or 'A Hmao'.[11] While closer to the Hmong language than any other branch of Miao (and classed in the same Chuanqiandian branch as Hmong by Chinese linguists), Hmao is nevertheless at least as different from Hmong as Italian is to French, and the two tongues are not mutually intelligible. I have several times seen a Hmong and a Hmo speaker struggling to understand each others' languages with no success; they do often discover some common and quite similar words, in different tones or with different pronunciations, and are aware of some sense of affinity. But they cannot understand each other, although quite often when members of the two groups have lived together for some time they learn the other language.[12] The Gu in the village spoke both Chinese and Hmong, though neither it was said very well.

Since (as we shall see) there were even legends still being told of how members of *other* Hmong clans could turn into tigers, it is not surprising that the Gu were regarded with some suspicion and contempt by most of the Hmong villagers. They said themselves that they had once been Hua Miao, but were now more or less the same as the Hmong through having lived with the Hmong and marrying with them. They seemed to have no sense of a distinct cultural heritage, and indeed appeared somewhat ashamed of their antecedents. They did stress however that they were local people who had always lived in this region, and seemed paradoxically proud of this. Some of the Hmong in Wutong, too, regarded the Gu as the original inhabitants of the area, and it may be that through the intermarriages which had taken place something of that process Graham (1937) referred to, of the absorption and assimilation of smaller local groups into the Hmong, was in the process of taking place.

Some information gathered in other places in the locality seemed to confirm this. Most of the Hmong villagers claimed they had originally migrated from 'Huguang', the Ming province of Hubei and Hunan which included parts of Guizhou, after having passed through Weixin county in Yunnan. Graham (1954:28) records a story of how the Hmong first arrived in Sichuan which tells how the Han Chinese

---

[11] A variant spelling of 'Hmo' is 'Hmao'.

[12] The Hmong however usually call the A Hmao 'Hmong Ntsaub'.

defeated the ancestors of the Sichuan Hmong in 'Guangdong', who were then forced to march to Sichuan with their wrists tied behind their backs, leaving the wrinkles which Graham was shown as proof of present day Hmong peoples' ancestry. Although claims of northern and central origins are widespread in southern China, the Ming militia certainly did include conscripts taken from ethnic minorities and these must have left descendants, and such stories, behind in the places where they helped the imperial troops to suppress rebellions and establish centralised order.

In one Hmong village in Xingwen county, the Ma family claimed to have inhabited the place for two hundred years, having originated from 'Huguang', and to prove the claim pulled up their sleeves to demonstrate these 'wrinkles' to me (not very remarkable ones).[13] It was these wrinkles which, as they saw it, distinguished them from the other main lineage in the village, the Gu, who they saw as the *original inhabitants* of the locality, and who were popularly reputed to be exceptionally strong and tall like giants.

And certainly there was a strong distinction between the earlier, and later, waves of Hmong settlers in the area, marked as we shall see by the historical suppression of the Bo rebellion. Sometimes seen as aboriginal inhabitants of the region who had become or were becoming Hmong, classified officially as Miao like the Hmong but not accepted as Hmong, the Gu were 'strange folk' unlike the other Hmong or Han in the village. Yet they had been accepted into Hmong kinship structures and rituals in a way that the few Han Chinese who had formed liaisons with the Hmong were not, and indeed they were somewhat grudgingly acknowledged as being in the process of becoming part of the Hmong community, although often seen as basically inferior to the Hmong. Here something of the enormous power of the local idioms of descent and affinity to incorporate and overcome, as well to affirm and reinforce, cultural differences, may be glimpsed.

While crucial differentiations of language and ritual were maintained and reproduced, and as I have tried to show here, the separateness of the Han and Hmong communities was most strikingly expressed in the general absence of intermarriage,

---

[13] Tapp (1996).

nevertheless the community formed a unity as a local economic and political unit, and its sense of interconnectedness was demonstrated not only in Hmong bilingualism, but also in a mutual participation in local ritual practices.

CHAPTER FOUR

SHAMANISM AS HMONG/HAN PRACTICE

The tendency towards a coalescence of Hmong with local Han cultural identities despite the continual affirmation of difference I have referred to was well illustrated in the Han employment of Hmong shamans. Xie Peijiang, the Chinese schoolmaster, was additionally popular with the Hmong since he believed in Hmong shamanism, and often consulted the shamans when a member of his family was ill. The story (laughingly confirmed by Mr. Xie) was that once while carrying coal, he and some friends had stopped off to eat at Li Peishu's house and got very drunk there. On the way home he fell over several times, and was convinced that he had suffered some awful calamity, and called for a shaman to be summoned to cure him—for which he had to sacrifice a whole chicken.

The continued practice of shamanism by Hmong in the village is an excellent instance, I would argue, of the strength of local cultural traditions to resist the incursions of the socialist state.[1] Shamanism here had not been reconstituted to satisfy tourist demand after the liberalisations of the early 1980s, as has been the case with many aspects of religion in China. Here it was an almost everyday practice, which had clearly been maintained or guarded throughout the great leftist swings of Chinese policy in the Great Leap Forward and the Cultural Revolution, and the subsequent campaigns against spiritual pollution and bourgeois liberalisation.[2] And although formulating an extraordinary vision of the cosmos and a spiritual order at apparently utter variance from the notions of moral authority enjoined by a secular state, and a ritual world in which a quintessentially Hmong identity could be posited, yet the practice of Hmong shamanism was clearly respected by at least some local Han Chinese villagers, and had met with their tacit consent and tolerance even where it was not actively patronised.

---

[1] There are other good examples, like the continued underground practice of Christianity by the Hua Miao for fifty years of socialism after their conversion by missionaries in the early years of the century.

[2] In 1983 and 1987.

Not everyone in the village believed in or practiced shamanism, and for example Yang Wanli's son said they only knew that a ritual had been performed the next morning or when they heard the beating of the shaman's gong, usually very softly and at night. This was at the time of a revival of the campaign against 'bourgeois liberalisation' in the aftermath of Tiananmen which particularly targeted religious practices, and memories of the Cultural Revolution when shamanism and other traditional practices were completely forbidden were still relatively fresh. Unlike ancestor worship, which received a certain amount of official understanding and tolerance, shamanism was firmly in the bracket of magical, superstitious, customs seen as 'backward' and not healthy. Although many households would resort to shamanism in crisis, particularly if a young child was ill, there was a constant fear of neighbours not too closely related, with whom one might have had some other difficulties, reporting on one to the authorities, so that the gongs were beaten very softly so as not to attract attention, and shamanism usually practiced very late at night so that it would be a fait accompli by the next morning.

Yet every clan in the village and neighbouring Hmong villages had at least one shaman in it, with more male than female shamans. As Yang Wanfang said, if you wanted any proof of the efficacy of shamanism, you could ask always Ma Jianqing's mother (at household number 75; their sister had married his first cousin's son) who had fallen down once in north Aijo, a hamlet across the mountain, and fainted when she had reached home. Ma Jiankang had gone out for help and met Xie Peijiang, the schoolmaster, on the way, and Xie Peijiang had told him to send for the shamaness, who 'took up the seven hemp leaves and two folds of paper and poured rice out of the water bowl by blowing on it and used the sickle and had a chicken sacrificed'. And (as Ma Jiankang did confirm to me) 'before she had even left the house my mother sat up, completely recovered, and she has never stopped thanking her since then'.

In this sense the *practice* of shamanism had paradoxically something of the classic elements of witchcraft accusation about it; a neighbour might accuse another of *inviting shamans*, who would then deny it. Oddly, though, the shamans themselves seemed largely unaffected by this official disapproval. Often they were lone and solitary figures, but they seemed to carry with them an authority which evoked some fear and respect in the locality. Hmong shamanism is classically not something one can help doing; it is an involuntary gift (or affliction), which cannot be acquired through tuition, and in that sense a shaman cannot be seen as fully responsible for his or her own actions. Moreover, it is not a solitary practice; shamanism must be practised on someone else's behalf, who has formally invited the shaman to their house to perform, and in that sense inevitably implicates a number of households whenever it is practiced.

When I first expressed an interest in shamanism, Yang Wanli's son suggested I should get someone drunk, and then invite a shaman on his behalf, since the shaman is always invited by someone other than the afflicted person, on the afflicted person's behalf. I did not do this, but my sponsor eventually succeeded in arranging a shamanic demonstration for me to witness, despite the dangers of doing this sort of thing where a foreign researcher was concerned. After this time I was able to interview the shaman, Yang Wanfeng, who practiced together with his wife, several times, and also to witness other shamanic sessions, which were very similar to those of the Hmong in Thailand and elsewhere, although they have incorporated many more elements of Chinese Daoist ritual.

With astute diplomacy, the villagers arranged for a large number of people to be present at the initial demonstration, implicating a number of people so as to make it more difficult for a complaint to be made or followed up at a later stage. Besides myself, my research assistant, Yang Wanfang (the shaman) and his wife Li Kaiyin, and Yang Qing Bai (my sponsor) who was the only one, having arranged it all, to leave strategically shortly after proceedings had started, there was Yang Wanqun's husband from Wangwuzhai, and the shamaness's brother who just happened also to be the deputy head of Yuhe township. Then there was also the Chinese villager Sun Huaixiang's daughter, and Yang Shingo (a teacher from Group One), besides Wang Zhongtang, who was the husband of the shaman's eldest daughter from Yuhe, and Yang Wanzhong, the first cousin of the shaman, besides the shaman's son with his own wife and two young children. The gathering was therefore not exclusively Hmong, and not exclusively of the Yang clan, and moreover not exclusively confined to the village, since it involved a high ranking official from Chengdu and a member of the local *xiang* government.

Much later, Yang Wanfang told me how he had inherited the spirits of shamanism through his *wife*'s family. His wife's father had been a shaman, and his father before him, since there can only be one in each generation of a lineage, and after their deaths his wife's elder brother first fell strangely sick. Another shaman was invited to exorcise him, and he was cured. Then his own wife became ill, with boils which lasted for twelve years. She went to the hospital but the X-rays revealed no internal damage, and eight shamans who they invited in succession to cure her all agreed on the same diagnosis; that there must have been a shaman in her family, whose tutelary spirits were now trying to 'find' (possess) her. Finally a (Ma) Teacher 'comforted' or 'assuaged' her, so that she became able to control the spirits for the benefit of others, but only together with her husband as, he said, it was difficult for a woman to practice by herself. So that thirty-eight years after her father's death, his tutelary spirits had been transmitted from the Otherworld to them. He was the only local Yang shaman, although another (Liu) shaman from Fenghuang was often invited to perform in the village.

This too is very typical of Hmong shamanism; the shaman cannot practice for the benefit of himself or his own immediate family, so that usually shamans from other lines of descent are invited. Nor can a shaman be taught (how to control the experience) by a member of his own descent group; Masters are sought among other surnames. However, the possessing spirits of a shaman are normally believed to descend in a direct ancestral line, so that while the gift itself, the innate capacity to perform, is patrilineally inherited (the capacity to become a shaman), shamanism also reaches out beyond the confines of the ancestral descent group, finding Masters from other lines and healing unrelated patients. It is probably this practice, of learning techniques from those unrelated to oneself, which has contributed to the uniformity of Hmong traditions of shamanism across wide distances.

As the shaman explained it, illness was caused by a variety of different categories of hungry spirit: for example, of those who died by drowning, by the knife or gun; of hunger, or of falling from a cliff. Different forms of ritual are demanded by the diagnosis of what type of spirit it is which is causing affliction. For example, a child who is sick may (be diagnosed to) have encountered the spirit of one killed by a gun, or by a knife where the form of spirit is very similar, since it takes the form of a whirlwind. If the child's 'life flame' is not so strong, his 'soul substance' (*pleg*) may have deserted him (trapped by the spirit) as a result of this experience, and the symptom of this type of calamity is facial bruising. A particular ritual is performed for this during the course of which the shaman takes a long pole with spirit paper streaming from the top of it which is wound around the child's head and shaken to release the dust and the whirlwind. Whenever you see a great cloud of dust rising in the air, the shaman told me, you know an evil spirit has departed.

Unlike the Hmong shamanism of South East Asia, where diagnosis tends to focus on what particular kind of *soul* has left the body of the sick and must be hunted for by the shaman and brought back, diagnoses among the Sichuan Hmong seemed to focus more on the exorcism of different categories of spirit related to types of death, which may betray the influence of local Chinese exorcistic rituals of a Daoist type on the Hmong shamans.

Graham (1954:37-45), who researched several of these villages in Gongxian in the 1930s, reaches a similar conclusion when he says that the work of what he calls the 'Ch'uan Miao magician' is in 'exorcising demons who are believed to be responsible for practically all diseases and calamities; the *tuan gong* in Chinese, or *do nun*[3] in Miao'. He also records rituals, as I was able to do, for specific demons such as those 'that cause pain in the nipples', or 'that cause boils', and rituals to 'remove bones and metal objects that have been swallowed'. There are the demons of women who died in childbirth, the 'demons that shed red blood', vomiting demons, malarial fever demons, hanging demons and water demons (that cause people to die by hanging or drowning), the 'naked demons' that make children cry at night, enticing love-sick demons and demons which cause abortion (Graham 1954).

But in fact (as Yang Wanfang explained to me) the Hmong know *two* kinds of shamanism: what they call exorcism (*xaav dlaab*, or in Chinese *song gui*), and also what they call 'healing illness' (*khao mao*, or *a neeb*), and this was similar to the White Hmong of North Thailand who practised two kinds of shamanism, one non-possessive

---

[3] This is Graham's idiosyncratic spelling. In RPA this would be *tus ua neeb*, the one (who) does (the work of the) spirits. In Chinese Hmong this should be *dol a neeb*.

and much like the exorcistic rituals I found in Wutong, the other the classic Hmong rites of full possession where, after a preliminary seance to diagnose the causes of illness, the shaman undertakes a journey into the Otherworld to rescue the afflicted *pleg* (soulstuff) of the sick.

Since it is often the same shaman who can perform both varieties, in Sichuan a combination of the two may have occurred, particularly since possessive shamanism, or *a neeb*, is itself divided into two sessions of diagnosis and cure/rescue. As I have said, I was able to witness both, and the possessive shamanism of the Sichuan Hmong was similar to that of the Hmong elsewhere and which has been well recorded.[4] I was more interested, however, to investigate the nature of the non-possessive shamanism which, although also specifically Hmong, appeared to be part of the same tradition as the exorcisms practiced by the local Han Chinese.

Yang Wanfang made a preliminary diagnosis of the nature of an illness by 'seeing the rice' in his own house, inspecting a cup of rice which had been brought to the shaman's house by the person from the patient's family who had invited him, by placing a cloth over the top and throwing the rice grains onto it to discover what sort of spirit is responsible for the complaint. This practice has much in common with those of Chinese village spirit mediums (*kan mi*), and is not commonly practised in possessive Hmong shamanism where diagnosis is performed in full possessive trance. However, he did then also visit the patient's house, as possessive Hmong shamans would, and on his second visit he would perform the full possessive shamanic journey or '*yin* rites' as they were known in Wutong, as opposed to the *yang* rites of preliminary diagnosis and exorcism.

Seated on a special bench before the altar known as the shaman's 'horse', with the patient seated on a low stool behind him, the shaman whose eyes are hooded to symbolise his inner vision, begins to rock back and forth as he chants in Hmong the long invocation to his tutelary spirits, the spirits of Old Saub, Madam Ntsaub and Lord Nas, the Original Ancestors, Siv Yis, the Founder of shamanic healing, the spirits of thunder and the waters, of the eagle and the buffalo, the spider and the centipede, the Chinese Masters of Iron

---

[4]   See in particular Morechand (1968); Mottin (1982); Lemoine (1987, 1996, 1997).

and Copper, the Dragon and the Parrakeet, the Lords of Herbal Medicine, the ancestral and the domestic spirits of the hearth and bedside, porch and gardens and orchards, to aid him in his flight across the twelve mountains and valleys of the Otherworld to locate the forces which have ensnared a wandering soul of the patient, to do battle with them or to bargain and deal, to guide the soul safely back to its home in the body of the patient, and to finally despatch his tutelary spirits with fanfare and respect, while his assistant (and apprentice/disciple) behind him continuously beats the bronze gong and the castanets on the shaman's fingers jangle ceaselessly to the rhythm of his violent rocking. Occasionally in the course of his sung narrative, which may last four hours or longer, the shaman lets out a wild cry and lets all his instruments fly away from him, or somersaults backwards over the bench.

A particular ritual of exorcism was performed by Li Kaiyin, the shamaness, for a wife who had suffered unexplained facial bruising. With her eyes closed, the shamaness diagnosed this symptom as having been caused by having encountered the 'spirit of one killed by falling off a cliff'. The *tos a neeb* (shaman) promised to get rid of what she called the 'bloody light' (the light of a bloody knife, the impending calamity) and to *txus shab tua ti dlaag* or 'kill the spirits'), so that the patient would be prevented from the fate which now threatened her, of dying from falling off a rock. During this long (two-hour) ritual, in which Li Kaiyin did go into a trance to invoke her tutelary spirits through chanting although this did not resemble possessive Hmong chanting, the patient was asked to blow on seven large cakes of glutinous rice folded inside leaves of hemp before the shamaness threw them away with the kind of loud exclamation ('Phaib!') often used by possessive Hmong shamans in the course of their trance, and declaimed the 'seven magic Hmong words' said to banish all spirits to their homes in rocks or trees. Two sickles were then furiously burnished together by the shamaness chanting now in Chinese;

> Yin *is the* yin *messenger* [soldier]
> Yang *is the* yang *messenger* [soldier]
> *you came from the fork of a tree*
> *you should go back to your forest*
> *you came from a crack in the rock*
> *you should go back to your rock*

you came from the root of a tree
you should return to the root of a tree.

The two sickles, said to cut the chains of the soul tied by the *yin* troops so that the afflicted patient can return to this, *yang*, world, were then cast by the shamaness out of the front door.

An extraordinary imaginary universe is pictured here, in which humanity is constantly threatened by the forces of the contingent and accidental, which are yet seen as natural forces. The landscape around the village was made up of boulders and rocks, clumps of trees and ravines, said to be the sites of malevolent spirits or where particularly unfortunate accidents had befallen members of the village who were still remembered by name. In the past the spirits of plague and pestilence had been even more common. Local history was interwoven with natural topography to form a living narrative in terms of which accident and misfortune could be comprehended and, sometimes, averted.

Sometimes, in an attempt perhaps to reconcile the theory of exorcism with the soul-loss theories of possessive Hmong shamanism, the ghosts of accident and misfortune (*dab qus*) were seen as actually scaring the souls of mortals out of the body, or capturing and imprisoning them, which the shaman would then have to reclaim and redeem for health to be restored to the patient.[5] Often, as the above example shows, ghosts were seen not only as the malevolent shadows of former earthly existences who had suffered unfortunate ends, and who therefore would have been unlikely to have had full funeral rites performed for them of the kind described in the next Chapter, but also harbingers of a fate which would afflict the patient in the future. But both these kinds of ritual were performed.

In one shamanic (*nqaig neeg*) ritual I witnessed for the rescue of the lost soul of the sickly (fifteen-year old) third daughter of a mother who kept dreaming of a white sow, the diagnosis was that the soul of this child had gone to 'the market of graves and mountains' to be reborn as an old white sow; a pig resembling this would have to be sacrificed, or else the child would die. The shamaness first

---

[5] I do not say 'client', since shamans always offer their services as a kind of grudging favour, and remuneration for these services is disavowed.

'descended into the world of *yin*', by entering into a trance with shut eyes and erratic movements. The shaman's stool had been placed before the table and altar, and was wreathed with paper spirit money, with more littering the floor beside it. The shamaness first threw the curved divination horns, made of buffalo horns, on the floor in front of her, until the *yang* and the *yin* of the horns were balanced (they must be thrown thrice three times in the same way to determine this; both of them facing down signifies imbalance, both of them facing up represents imbalance; one facing up with one down signifies that the soul in question has truly been located). After she had risen to sprinkle wine and meat in the 'five directions'[6] and drinking some of the wine herself, her acolyte spread a scarlet cloth across her knees and fastened a large white paper mask attached to two thin sticks to her head to make a horned mask, resembling those of the most ancient Chinese shamans (*wu*). Another pine stick tied to her waist represented a rider's whip (*npliav neeg*), since the shaman is seen as a heavenly rider, a cavalier galloping into the beyond to do battle with the forces of the unknown on behalf of the living. On her fingers she even wore the castanet bell-rings so, as she said, 'my soldiers will get ready to find the soul'. She then took the gong in her left hand and the shaman's bell in her right hand, and swaying convulsively, began to go into a possessive trance, chanting...

> *get onto the horses, mount up on the carriages, catch up, catch up, Ai ye tens of thousands of soldiers and horsemen, hundreds of thousands of heavenly generals and cavalrymen, accompany us and support us...the child is trapped in a lord's carriage, carried off into the world of* yin*, here it is that I see the mountains full of tombs, the valleys pitted with craters, and there I can see that old white sow wandering in the wild grasses, with one foreleg white, and one hindleg black, so let us kill, kill, kill that lordly pig! Ah! I have lost it, I can no longer see it, the poor child has been hidden away, somewhere very near here, I can feel it in my bones and in my flesh, my eyes reach out to search the gathering gloom, I call on the mighty Spirit of the Woodpecker who searches out the termites, I call on the Spirit of the Grasshopper who*

---

[6] Including 'the Centre'.

comes alive again in the eighth month, come to my succour, come to my aid, help me to find the cavern, rescue this child who is wandering in the tigers' lair, lost and alone, with no mother and father, no home and no garden to go to...and so we ride back to Yibin to get water for the horses, and for the mid-day meal, our carriage full of the souls of the living and yang *is leading the way, with the empty carriages, desolate of life, all following us...make way you fiends and demons for this carriage which leads the way, dare not to approach or attack us, we are approaching the city of Yibin accompanied by our entourage of the mighty heavens and earth, let us water the horses and take tea here, let us feast and enjoy ourselves, Ai you wretched people from the world of* yang *should give more, it costs as much as twenty cents to smoke tobacco, there's one old man here who's starving for a square meal but it costs sixty cents for just half a bowl of rice, thirty cents for barely a spoonful of rice, so eat up, eat faster, you Lords and Masters, spirits of ancestors and the home, Lord Father and Lady Mother, Siv Yis my Master, Saub who is kind to all beings, Lady Sun and Lord Moon, All Spirits of Thunder and Winds, of Rivers and of all Mountains, Green Dragon and White Tiger, Master Forgers of Copper and of Iron, Spirit of Noble Parakeet and Cunning Spider...my Carriage with the souls of the living goes on ahead, the grounds and parklands of this City of* Yang *, the Citadel of Mortals, are spacious indeed, do not stay to applaud us, but go on, on, ride ever faster, run ever quicker, we are returning to the home of this child who was neglected and was not watched, this child who is your very own future, the mountain veins of your children and grandchildren's children, long may they course in this world of valleys and mountains, may all Spirits and Masters be happy and at peace.*

The 'hungry old man' she had sung of was identified as her own Master, who had taught her how to control the spirits of shamanism, and was now 'ninety years old', she claimed the journey took precisely 49,499 miles altogether, from the spiritual 'market of graves and mountains' she had visited to the present-day city of Yibin, where they had stopped for a rest and refreshments. The references to the pig, and to money, were directions to the family of the patient as to what they should do, and how much payment would be expected. When she had finished she took off the mask and threw the divination horns again and again until she had received six favourable answers. This was an abbreviated shamanic session, since the sickness of the child was not severe, and it was said that she had not needed to travel too far across the Otherworld to rescue the soul; when a person is struck by the Thunder God their soul will depart to the entrance of the twelfth mansion, and a ritual of 'twelve knives' must be performed, but this may not succeed; once past the twelfth the soul cannot be retrieved, and the person will die.

In a simple non-posessive rite known as 'Crossing the Bridge', the shamaness' assistant had placed six upturned bowls on pieces of spirit paper in two lines leading from the front door to the altar, after first throwing the divination horns by each bowl to ensure that its position was appropriate. The shamaness then knelt before the table placed before the altar to burn spirit paper, and then used her shamanic wooden tablet to strike each bowl loudly, again throwing the divination horns for each bowl until a position of *yin* was indicated. Then she burnt spirit paper and incense in each of the four corners of the room, prostrated herself three times before the altar and again threw the divination horns on the floor in front of her until a position of *yang* was indicated. The entire company present then had to hop clockwise around the room from upturned bowl to upturned bowl, without touching the floor at any point with their feet, while the shamaness beat the gong wildly and her assistant struck the tablet a mighty blow on the table. After this all prostrated themselves before the altar and the tutelary spirits of the shamaness. This parlour-game like ritual was for the general protection of children; it was said that any child suffering an ailment would recover immediately after stepping on the bowls, and if all present were to tread the bowls this would ensure that the child would grow up to be strong and healthy.

In another ritual of exorcism for a family who were having repeated arguments and found themselves unable to agree on anything, which was chanted only in Chinese,[7] called to 'sweep and send away the flower tree', again the shamaness first burnt paper money under the table and, kneeling on a piece of paper, prostrated herself three times before it and the altar. Then she burnt more paper under the table and, taking up the gong, beat it twice, facing the Door, 'to inform the Masters and summon the soldiers to come'. Still softly beating the gong, she went to the Door and knelt down there to throw the divination horns on the floor. Returning to the table she burnt more paper before it, and prostrated again three times. Then from the bowl on the table she cast lustral water, wine and pork fat, in the 'five directions' of Heaven and Earth. Meanwhile her assistant was constantly stamping her shamanic 'seal' on the paper money on a table (in an invisible pattern). She then took lighted spirit paper outside the Door where three sticks of incense had already been set burning to each side of it, and returning to the table before the altar, dropped the shamanic tablet (a carved piece of black wood) in the bowl of water and added more lighted paper to it. With one stick of incense in her hand she then swiftly traced some magical charms on a strip of paper stamped by her assistant in a way which is characteristic of Daoist priests (see below), clapped both her hands together loudly, spun around three times until she faced the door, and put the lamp which had been on the table with one pair of divination horns on the ground before the door, chanting loudly

> *yin chuan shi zu* [her FFF]
> *yin chuan shi yi* [her FF]
> *yin chuan shi xiong* [eB; or *fu*; her F]
> *yin chuan shi di* [her B]
> *yin chuan shi tu* [F's apprentice]
> *yin chuan Ma lao shi fu* [Master Ma].

This is an invocation to her tutelary spirits, those of the ancestors, grandfather, elder and younger brothers, disciples and her own teacher, 'Master Ma'. Then again she threw the horns, prostrated herself, and cast burning spirit paper outside the door.

---

[7] Most Hmong shamanic rituals can be done in Chinese as well as in Hmong, and the better known Hmong shamans in South East Asia can do both. The Chinese spoken, though, is of a dialect which has not so far been identified.

The shaman, acting as her assistant, had meanwhile prepared 60 red and white cut-out paper figurines in a large basketware winnowing tray known as a 'sieve' which also held two plates, one with cooked rice on it, one with a large piece of porkfat of the kind used for cooking, and an small incense brazier with six lit incense sticks in it, and he placed this panier immediately in front of the door on the floor. The number of figurines, they told me, depended on how many spirits had been diagnosed. Facing the door,the shamaness repeated the chant above, and then sang nine times;

> *Here is good [dowry] rice and a fine piece of meat. Here also is wine, and the spirits of all those persons who died of hunger or from falling off a rock, who died from drowning or from working too hard, are all now planted in this 'flower tree' [huapan]. Here also we have 60 large coins and the small coins also are numerous, you will be sent to the cross-roads. Go ahead, the bloody light of all those who drowned, fell from rocks or are killed by guns, are all present in this flower tree.*

The shaman had meanwhile thrown the divination horns to indicate *yin* twice and burned more spirit paper beneath the table in front of the altar. The patient's family were then invited to sit down on benches and stools facing away from the altar, and the shamaness traced a line clockwise around them on the floor with her tablet dipped in ashes from the fire. Then she waved a great bunch of lit spirit paper over their heads, touching them each briefly with it three times 'to purify them', and then asked them to turn around on the benches to face the altar. With her hands clasped together in front of her body she then described an invisible circle around each of the patients, from their heads down to their toes, drawing out all the 'evils' which had afflicted them, and mimed emptying these evils out into the sieve behind them; then taking up the gong, beating it and stamping her feet wildly, she chanted raucously nine times;

> *If one spirit sees this, 9 spirits will be afraid,*
> *if 9 spirits see this, 99 will be afraid:*
> *the gong will cover your head and cover your body,*
> *when it covers your head your head will be released,*
> *when it covers your arms your arms will be released,*
> *when it covers your feet your feet will be released,*

when it covers your body your body will be released,
the sieve will protect your head and protect your body,
when it protects your head your head will be released,
when it protects your arms your arms will be released,
when it protects your feet your feet will be released,
when it protects your body your body will be released:
if one spirits sees this, 9 spirits will be afraid,
if 9 spirits see this, 99 will be afraid ...

Smearing wax from the three candles on the altar onto her ritual 'seal' to lend it additional spiritual power, she then 'stamped' each patient with it three times on the head, back, chest, both hands and both feet, while her assistant began to seal and fold pieces of spirit paper into small triangles.

Finally she blew out sprays of water from her mouth over everyone present and threw milled corn all over them from the box of it on the shaman's altar. Each of them was given one of the paper triangles to keep in an inside pocket as a protection against further spiritual attacks, and she then bent down by the tray by the door to throw the divination horns, demanding all spirits to depart immediately 'towards the West'. Then she told her son, who had been watching, to take the sieve outside and burn it at the cross-roads outside the village.

There is also a rite for the protection of the house known as 'Laying the Dragon to Rest' or 'Comforting the Dragon', which is usually performed some years after a house has been constructed if domestic animals and people in it frequently fall ill and suffer misfortunes. This is a non-possessive ritual (not *a neeb*) like 'Crossing the Bridge'. After the 'sieve' (the winnowing basket) had been placed by the front door, with a piece of beancurd, thirteen silver coins, two sticky rice cakes, two plates and two cooked eggs on it , a shaman prostrated himself three times before the domestic altar and threw the divination horns several times before a favourable response was obtained. Then he burnt spirit paper in each of the four corners of the room, in each of which one sheet of paper money, a bowl containing beancurd, an alight incense brazier and two lit candles had already been placed. Then he hit the table with a black tablet made of some rock and cried out to summon his tutelary spirits. Then he burned incense under the table and prostrated himself again three times, before dismantling all the paraphernalia which had been put in the four corners of the room. A box of corn and a set of stone mason's tools (including an axe, two hammers, a ruler and scissors) had been placed in front of the sieve, and the shaman then placed all of these on a table set before the altar together with the sieve, before burning spirit paper under the table yet again and kneeling down to the right of the altar to throw the divination horns once more until *yang* was indicated. Then the bowl of water from the altar, with pieces of burnt spirit paper which the shaman had purposely dropped in it, was offered to the family to drink while the shaman admonished the souls of the family members to behave like good children and not wander too far away from each other, and more spirit paper burnt outside the door.

The sieve used was composed to resemble a dragon (see Diagram 24).

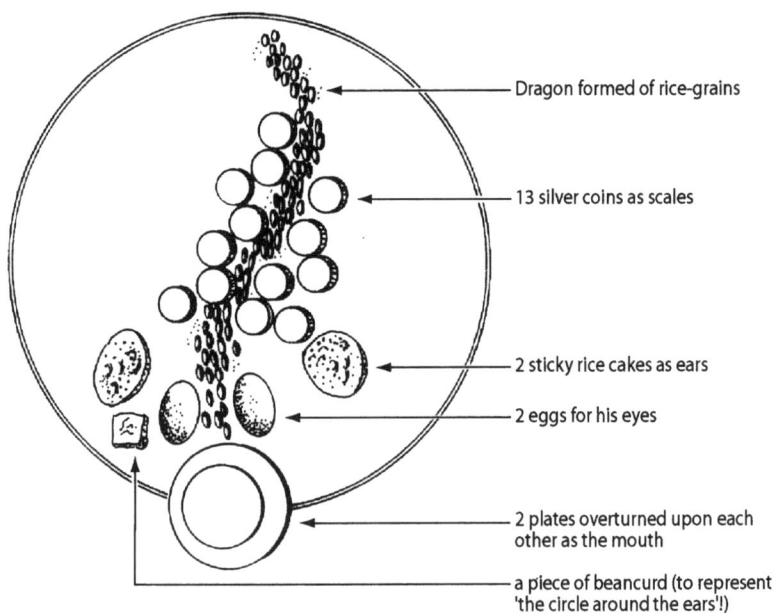

Diagram 24: A dragon sieve

As the shamans told me, the bowl used in this ritual, taken from its usual place on the altar, contained a liquid which was peculiarly powerful because what they called a 'thunderstone' (a meteorite) which had struck a tree dead, had been placed in it. This was a particularly effective rite of exorcism, which 'awakened the Masters', since the 'Five Buddhas' inhabited this bowl. When the table is struck with the thunderstone (the shaman's seal) all spirits are frightened into the sieve. When a new shaman is initiated, he drinks from this bowl together with his Master. Inscribing *fu* or mystic charms on a piece of paper which is then burnt, and the ashes mixed with water which is then drunk, is a common part of Daoist rituals.

Another ritual performed by local exorcists to cure a young boy or girl of an unsuitable infatuation was known as *song xiao shan pusa*, or 'sending the little Boddhisattva back to the Mountain', and required the family to pay the shaman ¥100 and provide both two chickens and a pig for sacrifice. The ritual centres around inviting a paper effigy representing the 'little Boddhisattva' to feast and wine on the flesh of the animals sacrificed, after which the effigy is borne off by the shaman to the back door and burnt. The name of the rite is said to originate from a Tang Dynasty legend about an Emperor Li and his Premier, Weizeng, who controlled Hades, and boasted to the Emperor that he could kill all the ladies at court. So the Emperor hid all his women in an underground tunnel, but the Premier drew a line to them with his sword, and killed them. Subsequently their spirits returned to beg the Emperor to redeem their lives, and he consequently made them the 'little mountain boddhisattvas'. Here the Chinese, and Buddhist, origins of local Hmong practices were particularly evident.

The most common household ritual performed, however, for the recalling of the soul of a sick member of the family, was the *hu pleg* or 'soul calling' which could be performed by an ordinary householder, and did not necessitate the intervention of a shaman or exorcist. Three sticks of incense and two candles are lit on a table set beneath the ancestral altar, and two small cups of wine and a plate of meat are offered to the ancestral spirits while the following is chanted;

> *Today is a good day; the great door has been opened, the high road is wide and vast, come Nphlaib's soul,[8] come quickly, come now, do not go behind the dark side of the*

---

[8] Nphlaib was the Hmong name (nickname in Sichuan) of the child.

mountain, where it is night, behind the dark side of the
mountain a great tempest is blowing, a mighty gale is
raging, the strong rains storm, the strong rains fall, mighty
gales have blown you there, great tempests have taken your
soul away, come back now, come home again, climb up the
steep and craggy mountain slope, descend again to the
mountain valley [khau dlis khau haa], come back to the light
side of the mountain, into the daylight, come through the
thickets of bamboo and wood, come past the beasts and the
birds, come into the orchards and plantations, oh come back
as one, Lady Soul return to Lord Soul, come quickly, come
home now, today is a good day, the door is ajar to welcome
Lady and Lord Soul to come back home together, come back
to rejoin your body, come home to rejoin your family, come
to join your mother and father, your elder brothers and
younger sisters, your mother's mother and your father's
father, come and live for a hundred years, you sons and
daughters, grandsons and granddaughters, may you live for
a hundred years.[9]

An egg is held up vertically in the clasped palms of both hands of the
supplicant; when it rolls to one side in the hands, this is a sign that
the soul has returned, and the chant may be ended. After the soul has
returned, paper money is burnt by the door of the house, and an
offering made to the ancestral spirits at the domestic altar..

This is a common Hmong ritual which we can find similar
versions of in any Hmong village from Thailand through Vietnam to
China, and the tune of the chant is similar. Indeed, soul-calling rites
for young children are performed throughout South East Asia and
South China.

Affliction then is dealt with by a number of local means; soul
recovery, exorcism, or shamanism (which is also a kind of soul
recovery), quite apart from the various ancestral rituals, New Year
and funeral rites.

---

[9] Although this ritual was otherwise all in Hmong, Chinese terms for the dark
and light sides of the mountain (*yinshan, yangshan*) and the female and male souls
(*yinhun, yanghun*) were used.

As we have seen, Hmong shamans were respected by local Chinese, and there is an interchange between the local rural Daoist traditions which appeared to be shared by both Hmong and Chinese, and the Hmong shamanic practices. Historically this has also been the case, as we see from the Daoist influences upon Hmong shamanism demonstrated by Lemoine (1987) and in the possibilities that Daoism itself may have originated from hybrid cultural practices in the southwest of China. Nevertheless the Hmong of Gongxian still preserve what they see as their 'own traditions', such as beliefs in deities like the benevolent *deus otiosis* Saub, the malevolent Ntxwj Nyug who decimates the living almost as fast as they appear, and Siv Yis the original shaman who all shamans 'become' in trance (see Part One). Yet many of these deities and otherworldly figures, seen by the Hmong and others as quintessentially Hmong, also go back to a historical time in which there seems to have been much more sharing of belief and cultural practice with others than is the case today. Lemoine (1972a) for example identifies Siv Yis with the legendary Chinese figure of Chen Yi, the Heavenly Archer who shot down nine of the ten suns at the beginning of time.[10]

In Sichuan they talked only reluctantly of these things, and as we have seen practiced shamanism covertly, to some extent fearfully; yet that it is practised at all, and to such an extent, is in itself an extraordinary indication of the complexity of cultural conditions in rural China, where party bureaucracy intersects with shamanic traditions in a uniquely fluid and flexible hierarchy of local authority, status and prestige. We have seen how a local government cadre may have a sister who is a practising shaman, we will see below how local cadres may also perform as funeral specialists. It is this sort of accomodation of apparently opposed interests, and the complex intertangling of kinship, economic and political relations with change and tradition, which makes up the vital web of village life, and which it is my concern to portray here.

Li Kaixiu's accounts of shamanism certainly had more in common with those of local Daoist-derived Han Chinese exorcism than with classic Hmong shamanism; she described how her family used to live in the impoverished Xanglo commune in the Wangliu

---

[10] These early folk motifs are very widespread among other minorities of the region. See Lemoine (1972b), and Dang (1993).

Mountains, and how difficult her life had been after she had married, how she had been afflicted with ulcers and sores and had seen a regular doctor who could not help her, and then went all the way to Didong for medical help which was equally useless.

There she had met a *noos tsa* ('rice-seeing') person (Ch.*kan mi ren*) or medium-diviner (an old woman) who told her her the soul of her (dead) father was looking for her husband to inherit his demonic spirits of shamanism, and this was why she herself had begun to learn both how to 'see the rice' (divine) and how to exorcise ghosts (*xaa dlaa*). Then she had achieved success reading the palms of a childless couple and prescribing herbal medicines for them so that they bore a child. Yang Wanheng and Yang Wanzhong had also consulted her about trouble they were having with their sons, and here she seemed to double as a geomancer (as Chinese spirit mediums often do), since she had been able to divine that the trouble was caused by their ancestral grave which was 'leaking rainwater onto their ancestor's eyes', and that they should repair it to overcome their illness. This had worked, and Yang Wanzhong had presented her with a red banner of thanks. While she claimed not to have *learned* what she practised, but to have been directly possessed by the spirits (they referred to possessive Hmong shamanism, or *a neeb*, as *yin* shamanism), she seemed to be more of a spirit medium in the Han Chinese mould, and she said that Pan Gu, the Chinese culture hero, had been the founder of her tradition, which had descended through the only one of his nine sons to have inherited the gift.

It was always her husband who practised the forms of Hmong possessive shamanism I saw; while his wife performed rituals such as one to help cattle delivery (which involved 150 pieces of paper money and 58 steps around the cow and scattering puffed rice on the land as offerings to the afflicting spirits), which are not normal Hmong shamanic activities. She said she could deal with such problems as swellings, childbirth and children's problems, and claimed she could enter the *yin* world , the spiritual world, and ask the spirit of her Father to diagnose illnesses; and she used a paper mask, rather than the cloth hood of the Hmong shaman. Her husband, on the other hand, was equipped with all the typical equipment of Hmong shamans, including the bells (*nees ju*), gong (*nruas*), dagger and horns (*kuab*) of the shaman.

While the shaman and shamaness appeared to practise both Hmong possessive shamanism and Han exorcism in entirely separate rituals, their audience probably had little idea which was which. At the New Year, all the proper shamanic rituals of inviting the possessing spirits and then returning them after three days to the Otherworld were practised, and the shaman had been initiated, like Hmong shamans elsewhere, by a special ritual sitting beside his Master, with an apron stretched over his knees as he sits on a stool before the newly made shamanic altar in his house to call '80 and 90 spirits', with two pieces of cloth, one stretching over a bamboo stick to the ceremonial door, one on the floor covering 24 bowls from the altar to the door, marking the earthly and heavenly bridges along which the possessing spirits will come and over which the new shaman must walk with his Master, before two cocks are sacrificed and their blood mixed and drunk to symbolise the sharing of the possessing spirits. Only Hmong can be spoken.

Possessive Hmong shamanism, then, contrasted strongly with some of the exorcistic rituals also practiced by the Hmong shamans in Gongxian. Moreover, special Han Chinese exorcisms were performed by the Hmong shaman to 'send the spirits back to Meishan' (*song Meishan*) in cases of lunacy and mental derangement, to 'send the spirits back to Shaoshan' (both historical centres of Daoist schooling) for unmarried girls who have died within their families, and for the souls of those who have died by hanging (*song diaosi gui*), to banish the spirits which specialise in such calamities.

In my interviews with shamans, Chinese technical terms were used as frequently as Hmong ones. As the shamans told me, no earthly medicines can cure those afflicted with disorders of the first sort, since it is their *fengtou*[11] or 'humour' which is out of order or irregular in the *yin*, spiritual world. A shaman (for which the Hmong term was always used; *tus a neeb*) must be invited to 'beat the mountains' by inscribing the appropriate mystical characters (*fu*),

---

[11] Literally, 'head-wind', the term is currently used to refer to 'a trend of events as affecting a person's circumstances', in particularly dangerous circumstances such as those surrounding the aftermath of Tiananmen, but as used locally had a more literal, quasi-ritual or medical significance, to which the best approximations I can think of would be 'humour' or 'atmosphere'; or 'malaise'.

and using the divination horns to communicate with the tutelary spirits (*shizu*)[12] to show that they are inclined to assist in the case. A piece of paper is placed on the patient's chest in such cases with Chinese characters inscribed on it (with incense) which will bring the 'soldiers, cavalrymen and generals' of the Otherworld to suppress the 'humour' or baleful influence.

If a shaman is not invited to perform the 'Shaoshan' exorcism in the second case above, it is believed that many other girls in the family may also die young and unmarried, because their *fengtau* has also been affected. The ghost which must be exorcised is addressed as *xiaoniang* or 'little' (younger) 'paternal aunt', is seen as still living and believed to speak to people from attics (where girls are often not allowed). As the shaman said, 'Nobody can replace them since they died unmarried, and so they will haunt the house as they are still alive'. A feminist gloss on this would be that a woman is not yet even allowed to die without having properly married (and having had sons). These are classic reflections of what one might call feudal patriarchal Chinese thinking, and sit a little oddly with Hmong kinship and ritual beliefs which commonly accord women (who are fully incorporated into husbands' lineages) a much more equal and visible status than that traditionally approved of in the formal Chinese kinship system.

The ghosts of hunger (and other violent deaths, particularly suicide) are also believed to be still living, and their presence is signified when female patients dream of handsome young men, and male patients of beautiful young women enticing them (that is, persistent erotic dreaming). Again in these cases a shaman must be invited to perform magical incantations and the family should prepare 'wax and incense' for the appropriate ritual, or more calamities will occur.

In the course of an exorcism against bad dreams I witnessed, three 'sweet and bitter' bamboos were planted in the ground outside the house, and a thread attached to these which led to a sieve which the young male patient, seated inside the door before the altar, held. Forty-eight *maoren* ('hairy people', or paper cut-out figurines)

---

[12] Lemoine (1987) notes the oddity of Hmong shamans calling Chinese tutelary spirits 'ancestors'.

previously prepared by the shaman were hung from the thread, and a gunman was stationed outside to the right of the door (stage left). At the climax of the ritual the shaman gave a great shout and the gunman literally seemed to shoot the thread away, whereupon all the paper figures started to slide down the thread towards the patient as if they were dancing. The patient is supposed to receive such a shock at this sight that he throws away the sieve he is holding and swoons away on the floor, and did seem remarkably surprised. Rough therapy perhaps, but one which focuses communal attention on the patient in a way which can be genuinely therapeutic, in which internal conflicts and subjectivities are objectified and personified in a performative dramatisation which literally takes the patient out of himself and into the embrace of a wider community which has expressed its concern about their welfare. I have tried to show, in the above, something of the dramatic, and even melodramatic nature, of these occasions.

These quintessentially Chinese rituals, almost certainly a bastard form of Daoist ritual and local folk custom, and with clear similarities to some of the exorcistic rituals reported among the Sichuan Miao by Graham in the 1930s and generally of the *tuan gong* or 'local wizards' of Sichuan, display a strange ambiguity in their diagnosis of the causes or symptoms of affliction, seen from an outsider's point of view. In the last case, for example, should we see the erotic dreams of the patient as a prime index or symptom of a deeper affliction, the ultimate cause of which is the restive ghost of one who has recently died a particularly unfortunate (violent) death, and which therefore presages or is harbinger to a precisely similar fate for the patient, should the affliction persist? Or should we see the main concern as being with the containment of the general malaise occasioned by such an unfortunate death as a hanging or suicide, which is likely to find symptomatic expression in further deaths of the same kind, *presaged* by troublesome (unacceptable, erotic) dreams? The ghost must be exorcised, yet the unfortunate event has already taken place.

The linking of the fates of the dead with the fates of the living is intrinsic to these formulations, and the sense of a community wider than the individual which is affected as a whole by the death of one of its members. Mueggler (1997) shows for the Yi how healing rituals can express an epistemology of origins which counters the dismissal of origin by the state modernisation project. Shamanism like exorcism in effect stretches the boundaries of selfhood so that the community is identified with it. So is the use of the notion of *fengtou* which seems to refer here to a concatenation of events wider than those surrounding a single individual, a kind of general 'malaise' which is seen as the root cause of misfortunes. The symptoms dealt with (boils, for instance, mental disturbance of some kind, or erotic dreams) seem almost incidental to these wider concerns with the well-being of the community as a whole, with its mental health and security and its continuance through 'normal' processes of marriage and childbirth.

Shamanism, then, was a performance which both united local Hmong and Chinese and yet expressed some of the differences felt between them. Moreover, it was a purely internal performance, signifying the adoption of an order of moral power which, it is tempting to say, had nothing to do with the secular order of the state, or at least was at variance with it. It has to do, not only with biophysical exigency, but also to do with the sense of local community and its sense of security in the face of external forces represented by challenges to the primacy of local conceptions and status rankings. Of particular interest in understanding the role of shamanism and shamans at the local level in a a socialist state must be the ambivalent identities of those who have specialised in such traditional vocations, the nature of the extraordinarily contradictory and conflicting demands which must be experienced, for example, by a party member who is also a funeral specialist, as we shall see in the following chapter. While there were specifically Hmong forms of possessive shamanism, Han were not excluded from these as patients, and the coalescence of Hmong with Han shamanism seemed to depict an identification of common local interests with the heritage of the past in a way which was quite explicitly recognised as running counter to the interests of the modernising state and had little to do with divisions of a cultural or ethnic nature.

CHAPTER FIVE

THE PRIMACY OF DEATH RITUALS

It is always through death ritual that conceptions of Hmong cultural identity as essence find their purest expression. In the melancholy of death, local communities mourn a past envisaged to have been of grandeur, and a purely Hmong profundity is expressed in these pre-modern narratives of loss. And it is in the details of how the rituals should be performed that Hmong ritual specialists insist on a specifically Hmong identification, and on the power of their own knowledge of these cultural forms.

Unlike Han rituals, Hmong death ritual does not usually include the entertainments and card games with which visitors pass the many days a funeral can take. Yet there are many elements which the Hmong funerals have in common with those of the Han, and more in Sichuan which have been recently borrowed.

On arrival at a funeral guests or visitors who have not bought maize and wine should pay some money (counted in odd numbers) at a desk set up for that purpose, and white cloth is wound around one's arm to signify that one is a gift bearer, which is a Han custom which has been adopted. At a funeral in neighbouring Fenghuang for an eighty-year old man, whose son-in-law was Yang Liping's nephew in whose house I stayed,[1] so that we were in the position of affinal relatives or 'MBs', no fewer than three bands of musicians had been invited—the suona together with leaf and pipes, horns and drum, cymbals and clapper—again a very Chinese touch.

A male deceased, I was told, should be dressed in an odd number of layers of ceremonial clothing, while for a woman an even number may be used. Even the number of threads used to weave the traditional sash which the dead must wear is also carefully calculated, and was locally said to depend on their age, so that seventy threads would be suitable for a man of seventy years old.

---

[1] See Chapter Seven.

The bereaved family don undyed hemp mourning clothes and white turbans.[2]

Immediately after a death there is the ceremonial shaving and cutting of the hair by the sons and daughters of the deceased, and enormous practical preparations to be made such as the making of the drum and the plaiting of a hemp rope. Two or more messengers, lineage relatives, are despatched to invite and inform relatives of the death, equipped with incense, paper money and bottles of liquor to toast those invited, and to invite the ritual specialists who include the Master of the Way and the players of the *qeej* and drum. Then there is the clothing of the corpse in the special clothes usually prepared many years before for burial, and the washing of the face by his or her sons (usually their wives). Then the bamboo divination horns (*kuam*) which will be used during the funeral by the Master of the Way, and then discarded, must be made. The special divination horns carved for the funeral by members of the family are of water-bamboo, and according to the specialists should be cut three fingers above the knot in it and two fingers beneath it, for a funeral, to distinguish them from those used at the post-mortuary rituals, which otherwise resemble the structure of the funeral quite closely.

A drum of cowhide is then tied up with rattan by the men of the house, to two green bamboo cross-poles strapped further together and suspended from the middle cross rafter beam of the house, so that the funeral drum hangs against the housepost on its stage left side, and it is here that the two, or four, players of the *qeej* reed-pipes which punctuate the course of the funeral dance. After the funeral the drum is thrown away and never used again.

Unlike in Thailand, and the more traditional Hmong areas, where the corpse is simply laid in the house exposed on a plain stretcher (almost as if just back from the battlefield), the corpse at a funeral in

---

[2] This account of funeral procedure is deliberately male-focused, since this is how it is seen by both Hmong men and women. The best of funerals, where all the rituals are correctly and properly performed, and which may last up to two weeks, are reserved for elderly men much respected in the community, with many descendants to support the funeral. The funeral of a young man may be finished in a day, and children often have none. The funerals of women reflect those of their husbands, but not so elaborately. A woman should not be without a husband; it is unfortunate if she dies before her husband, and disgraceful if she dies without having married, as it is disgraceful for a young man to die before his father, or without having produced heirs.

Wutong was eventually placed in a large black coffin with the lid half raised to expose the face, directly below the ancestral altar rather than to the left of it, and I was told it was important that the head should face to stage right of the house so that the dead man is not dazzled by the sunlight. Generally coffins are now used by the Hmong in the Gongxian area, on the Han model, although these vary greatly in size and in the cost of making or purchase.

During the *Qhab Ki* (*Qhuab Ke* in White Hmong), the great Song of Opening the Way for the soul of the deceased which we give below, which guides him back to the village of his ancestors from where he will be reborn as a member of the same clan, sung by a local Master of the Way who has been specially invited to the funeral, cooked rice and eggs are repeatedly offered by the Master (*mo*) to the mouth of the corpse. A bowl perched on the coffin or just above it has rice, eggs, and delicacies such as vegetables and biscuits placed in it, together with incense and spirit paper. Various ritual offerings are made by the Master during the *Qhab Ki* to the corpse, including a crossbow and a knife, a cock, a parasol and a pair of hemp shoes, and a candle in a bowl burns constantly under the coffin. After the Song is done the Master, in Gongxian, claps his hands twice, and ceremoniously sweeps over the corpse with paper money to purify it.

It is only after the *Qhab Ki* song that the corpse is ritually raised in its coffin and placed in a central position inside the central hall, and all the women begin to wail as the insistent drum which accompanies the *qeej* continues to summon neighbours and friends to the unfolding funeral process (messages have already been sent out to near and distant relatives). The *Qhab Ki* is usually recited towards evening of the first day of the funeral, whether this is reckoned from the day when the death took place, or the following day. As the corpse is raised, the *qeej* plays in turn the tunes known as the *kis laug*, *kis hmo* and *kis ces plaag*, and rice and wine are offered three times to the dead man, and incense and candles lit and paper burnt, both at the household altar and beneath the coffin, also three times by the nearest male survivor of the deceased.

There follows a ritual of the sacrifice of boar and cock to the ancestral spirits,[3] when rice and wine are offered three times three times to the corpse by the Chief Mourner as the *kis yuav ua cig* is played on the *qeej*, at the same time as his helpers (usually younger brothers and cousins) wind a rope from the front door through the drum to the coffin to represent the path the soul of the deceased will follow towards the Otherworld.

The liver of the chicken and pig or pigs after the cooking of the sacrifice is offered to the deceased (in the bowl beneath the coffin) at the noontime ritual by the Chief Mourner or his seconds, and paper money is burnt after this offering (*kis fantej*), as it is after each repeated rite At the funeral feast which follows this, the sacrificial pork should be placed in nine bowls, and the chicken which accompanies it in five; the chicken's neck should be cut from the left for a cock, from the right for a hen. The left wing is placed in the first bowl and the right wing in the second, the left leg in the third and right leg in the fourth and the buttocks in the fifth. This funereal meal is known as the funeral 'lunch' or mid-day meal, but it may take place very late in the afternoon.

If the deceased is male, all his patrilineal relatives (conceptually, the FyB and FeB) will now prostrate themselves three times on the floor as the *txij yig vaiv laug kis* is played. If it is the wife of the house who has died, her own relatives (affinal relatives to the household) will prostrate themselves first, as the *yiav dlaag* (MB) *kis* is played. But both lineage relatives of the deceased ('the sons') and affinal relatives of the deceased ('the sons-in-law') must perform these ceremonial prostrations to the ancestral spirits en masse. This is a spectacular occasion, which usually takes place near midnight, often at the end of the first day of a funeral (where the death has taken place on the previous day); in the darkness of the house, the white turbaned young men, sometimes thirty or forty of them at a time, prostrating themselves and lamenting aloud on the small space there is usually for them inside the house, as the *qeej* players whirl a martial reel, and the Master of the Way acknowledges these prostrations with cupped hands on behalf of the deceased he has been in communication with through the medium of the divination horns

---

[3] They used to use cattle, and this is more traditional, but this is unthinkable in present-day Chinese conditions. Hens are used where the deceased is a woman.

he constantly throws. There were 150 people crammed into the small house of one of the funerals we went to.

Whenever relatives arrive there are also welcomes, official announcements, offerings and presentations with playing of the *qeej*—and sometimes, if as they say 'the house has been too long without music', the *qeej* is played anyway, just for the sake of it (*qeej a si*). Important relatives or guests who come with important gifts, cloth banners and umbrellas, baskets of maize, chickens and wine, are additionally toasted (with an occasional reel known as the *tchauj kis*; the gift-bearer kneels at the door beside his gift and a special song is sung between him and the Chief Mourner or his second) at a special table set outside the house by the sons of the deceased, where orations are read and three plates prepared with special offerings—one of rice, two with sweetmeats—as the *kis yuav cig* of respect is again played (at the *a vaa*, or 'soul-releasing' ritual, performed thirteen days later, which repeats most of the form of the funeral, no meat is offered and the drum is beaten in two-time rather than three-time, so it is possible from a distance to know which is happening). Later the reader of the oracles will place a cloth over the coffin, which is constantly fanned by the woman relatives of the deceased..

At midnight of the day before the day of burial, the ritual experts of the *qeej* and drum are offered tobacco and toasted and feasted by the deceased's male relatives, in an offering known as the *txij qee txij nruas*, or the sacrifices to the *qeej* and drum. The three plaints of the *qeej* to symbolise nightfall, the *kis tsau ntos*, are also played in the course of the evening. A senior lineage representative appointed by the bereaved family should then invite representatives of the FBs and MB to discuss the affairs of the deceased, all seated at special tables set out in the central hall.

Well into the night, at one or two in the morning, when all the dead man's debts are judged to be settled, and the senior lineage representative has formally thanked the assembled company and praised the sons of the deceased, there are the three rituals for *kis xieshao*, and the burning of paper money for each one present. And the *yang yav kis* (plaint of yin and yang) is played on the *qeej*.

On the day of burial (often the third day of the funeral), the drum is first taken out and destroyed, then a person (who should not be a relative) will cut down the poles it has been attached to, and the coffin placed immediately before the front door.

At a funeral in Fenghuang, after the drum had been hacked down and the poles cut in two and thrown outside, while the coffin still lay lengthwise on benches in the middle of the room, a local Chinese *daoshi* or Daoist priest was invited, to exorcise the evil spirits which might have stayed behind. This is not part of a traditional Hmong funeral, and I was told was only done in the event of an unfortunate or accidental death. The Daoist I saw was an extremely tall man, dressed in an old white apron and robe, and while chanting, casting divination horns and burning paper money, he performed magical mudras with his hands and drew mystic charms (*hui* or *fu*) in the air with a bunch of lighted incense sticks, periodically clapping his hands together to frighten the spirits away from the body and through the front door. He also folded two pieces of blue and white cloth four times and then tucked it into the lintel of the door as a purification, and with a hatchet hacked down a chicken which had been trussed to the top of the door by a red and white string, then threw all his ritual paraphernalia, including a crossbow and his torch, with great panache out of the door after burying the chicken in a hole he dug with a sword in the floor of the house. None of the Hmong present had any idea of the meaning of all this, although they knew it was to purify the house of the evil influences caused by an unfortunate death.[4]

The coffin strapped up outside, the long procession starts to the burial site, where the Master of the Way conducts a special ritual to pay the spirits of the land for the 'purchase' of the spot. Offerings of a chicken, a crossbow, and a black umbrella held by a daughter of the deceased, together with paper and incense and offerings of food, are carried to the grave and placed within it.

The ritual process lasts much longer than the actual funeral (*pam tuag*). Immediately on return from the grave pieces of bamboo are sent back to the grave, green ones for a male dead and white ones for a woman, to enclose the grave. Six pieces of split bamboo are placed crosswise against six more to make a fence on two sides of the grave, facing out for a male, in for a female. 'Fire' (a torch procession) has

---

[4] It is quite common for Han congregations to have little idea of the esoteric meanings of Daoist rituals, as I found frequently at *dajiao* rituals in Hong Kong.

to be sent to the grave each evening for three days, and for three days a morning meal is also sent. The morning meal is sent all the way to the grave on the first morning after burial, halfway there the second day, and a third of the way on the third day. The meals (of rice and pork) are placed in three bamboo tubes and accompanied by water 'to wash the face of the deceased', and taken by the immediate family of the deceased.

On the third day after burial a special ritual is performed to invite the soul of the deceased to return home for the mid-day meal, and thirteen days after the burial the soul of the deceased is again invited to 'return' before its final despatch in a major day-long ritual which mirrors the structure of the funeral (*xw*). It was said that the divination horns which must also be made specially for this event, should be cut two fingers above the knot, and three below it. During the course of the *xw*, the 'dutiful sons' of the deceased take a cross-bow to the grave and encircle it three times, clockwise for a deceased male and anti-clockwise for a woman.

In many ways what was remarkable about the three funerals and one *a vaa* I witnessed in and around Wutong, by contrast with those in Thailand or Laos, was the elaborate welcoming and reception of relatives and visitors, which also takes place outside China, but with not so much attention paid to it, where the *Qhab Ki*, and the rituals of the *qeej*, remain the main focus of attention. This is an example of the greater Han Chinese influence on Hmong funeral custom in this area of Sichuan.

At one funeral in Wutong of an elderly man, the arrival of guests and relatives seemed endless. As the relatives arrive, mostly armed with paper banners inscribed with mournful Chinese couplets, they are said to *tsij*, or sacrifice. A tray with eight bowls of sweetmeats has been placed on a bench just beneath the drum. Another bench nearby holds a bottle of liquor and a bowl of wine. The leading mourner, usually a son or sometimes son-in-law acting for his wife, offers some of these to the bowl placed on top of the coffin. The Announcer recites the banner in a loud voice while the two kowtow, and when he has finished, burns the red-and-white banner beneath the bench as the tray is carried outside and the box of corn and incense returned to its place on a bench at the head of the coffin. The bowl of wine is poured onto the earth with burnt paper at the beginning of the rite, and then again with the burnt banner after the

Announcement is read. The gift-bearers as they prostrate themselves may express their sorrow in broken tones, or lament more loudly. Then the benches are all dismantled, and the *qeej* and drum are played, as four 'dutiful sons' representing the younger generation in the lineage of the deceased prostrate themselves before the gift bearers at the front door. Finally the *qeej* player, as he finishes, makes three lilting bows with sweeps of his *qeej* to the presenters of gifts. Then there is the singing of a special song to welcome the arrivals, the *tchauj kis*, in front of the door. And every time a relative's name is called out by the Announcer, at the beginning of the rite, the Chinese troupe of musicians all troop in, circle the drum and exit again, and each time they enter, the entire assembled company of men prostrates itself. Adding to this the offerings being made with low chanting by the chief mourner at the head of the coffin at the same time, the constant throwing of horns and invocations by the Ritual Master, the ceaseless keening of women, and the prostrations of present relatives on behalf of absent relatives as their names are called, and one may have some idea of the pity and the majesty of a Hmong funeral, of which this is but one small section, endlessly repeated, in a complex and elaborate ritual process.

The Qeej

The funeral is ordered not only by the long, several-hour chanting of the *Qhab Ki*, and the continuous arrival of relatives and guests with offerings who must be greeted and saluted, but particularly by the music of the *qeej players* and the beating of the drum.

The *Qeej Ntsaa*, as the music of the funeral is called, is divided by the musicians into twelve main parts: there is the *kis laug* (plaint of the old, for the Drum hung up to the main house post), the *kis mo* (plaint for the Founder of the *Qeej*) for the singing of the Opening of the Way, and the *kis ces plaag* (plaint of hunger) played in succession as the corpse is raised. These are performed three times three times altogether.

The *kis yuav ua cig* (of respect) is played as the sacrificed pork and chicken are placed in a bowl under the coffin. Then there is the *kis* of the *txij yis vaiv laug* (FyB and FeB), and then the *kis* for the *yiav dlaag* (MB), both of which are played, in the reverse order to this if the deceased is a woman. And the *kis* of the *txij qee txij nruas* (to offer to the Masters of the *Qeej* and Drum).

These are followed by the *kis sangshao* (for a funeral) or *kis xieshao* (where a post-mortuary service rather than a funeral is being performed); the *sangshao* refers to the donning of white turbans by male mourners, the *khawj roog* or (Ch.) *xieshao* refers to the doffing of turbans when an *a vaa*, the post-mortuary ritual. which ideally takes place three years after death, is being performed.

The *qeej* played when paper money is burnt is known as the *kis fantej* , but this accompanies all the other rites.

Then again, in succession, before the coffin is taken out of the house, and assuming the funeral lasts more than a single day into the morning of the next (as mostly they do), the *kis laug*, *kis mo*, and *kis ces plaag* are played. Finally, the playing of the *qee tcho* (of 'release') , also known as the plaint of *yin* and *yang*, finishes the proceedings, as the pole is cut.

But besides these twelve major laments, which run the entire course of the funeral, there are also playings of the *qeej* to mark the progress of each day; there is the *kis xaav ntus* at dawn (itself composed of three 'rites' and three chants), the *kis yuav tshaib* for breakfast, the *kis yuav shu* for lunch and *kis yuav hmo* for supper, as well as the *kis tsau ntos* at night, also composed of three rites and three chants.

Conceptually these are meals offered to the corpse, although mourners may eat at these times too; it is not so much the assembled company's ordinary procession of meals which is marked by these ritual and significant tunes, as that the corpse is ceremonially offered food at these times, with a spoon of rice and pork offered three times three times, and a small cup of water and one of wine three times three.

And there are also as I have said 'occasional' (but very frequent) playings of the *qeej* to mark each significant arrival of relatives with gifts (and for the musicians, and setting off of firecrackers), as the 'sons of the household' (including all male relatives in the same generation) prostrate themselves and paper money is burnt.

Most remarkable for me, at these funerals, was to find local cadres, officials, bureaucrats, and party members, not only attending as they must do by reason of their familial obligations, but actively participating in funerals as ritual specialists. The players of the *qeej* at funerals are as much ritual experts as the singer of the song of Opening the Way, since *qeej* playing requires a long and elaborate ritual apprenticeship. While the playing of the *qeej* is not limited to funerals; indeed *qeej* is played for fun, particularly at New Year celebrations, and where 'Miao' identities have been spectacularised with the visiting of tourists, and in expressions of publically acceptable 'Hmong culture', the *qeej* has become a particular emblem of a renovated 'Miao' identity. Although this was not the case in Wutong or Gongxian, an area rarely visited even by the occasional Chinese tourist, nevertheless Yang Dailu, the village (branch) party secretary, was also a *qeej* specialist, and was frequently to be seen with his friends at funerals, playing the mournful sounds of lamentation for the deceased on their passage back through time to the village of the ancestors and rebirth. Here we have a young man who sought to be as much at home in the technical practices of a distinctively Hmong cultural tradition as he did in the elaborate secular procedures of party bureaucracy and local politics. And he was genuinely respected for this; as a budding leader, who had the general approval of his elders, bearing the weight of Hmong cultural ability besides the weight of secular responsibilities entrusted in him by the state, and seeking for a traditional as well as a modern proficiency. Yet it is probably equally significant that the Master of the Way was not, perhaps could not be, such a man of all parts.

Some of the reasons for this may perhaps be glimpsed in the nature of this song, sung by the solitary Yang Wanfang (of the Yang Y3b lineage in Wutong, see Ch.7);

> *OPENING THE WAY FOR THE SOUL OF THE DECEASED*
>
> A bowl of water is placed by the dead man, together with two halves of horns and a cross-bow, hempen thread and a pair of straw slippers. The horns are thrown; the Master comes up and calls to the dead one,
>
> *Let us play* (now he calls the name of the deceased), *arise, arise, let us see and let us go to play*
>
> (Now he begins to dance and call the name)

(After calling three times like this, the Master recites the following);

Sub us uj, at daybreak came one walking from the edge of the sky, dressed up in beautiful finery and wearing a splendid turban on his head. I called you once and you made no reply, I called you twice and you did not answer, I fear that the one wearing beautiful clothes must be you, come to play

Sub yom yiaj, at daybreak came one walking from the edge of the sky, dressed up in beautiful finery and wearing a splendid turban. I called you once but you did not hear, I called you twice and three times but you did not listen, I fear that the one dressed in beautiful finery coming along the path is you, come to play

Sub us uj, at daybreak came one walking from the edge of the sky, dressed up in beautiful finery and wearing a splendid turban . I called you once but you did not hear, I called you twice and the third time also you did not reply, so the one in the road dressed in beautiful clothes must be you, come to play

prick up your ears and listen carefully to what the Master has to tell you, the Heavens were not flat (tiaj), the Earth was not even (tus), when spirits and people mixed together . In the past, when spirits and men died they changed their bones and could meet again, the bones of people changed into iron, the flesh of spirits changed into mud, so when fighting together, the people always won, the spirits always lost

Sub us uj, heaven was not flat, earth was not even, Nkauj Tsu Li Tus came down from the other side of the mountains and hills carrying an iron rod, and Nkauj Tsu Li Ntus came down from the other side of the mountains and hills holding a copper rod, they came down to beat the heavens and the heavens collapsed and the earth fell down. So the high heavens released 9 kinds of sickness onto the earth, let 8 kinds of disease fall on the earth, and in this world people *gagged and fell sick (*hnyav li hau vag*), and 9 healing herbs could not cure them of their sickness, 8 medicinal herbs could not heal their disease, so people of this world could not arise but went to become spirits, come to play*[5]

*Sub us uj, you will go to play under the heavens but first you have to leave the bedroom, and at the door of the bedroom the Lord and Lady Spirits of the Bedroom (*Poj Dab Txaj*), holding an iron and a copper rod, bar your way and will not let you take your fortune and go, so you say to them like this, 'Heaven released 9 kinds of sickness onto this world and 8 kinds of illness, so earthly beings fell weak and sick and their heads dropped, and 9 kinds of herbs, 8 kinds of medicines, could not heal them, so earthly beings could not remain alive, but arose to become spirits'. You say to them like this, and you can go slowly on your way, go to join the dance and play*

Sub us uj, the Master will give you some water to drink

*Sub us uj, prick up your ears and listen carefully to what the Master has to say to you now, the Master will lead you out of the kitchen (*cub; cooking fire*), but at the door of the kitchen the Lord and Lady Spirits of the Kitchen holding a rod of iron and a rod of copper will block your way to stop you leaving, and you must say to them like this; 'Heaven released 9 kinds of sickness onto this earth and 8 kinds of disease, then the people of this world fell sick in their bodies and giddy (*ntia ti npoo lev*), people felt sick and giddy in their bodies and their bellies (*ntia ti npoo txaj*), so the people of this world could not remain alive, but had to arise to become spirits'. You say to them like this, and you can go slowly on your way, you find the road to join the dance*

*Sub us uj, prick up your ears and listen carefully to the Master now, the Master will lead you out of the door of the hearth (*txos; large cooking fire for pigs*) . But the Lord and Lady Spirits of the Hearth, holding an iron rod and a copper*

---

[5] This refers to the Hmong story of the origin of things; cf. Lemoine (1972b).

rod, bar your way and prevent you from leaving, and so you should say to them like this; 'the Heavens released 9 kinds of sickness and 8 kinds of disease onto this earth, so people of this world fell sick and their heads lolled, and 9 kinds of shamans and 8 kinds of medicines could not cure them, so people could not remain alive but went to become spirits'. You say to them like this and you can go on your way, go slowly along your path to play

*Sub us uj, now the Master will lead you out of the Front Door (*niam rooj*), but the Lord and Lady Spirits of the Door block the way, with an iron rod and a copper rod, and will not let you go.*

You should say to them like this; 'Heaven was not flat, Earth was not even, Nkauj Tsu Tu and Nkauj Tsu Ntus came down with an iron rod and a copper rod and beat the heavens and the earth so they became flat, then the Heavens released 9 kinds and 8 types of sickness onto this earth, and people fell sick in their bodies and in their bellies, and in this world 9 kinds of medicines and 8 troupes of shamans could not cure them, could not heal them, so people could not remain alive but had to become ghosts'. And if the Couple who guard the Door still will not let you pass, you should say this to them; 'When those evil spirits beat and struck the earth, why did you not prevent them? When those spirits came to pound the earth, why did you not restrain them? Now people on this world cannot win when they fight against the spirits, they cannot hold on to their fortune, but must go to become spirits'. You say to them like this, and you can go slowly on your way, go to play

Sub us uj, prick up your ears and listen carefully now to what the Master has to say, now the Master will lead you out of the front door and onto the grassy plains, but nobody can find anything to put in your bowl for your midday meal. Where to find the seeds of crops and grains in this world? Where do the beginnings of crops and grains come from? Listen, it was said the seeds came from the country of Ntxwj Nyuj Laug, from the cliff of Ntxwj Nyuj Laug in the heavens, so Old Saub sent off a pes *bird (hawk) with a beak as sharp as a knife and feathers like arrows to fly up to the gates of heaven to find the seeds of life . The bird slept for three months all through the winter until the day of the tiger, and awoke in the spring when it could sleep no more. The bird pecked once, and one seed dropped, pecked twice, and two seeds dropped, pecked three times, three seeds dropped. In three days the bird flew down to earth and slept all through the winter, until the day of the tiger, could sleep no more and stretched and woke up, waking in the sunlight in a shower of rain (*nag tshauv*) and shook its feathers once, one seed dropped down, shook its feathers twice, two seeds dropped down, shook its feathers three times, and three seeds dropped on the earth and Saub helped them to take root in the ground, up came the shoots, with beautiful green leaves .*

There was one (seed) to bind the souls of sons and daughters, one to bind the souls of crops and grains, one to bind the souls of the domestic animals, one to bind the souls of the elders and leaders, one for marriages and weddings, one for the Yi and Han people, and one very little one left . Since nobody could find any food for the dead man's lunch, so I will use this one to give you your lunch . One spoon for your lunch, two spoons for your lunch, three spoons for your lunch, four spoons for your lunch, five spoons for your lunch, six spoons for your lunch, seven spoons for your lunch, eight spoons for your lunch, nine spoons for your lunch, ten spoons for your lunch, eleven spoons for your lunch, twelve spoons for your lunch and you can take your path and go to dance

Sub us uj, prick up your ears and listen carefully to what the Master has to say, now the Master will lead you to leave the plains and the valleys where your tomb is, but nobody on earth can find anything to make your coffin . Where to find the origins of bamboos and trees in this world? Where do the seeds of bamboos and trees come from? I heard say that the seeds came from the country of Ntxwj Nyuj Laug in the heavens, so old Saub sent off a pes *bird with a beak as sharp as a knife and feathers like arrows to fly up to the gates of heaven to find the seeds . The bird slept for three months all through the winter, and awoke in the seventh month when it could sleep no more . The bird pecked once, and one seed dropped, pecked twice, and two seeds dropped, pecked three times, and three seeds fell. In three days the bird flew down to earth and slept all through the winter, and could sleep no longer and stretched, awoke in the seventh month in a shower of rain and shook its feathers and its tail once, one seed dropped down, shook twice, two seeds dropped, shook three times, and three seeds fell to the ground where Old Saub helped them to take root and grow up with fine green leaves.*

There was one (seed) to bind the souls of sons and daughters, one to bind the souls of bamboos and trees, one to bind the souls of crops and grains, one to bind the souls of the domestic animals, one to bind the souls of the elders and leaders, one for marriages and weddings, one for the Chinese who came late, and just one little one left . Since there is no one else here to find wood for your coffin, I will use this one to transport you [6]

Sub us uj, come to play, prick up your ears and listen carefully to what the Master tells you, now your head hangs down, the Master lead you to leave the gates of the plains, to leave the valley of your grave, but nobody can find anything to guide you on your way . Where are people to find the seeds of the knowledge of fertility? Where do the seeds of fertility and the chicken come from? I heard say the seeds came from the country of Ntxwj Nyuj Laug, from Ntxwj Nyuj Laug's mighty crag in the skies, so old Saub sent off a pes *bird with a beak as sharp as a knife and feathers like arrows to fly up to the gates of heaven and find the seeds of life . The bird slept for three months, until the tiger day, and awoke in the spring when it could sleep no more.*

The bird pecked once, and one seed dropped, pecked twice, two seeds dropped, pecked three times, and three seeds fell

---

[6] Also refers to divination horns.

*out. In three days the bird flew down to earth and slept until
the day of the tiger (one week), could not sleep any more,
stretched and awoke in the sunlight in a shower of rain, and
shook its feathers and tail once, one seed dropped down,
shook twice, two seeds dropped down, shook three times, and
three seeds fell to the ground where Old Saub helped them to
grow and sprout green leaves.*

*There was one to tie the souls of sons and daughters, one to
tie the souls of crops and grains, one to tie the souls of
bamboo and trees, one to tie the souls of domestic animals,
one to tie the souls of elders and leaders, one for marriages
and weddings, one for the Han who came late, and just one
little one left . Since in this world nobody can find anything
to lead you on your way, this one will be used to guide you
on your way to play*[7]

*Sub us uj, prick up your ears and listen carefully to the
Master now come and dance for the Master will Open the
Way for you to go, when you were alive, you visited and
wandered in many places, ate and drank in many homes,
were warmed by many different fires, now we must give
thanks to all these places, so the Master puts the crossbow
on his back and takes the cock by wings and tail, to show you
the way and lead you (as an ox pulls a carriage) to mount
the ladder of heaven*

*Sub us uj, prick up your ears and listen carefully to what the
Master has to say, the Master puts the crossbow on his back
and takes the cock under his arm, to show you the way and
lead you to mount the ladder of heaven, you climb up 1,2,3
steps, the Master mounts 1 step, you climb 4,5,6 steps, the
Master climbs 2, you mount 7,8,9 steps, the Master climbs 3,
and you go up 10, 11, 12 rungs, the Master mounts to the
fourth rung*

*Sub us uj, now you have arrived at the country of Ntxwj Nyuj
Laug in the skies, you'll take a turn around his heavenly*

---

[7] Also refers to the cock.

*grounds, and the sky becomes scorching hot, a mighty tempest blows up (*nag xob nag cua*), but don't you fear or lament, the Master has an umbrella to give you, to protect you from the glare of the sun*

Sub us uj, the Master picks up an umbrella and gives it to you to shelter you from the sunlight, but now you will come across three wells (ponds), don't drink from the upper well, and don't drink from the lower well, these are for the Yi and the Han, but drink only from the middle well, of its bitter and filthy waters, to wash away the sickness and sorrows of earth, drink to the full and go ahead and play

*Sub us uj, prick up your ears and listen carefully to what the Master has to say now, the Master carries a crossbow on his back and takes a cock under his arm to guide you on your way, for your shadow to stride along the way, if you should hear another cock crowing and your cock does not crow back, that is the path for the Yi and Han people, but if you hear another cock crowing and your cock replies, then that is the road of your ancestors (*pog yiag*), you take the way of your heavenly Mother and Father and go and play*

*Sub us uj, prick up your ears and listen carefully to what the Master has to say, the Master bears the crossbow on his back and takes the cock under his arm to guide you on your way, and you will come upon three roads, one to each side, do not take the one to either side, one is for the Yi, and one for the Han, but take the road in the middle, with dirty footprints and hoofmarks (*khis ntsab khis hnov*), for that is your ancestors' road, that is the road for you*

*Sub us uj, prick up your ears and listen carefully to the Master, the Master carries a crossbow on his back and a cock under his arm to accompany (guide) you on your way, and now leads you into a deep dark forest, with great grasshoppers (*kab npliad*) wailing, don't take any notice of them, don't fear or lament, this is the sound of your own sons and daughters weeping and lamenting, you take your way and go ahead, go and play*

Sub us uj, prick up your ears and listen carefully to what the Master has to say, the Master again carries a crossbow on his back and a cock under his arm to help you on your way, and will lead you to a great river (dej dag), its waters seething and boiling, but don't fear or lament, the cock will carry you through the raging waters on its back, so you can find your ancestors' way, and go to play

Sub us uj, prick up your ears and listen carefully to the Master, the Master carries a crossbow on his back and a cock under his arm to guide you on your way, and you arrive at the flowery paths of Ntxwj Nyug Laug's mountain grotto on the skies, and now the Master will take you back down to the world to play, you descend 1,2,3 rungs on the heavenly ladder, the Master will come down 1, you come down 4,5,6 rungs, the Master will descend 1 more, you descend 7,8,9 steps and the Master will come down the third step, you come down 10,11 and 12 steps and the Master will come down four, so you can take your way and go and play

Sub us uj, now the Master has led you back down to this world again, prick up your ears and listen carefully to what the Master has to say . The Master will take you to a mountain of crawling worms and insects (kav nplam kab xyeb li kiab), as huge as tree trunks, as small as saplings, but don't fear or lament (so seev), the Master has a pair of hemp shoes to put on your feet, so you can trample them out of your way and go on your way, go to play

Sub us uj, prick up your ears and listen carefully now to what the Master tells you, the Master has led you back down to this earth, and now leads you across the mountain of knife-sharp dragon and tiger rocks, the Dragon and Tiger rocks will open their mouths like great basins to devour you, and stretch out their talons to catch you, but don't fear or lament, the Master will give you this twisted hempen thread to bind up their jaws tightly, to tie their claws firmly, so you can go safely on your way, go to play

Sub us uj, prick up your ears and listen carefully to what the Master has to say, Master has led you past the leaping rocks

*of Dragon and Tiger, the Master now takes you to your own
country to find the hillside of your grave (*toj ntxa;
graveyard*), that is your country and there is your land, to
put aside the breath of life, to go and play*

*The Master leads you to find your country and your land, the
Master leads you to return again along the flowery path of
revival (*kev paj kev sawv*) in the middle room (*nruag tag*),
you will hear the sound of the pipes like great crickets
wailing, and the sound of the drum like the mighty thunder
roaring, but do not fear or lament, for these are the ways
and the paths of your ancestors, your ancient Mother and
Father.*

In Sichuan these most significant of all songs were almost muttered
so as not to be overheard, rather than loudly chanted as in Thailand,
and it was most difficult to record them. In some versions I recorded,
in Yunnan and Guizhou as well as in Sichuan, the names of ancestral
figures or deities were deliberately mispronounced to counter
potential accusations of superstition. Then it could be claimed that
the funeral expert was merely responding to local demand, although
he of course knew better, and that such rituals were a part of local
custom and ancestral worship rather than a religious or superstitious
activity. Now that many aspects of Han ancestral worship are
permitted, Hmong death rituals can be a little more openly performed
than in the past, although this has been complicated by a recent
largely academic movement in China to reclaim shamanism as one of
the original religions of China as can be seen in the number of
publications about shamanism since the mid-80s.[8] Yet local funeral
specialists, like shamans, occupy a truly extraordinary position; as
guardians of local culture, as they are often seen, yet of a local
culture which is largely disapproved and discouraged by a wider
society, they have become melancholy and haunted figures,
somewhat like the esoteric Daoist priests who have maintained their
practices for centuries despite official persecutions.

At the same time, as we have seen, there are those who try to
combine some aspects of these roles, to participate in local cultural
settings while also representing state interests which are

---

[8] Such as Wu (1989) for example.

diametrically opposed to those cultural settings, which are painted in
cultural terms as 'being Hmong' or 'being Han' (or rather, and
significantly, as 'doing Hmong' and 'doing Han'; *a hmoob, a suav*).

In conversations with Yang Dailu and other local Hmong cadres,
it was often the sense of a double burden which was stressed, the
impossibilities of 'remaining Hmong' in a changing world where
advance depended largely on a wider outside society in which the
conventional identity of Han was largely assumed. It may indeed be
that it is on the mastery of what are perceived as two different social
cultural systems, two different types of identification, that effective
local leadership is believed or perceived to depend, but there is also a
personal angst here, a division of equivocal selfhood, which is not
easily overcome. It is how these sorts of identifications lead to the
adoption or assumption of particular cultural norms which is our
main concern here, in examining the complex dialectic of identity
and difference which mark Hmong-Han relations.

Despite the many features of funeral and mortuary ritual which
the Hmong share with the Han, and some which may have been
relatively recently adopted in Sichuan, it is particularly in the Song
of the Opening of the Way, combined with the playing of the various
qeej and the gentle feeding of the corpse, that a quintessential sense
of a unique Hmong identity and past is expressed. In the Song we
find an account of the separation of spirits and men, and of heaven
and earth, the origins of sickness and death, of seeds, of agriculture
and the forest and domestic animals. Armed with the crossbow and
the rooster which announces a new dawn, the *mo* leads the soul of
the deceased on a journey back to the origins of things, to the place
of the ancestors, the original Mother and Father, after ascending the
heavenly ladder and embarking on a series of ordeals through the
twelve passes of the mountainous Otherworld, and the descent again
which signifies a rebirth.[9] Throughout, a sort of unmarked, middle
category of 'Hmong' is clearly distinguished from that of the Mab
and the Suav (the Yi and the Han) as a separable and unique pathway
through this and the next world and the whole course of historical

---

[9] The term *mo* is not used by the Hmong of South East Asia, but has been
recorded for the Hmong of Sichuan and Yunnan through this century. A similar term
is used by other Southwest Chinese peoples like the Hani and Yi, and it may have a
Dai or Yi derivation.

time. And the melancholy which pervades the entirety of the funeral process, and particularly the singing of this song, brings to mind the many deaths and tragedies suffered in the past, and a deep nostalgia for a time of original blessedness, in which there was no sickness or death, the earth had not yet been shaped and the heavens not yet flattened, to which the dead return.

CHAPTER SIX

ANCESTRAL WORSHIP

In ancestral worship too there is the remembrance of a specifically and unique Hmong past with which present-day identities are connected, and this is of course intimately related to the idioms of patrilineal descent which the Hmong share with the Han (and may at some distant historical time have adopted from them or had imposed upon them). In the 'genealogical' model of descent in which Hmong and Han alike partake, differentiation (for example, of siblings) is expressed in terms of their roots in a common ancestry. In a similar way, as we shall see later, Hmong and Han cultural identities are sometimes expressed as those of a pair of siblings who have descended from a common father. Yet in many Hmong ancestral rituals, it is a specifically Hmong identity, and a specifically Hmong past, which is insisted on.

In a ritual which is taken to express the heart of Hmong cultural identity, performed periodically by distinct sub-lineages in remembrance of their ancestors' sufferings and hardships, and which since it refers to a passage over a 'great water' is often in South East Asia taken to refer to the passage of the Hmong out of China, where it is known as *ua npuas tai* or *ua tai*, to offer the (Tai) pig, but in Sichuan merely as *ua npuas roog* or offering the Door pig, no women or children are allowed to participate, and only Hmong is spoken. There is an absolute prohibition on any Han or other 'outsiders' being present. There are other verbal taboos, such as not saying 'not eat' or 'not want' or discussing the effects of the ritual. The ritual is usually performed after a period of several years of misfortune, when crops have failed, domestic animals or other members of the household have been ill, and the fortunes of the household in general are believed to be affected. The head of the family, usually after the diagnosis of a shaman, will make a vow to the spirits that if things start to go well, the ritual will be performed within a year, and then it must be. Two ritual specialists (*mo*) are invited, one as Master of Ritual and one as Ritual Butcher of the pig which is sacrificed to the Spirit of the Door. The Door, ritually known as the Door of Wealth (*txaijman*) must be kept closed all night after the ritual has ended, and only ritually opened, as at the New Year, when a person of some standing in the community, hence a person who is likely to be the harbinger of good fortune, comes by to visit. He will usually have been tipped off the previous day that he may be expected, and on the opening of the door will speak the 'Four Words and Eight Sentences' of congratulations to the family for having accomplished the ritual, and he will be invited to enter, toasted and feasted. The Door would not be opened if a woman, child, or unlucky person, chanced to come by.

During the ritual in which the Master invokes and thanks the ancestral spirits, the Door is ceremonially opened and closed three times. When the pig is sacrificed its bristles are burnt off its neck and later buried outside the Door as a sign (to the spirits) that the ritual has been performed. During the ritual of offering the pig to the ancestral spirits the Master holds a wooden spoon in one hand— which may also be a historic emblem of Hmong cultural identity, since for centuries the Miao were identified in south China by their practice of using a large wooden spoon to eat from a common bowl, and spoons rather than chopsticks are still mostly used by Hmong today—and a hemp rope to encircle the pig in the other. The carving of the pork, as in other Hmong rituals, is crucial; the first cut should be the chest, and then the tongue, then the kidneys, lungs, liver, stomach, bladder, small and large intestines. Then the external organs are attacked; the snout (in four pieces), the right ear (two pieces) and the left ear (in three pieces). Finally (the third cut) the left fore leg (in two pieces), the right fore leg (in two pieces), the left hind leg (in two) and the right hind leg (in two), and the tail.

The ordering of these cuts is a matter of ritual knowledge and expertise, since when feasting the different portions are supposed to be used to differentiate different grades of agnatic or affinal relationship. This is particularly important at funerals, where a specific part of the sacrifice must be offered to F,FeB, FyB, FZ, FZH and so on. But here three pieces from each of the three series of cuts are placed into nine bowls which are then placed on the parental bed, with nine tiny bamboo tubes representing nine cups of wine, in front of them. After the ritual is all done, these nine bamboo tubes, together with the spoon and the hemp rope, are placed in a bamboo basket which is hung from the top of the Door. The participants will eat the contents of seven of the nine bowls in their feast, but the first and last bowls are given to the host to keep in his bedroom, and are only taken out to be cooked and eaten seven days later.

Before this, however, in the main part of the ritual, the pig is dragged, bound and squealing, into the central hall and the Door closed. A rope is tied to its fore leg while the Master sings:

> *Long, long ago this Door could bring no riches*
> *long, long ago this Door could bring no treasure*
> *this Door would not look over the family*
> *this Door would not protect the people living here*
>
> *Today is a good day*
> *Today is an auspicious day*
> *The Door brings riches and treasure*
> *The Door will protect and look after the people living here*
>
> *We call the Spirit of the Door into the central hall*
> *according to the ways of the grandmothers and*
> *grandfathers[1]*
> *We summon the Spirit of the Door down into this house here*
> *following the roads of the mother and father*
>
> *We await the Door of silver and gold bamboo*
> *so the daughters and sons will be many*
> *We respect the Door of growing wood*
> *so sons and daughters will be rich and prosperous*
>
> *Setting the table we invite grandmother and grandfather*
>   *spirits to dine and wine*
> *according to the ways and customs of old*
> *pulling out the benches we invite grandmother and*
>   *grandfather spirits to sit first in the hall*
> *following the roads and paths of long ago*
>
> *The beautiful brace of silver pheasants*
> *flying over the mountain pass*
> *will be offered in respect to the grandmother and*
>   *grandfather spirits*

---

[1] *pos yiag*, FM and FF.

the beautiful brace of silver pheasants[2]
flying over the mountain slopes
will be offered in respect to the grandmother and
   grandfather spirits

We four people at this table (performing this offering)
roll up the sleeves and wash the hands in warm water
We four people at this table (making the offering)
call on the grandmother and grandfather spirits

Open the Door to the road of good fortune
bringing riches and wealth every day
close the door to ghosts and evils
bringing health and happiness every year
from this day on every day
from now on for always

May wealth and fortune stay with our masters
may the grandmother grandfather spirits bring wealth
   and fortune

As he sings, he ceremonially opens and closes the central Door three
times. It is after this that the pig is untied and placed on a bench to be
slaughtered, cleaned and cut. After the bowls and bamboo tubes are
placed on the bed the Master seats himself at the head of the bed and
sings a similar verse for each of the nine bowls. Finally he tells the
host to keep the remaining two bowls safely, chanting 'If in the
future you raise cattle they will be as mighty as the mountains, if in
the future you raise swine they will be as large as cattle, and silver
and gold shall fill your house and gardens'. Then all eat in complete
silence, so as not to break any taboos.

A similar ritual, in similar circumstances, can be prescribed for
the Spirit of Heaven (*cig ntos dlaag*), but here it is usually an old or
disabled sow which is sacrificed, and for the Yang and Yu clans the
hearts of the pig which they are forbidden to eat are offered to the
Spirit of Heaven. Again there is a taboo on any language other than

---

[2] This is in poetic reference to the boar.

Hmong, and this too is a ritual performed in fulfilment of a vow after a period of general domestic misfortune. It is also practised very late at night when everyone is asleep, since no women or children are allowed to participate, and a fire is prepared in the central room where the animal is to be cooked. A skirt is hung up over the door, said to be in remembrance of two small girls with no clothes who once accidentally happened upon the ritual. No bamboo or chopsticks are used for eating, only hands, and it is not allowed to refuse the food; anything left over must be taken away in a separate bamboo casket for each person, and given to other relatives or friends.

The animal is divided into 32 pieces, which should all be finished, and everyone should have some of each. This ritual, although rare, is more often performed than the *ua npuas roog*, which is usually only conducted once or twice in each generation of a patriline.After an old man dies and his sons separate, *ua npuas roog* should be performed 'to show independence', in which case the household head may decide to hold it without first consulting the shaman. We can see here how these specifically Hmong rituals act to symbolise the unity of distinct descent groups, affirming them as separate groups at the same time as recollecting their common ancestral past.

Simple vows of offering a pig in sacrifice by tying a rice straw around the neck of a pig, and vowing aloud to Yang Lao to send the pig as a sacrifice to Heaven if such an event goes well in the future can also be performed by individuals.

A particular story was told to account for the origins of this sacrifice to Heaven, also exclusively performed by particular patrilineal descent groups;

Once there was a Hmong leader named Yang Tw Kw Teem whose brother was Yang Suab, a very brave general in his army. Yang Suab always won each battle because he had a dragon heart (pleu zaag). *At that time, the Hmong people, led by Yang Tw Kw Teem and his brother Yang Suab, were struggling with the hordes of Han Chinese for possession of the land along the Yellow River valley.[3] In the battles, the Chinese troops used to cross the river by boat. Whenever*

---

[3]   The Yellow River may have been picked up from readings and generally accepted knowledge about the history of the Hmong.

the Hmong troops fought to the riverside, because Yang Suab had a dragon heart, he jumped into the river and the water would make way for him, so that then all his soldiers could follow him and cross the river as if they were marching across dry land. So each time he was able to defeat the Chinese armies. Eventually the Han soldiers realised they would never win the battles against the Hmong unless they could get rid of Yang Suab, the capable Hmong general. So they hatched a plot to trick the Hmong people through negotiating a false peace with them.

For a long time, the two sides maintained friendly relations with each other, and often the Chinese would invite the Hmong to feast together with them, and in return the Hmong too entertained the Chinese many times. And one day, the Chinese invited the two brothers, Yang Twb Kw Teem and Yang Suab, to a feast together. And because Yang Suab also happened to be a very good cook, he was asked to help with the cooking in the kitchen. After the dinner, some of the Chinese complained that they hadn't been able to find the pig's heart in the food. They were so fond of it that nothing could could substitute for it, and then they accused Yang Suab of stealing it. And so they told Yang Tw Kw Teem. And Yang Tw Kw Teem accused his brother, saying 'Brother, O my brother, we are such close relations. Why did you steal the pig's heart to humiliate me in this way?' And he was so angry with his brother that he killed Yang Suab, dug out his heart and gave it to the Chinese in return for their lost pig's heart.

As soon as the Chinese had got hold of Yang Tw Kw Teem's brother's heart, they launched a fierce attack on the Hmong. The Hmong were defeated, and the survivors, old and young, fled into the forests to survive. In their flight, they only took an old sow and a chopper with them. When they reached the forest, the old sow was too exhausted to move. They tried hard to lead it along, but it was all in vain. At last they had an idea. After the Hmong had been crushed in combat, Yang Tw Kw Teem had committed suicide by throwing himself into the Yellow River. Now the Hmong had nothing with them except an old sow which could go no further. So they decided to kill it, as a sacrificial offering to Yang Tw Kw Teem. However, they had no knife with them, and the chopper they had brought could not be used for slaughter. So they cut down a length of bamboo, made a sharp strip out of it, and toasted it over the fire until it hardened, and then they killed the old sow with this strip of bamboo. Unfortunately, nor did they have a pan with them with which to boil water to scald off the bristles of the sow. They had to burn the bristles off with the fire and then scrape it clean. Then each person cut one piece and cooked it to eat. After they had finished eating, they divided the rest of the pork amongst themselves; each person took one piece and ran off with it in different directions. Nobody could look after anyone else at that time.

During the sacrifice, the Hmong made bamboo tubes and asked children to blow them outside so that no tigers or leopards would come to threaten them. Also, during the sacrifice, no Chinese words could be spoken. Otherwise, the sacrifice to Yang Tw Kw Teem would have failed, because the Hmong felt such a deep hatred for the Chinese after their defeat.[4]

The story is particularly interesting because in it we appear to see a representation of historical divisions between the Hmong themselves, initially caused by the conflict with Chinese, which the ritual seeks to repair; an expression of Hmong unity, *despite* conflicts over and with the Chinese. A sort of desperate Hmong unity in the face of overwhelming adversity is predicated on the violence between brothers which is directly traced to the opposition between Hmong and Han. And there is a sense in which Hmong-Han conflict is felt to reach within the heart of the Hmong social system itself, since the name of one of the brothers is Suab which means 'Han' and suggests some innate relation between this heroic brother and their Chinese enemies in which one brother was suborned by the dominating Han (they took his dragon heart).[5]

Normal domestic ancestral rituals are also performed as with the Chinese on a daily and monthly basis, on the occasions of births and weddings, and particularly during the New Year celebrations, and these serve to carry much of the sense of what it still means to identify oneself as 'Hmong'.

---

[4]   Story told by Tao Xiaoping.

[5]   It was pronounced in a high level tone which I have indicated here through RPA -b rather than the Chinese system where the word would be written *shuad (55)*.

Hmong cadres

Local cadres practised and took part in domestic ancestral ritual as we have seen them do both with regard to the rituals of death and the rituals of shamanism. Indeed domestic ancestral worship, widely practised by villager Han, met with more tolerance from local authorities than either shamanism or mortuary ritual. Yet the practice of such rituals clearly reflected the ambiguous status of Hmong cadres recognised and recognising themselves as 'Miao'. What was happening here is quite different from the general situation of cultural hybridity and interblending in which the Hmong of Sichuan have found themselves for some time, since here loyalties to a particular locality (enjoining participation in local ritual affairs) are opposed to loyalties to the state (forbidding superstitious and healthy customs) in a way which parallels and yet does not entirely duplicate the traditional ambiguous relations between the Hmong and Han. I would argue that this kind of role incompatibility, in a still fairly traditionalist society, places a double burden on the individual trying to meet two contrary sets of cultural expectation, which is constraining rather than enabling.[6] Hmong cadres in the village were in a sense doubly alienated; from their home villages and backgrounds by their official status, and from many colleagues by their Hmong cultural identification. The latter alienation was however disguised by the extent to which they could 'pass' and be accepted as Han, which in the case of most ethnic minority cadres was considerable . A dual identity was often maintained, both as 'Hmong' and as 'Han', which the majority of the villagers also aspired to and to some extent achieved, and which was to some extent mediated by an assumption of the official classification of 'Miao'. It is this which may explain the minimal degree of conflict apparent between Hmong and Han living in the village, or between the business interests we examine in Chapter 8, managed by village Hmong but employing local Han labour. The question of a dual or divided identity of the subject is of course a complex one, related to issues of internal colonialism. Local structures of desire and identity, as Friedman (1990) puts it, of the type we have examined here, are

---

[6] Role incompatibility raises issues of the incoherence of beliefs (Skorupski 1978) and general problems of rationality.

inevitably connected with wider political and economic 'contexts', and it is the nature of these 'connections' and how they may place or arise from the sense of a local identity which should be among our prime concerns. In Wutong, as I try to show here, a sense of cultural identity as Hmong had been disguised rather than entropically 'lost'; and indeed we have seen that nationality policy has led to strong political and economic incentives for retaining ethnic minority status.[7]

Minority cadre ideology has come in for much discussion by those concerned with problems of the relations between the centralising state and local cultural identities. Recently both Litzinger (1995) and Cheung (1996) have stressed the 'inclusion of ethic subjects' (Litzinger 1995) in the writing of state historiographical projects and the creation of specific minority pasts, and examined some of the problems of 'voice' this raises. I would stress that, while this is true of the Yao and other groups of Miao, the Hmong (as 'Hmong') have not so far been involved in larger state projects in any significant way. Of the three main texts on 'Miao' culture, history and identity written by Miao officials themselves, none has been by a Hmong (see Cheung 1996). In this and in many other ways, the identity of the Hmong as a distinctive cultural group is hidden and obscured by more authoritative versions of a 'Miao' identity, narrative biographies constituting the Miao as a unique historical subject opposed to the traditional state. Of course all minority cadres, who are for most researchers their first introduction to *minzushue* (ethnology) in China, are agents of a state modernization process and are crucial in interactions between the state and local communities. Indeed in many cases ethnic subjects may have been historically constituted through the contributions of minority cadres. And Hmong cadres in the Gongxian area were not exceptional in this regard; they like other minority cadres were engaged in reconstructing a traditional culture in such a way that it might prove compatible with the dominant central state project of modernization and social and

---

[7] Dual identifications of this nature should not be assumed to allow flexibility of choice, and indeed the utilitarian paradigms of the past were very wrong to suggest that they might do so. With Leach (1954) and Bailey (1969), it was often assumed that conflicting 'norms' might allow actors some freedom of choice between them, or some ability to manipulate rules in forming the practical strategies constituting social organisation (Firth 1964).

economic development. Yet little attention has been paid to the mental agony of such individual elite men and sometimes women, the repression of primordial attachments called for by the commitment to a regulatory law, the constant attractiveness of appropriating that general regulatory law of the state to local (non-elite) purposes and interpreting it in novel ways, which in many cases may lead to neurosis and alcoholism..

In attempting to conform to ideal objectives of behaviour, which may be striven towards but never attained, actors even within the terms of their own cultural groups may suffer disappointments or exclusions arising from their perceived inability to fulfil cultural expectations adequately.[8] How much more this is so when ideal behavioural norms are available which are contrary, and which an actor nevertheless attempts to satisfy simultaneously. In most cases subjects in such positions are *not* like a post-modern surfer of identities and uncertain landscapes, nor like the classic middleman of entrepreneurial theory, bridging the gaps (like the anthropological 'culture-broker') between discrete systems to his own individual advantage (Barth 1967); the aspiring elite member may be torn between conflicting and incompatible role expectations, unable either to meet the expectations of his own (original, to some extent authentic) society or those of the cultural 'other', particularly where that cultural other (as in this case) is in a position of economic, political superiority and domination, as is the case with the Han in the modern multi-national state of China.

Some of the difference in our interpretation of these situations may be due to whether we interpret these sorts of cultural 'norms', or

---

[8] Holy and Stuchlik's 1983's elaboration of action, norms ('operational models') and representations ('representational models') has been one of many anthropological attempts to clarify the endless dialectic between social actuality and ideal, in which Bourdieu's engagement with strategy and rule has been central in formulatng a vision of the realm of 'practice' which attempts to go beyond internal or external representations of it. In 1960 Leach had talked of the actual, normative, and ideal models actors may have of their own society, which Barbara Ward (1965) advanced employing Lévi-Strauss's distinction between 'conscious', and 'unconscious' models, and distinguishing the home-made, immediate models actors have of their own societies as they actually are, from their 'ideological' models of how they believe their societies should be, and both of these from the 'observers' models' of others, whether these are the 'internal observers' models of other groups within the same society, or the 'external models' of, for example, external researchers.

regulatory law, as either actor-oriented, or society-oriented.⁹ In the former case, the subject has a set of different 'ends', a situation in which he may be expected to 'maximise' his advantage. The test here may be seen as one of utilitarian rationality; to what extent can an actor calculate the differential outcomes of alternative cultural strategies and 'economise' between them. But if such 'norms' are considered as social expectations of the individual actor, rather than intentionalities the actor seeks to fulfil, genuine choices may become impossible; how can I at once behave as a branch party secretary is supposed to behave at the funeral of my relative, and yet fulfil the traditional role expected of me as a 'dutiful mourner'? The choice may be impossible; I am more likely to succeed at one or the other, and while success at both might be possible, it is more probable that through trying to do both I do neither very adequately. In Guizhou province, a Miao who had cremated his own daughter in accordance with government policy was visited by group after group of Miao from long distances accusing him of being 'un-Miao' for not having buried her and lacking in concern for the fate of his daughter's spirit.¹⁰ It is hard to avoid a reading here in terms of the processes of displacement and absorption which have characterised discussions of linguistic colonialism; the mimicry of a paternal language, together with the displacement and absorption of native speech.¹¹

---

⁹ Sallnow (1990) makes a similar point on the *homo duplex*, contrasting Durkheimian collectivity-oriented approaches, which emphasise altruism, with Malinowskian individual-oriented approaches, which emphasise egotism. He further links the idealism of the first with an emphasis on structure and norms, and the utilitarianism of the latter with an emphasis on event and action. It is the more Durkheimian approach, then, emphasising the constraints of social facts on individual behaviour, which would lead to a view of the individual as doubly constrained by a position in different role systems/social structures/cultures—provided always that these are assumed to be discrete entities. As Butler (1993) puts it of gender norms, how are we to understand their compelling nature, 'without falling into the trap of cultural determinism?'

¹⁰ MacKerras (1998) gives similar examples with relation to Muslim cadres.

¹¹ See Pease (1992).

CHAPTER SEVEN

LINEAGE COMPOSITION OF THE YANG VILLAGE

Wutong village is thought to have existed for some four hundred years. The villagers, who are predominantly of the Yang clan, can list fourteen generations in the village back to the Ming Dynasty, and have an origin story of how they migrated there from Weixin county of Yunnan, where they recall a further seven generations living.

Much as the Yao peoples have traditionally invited a Chinese teacher to take up residence in their villages and teach some of their male children Chinese characters and culture, where circumstance and expense permitted (Lemoine 1982), so in the 1930s, when Graham was already describing the loss of traditional clothes-making skills and adoption of Chinese habits by the Hmong of Sichuan, the Yang surname of Wutong had invited a Chinese teacher 'to arrange their generations for them'.

Traditionally the Hmong have their own Hmong names although for as long as there are historical records they have adopted Chinese patronymics, and for at least four hundred years the Hmong men in China, or the more prominent among them, have been known by full Chinese names which consist of an initial patronymic, a middle name which indicated their generation, and a personal ending name.

The generations detailed for this group, which reached as far back as their own unwritten genealogies of that time could, were as follows; the Tian, Zai, Wen, Chao, Guo, Zheng, Xiang, Wan, Dai, Jia, Xing, Da, Yong, and the Guang.

Although the Yang of some other places had already reached the Yong and Guang generations, in Wutong the last four referred mostly to as yet unborn children, while Tian referred to the remembered founding ancestor. It was those of the Xiang generation in Wutong who had invited the Chinese teacher to name their generations, and since a number of these were still living,[1] it is convenient to think of the Xiang generation as great grandfathers of the village. The Wan generation which followed them accounted for most of the ageing but still active heads of household, the men who

---

[1] See, for example, households 27 and 28, 40, 67 and 68.

still ordered things in the village, and it may be convenient therefore to think of these as the grandfathers. The Dai generation were mostly younger men, some with young children or sometimes married children of their own—the younger fathers' generation. The Jia generation were not yet of very great significance in the village, except in a few cases where young men of twenty to thirty years old in the Jia generation had already started their own families, as in the 'O' lineage group in Group One of the village.

There were probably members of the Guo generation still alive at the time these generations were given their Chinese names, who were therefore remembering back a further four generations; to their grandfathers' grandfathers. The written genealogy which the Yang were in the process of constructing while I was in the village starts from the Tian generation.

They also recollected that there had been a further seven generations before the Tian; the Cha, Yi, Wa, Pao, Guan, Min, and the Zan.

There are therefore twenty-one generations stretching back from the present day, if we include those Yang elsewhere who had already reached the last named generations, and if we reckon twenty-five years to a generation this gives us a stretch of 315 years prior to 1989, or the year of 1674.

The Tian generation was largely recollected as the time they had left 'Fa Ta' in Zha Xi county, now Weixin, in Yunnan, which is quite probable, but this was also identified with the time of the war against the local aboriginal Bo state, said to be in the Ming Dynasty, which is most improbable since there is an established consistency in the dates given for this war from various sources of 1573; the Tian generation could have been some 200 years after this, if we estimate a rough birth date for the Xiang generation of 1900 and reckon each generation as twenty-five years.

This is one of a number of pieces of evidence which points (apart from the successive and continuous Hmong migration into the area, in which affinal relations have played an important part) to two main waves of Hmong settlement in the area, and strong divisions between original and later groups of Hmong settlers.

Of particular interest in the light of our concern with the position of the Hmong in Chinese society, and their relations with the Chinese state and people, it was said, as part of the clan history which was being prepared to attach to the written genealogy, that there had originally been seven Yang brothers of the Tian generation, but because their father left all his land to an *adopted* son who was Han Chinese, the eldest brother had left Yunnan to settle in Gongxian. A bronze gong had been severed into seven pieces for each of the seven brothers, so that their descendants would always be able to recognise their common origins.[2]

Most significantly, it was also said that the original founder of the lineage, in the Cha generation ('Cha Yi Er') had *not been Hmong at all*, but a Han Chinese of the Deng surname. After his ears had been cut off in warfare (a sign of punishment for rebellion?), he had taken refuge in the home of a Hmong family surnamed Yang, and begun to wear Hmong clothes and adopt Hmong customs. Eventually he married the daughter of the household and was adopted by the family, changing his surname to Yang, so that to this day the (Chinese) Deng and the (Hmong) Yang of the region cannot intermarry as they recognise they come from a common stock. This is similar to the processes Shepherd (1993) describes as occurring in Taiwan where an in-marrying son-in-law would bring up his sons as Chinese who might then gain control of aboriginal land which would otherwise have been inherited through a daughter.

It does happen, in Hmong as in the wider Chinese society, that an in-marrying son-in-law can adopt his father-in-law's surname and perpetuate his line, a practice which usually implies the father-in-law's lack of other male heirs and the son-in-law's poverty. But here we have a striking instance of what Barth (1969) saw as the constant flow of personnel across the boundaries of cultural units which can take place without affecting those boundaries It is also an apt example of the long, gradual process of the assimilation of individual Chinese into Hmong society which has been, and continues to be, a marked feature of their history, together with the converse adoption or recognition of Han Chinese values, customs and manners in a complex historical dynamic of exchange and interchange, interplay and reaction.

---

[2] In a somewhat similar way since the Great Leap Forward, different fragments of the Yang genealogy, some in written and some in oral form, had been entrusted to different members of the clan for safekeeping.

Many Hmong clans and lineages in South East Asia and China claim to have been formed through the marriage of a male Chinese with a Hmong woman whose children were brought up as Hmong, and one can find individual cases cases of this actually continuing to occur recorded throughout this century as well as directly observable in Thailand and elsewhere.[3]

In the account of the seven brothers of the Tian generation, there seems to be a suggestion that this kind of process—the assimilation and adoption of male Chinese—was leading to loss of land and birthright for the Hmong, forcing them to undertake their wanderings and migrations; an attribution of impoverishment and the loss of land directly to the influence of Han Chinese. The second version of the 'adoption' story, the acount of the Chinese lineage founder, however, appears to represent a claim by the Hmong themselves (sometimes known in Sichuan as Hmong Sua or 'Chinese' Hmong), of an original common ancestry with their Han Chinese neighbours, with perhaps also a veiled reference to recorded historical cases of the leaders of Chinese rebellions taking refuge among the Hmong and teaching them the arts of war (Mottin 1980).

As I say, it is likely that the ancestors of the Yang of Wutong migrated from Weixin in Yunnan in the Tian generation, or in about 1750-1775 (reckoning from a Xiang generation of 1900). Although it cannot have been this migration which was associated with the wars against the Bo, which took place as we have seen in 1573, the seven generations recorded *before* the Tian generation would take us exactly to 1575, or the time of the recorded suppression of the Bo. Probably two major migrations, therefore, took place, as I have said, in both of which ancestors of the Yang may have been involved.

It was also said that the generation immediately before the Xiang, the Zheng, 'had gone about everywhere begging', from 'Kaihua Fu' in Yunnan (probably Wenshan near the Vietnam border) to Gongxian, which points to a great dispersal and population movements of the Hmong around Guizhou in about 1875-1900.

---

[3] Tapp (1989).

The Yang

The village was known as 'the Yang village' for the very good reason that it was the Hmong clan of the Yang who had founded the village and still dominated it. To a remarkable extent, the internal lineage divisions of the Yang determined and defined the residential contours of village settlement, and it is through these internal fissions of the Yang lineage that we may understand the social relations maintained by the dominant Yang with the other Hmong surname groups of the Wang, Zeng, and Ma, with the Gu, and with the local Chinese groups of the Li and Xie, Sun and Huang. The recent history of the village was also largely understood as being constituted through the rivalries and alliances between Hmong clans, in particular the relations between what I have called Yang lineage segment Y3c and the three Zeng households associated with the family of the county party secretary. Chinese anthropology has been criticised for over-emphasising the jural structures of lineage and domestic arrangements (Sangren 1984), yet perhaps it should have more confidence in itself in this respect. For those with a lived experience of a Chinese village, the constant citing of these formal structures in everyday practices is very often a reality. The descent structures which the Han may share with a minority people are of particular interest in illuminating the nature of the processes and relations which define separable cultural groups. We do need, therefore, to examine the lineage composition of the Yang surname in some detail.

Diagram 25 shows most clearly the main lines and branches of the Yang clan represented in the village, and Diagram 26 how these were reflected in household settlement patterns in the village (Diagram 27 is a simplified version of the main lines and branches of the Yang clan, while Diagram 28 shows a simplified version of how these were reflected in the household settlement patterns).

ZAIYU (Y)

CHOUZHOU (Y3)

GUOSHI   GUOSHUN   GUOZHEN

XIANGWEN XIANZHOU

| WANLI 26 | LIPING | WANYUAN | WANLONG o. 59 | WANFANG 58 | WANHENG 19 | WANZHONG 15-18 | WANSHU o. | WANHE 5-8 | WANCAI o. | WANPING | WANTIEN |

Y3C

Y3B

DAIYU 81

DAIJI   DAIHE | DAIJIN 10 | DAIQUAN 9 | | DAIHE 74 | DAIPEI 72 | DAISONG 77-79 |

Y3A

| ZHAO 25 | HONG 24 |

| JIANEN 73 | JIAYUAN 78 |

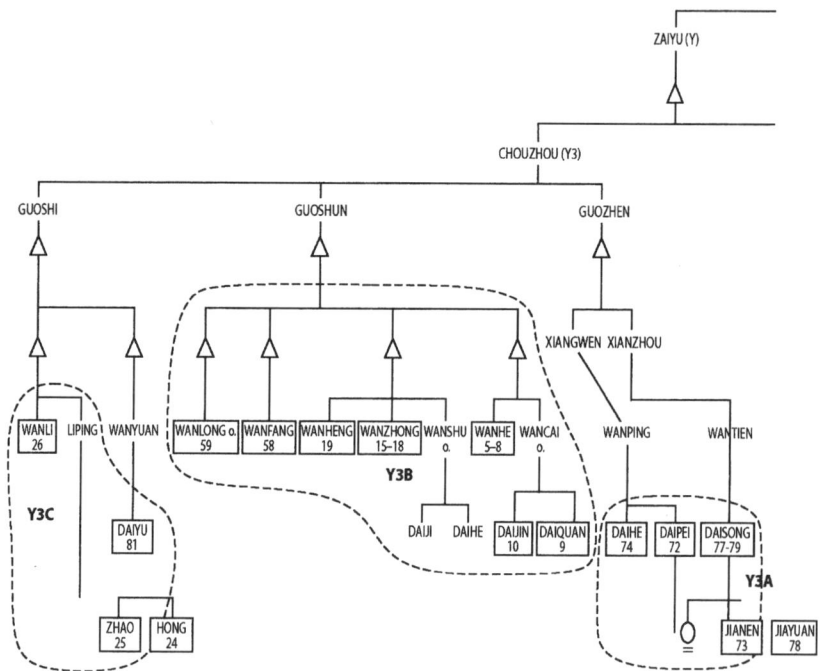

Diagram 25: Yang main branches

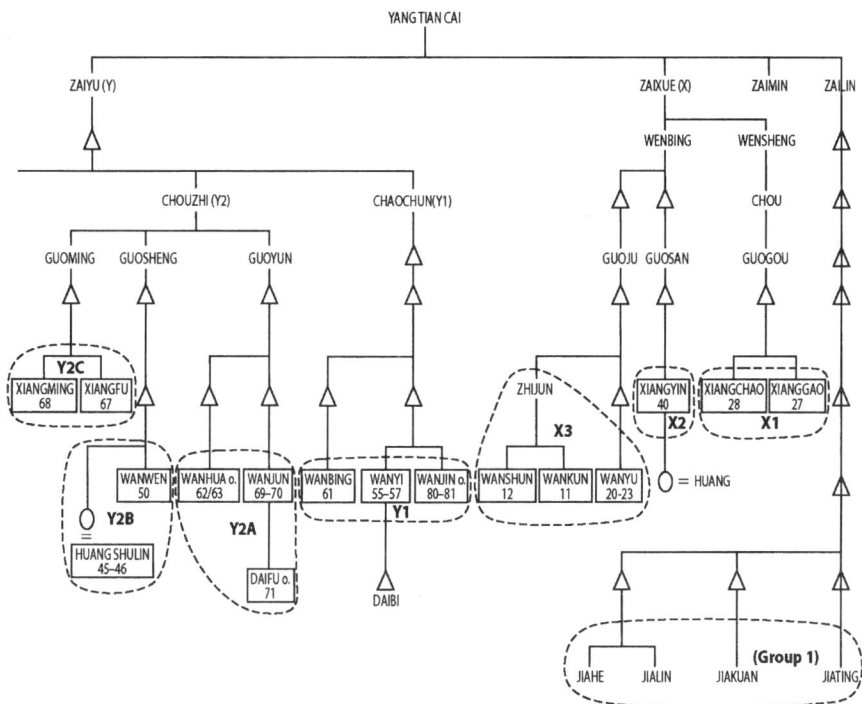

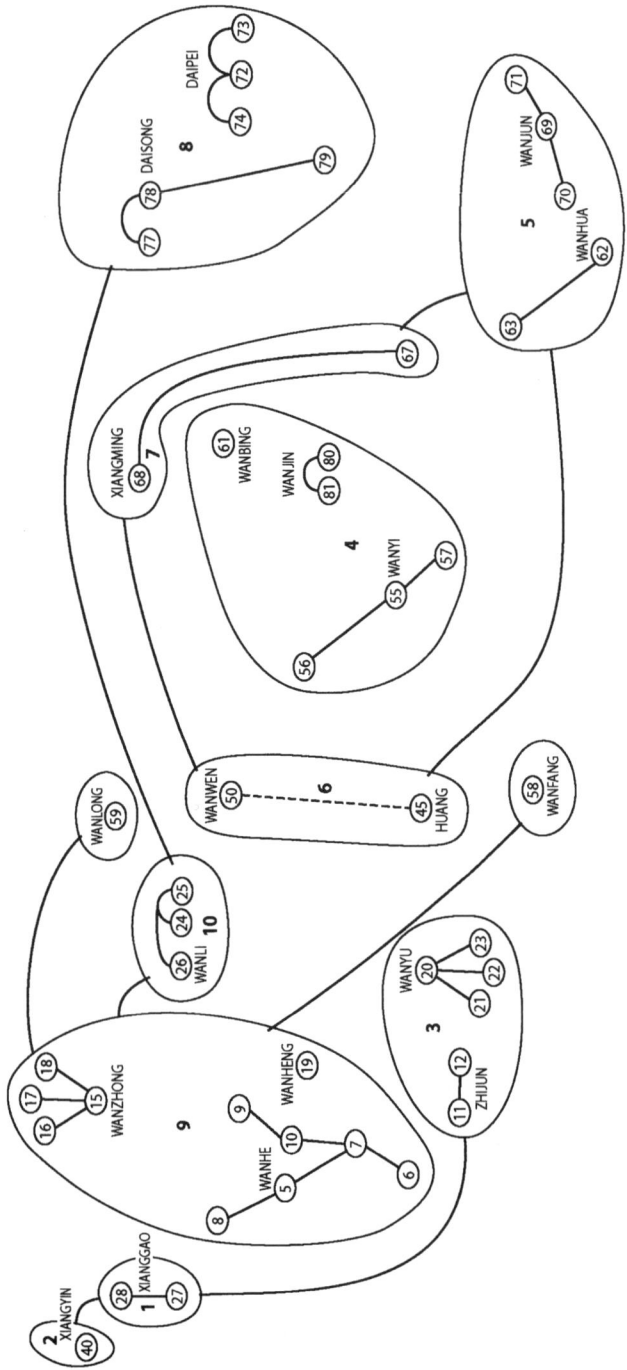

Diagram 26: Yang main branches on the ground

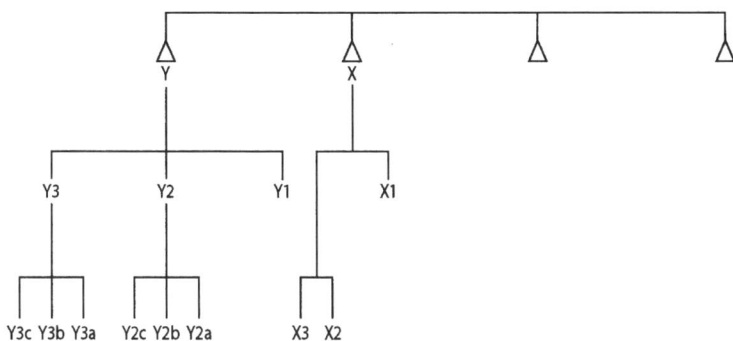

Diagram 27: Simplified Yang main branches

KEY (Diagram 27)
X1 : 1 (Yang Xianggao/Xiangchao)
X2 : 2 (Yang Xiangyin)
X3 : 3 (Yang Zhijun)

Y1 : 4 (Yang Wanyi)

Y2a: 5 Yang Wanhua
Y2b: 6 (Yang Wanwen)
Y2c: 7 (Yang Xiangfu/Xiangming)

Y3a: 8 (Yang Daisong)
Y3b: 9 (Yang Wanhe)
Y3c:10 (Yang Liping)

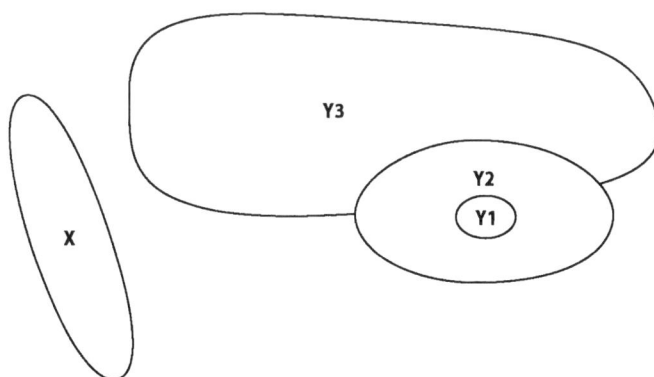

Diagram 28: Simplified Yang main branches on the ground

In the next chapter I want to provide a focal study of one family in the village (which I have called lineage Y3c on the diagram), and show how it was possible that this small lineage segment, represented really by only three households, had come to occupy such an important role in village affairs and indeed, beyond the village, a role quite disproportionate to their actual, somewhat marginal, position in descent structures and to their small numbers. In order to do this we need to understand their position relative to the other Yang segments and families living in the village, and in the following I therefore proceed by lineage segment, paying particular attention to marital relations with other groups and contacts beyond the limitations of descent..

Lineage X1

Lineage X1 was represented by the brothers Yang Xianggao (HH no.27) and Yang Xiangchao (HH no.28), who lived at the furthest northern point of the village in closest proximity with the other 'X' lineages (X2 and X3), with the Zeng households to their south, and those of the Wang III, Gu, and the Chinese Li to their south.

The two brothers' first cousin had married a girl cousin who was linked to the Xiong household in Group One by another first cousin relation, showing how the marginalised households of Group One were nevertheless attached through a number of kin and economic links with the main village in Groups Two and Three (and their mother had also been a Xiong). The three Zeng households in the main village had attached themselves to the various segments of the Yang clan through an astonishing variety of links, as we see in Chapter 9; Yang Xianggao's sister had married into the Wang II family who were connected to the Zeng; and Yang Xianggao himself had married a Zeng (the sister of the Gongxian party secretary). Yang Xianggao, although representing what I have called the great grandfathers' generation (the Xiang generation), was only 46 years old and had only had two sons, now teenagers, who lived with him and his Zeng wife. He was in sufficiently comfortable circumstances to have sent one of his sons, Yang Wangui, away from the village to study in Yibin, and had high hopes that he might join the Army.

Yang Xianggao's younger brother Yang Xiangchao (aged 43) had formerly had a wife surnamed Liu who had deserted him a few years previously, taking with her one of his only two sons, who like Yang Xianggao's were still teenagers. Although she had been marked as deceased on the Yang genealogy which the villagers were in the process of reconstructing (see chapter 8), this woman had in fact been a Han originating from Yibin. I gradually became aware of several cases where marriages between Han and Hmong had occurred, although often villagers were reluctant to talk about them at first, and generally denied that such marriages took place. They were seen as exceptional, dubious, and likely to end badly, and appeared to be a phenomenon which the general discourse of descent disguised. This woman had been one of several students sent down to the village during the Cultural Revolution in Maos's attempt to break down the barriers of class between the towns and countryside. It was not uncommon for these women to contract local marriages (known as 'desperate weddings') out of necessity. Most of these marriages were said to have broken up as soon as the reform process had started; Yang Xiangchao's wife had left the village and her husband as soon as she had been able to, after the reforms of 1979, and the two were now waiting for their divorce to be officially recognised.

Lineage X2

Lineage X2 was represented by only one household in the village— the somewhat distant (fourth generational cousin) of the two brothers in lineage X1, Yang Xiangyin, at household number 40. Yang Xiangyin, as Diagram 26 shows, lived across the slope of the valley from his two cousins, but closer to them than to any other Yang relatives, and closest of all to the Han households of the Li and the ambivalent households of the Gu. There was a reason for this proximity to Han and Gu households. Like his only brother, Yang Xiangyin, although aged 52, had only had the one daughter by his (Xiong) wife. And again a marriage with a Han had taken place, of a type which villagers preferred not to discuss too much. His daughter had married a Han named Huang Xuejun, who was said to be distantly related to the other Chinese Huang households in the village (HH nos.45 & 46), a member of whom as we saw in Chapter 3 had married the sister of another Hmong Yang in the village (Yang Wanwen in lineage Y2b). From the Hmong point of view, this marriage had been contracted for the sole purpose of perpetuating the male line of her father, since exactly as with Han practice in a case where a man has no male descendants, a daughter will sometimes marry a man who takes on the surname of his father-in-law to perpetuate the family line, or has one of his sons brought up with this father-in-law's surname. It had been Yang Xiangyin's, and his daughter's intention that one of her sons would adopt the Yang clan name of her father. However, she had had no sons, only three daughters, and her husband had refused to change his own surname to that of her father, so that it was probable that this 'line' would die out. We can see here just one of the mechanisms whereby Han may have been adopted into Hmong descent lines in the past, as indeed the founding origin myth of the entire Yang clan suggests, and imagine something of the way in which while individual Han were assimilated into Hmong descent structures, an assimilation of Han cultural values may have taken place among and within the Hmong.

Uxorilocal marriages of this kind generally took place where a bride's family had no sons and was short in labour, or where the groom's family was particularly poor or fleeing trouble, often political, from elsewhere, and the Hmong had special institutional procedures for dealing with this kind of situation which expressed themselves in a modification of the normal wedding routine. Instead of taking place mainly at the groom's house, as is normally the case, in the case of uxorilocal marriages the whole wedding takes place in the bride's house; and it is the bridegroom who is 'sent' to his wife's house with his 'dowry' and received by them, rather than the bride who is sent to her new husband's home. There are none of the rituals for presenting the branch and keys, or washing the face and feet, which we shall find are customary in chapter 10, and the other rituals are kept to a minimum. Nevertheless ancestors must still be respected; instead of the young couple paying respects to the ancestors of the groom together as is supposed to happen, it is the bridegroom has to pay respects to his wife's ancestors when he arrives, and on the wedding night the bride's father has to explain to his own agnatic relatives why the groom has come to live with them, and promise to be of assistance if possible to the groom's natal family. Even between the Hmong these marriages are not well thought of, and the in-marrying groom is particularly pitied, since it is known that he often ends up supporting his own parents as well as those of his bride.

Lineage X3

The cluster of households representing lineage X3 was much stronger than those of X1 or X2, and old Yang Zhijun who was the paterfamilias of this group acted as spokesman for the entirety of the X lineage. His two sons, Yang Wanshun and Yang Wankun, accounted for households 12 and 11 and his deceased brother's son Yang Wanyu lived with his own son (Yang Daiming) at household number 20, with three of Yang Wanyu's other sons (Yang Dailu, Yang Daihe, and Yang Daijiang) at households 21, 22 and 23. Yang Dailu was the branch party secretary of the village, and had nineteen people recorded under his name as comprising his economic household (see Diagram 29).

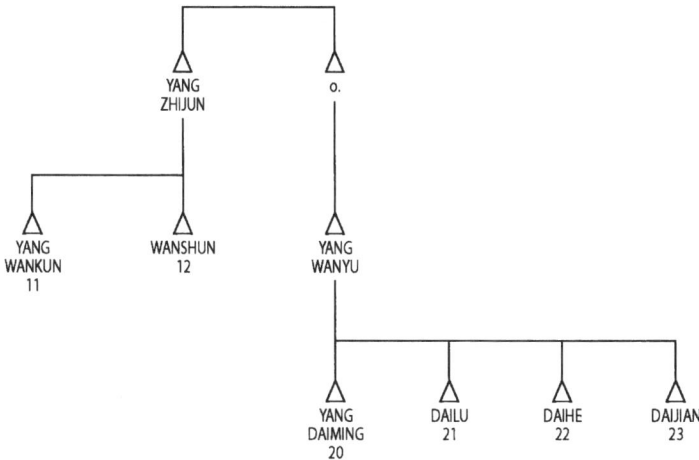

Diagram 29: Yang Zhijun's family

Yang Zhijun, a clear-headed, active old man of 76, was a funeral and ritual expert who was often consulted by younger members of the village on points of order. He was of course of the Xiang generation, but had changed his name to drop the 'Xiang' suffix as is quite often done following a series of misfortunes. He and his Wang wife had had one daughter who had already married out to a Xiong, and another son besides the heads of households 11 and 12; Yang Wanqian, who had married a Wang Rongzhang of Wangwuzhai and had moved there to live with his own five children.

Both Yang Zhijun's other sons still lived with him in an enormous courtyard house which had been Yang Zhijun's father's, but they shared the space with Yang Wanheng (household number 19, of the Y3b lineage) whose own brother *Yang Wanzhong* lived in another large courtyard house just across the valley.

So these two dominant representatives of the X and Y lineages (Yang Wanzhong of Y3b and Yang Zhijun of X3) confronted each other across the valley in a way which was entirely unhostile, as signified by the occupation by Yang Wanheng of Y3b of one of the wings of Yang Zhijun's X3 house. These apparently strange cases of co-residence, like Yang Wanwen sharing with Sun Huaixiang and Li Peixiang we saw in chapter 3, dated back to the days of the commune when some families were allotted with others for reasons of space or of production team membership, they had only continued to exist since the collapse of the commune where relations had been particularly amicable.

Immediately next door to Yang Zhijun was the large compound house of Yang Zhijun's brother's son Yang Wanyu and his four sons Daiming, Dailu, Daihe and Daijiang (effectively a single household of eighteen members rather than the four separate households of 9,4,3 and 2 members recorded for population purposes).

Yang Wanyu occupied a position of some prestige in the village, and it may have been partly for this reason that his uncle Yang Zhijun was so respected. Yang Wanyu had had one daughter (Yang Dai) who had married a Liu Guang and moved out of the village, and another two daughters (Yang Daizhen and Yang Daihui) who still lived with them. His eldest son (Yang Daiming) had actually left his Tao wife and three children (one studying in Didong) with his father, to go to work in Gongxian where he was the local Government Credit Bank accountant in charge of overseeing the many loans which had been made to the villagers; of Yang Wanyu's other sons who lived with them, Yang Dailu was as I have mentioned the party branch secretary for the whole village, and had a Wang wife and two young children; Yang Daihe had a Xiong wife and a young daughter; while Yang Daijiang had married a Yue wife who lived with them despite keeping her *hukou* (household registration) in her home village in order to retain rights to some land there. This too was quite a common occurrence in the new rural mobility which marked the late eighties and early nineties.

Lineage Y1

Lineage Y1, stretched across the centermost southern part of the village, was represented by the families of two brothers, Yang Wanyi (HH no.55) and Yang Wanjin (HH no.80), and their FBS Yang Wanbing (HH no.61) who lived at some distance from them, but still in the same part of the village.

Yang Wanjin (HH no.80) had recently died, leaving the home occupied solely by his Huang widow, who was one of the (Hmong) Huangs who dominated the nearby village of Fenghuang. Here again was an example of the flexibility of descent systems in accomodating those from outside, and ignoring strict biological rules of blood. Yang Wanjin's wife had only one daughter, who had married a Xiong, and rather than taking a second wife to assure himself of a heir, which used to be the most common case in the past, or asking a son-in-law or grandson to adopt his name as we saw above in the case of Yang Xiangyin, he had resorted to another approved means of perpetuating the descent line; he had adopted a son, Yang Daiyu (HH no.81) who lived with his Li wife and two children. His adopted son and his widow were on particularly bad personal terms with each other, and so lived quite separately and divided their fields and farmwork. Oddly, however, the adopted son was the actual FBSS of Yang Wanli (HH no.26) who represented the Y3c lineage, which we come to in chapter 8, at some considerable genealogical distance from lineage Y1. Adoption of a brother's son or father's brother's son is however quite common, often not reported or much remarked upon; it is possible that this one was only remarked because the lineage distance was somewhat unusual. In-marrying Han males, therefore, could have fallen into a practice commonly recognised and practised within Hmong lineages and lineage segments.

The other brother, Yang Wanyi (HH no.55), on the other hand, and his Wang wife, had had five sons and three daughters. The eldest daughter, Yang Daimei, had married Liu Guangming, a schoolteacher of Wangwuzhai village whose wedding is described later. Two of his sons had established separate households; Yang

Daiqing (HH no.56) with his Liu wife (Liu Guanghui) and two children, and Yang Daihong (HH no.57) with a Zhang wife from Yunnan and a young son. Yang Wanyi was left with his two younger sons, and another son Yang Daibi who had married the Zeng Gongxian party secretary's daughter, although in fact Yang Daibi with his family had now moved to Gongxian where he worked as an agricultural officer.

Again here was an excellent example of the incorporation of outsiders into descent lines, and the ways in which this may become disguised. For Yang Wanyi and Yang Wanjin had actually been half-brothers, rather than brothers as the Yang genealogy showed. Although the genealogy showed Yang Wanyi's father as having married twice, once to a Luo and once to a Xiong, we saw in chapter 3 how Yang Wanyi's mother had really been a Gu who had previously married a Xiong (the paternal aunt of Gu Yinshen at household number 44). Yang Wanjin had been this mother's child by her previous, Xiong, marriage, who had 'followed her' into her second marriage with Yang Wanyi's father. These two half-brothers, with their non-Hmong Gu roots, had nevertheless had been almost entirely adopted into the Hmong lineage, displaying something of the enormous flexibility and power of this system of incorporation. The reason Yang Wanjin had not adopted, for example, one of Yang Wanyi's sons, but instead one from lineage Y3c, probably lies more in the fact that his mother had been a Gu than in his genitor having not been a Yang, since the Gu connection was disavowed, as is shown on the genealogy, and in the location of the Gu at the opposite end of the village.

Lineage Y2

The four main families who represented lineage Y2 (Yang Wanjun at household number 69 and the family of his first cousin Yang Wanhua at household number 62 for the Y2a; Yang Wanwen at household 50 for the Y2b, and the brothers Yang Xiangfu and Yang Xiangming at households 67 and 68 for the Y2c) all lived in relative proximity to each other across the southern part of the village, encircling the Y1 lineage, although Yang Wanwen lived in the compound shared with others, and the two Y2c brothers lived particularly far apart from each other.

Lineage Y2a

Lineage Y2a looked like Diagram 30.

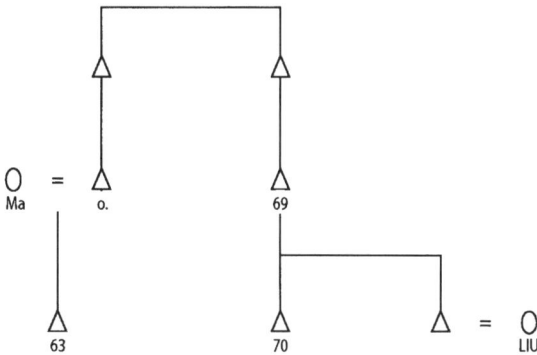

Diagram 30: Yang lineage Y2a

Although this segment was not particularly numerous in terms of households or population of households, Yang Wanjun at household 69 was a forceful old man of status and esteem in the village who managed to remain the effective family head of the group.

Like Yang Zhijun a ritual and marriage expert, Yang Wanjun was aged 64 and lived with his Wang wife and his two sons; Yang Daixiang, who had also taken a Wang wife and had two daughters who had not been listed on the household records and a son; and Yang Daigao, whose wife and son were similarly unrecorded. Nor was another of Yang Wanjun's sons, Yang Daizhong, who divided his time between his father's house and his second oldest brother, Yang Daiyun who lived at household 70 with his own Huang wife and a son and a daughter. Two of Yang Wanjun's other sons had died; Yang Daijiang, and Yang Daifu who had recently died of cancer, leaving his widow, Liu Qizhen (HH no.71), with a son and daughter in a small house on the outskirts of the village from where they had recently moved to Group One (where Yang Wanjun's half brother, Yang Wanchao, had lived, showing some of the attachments between the main body of the Yang and those in Group One). Widows' households were usually still counted as belonging to the surname of the deceased husband and grouped together with general membership of the Yang clan.

Another widow in this Y2a lineage was Ma Chenglian who with a son and a daughter still lived in the house (no. 62) of her former husband Yang Wanhua, the FBS of Yang Wanjun. They had had two daughters who had married out (to Huangs), while their eldest son, Yang Daiying (HH no.63), had also taken a Ma wife and had three children. Another son (not listed on household records) usually also stayed with the widow Ma, or between the two houses. Widow's houses were still important in maintaining existing kin and affinal networks, as we see here.

Lineage Y2b

We have already seen, in chapter 3, how the Han worker Huang Shulin had moved into the village after his marriage to the sister of Yang Wanwen, who was the sole representative of the Yang lineage Y2b. Yang Wanwen lived at household 50 with his Tao wife, a teenaged daughter and a son whose recent marriage to an eighteen-year old Xiong girl had not yet been recorded since she was only just legally marriageable. He had had two other daughters who had married out of the village. This house, as we saw, he shared with two Han families, those of Sun Huaixiang and Xie Peijiang. As the map shows, the household of Huang Shulin (no.45) and that of his son Huang Xijun (no.46) was situated just behind the courtyard house of Yang Wanwen, so that here was the sole representative of one of the Hmong lineage segments living practically surrounded by Han Chinese. Nobody seemed to find this at all odd, and I was assured that they all got on well together. Moreover, they cooperated together in sharing food and some farmwork. Yang Wanwen himself seemed to be well accepted as a lineage member by other Hmong Yang in the village, and was a hard-working, practical man who spoke good local Chinese. The close relations of Yang Wanwen with local Han Chinese, through his sister's marriage and his own residence, is only partly traceable to the days of collective production, which they had preceded, but were also due in part to his lack of close male relatives. Nevertheless, no further Chinese marriages had taken place, and this one was not well thought of by others. It was recognised that Yang Wanwen derived practical benefits from these long-established working and affinal relations with the Han families of the village (for Sun Huaixiang was connected to some of the Xie), and he was not blamed for this.

Lineage Y2c

Lineage Y2c was represented by two brothers only, forming the fourth main family in Y2. These were Yang Xiangfu at household 67, who lived with his aged mother (Wang Chaolian) and his one 21-year old son. He was 56 years old and his Wang wife had died. His brother, Yang Xiangming, was much younger than him, aged 34, and lived at household 68 with his Xiong wife and two very young children—a boy of eight and a girl of six. Such young children of relatively elderly parents were a relatively common feature of the household records and genealogies, and in some cases (as here) represented second families started after tragedies of the Great Leap Forward and Cultural Revolution, others extremely late marriages or births delayed by poverty and political turmoil. The two brothers lived not far from Y2b and Y2a but at some distance from each other, perhaps reflecting the difference of their ages.

Lineage Y3a

While the Y lineage itself greatly outnumbered the X lineage in population and strength, of all the lineage branches it was the Y3 which were the most dominant. We come now to the first segment of the Y3 lineage branch; Y3a, divided into two clusters of second cousins. This group (Y3a) lived at the northern extremity of the village, next to the Ma households, and is shown in Diagram 31.

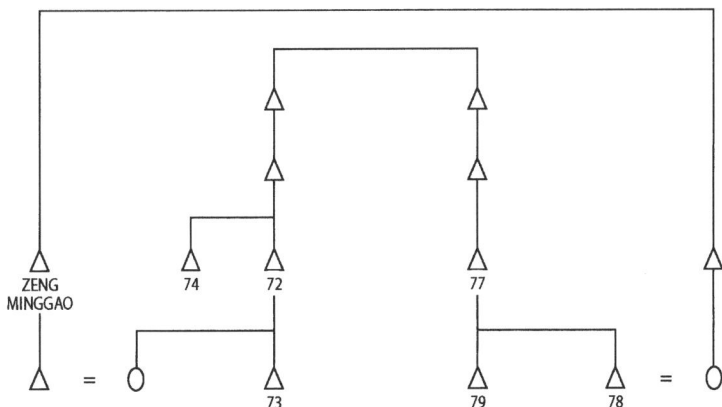

Diagram 31:Yang lineage Y3a

Y3a was an active and out-going descent group, well connected to the Wang and Ma families in the village as well as to the Zeng party secretary's family, headed by Yang Daisong (HH no.77) who at 52 years old provided them with capable leadership.

The family of Yang Daisong occupied a structurally pivotal role in village genealogies and inter-relationships. Yang Daisong himself had married a Ma Jianfen who was a classificatory 'sister' of the two Ma brothers who occupied households 75 and 76 nearby; one of his sons Yang Jiayuan had married a Zeng girl (the party secretary's brother's daughter); another son (Yang Jiahua) had married a Wang II girl—whose brother had married another sister of the two Ma brothers. As we shall see, the last Ma sister had married a son of Yang Wanshu in line Y3b (below), so that through the Ma and the Wang II, Yang Daisong's descent group had formed ambivalent relations of transferred affinity with their own patrilineal cousins in Y3b. Just as the members of Yang Daisong's group were located very close to the Ma households into which they had married, so the family of Wang Guoming into which his son Yang Jiahua had married were also located in the same part of the village.

As we can see, the households of Yang Daisong's nearest cousins, the brothers Yang Daipei and Yang Daihe (HH nos.72 & 74) and Yang Daipei's son, Yang Jianen (HH no.73), were located very close to that of Yang Daisong at households 77-79, in fact between them enclosing the Ma who provided these important affinal links with the Wang II and Yang lineage Y3b.

Yang Daipei and Yang Daihe, whose mother had been a Wang, were two out of five brothers; the other three had settled in another village; a sister and two of these brothers had all married Wang. Yang Daipei had a Huang wife and lived with her, two daughters and a son. One daughter (Yang Jiatsui) had married Zeng Wanshou (HH no.3, the party secretary's son), while the oldest son Yang Jianen (HH no.73) had married Wang Guoying. Yang Daipei's younger brother Yang Daihe (HH no.74) had like their cousin Yang Daisong, married a Ma, and had had three daughters and a son; the two oldest daughters were both studying in Chengdu. We begin to see here something of the way the Zeng families had allied themselves to various segments of the Yang clan in the village, and the crucial pivoting role performed by marriages with the members of smaller surnames such as the Ma and Wang II.

Lineage Y3b

We come now to the second descent group of the third segment of Y lineage (Y3b), which with 13 households outnumbered all other descent groups in the village. Just as the Y lineage households (35 in all) greatly outnumbered those of X lineage (with only 8), so the Y3 accounted for 21 of these Y lineage households, and of these 13 belonged to the Y3b segment. In terms of traditional village politics, this should have been the most powerful and dominant sector of the village. Yet we shall find in the next chapter how other factors had intervened to give this role to the small Y3c segment.

There are 5 main families to consider under lineage Y3b, all composed either of brothers or of patrilineal first cousins; *Yang Wanhe* (HH no.5), with sons at households 6,7 and 8, and brothers' sons at households 9 and 10; his first cousin *Yang Wanzhong* (HH no.15), with sons at households 16,17 and 18, and his brother *Yang Wanheng* (HH no.19); their first cousin *Yang Wanfang* (HH no.58); and the surviving household of a final first cousin, *Yang Wanlong* (HH no.59), who was deceased. It will be appropriate to consider the family of *Yang Wanshu* (also deceased), brother to Yang Wanzhong and Yang Wanheng, here, although they lived in Group One, since his four sons (households O,P,Q and R in Group One) formed an important part of the main Yang genealogy.

As the household map shows, the whole of lineage Y3b had settled in a fairly homogeneous group at the southern end of the village, around the households of Yang Wanhe (no.5) and Yang Wanzhong (no.15), with Yang Wanheng (no.19) at a little distance from Yang Wanhe, and the households of Yang Wanfang (no.58) and Yang Wanlong's widow (no.59) a greater distance away. Nearest to X lineage on the one side and the final branch of Y3, Y3c, on the north, Y3b's settlement pattern very clearly displayed its intermediary genealogical position between X and other lineage Y households (Diagram 32).

Some of their more prominent affinal connections with other villagers may be noted first here. Although they had not directly intermarried with the Zeng, as members of Y3a, Y2c, Y1, X1, and the 'O' lineage (represented in Group One by households L,M,N and their first cousin) had, particular liaisons had been forged with the Ma, Xiong and Gu, but most importantly with the Wang. Both Yang

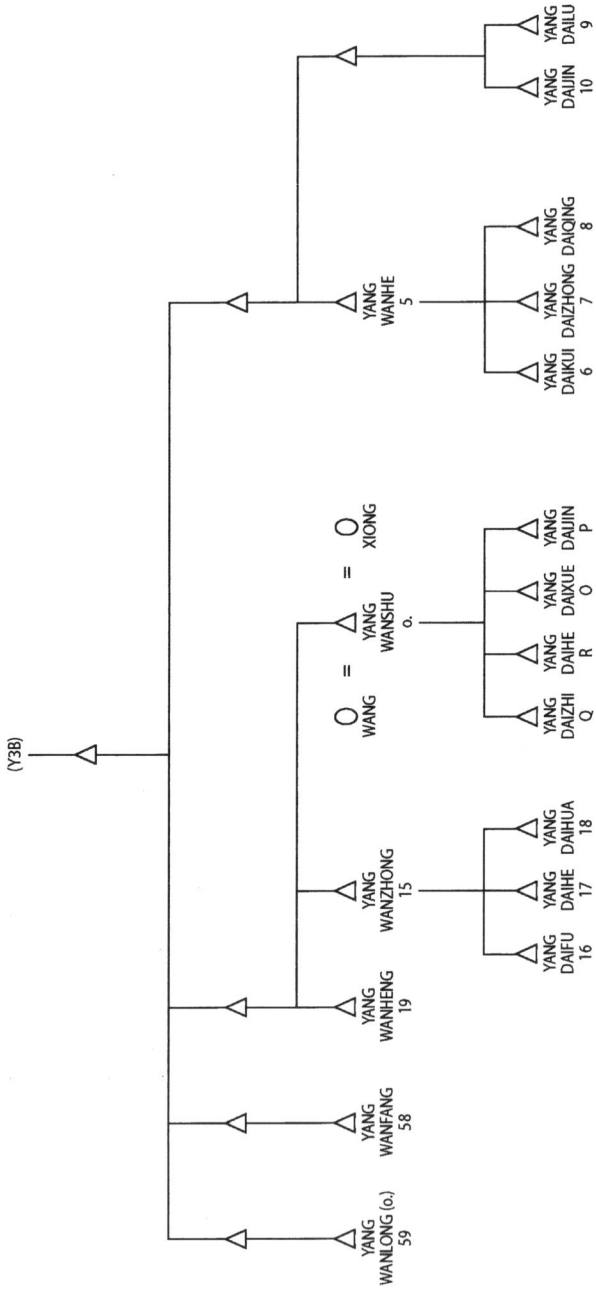

Diagram 32: Yang lineage Y3b

Wanzhong (HH no.15) and his first cousin Yang Wanhe (HH no.5) had married real Wang I sisters while the brother's son (Wang Zhongfu at household number 14) of those sisters had in turn married Yang Wanzhong's daughter Yang Daixiu (and a brother of Wang Zhongfu brother had in fact married one of the Zeng girls). This Wang I family had been originally helped to move in and settle in the village by Yang Wanzhong, and this was a fine example of the importance of such 'brother-in-law' and 'son-in-law' ties in establishing settlement, forging economic reciprocities and dependencies.

It was the sister of another of these first cousins, Yang Wanfang, who had married the brother of the non-Hmong Gu Yinshen at household 40 as we found in chapter 3, so that the Gu were related not only to the Hmong Yang Y1 line but also to this Y3b segment, while it was the sister of another parallel patricousin Yang Wanlong at household 59 (Yang Wanfen) who had married the first cousin of Wang Zhailing (of the Wang III line) at household 30.

Finally, the deceased Yang Wanshu had married the first cousin of Xiong Dingchao at household C in Group One, while a son of his, Yang Daizhi, had married one of the sisters of Ma Jianqing and Ma Jiankang at households 75 and 76 (another of whose sisters had married a Wang II brother).

Imaging this diagrammatically, we have Diagram 33.

Although the Wang II were more nearly related to Yang Daisong's family in lineage Y3a and to Yang Xianggao of lineage X1, as we have seen, they in fact worked for Yang Wanshu, and it is possible that other marriages had taken place between the Wang II and members of lineage Y3b which were not revealed by the genealogies. We can see here the close relations established with the Xiong of Group One where the sons of the deceased Yang Wanshu were settled, as well as with the Gu and Ma of Wutong, and above all with two of the Wang families, Wang I and Wang III—relations which in fact included all the non-Yang Hmong surnames in the village except, directly, the Zeng. Indeed this had been the general strategy of this pioneering section of the lineage, which by forging affinal relations with the members of poorer surnames had traditionally dominated the village.

In the following I consider each of these five main cousinly households of Y3b in turn.

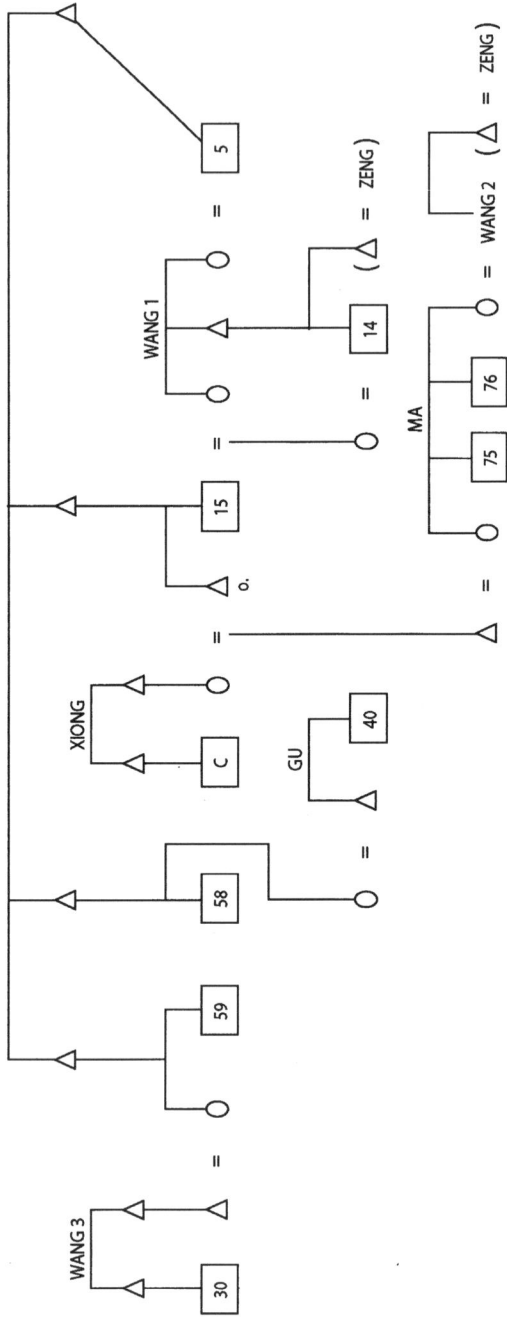

Diagram 33: Y3b and the Wang

Yang Wanhe at household number 5, aged 61, lived with his unmarried daughter of 18 years old and his three sons aged 20, 16 and 13, but had also had four other children who had married and moved out; three sons, and a daughter (who'd married a Yue). His oldest son, Yang Daikui, aged 35 with a Liu wife, son and daughter, lived at household 6; his second son Yang Daizhong, who had (like his father and father's brother) married a Wang and had two daughters, accounted for household 7; and then another son, Yang Daiqing, again with a Wang wife and a son, was at household number 8. In fact the latter remained with his family in his father's house, a single household with 9 members (rather than two of 6 and 3 members as listed in the household records). Yang Wanhe's older brother, Yang Wancai (who had died) had left his two sons; Yang Daiquan, again with a Wang wife, son and two daughters, to make up household 9, although they mostly lived and worked at the Furong coal mine, and Yang Daijin (HH no.10), aged 34, with his widowed Tao mother and his Xiong wife, bedridden elder sister and three children. Another sister had been married out to a Huang. There was an exceptional predominance of marriages with the Wang and Xiong here.

Yang Wanzhong, first cousin of Yang Wanhe, was the leader and spokesman for this entire descent group. Yang Wanzhong, as we have seen, had married the Wang sister of the wife of his first cousin Yang Wanhe, and therefore received strong support from the Wang I family, and one of his own daughters had married back into the group. Yang Wanzhong lived officially at household 15 with his Wang wife, a nineteen-year old son and one unmarried daughter, but his other sons' families (nos.16-18) all still lived with him in a large courtyard house[4] making this a single household of 10 people. Wang Zhongfu, his son-in-law and nephew (whose brother had married the Zeng) lived next door, which was convenient for working relationships. Yang Wanzhong was also a wedding go-between and specialist, as perhaps befitted one who had had three older daughters, all married. His eldest son of 32 years, Yang Daifu (HH no.16) had also married a Wang, and had a young son and a daughter of his own; the second son, Yang Daihe (HH no.17), had just married a

---

[4] Rather than 4 households with 4,4,1 and 1 member respectively.

Xiong and planned to move to her home in Luobiao. His third son, though, Yang Daihua (HH no.18), was yet another Hmong male who had taken a Chinese wife (a Luo). This marriage had been freely made, and although it had been against the wishes of his family who did not approve of marriages with Han, they had gone along with the wishes of the young couple. But his case was held up as an example of what was wrong with these Han marriages, and what was likely to happen when such marriages were made, because she had left him very shortly after their marriage (and the Yang genealogy consequently did not include her name).

Yang Wanzhong's own brother *Yang Wanheng* (HH no.19)—who had married yet another Wang—was the village *mo* or funeral specialist, Master of the Qhab Ki or 'Opening of the Way' ritual chant of the dead (see chapter 5). Besides the two sons and two daughters who still lived with him and his wife, he had also had an elder daughter who had married a Huang and moved out. This ritual specialist, who lived closer to his cousin Yang Wanhe than to his brother Yang Wanzhong, was a gloomy, solitary, hard-working man who lived in a reasonably sized but extremely traditional, wooden Hmong house (quite unlike the large courtyard type of his house occupied by his brother) which was surrounded by fruit orchards, white mulberry trees and herbal gardens, and was also much poorer than those of his brother and cousins..

Although not part of the main body of the village in Groups Two and Three, we should consider here also the deceased *Yang Wanshu*, another brother of Yang Wanzhong and Yang Wanheng, who had formerly lived in Group One.[5] As we have noted, Yang Wanshu had married a cousin of the Xiong household (C) in Group One, but he had had two wives; he had also married a Wang related to the Wang II family who worked for him.

In this more marginal section of the village in Group One, Yang Daizhi and Yang Daihe at Q and R were his sons by the Xiong wife; Yang Daixue and Yang Daijin at O and P were his sons by his Wang wife. Besides Yang Daizhi (Q) who had married the sister of the Ma brothers and had a son and a daughter, and Yang Daihe (R) who had a Xiong wife and a daughter, Yang Wanshu's Xiong wife had given

---

[5] The three brothers had also had one sister, who had married a Huang.

him five older daughters, two of whom had also married out to Wang.

Yang Wanshu's Wang wife, besides Yang Daijin (P) with a Tao wife, son and daughter, and Yang Daixue (O) who was as yet unmarried, had also produced a younger son and daughter, and an older daughter who'd married a Liu Qizhou. The youngest son, Yang Dailan, had 'fled' the village after helping Yang Wanchao (half brother to Yang Wanjun in Y2a) burn down the house of a family who had refused the latter their daughter in marriage.

Yang Wanzhong, as I have said, was really the kernel and nucleus of this whole group; while this older brother of his, Yang Wanshu, had taken both a Xiong wife and a wife from the the Wang II who worked for him, he himself had married a sister of his older cousin Yang Wanhe's Wang I wife who worked for him; they had overseen, in the next generation, the further cementing of alliances with the Wang I through the marriage of his own daughter, and with the Ma, who had also intermarried with the Wang II, through the marriage of his brother's son, while two of his junior cousins (households 58 and 59) had obtained Gu and Wang III sons-in-law respectively. These 'brother-in-law' lineages of the five descendants of an original four brothers in lineage Y3b, then, comprised the Wang I, Wang II and Wang III, the Xiong, Gu and the Ma, providing a valuable source of moral and economic support outside the Yang lineage for the Y3b descent group which centred on the sunny, active figure of Yang Wanzhong.

At household number 58, a considerable distance away but still conceptually in the same zone as his lineage brothers, lived the village *tos a neeb* or shaman, *Yang Wanfang*, first cousin to Yang Wanzhong and Yang Wanheng, who like Yang Wanheng the ritual specialist lived in a smaller, traditional, largely wooden house by the side of a waterfall and beneath the shade of spreading walnut trees. It was his sister, Yang Wanliang, who had married the Gu brother, but the Gu were more clearly established with Yang Wanyi's group in lineage Y1 than to this line of the Y3b.[6] Yang Wanfang and his Li wife (through whom he said he had inherited his exorcistic spirits;

---

[6] Yang Wanfang (and all his cousins) had had another FB who had married a Gu; he had also had a younger brother who had married a Xiong, but lived elsewhere and had no children.

chapter 4), had three other unmarried children, besides Yang Daikui who had just married a Tao girl and was about to move out. His eldest daughter (Yang Daihua), like so many of his relatives, had married a Wang—Wang Zhongtang, who was related to the Wang IV.

It was possibly because of their traditional dominance in village affairs, achieved as we have seen partly through contracting strategic marital relations with poorer lineages, that this lineage segment of the Y3b were able to act as a kind of umbrella for less advantaged groups and individuals, and in a sense provide a shelter for the ritual experts and shamans of the clan.

Finally, also well distanced from the others, lived the Tao widow of *Yang Wanlong* (HH no.59), the last of this group of four first cousins, whose sister had married into the Wang III family, and whose mother had also been a Wang. With five daughters whose father had only recently been killed by an avalanche which had become the site of mortuary rites, this was a household of tragedy; but they did receive assistance from their other paternal cousins, as we see in the following chapter.

CHAPTER EIGHT

THE FAMILY OF YANG JUNMING (LINEAGE Y3C)

Last but not least, we come to the final lineage of the Yang settled in the village, Y3c, settled strategically at the centre of the village, not far from the primary school, between the clusters of Y3b, Y2b, and X3. Since they were only represented by three households, two of which in fact lived together, this in terms of sheer numbers should have been among the weakest and most insignificant of the Yang descent groups in the village, but as we shall see, this was far from being the case.

The household group in the village was composed of two brothers. One was *Yang Liping*, a 62-year old with a Tao wife who lived at the household classified under the name of the son who lived there with him, Yang Hong (HH no.24), 28 years old with a Ma wife and an infant son; a large courtyard house, in one wing of which lived Yang Hong's younger brother Yang Zhao (HH no.25) with his own Ma wife and infant daughter. This then was one household of 8 members rather than two of 5 and 3 (as recorded). The other was their father's younger brother who lived close by, in a long extended whitewashed cottage house; *Yang Wanli* (HH no.26), with a Li wife and four sons, one with a newly wedded Wang wife.

Although a father's brother's son of Yang Wanli and Yang Liping had had a son who also lived in the village named Yang Daiyu (HH no.81), as we saw in chapter 7 he had been adopted by a member of the Y1 lineage and so did not properly constitute a member of their descent group. However, relations with him were still close and amicable, and therefore also with the other members of lineage Y1.

While well placed within the village, the Y3c households (effectively two; those of Yang Liping and Yang Wanli) were more important for their relations and connections outside the village, as we shall see.

Their father, Yang Junming (neither he nor any of his four brothers, who were in the Xiang generation, had adopted the generational terms used by the other Yang lineages), had had two Li surnamed wives, and the two sons of one of his brothers were settled in Wangwuzhai, representing the Yang of that area. So the Y3c Yang were importantly connected, through first cousins, to the main area of Hmong settlement in Gongxian, Wangwuzhai, where a number of marriages had taken place with the Wang.

Yang Junming by his two Li wives had had two daughters, one of whom had married a Xiong and the other a Huang. There had also been four sons; *Yang Wanliang* (the oldest), *Yang Qingbai, Yang Liping* (who remained in the village), and *Yang Wanli* (who also remained in the village The latter was a child by the second wife of Yang Junming, although all the brothers were close.

Apart from Yang Liping's two sons at households 24 and 25 (Yang Hong and Yang Zhao), he had had three daughters, the eldest two of whom had respectively married a Wang and a Xiong. Their youngest daughter (Yang Xiaoxin) was now studying in Yibin.[1]

Yang Wanli, as we have seen, had had four sons, the oldest of whom had a new Wang wife. While two of the four brothers (Yang Wanli and Yang Liping) remained in the village, Yang Liping having returned previously from a long spell away in Nanchang, it was their two elder brothers who represented the most famous members of the Yang clan, since the eldest brother, Yang Wanliang, had supported the Guomindang during the Anti-Japanese War prior to the Revolution (when all the local villagers had been required to send up one person or the whole clan), and during the fighting immediately prior to Liberation, had fled with other Guomindang remnants first to Burma and thence to the hills of Northern Thailand (also populated by Hmong whose language he would have understood), from where he was airlifted, in 1954, to Taiwan.

There are many accounts (such as McCoy 1972), of how the remnants of the Guomindang's Third and Fifth Armies under Generals Li and Tuan, were initially informally permitted by the Thai Government to reside in what soon became a Chinese Guomindang encampment along the Thai border with Burma, how in the early years after the Revolution they were used by the OSS (precursor of the CIA) to mount forays into 'Red China', and then later provided a bulwark against the emerging communist insurgencies in Thailand and Laos; and how they were permitted to monopolise the incoming trade in opium to subsidise their activities,

---

[1] So she does not appear in household records.

until international alarm and awareness of their situation led to the UN-supervised transportation to Taiwan in the mid and late 1950s. And it is well known that many of the Chinese Guomindang soldiers and officers did not go but stayed behind, and in some cases paid members of the Hmong and Lahu and Lisu[2] minorities in northern Thailand to take their places, so that to this day there is a group of North Thai tribespeople settled in Taiwan. Yang Wanliang was not one of these—he went, usually disguising his own Hmong identity and posing as a Sichuanese Chinese and accepted as such, first by his Guomindang compatriots and then by the Taiwanese he came to know.

He must have been aware of the other Hmong in Taiwan and probably knew them and had contacts with them. However, he continued to assume a Chinese identity, taking a Chinese wife surnamed Fang and having two children, a boy and a girl, to whom he gave their appropriate Hmong Yang generational names—Yang Daijin for the boy, and Yang Daiyun for the girl. And indeed he prospered in Taiwanese society, working in the Taiwanese postal service at a time when it had something of a reputation for sharp practice, and rising steadily until he became not only a General Postmaster but also, by Taiwanese standards, extremely rich.

Yang Qingbai, the second brother, had also thoroughly assimilated into Chinese society, but in the opposite political direction, like his older brother marrying a Han woman, surnamed Wei, and having two sons and a daughter none of whom had grown up to speak Hmong. Yang Qingbai had early been politically active and noticed by the cadres, so that he was selected for political training at an early stage and sent to study at the Southwest Nationalities Institute in Chengdu, where he became a party member and did so well that he joined the Sichuan Minority Affairs Bureau (the main government agency in charge of affairs regarding ethnic minorities) as a cadre. Extremely astute, capable, and diplomatic, he was then promoted and posted to Beijing where he became a member of the Central Minority Affairs Bureau, and also a Central Party Committee member.

---

[2] The Lisu are closely related to groups classified as Yi in China, particularly the Nosu (Lolo).

During the Cultural Revolution (1966-76) he fell into disfavour, and his two brothers back in the village also suffered, since their family had been that of a relatively prosperous minor landlord. Yang Qingbai was demoted and sent back to Chengdu. But he still remained an important provincial personage, with his good communicative connections (*guanxi*) in Beijing, a high position in the provincial capital of Chengdu, and above all a knowledge of the wider world and of political affairs which none of the other Wutong villagers could remotely aspire to.

This inevitably reflected on the standing of their two younger brothers in the village, Yang Wanli and Yang Liping (who had himself gained some local prestige through working outside the village and travelling overseas before returning to the village). Although they did not appear to take overt advantage of their wider connections, in Chengdu, Beijing, and overseas, the other villagers did pay them considerable respect, and were clearly aware of the importance of these familial connections. Yang Wanli was a hardworking, not particularly intelligent, rough mannered farmer who was also the boss of the local *xiang* semi-government construction enterprise, employing workers in Didong and from the village under contracts for building work in surrounding villages and towns. His wife told me his 'studies had been interrupted' early; he had not been able to leave the village, but had had to 'get up very early' and 'work very hard'. This was in the nature of an explanation for his always having remained in the village as a farmer, until recetly he had become an entrepreneur. Yang Liping, his older brother, was a bookish, clerkly, kindly older man whose knowledge of Chinese characters (though by no means excellent) was widely respected in the village. Like Yang Qingbai he had joined the PLA when young, at the age of 20, and had stayed with the army, spending 3 years in Korea, until he was 28, and then spent a further 4 years working at the Nanchang Iron Factory 'to make money for his family' before returning to the village with retired cadre status. He had married a girl from Junliang while he was in the army. When asked if he did not regret having returned to the village in his thirties, Yang Liping said, 'Well both have their advantages and disadvantages. Living here in the country I can see all my family whenever I want'.

But it is in the light of their wider connections beyond the village that the deep-rooted hostility between lineage Y3c and the three Zeng households of the Gongxian party secretary, Zeng Minggao, can be understood. This hostility dated back to when a FZ of Zeng Minggao had married the Yang brothers' father's eldest brother (Yang Xisan)'s adopted son, Yang Wanyong, but had then run away and deserted him (the Zeng said he'd constantly beaten her for no reason, the Yang said she'd cheated on her husband). Later their FB had remarried and had a real son named Yang Wanyuan, whose own son Yang Daiyu was as we saw above adopted by lineage Y1.

Yet the hostility between these two families had as much to do with their official class categories and backgrounds as with this affinal connection. Prior to Liberation Zeng Minggao's family had been desperately poor, landless labourers, while Yang Junming, the father of the four brothers in lineage Y3c, had been a minor landlord, owning his own farmland and employing some seasonal Han Chinese labourers. This meant that after Land Reform Zeng Minggao had been particularly favoured; starting as a communist youth league member, he had been able to join the party, and he too had been sent to the Southwest Nationalities Institute in Chengdu to study. However, he had behaved so 'inappropriately' there (excessive drinking and womanizing) that no further positions in Chengdu were forthcoming, and so he had been despatched back to his local district, where he eventually succeeded eventually in becoming the county party secretary. In that position he was able to channel some of the government assistance designed for the district as a whole to benefit the development of his own village, which as a result unusually had both a water supply and electricity, and a fair proportion of its teenagers now studying in Gongxian and Didong, and even in Yibin and Chengdu.

But Zeng Minggao was a local power only, and his remit and connections did not extend much beyond his own village and the county seat of Gongxian. Yang Qingbai, on the other hand, who had left the village for Chengdu in the early years after Liberation, and thus evaded the effects of Land Reform, had been steadily progressing and rising in the party bureaucracy, quite detached from village or even local county affairs, while Yang Liping had struggled equally hard to overcome the stigma of his family's Guomindang background through studying; this generally meant political study, but he was also able to study some literature and science.

While the two Yang brothers who had been left behind in the village were criticised during the Great Leap Forward and openly attacked by the Zeng during the Cultural Revolution on account of their family's class background and their older brother's Guomindang (KMT) affiliation, they never suffered as much as they might have done, and this was in large part due to the general knowledge that Yang Qingbai, their older brother, was far more powerful than Zeng Minggao, and in a crisis would be able to protect his brothers.

Indeed Lineage Y2a had joined in the criticism of Y3c during the time of the Great Leap Forward, with Yang Wanjun claiming to have been a servant in the Yang brothers' home (which they said he never had been, but had just come to help of his own free will) and accusing them of having hordes of silver stored there. Yang Shaozhen, however, the grandfather of the Yang brothers, had been astute enough to admit to this (although it was not true), since if he had tried to deny it he would certainly have been beaten. But in addition he had accused Yang Wanjun of now breaking a solemn oath they had all sworn, to keep the matter of the silver which was to have been shared between them secret. Not long after this, Yang Wanjun's son Yang Daifu (HH no.71) died and so did his daughter, which people attributed to him breaking the oath he was supposed to have taken, leaving all the villagers afraid, and nobody very sure exactly who had had a share in the (mythical?) silver. But it was the Zeng who had been instigators of these criticisms, and this was not lightly to be forgotten.

There was thus a very long-standing tension between the Zeng family of the local party secretary, who had risen from the ranks and was in the ascendant during the Cultural Revolution, on the one hand, and the Yang families of Y3c on the other, with their relatively affluent background, overseas connections, and a brother high up in the party hierarchy, whether he was stationed in Chengdu or in Beijing. Yang Qingbai was perceived as the man who had made it, athough he had been demoted from Beijing to Chengdu (Chengdu still remained the apogee of most villagers' aspirations) and was a relative stranger to the village; Zeng Minggao was seen essentially as a failure, who had not been deemed sufficiently capable to stay on in

Chengdu, a kind of 'Ah Q' figure who became in his frequent drunken bouts a figure of fun, yet whose efforts to assist the village were also appreciated.[3] In many ways Zeng Minggao was perceived to epitomise the worst of local government officialdom, yet it was also recognised that he was a useful local representative.

While the fortunes of the two Yang brothers in the village suffered a decline during the Cultural Revolution, with the demotion of their brother from Beijing, after 1981, as the effects of China's economic—and political—reforms began to be felt in the county, their status and conditions dramatically improved. Locally this was reflected in the entrepreneurial success of Yang Wanli; the kind of construction enterprise he part-managed was typical of the TVEs (township & village enterprises) which began to emerge, and then flourish, in the early 1980s, often based on older commune industries, but now with an effective degree of private management and profit-sharing arrangements between local enterprise and local government.

The enterprise Yang Wanli managed was the Yuhe Miaozu Xiang Construction Team, which currently employed seventy workers (*pugong*) and technicians (*jigong*), mostly from Wutongcun, and which was responsible for most of the new constructions in Didong and the surrounding villages. The labour force was almost exclusively male, with only four women. It had started as an unofficial village enterprise in 1970; since 1978 they had been allowed to engage in formal contracted work, and now that management autonomy was officially recognised, business was booming. Yang Wanli complained he didn't have time for his fields, although actually he still spent a large proportion of his time inspecting them, doing odd jobs, and organising the labour of his wife and children and some hired help, on them. Yang Wanli estimated the enterprise brought in ¥250,000 annually, which was banked at low interest rates; of the three similar enterprises in Didong his had been the most successful. One of the disadvantages of the new policies was that while in the old days they had been free to go virtually anywhere to work, since 1978 when the enterprise had been formally registered they had been restricted to Didong.

---

[3] Ah Q is a famous literary hero and buffoon by Lu Xun, notable for his irrational optimism, sometime taken to caricature Chinese officialdom.

The enterprise was largely based on the existence of local *guanxi* and its manipulation . Yang Wanli had been helped to establish it by his elder brother, whose Minwei position and party membership led to excellent contacts with the party and government officials in Gongxian, and the fact that the village was an 'advanced' one owing largely to the efforts of the county party secretary also helped the initial establishment of the enterprise. Since that time however Yang Wanli had cultivated his own contacts with district officials which resulted in the awarding of contracts, and with the district population as a whole which meant that he could employ labour in the district town as well as from the village . One sees here how crucial the importance of networks of friendly and warm local *guanxi*, in addition to those of kinship, are for the establishment and maintenance of enterprises . Villagers regularly visited the market at Didong and so other personal relationships were initiated and kept up. At the same time the *guanxi* which may support an enterprise economy cuts across and meshes with the official structures of the party and the state in an instrumental way. The enterprise had begun as a brigade venture, and relied on support both from local party officials and Minwei for its establishment on a private basis .

It was highly appropriate, then, that as China began to open up to the outside world after 1980, the Yang brothers, through Yang Qingbai's extensive external contacts, should have tried to re-establish contact with their long-lost brother in the Taiwanese Post Office, Yang Wanliang. It was not so remarkable that they should have tried to contact a brother who, after all, had supposedly fought on the opposite side to them. In the years before 1949 the whole area had been riven with conflicts between the KMT and CCP forces, and although brothers did fight against brothers and whole families were destroyed in these wars, in most cases the Hmong of south Sichuan, very like the Hmong in similar conflicts in Laos and Thailand and perhaps like many other peasants in China, had simply supported whichever side seemed like winning without any real wish to be involved. Accident and historical contingency, much more than ideological commitments, determined who had fled to the Guomindang and who had stayed behind to become a patriotic citizen of the new China. Ma Yinggao, for example, the father of households 75 and 76, was well known to have 'escaped' from the Guomindang, and there were other cases of past Guomindang support in this and neighbouring villages. I had not quite realised how extensive local support for the Guomindang had been until the day I was approached by a group of several Hmong on a visit to another county who asked me if I could help to redeem tens of thousands of KMT issued dollars they had been hoarding ever since the early 1950s. I was told that the Hmong in Gongxian had basically supported the Guomindang until the Revolution or very shortly before, and only then the PLA. Certainly it was the case with the Yang brothers that they had been divided by historical contingency rather than by personal convictions, and they were now eager to re-establish familial contacts.

In this they did no more than express the spirit of the times, since it was from the early 1980s onwards that Deng Xiaoping's policies favoured economic development over political struggle, a measure of petty capitalism was restored to the local economy in a way which privileged the household as the basic economic unit, after China formally established diplomatic relations in 1979 with the US, long-time ally of the Nationalist Chinese in Taiwan.

Yang Qingbai had succeeded in the attempt to contact their oldest brother, and two years before I went to live in the village with my wife and six-week old son, Yang Wanliang had made an officially blessed return to China, to Sichuan, to Gongxian, and to the village of Wutong, and this two week visit must have been an extraordinary social event, since the village and local government offices in Gongxian were full of photographs of this elderly Taiwanese businessman garlanded with flowers and surrounded by his family, stepping out of cars and being toasted at banquets, being ceremoniously welcomed to the village with Yang Qingbai at his side, and meeting all the important government and party dignitaries in Yibin and Gongxian.

For Yang Wanliang was rich—not only in village terms, but even in Taiwanese terms, and he was to become a major benefactor to the county and particularly to the village. This was the reason for his official reception by party and government dignitaries, and again this was entirely in acord with official Chinese policies which were not only explicitly encouraging some to become rich before others (like Yang Wanli) , but also sanctioning and seeking just such donations and support from foreign and overseas compatriots. In fact, at the time arrangements for the visit were initiated, it was by no means clear that there would be official approval of these sorts of donations and investments by overseas Chinese, particularly those in Taiwan; the policy was just being formulated. The visit had been astutely orchestrated by Yang Qingbai , who had insider knowledge of the current policy developments, and had proved a success in every respect.

Large amounts of largesse were distributed into private pockets. Token donations had been made to local schools, hospitals, clinics, road-building and other constructions, and for the support of needy individuals of the Yang clan, not only in Wutong but also in many of the surrounding villages. Although in many cases these amounts were small, they were most significant at the village level, reinforcing the dominance of the Yang clan and in particular the strategic importance of the members of Y3c. And much more was on the way, or promised.

My own entrée into the village was as a direct result of these events, and was in fact really a single moment in the developing engagement of the region with the Taiwanese entrepreneur. I should describe this here, in order to convey something of the real context in which research is often organised in China, the context in which research should be understood against a local background of economic and political realities. For after the highly successful, state-like visit of the long-estranged brother to his native town (*xiang*) in 1987, there was a need for further visits, contacts and meetings to organise the distribution of further funds. In particular this required a visit by Yang Qingbai to Hong Kong, where I was working, to meeet his brother from Taiwan. The most convenient way in which this could be arranged was for Yang Qingbai at the Nationalities Affairs Bureau in Chengdu to take an interest in the approval of my application for research permision. The original application had been made with the help of my Department in Hong Kong which maintained its own programme of ongoing relations and exchanges with the Minorities Research Institute which was part of the Bureau. It was as a result of my invitation that later a reciprocal invitation from Hong Kong could be issued to Yang Qingbai and others from the Bureau to visit Hong Kong.

And so it was Yang Qingbai, as the only Hmong at an appropriate level in the Commission, who facilitated my research permission, and did much more than this, arranging permissions for us to stay in his own home village in the home of his younger brother, Yang Wanli, acompanying us from Chengdu to Gongxian by train, around the time of Tiananmen, introducing us to local officials and to all his family and friends in the village, arranging interviews and visits to other villages and other areas and even, as we have seen, enabling me to witness shamanic sessions. Initally I was afraid that Yang Qingbai would prove to be a hindrance of the kind often encountered by foreign researchers in China, and took pains to arrange my own research assistance from an entirely separate institution, but this was far from being the case.

Yang Qingbai, like some other local *xiang* Hmong officials we met, had his own genuine interest in, and respect for, what he saw as the Hmong cultural heritage, and indeed throughout the years had collected tapes of Hmong music, legends and wedding customs as many minority officials have done since the 1980s and even before that time.[4] In the village he was solely concerned to discover exactly what I wished to do, and then to facilitate it by every means possible. At first he attended interviews and ritual occasions with me (and surely he must also have been concerned that I would not act in some unforgiveably inappropriate way), but soon he was content to let me work alone with my research asistant, and only appeared when requested. I believe he had a genuine interest in my work of, as he saw it, understanding and recording the local Hmong culture; at the same time my own visit should be understood as part of a reciprocal process of exchange with the outside world in which Yang Qingbai was personally involved.

My own part in all this, which I describe here for reasons of general interest in the conditions of fieldwork in China, was minor and subsidiary, merely facilitatory; what was really important was the developing economic progress of the village and its neighbouring region, the input of local funding from an 'overseas Chinese compatriot' who was in fact ethnically Hmong, and most importantly

---

[4] All this material, as well as more collected in Gongxian, remains untranslated and untouched, and this is a common situation across China. There is an unbelievable wealth of local cultural materials which have been carefully and individually collected and recorded, which only a very few anthropologists and historians from outside China have been able to tap into only a very small proportion of. The situation cries out for major research funding and nationally directed programmes of translation and editing.

the effect this was having on the local culture and ethnic profile of the area. In turn we should understand this as occurring within the context of Chinese economic marketization, accompanied by the decentralisation of social services, internal labour migration and a certain retreat of the state from everyday life resulting in the greater marginalization of economically 'backward' areas. For together with these sorely needed foreign funds, and the expanding openings for local entrepreneurial activities, a kind of local cultural renascence was taking place, associated with an expanding awareness of a much wider outside world in which Hmong culture and relations reached from Taiwan to Thailand and the US, and clearly also based on the introduction of electricity and the influence of television (three then in the village), in which my own role as—external—researcher and inquirer into the niceties of Hmong culture and local history proved to be entirely and throughly appropriate.

Most significant in this respect, and in terms of the 'portrayal and understanding of local/global historical encounters, co-productions, dominations and resistances' (Clifford 1992), apart from the increasing interest by some local officials—by no means all—in collecting and printing editions of Hmong folklore, and the increasing—albeit still wary—confidence with which ancestral and funeral, geomantic and even shamanic rites were being practiced— was the reconstruction of clan consciousness which was taking place among the Yang. It was in the 1930s, during a period of relative calm in the region, that the Yang had last been in the position of being able to invite a Han Chinese teacher to draw up a genealogy and set generational terms for them. This was only the second time such a thing had been possible, and the more extraordinary for coming after 40 years of socialist rule Most remarkably, a clan assembly, composed of the representatives of all the leading households in the different lineage segments of the village, had been formed, and the Yang genealogy, most of which had beeen destroyed in the Cultural Revolution, was in the process of being reconstituted and written down under its direction.

We must remember that the Hmong have traditionally had no form of writing for their language, and so have not been able to possess written genealogies. Nor, in traditional Hmong society (even in the comparatively advanced Gongxian or Sichuan region) had there ever been anything like a Chinese-type 'clan hall'. Yet now, under the influence of Yang Wanliang's visit from Taiwan and the new prosperity and status this was leading to (and certainly in the context of the new political and economic conditions prevailing in the country), there were even serious plans for the Hmong Yang lineage to establish its own clan 'ancestral hall', on a thoroughly Han Chinese model.

The Yang genealogy was not yet complete, and was being slowly and carefully compiled, as Yang Wanliang had suggested, by research and interviews and meetings with elders and visits to Yang relatives further afield. My own work on the Yang fitted well into this, and it became something of a joint venture.[5] In the form I found it, not only was the genealogy incomplete—although already very extensive—it also suffered most of the classic faults of genealogies; some collapsing of generations had occurred with the omission of non-apical or disgraced ancestors, the deaths of young children were not usually recorded (Yang Qingbai for example had had two younger brothers who had died as infants from 'dysentery'), males tended to be recollected more easily than females, particularly in ascendant generations, and disgraced lineage members like murderers and suicides were being entirely omitted. We had discussions on these points, and some of this was corrected (they took the points about women being left out very well and were trying to include them all, but I suspect disgraced members may never reappear). Still it was a remarkable endeavour, and taken together with the plans for an ancestral hall which would have marked a completely new departure for Hmong society, a really extraordinary sign of the renewal and reconstructed forms of cultural identity with which economic progress and political liberalisation appeared to be inevitably associated.

The minor local cultural revival represented by the construction of genealogies and the formation of a clan assembly was clearly connected with the ability of the Yang brothers to have re-established contact over the political breaches of the past between Taiwan and China, signifying the political spirit of the times, and with the subsequent flow of petty investments and donations into the district.

---

[5] For the previous section I have been able to largely follow this genealogy, checked against the genealogies I collected in household interviews, which were more extensive for recent generations.

Whether such transnational alliances would in time result in a greater integration of the region into the Chinese polity, with as Appadurai (1993) put it, the release of the nationalist 'genie' out of the bottle of the state, remained to be seen.[6] In the last year the district had received over ¥100,000 of Yang Wanliang's money, or about £10,000. In addition to this, his brother Yang Liping in the village had received ¥40,000, and a further ¥40,000 had been paid to the local Minwei offfice. Besides this ¥20,000 had gone to the Yibin area, and 15,000 was about to come to Gongxian.

Of the ¥100,000 which was in the charge of Yang Qingbai, ¥30,000 had been paid to the Foreign Affairs Bureau of Yibin (for the Education Commission), and ¥70,000 had gone to his brother Yang Wanli for the repairs and redecoration to his house. ¥60,000 had been paid to the brothers' sister in Yibin for her apartment there (her children, although by a Chinese father, had adopted Miao nationality). Some money had also gone directly to local schools; Wutong primary school had received two payments of ¥1,000 each, the primary school at Yuehue had also had two direct payments, of ¥2,200 and ¥500, and the Miao primary school at Fenghuang village, further upslope behind Wutong, had also had payments of 1,000 and ¥500 and another was due. The amounts were small, but taken as a whole, significant. This year it was planned to establish a book fund of ¥15,000 specifically for the Yang clan, to encourage the young Yang children to study, besides scholarship funds for Yang children to attend middle school, and a vacation class for coaching backward pupils. And prizes were to be established for all pupils, not just the Yang; for example, at primary level, a prize of ¥50 would be presented to every child who got 60% for their years' schoolwork, rising at ¥5 per additional mark to 70%; at middle school, ¥10 would be awarded per mark from 71% up to 80%, and then ¥15 per mark up to 90%. Personal grants had also been made to older clan members and the leaders of other descent groups, such as to Yang Zhijun of lineage X3 and Yang Wanjun of lineage Y2a.

Grants were not to be limited, though, to Yang clan members alone, and Yang Qinbgbai and his brothers were very clear on the need to be careful not to create local jealousies and antagonisms;

---

[6] Cf. Christofferson (1993).

their daughters and sisters' children, for example, could also benefit through a general charitable fund being established, to be known as the 'Shaozheng Fund', after the name of the their father's father.

Besides these sums, an additional ¥60,000 had been given to construct a stone road from the village to Gongxian, to match ¥60,000 provided by the local government. The impoverished members of Group One were taking no part in the construction of this road, since as they saw it it would not directly benefit them. Most importantly, there had been a plan to establish a local clinic, although this was temporarily on hold for fear of competing with the private clinics already established in Gongxian, and an additional sum of ¥200,000 had been put aside to establish an entirely new vocational training school in Gongxian in Gongxian, under the name of (Yang) Shaozheng, with three classes for ethnic minorities and one for the Han, and with 30 *mu* of land donated by the local government. This project too was pending in the uncertain time following Tiananmen (referred to as 'the Beijing Event'), but the funds had already been allocated.

The sum is not very much in terms of international development assistance, but a small personal fortune was being annually disbursed which had a most significant impact locally, and we must remember that other expenses had also been incurred, and that that if anything these officially disbursed sums represented an under-estimate of all the funds which had been received. This was an initial stage of local investment, and there were plans for much more. As we walked around the nearby village of Fenghuang, for example, we often met people who had been informal beneficiaries of the Yang brothers' generosity; one old man of the Li surname without an immediate family had had ¥150, another Wang family with a preponderance of daughters ¥200, and a Xiong widow with a large family born as a Yang (Yang Qingbai's FBD) had had ¥5,000. Most of the widow households in Wutong who might previously have expected some form of support from the commune had benefited. And we can see how carefully and strategically the major funds had been disbursed; some to local government, some directly to villagers, some to schools within the villages, some to individual villages, much to Yang lineage members, some to those who were not.

The strategy of not distributing solely to the Yang families was clearly working almost too well, since some of the local villagers complained that Yang Wanliang cared more about the area as a whole than about his own family.

While in many ways, therefore, as we saw in chapter 7, it was the lineage members of Y3b, through a network of paternal first cousins and affinal alliances formed with 'son-in-law' lineages, which dominated the internal composition of the village, its internal political disputes and affairs, the two brothers representing Y3c in the village had acquired an influence over village matters quite disproportionate to their marginal position in the lineage structure and their small numbers. Meanwhile the close-knit Han families of the Xie and Li, and the disadvantaged residents of Group One, occupied thoroughly peripheral positions to the main body of village life focused on the Hmong Yang clan members. The Yang brothers of Y3c had been able to acquire this privileged position despite a more privileged class background, largely through their mastery of a wider social world in which the village was inserted (as has often been the case in the emergence of local entrepreneurs since liberalisation).

A closer look at the genealogy of the two village brothers shows how widely beyond the village their family ramifications spread (Diagram 34).

We note the number of marriages with Han which had taken place (Yang Qingbai and his brother in Taiwan as well as their sister in Yibin), their desire to distinguish themselves from other members of the lineage by *not* using the generational terms favoured by them, and the number of young children embarking on an education.

Their main rivals in the past, in terms of access to a wider social context which determined the position of the village, had been the family of Zeng Minggao, who had been able to become the county party secretary and for more than a decade prior to 1978 had acted as the main patron of the village and the villagers within it. We can see here how, through both the entrepreneurial activity of Yang Wanli and through the visit of their estranged older brother from Taiwan and the funding which they directed, the Yang brothers were in effect reasserting what had been the traditional dominance of the Yang in the region. Throughout the 1960s and 1970s it had been largely due to Zeng Minggao that Wutong had benefited to the extent it had, but now the very considerable funding being channeled through the Yang brothers had virtually eclipsed the importance of the benefits

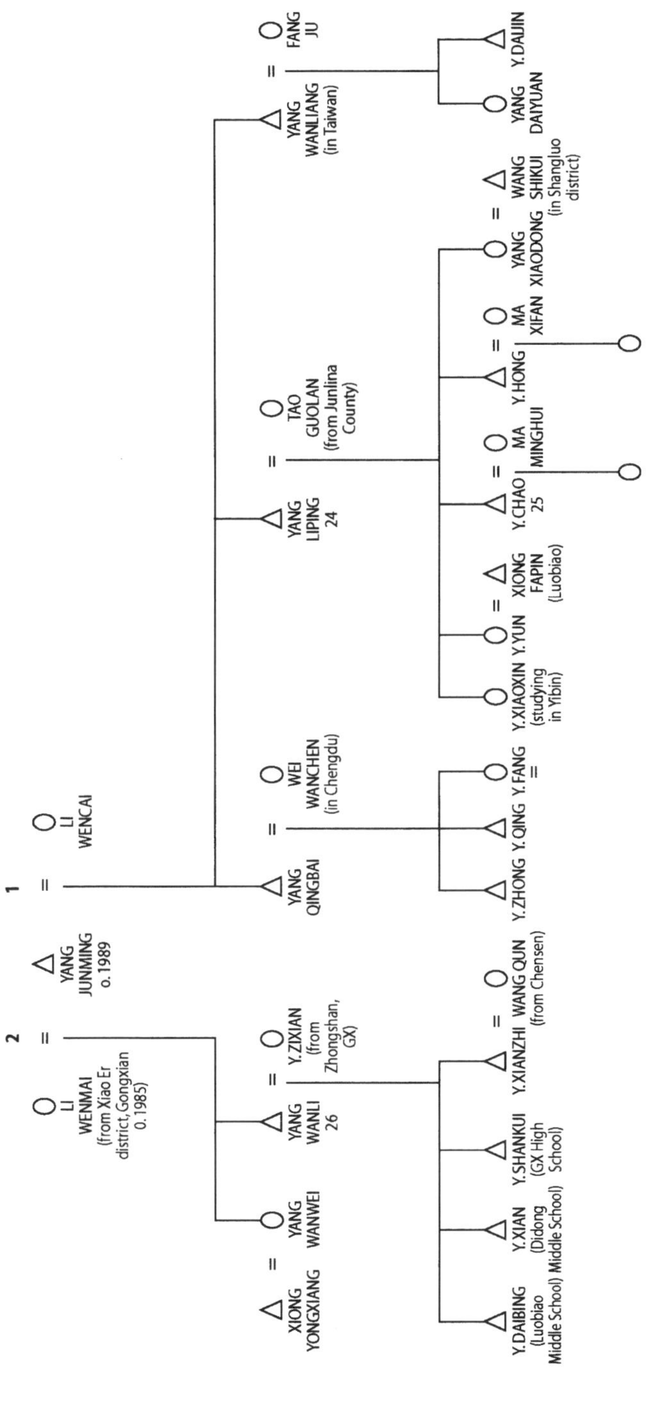

Diagram 34: Lineage Y3c

secured through the party secretary's previous activities (in water, electricity, and scholarships to schools particularly).

The Minority Affairs Bureau had for years funded an ethnic minority class in the No.28 Middle School in Chengdu, and every year young members of the minority elites from the Tibetan areas such as Gansu and Aba, and Yi from Liangshan and the Miao from Yibin, were recruited, usually about three or four students for the whole of Yibin, competing for a limited quota of places which were circulated between the various counties. In the previous year Gongxian county had been allotted one place, which was given to a student from Wutongcun in the Gongxian junior Middle School. Coordinated between the Gongxian County Education Commission and the Minority Affairs Bureau, it was this sort of decision which the the county party secretary had previously been able to influence, and through such patronage the general course of development in the county and the village.

Development and Revival

'Development' may be said to have taken place in Gongxian through a number of factors, closely related to processes of acculturation and adaptation, reverse assimilation and the re-formation of traditional culture. It is important to distinguish between three quite different types of social change, all of which are perceived locally as amounting to 'development'. The first of these is the very long historical process of cultural 'Sinicisation' which we considered in Part One, and which has been noticeable in Gongxian for nearly a century. It will be remembered that Graham had remarked on the disappearance of traditional Hmong weaving patterns and techniques in this area before 1910, and Han acculturation had affected language and costume as well as house design and, as we shall see below, marriage practices. In linguistic terms the villagers of Wutong were bilingual in the local Han dialect and could easily communicate with local Han in this (Chongqing dialect of) Sichuanese. Besides earlier strata of words shared in common with Chinese and early loans from Chinese, much more recent loans from Chinese and compounds had been incorporated into local Hmong everyday speech . Widespread examples of these were the compound, *tsi ma wenti*, for 'no problem' (a common Han expression), the first two words of which ('not have') are Hmong, the latter, 'problem', Chinese; and the use of the Chinese term *jua kung* for mother's father, which is generally shared by the Hmong of Sichuan and Guizhou (Appendix VII). Literacy in Chinese was widely sought in Wutong, and those in possession of it enjoyed a respected position in the community . Costumes and clothes had already changed before 1949, becoming less elaborate and complex, and approximating more to Han standards. The lack of silver among the Hmong in most parts of China leads to obvious differences between their costume and the more traditional costumes to be seen in Indochina. What had survived until fairly recently in China were traditional womens' costumes, and particularly the headware which continued to act as the main marker distinguishing local cultural traditions between different groups of Hmong. Again, improved communications and intermarriages had recently led to a lessening of these cultural distinctions between groups of Hmong, a process furthered by the party policy of ignoring sub-cultural differences within national minorities which has paradoxically had the effect of increasing the sense of overall Hmong ethnicity and brotherhood as we saw in chapter 2. What is certain is that the adoption of Han ways and manners has been immeasurably hastened by the process of Liberation, Land Reform and the Cultural Revolution. Songs praising Chairman Mao have blended with songs complaining of the hardships of married women, and it is common for the older men to mix socialist rhetoric with their explanations of traditional custom. Thus the bride is exhorted to be diligent and increase production. One sad wedding song, sung by Yang Wanjun as night fell, went as follows:

> *We Hmong who live in the mainland of China*
> *we have a history of 5,000 years*
> *we Hmong had no writing*
> *passing our time only eating and drinking*
> *since the days when Huangdi lived in the Yellow River valley*
> *and Chiyou was driven to the southwest*
> *we were driven up to the high mountain places*
> *grieving and in lamentation*
> *we must read Sun Yatsen's books*
> *and study Mao Zidong's works*

and in the future our sons and daughters will be sent
  far away
to learn and study to a high degree

But we do need to distinguish these types of long-term cultural
change and exchange, although immeasurably accelerated recently,
from the social and political changes resulting directly from 1949,
which have also largely been externally inspired. The *bao-jia* system
of local administration, which itself was not a traditional Hmong
form of social organisation but rather a measure of their integration
into the local administrative hierarchy, has now been transformed
into the administrative system centred on different levels of
bureaucracy such as province, county and township which basically
covers all parts of rural China. As we have seen, there are party
members at the village level, and the village is integrated into higher
hierarchical structures through the *xiang* administration and the party
network. These socio-political and cultural changes, which are of
course inter-related, must be taken into account in any description of
social change in the area, but they leave the role of economic
development in its relation to these social and cultural processes
unexamined. The spread of literacy may be seen as related to long-
term cultural processes of assimilation as much as to the effects of
political developmental campaigns under socialism, while the
material improvements often pointed to by local officials and
villagers as signs of obvious progress, such as better seeds, chemical
fertilisers, mechanised mills, and electricity in some villages, are
more easily and unambiguously related to the social and political
changes brought about by the socialist revolution .

   But we have seen here how a third type of economic,
development, was now taking place in Gongxian and similar regions,
based on a local type of individual enterprise now partly freed from
state intervention. This kind of development, which we may
distinguish both from long-term cultural processes aimed at social
betterment, and from the directly state-inspired efforts in education
and health, sanitation and infrastructure, productivity and population
control, was in Gongxian both clearly related politically to China's
current national and international position, and also adopting the
form of a local cultural movement in which *relations between the
Hmong and Han, and the burden of Hmong cultural inheritance,
were beginning to be resignified in quite novel ways*. As we have

seen here, a road was being built to Wutong (and many other inputs made) by the local government with the assistance of funding received from the oldest brother of a leading villager, who had lived in Taiwan since supporting the Guomindang prior to the Revolution, in honour of the deceased father of the brothers.[7] And really this is an extraordinary case, of a national_minority without the concentrated power of for example the Hui, employing Taiwanese funds for local development in commemoration of a deceased ancestor, after a very 'Chinese' model.

Now the position of the party secretary, and with it that of his Zeng family, had become well overshadowed by the gifts and contributions emanating from Taiwan, for which the Yang brothers acted as intermediaries. And at the same time fragments of former cultural practices were being 'recycled' in novel forms, as Siu argued generally for the resurgence of cultural traditions in China. In this too the Yang brothers who had re-established Taiwanese contacts and invited a foreign anthropologist played a pivotal role, sponsoring a clan assembly and the drafting of a genealogy, and even formulating plans for an ancestral hall. Now what makes this a 'recycling' of 'fragments', rather than a revival of traditional forms, is that while clearly expressing a sense of local Hmong specificity and particularism in the present, these attempts did not correspond to the cultural essentialisms of the past; neither written genealogies, nor clan assemblies, nor ancestral halls, have ever been specifically 'Hmong' practices in the past, but they are, on the contrary, very marked features of Han Chinese social organisation. And this is not a matter of ethnographic purism; writing and ancestral halls may almost be said to be emblematic of Chinese identities by contrast to those of the Hmong, who indeed often define themselve precisely by the absence of these things.

So how, precisely, may one characterise or understand this recycling of cultural fragments in fact borrowed from a neighbouring, and more dominant, culture, this resignification of iterative practices? It would be easiest to understand these phenomena as one more step on the long road of the Hmong towards

---

[7] The extent of Taiwanese investment in China is now well-known, and it is known that this often adopts a sentimental or familial form, yet there are few studies of how this is brought about at the local level.

the 'Sinicisation' stressed by so many previous writers on ethnic minorities in China and Sinologists. In Chinese terms, which often blur distinctions between 'culture' (*wenhua*) and 'development' (*fazhan*), the local development of schools and transport which was taking place in the county through the patronage of a Taiwanese kinship connection, the entrepreneurial activities of some of the villagers, and the apparent adoption of such emblems of traditional 'Chinese' culture as genealogies and ancestral halls, are all of a piece; here is a village which is progressing, adopting symbolic markers of Chines-eness at the same time as economically developing. Since in Chinese evolutionary theory, the Han remain at the vanguard of social development as the most 'advanced' of *minzu*, it would appear natural for the members of 'backward' national minorities to adopt what are seen as Han characteristics in an attempt to modernize. A classic diffusionist would also be comfortable with the notion that a peripheral cultural group should in this way slowly be absorbed into the mainstream of a cultural centre. Yet at the same time, it was a Hmong identity which was being expressed and articulated, cited through these means; and even if we were tempted to put this down to a simple case of acculturation without the loss of a sense of ethnic identity (since there are other cases of minorities in south China adopting Han cultural practices as cultural markers), what then are we to make of the attempts to record and publish fragments of Hmong culture in the form of love songs, legends and ballads? the continued practice of shamanism, the study of the *qeej* by local cadres? Should we then adopt the optimistic diffusionist view of cultural interaction, that a kind of indigenization of more global (at least national) influences is occurring through these developments, a kind of appropriation of dominant cultural forms for intentions other than those originally associated with them, a counter-hegemonic trans-coding of signifiers with new, potentially subversive meanings? Is it sufficient to say that these cultural forms have merely become uprooted, 'dissociated', from their original social contexts so that they can be used in new ones?

It is in an understanding of the local constructions of difference and otherness, kinship and identity, that the answers to these questions lie. Besides the paramount distinctions made, and as we have seen partly overcome, at the village level, between being 'Hmong' and 'Han Chinese', there are also compulsive and immediate distinctions between the identities of ordinary Hmong villagers, and those of Hmong cadres who are in the position of state agents, which we have attempted also to consider. But of most relevance in traditional social life, and consequently of great interest for us in their present-day setting, is the ideology of descent and alliance which operates for the Hmong at the village level in much the same way as it does for Han Chinese, by painting distinctions between groups of agnatically related men which are seen as overcome or mitigated through the network of affinal ties crosscutting these divisions, and which are expressed in the rituals of wedding.

Let us continue, then, to examine with some care the precise nature of the alliances formed by the Yang with other Hmong clans, in the case of the Zeng family of the county party secretary whose rivalries with the Yang of Y3c we have already witnessed.

CHAPTER NINE

OTHER HMONG CLANS

The Zeng

The village map shows how, as we move towards the boundary of the northern and southern parts of the village we come across the three Zeng households of Zeng Wanshou, Zeng Wanlu and Zeng Wanpei (Tao Lian Juen), who all actually inhabited one large extended courtyard house.

The relationship between these three 'households' was that Zeng Wanshou (HH no.3)'s two FBS were Zeng Wanpei (HH no.1) and Zeng Wanlu (HH no.2), as we can see in Diagram 35.

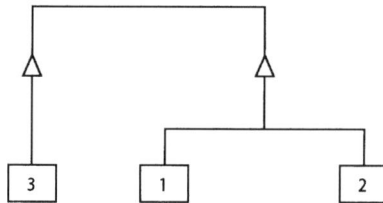

Diagram 35: The three Zeng households

Zeng Wanshou at household number 3 had married Yang Jiatsui, the daughter of *Yang Daipei* (HH no.72), and lived with his wife and three young daughters. Zeng Wanshou's father was Zeng Minggao, the party secretary in Gongxian and therefore as we have seen one of the pivotal figures in the local hierarchy of power. His wife was Wang Wenhua, and his paternal grandfather had also married a Wang. Zeng Minggao's younger sister had married *Yang Xianggao* (HH no.27, of the X1 line), just as his FZ had married another Yang, the (adopted) first cousin to the Yang brothers of Y3c; and here we begin to see something of the importance of the alliances the small Zeng clan had formed with members of the other Wang and Yang clans in the village. Zeng Minggao's brother was Zeng Minzong, whose two sons Zeng Wanpei and Zeng Wanlu accounted for households 1 and 2.

Zeng Wanshou (at household 3) in fact had three younger brothers who had all left the village; Zeng Wanshi, who worked in Gongxian at the electricity depot, Zeng Wanyun who was in Gongxian at school, and Zeng Wanfu, who was in the army post in Gongxian. Their sister like their father had also married a Wang; *Wang Guoming* (HH no.65).

And Zeng Wanpei, at household 1, was working in Gongxian as a teacher, leaving his Tao wife and Li mother with two younger daughters in the village, while a third daughter (Zeng Daiyong) had married the party secretary of Chengsen *xian*, Yang Yuqin. The predominance of party secretaries, teachers, scholars and soldiers in the family are an index of the way in which a new elite in the countryside was formed prior to the ending of the Cultural Revolution, which has formed new alliances with local economic interests and emerging business concerns since then.

Zeng Wanpei's brother Zeng Wanlu (at number 2) had however not been so fortunate as the rest of the family; he had been imprisoned after murdering a man in Yibin in a brawl, leaving his wife *Yang Daiyun* with three daughters in the village. One of these daughters had recently married *Wang Zhongping* at household number 13 (the brother of Wang Zhongfu at 14), but was still at home waiting for a new house to move into.

To show the strength of village endogamy between Hmong clans particularly involving the Zeng, these two brothers, Zeng Wanpei and Zeng Wanlu, had a sister (Zeng Wanfeng) who had married *Yang Jiayuan* in Group One (whose first cousin's daughter had married Ma Jianqing in household number 76), another sister (Zeng Wanrong) who had married Yang Daibi the son of *Yang Wanyi* (HH no.55), another sister (Zeng Wanhui) who had married Yang Jiayuan (HH no.77) the son of *Yang Daisong* (HH no.78), and another sister (Zeng Wanxiu) who had married *Yang Jiakuan* in Group One (at the local grain depot), besides two other sisters who had died young.

Imaging those affinal relations which concern us here, we would have the situation of Diagram 36, which shows all Zeng-Wang-Yang relations.

One notes that a particularly close interweaving of Yang, Wang and Zeng has occurred here; Zeng Minggao's daughter has married a Wang whose mother's brother (Yang Xianggao) married Zeng Minggao's sister (Diagram 37).

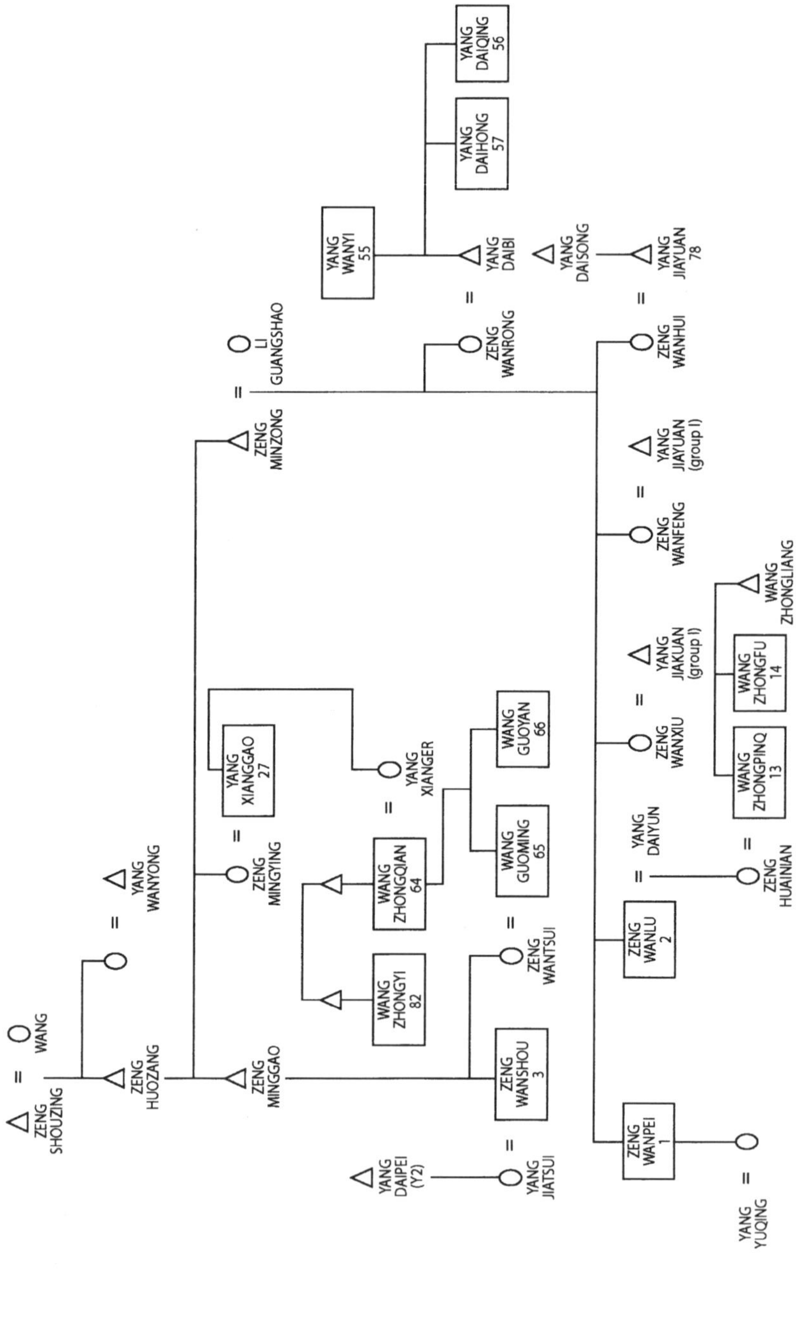

Diagram 36: All Zeng-Wang-Yang relations

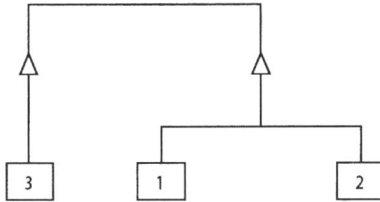

Diagram 37: Zeng Minggao's family

To employ a mode of analysis appropriate to the way in which these relations are actually phrased in the village, the diagram shows how the Zeng have been 'wife givers' to both the Yang and Wang, while the Wang have been 'wife-takers' from both. More importantly, while the Yang and Wang are themselves affinally related, both are in addition affinally related to the Zeng. It is clear that the Zeng have taken care to relate themselves to both the dominant clans in the village, and play a particularly pivotal part in the relations between these other two clans, since the Yang and Wang have formed relations of double affinity between themselves, rather as we have seen occurring within segments of the Li and Xie Chinese surnames, through the medium of alliances with the Zeng. Zeng marriages have allowed the Yang and Wang to forge a sense of identity between themselves beyond their own relationship of affinity, since both can and have married the Zeng, and this reinforces the centrality of the Zeng in village genealogical structures, emblematically expressed in the party secretaryship of the Zeng.

The Wang

To some extent we have considered the relations formed between the Zeng, Yang and Wang, but we may understand these more clearly if we adopt the vantage point of the Wang families settled in the main part of the village. The Wang form the crucial bridge between our consideration of the Zeng and the consideration of the dominant surname, the Yang, already undertaken. There were in fact three distinct and unrelated Hmong groups of Wang in the main village, all of whom had quite separately attached themselves to the dominant Yang in much the same way as the two Chinese Xie segments had attached themselves to the Li, and a further Wang lineage settled in Group One

The Wang I

Two of the three Wang groups in the main village had formed alliances not only with the Yang, but also with the Zeng. To deal first with the family I shall call Wang I, Wang Zhongping at household number 13, whose brother Wang Zhongfu was living at number 14, had married the daughter of Zeng Wanlu (Zeng Huainian) at number 3, who was Zeng Minggao's brother's son. The brother of both Wang Zhongping and Wang Zhongfu was Wang Zhongliang, who had lived apart from his two brothers for some time; their household was located further towards the centre of the village, downslope over the crest of the hill on the other side of the path. 38-year old Wang Zhongfu had married a Yang girl, the daughter of *Yang Wanzhong* of the Yang lineage Y3b and had one daughter. One of his father's sisters had married the cousin of Yang Wanzhong, Yang Wanhe, and another had married Yang Wanzhong, so that his own marriage was a real FZD one. His brother Wang Zhongping, aged 21, had as we've just seen married a Zeng, and was in the process of moving out of Wang Zhongfu's house to join his older brother Wang Zhongliang, his Zeng wife still not having moved in.

This was essentially a son-in-law lineage of Yang Wanzhong of Y3b lineage, who had helped them move recently into the village from Chengshen.

The Wang II

Another family of Wang, whom I call the Wang II, was represented by Wang Zhongyi (HH no.82). Wang Zhongyi lived in the south part of the village well over the hill from his FBS Wang Zhongqian (HH no.64), who lived with his two sons, Wang Guoyuan (HH no.66), and Wang Guoming (HH no.65) who had married the sister of Zeng

Wanshou (HH no.3).[1] So that both these two Wang families (Wang I and Wang II) had married Zeng girls, and we shall see that in both cases an initial affinal relationship with the Yang had been followed by a more strategic alliance with the family of the Gongxian party secretary. These Wang II had originally moved into the village as labourers just after the Liberation to work directly for *Yang Wanshu* (the elder brother of *Yang Wanheng* at household 19 and of *Yang Wanzhong* at household 15, of the dominant Y3b lineage) in exchange for land prior to land redistribution. They had effectively followed the Wang I into the village, who were already related to *Yang Wanzhong*, making use of their own brother-in-law relation with Yang Xianggao of lineage X1 but following the Wang I in entering into a relationship of economic support and dependency with the family of *Yang Wanzhong* and *Yang Wanshu* in Y3b. Like *Yang Wanshu's* family, they had lived in Group One until Land Reform when their position in the village improved.

Wang Zhongyi himself (HH no.82), aged 48, lived together with his Xiong wife and five young children (the eldest boy at school). His first cousin Wang Zhongqian (HH no.64), whom he had followed in moving into the village, had married the elder sister of Yang Xianggao (HH no.27, of the X1 lineage) (who has as we have seen married Zeng Minggao's sister, while Wang Zhongqian's son had married Zeng Minggao's daughter, so that relations were particularly close between these three families). Although Wang Zhongqian was recorded as living with his Yang wife and four children since his two eldest sons are listed as separate households (HH nos.65 and 66), in fact all three of these Wang households still remained together under the same roof.[2] Another daughter had married out to Yang Daisong's son (in lineage Y3a), and his son Wang Guoniang had just married Ma Jianzen, sister to households 76 and 75, as we see when we consider the position of the Ma. Wang Zhongqian had settled uxorilocally in the village after his marriage to Yang Xianggao's sister.

Like the Wang I, then, the Wang II had attached themselves both to the Yang and to the Zeng through marriages, and had moreover

---

[1] One household of 14, not 3 of 4, 4 and 4.

[2] Transforming these three households of 6, 4 and 4 members into one with 14.

attached themselves to two different segments of the Yang; both X1 and Y3a. And similarly to other cases we have considered, we see a kind of dual relationship being formed with the Zeng through the marriages of Wang Zhongqian and his son Wang Guoming. While a direct relationship of affinity with the Zeng had been formed through the marriage of Wang Guoming with the Zeng girl, his father had married into the same Yang family his daughter-in-law's family had married into, so that a relation of resemblance had been formed between the Wang II and the Zeng, who had both married into the same family of Yang Xianggao.

Moreover, Wang I and Wang II had established a similar relation of solidarity as well as of transferred affinity to those we have seen among the Chinese Li and Xie between themselves, through their marriages with different segments of the Yang, Wang I marrying into Yang lineage Y3b, Wang II into Yang lineages Y3a and X1.

The Wang III

The third Wang family in the main body of the village, the Wang III, was represented only by Wang Zhailing with his (second) Yang wife and son Wang Yingchen (who had a Ma wife) in households number 30 and 29 (again in fact in one house), located strategically between the two branches of the Chinese Li.[3] A mentally ill unmarried elder brother of Wang Zhailing, Wang Zhaiquan, also lived with him. Although the Wang III had no direct kinship connections with the other Wang families in the village, they addressed the Wang II respectfully as their *vaiv yig*, or FyB.

As the central position of the Zeng in terms of their affinal connections with the other groups in the village was reflected in their central location of their settlement, so Wang Zhailing's somewhat distant kinship connections with other groups was reflected in the peripheral position his house occupied in the village. One firm and important original liaison had been formed with a member of the Wutong Yang (as Diagram 38 shows), but otherwise the Wang III had more relations with the Yang of other villages in Gongxian.

---

[3] Since these two 'households' remained together, again two households of 3 and 7 members have become one with 10 (one unregistered) members.

Wang Zhailing's family had moved in to Wutong 60 years previously from the village of Fenghuang after their six lineages formerly living there had divided owing to their extreme poverty (each family had only a small patch of rice, they said). Wang Zhailing himself,[4] had married a Yang Guangshu of Fenghuang village, whose brother Yang Xuwen had married his first paternal cousin,Wang Xingnian. Again a kind of symmetrical 'sister' exchange had occurred here. And Wang Zhailing's sister, Wang Zhaizheng, had married *Yang Wanquan* (of the distant, 'Guotai', X4 line of the Yang genealogy). But it was his first cousin Wang Xingwen (the son of Wang Wunquan) who had married the elder sister of *Yang Wanlong*, one of the Wutong householders (HH no.59), FBS to *Yang Wanzhong* and *Yang Wanshu* of the Yang lineage Y3b. And their son Wang Yuanping had married another Yang girl of Fenghuang, Yang Xiyong. So Wang Zhailing, representing households 30 and 29, had formed a number of separate connections with the dominant Yang in the village. The Wang III, then, had particularly few affinal relations with the other Hmong surnames in the village; the main connection was with the dominant Y3b lineage of *Yang Wanlong*, and other connections with the Yang were more remote. Yet the Wang III had joined the village in exactly the same way as the Wang I and II; as impoverished sons-in-law to lineages of the dominant Yang. Indeed it was the Wang III who had made the first move, and the other two Wang families had then followed them. Surnames are closer with the Hmong than with the Han; all those with the same surname in the same generation are conceived of as brothers and sisters; the 'sisters' cannot be courted, but the 'brothers' may be asked for hospitality. These Wang groups, had originated from different places and could find no known ancestral bonds; nevertheless there was a sense of brotherhood between the Wang in the village which had been one of the reasons for their original settlement together.

Diagram 38 shows the relations of the Zeng and Wang to the Yang segments we have already considered, while Diagram 39 presents a simplified version of this. Diagram 40 presents an amended version of the Yang household settlement patterns

---

[4]   Wang Zhailing's son Yingchen had another son not recorded on the registration, bringing the population of their household to 11 rather than 10.

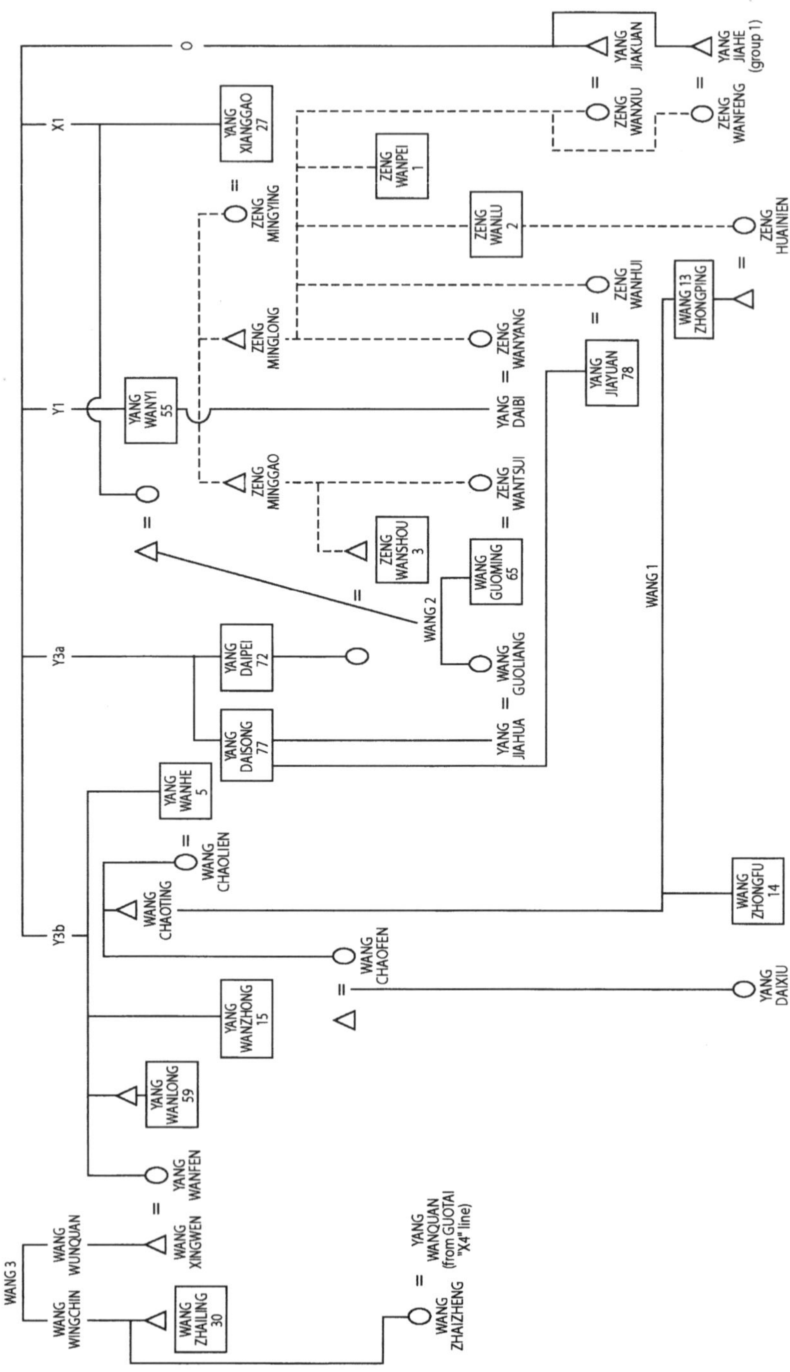

Diagram 38: Relations of the Zeng and Wang to the Yang

displayed in Chapter 6, showing the locations of other surnames in the village.

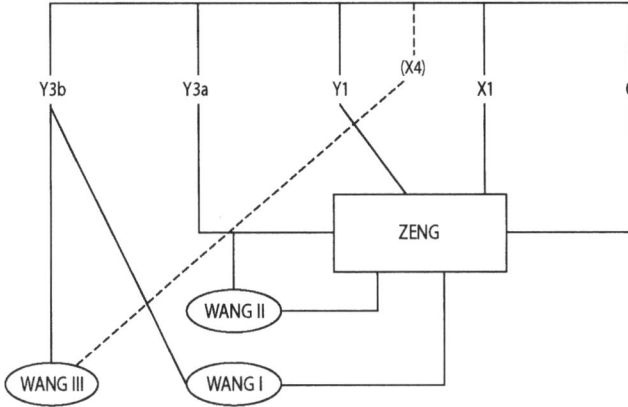

Diagram 39: Simplified version of relations of the Zeng and Wang to the Yang

KEY (Diagram 39)[5]
Wang Zhongfu: I
Wang Zhongyi: II
Wang Zhailing: III

The Wang were of particular interest in illustrating the process whereby impoverished Hmong lineages, through 'son-in-law' marriages, had moved into the village to strengthen the position of the Yang clan there, and particularly of its Y3b segment. But the nature of the inter-alliances they had formed also show the way in which relations of resemblance (through marrying into the same families as others) are conjoined with relations of contrast (through directly marrying them)[6] as part of a general strategy in the dialectical intertwining of identifications and differences, expressed through the medum of kinship and wedding ritual.

---

[5] The family of Wang You Cai in Group I have called Wang IV.

[6] Again see Kelly (1974).

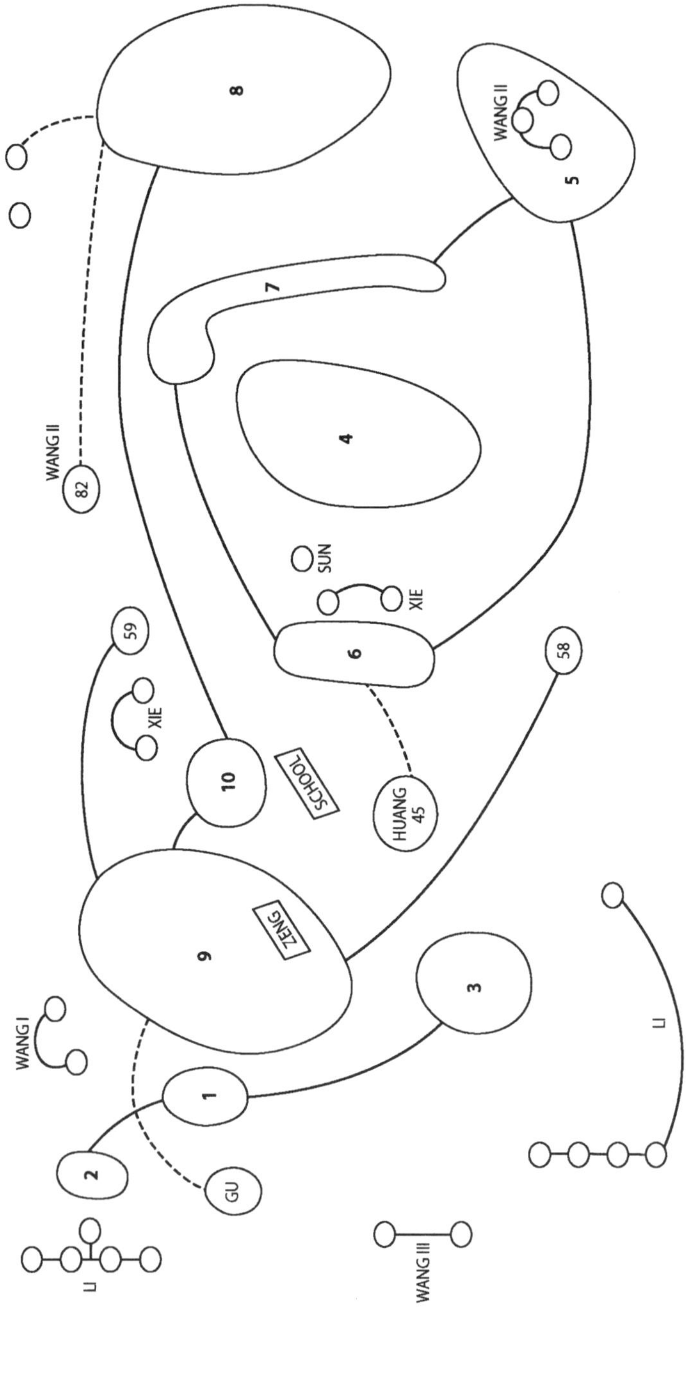

Diagram 40: Household settlement patterns

The Ma

The remaining Hmong surname in the main village was represented by the households of the two brothers, Ma (Muas in Hmong) Jiankang (HH no.75) and Ma Jianqing (HH no.76). Again close affinal relations had been formed between the recently incoming Ma and three segments of the Yang and one Wang family. While Ma Jianqing himself had married the daughter of Yang Jiating (L in Group One), his sister (Ma Jianying) had married the son (Yang Daizhi) of Yang Wanshu (of lineage Y3b, who had married into the Xiong family in C of Group One). Another of Ma Jianqing's sisters (Ma Jianzen) had married the brother of Wang Guoming at household 65 (Wang Guonian)—in the Wang II family—whose own sister (Wang Guoliang) had married the son (Yang Jiahua) of Yang Daisong (HH no.77). And another Wang II relative had married Ma Jiankang. Diagram 41 shows this.

Again this shows how the Y3b lineage of the Yang had been instrumental in facilitating the immigration of an affinally related surname, and although the Ma households were closest to Yang Daisong's own home in the village, they were not far from other households of the Y3b lineage or from the Wang II settlements, and also maintained close relations with the surviving sons of Yang Wanshu in Group One (O,P,Q and R).

Ma Jiankang himself, aged 37, who lived with his widowed mother who had been so grateful to the shamaness, had married a Wang Guoqin who was a cousin to his sister's husband, so that we find here a simple sister exchange (even if a classificatory one) with the Wang II, who were 'son-in-laws' to Yang Daisong in Yang lineage Y3a, at the same time as the Ma themselves had become 'son-in-laws' to the Y3b lineage of the Yang.

This was Wang Guoqin's second marriage; she had previously been married to another Ma, Ma Jianchuan, one of Ma Jiankang's FBS who had died young, so that this was a case of levirate within the lineage, explicable in terms of Ma Jiankang's poverty at the time of his marriage. She had brought with her into the marriage a young child of her own who would be brought up as effectively one of Ma Jiankang's own, again showing the enormous flexibility of the lineage system with regard to the transformation and disguise of individual identities.

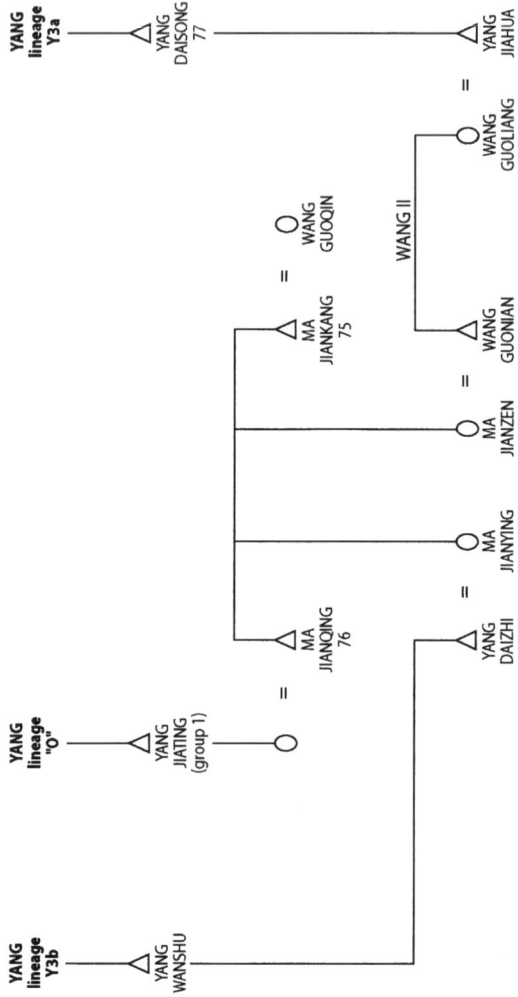

Diagram 41: Yang relations with the Ma

Ma Jianqing (HH no.76) lived with his Yang wife and two sons in close proximity to the house of his brother Ma Jiankang. Ma Yingao, their father, who had married a woman surnamed Han and had a Xiong mother, had moved into the Gongxian area from Junlian in 1944. I was told he had been 'escaping' from the Guomindang troops who had 'captured' him, but it is more likely that he was in an area which had fallen under Guomindang control, or was perforce a supporter of the Guomindang who had changed sides strategically. His widow took some pride in recounting a life of amorous adventures her husband appeared to have had before moving into the district, and claimed that he had really been fleeing from the relatives of a woman he had had an affair with who had been trying to beat him black and blue. It was his son Ma Jiankang (HH no.75) who had subsequently moved into the village to join his wife's Wang II relatives, and also to join the relatives they shared with them (Yang Daisong), and the other Yang of O and Y3b lineages (Yang Jiating; Yang Wanshu and Yang Wanzhong) they became related to through his sister's and brother's marriages.

There had been extensive marriages with other local Yang; Yang Zhao (HH no.25), the son of Yang Liping, had a young Ma wife as had his brother Yang Hong, and the whole of this Y3c lineage of the Yang addressed the Ma respectfully as their FB's WB ('uncles'). Yang Wanhua (HH no.62) had also married a Ma, as had his son Yang Daiying.

In particular, though, both Yang Daisong (HH nos.77-79) and his second cousin Yang Daihe (HH no.74), all of the Y3a lineage, had married Ma; Yang Daisong had married a Ma Jianfen and Yang Daihe had married a Ma Shaoxian, who were FBD of the two Ma households in the village.

This emphasises the particularly close relations of the Ma brothers to Yang Daisong's own Y3a group, which they had settled beside in the village. The Wang connection confirmed this, and their present relations with Yang Daisong's family eclipsed the significance of their other sister's marriage to Yang Wanshu's son of the Y3b lineage in Group One which had originally enabled them to move into the village as a 'son-in-law' lineage to the strong Y3b segment of the Yang. Not only had Ma males married Yang women extensively, but the reverse was also occurring. Diagram 42 shows the linkages between the Ma, Wang and Yang.[7]

The same general pattern of doubly confirmed kinship links we have seen elsewhere also asserts itself here; the Ma were brothers-in-law to the Wang II who were brothers-in-law to the Yang, as well as being brothers-in-law to the Yang themselves. The Ma thus affirmed through kinship links a sense of *identity* of a descent type with the Yang, through marrying into the same family the Yang married, at the same time as affirming a sense of affinal *difference* from the Yang through undertaking their own marriages with them.

In this chapter, we have seen something of the strategic nature of the alliances formed by the Zeng with other clans, as well as how the general dominance of the Yang has been expressed and confirmed in the way other clans had attached themselves to it through affinal ties.

In terms of the divisions of lineage expressed almost exclusively in ethnically Hmong terms in the village, and the pattern of alliances with other Hmong lineages which stretched out beyond these divisions, and considering the wider differences expressed between the Hmong and Chinese which are nevertheless ironically contradicted through the adoption of individual Han Chinese into Hmong lineages at critical junctures, it is of particular significance, as we saw in Chapter 2, that affinal alliances had beeen formed with the Gu, an aboriginal non-Hmong group of Miao nevertheless similarly defined in terms of a contrast to Chinese cultural identity, since here we may glimpse something of the importance of the local sense of history which is mustered to support present-day cleavages and identifications.

In the following two chapters, I attempt to show something of the intertwining of recollections of the past with the solidarities and rivalries of the present, through examining the rituals of wedding which bound certain segments of the Hmong of Wutong village with the Hmong of Wangwu, the main local centre of Hmong settlement.

---

[7] It was not possible to confirm all these linkages, in particular where Ma FBD relations were confirmed without further specification.

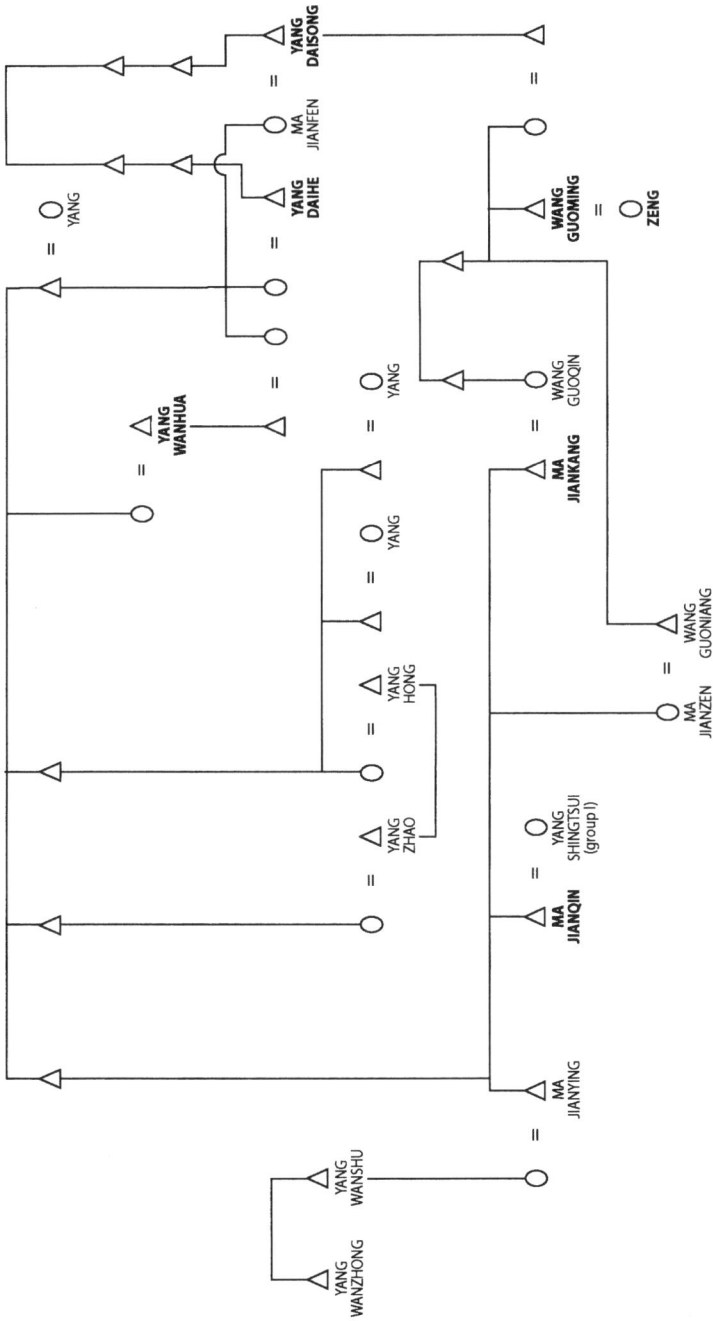

Diagram 42: The Ma, the Wang, and the Yang

CHAPTER TEN

THE WANGWUZHAI WEDDINGS

SONG OF THE GO-BETWEENS

First morning
We come here for no other reason
the Mother lives in the side room
and the Father lives in the middle room of the house
the Mother is honest and truthful in character
and the Father also has an upright temperament
the Mother could not sleep under a woollen quilt
and the Father slept badly under a silken quilt
the Mother thinks of the road of fortune that can link their
relatives
and the Father thinks of the way that their relatives can be
joined in marriage
the Mother arises at daybreak
and the Father gets up at first cock's crow
the Mother scatters rice to feed the chickens
and the Father calls the fowls to come and eat
the Mother catches a hen
and the Father seizes a cockerel
the Mother prepares food for the breakfast table
and the Father invites the go-betweens to be seated
They invite the two go-betweens to come and eat
the Mother has prepared the breakfast for us to eat
the Father has fetched water for us to drink
We have come here, bearing the golden umbrella
and carrying the quilt which is made of lambswool

We crossed the flat basin
and climbed up the steep bamboo slope
and walking down the slope into a fair valley
passed many villages of the Han people
and many homesteads of the Yi people
but those villages were unfitting to stay in
and the doors of their houses were not well matched

and we came to the forest of mulberry trees
and climbed nine ranges of mountains
to where the view was wide and far
so that we could see your good family in the distance

Well-tended gardens surround your house
and a beautiful sunflower grows in your home
virgin land is spread out behind your house
where grows a sunflower of silver and gold
within the pavilions and courtyards

We carried a bamboo sapling with us, clean and fresh
and placed it against the dragon door of your family home
my first leg crossed the porch of dragon veins
and I carried the quilt on my back
and my second leg crossed the dragon vein porch
and I carried the umbrella in my hand[1]

We came to the house of this noble family
for the purpose of marriage and wedding
we came to pick the golden and silver flower
to plant in the centre of the field
for the boy matches the girl
and the girl well suits the boy
as flowers blossom in couples
and fruit also ripens in pairs
we take them back as the roots and the seeds
for their descendants to multiply and prosper
and succeed the old ones generation after generation
they will boil water for the old ones
and offer tea to the elders

Second morning
(Ditto, ending) *We have been here for one night and two*
  mornings
and we stayed with this family
and must give them some trouble

---

[1] The 'dragon' metaphors emphasise the geomantic auspiciousness of the place.

—one more guest, one more bowl of water
one more guest, one more pinch of tobacco—
we came here for a purpose, hoping for an answer
which the Father's Brothers may discuss
when we came, we carried the bamboo sapling in our hands
and when we return, we shall decorate our heads with
flowers[2]
and we will send the message back to the boy's family
so they may be calm of heart

Third morning

(Ditto, ending) *We have been here for two nights and three*
mornings already
the reins (halter) of our horses are still fastened to the tree-
trunk
while we were here, we have troubled our host a great deal
—another chicken needs more grain
another duck needs yet more meal—
the host prepared the food for us to eat
but better keep it until May and June[3]
and we hope the girl's mother and father
will agree all things with the girl's Father's Brothers

In the best and most concise account I received of the formal structure of the wedding itself, it was summarised as follows;

1. The parents of the bride, as well as those girls who will accompany the bride, will all don new clothes. Then there will be a banquet before the bride's mother leads her weeping (quav tsoom) *out of the inner room, and the* zaa xaav ntxhais *(song of sending the bride) is sung.*

2. Paying homage (pe pu yiag) *to the ancestors by the bride before her departure* (faiv nas faiv txi)*, and her Grand Manager throws the rice out of the door to symbolise her departure. Then the umbrella* (tsoo kaum) *is held over her head, and her face will be covered with a piece of cloth.*

---

[2] The ritual of dressing the groom which takes place in the groom's house the night before he is to be married.

[3] The time for weddings.

3. Lunch is eaten halfway to the bridegroom's home (nosu). *This is a ceremonial lunch, which constitutes the part of sending the Bride to the Bridegroom's house, and the evils of the halfway are beaten back* (ntau xee). *And a bamboo sprout* (rhuv ntxoov) *and a branch of tung tree will be taken to be tied together, and a song to represent this is sung at the same time. The chief sender takes some rice out of the basket and gives it to the bride to eat, as does the Grand Manager*

4. Then there is the receiving of the bride's team near the bridegroom's home (quav tau). *The bridegroom's family build a fire* (hlua tes) *near or at some distance from the house. The bride's team stops then. The hosts of the bridegroom's family and the matchmakers offer tobacco* (nrua yeeb). *After beating back the spirits at the door of the house, the hostess (the groom's father's sister) comes out to receive the bride and her accompanying girls. The bride's older brother holds the main umbrella and her younger brother takes her hand. The aunt take the umbrella* (txaiv kaum) *from them. Then they enter the room. Different clans have different customs. Some will pay respects to the ancestors. Others just go around the fire in the central room* (tang)[4] *and then go to the hearthside* (qhov cu) *for a bit* (ib ntshi). *As for the men in the bride's team, first, they go around the fire in the house. Then two special tables are set out to entertain them* (tau ki). *First, tobacco is offered to each, then they drink some wine.*

5. At this time the Keys are given.. The Grand Manager (hauv tsoo) *of the bride's side will present keys to the Grand Manager of the bridegroom's side. Then a dialogue between them will occur* (haj zaa jiao ntsog). *Then members of the bride's family will make up a bed for her.*

(This is the end of the Sending of the Bride)

6. A great lunch (noj su) *is prepared for the bridal sending* (xaav tsoom) *team. Separate tables are laid for men and (later) the women. After this lunch, there will be time for fun and rest.*

---

[4] This is not always the central hall; at one wedding it was the right-hand side room of a tripartite house. That is, the Hmong traditionally had no concept of 'village', but defined local groups according to the descent groups they belonged to.

7. As evening falls, there will be a special supper (nao hmo) *at which words of unity are spoken. In some other places small boys and girls are allowed to take part in this meal. But here there are only seven from the sending team (as well as the bride).*

Women from the bridegroom's family also take part in this meal, at the same table. The bride's side offer a cock. The bridegroom's side present a hen. After they are cooked, divination by chicken tongue (sua qas nphlaib) *will take place. If the tongues are not damaged in any way, the signs will be very lucky. More feasting continues (and the cooks come out to see if the meal is alright, and are given some coins).*

8. Late at night there is the ceremonial washing of the bride's feet (ntxua teb). *More songs* (hub nkau) *may be sung, by both men and women.*

9. At midnight (xaav ntos), *payment is made by the bridegroom's family to the porters of the bride's wealth* (tua ntsauj).

10. After more festivities on the next morning, the bride's team return (nov des tche), *to give thanks to the bride's family, singing songs of the way* (haj zaa mus ki)...
(Yang Zijun)

Wutong village maintained its most extensive relations with the outside world, not through economic and trading links, nor through the political structures of party and government administration, but rather through networks of kinship and affinity which formed the basis of social relations both within and beyond the village, and through which a specifically Hmong identity was defined. This chapter concentrates on the Hmong of Gongxian as a wider community than that confined to a single village, through showing some of the relations which connected the Wutong Hmong to those of Wangwuzhai, the main centre of Hmong settlement in the region. It was in Wangwu that the sense of a local history shared generally by the Gongxian Hmong, and many local Han Chinese settlers, was most clearly mobilised in the form of varying appeals and claims upon it made by cleavages and divisions expressed in the rivalries between and within patrilineal clans which weddings attempted to overcome, only to reassert.

In the old Morganesque metaphors of blood and soil, which continue to inform academic discourse in China, the shifting cultivation historically practiced by Hmong and definitive of their identity by contrast to others is seen to privilege the fluidity of blood over the fixity of soil, since the territory of shifting cultivators is unfixed and impermanent, while it is mobile descent-defined lineages which form the stuff from which local identities are largely made. It was Cooper (1984) who first pointed out how unreal a concept 'village' (*zos*) has been for the Hmong; under the system of shifting cultivation, 'villages' tended to be established by the members of a single local descent group, and it has really been only under modern conditions of development that villages containing several surnames have emerged in Thailand and Laos.[5] When questioned about the reasons for this in South East Asia, Hmong men usually say that having many surnames living in one place together makes *courting and wedding* easier than in the past, when you had to travel long distances to find brides. However, the most important unit of social action for the Thai Hmong, at the local level, is still the local lineage segment, which is rigidly patrilineally defined and exogamous and extremely widely distributed, and determines the affinal relations which may be formed. It is often said that a Hmong surnamed Wang from Thailand would expect to be treated as a classificatory brother and receive hospitality if he were to visit a Hmong surnamed Wang in south China, and to a large extent this is true.

Despite the fact that the Hmong of Sichuan have been permanently settled for at least two centuries, this idiom of extensive patrilineal descent, seen as specifically Hmong, still prevails among the Hmong of China, and it has been partly the intention of some of the previous chapters to show how this is so. 'Blood', one might say, is not yet entirely bound to the 'soil'. In terms of 'Chinese religion', a contrast between domestic ancestral worship and the institutionalised worship of territorial deities (Feuchtwang 1992) has framed classic discussions of the opposition between principles of kinship and of territory. Among the Chinese Hmong there are as yet no Chinese-style temples or ancestral halls which might serve as the

---

[5] That is, the Hmong traditionally had no concept of 'village', but defined local groups according to the descent groups they belonged to.

focus of communal worship by a local lineage, nor are there yet any local territorial deities (*tutigong*, *tutipo*) who should be sacrificed to, as there are in the Han villages. However, Hmong intentions to establish such ancestral halls were being expressed, as we have seen in the case of the Yang of Wutong village, and the Hmong in Gongxian did indeed pay their respects to a little shrine of the Chinese deity Guan Yin perched atop a nearby mountain whenever they passed by it. The sense of attachment to, and identification with, a local place was much more evident among the settled Sichuan Hmong than it was among the more migratory Hmong of Thailand, Laos or Vietnam, and in Gongxian this sense of place was most clearly expressed by the Hmong of Wangwu, which claimed to have been the original site of Hmong settlement for the whole region. At the same time relations with other Hmong clan and lineage members were still known and maintained across wide distances within Sichuan and across the borders into Guizhou and Northwest Yunnan, much as they are in South East Asia, although some striking differences of specific marriage practices had emerged between the different areas of Hmong settlement in China.

A transition from a classic system of bridewealth systems to a more complex one of reciprocal marriage exchanges and inheritances was slowly taking place for most of the Hmong of China which was in evidence in Gongxian and neighbouring counties. In Gulin county, a more traditional area, the importance of true bridewealth still outweighed that of either direct or indirect dowry payments,[6] while in Gongxian a system focused more on gifts of imperishable goods by the bride's family to the new couple, on what is seen as a traditional Han Chinese model, was widely practiced. Yet marriages regularly took place between these two counties, and wherever they did, the patriarchal androcentrism underlying both these systems prevails; it was the 'customs' of the *bridegroom's* area which had to be followed. So that in these marriages (although this is not recognised), there should in fact be a constant flow of the majority of goods and wealth into Gongxian, the richer region, out of Gulin, the poorer region, even when, following the dictates of post-marital patrilocal residence, a Gongxian woman goes to live with her

---

[6] Goody (1973).

husband in Gulin. It may indeed be in such unintended and unrecognised effects of localised cultural systems that history has witnessed a general transformation of bridewealth into more complex systems of marriage exchange, associated with wealthier regions and classes. Although traditional Han dowry systems may have disappeared under the impact of agricultural collectivisation and the abolition of wealth differences to become something more like the bridewealth system generally practised by Hmong,[7] the trend towards dowry-giving following economic reform in Gogxian would seem to confirm the association of dowry-oriented systems with 'wealth-based status competition' argued by Harrell and Dickey (1985). Wangwuzhai, however, was also in Gongxian county, and marriage practices were similar in the two areas of Wangwuzhai and Wutong.

The establishment of firmer patterns of settled sublineage co-residence must have been complicated by the wars between the Guomindang and CCP, and the mobility of landless peasant labourers before 1949, and by the Land Reform campaign (which was considerably delayed in this area). Thus as we have seen a number of households in Wutong had moved in as peasant labourers during the Kuomintang era or been granted land there in the 1960's. Yet with both less geographic and social mobility since then, some more traditional tendencies towards lineage co-residence had reasserted themselves, and we have seen this very clearly in the patterns of co-residence expressed in the settlement of Wutong; whenever possible and wherever given the chance, it seemed, members of the same descent group or even surname had chosen residential proximity, while their descendants had as if naturally settled nearby, and this was not always very difficult since while the members of a single sublineage may have dispersed into several villages, these villages were usually not very far away from each other. So that with natural increase and some individual relocation, a tendency not so much towards single-surname villages as towards villages in which one surname was clearly dominant had become apparent among the Sichuan Hmong generally (as among those in the nearby areas of Yunnan and Guizhou). Wutong village was perhaps

---

[7] As Parish and Whyte (1978) showed in Guangdong.

exceptional in the extent of its overwhelming domination by members of the same surname, which had been achieved through a number of contingent means; a strong local leadership, a high rate of natural increase, and the official amalgamation of part of a neighbouring village where the majority shared the same ancestors as the majority in Wutong, but in general most Hmong villages in the region did show a clear domination by a single surname. What was not found among the Hmong of Wutong and neighbouring villages was an elaborate systematisation of intermarriages with members of different surnames in the same village of the type for example which has become increasingly common among the Hmong in Thailand as settlements which used to be shifting have become more permanent. Although we have stressed the importance of the affinal relations formed between different Hmong surnames within the village, in some ways this is misleading; their range of affinal relationships stretched much more widely than this, across the whole county and even into neighbouring counties and provinces, as this chapter may show. Yet there was also a tendency for a cluster of marriages to occur between different surnames in particular villages or areas somewhat wider than officially recognised villages; particularly strong bonds of affinity united the Hmong of Wutong with the Hmong of Wangwuzhai, and social visits and ritual relations were common between the two villages.

This wide geographic extension of Hmong affinity was in strong contrast to the affinal patterns demonstrated by the Han Chinese in the village of Wutong, which showed very clear tendencies towards village endogamy, although notably few alliances between themselves and the Hmong. I think we may suggest that this was because the clan-lineage has remained a basic unit of social intercourse for the Hmong in a stronger sense than it has for the Han. And the clan-lineage unit has become as particularly marked for the Hmong who are highland swiddeners in Indochina as it has continued to be for the permanently settled Hmong of Sichuan. The patrilineal Hmong clan in the highlands of Indochina has remained strictly exogamous in a way it has not for the highland Yao of South East Asia, whose kinship system has become virtually bilateral (Miles 1989). Marriages do now generally take place between Han Chinese members of the same surname who have no recent common ancestor, but they still do not for the Hmong of China, who are in this respect unlike other Miao groups such as the Hmu of Guizhou or the Gho Xiong of Hunan (who have only recently adopted a unilineal system of descent on the Han Chinese model). Yet the kind of long-term permanent settlement which the Hmong have undergone in Sichuan since 1573 might have been expected to privilege particularistic patches of soil over wide-ranging ties of blood, and lead to more tendencies towards village endogamy.

This Hmong perpetuation of more wide-ranging systems of affinal connection than is common among the Han is a 'sign' which can be variously interpreted; it could be taken as simple evidence of the less advanced stage of social evolution represented by such an ethnic minority, a clinging to primordial ties of descent and affinity of the type largely dis-avowed by the more urbanised Han—as the more traditional of Marxist Chinese ethnographers would undoubtably claim; or (since the wide extent of these Hmong affinal relations is mostly unrecognised by Chinese scholars) the wide-ranging networks of Hmong affinity might be considered an aspect of resistance to that state hegemony of which the culturally Han Chinese claim to be the bearers. For localisation is in fact an aspect of both state and nationalist strategy,[8] and an affinal strategy which continues to challenge that colonialist attempt to administer on the basis of tying specificied cultural essentialisms to particular localities of place may be seen as a tactic which represents an (implicit, potential) challenge to the kind of homogenisation of social identities demanded by a modernizing nation-state at local levels; a refusal to be pinned down to a fixed identity, associated with a specific ('national minority') locality which can be treated in specific ways, according to specific policies; on the contrary, such affinal networks may be seen as reflecting a demand for cultural fluidity and social independence, transcending of the bounds of (state-defined) 'local territory' in favour of a wider notion of identity which, as 'Hmong', is seen as of a higher order than the specified and fixed localisations of identity demanded by the modern state

Wangwuzhai, where many of the Wutong villagers maintained kinship links, a stockaded encampment running from 900 to 1,500m. above sea level, was made up of two official villages located in

---

[8] As perhaps only De Certeau (1984) has clearly seen, in his consideration of the construction of a category of 'folk-lore' by scholarship in 19th.century France.

Luobiao *xiang* (Xinhua and Xinzhuang) and three more in that of
Luodu (Paofang, Nanmu, and Caomen), and had a mixed population
of Hmong and Chinese numbering 4,002 in all. The Hmong
surnames represented in the village, in order of their numerical
strength, were the Wang, Tao, Li, Xiong, Liu, Yang, Ma and Zhang.
It was Wangwuzhai where the missionary scholar and collector
Graham had mainly worked during the 1930s, at which time there
had been significant Christian conversions, and Graham was still
remembered by the older villagers, as was his daughter who had
revisited the area in the early 1980s. The first of five primary schools
for Hmong in the district had been established here under Christian
auspices, in 1931, and was still running. Wangwuzhai enjoyed
particularly close relations with Wutong, and there were regular
intermarriages between the two areas.

We had come to Wangwuzhai to see two marriages, and recorded
the main part of the first from the bridal parting to the bride's
procession and reception at the bridegroom's house, and the rituals
on the previous evening at the groom's house at the second as well as
attending some parts of the later rituals in the groom's house at the
second wedding. We were accompanied by a crowd from Wutong
including Yang Qingbai and my research assistant, Mr. Peng
Wenbing , as well as Yang Wanheng (of the Y3b lineage), Yang
Dailu, branch party secretary (*dangzhibushuji*) and *qeej* player of
Wutong, whose father Yang Wanyu was the brother of Yang Zhijun
of the X3 line, and most importantly by old Yang Wanjun of the Y2a
lineage, who was a wedding specialist and 'Grand Manager' of the
first wedding and, apart from Yang Qingbai , who was as we shall
see being appealed to to resolve a number of village disputes, the
most seminal figure in both weddings.

The Process of Betrothal and Wedding

In this section I present a composite account of the wedding process,
drawn mainly from the wedding of a girl called Yang Dainiang from
Wutong to Liu Fucheng of Wangwu, and of bride Zhou Damei to
groom Wang Zhongqin of Wangwu to whom the Yang of Wutong
were related. The stylized, mannered way in which the Hmong view
their own customs and traditions, will be apparent and it is
something of this I have tried to convey here. While the weddings we

saw did not correspond in all details to the ideal process as described, nevertheless they approximated to this model and deviated from it only reluctantly, by mistake, or because of expense and accident, although there were occasionally significant differences of clan or locality. Of the many accounts I received of the long process, taking sometimes many years, of betrothal leading to wedding, the following was undoubtably the fullest;

'If a man wishes to get married in this district, before the formal matchmaking[9] a visitor must be sent to the girl's family to see whether or not they are willing and to return to the boy's family to say that if go-betweens come, they will not be refused.[10] And before these matchmakers (tus qau), who should be people trusted by both families) can be chosen, the suitor must have invited them both to a feast in his home and have kowtowed to them in the middle hall of his house. Then the two go-betweens are sent to the girl's family, carrying between them two bags of sugar bound with red-threaded embroidery for the girl's mother, a pair of buffalo horns to drink from, two bottles of wine for the girl's father, and two sheets of tobacco and an umbrella which they will leave there. Usually the family will ask them to return after one month to give them time to consider the match.

One month later, if there is no objection on either side, the matchmakers will return again to the bride's house, bearing with them the same gifts. The purpose of their second visit is to get the parents' consent to the proposal. Again they bring two bags of sugar, two bottles of wine and also two pieces of cloth—one for a blouse and the other for a skirt. If her parents favour the match they will accept the gifts and tell the matchmaker they will ask their daughter after they have gone.[11] The match is decided at this time.

---

[9] too hmoo.

[10] In Weixin this first visitor should not be a go-between, but in Gongxian it usually is.

[11] Before Liberation arranged marriages were the norm, claimed several informants, and boys and girls could not be married without their parents' permission. This is certainly the Han practice. They used to have marriage by capture but now very seldom. This is still practised where the bride's family don't approve of the match; she will steal away to her lover's house, and later present a basket of corn and wine to her parents, and register the marriage.

The third time their gifts are the same, but this time the boy accompanies them to meet the girl.[12] *The matchmakers may still be asked to come back again later to settle the marriage payments. If no date has been set for the girl to visit the home of her husband-to-be on the second visit, then a date will now be set.*

On the main, second visit, they have to enter the girl's house by the main door. They should try to arrive from an easterly direction, so that if the girl's house already faces east there will be no problem, but if it faces south, they may have to go around a bit. On entering, they will find their bags hung up on the eastern house-post, and the umbrella on the eastern middle post, the ncej taag.

When the bridal side hang up this umbrella, made of 'sweet-and-bitter' bamboo, in the central hall of an unmarried girl's house, it is a sign that they are willing to entertain the marriage being proposed; arrangements cannot proceed further unless the umbrella is hung. Later this umbrella will be presented to the bridegroom's party when they finally leave the bride's house during the course of the wedding.

The girl's father and mother and family will receive the two go-betweens, and some wheat is fried for the girl's family. They stay with the girl's family for three nights. On the morning of the first day, the go-betweens bring some wine and tobacco to the bedroom of the girl's parents and sing the song of marriage before the bed. If the parents favour the marriage, they will then prepare a feast for the go-betweens.

After this meal, the go-betweens carry tobacco and wine around the village to visit the villagers, and sing songs at each house. Then they return to the girl's home for the second night. The next morning they again present wine and tobacco and sing the second song at the parent's bedroom, and again go around the village singing. That night they again stay in the girl's home. And the third morning is the same, when the third song is sung. And if the girl's parents agree to the engagement, they will try to find their own two go-betweens to discuss affairs with the visiting go-betweens.

---

[12] In Gongxian the boy accompanies the matchmakers on their first visit.

But usually it is only women and children who come to visit the girl's family to start with. They make some excuse for dropping by, such as having lost something or wanting to borrow something from the girl's family. And whenever anyone comes in, the groom's two go-betweens have to offer them both wine and tobacco, and sing the third song to them. And according to whether these visitors' impressions are favourable or not, it will be decided whether to invite go-betweens on behalf of the girl's family. The visitors report to the girl's go-betweens, and then they can agree to come to the girl's house.

Either on this visit, or on the third visit, the boy's relatives including his fathers' brothers visit the girl's home with gifts for her relatives, including her mother and father, mother's brother, father's sister and father's sister's husband. They also bring a cock and a hen, tobacco, clothing and pork, and place all on a ceremonial table. Two go-betweens now represent the girl. The boy's go-betweens sing a song and offer wine and tobacco to the girl's go-betweens, who respond. There is a kind of competition of songs, between the two pairs of go-betweens, the boy's go-betweens pleading with them to accept the marriage, the girl's go-betweens again and again refusing, until finally they agree.

The boy's go-betweens will ask to speak with the girl's father's elder and younger brothers, but they don't come, the girl's go-betweens represent them. After the boy's go-betweens have ritually saluted (ua yim) those of the girl, the girl's go-betweens will ask the boy's go-betweens in song, when coming there, had they seen a peacock (tus ncag)?[13] *They will answer, yes, they saw one—and that is why they have brought two chickens to be sacrificed to examine the tongue-bones for omens of the marriage. If the omens are good, the girl's family will prepare a table of wine and they will all ceremonially drink together what is known as the 'consenting cup', at the 'feast of consulting the omens' (noj qab sau nphlaib). Two tables are put together for this, with the boy's go-between seated to the east and the girl's go-betweens seated to the west. And the boy's go-betweens will*

---

[13]   ua yim refers to a ritual bowing of the body and offering of cupped hands; ua pe is the full prostration, repeated thrice.

*place some cash under a leg of the table to keep it steady; this money
will be kept by the girl's go-betweens.*

*And the girl's go-betweens will ask in song, when you came here, did
you cross over or under or through the bridge? If they crossed
under, it means that the boy's generation is younger than the girl's;
if over, that they are older than the girl's; if through, that they are in
the same generation.*[14] *And they will sing, did you come by road or
across the fields? 'By road' means the two families are already
related; 'across the fields' means they have no relations.*

On the table there are two bottles and four cups.

*The girl's go-betweens also ask in song, did you see a big flat stone
on the road? Were there four holes in it? Was there any water in the
holes? When they sing like this, the boy's go-betweens must
replenish their cups.*

*And they will ask, did you see many leaves on the trees on the way?
If you saw many leaves, you should collect some so we may sit down
on them and discuss things. This riddle refers to the amount of
money which the boy's family should give.*

Each riddle is one song.

*And they will ask, if it was raining, did it rain heavily or only a little?
If heavily, it means they are really willing to marry.*

*The girl's go-between will ask the groom's side to prepare meat and
wine for the wedding feast, and skirts and clothes,* siv *and* sev *(belts
and aprons), head-dresses and pairs of shoes. This is the* kua mis
*(tears and milk; bridewealth), the part of the bride's dowry which
the boy's family must pay, and how much it has to be must be
negotiated between the four go-betweens. Here we usually ask for
'wet gifts' of 60* jin *of wine, 120* jin *of meat, sometimes one pig, and
'dry gifts' of six 'sets'* (chim) *of clothes, but sometimes for 80* jin *of
wine, 160* jin *of meat, and eight sets of clothing. All must be
embroidered, with three arm-bands, and also there should be two
sets of silk clothes, also embroidered and with three arm-bands,*

---

[14] To be in the same generation is most important. In terms of personal age,
brides may have generally been older than grooms in the past, but not today.

which are used to dress the dead. If there are eight skirts, with aprons, at least four of these should have batik and embroidery. One skirt, takes 24 chw *(feet) of cloth. The white belts are 0.3* chw *wide and about 4* chw *long. There should be one plain and one embroidered turban,and half the belts should be embroidered and with batik, and half the aprons too. And two pairs of white leggings, 24* chw *long, 1 pair of shoes with iron studs, 1 pair made out of cloth. The groom must also give some clothes to the bride's family's in-married women, to her mother, her mother's mother and her father's mother.*

At this meal the boy's go-betweens also tell those of the girl the amount of wine, pork and sugar for the feast they have already brought, and what is for whom, after which the girl's go-betweens count the betrothal gifts and take them away. Before they finally depart, the go-betweens should also meet around the table to finalise all the arrangements for the sending off and reception of the bride; if we have sent a buffalo or a sheep to your family, what do you have to send with the bride, besides her mother's brother and father's brother? After agreement has been reached, the matchmakers all ua yim *to each other.When all is settled, meat and wine, clothes and skirts, the boy's go-betweens will return home to inform the boy's family what has been resolved.*

So then they will prepare all these things.

After all the clothes have been made and sent to the bride, and the bride has visited her new home, a wedding date is fixed to 'receive the bride' (thov nyaa*).*

And the Chief Sender (bridesmaid) for the bride must be invited long before the date for the wedding is set; at least ten days before.

So that the boy's side must choose an auspicious date for the wedding and prepare meat and wine and go to inform the girl's family of the date (this is the third visit of the go-betweens). And after the girl's parents have agreed to the date, the boy's go-betweens will return to the boy's family to tell them that the date has been agreed.

On the evening before the bride comes to her new home, there are three procedures which take place in the groom's house. First there is the tcauv paa *('putting flowers on the groom'), which is the donning of all the layers of wedding clothes by the husband-to-be. And there is the* pej ta yiag hau ciag *('groom offers wine to the elders'), which he must do before the ancestral altar to every category of relative, whether they are present or not, as their names are called out, as he dons his new clothes. And also there is the* yiav nbeig pes hab trau *('friends or young relatives of the groom play jokes on him'), some teasing and horseplay as his friends and relatives call out advice for the marriage.*

The day before the bride is received into her new home, the groom's side sends wine, pork and sugar for the feast to her home. These senders are feasted by the bride's family after their gifts are received, and homage is also paid to the bride's ancestors with these gifts on the table.

On the lucky day, the boy's family prepare food and wine and carry it to the girl's home. Again they must arrive from the east. The girl's family will place everything in the middle room, in the ancestral place. They have prepared two tables in the middle room with plates of walnuts, chestnuts and edible seeds and cups are put out. The girl's father's brothers and other close relatives will join the meal to represent the girl's family.

After eating and drinking, they will spend the night there, and in the evening the girl's family should give them a big feast, and after the feast the girl's ceremonial managers have to place two tables with matching grains in the middle room, and lay out all the food and wine they have brought with them on the table, and put everything on the table as well as wine in four cups, to be offered to the bride's mother and her father, her father's elder and her father's younger brother, as they sing a song inviting them to come and eat, the song of the 'origin of the wedding table'.

They also should have prepared some suger sweets, wine, sunflower seeds and chestnuts to send to the girl's kwtis *(lineage relatives) on the next day. On the second day, the bride's father's brothers will send these to other families in their lineage.*

And the girl's masters of ceremony and her father's brothers have to count everything, to see if it is all correct, and then agree to receive the gifts. And the girl's family will give them a small banquet, and one day later the cooks will be entertained by the boy's family, presented with some tobacco and wine and paid respects to and thanked for preparing the feast. And also they have to argue about whether the knife should cost 1.2 or 2.4 yuan.

When the boy's family brought all the meat and wine to the bridal house everything had to be in even pairs.

On the second morning at the bride's home, the girl's father's mother will prepare breakfast for the boy's party—for not only the boy has come, but also his father's brothers and at least four people to carry everything, so there must be eight or ten people in their party altogether, usually including his father.

After this breakfast, the girl's father's brothers invite the boy's father's brothers to go out with them and party with their neighbours. But the boy's side will say that they have to go back now, so the girl's father's mother and father's brothers will prepare more wine on two tables with cups for everyone, and they will have the 'sending off the guests' (xaa qhua) ceremony. And then the groom's party return home.

As they prepare to depart from the girl's home, the boy's father's brothers will ask the girl's father's mother to come out of the house, and the father's brothers will have the boy prostrate himself to her; from this time on, the boy should address his wife's parents as if they were his own. Then the bride's parents will ask the boy to stay with them for a few days. When he says he cannot and must return home, the girls' father's mother will prepare a new set of clothes to give to the boy. If they haven't prepared such a suit, they will give him ten or twelve or twenty yuan for new clothes. And as they leave the girl's house, her sisters will have prepared some clean water to sprinkle over the boy's family, signifying that the bride has been given. Even if the boy stays, they still sprinkle this water.

Some lineages have the boy's mother wave a rooster three times around the new bride's head before she enters the groom's house to dispel her evil influences'...[15]

---

[15] Most of the latter part of this process can actually be accomplished in three days, with the main visit of the go-betweens on the first day, and the sending of meat

The complexity and elaboration of the detail, the punctilious etiquette which, it is felt, should be strictly followed if the occasion is to perform its performative task, is particularly clear in this account. The whole process leading up to wedding, like the wedding itself, is carried through and conveyed by songs which mark each important moment. An example of the antiphonal songs which can be sung before the groom's party leaves the bride's house was recorded at a village near Wutong, Fenghuang;

> The Groom's Side: *This girl's family have put a lot of wine and meat on the table to invite us here, this family intends to invite us here and has placed much wine and meat on the table, this family doesn't wish us to leave, why have you killed pigs and prepared wine, and sent so many people here?*

> The Bride's Side: *We know you have come here wanting to pick a flower, you just tell us about it all frankly, and if the girl's Father's Brothers speak words of agreement, then we can all open our mouths and speak together*

> The Groom's Side: *The Lady and Lord (we represent) live in a great house, in a mighty room, the Lady has so many relatives and the Lord has so many kinsfolk living with them, so we have carried goods and treasures to the girl's noble family to send tidings of wedding to this family, it seems this marriage will be an excellent one, it is the wedding of the girl daughter, so we will mark this wedding with a cup of wine, and we ask you to persuade the girl's mother and father, to consent to this matching of mates*

> The Bride's Side: *Aye, when you begged us for this match, you spoke sweet and pleasant words, but if we agree that this*

---

and wine for the feast to the girl's house, their departure the following morning as another team from the boy's house sends the clothes and skirts, which will be counted on two tables at a banquet at the girl's house that evening while the groom also has a banquet in his house (the 'donning of flowers', and the collection of the bride on the third day.

flower should bloom within your household, we do wonder whether she will be treated fair and well

The Groom's Side: *Have no fears on that score, we will treat her well indeed*

The Bride's Side: *You come here from the boy's family, you carried the umbrella and many things with you, when you came here did you see a big flat stone? Did it have four holes in it? Did you see any water filling those holes?*

The Groom's Side: *We crossed the low valleys, and scaled the high mountain, past a great stone rock, with water more than filling up its four holes*[16]

The Bride's Side: *When you came here, in the middle of the way, on the side of the mountain there were many horses and cattle grazing, did you see if they had lost their shoes, and were the mules' and cattles' feet uneven?*

The Groom's Side: *There were many cattle and horses grazing beside the mountain paths, my eyes could not cover them all, all sure-footed and of upright stance*[17]

The Bride's Side: *When you came here, in the middle of the way, on the side of the mountain there were many bamboos growing, with many sections, was it us who asked you to cut them down, or did you ask us to cut them down?*

The Groom's Side: *Together we cut down the many bamboos growing in the middle of the path, together we go foward across the mountains*[18]

---

[16] This means the boy's go-betweens should stand up to replenish their cups, which they do.

[17] This means the boy's go-betweens should put some money under the legs of the girl's go-betweens' bench to steady it, which they do.

[18] The bamboo is always green, and grows very quckly, and from one branch can grow nine, which is why it represents growth.

The Bride's Side: *When you came here, in the middle of the way, did you see the swallows with no feathers on their backs? Did you see the partridges with no feathers in their plumage? We shall see how you can put the feathers back on their backs again*

The Groom's Side: *Feathers coating the backs of the swallows, plumage covering the backs of the partridges and wood-fowl, silver and gold filling up the wooden chests, and a beautiful sunflower growing in the gardens*[19]

The Bride's Side: *Nine days you have come here to ask for this marriage, and ten days you have come here to take the bride back to your home, if you wish to do so, you may take her back to your home*[20]

The Bride's Side: *When you take these bamboo horns back home, where will you keep them? Will you put them on a high place, or place them in a low place?*

The Groom's Side: *Yea, we vouch to you that when we take these bamboo horns back, we will keep them in a high place, we will put them in a good place. Please tell the girl's Mother and Father to have no fear...*[21]

On leaving the Zhou bride's house in Wangwuzhai, on the morning of the wedding, the groom's Grand Manager, Wang Xaojin, sang:

We come to the host's family, today we will return to the city and say farewell to the host. We brought our brothers here for more than a day and more than a night. If we have spoken any improper words, we beg the host to pardon us, to forgive us

---

[19] This means the boy's go-betweens should give some money to the girl's go-betweens, which they do.

[20] Now the girl's go-between take their pair of bamboo drinking horns and present their handles to the boy's go-betweens.

[21] It is my great regret that I cannot reproduce here the music, and the gestural actions, which accompany these partly improvised recitations.

The bride's Second Manager, Zhou Xaozhen, sang:

> *You distinguished guests came here, we have good guests but there are no good hosts here*

Then the bride's matchmakers called out:

> *take out the meat! light the incense and the candles! ask Zhongqin (the groom) to come! this family's mother and father, the bridegroom* ua yim *(pay homage)! Host, matchmaker, bride's father's elder and younger brothers, come here!*

Then Wang Xaojin sang:

> *We have stayed here for one day and one night. It seems that the time has come: we plan today to go back: we raised the dust on the host's floor: after we leave the host will sweep three times with the broom to the stove: sons and daughters filll the house to catch up with your forebears: sweep three times to the central hall: sons and daughters fill the house and endure for a hundred years*

And Zhou Xaozhen declaimed:

> *Things are like this, we have good guests without good hosts, take away the good words, the bad words discard halfway*

Then Wang Qijun, the bride's Grand Manager, chanted:

> *To plant an umbrella in the valley, it will have branches and bud: to plant it in the fields, it will also have branches and bud: flowers bloom in pairs: seeds grow in couples: both families have their places for wine and for meat, and their places for the bride and bridegroom to come and go (to visit): may their children prosper and be strong*

Before the groom's party leaves the bride's home preparatory to the bridal procession which departs later for the groom's home, the *bride's txiv yig vaiv laug* (representatives of her father's elder and younger brothers) are called over to stand in a row to be prostrated to, and the song thanking the hosts for their hospitality is sung.

Informants concurred that wedding Officials should include the Grand Manager (*hauv tsoo*), the Lesser Manager (*la tsoo*), External and Internal Masters of Ceremony (*ntchauv tsej*), the Offerers of Tea and Tobacco, the Cook or Cooks, the Couple in charge of Grain, the Couple in charge of the Loft (where the gifts are stored), the Two Book-Keepers, the Couple in charge of the Fire, the Couple in charge of the Wine, and the Couple in charge of Cups, Bowls and Chopsticks. Inevitably, not all these roles are precisely allocated to separate individuals in a consistent way. But the offices of Grand and Lesser Manager must be strictly allotted, both for the groom and the bride, and often these roles are fulfilled by those who have been go-betweens during the process of betrothal. Permission for the marriage is supposed to be granted first by the bride's parents (*nas txi*), then by her brothers (or their wives) (*tisveij*), and finally by the lineage (*kwtis*) as a whole, and this is a pattern generally followed. Traditional Hmong marriage is not generally arranged by families prior to the couple meeting; it is the result of a couples' own inclinations, following a period of courting. In the Gongxian area there had been tendencies towards the arranging of marriages on a Han model in the past, but these had lessened with socialist reforms. Now most matches did result from the wishes of the couple concerned, although opportunities for free courtship were much more limited than had been the case in the past.

The symbolism of the parasol, which haunts also Hmong death rituals and is often said to symbolise the tiers of heaven, is particularly important at weddings, and as the groom's party departs from their final visit to the future bride's home the parasol originally presented to the bride's family during the course of betrothal will be ceremonially returned to them. The following verses sung on this occasion were recorded from Yang Dainiang's wedding in Wangwu.

ZAA KAUM *(GIVING THE FIRST UMBRELLA TO THE GROOM'S PARTY ON THEIR DEPARTURE)*[22]

This umbrella is made of bamboo,
standing for the basis of match-making,
today this umbrella will be returned,
sent back to the house,

---

[22] To *ha zaa* is to sing a song when giving gifts, on celebration, while to *hu nkauj* is to sings a song for mourning or instruction. They are sung on different occasions, and have different notes and tunes.

placed in the central hall,
planted among the flowers and the fruits

when the flowers are in blossom they are in couples,
when fruits ripen from their seeds they are in couples,

like the waves of the Yangtse River,
like the Great Bridge of Nanjing,
stamp on it and it will not break,
trample on it and it will not collapse,
like the great Queen Bee,
the descendants will multiply and live long lives,

great good fortune will be accomplished,
high wealth and status achieved

As Yang Wanjun, the Yang bride's Grand Manager, repeated this song, he cast spoonfuls of puffed rice out of the bride's house through the front door to symbolise the casting out of the bride's future fertility, finally toasting her mother and father.

As the bride at this wedding finally left her home together with her own bridal party, weeping and with a cloth covering her face, accompanied by her procession, it was the bride's elder brother who held the main umbrella in front of her; she took hold of his waist, and her younger brother helds her hand. Again, at this point her parents or father's brothers may pretend to stop her leaving, as the song for the 'sending of the bride' is sung by one of the Managers.

ZAA XAAV NTXHAIS (*SONG OF SENDING OFF THE BRIDE*)

The Sun has come, already lighting up the Host's central hall, the Bride who has married out is already outside, the Sun has come out to shine on the high mountain, today the Bride will depart to the South, the sons will be sent off to study, while the daughters are taught to weave cloth and sew dresses, the sons will inherit the clan, while the daughters will marry and leave their homes, sons study how to raise the pen and write, and the daughters will marry out to the South,

*today is a good occasion, a great day, the couple will live
out all their days together*

*Today the hour is good, I will sing a song, this song is a
song to send the bride, this year for Raug Cub Fua Tai (the
Emperor Raug Cub) the festivals and the hour is good, Raug
Cub Fua Tai is ready to send daughters for celebration.
Working, Raug Cub Fua Tai watched two sides, he wanted to
buy 'horses and cattle' this year to send his daughter, Raug
Cub Fua Tai was busy buying horses, engaged purchasing
cattle, horses and cattle will be brought back to be tied in the
house or in the stable, wait until the time comes, he got
ready to complete his daughter's wedding, there is a person
who cannot understand who comes and asks, whyever did
you buy horses and cattle? How did you know this year is a
good year? Raug Cub Fua Tai wants to send his daughter,
and horses and cattle will be given to Raug Cub Fua Tai and
his daughter to ride on to get married, when Raug Cub Fua
Tai's daughter is married this can earn her family glorious
fame, in order to send his daughter, the Matchmaker, the
Grand Manager and relatives and friends will all be invited.
And persons who beat the gong and blow the sauna horn,
3,000 persons who blow the trumpet, 3,000 carrying flags,
3,000 beating gongs, are also invited to send Raug Cub Fua
Tai's daughter to go and get married. Raug Cub Fua Tai
sends his daughter as well as 3,000 persons who hold
banners, 2,000 who blow trumpets, 3,000 who blow horns,
3,000 who beat gongs, 900 blowers, together away to the
side of the boy's family, Raug Cub Fua Tai sends them here,
Grand Manager of the groom's side comes out to receive the
guests, women also come out to receive guests, Raug Cub
Fua Tai's daughter was received to descend from the sedan
chair, and welcomed into the central hall, where the bride
and bridegroom pay respects together to the protective
ancestral spirits, after Raug Cub Fua Tai's daughter and
groom paid respects to the protective ancestor gods, they
also pay their respects to relatives and friends, altogether
there are 3,000 people, showing that they have got married,
after Raug Cub Fua Tai's daughter and the groom have*

finished paying their respects, they enter the bedroom, in the future this married couple will give birth to boys and girls, like the Queen Bee in her Hive, people and wealth will flourish together, they will live in happiness their whole lives, well, well, well, this very good song is finished

It is the bride's Father's elder Brother's wife (*nas laug*) who most importantly accompanies the bride on the procession to her new home; if there is no *nas laug*, then her Father's younger Brother's wife (*nas ncius*) is supposed to stand in.[23] She is the chief sender, representing the girl's parents (*ua nas txi*). Altogether there are seven women who accompany her; divided between inmarried women of her parents' generation ('father's brothers' wives'), and those of her own surname in her own generation ('sisters', but with these may be grouped her first maternal cousin, the Mother's Brother's Daughter). If there are no other inmarried women of the preceding generation available apart from the main one representing them, her own younger and older brothers' wives can replace them, so that she is accompanied by her brothers' wives and her own sisters. Altogether, it was said, there should be thirty-two people to send the bride; in fact there were invariably eight in the bridal party, including the bride.

After the bride's sending group leaves, the bride's parents stay at home, clear up the house, entertain guests who come to congratulate them, and wait for the party to return in a few days, or some time later (depending on the distance and how the families have arranged things). Shortly after leaving the bride's home, the song of 'meeting people on the road' can be sung by the Grand Manager who accompanies the bride.

ZAA TAUS KI (SONG OF THE ROAD)

Every song has this beginning, listen to me, the beginning has started; this year the sun has come out, the tree leaves and bamboo leaves all begin to bud, this year the rain has fallen and the tree leaves and bamboo leaves also begin to

---

[23] The role of the bride's mother is to prepare the dowry; she gives most of the responsibility to her sister-in-law to inspect the gifts, but helps to entertain the guests.

bud and grow, just like this year a new couple formally accomplished the wedding's arrival, this year is a good year, in order to accomplish the great event on the female side Txws Tchwb came, in order to accomplish the great occasion on the male side the daughter of Txws Tchwb has accomplished the wedding, Txws Tchwb sends his daughter to his own relatives all the way to the house of Ntxws Tchwb, Txws Tchwb saw Ntxws Tchwb putting out the stools and tables, ten tables to receive Txws Tchwb's relatives, Ntxws Tchwb has good manners to receive Txws Tchwb's good guests, when Txws Tchwb sent them to Ntxws Tchwb's house they saw Ntxws Tchwb's house had invited helpers to put out ten stools and ten tables to receive the guests, Ntxws Tchwb has put out ten stools and ten tables, ten tables set with ten small bowls, Txws Tchwb's relatives saw that on those ten tables would be placed a vase of wine and small cups, Txws Tchwb asked where did the vase of wine and the cups come from, Txws Tchwb's relatives were drinking wine at the ten tables, eating pork at the ten tables, Ntxws Tchwb had set out all the tables and stools, and vases of wine, wine and meat on the tables, Txws Tchwb's children could not understand the meaning of this, and the elders told them, you are but a small child, you don't know where this vase has come from, these small cups, and bowls, they come from, this vase and small cups and bowls all come from the Col of Nanguang River[24]—vase, and bowls, were all loaded on the boat to be carried here, vase, bowls, small cups, were all carried here by boat, and the people were happy to see this and their faces brightened, this year the Sun is very good, Txws Tchwb had also invited relatives, his elder brother and younger brother, to send Txws Tchwb's daughter, this year the sun, the rain are in good harmony, this year there are good festivals again, Txws Tchwb informed his relatives and friends to arrange his daughter's wedding, Txws Tchwb's relatives and friends sent Txws Tchwb's daughter to Ntxw

---

[24] The river of Gongxian, a tributary of the Yibin River.

Tchwb's house, they saw their brother-helpers, and all of them out to receive them

Txws Tchwb saw that Ntxw Tchwb's house had planned the wedding carefully, they had good manners to come and receive Txws Tchwb's relatives, Txws Tchwb's sisters sat at the table and saw were four corners to the table, they saw also that the table was in four parts, and on the table there were a vase, bowls, small cups, small bowls, Txws Tchw's senders were drinking wine and eating meat at the tables, they saw these four corners, and these four parts, and one small child didn't understand and asked, where did these cups and bowls at this table come from? Ntxw Tchwb had a person capable of explaining, talked to the small child and said, Ntxws Tchwb's vase, small cups, small bowls, are all from the Col of Naguang River, from the place of the Col of Nanguang, this vase, these bowls, they crossed ten great rivers, the vase and the bowls come from the boat on the muddy river, and the small cups and the small bowls also crossed ten great rivers, were placed on the deck of the boat to be carried here, the vase and bowls here are just as if they were placed on a plank, the small cups and small bowls are just as if they were placed on a boat to be carried here, the vase and the bowls look so beautiful, the small cups and the small bowls soften the heart, Txws Tchwb's senders will raise their spoons at the table, will take the wine and pork from the small cups and small bowls to eat and to drink, Txws Tchwb's senders will pick up Ntxw Tchwb's relatives' meat from the table to eat, to show the accomplishment of the wedding between men and women, to get Ntxws Tchwb's wine to drink and pork to eat.

During the course of the procession of the bride to the groom's house, which in the past and still today may necessitate a journey of a day or some days, a 'sweet-and-bitter' bamboo is picked along the wayside . After replanting, it is said, it can grow many shoots and form a bamboo grove, meaning that the couple can have many children. Also, a branch of the *tung* tree is picked to stand for the

first marriage ever performed.²⁵ So that, as Yang Wanjun said, when
the *tung* branch is tied to the bamboo, this couple will not be
separated but will have many descendants.²⁶

ZAA YUAV TSAB TXOO *(SONG OF TAKING THE BAMBOO AND TUNG BRANCHES)*

*Planting bamboo, grows the bamboo shoots, planting water-
bamboo, grows the water bamboo shoots, cutting bamboo
makes a basket, cutting the water bamboo makes a
winnowing tray, winnowing the chaff, sifting through the
broken husks to feed the chickens and the ducks, the bridal
family raised up nine styes of pigs, the father stored nine
pots of silver, the mother raised a daughter in her home,
when grown up she's sent to study, come of age to set up her
own home, this year this girl changed her attire and put on
new clothes, it cost her mother and father's silver greatly,
this daughter wearing flowers of gold upon her head,
exhausting her mother and her father's care, the young don't
know how many herbalists and shamans were sent for to
cure all their colds and illness, until now she is all grown up,
and will marry out into her husband's home to conduct his
household affairs, cutting green fodder for the pigs, feeding
all the pigs and household animals, going along the dykes to
farm in the fields, to marry out a daughter, is an ancient
custom, and so we come to the stone where the bamboo
sprouts; pick up a bamboo shoot, come to the great field,
pluck a branch of the tung tree, bamboo shoots and tung tree
plucked together, this is to say, to bear a boy, to raise a girl,
to pass on the clan and continue the generations, plant it in
the valley and it will sprout and bloom, and bear fruits, one
branch will study to a high degree, will have fame, will wear
the headgear of high officials, will travel to Beijing, one
branch will grow more sprouts in the countryside, like the
spring, as the spring comes, thousands of sweetly scented*

---

²⁵ Since *tung* sounds like the Chinese *tong-zi* ('lad') and the *tung* is also very
fruitful.

²⁶ Date can also sometimes be used, which is equally fruitful.

flowers, wait until the daughter sets up her family, families from both sides will come and go, the bridegroom, the bride, will never forget their parents' loving kindness, to come and go (visiting) often, mothers and fathers from both sides, drinking the wine and eating the meat is ahead of us, we send you a daughter with nothing at all, only with the least of gifts, to give to our host's ancestors merely as a token of our esteem

After the song of 'taking the bamboo and tung branches', there is the *zaa noj su* (song of lunch). This should be sung halfway on the way to the groom's house, and at the Yang wedding in Wangwuzhai it was, as they paused to re-tie the bride's leggings:

The Sun comes out in the east and sets in the west, shining on the side of the host's family. I send the host's daughter to the halfway point to part, the lady's ancestors will return to the lady's house, the lord's ancestors will come out to welcome them. The nine dragons in the nine valleys, and the ten horses and cattle on the ten mountain slopes, the mighty dragon comes, and will return to the oceans, the horses and cattle are ready to return to the mountains, to suppress all monsters, spirits and ghosts—beat them back, all will be close together and make wealth prosper, one hundred things will go well, the sons will be sent to study, daughters are married out to sew clothes, the sons in future will pay their respects to the protective ancestral spirits, the daughters in the future will marry out of the gate, one at the halfway place will beat back the spirits, one hundred things will go smoothly, everyone come together to enjoy this luncheon meal

Yang Wanjun, the bride's Great Manager, scattered cooked rice all over the assembled party and the Chief Sender (her paternal aunt) then presented some of this in a bamboo plate to the bride. Only one person in the bride's party, I was told, should carry the ceremonial meal for her, consisting of a casket of cooked sticky rice and a cleaned but uncooked hen.

'Lunch' is in fact eaten three times, once before the bride has left her home, once halfway on her way to the groom's house (although this is usually only a token lunch where the distance between houses is short), and once after arrival at the bridegroom's house.

Mus Txaij Nyaa Nqaig Tsej *('Going to Receive the Bride to Enter into the House')* and Cuav Xaab Tau Do *('They've Arrived!')*

At the Zhou girl's wedding in Wangwuzhai, the groom's relatives had stuck a piece of burning wood into the ground some distance from the groom's house to meet the bride's sending team. They halted there, and the bridegroom's Grand and Lesser Managers (Wang Xaojin and Wang Xaoshen) came out to greet the men of the party and offer them tobacco *(nrua yeeb)* and tea. The groom is supposed to send as many women as are in the bride's party to meet them, and his helpers all come out to bring the furniture into the house. Meanwhile, the Bamboo and Tung picked on the way (by a crowd of struggling young men who drew laughter as they fell down in their efforts) was taken into the central hall and placed in a corner. It must not be destroyed. The song of 'offering tobacco' by the groom's side to the bride's senders was sung as they arrived.

ZAA NCUAV YEEB *(SONG OF 'OFFERING TOBACCO', BY THE GROOM'S SIDE TO THE BRIDE'S SENDERS AS THEY ARRIVE)*

Today the hour is good, the day is good, today the weather, the climate is good, everyone is smiling with bright faces and begins to sing songs. First sing the origin of the song, men are needed to begin the song, from the very beginning the song is begun, one woman cannot be without a man, one man cannot be without a woman, they are united together, united together they can give birth to sons and daughters, then the lineage can be passed on and the generations continued, there are no men without any women, and there are no women without men, just like the sunny day and the rainy day, as day and night are needed, so everything can grow, this couple will both look for good seeds to sew, in the future offering tobacco is needed for the opening of relations between relatives and friends in the neighbourhood, where did the male tobacco come from? where did the woman tobacco come from?[27] *at first male tobacco was in the bud, at first woman tobacco was shaken from the bud, wrapped in papers and placed in the tobacco basket, male tobacco is mixed with ash, woman tobacco seeds sewn in the earth, when winter comes male tobacco also lives in the earth, and woman tobacco when winter comes also living in the earth, does not grow, male tobacco and female tobacco join hands together to sleep peacefully in the earth to pass the winter, wait until the spring, the weather is warm, male tobacco will grow buds, woman tobacco when spring comes and the weather is warm also begins to grow buds and have leaves, male tobacco will form a small seedling, female tobacco also grows gradually step by step for the small one to grow up, wait until two or three months later, male tobacco will grow up, female tobacco also will grow up, women will cut this grown up male tobacco and carry it home in a basket, and the female tobaco will also grow up in three months, also women will cut it and carry it home in a bin, cutting the male and the female tobacco together and carrying it home, plan to tie the male tobacco with ropes, use vines to bind the female tobacco, binding with ropes completes it, wait until the sixth month, the time of the Great Sun,*[28] *male tobacco will be tied with ropes to be aired in the sun, in the sixth month Great Sun female tobacco is tied with ropes and aired out in the daylight, after male tobacco and female tobacco are aired Lord and Lady Tobacco are bound with guava leaves—use dry rice straw to tie them into a large bundle, place it in the attic for storage, the male and the female hosts will store this tobacco to select an auspicious date, now they have selected this year which has an auspicious date, it is sufficient for the man's eight characters and the women's eight characters, to select an auspicious date to finish the greatest event of the son's and daughter's lives, it seems that this year the time is coming, men and women plan to take out*

[27] The terms for 'mother' and 'father' are used to prefix tobacco, to title and humanise them, throughout. These can be variously translated as 'Mother Tobacco, Father Tobacco', or 'Lady Tobacco, Lord Tobacco'.

[28] Reference to leap years.

*the aired tobacco to complete the man's and the woman's
greatest event of marriage, Lord Host and Lady Host hold
the tobacco in their hands and give it to the bridegroom's
matchmaker, women will give tobacco to two women who
can be trusted, to offer Sir and Madam Tobacco by the side
of the house and in the central hall to receive the guests,
male and female hosts together take the tobacco out and
offer it to the senders' and relatives' friends to complete the
son's and the daughter's greatest occasion, so that tobacco
is the first prime knowledge used to receive the guests, well,
well, well, good, good, good, this song is beautifully sung.*

After washing outside the groom's house with water which is
brought to her by members of the bridegroom's family, the bride at
this wedding changed into new clothes. The groom's family who had
come out to welcome them were now presenting wine and tobacco to
everyone—first to the bride's Grand Manager, then to her father's
brothers and to all the 'thirty-two' people accompanying her.

By the door of the bridegroom's house (just outside), the boy's
Grand Manager had placed two tables with two bottles and many
cups, and he invited her party to be seated and to drink. This was the
'first reception' for the bride's party. The major table (stage left of
the door) was for the bride's chief sender, matchmakers and two
managers, the other for her two brothers, her Father's elder and
younger Brother. Two people from the groom's party entertained
them at each table, the groom's two matchmakers at the table on the
left. Her other senders and helpers were entertained at four other
tables set slightly further away from the house.

There were more tables just inside the door where the girl's
family had placed two of the four chickens they had brought with
them. The groom's family had also placed two of their own. Each
pair had to be a brace (a cock and a hen). The *ntau xeeb* ritual
(sending back the spirits) was then performed at the table set up just
inside the door on which there was a *sheng* (litre) of rice, a piece of
meat and some boiled eggs as sacrifice. While chanting the song, the
ritual expert threw unhusked rice away from the front door of the
house, chanting to beat away the wild spirits which may have
accompanied the bride from her own patrilineage away, and the

chicken bones were also read for auspicious omens while the two tables blocked the door.[29]

If this *ntau xee* is not performed, as Yang Wanjun and others informed me, the soul of the bride will not be settled, and she will often get sick, vomit and have headaches.

NTAU XEE *('BEATING THE SPIRITS')*,[30] OR, NTAU DAAG ZOO DAAG ZUAG *('BEATING THE WILD SPIRITS')*

Hawm, this day is good, this hour is good, the bride comes here, the carriage returns home, on both sides there is a bowl of meat, a bottle of fragrant wine (meijiu)*: also some pork breast is needed, and a brace of mandarin ducks to accompany the Phoenix; two bridal carriages are invited: many couples accompany the invited guests to the bridegroom's family: in my humble hands I hold a cup of wine: to pay respects to the Immortals (I offer) fragrant wine to the ear-rings:*[31] *the carriages of the two families come here to receive (it): the Four Corners are invited: I hold a spoon in my hand to distribute to different parts: one part is to wish the bride's family prosperity and wealth as long as Heaven and Earth endure: secondly to wish the bridegroom's family prosperity and wealth as long as Heaven and Earth endure: thirdly for the bridegroom's family to be free of care and free of ghosts: fourthly for the bride's family to be free of care and free of ghosts*

With no heavenly prohibitions, no earthly prohibitions, no yearly or monthly observances, no daily or hourly observances, Jiangtaigong (in charge of spirits) commands

---

[29] 'This has been regarded as a superstition but is actually a traditional custom', I was told.

[30] In Chinese this is known as the *hui che ma*, 'returning the bridal carriage'.

[31] A reference to spirits.

all spirits of heaven and earth to retire, hawm, hawm, hawm
(yea, yea, yea)[32]

*Flowers in bloom have their places, flowers in seed burst
forth. Relatives of both sides, one family for the boy, one
family for the girl, today is a good day for the
accomplishment of the wedding, all evil stars will be
suppressed, and the new couple will be forever safe; we have
come to the family of the host, the wine and meats have not
yet been eaten, for first we must get rid of all evil stars,
suppress all monsters, spirits and ghosts; on the girl's side
we suppress the evil stars of the girl's side, on the way we
suppress the evil stars of the way, and coming to the family
of the host, we banish the evil stars from the host's family,
the nine dragons which came to drink water, the ten
monsters which came to cause pestilence, my hand will hold
the spoon, we ask Taibaixing (Venus) to suppress the nine
dragons and wipe out the ten monsters, for sons and
daughters will be sent away to study, and these sons and
daughters when they are grown fully will establish families
of sons and daughters, the sons will pay respects for the
protection of the ancestors, the daughters will marry out and
leave the family, this is the ancient tradition of the past and
future, naturally these ways will long exist*

*When the matchmakers of the girl and the matchmakers of
the boy arrive at the porch of the host's family, all welcome
them into the house, come to the porch, welcome to the
central hall, both sides decide the wine and the pork, the
meat is 80* jin *and the wine is 50* jin, *from now on the
greatest event of all, the marriage, will be decided, the men's
side will set up a family for the groom, the women's side will
set up a family for the bride, from now on make wealth and
make fortune, so that greatly the family may prosper*

*One gave birth to a boy and a girl, the one named Xee, the
other named Kaum, the one named Xee, the other named*

---

[32] This introduction is sung in Chinese. The remainder is in Hmong.

Sau,[33] *they knew how to blow the* qeej,[34] *they knew how to beat the hanging drum, they could remember their ancestors, knew how to make the* qeej, *when seven characters were placed in seven tubes, to memorise their ancestors for ever*[35]

The father can raise nine boys and nine girls, and the mother can raise ten sons and ten daughters, having a daughter is like a gaggle of geese, ten sons are like ten chickens, they can win their father's heart, sons will replace the father's labour, daughters will substitute for the mother's labour

Men will carry hoes and ploughs up the mountain side, women will cast seeds on the mountain slope, wait for those seedlings to grow up, blossom and have seeds, (when) ripe the harvest (taken) home, taken to the brewery, and brewed into wine; in the future the happy occurrence will come to the boy and girl, everyone is delighted, singing songs, drinking wine, can make some of the younger boys tipsy, everyone amuses themselves by the fireside

On the women's side the girl goes riding horse and mule, dressed in silk and satin gowns, her hands clutching the mane, she is married to the boy's side, today they will meet the man's forefathers, and see his mother and father

The daughter riding on the horse and mule, comes to the man's side, to meet the ancestral spirits of protection, to see the mother and the father, to meet the groom, in future both should work hard, and both should make wealth, until the sixth day of the tenth month, the women will come to take back the bride and groom, to take the couple merrily back to the family of the girl, this is my ntau xee, *let noboby mock, today after the* ntau xee *there will be* noj su *(lunch)*

---

[33] This poetic doubling and transference of names is very characteristic of Hmong poetic discourse.

[34] The famous Hmong reed-pipes.

[35] There seems to be a reference here to a widespread 'Miao' legend about the origin of people from the pipes of the *qeej*.

Then the two tables were pushed away to the sides of the door, and the house could be entered. A procession conducted the bride's party the short way to the very door of the boy's house, the boy's two sisters shading the bride's head with two umbrellas. The bride's elder brother walked in front of her, and her younger brother behind her, and they also held umbrellas for her, so that there were four umbrellas altogether, just as (it was said) there should be a minimum of four young girls to accompany her.

First to enter was the girl's Grand Manager, bearing the bamboo and tung branch, then the bride's elder brother, then herself, then her younger brother. There has to be a couple at the door to receive them, such as the boy's brother and brother's wife, or even better his father's younger brother and father's younger brother's wife (as at the Yang wedding). And some clans, like the Yang, still have the groom's father's sister[36] wave a rooster three times round the new bride's head to call her soul (WM *hu plig*; GM *nqaiv pleg*), after which she takes the umbrella from the bride's younger brother, gives it to her husband, then leads the girl into the house.[37] At this point, I was told, the bride should not cry; she should only cry (if at all) on leaving her own home. The Yang girl, however, howled like anything, and this was considered rather bad manners.

The furniture which had accompanied the Yang bride was now carried into the central room of the groom's house (not into their bedroom), and it was now carried by the groom's helpers (not by the bride's).

Some bridal parties still practise the local Hmong way of respecting the ancestors by processing around a fire lit in the middle of the hall[38] with the groom's father's sister leading the girls, before

---

[36] WM *phauj*; a relative with special powers to curse and change lineage custom, the subject of respect and avoidances.

[37] This widespread Hmong custom of *lwm qaib* or banishing the girl's evil influences appears to have been largely replaced in Gongxian by the *ntau xee*. One wedding Grand Manager said firmly that 'the girl has no soul'. Most agreed, however, that the *ntau xeem* was to 'return spirit' or send back the girl's clan spirits as well as evil things in general. Before a girl marries, she belongs to her father's lineage, and after marriage, to her husband's, which is why they call her name at ancestral rituals after her death. Her name will be called in her father's household if she dies before marriage.

[38] *zoutang* in Chinese.

the bride with her elder and younger brother retire to the hearth in an inner room. Others follow the Chinese custom of paying respects before the ancestral altar to Heaven and Earth (*bai tiandi*). Sometimes both are done, as happened in the Zhou wedding, with the prestigious Chinese ritual first. A song can also be sung to celebrate this;

> *From the East a red cloth comes: a red cloth flowers in the West: the two red cloths meet together to welcome the new one, the bride to descend from her sedan chair. When the peach blossoms, it is the time of the Phoenix:*[39] *when the bride goes to the bridegroom's house they are well-matched: when the Cowsherd and the Spinning Girl meet each other on the Magpie Way:*[40] *when the bride and bridegroom bow (pay their respects) to the exalted parents in the central room*[41]

At the (Chinese-style) rite to pay respects to the ancestors in the central hall (*pe pu yiag*) which was performed at the Yang wedding, a quilt was spread out on the ground and the groom's uncle stood at the table set before the altar to preside over the ritual. The bride and groom stood side by side, the bride bowing and the groom kowtowing three times on the quilt, first for Heaven and Earth, then for the parents and ancestors of the groom, and then to each other. Then the quilt was taken away as two elders representing the boy's Mother's Father and Father's Brother addressed the couple and said words to the effect that that today was neither a festival nor the New Year but a wedding, for this couple were to be married, yet the wine had not yet been drunk, nor had the meat been eaten, since before eating they should offer this to the ancestors (putting rice and meat in eight bowls and four dishes on the table before the family altar). This was known in Hmong as *pe taag daag*, or paying respects to the spirits of the central hall. Only after this is performed are the couple allowed to enter the 'new room' (the bedroom).

---

[39] In Chinese the phoenix symbolises the union of male and female in wedding, *feng* representing the groom and *huang* the bride.

[40] That is, the middle day of July.

[41] *Baitang* (Ch.), signifying to be married.

After the bride and groom leave the central hall, the groom's parents are asked to come in to the middle of the central hall. Now, the bride's Grand Manager ceremonially presents them with the bamboo sprig tied to the *tung* sapling, as happened in all the weddings we witnessed. The boy's Grand Manager will ceremonially accept the Bamboo and Tung on their behalf and carry it further inside the room and place it on tables to the left of the central hall (the east side).

ZAA YUAV NTSOO TCHAUJ/TSA TSOO *(SONG OF PRESENTING THE BAMBOO AND TUNG)*

Oh host and hostess, the bride's parents are poor, and cannot arrange anything at all, today we have come to the Bridegroom's house, and see how the male side is rich, can make eight suits of clothes, ten dress suits to place in the central hall, yet in the great valley below, we are unable to find eight suits of clothes, ten dress suits, and are overcome with humiliation, elder brothers and younger brothers alike, nobody has the temerity to look on the faces of all these relatives and friends, we have only one daughter to send away, we have nothing at all to give but one ornamental umbrella

We have come to the host's family and can see, the host's family can prepare clothing, goods and treasures, filling up the table, yet my side, in the great valley below, this humble visitor cannot prepare any clothing at all to place in the central hall, in the central hall nothing at all can be put, when our host sees this, his heart is chilled within him, there is nothing to place upon the table, the host sees this and he is grievously disappointed, we have only a daughter to send you, please forgive us

The mother and father of the bride, have raised a daughter in their home, and the mother and father become concerned, nobody has proposed to her yet, the father only asks his eldest son to go to spread the news, and the mother only asks the father to go to her (own) family to send this message, for the mother will follow her brother,[42] and so now this daughter has grown to maturity, she will marry out, like the Sun, men here can go to Gongxian, to arrange the dowry, like the Sun, some women are able to go to the streets of Gongxian to prepare a dowry to offer on her behalf, but in the great valley, this mother and father have no prospects at all, unable to go to the market in Gongxian, unable to buy quilts and clothing, silks and satins, they are unable to go to the market in the street of Gongxian, can find no dresses or dowry to offer, we send a daughter here, without anything at all, poor in silver and gold, and although there is some clothing and it cost some wealth, we regret this deeply and apologise greatly to our hosts

Like the Suav (Chinese) who can ride on the trains to Chongqing and the Mang (Yi) who travel to Beijing, some Chinese and Yi people can do business and trade in Yibin and Chengdu, the Chinese and Yi are so wealthy, when they marry out their daughters, they will give silks and satins, but our Hmong families are so poor, dressed only in hempen rags, yet we can see that this host's family can go to the markets in Xingwen and Zhoujiaxiang, can get chests of drawers and wardrobes, full of goods and wealth, where we can only afford to put two wooden boxes in the central hall, Oh host please pardon us, kindly ask some helpers to help carry them into the central place, we have sent an umbrella here without anything else at all[43]

The bamboo, the tung branch and the keys are actually supposed to be ritually presented three times; first when the bride's party has just arrived, as they are being entertained or just afterwards, which is also

---

[42] A reference to FZD marriage, where the *daughter* follows her mother's brother to marry his son.

[43] Actually the meaning of the *haj zaa* when giving the bamboo and *tung* relates to the origin of the *umbrella*. An umbrella is made of *bamboo* and bamboo comes from its shoot. The couple cannot be separated from each other, just like the close tie between the bamboo branch and the *tung* tree, without marriage there will be no offsprings.

known as 'drinking the wine to welcome the travellers'; then again, after the first 'lunch' (usually quite late in the afternoon) in the groom's home, and finally after supper on the same day.[44] The tripling of sequences is also a common feature of Hmong ritual process, but in the festivity and drinking this precise scheduling of events often slips askew.

After the wedding is completed, the bamboo and tung is hung up on the wall inside the central hall of the house until the bride gives birth, when it is discarded because it has 'borne fruit'.

After the formal presentation of the bamboo and tung has been made, to the accompaniment of many libations and toasts, the bride's chief sender has to present the keys ('on behalf of the girl's father's brothers') for the opening of the dowry to the groom's *mother*, which is also marked by a ritual singing. No actual keys are presented, however; this is what is called a 'ceremonious' presentation.

ZAA JIAO NTSOG *(SONG OF PRESENTING THE KEYS)*

Clothing and other gifts are not so much, to express a happiness to the Bride, as in days of yore, when Li Laojun was still living, he raised a hammer in his hand and beat, he used his mouth for a bellows, on the same day as keys are forged, luck too can be forged, and today these are given to the host's parents, as when Spring comes there is the sweet scent of a thousand flowers, on the sixth day of the sixth month, the Sun comes out to shine across the mountains, open all the cupboards with these keys of silver and gold, take out all the clothes, let them be aired in the sunlight, high mountains can make a happy wedding, flat plains can bring about the weddings of men and women,[45] the host's mother and father open up the cupboards with these keys of silver and gold, take out new clothes to air them when the flowers

---

[44] If the groom has no living parents, or they are in mourning, their place is taken by paternal relatives. At Liu Guankui's sons's wedding in Wangwuzhai, neither he nor his wife came out to receive the branches and keys since his own mother had died less than three years before and they had not yet performed the mortuary rite of *a vaa* for her. Instead his brother and sister did so.

[45] That is, a good wedding can be accomplished in an auspicious combination of fertile plains and protective mountains.

blossom in June, to dress your daughter-in-law for many future happy occasions, workers, relatives, friends, all praise, this is a good couple, may their descendants multiply, may men and wealth both prosper

Since the dowry was locked when it was brought in, it is said, the girl's fathers' brothers have brought these keys for the boy's parents so that they may unlock it.

The father of the Zhou bride was a widely travelled man, who had been able to compare wedding practices in many different Hmong regions. According to him, in an exemplary statement,

a wedding should cost 5,000 yuan, or 200 nyiaj (silver coins), just for the clothes, meat and wine. But here some people can only afford two or three hundred yuan. Down in Wenshan (near the Vietnam border) it is different. There, if the girl is very beautiful and the man is very rich, the price must be very high, but generally it's not like that here, it's very low. The Hmong of this region have generally not used much cash or silver, unless there was no meat or wine or clothes, although before Liberation, it is said, when landlords got married, 2,000 silver coins were given.[46] In the recent past anyway, not much could be afforded. 'Wet gifts' acounted for most of the presents, and if 100 jin of wine and 100 jin of pork were given to the bride's family, no clothing was needed. But now 'dry gifts' like furniture have become the major part of wedding payments. These are decided by both sides, but the amount of 'wet gifts' is decided by the groom's family, such as 10 jin of pork, and 10 jin of wine.[47]

The boy's family also give some money to the girl's family, and the girl's family also prepare some dowry, for example including a bicycle or tape-recorder or sewing machine. What the girl's family gives in Gongxian is now more than the boy's side gives, but the

---

[46] As Yang Hoov Cheeb of Weixin pointed out, the practices of Hmong Lees, Hmong Sib and Hmong Daus, are different.

[47] The Hmong of Gongxian were in the process of transition from a traditional bridewealth system to a more traditional prestige Han-like one of indirect dowry. In the neighbouring county of Gulin, bridewealth was still largely practiced (as it is in Wenshan), and the wedding proper only takes place when a child is expected. In intermarriages between the two regions the groom's customs were adopted, so there was a net inflow of cash into Gongxian from Gulin whether dowry or brideprice was paid. See above.

majority of this 'dowry' is often already paid for by the boy. The groom's side give clothes, wine, pork, sugar, cash and a suit for the girl's father and a suit for the girl's mother, but the bride's family, it was said, should be seen to give much more, since this is to be her inheritance.[48] We might see this as a system of indirect dowry, directly transitional between a former system of bridewealth and aspiring to one of true dowry.

The bride's parents must make some clothes and furniture before she gets married, such as a wardrobe, cupboards and chests of drawers. There used always to be a cow or at least a pig for her 'dowry', but now most parents only give her two chickens to take to her husband's home. When she comes back to revisit her parents, some days after the wedding, she is supposed to take one of these back with her. In fact however her husband's family usually give her a small amount of money to take back to her parents in lieu of the chicken (one or two *yuan*), because (as they said) it's easier to raise two chickens than one.

The groom's gifts are given to the bride's family, and their distribution is then decided by her family. They will try to ensure that about a third goes to the parents, with the majority going to the bride. The clothes given by the bridegroom's family tend to be for the bride; the wine, pork, sugar and money (often only 100-200 *yuan*) goes to the parents, who may use most of it for the feasting. Since it is the bride's parents who make the furniture for her, the amount of money paid by the bridegroom depends on how much furniture has been made. If they can, the bride's family will still give a cow, pig and a chicken. This happens at the wedding—and when the bride's father dies, her husband's family will (also) sacrifice a pig at his funeral if they can.

At the Yang wedding in Wangwu, the groom's mother's brother had also given him corn, rice, beans, money, two guns and embroidered clothing. The girl's mother's brothers also have to give presents to the girl. And the girl's father's brothers sent presents (in

---

[48]   The bride's side at one Gongxian wedding gave: 1) cow, pig, chicken; 2) cupboard, desk, drawers, 4 stools, 1 table. A shelf for basins, 2 basins, 2 quilts, 2 mosquito nets, 2 pillow cases, 2 pillows, 1 door-cloth to hang on the door, 2 bedcovers (if it's not such a good marriage, only 1 can be given), 2 trunks and 2 sheets; 3) 8 dishes, 8 saucers, 8 cups, and 8 bowls for a table of 8 people. This is of course less than it seems where the groom actually pays for the cost of the furniture.

the dowry) specifically for the boy's parents, his brother and sister, and his father's sister.

After the preceding procedures, the two Grand Managers should be seated in the main hall in the 'ancestral position' (immediately in front of the place for the altar, facing outwards towards the door of the house)—the girl's Grand Manager on the right of the hall, and the boy's Grand Manager on the left. These equivalences between the left, the east, and the male, as opposed to the right, the west, and female, are entirely in conformity with Han usages and practice.[49] Everyone else sits or stands ranged around the walls of the hall, and there was usually a great press of people at this point with children hanging from the rafters and looking out of lofts..

The boy's Grand Manager calls the four people who have been offering everyone wine and tobacco all this time—two by two—to come inside from outside the door; and they must prostrate themselves to all the people in the room. Two have the tobacco, and two have the wine. After kowtowing to the ancestral altar at the porch of the door, they come right inside the room. One couple (with wine and tobacco) is directed to go to the Grand Manager seated on the right side of the house, and the other couple to the Grand Manager on the left side of the house. Then the two on the left will serve all members of the formal party on the left of the room (that is, those formally seated at tables rather than those milling about, though some of these may be offered to as well), while the two on the right will serve the party on the right side of the room, and then all four servers prostrate themselves again at the porch and leave to serve those outside.

And this all happens again, and then again. At some point after the second time, the boy's father's elder brother and father's younger brother take up midway points on each side of the room. These two pay respects (prostrating themselves) to the Grand Managers, and ask loudly 'Who is the girl's Father's Brother?' Then the girl's father's brothers come forwards to identify themselves, are toasted, and are invited to sit together with the Grand Masters at the top of the main table set beneath the altar.

---

[49] See for example Hertz (1973).

The boy's father's brothers are now supposed to offer tobacco to the girl's father's brothers. Then they offer tobacco to the four brothers of the bride and groom seated in the middle of the table. At some weddings this is done very traditionally, with sheets of tobacco which nobody seems quite sure what to do with; at both the Yang and Zhou weddings packets of cigarettes were used and cigarettes offered in pairs. Then these four in the middle will offer tobacco and wine to all present. Ideally, the two elder brothers sit together at the table; and the two younger brothers sit together at the table. The boy's elder brother should serve the girl's elder brother, and the boy's younger brother should serve the girl's younger brother, and so on. Very often an exact kinship relative is missing and his or her place is taken by someone else, but usually there was some strictness about trying to do things in threes, for example, or having made the right offerings to the right kind of relative.

I was told that this might go on for several days!

After this, at the Zhou wedding, four more tables were placed before the 'altar', and an attempt was made to seat everyone of importance for the wedding luncheon. Each formal meal, at which men and notables picked at small bowls of food and toasted each other simultaneously, was followed by a real meal when more food was brought out and everyone ate with gusto and not much decorum. The wedding lunch is appropriately followed by the wedding supper, usually much later in the evening, and as soon as these meals (lunch or supper) are over more food is brought out (where families have it) so that 'unimportant' women (that is, those without any formal role in the business but who nevertheless have probably done most of the work) and children, often running around or on laps, can eat. In effect this adds up to a constant process of formal and informal banqueting and toasting, punctuated by ritual songs. It is at this point that the song of the wedding table, which can also be sung in the bride's house before her departure, is sung.

SONG OF THE ORIGIN OF THE WEDDING TABLE

Eh, in ancient times, where was the table to be found, it was hiding in the dark forests, it had not yet come here, and who were they who cut it and brought it here? The table comes into the great hall, beneath the ancestral altar, according to the ancient way of the Hmong, the way of the middlemen and go-betweens, the table shall be set here, here in the central hall.

Eh, this wedding table, that table is made of bamboo, but this is a table of wood, that table is a round table, but this is a square one with four corners, suitable for forming plans and designs, this is a table indeed for daughters and sons. Now that the table has arrived, now that the table is laid and prepared, we await the (paternal) spirits of grandmother and grandfather (xee pog xee yawg)[50] at the ancestral altar. we await their arrival in the ancestral hall, we will offer them bowls and bowls, we will lead the bride and groom to sacrifice to the ancestral spirits, we four middlemen will perform the sacrifice to heaven, and we will present the honourable offering to the affinal relatives

Eh, we four middlemen have not enough hands to help us, the left hand will take the new ladle for soup, the right hand will take the knife to slice out the liver of the pig, the left hand will take the spoon for the unhusked rice, the right hand will take the entrails of the chicken, and we will call the spirits of earth and place (xee teb xee chaws), the spirits of grandmother and grandfather, to come and dine with us, to open the road of wealth and fortune, of marriage and relations, for bride and groom

---

[50] I have generally used the system for transliterating White Hmong developed in Heimbach (1979) known as the Romanised Phonetic Alphabet, in which doubling of consonants indicates final nasalisation, and final consonants indicate tone values. Tonal values in the Gongxian dialect however differed dramatically from those in all other recorded Hmong dialects, and I have tried to indicate this where possible. It does not always work very well to convert directly from the standard Chinese system for writing Hmong to RPA although they are based on the same model. For example, in the Chinese Hmong transcription, 'we' is written 'bib' which should convert as 'pib' for Thai White Hmong (since the tone is unaltered), but in fact the Thai White Hmong is 'peb'. Moreover, in Gongxian this is pronounced more like 'piye'. Again, the Chinese Hmong for 'paternal grandmother' is 'bos' which should be converted to 'pug' but Thai White Hmong is 'pog' so no conversion of the vowel is actually needed here. Nor are the tonal changes as consistent as one would expect, and pre and post nasalisation can occur quite randomly. There are therefore some inconsistencies.

We four Masters all by ourselves, the left hand takes the new ladle for water, the right hand holds the liver of the pig, the left hand takes the unhusked rice, the right hand takes the liver of the chicken, and we call all the spirits of earth and place, the spirits of grandmother and grandfather, the locality and ancestral spirits of Weixin,[51] to eat together and offer to Saub,[52] that this couple in marriage may trade and prosper, thrive and be well, following the customs and traditions, that their crops and harvests flourish and bloom and their grandsons and grandaughters multiply and increase, that they may eat and drink without ever ending

We Yunnan Hmong, we came from afar, now we will wine and dine, set the table of silver and gold, set the firm and strong table for the daughter and son, and one hand will take the new ladle for soup, the other will take the spoon for rice, one hand will hold the chicken's liver, the other the liver of the pig, as we call the spirits of earth and place, of grandmother and grandfather, to join us and eat fully, for the bride and groom to be wedded, have many children, for the go-betweens and middlemen, for the road of fortune and wealth to be opened for them

Having spoken like this, and arriving at this stage, our left hand takes the turtle spoon, our right hand takes the liver of the pig, the right hand offers rice, the left hand holds the liver of the chicken, and we call the spirits of earth and place, of grandmother and grandfather, of the locality and ancestral spirits of Zhaotong, etc.

And now this is done, now that is completed, let us speak of the way we have taken, we crossed nine long passes, 99 roads as wide as they are long, 99 feet in width, choosing the

---

[51] These sacrifical verses (*laig dab*) are widespread in Hmong areas, can be chanted or more simply said and their content may be varied for the occasion of the New Year, for example, or a birth. Commonly ancestors are called by name for three generations.

[52] The benevolent ancestral deity of the Hmong.

*road to Weixin county, and passing through Weixin, we call the Earth and Place spirits of Weixin, the grandmother and grandfather spirits of Weixin, who eat the ghosts and evils, call the spirits of Waters and Valleys, the spirits of relatives and marriage (*xee neej xee tsa*), the spirits to come for Saub's way, so this couple may marry and follow the road of fortune and prosperity, and their children multiply generation after generation*

*We have crossed Nine long roads, traversed Nine lengthy ways, passed over the mighty Shuang He River, calling the spirits of Earth and Place of the Shuang He River, we will feast and dine, and we invite the spirits of earth and place to eat meat with us, the grandmother and grandfather spirits to drink wine with us, we call all grandmother grandfather spirits, all the spirits of earth and place, the devourers of ghosts and evils, the grandmother spirits to eat fully, the grandfather spirits will eat fully, to offer to Saub on high. The grandmother and grandfather spirits will make the bride (*nkaum laaj*) and groom (*tub nraug*) join in the road of wedding, eat up, grandmother and grandfather spirits, grandmother and grandfather spirits will make the bride and groom, united in marriage, have children and grandchildren, make the bride and groom grow in riches and wealth, reap harvests from their crops (*qoob looj*), with food they can never finish, drink that can never end*

Having reached this point, and now the table is fully prepared, we invite all sons and daughters, the father's elder and younger brothers, go-between and middlemen, elder and younger sisters, to the table in the central hall of the house, and the left hand takes the ladle for water, the right hand the meat, the right the chicken liver, the left hand holding the spoon for rice, takes the liver of the pig, and we summon all spirits of earth and place, of grandmother and grandfather, to eat up the ghosts and evil influences, and open up the way of fortune and wealth for the bride and groom

having reached this point, we eat the meat, we drink the
wine, and invite all spirits of earth and place, grandmother
and grandfather spirits, spirits who devour ghosts and
miasmas, so now the bride and groom will return to our
house, with boxes of seeds to plant in the fruit gardens
around the house, will have sons and daughters, will
multiply (npau) *and prosper greatly*

Yo! We have arrived here, at the house of the mother and
father, now it only remains for them to come into the central
hall, and eating our left hand takes the new ladle for soup,
our right hand holds the liver of the pig, our left hand holds
the spoon for rice, our right hand holds the liver of chicken,
we will call all the spirits of earth and place, of grandmother
and grandfather, so that the bride and groom will come
together and have sons and grandsons, one granary
becoming ten thousand granaries, their one cow will give
birth to nine, and nine to ten thousand bulls, good, good,
good, now we are all here, in this great house, the family of
the bride and groom will grow and increase, as they will
have ten thousand bulls and pigs; the pig you feed is locked
in the pen, giving birth to nine piglets, all male ones.

In ancient times, the heavens and earth were all dark, no
humans lived on earth, the ancestors of people came to earth
and had no food to eat nor clothes to wear, could only eat
the bark of trees and roots of grass, they found the seeds of
grain and seeds of crops from Heaven, from then on people
had food to eat and clothes to wear, and the people
multiplied and grew in number, invited blacksmiths from
Huguan and Jiangxi, who helped to find iron and copper for
them, and made knives and swords for them, so they could
cut down the trees, to make this wedding table.[53]

At the Yang wedding in Wangwuzhai the girl's 'father's sister's
husband' was originally seated with the boy's 'father's sister's

---

[53] Song recorded from Xiong Hua Jie. This can also be sung at the bride's house
preparatory to the wedding.

husband' at the left side of a central table and the boy's 'father's brother' seated with the girl's 'mother's brother' on the other side. That is, while the groom was represented by no maternal relatives, nor was the bride by any direct paternal relatives, and only men were seated. At supper later this was repeated, with the order was reversed. For the formal luncheon, four main tables were set out in the hall with eight people at each, the boy's and girl's 'older paternal uncles' seated together at the top left of one table (in the upper left portion of the hall), facing their 'younger paternal uncles' at the top right of this paternal table, and the boy's and girl's father's sisters with their husbands seated at the bottom left of the other table (in the upper right portion of the hall), facing the boy's and girl's 'mother's brothers' and mother's brothers' wives at the bottom right of that table for cross and affinal relatives.

There was wine on the table, but first pork trotters were ceremonially presented. The upper haunches were offered with some care to the two upper people at each table, and then these two each had to place ¥1.2 on a plate ('for the cooks'). Only the skin was picked at, not the flesh, and then the plate was returned to the cooks. There were nine dishes to each table.

It was only at supper that the bridegroom was placed at the top of the table, with his elder brother to his right.

And a table of food had also been laid inside for the bride. On the tables set outside the door for the large company there, there were two or four bowls and wine on each, with plates of sunflower and walnut seeds, and the other tables inside were laid in the same way. The second time wine and tobacco was offered outside, the bride's elder brother and younger brothers left the inside room and joined the party outside. The boy's mother's brother and father's sister's husband, after visiting the bride and her party in the inside room, then joined the honoured guests at the top of the hall, as there were supposed to be inside only women inside, and only men outside.[54] Then the boy's own sisters were invited to join the bride and her four bridesmaids inside, making eight women altogether, all inside the inside room. Men were also supposed to stay on the right side of the

---

[54] This is the case in Wangwu; in Wutong, however, the bride returns to the main hall after visiting the fireside, where she sits at one of the tables and helps entertain the guests.

central hall, while women were supposed to rest on the left side, and when formal rituals occurred, there was some attempt to ensure this.

Noj Nag Hmo ('The Evening Meal for Family Unity')

When it became dark, at the Yang wedding, a special meal 'for women' was served for eight women (one representing the groom's side, the other seven were the bride and her chief sender and five others of her party), while a troupe of local musicians played in a right side room. The use of professional musicians is often a feature of Han weddings, and better-off Hmong families in the Sichuan area also did this. This meal was only for the women, the other two chickens the bride's party had brought were now used. The bride's side had cooked one *sheng* of sticky rice and killed one chicken (with its internal organs removed) for this meal which had been carried to the groom's house in a basket by a helper. The bridegroom's side had done exactly the same, and they were all re-heated together and put on the table. There are proper ways of positioning the chicken's head, wings, tail, legs and so on, I was told, so that it looks (as it did) like a complete bird in the bowls. The two bowls of chicken were placed on the upper half of the table. Then the old woman representing the groom's family should pick up one part of the hen and give it to the bride's chief sender (the right wing and leg, which should be eaten by the bride two mornings later). And the bride's chief sender should give one part of the cock to the old woman (the left leg and left wing, which should be eaten by the groom two mornings later). And the groom's go-between presented the bridal side with the head for the bride's father. The other women who received legs again had to place 1.2 *yuan* on a plate for the cooks. But while before there were eight bowls of rice for the eight people at table, now there were ten; two extra. The boy's 'father's brother's wife' is supposed to put the additional two beaks in the extra two bowls and send them later for the boy's own mother and father.

Then the two Grand Managers and the boy's and the girl's father's brothers all went outside to discuss the arrangements for the Midnight Meal...

At midnight, a discussion of the 'return money' (*tua ntsauj* 'remuneration for the bride's senders by the groom's family') was held at all the weddings we saw over many cups of wine at the table in the central hall over the payment for the bride's senders and helpers. At this meal the girl is represented for the first time as the wife of her husband. The groom's managers and matchmakers, and the bride's Grand Manager and matchmakers and chief sender sit together, drinking. The bride's side present the groom's side with a list of all the helpers and their payments.

At a Yang wedding in Fenghuang, the total payment to the bridal sending party was 156 *yuan*;

Nqe tais[55]: 24
Chief Sender: 8
Bride's brother: 3
First Manager: 3
Second Manager: 3
Two people who led the bride: 6
Five other persons who accompanied her: 15
Four cupboard carriers: 8
Two carriers: 14
Two Sewing-machine carriers: 4
Washing-basin shelf carrier: 4
Two chest bearers: 4
Two desk bearers: 8
The person who carried the basket with the bride's meal: 3
The person who carried her lunch for the halfway stop: 3

Generally the payment was decided by the number of things the bride's side had brought; it is seen as the cost of the helpers' work.[56] Usually reckoned in (multiples of) 1.2 or 2.4 *yuan*, since it must be exact and evens are lucky at weddings (as with Han), it will be paid at the ceremonial meal before the bridal party leaves the next morning, first to the girl's 'brother's wife' and her 'father's brother' and her brother and then to her four bridesmaids and all the porters.

---

[55] *Yangjia* in Chinese; tea-money ('tobacco money') for the bride's parents.

[56] At Han weddings, this money is given as soon as the furniture is put on the ground outside the house, and then carried into the house. At Hmong weddings, the furniture is first brought into the home, and then the payment is discussed at night at the table. The money is given directly to the helpers for their work, not to the bride's family or anyone else.

The Midnight Payment Meal

This is another formal toasting banquet which follows the practical reckoning of accounts. At the Yang girl's wedding, it was introduced by a formal exchange between the two sides. Liu Guangtsai, the groom's Manager, declared:

Hanging this umbrella in the central hall, farming in the fields and going along the ridges, the marriage of men and women has its own proper customs and traditions, Manager and Matchmaker, if you have some procedures or formalities, please speak out now

The bride's Manager, Yang Wanjun, returned this by saying:

Oh Great Manager, Father's elder brothers and Father's younger brothers, if you do not ask I will not speak, (but) since you ask me I will speak, I say we want no (special) procedures or formalities, and our Host also says, do not ask for any procedures or formalities; because the gifts of the host of the female side are very few, just like the Sun, as the Sun is shining in the middle of the sky, on behalf of my hosts I cannot ask for 'happy money', but the old customs have laid down that we should ask for nqe tais *(payments to the bride's parents), by which the wedding can be accomplished, I beg the host and the host's younger and elder brothers to consider this*

To which Liu Guangtsai (pouring more wine) responded:

The bride and the bridegroom will become one couple, the host of the bride's side has the least of gifts to pay, this matter will be settled tonight, to form the waters of the Yangtse River and the Bridge of Iron Slabs, from now on the sons and grandsons will prosper and multiply

And Yang Wanjun, not to be outdone, said:

We have eaten and we have taken away many goods, we apologise deeply to the host

But Liu Guangtsai returned:

Very little—please excuse us, it seems there are still seven days left to play in, we sincerely ask the hosts to stay here and play (enjoy themselves) for several days

And Yang Wanjun (for the bride) insisted:

*The time has come, the Sun and Moon have completed their circuit,
tomorrow we will return to see another place*

So that Liu Guangtsai and Liu Chiluo (together) inquired:

*the evenings are drawing out, we have good guests but not good
hosts, since our guests must go to see another place, when will you
come back again?*

And Yang Wanjun, seeming to tire, simply replied:

We have troubled you so much

At which the two Liu shouted out:

Bring two bottles of wine! Drink up, everyone!

Also at the Yang girl's wedding, a song of washing the feet was
sung. I was told there used to be a custom whereby two men from the
groom's house washed the feet of the men in the bridal party, but that
this had now practically died out. Two women from the
bridegroom's side (who should be his younger sisters) still prepare
hot water to wash the feet of the female members of the bridal party,
first presenting two basins to the bride and to her father's brother's
wife. . But now actually (I was told) they only wash the bride's face
and hands, and actually (as I saw) she mostly does it herself, but she
should and still does give some lucky money (1.2 *yuan* each) to the
'sisters' who serve her, and to the 'sisters' who serve her 'older and
younger brothers', while the song for washing the feet can be sung.[57]

ZAA NTXUA TES *(SONG OF WASHING THE FEET)*

*It was dark already, Heaven and Earth turned dark with no
light, the host's family in order to receive the new girl is now
making all the preparations to boil water to bathe the feet,
guests everyone please come to listen to me singing this song
for the bathing of feet, it becomes dark, now it is dark again,
the Earth rotates and rotates to darkness, very soon the
host's family will prepare to wash the feet, the host's family*

---

[57] This song can also be sung when the bride arrives at her new home, when
water is also presented to her to bathe her hands and feet.

would prepare the basin and towel to get ready to wash the feet, it is dark, it is dark again, in the sky the weather has already changed, the rotation of Earth has already changed, and darkness came again, preparations have been made of the water for washing feet to receive the relatives of the senders, now the water is hot enough, the foot-basin and towel are all ready, and the host's family have invited two persons to come to wash the feet, they will wash the feet of the sending girls, first to wash the feet and legs, second to wash the hands and arms, to wash them clean, the host's family has invited two girls to wash the feet of the sending girls (bridesmaids), two men have also been found to wash the feet of the men senders, the girls will wipe the feet dry with towels, to put on new cloth shoes, men will also wipe the men senders' feet and legs, hands and arms, wipe them clean with towels, at the same time as the women senders will be washed clean, to put on new cloth shoes, will wash the men's hands and feet with the towels, together put on new cloth shoes, this evening everyone will sing songs and have amusements, now this song has finished, together put on new shoes, the completion

The groom's helpers who carried goods to the bride's family before the wedding and the bride's helpers who have sent her to the groom's house and carried the wedding goods must be asked to stay the night, and they are put up either in the homes of relatives of the bride (for the groom's helpers) or in the homes of relatives of the groom (for the bride's helpers) if, that is, they sleep at all, as these proceedings can stretch well into the small hours.

Xaiv Rov Mus *(Sending off the Guests)*

At dawn (*po kis*) the next morning the bride's party, ideally and in all the weddings we saw, after washing their faces, is entertained again at a ritual called the *rao tua ntxais* before they return home. Two tables are laid in the central room. The girl's company should enter from the left, and the boy's party should come in from the right, and the boy's mother and father (or their representatives, often a mother's sister or father's brother) must also come into the central hall, and the boy's and girl's father's brothers are also invited. On each table there are two bottles of wine and four bowls of pork, and tobacco. Pork ribs are presented to all the go-betweens, and they are thanked.

At the meal, the bride's party express their gratitude to the groom's family and bid them farewell. Both sides express the hope for more dealings with each other in the future, since bonds of amity have now been established between them.

The girl's father's brothers (or the matchmakers on their behalf) will sing or say words to the effect that the girl they are leaving has grown up in her parent's home elsewhere and may well know nothing worth knowing, and beg her new family to forgive her if she does anything wrong. They say that if the bride should be guilty of some fault, her mother and father-in-law are welcome to come to the girl's mother and father to complain of it, but that they should not listen to any gossip by others about her. Then they express good wishes for the length of the marriage, to the groom, and tell both the groom and bride to respect the groom's parents.

And they beg the boy's father's brothers to help the couple out if they should cause any pain to their parents or suffer disagreements with each other. And the boy's parents (through their own matchmakers) sing back of how their son's bride is now like their own daughter to them, and they will treat her as one of their own. The tables within the room are then turned so that the grain of their wood runs towards the door, to 'smooth the way' between their homes, and a place must be reserved to the left of the room for the women to watch the final proceedings.In the course of drinking, the hosts and guests swap places, and the hosts offer wine to the guests to send them off.

On leaving the house, when the 'Song of Farewell' is sung, one of the girl's father's brothers carries the umbrella and pays respects (*a yim*) to the boy's father's brothers and thanks them. The boy's mother and father, or other relatives, should try to stop the girl's party from leaving, as also occurs at Han weddings, so that everyone has to come back into the two inside rooms and apologise and say they have another pig that they should kill for the boy's family. Again they will try to keep them, and the boy's and girl's father's brothers will retire to their places to discuss further about the pig. If they agree, the pig will be killed at once, and the party may stay another night before they finally leave. This is what should ideally happen; in the weddings we saw, this was rather cursorily done, although the departing guests were enticed back briefly at one.

YANG WANJUN: (SONG TO BID FAREWELL TO THE GROOM'S HOUSE)

We have already stayed and played here
for seven days and seven nights,
now we plan to go back again
to the great valley of Paofan village to see another place
We have stayed here for seven days and seven nights
and the central hall of the hosts has been put into an
*   uproar by us,*
after we go back to our lordly home,
the host will sweep three times with a broom to the stove,
and sweep three times with a broom to the central room;
then all the families will prosper,
and the sons and grandsons will thrive;
we send our niece (the bride) here,
we have been so warmly entertained by the host,
and the host's elder and younger brothers,
Oh Lord and Lady Hosts,
we express our gratitude to you,
our niece in your house,
we hope you may treat her as your own Daughter
because she has only the knowledge of a very small child
we hope the mother and father (of the groom) will
*   educate her,*
and from now on this married couple should live
*   well together*
and be in accord in all things
raising the crops from the fields
and increasing the silver and gold
and making their fortunes through working well.

On the final departure, the Managers cry

there is wine in the bottle, you can have your son
those who blow the suona horn should get ready!

But before the departure of the bridal party, the groom's side should have inquired about the date for the bride's first return to her parents' family. In Weixin she will only stay with her husband for two to three days. In Gongxian, usually, 13-15 days after the wedding, two of her family, usually her brothers or father's brothers, will come to collect her. The husband's sister may seek to prevent them from leaving. They may be given a piece of cloth or another gift (not money) by the groom's family when they come, but the bride needn't take any gifts home at this time, and can stay at her parents' (often with her husband) for a week to a fortnight, or perhaps three weeks if it is at the time of the New Year festival, after which she will return to her husband's family.

And as Yang Wanjun summarised what he saw as the essence of the marital customs:

In this world there are both yin *and* yang. *Men are* yang *and women are* yin. *Only through marriage can there be parents. Men are women inside their bodies. Man stands for feelings and woman for rain. By feelings and rain, there will be a completion. Men without women will be just like a drought. Sons without daughters will be single*

To me the Han influences on these Hmong weddings were particularly apparent. The minimisation of bridewealth, the use of Grand and Lesser Managers, the employment of musicians, the written lists of expenses drawn up, all recalled Han weddings more than traditional Hmong weddings I had seen in Thailand. Yet to a large extent,as we have seen, these marriages excluded Han and were crucial in forming wide-ranging networks of Hmong affinity which contrasted with the close-knit nature of Han descent structures. The kinship relations posited and displayed in the Wangwu weddings were of particular interest, as we see in the following chapter, in illustrating local clan conflicts and cleavages, the complex shared local history of the region, and the flexibility of the descent system as a whole in expressing and incorporating shifting and changing relationships of difference and resemblance.

CHAPTER ELEVEN

HISTORY AND CONFLICT

We can illuminate the nature of some of the tensions and conflicts of the village which were expressed in these weddings through finally examining something of their historical background. The villagers of Wangwu shared with the Hmong of Wutong and other villages in Gongxian historical memories of the suppression of the Bo people, which was inscribed in the surrounding landscape as a living and felt history. In one local account I was given by an educated young man of the village, which I reproduce here in full, the inscription of a legendary history in the contours of a local landscape and everyday life, as well as the appeal to local scholarly sources, was particularly evident:

The Story of the Ha Kings

This is the story of the First Ha (or A King) (A was a surname used by the Boren, as we know since in 1983 in Luobiao a hanging coffin was discovered to have had wooden (chopsticks) with the name A Mu Dan on it).[1] This first Ha King was able to fly in a dustpan,[2] and he established a city known as The City of the Nine Silk Threads. The first site he chose for this city was in Feiyingzai (Flying Eagle Village), where there are now two hamlets, and although it took as much as 3 liang *of silk threads to encircle the site, it was still too small for him, so he chose a new site which required 9* liang *of silk threads to encompass. At that time there were two Ming generals, Zongping Liu Xian and Xuenfu Zeng Xingwu who in 1573, which was the first year of the Wanli reign, led an army to attack the First Ha King and the Second Ha King, who was his brother. But the*

---

[1] The Chinese character used for this is pronounced 'Ha', but the local Hmong always said 'A'.

[2] I translate the Hmong term used here, *ciblaug*, as 'dustpan'; it is a kind of three-cornered basket used for throwing rubbish and ashes out of the house. In Chinese versions it may be a *baji* which is referred to, the meaning of which has some variations according to locality; Graham's informants may more poetically have talked of *baji* meaning 'winnowing baskets' as his translations have it (which in Hmong would be quite different from a dustpan; *vab*).

generals were unable to defeat the Ha Kings because the City of Nine Silk Threads was so strong. So fnally Liu Xian took advantage of the Double Ninth, the Ninth Day of the Ninth Month, when the Bo were worshipping their gods (this is also the Chinese festival of chongyangjie *when people climb high mountains to visit their ancestors), and they attacked on that day.*

Only one road led up the mountain but Liu Xian got his soldiers to pile up wood behind the mountain, and one of his spies among the peasant soldiers sent a signal to him when they were all drunk, so then they set fire to the wood and the Bo all ran out, and there are fossils of burnt rice to prove it. After the city was taken and the First Ha King had been killed, he picked up his head and flew in a dustpan to a place where he saw an old woman, planting vegetables. And he asked her, 'You are planting vegetables. If vegetables have no heads, can they still live?'

And the old woman replied, 'Without heads, they cannot live'. After hearing this, he stamped on the ground, threw away his head, and died—and that is why the place is called Boxiaxiang, and you can still find the footprint there where he stamped at Jiubanyan (Footprint Rock).

The second Ha King also rode away on a wooden 'horse' to the border of Gongxian and Xingwen and two other xiang *(Jianwu and Shibei) where he was also killed by the Ming soldiers, so that place is called Xiarengou (the Vale of Death). According to the Gongxian chronicles, the second Ha King was actually killed in Liupansan, Guizhou; according to the chronicles of Gongxian and Xingwen, the Ming soldiers captured more than 300 Bo prisoners, and some surrendered and joined the Ming army but others were released and no one knows where they went. The chronicles agree on the dating but disagree on the content.*

The Hmong came here after the conquest of the City of Nine Silk Threads. There were some Hmong here before then, but they were not permanent settlers because there was so much fighting. Wang Wu was not Hmong, but married a Hmong women.

Liu Xian's son was called Liu Ting. He was not an important participant in the battle, but his name is written at the bottom of the memorial tablet in Jianwu Qu (nearby), so he is buried in the earth.

He was so angry he kicked over the tablet but vomited up blood and died.

My own hometown is called Caoying because one of the Ming generals named Cao who besieged the City of Nine Silk Threads camped his soldiers there.[3]

I live in Group (Hamlet) 3, Xincun (Xin village), Caoying xiang (Caoying township), Gongxian. This hamlet is also named Makan (Horse Ridge), because the First Ha King's hometown was in 1) Luobiao xiang 2) Matangba, but the city he founded was in Jiusicheng (the City of Nine Silk Threads) which was very far away so he had to travel to work everyday. From Makan to Jiusicheng ran a cave called Makuadong (Horse Leap Cave) with the hoofprint of a horse. Under the cave was a valley called Taojiawanzi (the Tao Family Valley) and so whenever he left the cave he would ride across this valley, and that is why it was later called Makang.
(Tao Xiaoping)[4]

Such stories, signposted by the metaphorical riddle of the vegetables, form part of a genre of stories common in south China, which often employ geomantic idioms to express a discourse of rebellion against the sovereignty of the Emperor (Faure 1990; Tapp 1996). The theme of local Kings who survive decapitation to re-emerge reflects historical struggles against centralised Han authority, and I consider more Hmong stories in this vein in Part Three.

It was particularly significant that the above raconteur, of the Tao surname in the village, besides associating Hmong settlement in the region with the historical suppression of the Bo, should have denied that Wang Wu, the supposed original founder of the village, and ancestor of the dominant Hmong clan of the Wang in it, was Hmong. A locally published account, by one of the Liu clan in the village, which attributed the suppression of the Bo directly to Wang Wu, also depicted Wang Wu as Chinese (rather explicitly!).

---

[3] *Ying*, billet; hence, Cao's Camp.

[4] Graham (1954) gives three similar stories on the Ha Kings, but only dealing with how the imperial Chinese troops suppressed them.

Wangwuzhai Stockaded Village

> Wang Wu was a Han Chinese. His home was in Fujian province. During the Wanli Era of the Ming Dynasty, he distinguished himself by putting down the revolt led by the Bo leader, King Ha. After which, he travelled from Jianwu (now in Xingwen county) to the mountain behind the Luoxingdu ferry point. Later he married a young Miao girl. The couple were very much in love and agreed on this: should the husband pass away first, their descendants would become Miao people, and should the wife pass away first, then their descendants would be Han. In the end, it was Wang Wu who died before his wife, so that all their descendants became the Miao people.
>
> And the stockaded village built by Wang Wu came to be known as Wangwuzhai.[5]

We should remember that these stories refer to real historical events, since the remains of the 'Bo' people around Gongxian and Weixin of Yunnan have attracted considerable historical and archaeological attention. Early records such as the *Lishi Chunqiu* depict the Bo, who were often carried off as slaves, as a part of the ancient populations of the Di and Qiang during the Qin dynasty, at which time a Bo principality was established in Yibin. In the Han dynasty a Bo prefecture was established whch covered Dianchi in Yunnan and Xichuang in Sichuan. Tang dynasty records referred to the 'Bo Man', using a character which is now pronounced 'Bai' (in standard Chinese; in the southwest it is pronounced 'Bei'), and during the Yuan period their practice of hanging coffins was referred to in the *Yunnan zhilue*.[6] The consensus of general Chinese academic opinion is that they were ancestors of the present-day populations of the Bai, who are among the more sinicised of China's southwestern minorities.

The dominant Wang clan of Wangwuzhai, who traced their descent from Wang Wu, like the Yang of Wutong to whom they were closely related, did have a clan ancestral legend which pointed to an originally Chinese founding ancestor, and in all probability the Hmong Wang had some hybrid origins in which their ancestors had taken the side of the Chinese against the native peoples. Yet they

---

[5] By Liu Guanqing, in Fan Zhongchen 1988:83. I have published a preliminary consideration of this in Liu and Faure (1996).

[6] *Zhongguo da baike guanshu* 1986:54.

insisted that Wang Wu himself had been Hmong, and that it was his wife who had been Han, as in the following oral account by a Hmong Wang of Wangwuzhai:

In the second year of the reign of Wanli, Wang Wu joined the army to suppress an uprising of the First and Second Flower Kings (hua da wang and hua er wang). He went to southern Sichuan, first to Xingwen, and the army conquered this place. He left the next year and settled in Wangwucun (now Jianwu in Xingwen).. His wife's surname was Li, a Han who had married him before he arrived in Sichuan. Wangwu found Xingwen was not a suitable place to live in because the mountains were too high, and the water was too cold. So he decided to move to Fanjiadong, Luodu. Later their descendants moved here, which was named Wangwuzhai after their founding ancestor. Here the Wang family cultivated land and settled permanently.

The difference between the Tao and Liu accounts of Wang Wu as a Chinese, and the Wang insistence that he had been Hmong (although they had had other Chinese ancestors) arose from the historical rivalry there had been in the area between the Wang and members of other surname groups.

There had been a very serious conflict in Wangwuzhai for some time between the Wang family there, who had campaigned for Wangwuzhai to be declared an autonomous minority *xiang*, taking the name of their famous ancestor, and the other families who disagreed on the grounds that Wang Wu had in fact been a feudal despot who had suppressed a peasant revolt.

And this academic, historical, and political dispute of course reflected the fact that the Wang had been major landlords and hirers of labour in the area prior to 1949, by contrast with the other surnames in the village who had been poorer. The Wang family and the Liu, in particular, had been rivals for a very long time. Before 1949 the Wang family had boasted several big landlords who had been exceptionally wealthy in local terms, and the great tombs of the Wang family behind Liu Guangyong's house in the village bore witness to this. Some of them, I was told, had even been dug up by 'thieves' in search of treasure. Historically, the Wang had always surpassed the Liu both in numbers and in terms of local power.

Currently the Wang had reacquired some of their traditional prestige, and were proud of having two members in the county government[7] besides a number of teachers both in town and village schools, while the Liu family despite a former party membership and one important town position, were otherwise mostly only village teachers and officials.

The biggest problem lay in the founding of the 'Autonomous Miao Xiang', as it was known. The Wang family wanted the new *xiang* to be named after their illustrious ancestor, Wang Wu, who had founded the village and suppressed the Bo, but the Liu held that he had been a feudal army general and it would impossible therefore to name the *xiang* after him (they wanted the whole place to be called Jiulongshan, Nine Mountains, after the nearby range). What the Liu family, particularly the local Liu teachers, most feared was, as they said, that after the new *xiang* had been established, most of the important positions would be taken by the Wang, and the Liu would again fall under their domination. So educated people on both sides had written a number of reports to the relevant organisations, and they had even asked Yang Qing Bai, because of his position in the provincial Nationality Affairs Commission, to help. And there had been heated arguments over the site of the new *xiang* government and whether all the villages in Wangwuzhai should combine to form the *xiang*. Because of all this dissension, the new *xiang* had still not yet been approved.

So that the attempt to declare Wangwuzhai a minority *xiang*, which would in fact have carried considerable benefits for all its residents as most of them recognised, had been held up by the fierce conflict between the Wang who wanted it named after their heroic ancestor, and the Liu and other clans who opposed this and wanted it named after a nearby mountain. This war of names, reflected in a historical debate about whether Wang Wu had really been a peasant hero or a feudal oppressor of peasants, expressed a more deeply rooted conflict over the traditional political dominance of the Wang, who had been the pre-revolutionary landlords in the area and were still numerically strong and well represented in local official and government circles. Pitted against them, rather as the Zeng had been

---

[7] Wang Fuzhang at the Gongxian Agricultural Bureau, and Wang Shuizhang at the Bureau of Culture and Education.

opposed to the Yang in Wutong, were in particular the Liu, with a
pre-revolutionary background labelled as 'poor peasant', who had
'come up' through a party membership in the 1950s and 1960s, and
now also occupied a number of significant local administrative and
educational positions. Mostly the Liu were teachers, but Liu Guanqin
was chief of the Bureau of Civil Affairs (*minzheng ju*). The struggle
was essentially about local dominance, and the number of positions
in the newly proposed *xiang* government which members of the
different lineages would occupy.

It is most significant that Yang Qingbai, as a high-ranking Minwei
cadre from Beijing, who had recently achieved further fame in the
district through the visit and largesse of his oldest brother from
Taiwan, and who accompanied us to the weddings in Wangwuzhai,
should have been asked to mediate in the conflict in this way, since it
shows the prominent position this Y3c Yang lineage segment of
Wutong village had acquired locally through their overseas and
external connections in the district as a whole.

Feelings ran deep in this struggle for local dominance between
patrilineal clans, since the Liu and Tao had their own claims to the
original founding of the Wangwuzhai area, as this account shows:[8]

> A Miao, Liu I Mbai (the 'I' usually signifying a founding ancestor)
> came and reported to the official that he would occupy Shih T'i Chai
> (Strong Ladder Stronghold) and make clearings. Another, Tao I Guai
> (or Kuei) also went and reported about the wilderness and occupied
> Ch'iao Ch'ang Pa (Long Bridge Flat). This was certainly at a very
> early time. Later, in the first year of Wan Li (AD 1573), they went
> again and reported (that they would occupy the wilderness). In the
> third year of Wan Li the Chinese came and conquered the Miao at
> Chiu-Shih-Ch'eng near Hsin Wen Hsien. At that time Ha Ta Wa and
> Ha Er Wa rebelled. Ha Ta Wa at Chiu-Shih-Ch'eng put yellow clay
> inside bamboo tubes. He said 'This is what I passed out of my
> bowels'. He used leather four feet long to make leather shoes and told
> people these were the shoes he wore. He could put two winnowing
> baskets under his armpits and fly. He used a broom as a tail. In the
> second year of Wan Li he was killed. His two winnowing baskets fell
> below Chien Wu Ch'eng, and that place is called Po-chi-hsin
> (winnowing-basket gorge).

---

[8] Graham (1954:360; 'When the Miao came to Wang Wu Chai').

Here it was the Miao who were conquered by the Han, and some relationship between the Miao and the rebellious Ha Kings sems to be implied. It may well be that there was a historical division between incoming Hmong such as the Wang who had taken the side of the imperial troops, and other Hmong families, settled earlier in the region, who had been caught up in the general unrest, of the type generally depicted by the Chinese between the 'raw' and the 'cooked' minority groups. It is however also possible that Wang Wu had been a Han Chinese, who had married into a Hmong household and whose descendants had formed the local Hmong clan of the Wang, as indeed their clan ancestral origin legend declares had occurred at other points on the tree.

The Tao and Liu

Yet lineage conflicts at Wangwu were not limited to the traditional rivalries between the Wang and other clans. The Liu were also involved in a serious dispute with the Tao, and in particular with Tao Yuankao, director of the local clinic, who had married the sister of Liu Guanyuan, headmaster of the primary school started by Graham, and of Liu Guankui, one of the teachers, whose son Liu Fucheng was marrying a Yang girl related to the Yang of Wutong village and whose wedding I have drawn on in the preceding chapter. For one thing, Tao Yuankao (whose son Tao Sen, another teacher, had married a Li girl whose mother was also a Yang related to Yang Qingbai) had recently accused his Liu brothers-in-law of stealing and copying and illegally selling a geography school textbook, and had had a furious row with his Liu father-in-law about this. This seemingly trivial affair in fact reflected a more long-standing enmity between the Tao and Liu, which Tao Yuankao's marriage had failed to resolve. This had been expressed in a geomantic dispute over Tao Yuankao's mother-in-law's grave (that is, the mother of the Liu brothers, who had also been a Yang, very closely related as we will see to the Wutong Yangs, as Yang Wanjun's half-sister). Tao Yuankao had wanted to shift his Liu wife's Yang mother's grave from its current location, which he considered unfavourable for his own children, to a more auspicious site, but was firmly opposed in this by his Liu brothers-in-law and their father, as well as by members of the Yang Y2a lineage in Wuting who were related to Tao Yuankao's Yang mother-in-law (Yang Wanjun's half-sister). The Liu further resented Tao Yuankao's opinions in this case since he was only their sister's second husband; her first husband, despite the general rivalry between the Liu and Wang, had been a Wang Xaohua, who had been executed for taking part in the landlords' resistance, locally described as the 'bandit's rebellion', of 1951-2.[9] It was after Wang Xaohua's execution and disgrace that the Liu had begun to prosper at the expense of the Wang.

In the account I had from one villager who knew the case well:

In February 1989 Liu Guanyuan and Liu Guankui's sister named Liu Guanyin (not Tao's wife), who had married Yu Faquan and lives in Lushai qu, Fuxin xiang, came to invite her father (Liu Yunzhou) to her house for a xi (post-mortuary ritual). Tao Yuankao's wife (her sister) also came with her father to Fuxin. Later Liu Guanyin's husband (Yu Faquan), sent his father-in-law back home (and Tao Yuankao's wife must have gone back with him). When they got to Luodo, they decided to stay the night in Tao Yuankao's house (after which old Liu Yunzhou would return to Liu Guanyuan's house where he lives. He lives with his son; his wife used to live with Liu Guankui but later died). That night at Tao Yuankao's house, Tao Yuankao got drunk and said some evil things; he said that his brother-in-law Liu Guankui had borrowed a geography textbook from him and given it to Liu Laoba (a first cousin of Liu Yunzhou's), who had given it to some other people to copy and then they had sold the copies on the streets. Tao Yuenkao cursed Liu Laoba three times and called him a gouxide. So Liu Yunzhou was furious and said, 'You said Liu Laoba was a dog-fucker, so I am a dog-fucker and my dog-daughter got married to you and you already have puppies. I don't want to stay the night in your house; I will go!' Tao Yuankao dragged him back to the house twice but failed; in the end Liu Yunzhou spent the night at Yang Wanqun's (who used to be called *Tao Yungui).*

Tao Yuankao knew a bit about geomancy and had decided on a grave-site for his wife's Yang mother (who used to live with Liu Guankui), but Liu Guankui moved his mother's grave to another

---

[9] She had had one daughter by her first marriage, and several by her second husband before giving birth to Tao Sen.

place. This upset Tao Yuankao and he said, 'you have moved my mother-in-law's grave-site, this year a disaster will befall you, it is bad baoyin *(karma). So your daughter was tricked into going to Jiangsu (i.e. sold into marriage)—this is bad fortune', so both the Liu brothers were extremely angry and eventually Liu Guanyuan too quarreled with Tao Yuankao.*

Diagram 43 presents a simplified version of these relations.

We can now sense something of the complex history of conflicts and tensions which lay behind the Yang girl's wedding in Wangwuzhai. As we shall find shortly, the bride's father had rejected his own upbringing as a Tao and reclaimed an original Yang identity as a mark of his solidarity with the Liu, while Tao Yuankao's family, including his Liu wife and his son's affinal Yang relatives, boycotted the entire part of the wedding of Tao Yuenkao's wife's brother's son to the Yang girl which took place at the Liu house on account of his continuing quarrels with his Liu brothers-in-law.

Geomantic Conflicts

The geomantic system, as Freedman (1966, 1968)and Feuchtwang (1974) both showed, tends to act as a focus for sibling rivalry within lineages and indeed as an expression of social conflict generally (Aijmer 1968). Geomancy is a ritual and poetic system shared by the Chinese and the Hmong, as I have shown elsewhere (Tapp 1989), in which the siting of ancestor's graves on 'strong' points of the landscape, where the natural energy or *pa*[10] courses, is believed to benefit the fortunes of particular lines of descendants. While the Wang-Liu conflict between lineages had been expressed in terms of a *historical* debate, in the case of the Tao-Liu dispute between 'brothers-in-law' lineages it was the *geomantic* system which was appealed to. Another geomantic conflict, this time involving the Yang clan of Wutong with Wangwuzhai, illustrated the more classic use of geomancy to express sibling-like rivalries *within* a patrilineal lineage.

---

[10] The *qi*, in Chinese.

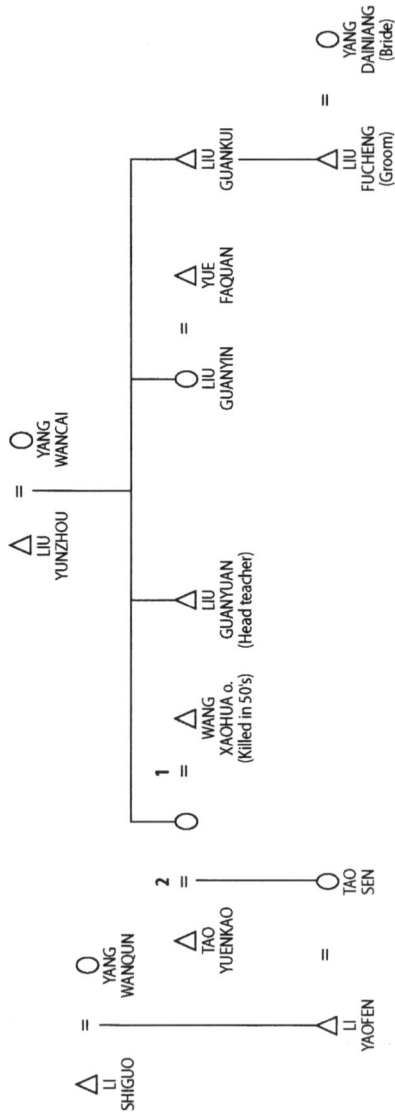

Diagram 43: The Liu family (simplified)

For in Wangwuzhai there was also a conflict between Yang Qing Bai's first cousins who lived there (Yang Wankui and Yang Wanwen, descendants of the same Liu paternal grandmother as Yang Qingbai) who wanted to bury their own (Huang) mother in the same site as their paternal grandmother, in order to share in some of the good fortune of Yang Qingbai and his brothers in Wutong. Again Yang Qingbai had been asked to intervene in this local dispute, and in this case had been specifically requested to write a letter to his elder brother in Taiwan to ask him to mediate in the case. The burial site in question was a particularly auspicious one, and the story of how the Yang had first acquired it reflects the particularly close relations which this Y3c lineage of the Yang clan of Wutong village (Yang Qingbai's) enjoyed with the villagers of Wangwu.[11]

Yang Junming, as we saw in Chapter 7, was the father of the Yang brothers in Wutong, and had another brother (Yang Shuran) who had settled in Wangwuzhai, where his two sons still lived.. One day, long before 1949, when Yang Junming was visiting his brother in Wangwuzhai, his brother had told him of a special place he knew in the mountains near Wangwu. The cattle always rested here, both in the heat of summer and in the cold of winter, since it remained cool in the summer and warm in winter, and there never seemed to be any flies or mosquitoes there. A thin topsoil covered the limestone base, and it appeared to be a very special place, surrounded by mountains in four directions. To its west, there were five mountains (geomantically representing the Four Ministers to either side of the Emperor). To its east, there rose a small hill, seeming to embrace and protect the whole area. To north and south there were also mountains, so that the hollow in the middle resembled a lotus emerging out of water. The place was known locally as the 'Five Sons' Attainments'.

This piece of mountainland, however, belonged to the absentee *Han* landlord family of the He, who many of the local Hmong worked for at the time. Since Yang Junming had a good knowledge of geomancy he was determined to acquire the place as a burial site, and tried to buy it from the He family, but he took great care not to

---

[11] Liu Guanyong, himself related to the Yangs, had this story from the elder brother of Yang Junming.

tell them exactly which plot of land he wanted in case they should guess that the land had geomantic advantages and wish to keep it for themselves. Some of the He lived in the village, but most of them were in Chengdu and knew nothing about the deal Yang Junming proposed. The He in the village agreed to sell most of the land, including the plot which Yang Junming wanted; they first excluded the best farmland and pasture, and then they asked Yang Junming to specify which part of the remainder it was that he wanted. But Yang Junming had been too clever for this. He refused to specify which piece of land he wanted, but insisted that a contract first be drawn up for the whole of the land, allowing him to buy whichever smaller part of it he wished at a fixed price, and signed. Since he was prepared to agree a particularly high price, the local He family finally agreed to let him have the land he wanted, but then some of the absentee members of the He family had returned to the village and refused to agree to the sale since they realised what Yang Junming was up to. They eventually had to go to court over the ownership, where Yang Junming won because of his signed contract. And this was where he buried his father's mother, who was a Xiong, transferring her bones from Wutong where they had previously been interred, and later his own mother, who had been a Liu.

But he had had another furious altercation with his own geomantic teacher about the exact siting of this grandmother's grave. His teacher had wanted the grave located in the north, facing south, but he insisted it should be in the east facing the west (towards the 'Mountain of the Emperor'. In the end the teacher was so infuriated by his recalcitrance that he had refused to instruct him any further (see Diagrams 44 and 45).

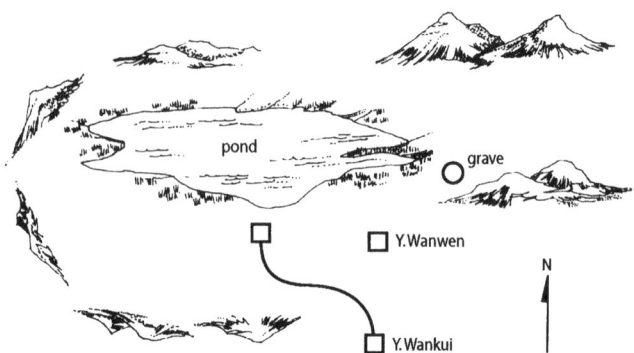

Diagram 44: The geomantic site

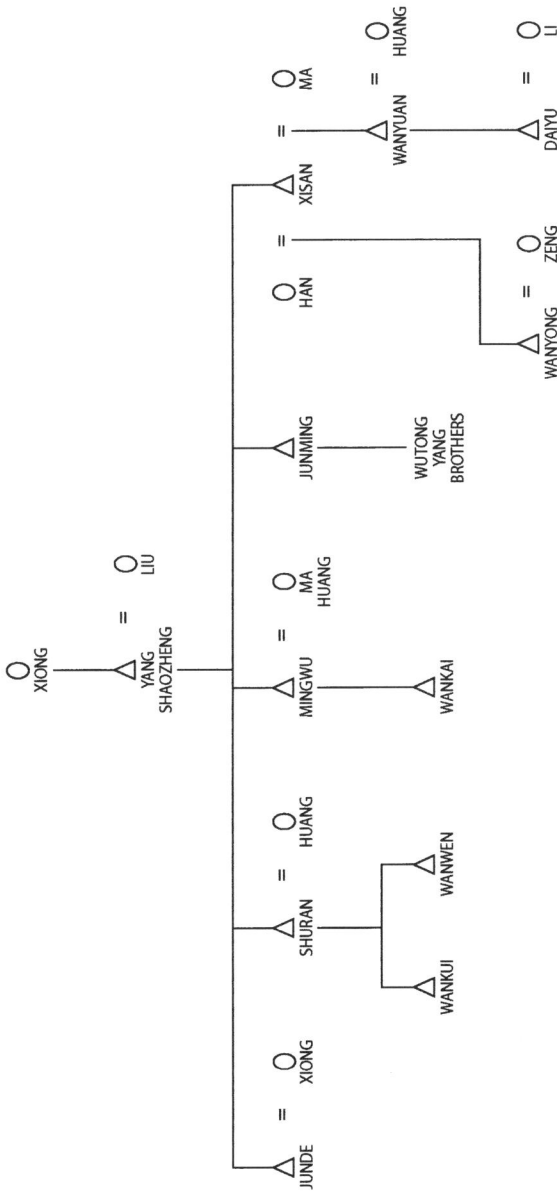

Diagram 45: Yang Junming's geomantic relatives

Now Yang Wankui and Yang Wanwen wished to bury their own (Huang) mother in this grave in order to benefit their own line, but their first cousins Yang Wanli and his brother Yang Liping in Wutong were both against this, and here again their elder brother Yang Qingbai had been asked to intervene, in this case specifically to appeal to their oldest brother Yang Wanliang in Taiwan. There was no dispute about these cousins' common paternal grandmother's *Liu* grave.

This was a remarkable case, not only in showing how geomantic disputes can mirror the rivalries *within* lineages as well as between them, the importance of maternal ancestors in the geomancy practiced by the Hmong, and the persistence of geomantic practices under socialist rule, but also in showing that local lineage disputes involving burial practices and geomantic beliefs may necessitate an appeal to the adjudication of external and high-status relatives far removed from the village, in this case as far away as Taiwan. It also of course demonstrates the very common rivalries between Hmong and Han which are so often expressed in tales of geomantic trickery and competition.

A very common Hmong story, which I heard in Thailand and is also given by Graham (1954,p.27), relates how the Han and Hmong were originally brothers but worshipped at the grave of their father at different times of the year, so that in time their descendants grew apart from each other and were unable to understand each other's languages (see Appendix IV for a hybrid version of this).

Affinal Tigers

Despite the many intermarriages between patrilineal clans, there was still considerable mistrust expressed between the members of Hmong clans, and these were reflected in China as in South East Asia by tales of lycanthropy, tales of transformations into beings unlike oneself. . I was told (by young male members of the Wutong Yang) that it was still quite common for members of the Wang clan to turn into tigers, and particularly common were cases where an elder brother became a tiger, while his younger brother's wife (often as we have seen Yang) became a tiger's wife. The corpse of one of the Yang girls, Yang Daiqin, from Wutong, who had married a young Wang in Fenghuang, was said to have disappeared three days after her death, leaving behind a foul animal stench. Her father's two elder brothers were both good hunters, so they had set off to hunt the animal; they succeeded in finding it, and shot it, and even removed its skin, but then it again vanished, and that night the tigresss appeared to them both in a dream, reproaching them for having shot at it, since it had not tried to eat them. Such stories are told in a semi-jocular way, as one might tell ghost stories, but children believe them, and adults may half-believe them. When is a belief not a belief? When you are telling stories about your in-laws, and their designs on your sisters.

There is a delight in such stories.[12] Yang Qingbai once told me, almost seriously, that *most* of the closely interconnected Tao and Xiong men also become tigers, and that their wives then become the lovers of tigers, and that this was hereditary among the Tao and Xiong. Once, he said, Tao Geliang's family in Junliang killed a tigress, and then a Xiong family came to see them to beg them to return the bones to them (shades of geomantic practice here). And they had to build a special statue of a tiger on a hill to show that the tiger's bones had, indeed, been returned. This was why there is still today a shrine with a statue of a tiger inside it, on Wangwuzhai mountain where a stream marks the boundary of Luodu with Luoyi *xiang* in Junlian.

And then somebody told another story, of how a couple were once working in their fields when a tiger caught the wife and took her away to the mountains. The husband searched high and low to find her, blowing his flute, until one day he spied his wife among a group of tigers beneath a rock, embroidering as a good wife should. He kept spitting down onto the cloth she was embroidering, to let her know he was up there, but she kept thinking it was birdshit, and wiping it away (this is the bit that gets the children).Eventually she catches sight of him, and warns him not to come up to her straight away or the tigers will eat him, but to wait until the tigers return from hunting and then shoot them, which is what he did. But in that place you can still hear the song he played on the flute, and the echo of her words, 'Don't look for me, tigers have borne me away'... We turn to

---

[12] See Appendix III.

a more analytic consideration of these stories at which the Hmong excel in Part III.

Some Genealogical Complexities

With this understanding of how some of the major conflicts and cleavages in the history of the village had taken concrete form in arguments about the founding of the village, geomantic burial siting, and geography text-book sales, we can now return to consider some of the ways in which the two weddings which were the subject of the previous chapter expressed a dynamic situation of constantly shifting change and the reciting of relations. The first wedding at Wangwuzhai was that of the not so young 'Yang' 'girl', Yang Dainiang, to Liu Fucheng who was the son of Liu Guankui who, as we have seen, was in dispute with his Tao brother-in-law both over a matter involving the sale of geography textbooks, and over the geomantic siting of his own (Yang) mother's grave.

Yang Wanjun was the Grand Manager on the bridal side, seconded by Yang Wankai, a FBS of Yang Qingbai. The rivalries of the past (Ch.8) between these two Yang segments of Wutong had been largely overcome, particularly where the occasion of a Yang marrying a Liu united different Yang segments together in a segmentary fashion.

This wedding of Yang Dainiang had a number of remarkable features, which is the reason we consider it here. In particular, the bride's father (Yang Wanqun) had only recently reconverted to being a Yang, having been adopted and brought up as a Tao and previously known as Tao Yungui (as we saw in the story of the Liu-Tao quarrel over the textbooks above, old Liu Yunzhou had left his Tao son-in-law's house in a rage, to spend the night in Tao Yungui's house, who had deserted his Tao clan of adoption at the time). After his own, Yang, father had died, his Tao mother had returned to her natal family in Wangwu where he had been brought up as Tao. But he had been ten years old at the time his Yang father had died, and still conscious of his Yang affiliations. The Liu family in Wangwu had played on this and involved him on their side in their dispute with Tao Yuankao; he had become a good friend of Liu Guankui, whose son his daughter (by a Wang wife) was now to wed, and had reverted to his original, Yang, clan identity in what was seen as a public expression of his support for the Liu in their quarrels with the Tao.

Not only was this bride's father of such an equivocal clan affiliation; he was also first paternal cousin to a female, Yang Wanqun[13] whose Li daughter had married the son of Tao Yuankao, who was on such bad terms with his brother-in-law, the Liu groom's father.

This Yang Wanqun line was distantly related, as classificatory FBS, to the line of Yang Wanli and Yang Qingbai (Y3c) in Wutong, and Yang Wanli had in fact acted as 'parent' (*natxwv*) for the recent marriage of the (female) Yang Wanqun's daughter to Tao Yuankao's son, since her own husband (Li Shiguo), had died.

Most extraordinarily, though, was that old Yang Wanjun from Wutong, here representing the Yang bride as her Grand Manager in her wedding to a Liu, quite apart from the fact that he was in any case related to the Wutong Yang brothers as a member of another lineage (Y2a) of the Wutong Yangs (Ch.7), was himself the half-brother of the Liu bridegroom's FM, who had been a Yang.

Diagram 46 shows the full version of this.

In effect, then, the Yang bride (Dainiang) was one of the groom's FM's half-brother's classificatory 'daughters', being of the Dai generation rather than the Wan generation among the Yang, and the daughter of a cousin of Yang Wanjun's. In general care was taken to avoid marriages between equivalent generations of different surnames who were co-residential, although sometimes these did occur (as when Yang Daisong, in chapter 9, had married a Ma girl of the same generation as the Wang family his son had married).

The groom's Grand Master was Liu Guangzai and the Lesser Master Liu Chiluo. The second marriage we took part in at Wangwu was that of groom Wang Zhongqin to bride Zhou Damei, and this was in fact the wedding I had been particularly invited to. The Wang wedding was beautifully organised and orchestrated by members of the dominant Wang clan of the village, much as in the ideal order of wedding ritual given in chapter 10, although owing to the various tensions we have considered of the Wang with the Liu and Tao on the one hand, and between the Liu and Tao on the other hand, my

---

[13] Unfortunately these two paternal first cousins, one male and one female, had exactly the same name.

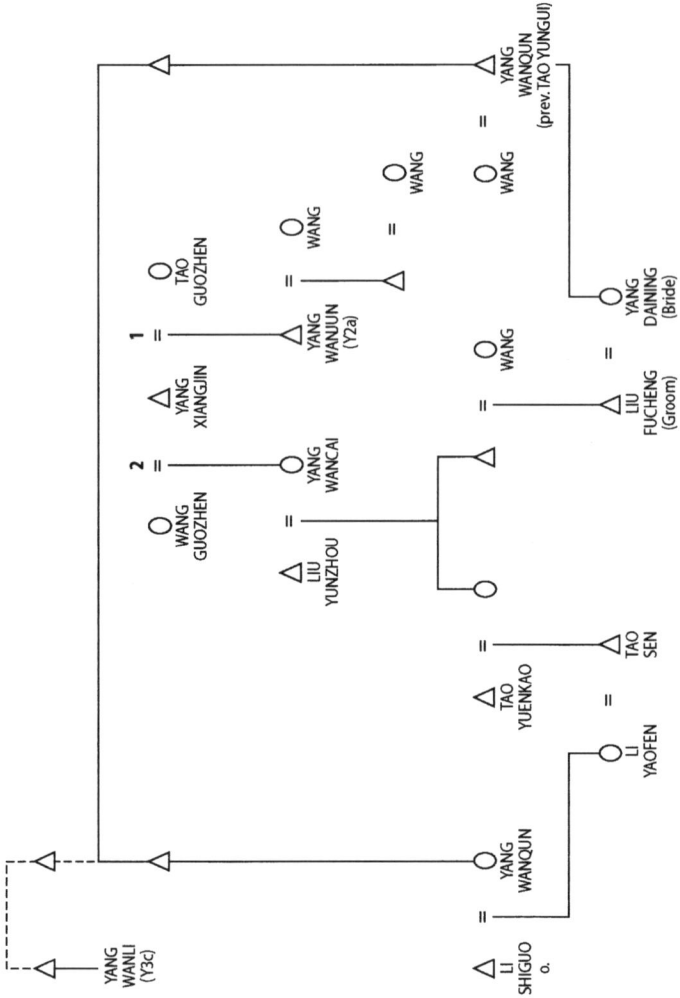

Diagram 46: The Liu family

Yang companions from Wutong, mindful of their own intricate positioning in this mesh of affinal alliances, had to take extreme precautions to avoid offending anyone. All attentions and gifts had to be equally and nicely distributed, and it was even necessary to change the clan of the householder we stayed with each night for this reason.

For the Yang of Wutong were also related to the marrying Wang family, and had to remember their proper genealogical positioning at every turn. The Grand and Lesser Managers for the Wang groom's side were Wang Xaojin and Wang Xaoshen, and on the Zhou bride's side, a *Wang* Qijun and Zhou Xaozhen. Again (like the Yang bride's family at Wangwuzhai, and two of Yang Qingbai's own cousins), this Wang Qijun, who acted as Grand Manager for the Zhou bride, had actually been born a Zhou himself, so that it was still thought appropriate for him to act on behalf of the Zhou; he had taken on his mother's natal Wang surname after she had been widowed while he was still young (just under eight years old). These quite frequent adoptions and changes of surname, whether occasioned by an impoverished son-in-law marrying a richer girl with no brothers to carry on her father's line, or through young children after their fathers' deaths assuming either their mother's maiden surnames or the surnames of their step-fathers, contributed to a fluid and dynamic, volatile *process* (rather than a 'system') of kinship, a very practical kinship *situation* in which identities were often changing and evolving. Adoptions, second marriages, and the assumption of father-in-law surnames, were not so much exceptions to a general standard of behaviour, as may be the case in Han communities (Watson 1982), but part of a more volatile patterning of kinship identifications.

Old Yang Wanjun, bridal Grand Manager at the Liu wedding, was also maternally related to the Wang groom in the Wang wedding, since this Wang groom's father (Wang Xizhong) had married Yang Xiangmei, whose FFBSSS was Yang Wanjun himself. Moreover, the Wang groom's father's own FB was Wang Puzhang, and Wang Puzhang's daughter (Wang Yongcui) had married Yang Dailu, the branch party secretary of the X3 line from Wutong who also accompanied us.

In fact Yang Wanjun had particularly close Wang connections; he, his son, his brother and two of his brother's sons, had all married

Wang who had some connection to the Wang of Wangwuzhai. So, while Yang Qingbai played a seminal part in the Wangwuzhai weddings as the politically well connected outsider, Yang Wanjun played the pivotal role as the master of marital customs and genealogical relations at both these weddings. He knew all the lengthy and vibrant strings of kinship connections involved as well as the traditional Hmong wedding procedures which had re-emerged in the early eighties, and, as a wedding specialist and elder kinsman, was treated with as much respect at the Wang wedding as at the Liu wedding where he occupied the formal role of bridal Manager.

The geomantic dispute (in which Yang Qingbai had been invited to intervene) between the Tao and the Liu clans involved the grave of the Liu brothers' mother, who was mother-in-law to the Tao. We may see that this was actually the grave of *Yang Wanjun's half-sister*, who was considered as a real sister in every respect, since distinctions between the children of different mothers are normally completely ignored.[14]

Given the serious conflict between the Tao and the Liu brothers over the placing of the latters' mother's grave, and particularly since Tao Yuankao's fierce argument over textbooks with his old father-in-law Liu Yunzhou, it is understandable that the Tao (that is, Tao Yuankao with all his children and his wife, even though she was the groom's own paternal aunt, and thus should have played an important part in his wedding) should have entirely boycotted the Liu part of the Liu-Yang wedding; the departure from the house and the reception of the bride at the groom's. But so did (the female Yang Wanqun), although she was the Yang bride's father's paternal cousin and another of the Wutong Yangs, Yang Wanli, had officiated at her own daughter's recent wedding. This was because her daughter had married Tao Yuankao's son; as a widow she had moved in to live with Tao Yuenkao and her daughter, and did not wish to upset the new Tao in-laws she now lived with.

---

[14] This may seem odd to those familiar with the notion of 'half' sisters or brothers, but it is the case that these children are usually brought up equally in every way, and taught to ignore their differences of birth, and only very rarely that a mother is sufficiently irresponsible to favour her own children over the other children of her husband.

In this Liu-Yang wedding, we might see the Yang as celebrating a kind of victory over the Tao, since the Yang bride's father had rejected his Tao affiliation and returned to the Yang fold, while the Yang were after all 'giving' a bride to the Liu who had themselves fallen out so badly with the Tao, both in a geomantic dispute which involved a Yang grave, the grave of Yang Wanjun's own half-sister, and over the recent more trivial, but still rankling, affair of the textbooks. We can understand even more clearly, then, why Tao Yuankao felt humiliated by the wedding of his Liu brother-in-law's son to one of the Yang girls, who should moreover have been a Tao herself if her father had not changed clans.

While the Liu brothers had as we have seen had a *Yang* mother, they had also had a *Wang* MM, and so old Yang Wanjun, with his own close Wang connections, was in a particularly strange relationship towards them. He was seen by them as a kind of MB since he shared a Father with their own Mother and yet, in a semi-paternal way, as one of the Wan generation of the Wutong Yangs, he was sponsoring the marriage of a young *Yang* girl to one of their sons, which put him doubly in an affinal position towards them, but this time at their own generational level (more like their son's bride's FB than their own MB); doubly affinal, then, through their parents and their children.

The marriage was locally recognised as an MBD type one; in Hmong, *raw muas nyaa* (Ch. *sui mujao*), or where a girl follows her FZ (our MBD marriage, since the Hmong and Chinese are more female-centred in their analyses!). MBD matches were more common in the region, and FZD disapproved of. For example, Yang Wangkun in Wutong, son of Yang Zhijun, had had three generations of real MBD marriages, he, his father and son all marrying Wang of the same family. These sorts of marriage are distinguished from simple exchanges arranged between clans where bride and groom were not already well acquainted known as 'shoulder-pole weddings', which had been becoming more common in Gongxian in the past, and the occasional direct exchange marriage (where a brother may marry the sister of his sister's husband), which was known as 'cutting off the water' marriage because it seems to rule out the need for further exchanges between the two families. The dowry and rituals and matchmakers are all said to be 'returned', and these marriages usually take place on the same day.

Conceptually (since a half-brother is involved, although this is not seen as significant), one of the Liu brothers' sons is marrying their own MBD; furthermore, this more-or-less (half) and doubly (ascendant and descending) Mother's Brother's *own* Mother was a *Tao* (Tao Guizhen). From the point of view of Liu Guanyuan, the local headmaster whose nephew was the groom, his sister had married one Tao, his marrying nephew's new father-in-law had been brought up as a Tao, and his own mother's half-brother's mother (like a kind of MM) had *also* been a Tao.

Yang Wanjun, then, whom we accompanied from Wutong, was the *epitome* of the ambivalent and equivocal affinal relative, representing at the same time the Liu brothers' mother, their sister's husband, and their son's wife, all in different ways (as their mother's Yang half-brother, as a half-Tao like their own sister's difficult husband, and again as a Yang in a paternal relationship to the girl their son was marrying -or was she really to be considered a Yang? was she not, perhaps, still a Tao manque?). We can see here something of the intricacies and complexities of the real kinship and affinal relations which the Sichuan Hmong play out in their interactions with other Hmong, with their capacity for change and transformation, which defeat and ridicule formal models of kinship.

Identity and Difference

Throughout Part II we have witnessed a complex dialectic of Hmong/Chinese similarities and differences, expressed in an idiom of patrilineal kinship shared by Hmong and Han, which allows for intermarriage (and assimilation through adoption) between the two, but in which it is notable that the male is always privileged.

Ethnic difference may be figured in the rivalry between two brothers typical of the patrilineal descent system, as when stories such as that given above are told of two brothers of a common ancestry whose descendants then diverge to become respectively the Han, or the Hmong, or in the story given in Chapter 5 of the Hmong brother who killed his (partly Chinese) brother (see Diagram 47).[15]

---

[15] See also Appendix IV.

Diagram 47: Diverging descent

It may however be figured, in the case of particular Hmong patrilineages, by the *absence* of male descendants which has necessitated the *presence* of an affinal, Chinese son-in-law—all or some of whose descendants have then *ignored* the principles of patrilineal descent, to follow their *mother's* ethnic affiliation, in assuming a Hmong identity. Here, Hmong identity is still given as prior; the Chinese intervention has been an unfortunate necessity, swiftly disavowed by the re-assumption of a continuist Hmong identity by at least some of his descendants, a re-assumption which resumes the fiction of patrilineal descent despite the intermission of the *mother* who, in this case, occupies the place which *should* be occupied by a (Hmong) father (Diagram 48). Yet there is also a claim to a common ancestry with the Chinese implied here, as in the story of the two brothers but inverted (Diagram 49).

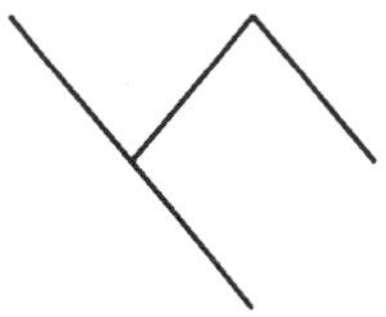

Diagram 48: Intervening descent

Diagram 49: Convergence

The legend of Wangwu given in this Chapter is extraordinary in that it seems to imply a *choice* of ethnic identity by the descendants of a mixed marriage, although indeed this is quite often the case for the children of such mixed marriages in China today, and must indeed have been so to some extent in the past. What is surprising, in this story, is the overt recognition of these optative choices, in what one would otherwise assume to be a situation of ethnic exclusionism and essentialism. For indeed Hmong and Han cultural identities are very much essentialised at the local level, as we have seen (Diagram 50).

Diagram 50: Convergence and divergence (optation)

And then there are adoptions, which are also relatively common between the members of different ethnic groups in south China. Adopted children, like the children of different mothers, are brought up in every way as equal to natural children, and no differentiation is made between them. Thus the origins of an adopted son (I have never heard of the case of an adopted daughter) are altogether disavowed; it is unusual that sons would be adopted beyond the age of puberty, and usually children who are adopted, like the children of two wives or indeed the children of a remarried widow, grow up with no consciousness of their natural origins. The result of adoption is then the same as that of the in-marrying son-in-law (Diagram 51).

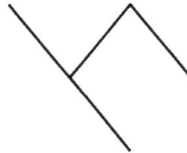

Diagram 51: Adoption

Sons are most usually adopted where male heirs are lacking, and in this sense the adoption of a Chinese son as in the Yang origin story given in Chapter 7 does resemble the acceptance of a Chinese son-in-law. The effects of these two processes are then similar, in that descendants might or might not assume a Hmong identity (Diagram 52).

There is never a Tallensi-type claim to differential descent through ethnically different mothers (two wives), as there might be given ubiquitous Hmong polygyny and the occasional but highly significant marriages with Han (e.g. Diagram 53). The reasons for this lie both in the strong ideology of descent which disavows half-brothers, and in the historical fact that it has almost invariably been Chinese men who married Hmong women, rather than the reverse.

Diagram 52: Optation

Diagram 53: Divergent filiation

While the Yang clan origin story in Chapter 7 (of the adopted Chinese son who took the Yang lands) points to some recognition of a long historical process of the assimilation and adoption of Chinese leading to a loss of patrimony, the other story (of Hmong descent being traced through a Chinese son-in-law, leading to both descent from Hmong (maternal) and Han (paternal) ancestors does as we have said contain an implicit claim to common ancestry with the Chinese, and is therefore closer to the story of the two brothers whose descendants diverged to become the Hmong and the Han (Diagram 54). Repeatedly in these stories, one finds the statement, 'we are *not* like the Han, though we *are*'! Similar to this was the repeated denial by villagers of marriages with Han despite the fact that they did take place. We consider the implications of this in the Conclusion to Part III.

Diagram 54: Common ancestry

Conclusion

This is intended as a partly experimental work, where an attempt has been made to involve the reader in as much of the process of research as possible, in a similar way to the researcher. This is why we have concentrated on household composition and lineage structure as much as we have, why the Wangwuzhai weddings have been gone into in such detail, and why I have tried to show how my own research fitted into a larger local context (Chapter VIII). Of course this may also be what Malinowski had hoped to do, in rejecting the larger, abstract theories of evolutionism and diffusionism of the day in favour of the 'minutiae' of daily life derived from the experience of fieldwork. Fieldwork can indeed be thought of at that time as a novel means of introducing a personal experience and *perspective* into what was overtly presented as a 'scientific' undertaking.[16] The structuralists who followed these early functionalists were particularly concerned to present theoretical adumbrations of 'other society' viewpoints which would communicate something of their 'rationality', a larger intention they shared with Malinowski. It was Firth who in 1964 first drew attention, drawing on Cassirer, to the problems of 'observer effect' which had begun to concern the physical sciences, problems of interpretation we now recognise as inherent in the personal nature of fieldwork.

But as Merleau-Ponty, whose Cézanne we briefly introduced towards the end of Part I, had (like other visionary philosophers) already so clearly seen, an apparent perspective-lessness in the paintings of Cézanne was in fact the result of the awareness of a plethora, a multiplicity, an ambiguity of perspectives which could not (should, need not) be reduced to the fascistic univocality of a merely 'single' interpretation—an attempt to encompass the all. So it was Cézanne's genius, that 'when the over-all composition of the picture is seen globally, perspectival distortions are no longer visible in their own right but rather contribute, as they do in natural vision, to the impression of an emerging order...' (Merleau-Ponty 1965:14).

---

[16] See Fardon (1990) on how the fieldwork experience has provided a relatively timeless paradigm of truth, unlike the shifting models of theory, despite its embeddedness in writing.

And so, of course, particularly in the light of re-appraisals of famous anthropological studies which have shed a quite different light on their interpretations, and the increasing questioning by formerly unvoiced subjects of the interpretions of themselves authorised by others, a reflective acceptance of the role of subjectivity in the fieldwork encounter with 'others' has now become standard. This does again raise general problems of interpretation, and the contexts in which particular interpretations are made, which will be the topic of Part III. In the preceding, through focusing on the composition of particular villages, and considering some of the religious and kinship practices through which Hmong encounters with others are locally framed and defined, I have tried to bring to life those aspects of the local setting which form the recognised context of social action, while at the same time not wishing to insist that this provides a sole, authoritative, context which would exclude other contexts and lead to different interpretations. We cannot maintain, as Hobart (1986) aptly puts it, that 'context can only play at the feet of the towering structure of culturally essential beliefs'.

The presumption of a 'completed synthesis', on which a real knowledge of the world could be based, is as Merleau-Ponty points out, impossible, because of the very nature of the perspectives which have to be inter-related, 'since each of them, by virtue of its horizons, refers to other perspectives, and so on indefinitely' (Merleau-Ponty 1965:330). When I speak of 'context', to which we return in Conclusion to Part III, I mean something very similar to what Merleau-Ponty had in mind when he spoke of 'horizons' and 'perspective'. The ideal synthesis of horizons is, as he also points out, essentially a temporal process; if a complete synthesis were ever actually achieved, and the world defined from no point of view, then nothing at all would exist; 'I should hover above the world...and would be involved nowhere'.

In Part Three, I move away from the level of individual social action and the local village setting, defined in its economic, social and political context, towards a consideration of cultural forms which express a trans-personal and non-individual sense of agency in a way which the tacit understandings of everyday engagements cannot do fully, through an examination of those myths and legends in which a particular sense of history and cultural identity is posed. We have already seen something of this in this chapter, through the painting of local differences and identities in Wangwuzhai in terms of a contested local history involving others besides the Hmong. We shall now see how a particular series of legends, not specific to any one locality, but associated generally with ideas of marriage and the transformation of fixed identities, speak of salvation in hybrid and utopian terms, before returning finally to the problem of context and identity.

Part Three:
Notions of Heroism and Agency

Introduction

In the irreconcileability of analyses based on analyses of 'meaning' with those based on analyses of 'power' which used to characterise social treatises and arguments over 'representation', it seemed almost as though we were confronted by two alternative universes of thought. Indeed, a sense of the incompatibility of these two universes, of meaning and of power, haunted me through my first fieldwork with the Hmong of Thailand; there appeared to me to be one 'universe' in which expression, articulation, representation in the aesthetic sense, was all-important, and another quite different one, in which the glaring inequities of power and access to resources in a world of what I took to be 'real' social relations, the lack of representation in a political sense, seemed to mock a universe of mere comprehension and imagination.

Although this kind of distinction between the semantic and the material is still often insisted on,[1] generally today there is a more sophisticated awareness of the 'politics of culture', of the symbolic construction of relations of domination and submission, of the powering role of imagination in the realm of social relations. Again however the thorny issue of 'representation' raises itself, since so often the relationship of such cultural products to some unmediated empirical experience of the world is questioned. And again, we have to remember that there can be no *literal*, or realist, appreciation of this world; the world itself is a kind of text we, and the Hmong, work ourselves out in. It is worth re-emphasising here that there can be no 'understanding' which is unmediated by its cultural context, since language is itself rooted in signs and the essentially figurative nature of language. Yet if that apparent disjuncture, between universes of political economy and cultural discourse, was so difficult for theoreticians of the past to overcome,[2] why should it not be equally difficult for many Hmong to experience a similar discomfort and unease, a similar inability to translate, say, the symbolic language of

---

[1] See Bloch (1986) for example, on the relationship between 'ideological' and politico-economic' phenomena.

[2] See Steiner (1975) on 'culture' and the enjoyment of Beethoven by Nazis in the concentration camps.

the supernatural and the ritual village of the ancestors in which a specific historic identity is asserted, into the commonplace language of everyday *realpolitik* or economic necessity? It is largely through historical constructions of cultural difference and identity, as I have tried to show in Part II, that Hmong villagers in Sichuan today can achieve that active 'suspension of disbelief' through which the the 'real' can be imagined and the 'imagined' realised, and this is well reflected in the genre of everyday tales which we examine here.

It is always History which links such apparently ill-fitted worlds of the cultural imagination and of a positivistic reality (which is itself imagined and imaginary), since 'history' is itself a symbolic construct ultimately intending always to refer to a current reality. If the ancient battle between poetry (which I take to cover metaphor, fiction, and narratives with the capacity to alter 'the truth') versus philosophy (as science, or accurate depiction of 'the truth') has already been well won in our philosophical discourse by poets as Clifford (1988) claimed, then that must be why it has primarily been the 'poets' or spinners of tales among the Hmong that I have found myself most interested in. It may well be the complex nature of the way in which the entirety of the Hmong social system has been politically inserted into the highly stratified structures of historical Chinese civilization which partly explicates the richness and resonance of their poetic visions of the universe and the mysteries of death and life expressed in them. Similarly, this richness and resonance of cultural 'connotations' might be said to have enabled the complexity of that historical social insertion.

As my stress on the importance of the historical relations between the universes of political economy and cultural discourse in the final chapters of Part Two may have shown, moral questions of the ultimate effects of culture on a realm of social practice divorced from it of the type Mathew Arnold might have posed, or which are still often raised in debates about the effects of pornography and screen violence, become irrelevant. A compartmentalization of experience, or some inherent moral ambiguity and dualism, can only form a part of our answer to such questions as the appreciation of 'high' art by the Nazis. Our answers need also to consider the extent to which different aspects of experience are either imaginatively articulated to form part of what appears to be a single, seamless whole, or fragmented into diverse and scattered practically rooted understandings, which work to constitute a world we find acceptable.

Poetry is potentially *liberating*, rather than necessarily mystifying (and we all have it!).[3] Despite Culler's view of the ultimate pessimism of Foucault's thesis on 'discourse', Foucault's exposure of the confines and determinism of discourse can also be seen as a potentially revolutionary liberation of the *infinite possibilities of discourse* (cf. Ginzburg 1980), and of the fact that it is always possible to shape the world in new ways. As Chomsky even earlier (1957) stressed in his attempt to deal with 'the problem of rule-governed creativity in natural language', a sentence never in the history of the world heard before may at any moment be generated by any one of us (and that sentence might be a world-making one).

It is this infinitely creative capacity, and the possibilities of liberating it, which is at issue here, and which is my main concern. It does seems to me enormously important to reinstate a new vision of agency, not necessarily at a personal or individual level, as creative, and to be able to relate this to historical potentiality and the power of the imagination. How, then, are we to fully recognise the power of human agency, not necessarily at a purely individual or physically 'embodied' level, of which we so often speak, and so often deny?

Given the extent to which our understanding of the very social rules by which we lead our lives remains problematic, and inasmuch as our practical comprehension of the world in which we are immersed remains inarticulate and inarticulable, as current social theory has shown, it may indeed be in the cultural realm of largely taken-for-granted *tellings and re-tellings of the past*, that the capacity to imagine or posit alternatives, to step outside a current social conditioning and move towards a potentially liberating future, is best realised. Bloch's capacity to step outside one's own social conditioning, the determinism of a culture, the constraints of a particular language, is in fact a fictive and imaginative capacity; the linguistic capacity for *conditionality* and *alterity* as Steiner (1975) put it. This, indeed, is the source of human agency, as we shall try to show; the capacity to alter a 'discourse' which otherwise must define and limit us. As Ricoeur, again, put it; 'May we not say that

---

[3] See Part I. My use of 'poetry' is clearly not Bakhtin's; indeed, the folktales considered in this Part are more novel than poem in his sense.

imagination—through its utopian role—has a *constitutive* role in helping us to *rethink* the nature of our social life?' (Ricoeur 1986).

If we are to find the traces of agency, the source of human creativity and potential anywhere beyond the notion of an 'individual' constituted by contrast to 'society',[4] it may well then be in that very realm of cultural production and particularly in the stock of proverbs, folk wisdom, legend and myth, superstition and remedy, which have formed the object of so much—and so much criticised (Bloch 1977)—anthropological and local historical attention, and of which the Hmong furnish us with so particularly a fine example. As Levi-Strauss so clearly saw, there is a *logic* and a *thinking* in this body of myth and legend, which speaks of, and to, the conflicts and contradictions of everyday life.[5] Clearly it cannot do so in any simple or uniform, or easily intelligible way, but that it does so or can do so should not in any sense be in doubt, since otherwise it does make a nonsense—not so much of past anthropological or folklorical endeavour as Bloch argued—but also of the very deep appeal and workings of these cultural productions in the workings of the human mind and to the consciousness of a past which is invoked in the imaginative construction of a common identity.

This realm of a practical or commonsensical knowledge, which like Gramsci I would prefer to couple with the world of myth and legend, has at times been considered as a kind of 'ideology' (Geertz 1983, when he considers what he calls 'common sense' as a 'cultural system') or denied a purely 'ideological' or mystifying role. Such questions, in the light of the foregoing, need no longer concern us, except insofar as they refer to the extent to which such utterances and evocations may be relatively *structured*, or lack in such formal organisation.

Wedding procedure and funeral protocol, shamanic practice and ancestral worship, are areas of restricted and constrained behaviour in which individuals may excel and specialise. They so clearly

---

[4] The problem with the 'habitus' is that there's no such thing; it is an entirely heuristic construction.

[5] By 'mythology', I mean something quite different to Barthes' description of 'myth' in late capitalist society, where his use of the notion of 'connotation', which relates to the infinite extensibility of meanings, attempted to relate a basically Saussurian schema to a wider socio-cultural *context*.

express the force of conservative tradition and the distinctive nature of the Hmong as a separable group that they too easily become the target of political campaigns and contention between older and younger generations, traditionalists and modernisers. It is only in the area of what Coleridge called Imagination, rather than Fancy,[6] that a creative interplay between the exigencies of the present and the boundless possibilities of the future can be expressed in a historical context which is apparently anybody's domain, contentionless because it claims and declares nothing, open to endless reconstructions and redefinitions of a creative and evolving identity which are the genuine signs of an agency which cannot be repressed. This too came under fierce attack and criticism during the Cultural Revolution, when 'Han' became landlords, and 'Hmong' peasants, and historic Hmong resistances to central state encroachments became reinterpreted as struggles against feudal oppression, but as a form of domestic legend, usually told at night, and not written down, far less so than other more visible forms of cultural production. As (until recently) barely recognised aspects of cultural production they are *more* difficult to contest than those which are more obvious. In this sense they are somewhat similar to the unreflective use of domestic space in Shaanxi cave dwellings during the Maoist revolution remarked by Liu Xin (1998).

Experience, inasmuch as it is culturally or linguistically mediated, is metaphorically understood, and if there is another, unmediated, *experience or understanding* to which we still aspire, it is either at a level so far beneath the level of conscious articulation that a scream or laugh becomes the best kind of poem, or so far off in an unrealized potential future of what Bloch (1918) called the 'Noch-Nicht', that all our cultural productions can merely whisper of it.[7] Indeed, it may be this kind of unmediated experience we shall find the Orphan tales of the Hmong pointing towards, through means other than metaphor.

In this area of 'free play' (from which the symbolic function itself may be seen to emerge), men, women and children have near equal voices with men, unlike the more formal domains of kinship and

---

[6] Cf. Peirce on 'Play'.

[7] Indeed, Derrida (1982;285) wittily demonstrated that philosophy was more in metaphor than metaphor was in philosophy.

ritual we have examined; this domain of folk-tale most perfectly fulfils the Chomskyian vision of an unconscious linguistic competence as potentially infinitely creative.[8] It is in this realm of what the Elizabethans knew as 'Delight' that moral homily becomes irrelevant and education unimportant; this is intentionless, irreducible fun for the sake of fun (as Bhaktin saw narrative); there is nothing here which is sober, prosaic or purposeful that is not laughable, and there is no possibility of ownership or private claim to such tales, which are of their very nature capable of infinite future reinterpretations; there is no 'utilitarian' design to this sort of tale, apart from that of sheer entertainment and enjoyment.[9] It is through this genre of *folk tales* that Hmong raconteurs, and perhaps similar raconteurs the world over, most openly express those things which in an everyday context are sensed as most important, for it is only in this semantic realm that it is literally possible to do almost anything, and the anchorage with any assumed, or accepted, conventional reality becomes entirely adrift.

While there is no necessary or needful relationship between social structure and ideology (or may we say between social practice and cultural structure, in a Saussurian way?)[10] in the folk tale, at the same time it is impossible to separate them, since present realities are twisted, distorted, faithfully reflected, played with, turned upside down and righted again, in that unimaginably inventive way which has delighted children and adults through the ages. Largely through echoes and allusions, in a way to which Levi-Strauss' Marxist presuppositions were perhaps too rigid to be so formally applied (for he always saw himself as applying analytical methods to those areas beyond the political economy which Marx had left to others), the everyday myths and legends of the Hmong in Sichuan, which are only told in an informal setting, speak of general concerns, typify historical aspirations, and 'think' through conflicts and problems of identity and difference, resemblance and imitation, in a way which is no less illuminating for being, ultimately, playful.

***

---

[8] It was the 'creativity of language' which Chomsky (1957;52) saw as the 'most striking feature' of linguistic competence.

[9] Cf. Bakhtin (1979).

[10] Friedman (1990).

In the interpretation of myths and legends such as those of the Hmong, it is even more important than in the interpretation of 'real social relations' of the type displayed in Part II to avoid interpretive determinisms and reductionisms of the kind which would, for example, trace an elemental struggle of man against the environment in agrarian legends, see feudal despotism in stories of princely weddings, or unconscious motivations in images of Jack and the Beanstalk. We must indeed listen to what these kinds of story have to say with a sensitivity which is not often amenable to rigorous principles of selection of the kind Lévi-Strauss or Dumézil attempted, but which has more to do with the kind of cultural understanding, aesthetic sensibility, and poetic imagination which so many Hmong do so exemplarily display. It also importantly has to do with an appreciation of *context*, which I come finally to in Conclusion.

Since society may be composed of so many and such dissonant voices, as the argument we owe largely to the feminist and post-structuralist movements has established, it has become impossible to take the myths and legends of a society as representative of a society's 'thinking', since that 'thinking' must be disunited and not at all a 'chorus of harmony' (Leach 1960). But it is in the very variety of myths and legends, in their capacity for infinite multiplication, revision and variation, as we may see here, that this polyphonic dissonance of social voices is itself reflected, and precisely through these means that myth manages to convey that alternative sense of history and future potentiality which is fundamental in the formation and transformation of identities. It is fundamental, too, in the transformation of a material situation such as that described in Part II, through the capacity of such myths to construct new contexts which are in theory boundless, through the very 'unlimited semiosis' feared by Eco and the pragmatists.

We can therefore anticipate a mixture of Hmong with other voices in the re-citations of the past which follow, as was also true of the descriptions of Hmong social practices in the village which formed the stuff of Part II. The stories collected here and in some of the appendices were told in Hmong in villages in Sichuan; they were recorded both by myself and by others, and many have also been published in Chinese in a local work called the *Gongxian Miaozu minjian gushiji* (1989). As a first example of this genre of folk-tales and historico-mythical legend, let us consider a very typical story of the Hmong hero, seeking salvation through marriage, told in the guise of an account of the origin of the Echo:

THE ORIGIN OF ECHO IN THE MOUNTAINS (LEGEND 1)

Once upon a time, there was a couple who had a son of great strength, but he ate quite a lot. In one day he could eat two sha *(sheng, one litre) of rice, and four* sha *in two days. In five days he could get through one* daib *(dou, decalitre) of rice, and so the couple were unable to support him and made up their minds to desert him. One day, his mother led him to a place. 'Have you ever been here before?' she asked him. 'Yes, I have' replied the boy. Then they came to another place. Again his mother asked the same question, and again the boy gave the same answer. They walked on and on, and finally arrived at a distant place. His mother asked again, 'Have you ever been to this place?' 'No' the boy answered this time. 'You've never been to this place?' said his mother, 'then you stay here and amuse yourself. I'll come back later'. After she said this, she went away. Later she took off her straw sandals and put them on again back to front and returned home, leaving the boy there. The boy stayed in the same place all the time, waiting for his mother to come back,* but she didn't.

When it got dark, a big tiger came, wanting to eat up the boy. There was a terrible fight between the boy and the tiger. Finally the tiger was killed by the boy. Then the boy chopped down some sticks of firewood, and tied them togther with the tiger inside. At dawn, he put the bundle on his back and found his way home. When he got back, he said to his Mother and Father, 'Mother, Father, if you don't want me, leave it at that. Last night I caught a mouse, and I'll give it to you. You can sell this mouse. With the money, please make a 1,200 jin *iron fork for me. Then I'll go off to find food for myself, without your support'.*

His mother and father took the tiger away and sold it. Then they had a 1,000 jin *iron fork forged, and they took this fork home. But their son said, 'This fork is too light. I want a fork of 1,200* jin—*this fork will have to be reforged'. So his mother and father had to go and get it reforged again. And after the boy had taken the 1,200* jin *iron fork, he went off with it to find food for himself (make his own living). On the way he met a strong man, who was digging a ditch to a weir. 'Where are you going, young man carrying an iron fork?' asked the strong man. 'I'm going to a distant land to make my living', answered the boy. 'Well, I'll come with you', said the strong man. 'You want to come with me? What skills do you have?' asked the boy. 'I have great abilities' replied the strong man. 'Then show me your abilities', said the boy. The strong man picked up his hoe (hlaw) and in no time at all had dug out a deep ditch. 'Yes, you do have abilities', said the boy, 'so come with me'. And the two set out together.*

Later they met a man who was reclaiming the wasteland. 'Young men carrying a hoe and an iron fork' he shouted to them, 'where are you off to?' The boy and the strong man told him they were going to a distant land, to try to find food for themselves. 'Well, I'll come with you', said the man. 'You want to come with us?' said the boy, 'and what abilities do you have?' 'I have great talents' said the man. 'Then show us your talents', said the boy. And the man opened up a huge area of wasteland in no time at all with his knife. 'Yes, you do have abilities', said the boy and the strong man, 'so come along with us'.

The three men set out again. A long time later they arrived at the foot of a mighty forest. There they built a hut for themselves and settled down. On the first day, the man who had been reclaiming the wasteland was left at home to cook, while the boy and the strong man went off to search for food. When he had finished cooking, he went out of the house and called, 'My two friends, please come back and eat'. He heard an answer from halfway up the hill on the other side. Then a tall, old man appeared, with his mouth as big as a basket and his teeth like sticks of ginger. The old man devoured all their food. Before he left, he dealt the man who used to reclaim wasteland a great blow, who fainted right away.

When the boy and the strong man came home and found no food, they asked the man what had happened. 'You stayed at home to do the cooking, where is all the food you cooked?' 'After I called you', said the other man, 'a wicked old man (an ogre) appeared. He was very tall. His mouth was as big as a basket and his teeth were like pieces of ginger. He ate up all our food in a trice'. Although he tried to convince them of what had happened, they did not believe him.

On the second day, the strong man who used to dig ditches stayed at home to do the cooking, while the boy went out with the man who used to open up wasteland to find food. When the strong man had finished cooking their lunch, he went out of the hut and called out 'My two friends, please come and have your meal'. He too heard a reply from halfway up the hill on the other side. The tall old man reappeared. His mouth was as big as a basket, and his teeth were like sticks of ginger. When the old man had finished eating up all their lunch, he again gave the strong man a mighty blow, who fainted dead away.

When the other two returned, again there was no food. They asked the strong man what had happenened. The strong man's story was the same as on the first day. He told them how the wicked old man had came and eaten up all their food. He had passed out after the old man had hit him. The boy who carried the iron fork was clever. He said, 'There is no such strange thing as that. I don't believe what you say, you must be telling lies. You must have gone out somewhere to play. Tomorrow I shall stay at home and cook our food'. So, on the third day, he didn't go out while the other two went off to search for food. While he was cooking, he cut some bamboos to make into a basket. And when the meal was ready, he went outside to ask his friends to come back for supper.

Again there was a reply from halfway up the hill opposite. The boy took no notice of it and sat outside the door, still weaving the basket. A moment later, the old man appeared. 'Why are you weaving a basket, young man?' asked the old man in surprise. 'I want to keep my parents in it', *replied the boy. 'Why are you making it so big? Are your parents so tall?' asked the old man. 'My mother and father are as tall as you and as large as you', said the boy. 'I can't believe it' the old man said. 'Well', said the boy, 'I don't have a size (model) for it. Would you like to crawl inside it and have a try? If the basket is big enough, I can stop weaving it', suggested the boy. The old man crawled into it and had a try, but it was still not long enough for him. So he came out and sat beside the boy, watching him weaving the basket. After some time, the boy suggested that the old man should have another try. When the old man crawled into it again, it fitted him exactly. The boy quickly sewed it up tight. The old man could not get out. 'Why have you sewn me up in your basket?' shrieked the old man. 'No matter', said the boy, lifting up the basket and throwing it into a corner near the bed.*

When the other two came back, they found the meal was all ready, and not eaten up by that old man. The boy put the blame on them— 'you're always telling lies', he said. The other two insisted they had told the truth. 'Well', said the boy, 'there's no point in arguing about that now. After the meal, I'll take you there to see the old man. I've already caught him and thrown him into the corner by the bed'. The other two were impatient to get the old man out immediately and beat him to death. 'Don't worry', said the boy, 'we'll have plenty of time after we've finished our meal'. When they had finished their meal, they dragged the old man out, and were about to punish him cruelly. But the old man was terribly frightened and begged them not to beat him; 'I have seven daughters. If you set me free, I'll give you three of them to be your wives'. *The three men agreed to this, and they released the old man, who went back to his own home.*

The very next day, all three of them went off to see the old man, to ask him to give them his daughters in marriage. But on hearing the news of their arrival, the old man shouted, 'Daughters, daughters, bring me my fan (ntxo) *quickly and I'll fan my sons-in-law'. His daughters brought him out a fan, and he waved it just once. In a moment, they were fanned all the way back to their hut. Realising how powerful the old man's fan was, the three of them then made another fan, which looked exactly like the old man's. On the second day, they stole quietly back to the old man's home with the false fan they had made. When they arrived they found that the old man was out. So they called out, 'Little sisters, your father has such a powerful fan. Please let us have a quick look at it. We only want to see what it really looks like'. Not realising they were being tricked, the girls brought out the fan and handed it to them. While they were looking at it, they secretly exchanged it for their own false fan.*

On the third day, they went there again to ask the old man to give them his daughters in marriage. When he heard them coming, the old man shouted, 'Daughters, daughters, quick, bring me my fan! I'll fan my sons-in-law!' *His daughters brought out the fan and the old man fanned them once, but they didn't move. Then they took out the fan they had stolen from the old man's daughters and fanned that once. The old man was fanned up onto a rock, and could not come down*

again.The old man was furious and said, 'So this is how you treat me. In future, whenever you speak, and whatever you say, I'll always repeat your voices'. In the end, those three took his daughters away. And now, when you go shouting in the mountains, you'll still find that that old man is imitating you.
(Muas Xis Xyang)[11]

One observes in this typical tale the repetition characteristic of the story-teller's art everywhere, and that curious simplicity of utterance, devoid of complex metaphor and trope, which is so often found in folk tales, because what is being recounted is literally, almost pure narrative, which therefore loses little or nothing in translation. It may indeed be the purity, the naive nudity of the narrative in these legends which explains their rapid migration across great cultural distances.

Through the very banality of much of the language, again the story is typical of folk legends in its nonchalant description of what is accepted as normal life (the search for food, the forging of iron forks, the weaving of baskets, the difficulties of supporting children, the constant working in the fields, the capacity of men to give away their daughters in marriage, the need for cooking every day...) But at the same time it falls into epic mode when describing the superhuman attributes of the insouciant hero in a similarly naive casual fashion—the hero refers to the tiger he has killed as a mouse, and effortlessly tosses the giant into a corner of the room; and, in a more complex way, still refuses to believe his friends while apparently accepting as normal the appearance of the ogre!

And it is through the themes of trickery and deception which so strongly characterise all these genres of story, through plain counter-factuality and fiction rather than rhetorical device, that the story reveals the kind of creative fictiveness that may seem to support Steiner's (1975;226-232) contention that 'language is not only innovative in the sense defined by transformational generative grammar, it is literally creative'—through its capacity for counter-factual statements, the 'dialectic of alternity', metaphor, conditionality and the hypothetical. Moreover, the world which we are able to set aside through such statements is itself largely 'a

---

[11] My emphases throughout.

linguistic construct' (Bloch's world of social determinism). Steiner asks when it was that man first learned to lie, to 'say otherwise', and suggests that this linguistic capacity for 'fictive genius' , for counter-intuitive imagination, may have been primary in evolution and biological survival, and *the only genuine site of 'free will'*.

Therefore it is inaccurate to assign to the development of speech 'a primarily informative...communicative motive'; it is the 'masking functions' of language, the 'grammers of the future', the 'capacity to conceal, misinform, leave ambiguous, hypothesize, invent', which are 'essential to the sanity of consciousness', and linguistic evolution is inseparable from the impulse to concealment and fiction. Steiner is here contributing to a debate raised by Chomsky's (1971;19) remark that meaningful use of language 'need not involve communication or even the attempt to communicate' (see Chomsky's 1975 attack on Strawson and Searle's assumption that 'the purpose of language is communication'). Steiner argues for 'non-truth or less-than-truth' as a primary device in the creative use of language, and points for proof of this to the beginnings of mature speech in 'shared secrecy' between the members of a group, before what he calls 'linguistic exogamy', the multiplicity of languages and the development of pidgins. (1975; 226-232).

The story is also typical of many folk legends collected in the Gongxian and south Sichuan area in showing *a blending and fusion of Han and Hmong sources* (cf. Appendix IV) in keeping with the *culturally hybrid* situation we have examined. While fitting well with a category of folk tale about the origin of mountain echoes quite common in south China, the story also fuses elements of traditional Chinese cosmology (in particular the seven daughters, or seven sisters, of the Northern Dipper, or the Pleiades as is often thought, important in Daoist worship), with a series of traditional Hmong folk tales about Xob, the God of Thunder, who is trapped and bound by brothers through trickery and deception at the beginning of time, and sometimes associated with the coming of the Deluge.[12] The clearing of the 'wasteland' by one of the supernatural helpers seems also to refer to a distant historical time, the beginning of cultivation or of legal settlement..

---

[12] See Nusit Chindasri (1976); Mottin, *Contes* (n.d;23).

But most importantly for our purposes here, we meet for the first time the figure of the Orphan who is so significant in Hmong legend and present-day story-telling, since right at the beginning of the tale we are seen the hero deserted by his parents, and shown his mother turning her sandals back to front, which to anyone familiar with Hmong funeral rituals (Ch.5) would signify her death. The orphan then reverses this original desertion by himself leaving home, which as we shall see is also a common theme in the important cycle of Orphan tales.

The supernatural strength of the hero, and his two supernatural helpers, are of course common legendary motifs, but the violence expressed towards parents ('I want to keep my parents in it') is not common, although it does appear in other Hmong Orphan legends (cf. Tapp 1989 p.133; again violence directed towards the mother; and 1996 p.91). But in the context I would like to emphasise here, since it is particularly significant for the Hmong of Gongxian, what is important is the figure of the supernaturally gifted Orphan, who overcomes all obstacles to achieve ultimate success, and the fact that *marriage* is seen as integral to this.

Another story best typifies the 'rags-to-riches' nature of many of the Orphan tales, and shows the inspiration of the Orphan by the main divinity of Hmong cosmology which marks him as the figure of a specifically Hmong identity.

THE ORPHAN AND THE WILDCAT (LEGEND 2)

Once upon a time there lived an orphan. People called him Laus Ntsuag. He wore nothing but rags, and was so very poor that he went hungry all the time. One day, since he had nothing better to do, he went off hunting, high up in the mountains. He set up a trap of ropes in the forest, and then returned home. Early in the morning of the next day, he climbed up the mountains again, but found only a tiny wildcat was caught in his trap. A sudden shudder gripped his heart. He started beating the wildcat with his stick. But all of a sudden the animal started to talk, saying 'Laus Ntsuag, stop beating me. If you agree to take me home with you, I can sing on the streets for you. Certainly you will grow rich in this way, and have food and clothes forever in plenty'. Laus Ntsuag was astonished to hear this, but thought there would be no harm in trying it. So he asked the wildcat to give him a demonstration of its performance. And the wildcat began to sing, 'La de da le ma da le, may all tigers, leopards and jaguars be struck dead, and the small wildcat will bring you happiness. Your life will flourish like a flower, the small wildcat can make the spring flower stay to bring good fortune to earthly people— forever spring!' Laus Ntsuag was delighted to hear the wildcat singing. What a marvellous wildcat, thought the orphan, and he leashed the animal and took it home with him.

As the sun arose from the east on the following morning, Laus Ntsuag put the wildcat on a lead and hopped and skipped his way to the market. Along the way they passed some people who sold salt, and some people who sold cloth. There were porters and coolies too. All were most surprised by the sight of Laus Ntsuag leading along a wildcat. So they gathered around him and asked 'Why are you walking this wildcat, young man?' 'Because it can perform on the streets', answered Laus Ntsuag. The people around were perplexed; 'Stop this nonsense,' said one, 'You can have my bag of salt if that wildcat can really sing'. And another said, 'If your wildcat could really sing you could have all the salt I am carrying'. And then the porters joined in too, promising to carry all the goods home for him if the animal could really sing. Laus Ntsuag accepted all the bets and told the wildcat to start singing. And the animal, waving its tail, began to sing, 'La me bai, da le lai, may all tigers, and leopards, and jackals be struck dead, and the wildcat will bring you happiness and fortune, your life will blossom like a flower, the small wildcat will cause the spring flowers to stay so spring will be forever on the earth'.

'Heavens, how wonderful! All my cloth now belongs to you', said one of the onlookers. 'And my salt is also yours', said another. Everyone who had betted on the wildcat handed their belongings to the orphan. Even the porters were as good as their word, and carried everything back home for him. And from that time on, the orphan started to become wealthy and prosperous.

Then one day, a Zhou Duosou, who knew the orphan very well yet despised him terribly, rode past the back of the orphan's house. The orphan invited him in, saying 'Come in and smoke a pipe before you go on'. But Zhou ignored him, saying 'You are so poor you barely have roof over your head or room beneath your feet. Your poverty is like dry tinder, yet you still have the nerve to invite me in for a smoke. You are surely not in earnest'. And he rode on past without even dismounting. But when he rode back again that afternoon, the orphan invited him in again. Just at that moment the horse stumbled and rolled down the gutter at the back of the house. Zhou took the opportunity to dismount, and with great strides, strutted his way towards the orphan's house, muttering to himself, 'So many warm and friendly greetings—I'll just see what good things you can treat me to! I'm sure I'll not get as much as a sniff of his fart'. But the orphan took no notice of his guest's evil thoughts. As soon as he saw his friend he took a chair out of his house and begged him to be seated. Then he began to prepare the tobacco and the wine for his guest. The tobacco was about as big as the droppings of a mouse. Zhou was mightily displeased, and started to complain, 'How can this much tobacco be enough for me?' The orphan hastily apologised, trying to smile, 'I am sorry. You just take this first. I'll fill your pipe up again when you have finished this'. And Zhou was most surprised to find that the tobacco lasted for more than two hours. In the end he had had more than enough, and had to stop smoking.

As soon as he had finished, the orphan offered him a cup of wine and some plates of food. Zhou looked contemptuously at what he was being offered—the cup was no larger than the eye of an ox, and the dishes were no larger than silver dollars. Again he began to complain; 'If you really have so little, you need not bother to treat me. How can you think that what you have here is enough for my stomach?' Laus Ntsuag hastened to reassure him, saying 'My friend, don't be angry. There is more to come after you have finished'. But Zhou was never lucky enough to have his dishes and cups replenished, since he was quite unable to finish what he had first been offered. So Zhou began to change his manner. He even addressed the orphan in a much more friendly way: 'You were so poor before. How is it that, all of a sudden, you seem to have become a rich man?'

Sighing, the orphan told him, 'It is all because Heaven pitied me. At first I was going to hunt to make a living. But I could find no animal other than a wildcat. I hated that animal so much I nearly beat it to death. But then I was astounded to find that not only could it talk, it could also sing. Now all that I have has come from its singing'. 'Was that really how it was?' Zhou could hardly conceal his surprise. The orphan reaffirmed that it was. Then Zhou's eyes took on an evil glint, as he asked 'Could you lend me your wildcat tomorrow, so that I too can make a small fortune?' 'Fine,' said the orphan, 'but you had best first return home and dispose of all that you have—your farmland and property, otherwise the wildcat will bring you no good fortune'.

So Zhou quickly got back onto his horse and galloped all the way home. Everything he had, he got rid of, and then he went back to see the orphan so that he could borrow the wildcat. He leashed up the animal, and took it walking around the streets. Everybody gathered around him to ask, 'Sir, why are you leading this animal around?' And Zhou told them that it could perform on the streets. The traders started to lay bets on the beast's abilities, exactly as they had with Laus Ntsuag. They said they would give him everything they had if the animal could really sing. And Zhou's heart was almost bursting with delight to think of the fortune he would soon have. So he ordered the wildcat to start singing at once. But the animal only came out with a series of noises, 'Lei lei lei lei!' There was no song. Enraged, the traders and the porters beat Zhou almost to the point of death. It was midnight when he finally found his way home.

On the following day, the orphan visited Zhou to retrieve his wildcat. 'Look what your wildcat has done to me,' Zhou told him, 'I have lost everything because of your animal, and nearly died. I have beaten it to death and thrown its corpse by the river'. The orphan was filled with sorrow. He went looking for his wildcat, sobbing all the way, until he reached the side of the river. There he rescued the body of the wildcat, and he buried it beneath a raised grave mound.

Three days later, the orphan went back to the grave again. The mound where he had buried the wildcat had shrunk in size, and a tiny tree had grown up in the centre of it, glowing silver. He hugged the tree in great glee. To his surprise, another wonderful thing happened. When the tree was shaken, treasures of gold, silver and precious stones fell down from it. The orphan took all the treasure home, and became still more rich.

Some time later, Zhou again rode by the orphan's house. The orphan greeted him cordially, and for a second time Zhou visited the orphan's house. This time he was surprised to see the house was full of new furniture, and he asked the orphan how he had come by all this. The honest and inarticulate (uneasily spoken) orphan told him the secret of his young tree. Zhou asked, again, whether he could borrow this tree for a while, and the orphan agreed to this. Following the orphan's directions, Zhou succeeded in finding the tree. And as the orphan had told him to, he spread out a sheet and wool blanket beneath the tree while shaking it vigorously. But only pig shit and dog droppings fell down from the tree—no gold, no silver, no precious stones at all—completely ruining his sheets and woollen blanket, and covering Zhou with filth all over. In a terrible tantrum, Zhou chopped the tree down with his axe.

The next day the orphan visited Zhou, saying 'Yesterday I lent you my wonderful tree; I would like to have it back so I can use it today'. And Zhou said, 'What a wonderful tree you had indeed! All I got out of it was filthy shit, ruining all my sheets and blanket, and no gold, silver or precious stones at all. I had to throw out all my sheets. I was so angry I've chopped your precious tree down. Go and look in the yard outside'. Sobbing with grief, the orphan left to look for his tree. When he finally found the dead tree in the yard behind the house, he chopped it up into smaller pieces, and took the heaviest ones home to make a trough for his pigs out of them. Soon all his piglets grew into fat, heavy pigs. After only a few months they were ready to leave the sty.

One day later, Zhou again passed by the orphan's house, and again the orphan, being of a very kind nature, greeted him warmly and invited him to come in. Inside the central hall Zhou saw there was lots of hanging dried meat. He asked the orphan how this had come about, and the orphan told him frankly how the meat came from the fat pigs who were feeding from the wooden trough made out of the timber of the young tree. In no time Zhou begged the orphan to lend him his trough to feed his own pigs for a while. The kind orphan agreed that Zhou could borrow his trough. As good fortune never befalls the evil-hearted, when Zhou used the trough he had borrowed to feed his pigs they all died or became sick or contracted favus of the head within a few days. Zhou was so angry that he took up an axe and chopped that trough up into firewood. When the orphan came round to collect his trough, Zhou told him what had happened. The orphan was so sad to hear this that he began to cry. Still weeping, he went over to the stove where the firewood was now burning. He ran his hands through the tinder inside the stove, still crying. Then he spied a small red ember and picked it out carefully with a pair of tongs and carried it home with him. But on the way, he accidentally dropped the glowing ember into an earthen dyke in a field, and the fire died out. He tried to scoop it out again, but when he succeeeded in getting it out, it was not an ember any more, but a pair of beautifully made scissors, which gleamed in the sunlight. The orphan tucked the scissors into his breast and ran all the way home. There he kept the scissors in his work box before leaving for the mountains to work.

Laus Ntsuag worked hard every day, from morning till dusk. And every day, when he came back from working, he was surprised to find that the whole house had been cleaned and a full meal was prepared for him—but there was nobody to be seen. *And he was astounded to see that two new suits of clothes had been specially made for him and laid out. Who would wish to help a poor orphan in this way? After he had eaten the excellent supper, he hurried off to ask Old Saub who it was who had been there helping him. He knelt at Saub's heavenly door and called 'Saub! Oh Old Saub! Please tell me who prepared this meal for me? Who swept all the floors for me, made all the clothes for me?'*

Saub heard his prayer, and answered him in a song, 'Well, well, Laus Ntsuag who is kind-hearted and hard-working, the wildcat is a fair lady in disguise. *Of her own will she has brought you happiness and fortune, you will enjoy all fame, glory and wealth; suffering and poverty will desert you forever'.*

Saub advised the orphan to pretend to set off for the mountains, but then to turn back and hide inside the house. As soon as the maid appeared, Laus Ntsuag should seize her tight.

Laus Ntsuag followed Saub's instructions. After making his preparations and placing the broom in a new position behind the door, he pretended to leave for the mountains. Thinking Laus Ntsuag had left, the small pair of scissors leapt out of the work box, landed on the floor with a ring and turned into a beautiful girl. She swung her left arm around and moved her right arm, and at once a blouse, skirt and coloured sash came into the room. The lady had a pink face

and a slim, graceful figure. She looked even more beautiful in her
flowered blouse and the brightly coloured skirt and sash. Laus
Ntsuag stared at her in fascination, nearly forgetting the things
which he should do. Only when the girl began to look for the broom
did Laus Ntsuag wake up. With giant steps he strode up to the girl
from behind her. He seized hold of her and, holding her tightly,
would not let go of her.

After that time, Laus Ntsuag and the spirit *became husband and wife*
and lived happily together. The husband tilled the earth, the wife
weaved at home. They made the best kind of life on this earth by
working hard. They built a great mansion with red walls and yellow
tiles upon the roof. And they dressed in silks and satins they had
made themselves. Their life became more and more wonderful.
(Xiong Zhenmei)[13]

A much shorter and more unpleasant version of this tale is included
in Appendix V. While the language of this story is more embellished,
less stark and generally livelier than that of the preceding one, it
announces its essential character as an oral legend through its use of
the device of frequent repetition and the tendency for things to
happen in threes, and of course in the near-universal theme of the
magical housecleaning by invisible helpers (as in the Grimm
Brothers shoemakers story, for example, and which we meet again in
Legends 6 and 7, below). As in many of these stories, the raconteur
breaks into song or onomatapeia from time to time in the Hmong
version in a way which it is impossible to do justice to here, but
which illustrates the nature of these tales as performance.

The Hmong nature of the legend is stressed through the
introduction of Saub, the legendary divinity of Hmong myth who
appears at the dawn of time and then retreats (a *deus otiosis*), to be
appealed to at times of need. Saub[14] is a kindly and benevolent figure
who has the best interests of humanity at heart, and is often pictured
as an old man or sage, contrasting to the malevolent deity of the
Otherworld Ntxwj Nyug who devours people almost as fast as they
are created through sickness and death. In the messianic legends of
the orphan common in Yunnan, Vietnam, Laos and Thailand, the

---

[13] My emphases throughout.

[14] Pronounced 'Sub' in the Death Chant given in Part Two.

hero—or very often in real messianic uprisings hs earthly representative who leads a political movement—is presented as being in mystic communication with Saub in a way which validates and legitimates him. Sometimes a new form of writing for the Hmong language is discovered or invented by such leaders which acts as evidence of his supernatural sanction. It is significant in terms of these other stories that this relationship between Saub and the orphan is recreated here.

This account brings out particularly clearly the moral goodness of the orphan hero—he is kind and generous, hardworking, honest and inarticulate. Like Peredur of the Arthurian cycle, and perhaps the nature of the folk tale generally, the fictive functions of language, the capacity for speechifying and nice/false speech, is seen as irrelevant to the search for ultimate salvation. These moral qualities are firmly opposed to the jealousy, greed and boastfulness of 'Zhou', in a contrast which is at the same time an envious and desireful contrast between the poor and the rich. 'Zhou' seems to be seen here as Chinese, while in other stories (App.V) he is seen as the older brother of the orphan (and appropriately to this other related stories tell of the older brothers of Hmong cultural heroes being Chinese, see Appendix IV). Good fortune is unambiguously linked with these moral qualities, and misfortune expressly attributed to the evil-hearted.

(In a comparable Hmong legend from Thailand, one of three orphan tales collected by Mottin, the orphan (Nraug Ntsuab) escapes from his wicked brother and wife who have blinded him to hide in a tree where he overhears a bear, a boar, a tiger, a leopard and a wild cat, discussing the three pots of silver and three pots of gold they have each found in an old man's house, which he takes and thereby becomes rich. The older brother tries to emulate him, and so is blinded, but is discovered by the five animals when he tries to overhear them, who assume it is he who has taken all their riches, and kill him! The wild cat figures in all Mottin's orphan stories, and in one of them the orphan becomes Emperor (*Huab Tais*) (cf. Charles Johnson, How an Orphan Boy found the Animal's Buried Treasure', 245-257, & 385-395,1985).)

The wild cat is an indigenous Hmong motif, appearing in many Hmong tales. As Eberhardt (1954) says in his comments on

Graham's stories, there are very few stories in China about the cat, which seems to have been introduced there through India.

In an interesting conclusion to this tale, the simple life is praised, in a way which is as true to the original spirit of Daoism as it may have been to aspects to Maoist thought- the life of self-sufficiency, of equality between man and woman; an idyllic, pastoral restoration of abundance which forms a kind of resolution (although this need not be taken in a strict, Levi-Straussian sense) to the conflicts between rich and poor, immoral and moral, which the story explores.

And yet it is a *passage* which is spoken of here, a *transformation* of poverty to wealth, of misfortune to fortune, and this passage is ultimately achieved through the mystic marriage with a lifelong helpmeet. While the theme of the orphan overcoming all odds to achieve a supreme triumph has a particular historical significance for the Hmong in general cultural terms, which has often been interpreted and expressed in political terms, here I think the immediate significance—and effect—of the story lies in the vision of marriage and union with another it conveys, as a solution to the problems of poverty and hardship, loneliness and sorrow.

And there may also be a sub-text here, on the nature of the ideal marriage, in which the wife's essential role is one of supporting and helping her husband, loyally and devotedly, so that he can achieve success. In terms of the legendary characteristics of the tale, what is important is the linking of the supernatural animal helper (the wildcat) with the notion of the mystic marriage, which we find also in many other related legends.

Several other stories elucidate this notion of the orphan's mystic marriage, and who it is who originally oppresses him:

THE STAR GIRL AND THE ORPHAN (LEGEND 3)

Long, long ago there lived an orphan, Laus Ntsuag, whose parents had both died. He had neither food nor clothes, and lived by himself in a cold shack meant for dogs. Even at the age of nineteen he still had not been able to find a wife for himself. He was so poor. Each night he would come out to enjoy the moonlight, look at the stars and moon in the sky, and cry out, 'Oh stars and moon, we would like you to come down, oh stars and moon, come down and we will get married'.

For three nights he cried like this. And on the third night, a lady descended from Heaven. She said to Laus Ntsuag, 'You cried to the stars, and now I have come'. As soon as he set his eyes on the star girl, Laus Ntsuag said, 'Let us be married'. The star girl agreed to this. Then she asked him, 'Have you eaten yet?' 'No, not yet'. 'Do you have any rice?' asked the star girl. 'Wherever could I find some rice?' asked Laus Ntsuag. 'Well, if you have no rice', said the star girl, 'go and get a bucket of water and boil it'.

So Laus Ntsuag went out to fetch a bucket of water and put it on the fire to boil. The star girl gave him a single grain of rice and said, 'Take this and cook half of it'. As she had told him, Laus Ntsuag cooked the half grain of rice. And the more they cooked, the more rice there was, until it filled the whole bucket. They made a full pot of rice out of only one grain of rice. The two then sat down together to have their meal. When they had finished eating, the star girl said to Laus Ntsuag, 'I'm going to set this house of yours to rights. You just stay quietly in bed this evening. Don't move when the heavy rain pours and the strong wind blows. You must lie still even when the thunder strikes'.

Laus Ntsuag went quietly to bed after the meal. In the middle of the night, the rain poured heavy and the wind blew strong. There was also the heavy roaring of thunder. Laos Ntsuag obeyed the words of the star girl and kept on sleeping quietly in his bed. He only opened his eyes when dawn broke.

Heavens! The shack was gone. Laus Ntsuag was lying on a double bed, with beddings and counterpane for two people. Above him there were new tiles and rafters. The roof was very high. Laus Ntsuag jumped out of bed, pulled on his trousers and went outside to have a look. What a big stone house it was! The whole place had been beautifully rebuilt. Now it was a mansion of many chambers with a central courtyard, and additional rooms on two sides of the house built on raised platforms. They could pound grain under the terrace and raise geese on the terrace. What a wonderful life they would have!

'What do you think of this house?' asked the star girl.

Laus Ntsuag laughed with tears coming to this eyes. 'It is a marvel! Wherever could I have hoped to find such a house?'

From that time onwards, Laus Ntsuag always had food, money,
clothing and a house of his own. He and the star girl worked hard
and lived happily together ever after.
(Yang Xiao Zhen)[15]

The 'have you eaten rice yet?' question after Laus Ntsuag's proposal
has been accepted is not *quite* the bathos it appears as since it is such
a common turn of phrase signifying intimacy and friendliness.

In this rudimentary tale the theme of the mystic marriage from
which abundance results is revealed particularly clearly. What
appears to have happened, with regard to ultimate sources, is that the
Hmong sagas of the Orphan have combined and blended with a cycle
of Chinese folk tales about earthly weddings with stars, in particular
the seven sisters of the Pleiades, or with the moon-girl. Again we see
here that the industrious nature of the orphan, his hard working, is
stressed. And what is most clearly shown in this story is the peasant
vision of abundance which the orphan obtains through his mystic
marriage—the half grain turning into a full pot of rice, as in the
previous story where the orphan's wine and tobacco are perpetually
replenished. This is a vision of *abundance* which is classically
related to prophecies of messianic salvation, and a Hmong audience
would understand this.

A similar vision of abundance, similarly resulting from a mystic
marriage, is shown in another orphan story:

LAUS NTSUAG THE ORPHAN (LEGEND 4)

Ha!
Mother of Laus Ntsuag, she ate an unfertilised egg
Mother of Laus Ntsuag, she passed away
Father of Laus Ntsuag, he ate a hard egg
Father of Laus Ntsuag, he passed away.
They both left me behind.
I, Laus Ntsuag, had no choice
I went to live with my father's younger brother and his wife.
My uncle went away on a long journey selling cattle
And I stayed with my aunt.
Ha!

---

[15] Also recorded in GMMG 317-18.

My aunt fed me bitter crusts of buckwheat
Bitter, bitter, so bitter.
I had nothing to choose. I, Laus Ntsuag, can only cry to the heavens.

After the morning meal, Laus Ntsuag went out to till the fields. He worked from one end of the field to the other. He let the cattle graze. Then he sat and sighed. Every day he did the same.

One day, after he had finished singing, he saw a maiden step out from a cave. She looked out, and she said to Laus Ntsuag,

Listen to me, Laus Ntsuag,
Your aunt fed you with bitter crusts of buckwheat,
Bitter, bitter, O so bitter.
Go home now and make a rope of eighty-eight strands
And I will marry you.
Laus Ntsuag, will you or won't you?

So Laus Ntsuag returned home and began to weave the rope. By dawn of the next day, he had completed forty-four strands of the rope.

The next morning, his aunt gave him bitter crusts of buckwheat to eat. He let the buffalo rest and began to sigh. The maiden in the cave heard him sighing, and asked 'Have you finished the rope yet?' 'Only forty-four strands', said Laus Ntsuag.

The next morning when Laus Ntsuag had finished the bitter crusts of buckwheat his aunt gave him, he went off to plough the mountain land. He ploughed three times in one direction and then three times in the other. When he had finished, he let the buffalo rest, and again began to sigh. The maiden peered out of the cave and said, 'Throw me the rope of eighty-eight strands, and I'll run off with you'. He threw the rope up to the girl. She climbed down the rope and they ran away together.

On the way they met Laus Ntsuag's uncle, returning from his long journey. 'Where are you going?' asked his uncle. Laus Ntsuag told him:

Ha!
My mother ate an unfertilised egg
and so she died

My father, he ate a hard-boiled egg
and so he passed away.
Only I am left behind.
I had nothing to do but
to stay with you uncle and aunt.
While you were away trading cattle in a distant land
My aunt fed me bitter crusts of buckwheat —
bitter, bitter, so bitter.
I ploughed the land, right up to the high mountain.
I told my sorrows to the spirit lady.
I rolled a rope up of eighty eight strands
so as to take her home and marry with her.
I shall never come back to your home
I, Laus Ntsuag, must live also like a man.

After saying this he went into a big forest. As night fell, there the couple slept. At midnight, the girl said to Laus Ntsuag, 'I'll summon my sisters to build a house for us. Keep calm when the rains pour and the winds blow. Stay still when the thunder strikes. Just lie still in bed, and don't move'.

And Laus Ntsuag went to sleep. The maiden went outside and cried out, 'Sisters, come out and build me a house!'

In a trice seven sisters appeared. The winds blew strong; the rains poured heavily, and thunder roared. After the winds, rain and thunder had all stopped, out came the moon. There by the light of the moon could be seen a magnificent mansion with a central courtyard and many chambers. 'What a big wonderful house!' exclaimed Laus Ntsuag.

And when he awoke in the morning, all the forest had gone. Before him were plentiful wet rice fields, with terraced fields one on top of the other stretching up the mountainside. Cattle, horses and sheep were grazing peacefully at the edge of the woods. Chickens, ducks and geese were running around everywhere, noisily pecking grains from the ground. The large stone house, with its central courtyard and many chambers, looked marvellous. 'All these are ours' laughed

the maiden. Laus Ntsuag and the spirit lady lived together very happily.
(Yang Shaoan)[16]

As in the previous story, Laus Ntsuag has to stay still while the heavens are moved, and is fed bitter buckwheat as in Appendix VI (a similar but fuller version of this story, which does not bring out the ill-treatment of the orphan by his uncle so clearly, but does have him also killing a tiger). Again the rudimentary outlines of the myth appear clearly—the original mistreatment and poverty of the orphan, and the superhuman ordeal he must undergo before the mystic marriage brings prosperity and fortune, in a peasant vision of agrarian abundance. In this version, the mystic marriage is unambiguously related to the Seven Sisters of the Pleiades, and as in many versions, the source of the orphan's misfortunes lies in his father's younger brother and particularly his wife.

The strange theme of the unfertilised egg leading to his mother's death serves to reinforce the notion of the orphan's spiritual, otherworldly origins—not human or social, since he is parentless and therefore remains outside the normal kinship system (see Legend 9 below). Miraculous births, of the kind given in the Thai Hmong messianic myths of culture heroes, are not uncommon among Chinese cultural heroes; the semi-legendary Laozi for example is often attributed with a miraculous birth. Indeed, this is the 'meaning' of the Orphan I would favour; the orphan with no name, or speech, is posited as prior to the Lacanian Symbolic realm of the kin relations guarded by taboo and sanction and regulated by the 'law of the father' and the incest prohibition (Butler 1993;72), through the image of the unfertilized egg. Yet if this is our 'reading' of the Orphan, this is indeed where the site of a critical agency should be situated, for as the nameless and ungovernable, the Void or empty chasm of meaning, the symbol at once epitomises the unbounded potentiality of the transformation of identities and achievement of supreme success. He is indeed intermediary between the two realms of the named and the nameless, as the images of the overcooked and under-developed eggs suggest; essentially equivocal and unfixable.

---

[16] Also recorded in GMMG 322-24. My emphases.

Another fable laments the death of the orphan, although in others he is resurrected (as in Appendix II) and the story is linked to another well-known Hmong myth about the first cock's crow, while the source of oppression has been transferred from the figure of the father's brother to a wife's father (as in the first story above):

THE MARRIAGE OF LAUS NTSUAG (LEGEND 5)

Laus Ntsuag was an orphan. Both his parents had died, and he lived with his father's younger brother and his wife. They had no children of their own and were very kind to Laus Ntsuag. However, they were wretchedly poor and life was very difficult for them.

For eighteen years Laus Ntsuag lived with his uncle and aunt. It was time for him to find a wife, but his uncle and aunt could not afford any money for a wedding, and were so worried about this that their hair turned quite white. Laus Ntsuag felt very disturbed to see this. So he said to both of them, 'You have looked after me for eighteen years now. Now you are worrying about my marrying. So I feel anxious. We are so poor that there is no money to get married. I shall leave for a distant place, to find a wife for myself'.

His uncle and aunt could not prevent Laus Ntsuag from leaving them so he could find a wife—nothing they did was of any use. In the end they made some bread out of buckwheat for him and asked him to save this food for his journey. And Laus Ntsuag put his belongings in a bag and set out for his journey. His uncle and aunt came out quite a long way to see him off.

And then he walked and walked and walked. After several nights walking, at last he reached a great forest. Night fell, and all the birds returned to their nests. But Laus Ntsuag still went on walking. Soon he saw a light in the distance. When he came closer, he saw that it came from a thatched hut. Up he walked to the door and made himself known, hoping to sleep there for the night. A cunning looking old man opened the door. Laus Ntsuag said to him, 'Nuncle (FeB), I am going to a very far away place. Since it is now dark, may I spend the night in your home?' But the old man said, 'No, you can't stay here. My place is too small and there's no room. You can't stay here'.

Just at that moment two women came home, each carrying a hoe on their shoulders. 'What's this young man doing here?' asked the older daughter. The old man told her, 'He is on his way to a distant place. Since it is late, he would like to spend the night here'. Seeing that Laus Ntsuag looked handsome and purposeful, the two women said to their father, 'Father, it is nearly dark. There is nowhere else here he can spend the night. Why not let him stay?' The two women were very kind, and so at last the old man agreed that he could stay the night. Laus Ntsuag had to sleep under the dry eaves of the house, while the father and his sons (sic) slept inside the house. The two women were sisters. The elder sister was called Oucai and the younger one Ouniang.

The next morning, Oucai lit the fire at the front of the stove and Ouniang cooked behind it. When all the food was ready, Oucai secretly handed Laus Ntsuag a bowl of rice, fearing her father would beat her if he knew. After breakfast, the two sisters told their father they were going out to work, and asked him to stay at home and look after the house. After they had both left, Laus Ntsuag said to the old man, 'Nuncle, I will go too. If I cannot find anywhere to stay at nightfall, I must return here to spend the night'.

Laus Ntsuag followed the two sisters. They were out there clearing the land. They finished ploughing some furrows in the field. Laus Ntsuag went up to them and helped them to turn the soil over. He was strong and he dug fast and worked well. The two women started to like him very much. That evening, he went back to the house with the two young women.

After a few days, the old man began to be very suspicious of Laus Ntsuag. What was he up to? He started to develop evil thoughts against Laus Ntsuag, and decided to poison him to death. But Oucai said to Laus Ntsuag, 'Tomorrow morning we will get up early to cook some rice for you. Be careful not to take any food my father gives you'. And the next morning, after he had finished the rice Oucai had given him, Laus Ntsuag set out again with the two sisters for the fields. The old man continued to hate him.

They went on working hard in the fields, and all the crops grew well. More and more Oucai and Laus Ntsuag liked one another. And the more the two sisters liked the orphan, the more the old man hated him. One morning, the old man got up very early to cook the food. After the two sisters had finished setting the table for Laus Ntsuag, they left the house. The old man would not let go of Laus Ntsuag and insisted that he take a bowl of his rice. Laus Ntsuag had to eat it. The poison got into his stomach, caused him excruciating pain, and was the end of him.

Night fell. The sisters came home, only to find Laus Ntsuag was dead. 'Why did you kill him?' said Oucai to the old man, 'he was kind hearted and could do heavy work—he worked for us every day. What are we to do, now that you have killed him?' She cried and cried and cried. She cried with such sorrow that the winds began to blow and the rains began to fall. At length Oucai said to the old man, 'Now that you have killed him, we shall bury him in your own big black lacqueur wood coffin'. Seeing how angry his two daughters were, the old man was afraid they might run away, leaving noone around to work for him any more. So he let them bury Laus Ntsuag in that big black lacqueur wood coffin of his.

The two young girls bore off Laus Ntsuag and placed him inside the coffin. And to the head of the coffin they tied a cock. Then with all their strength, they heaved the coffin out to the open field. At the foot of the slope in front of their house there was a river flowing. The two sisters carried the coffin to the side of the river, but it was so heavy that they could go no further. Then Ouniang suggested, 'Let us put him in the river and the waters will bear him home'. 'Bravo', said Oucai. And they lowered the coffin down into the river. Suddenly a big wave washed the coffin right to the middle of the river, and the river carried the coffin downstream for three nights and three days. The coffin spent three nights in muddy waters and three days in clear water. After that, it finally arrived back at Laus Ntsuag's home.

It was well past midnight. The cock which was tied to the head of the coffin then began to sing, 'Kuku kuku, Laus Ntsuag left for a distant land to try to find a wife, and he found himself arriving back here in this place, Mother of Laus Ntsuag, Father of Laus Ntsuag, Laus Ntsuag is back from finding a wife'.

As soon as Laus Ntsuag's aunt heard this, she called out to her husband, 'Eh, quickly! Do you not hear one shouting that Laus

Ntsuag has come back with a wife? Let's go out and see for ourselves!'

But Laus Ntsuag's uncle just answered, 'He cannot be back. You miss him so much you are dreaming'. But just then, the cock sang again, 'Kuku, kuku, Laus Ntsuag went to the land high above looking for a wife. There was a wicked old fellow, who poisoned me to death. The cock led the way to show me the way home'.

His aunt pulled his uncle out of the bed; 'He is really back! You must get up quickly!' His uncle pulled on his gown, saying 'It is well past midnight. Where did you hear this? Where?' And the cock started singing again, 'Kuku kuku kuku, Mother of Laus Ntsuag, Father of Laus Ntsuag, Laus Ntsuag went to the land high above looking for a wife. There was a wicked old fellow, who poisoned me to death. The cock led the way to show me the way home'.

The uncle was scared out of his wits to hear this. He picked up a hook and headed for the river. Heavens! He saw a big black wooden lacqueur coffin, washed up by the bank of the river. To the top of the coffin a cock was tied.

When the cock saw the uncle and aunt of Laus Ntsuag approaching, it flapped its wings several times, and a thin mist appeared on the surface of the river. With a loud wala *(gurgling) sound, a beautiful girl arose out of the waters. She looked at them both for a moment. And the faint sound of the reed pipes could be heard. The girl's face looked very sad. Soon they heard her singing softly through the gathering mist,*

> *'Heaven, O Heaven!*
> *Laus Ntsuag travelled to a place higher up*
> *looking for a wife*
> *and there he found a wicked old man*
> *who poisoned me to death.*
> *It was the cock which showed me the way home.*
>
> *There was an elder sister who was very kind-hearted*
> *and a younger sister who was kind and nice*
> *they put me inside a black lacqueur wooden coffin*
> *and it was the cock which showed me the way home.*

The kind-hearted sisters were ill at ease
putting me into the black lacqueur coffin
the yellow water carried it away for three nights
and the clear water bore it along for three days
it was the cock which showed me the way home.

Coming back home, Oh returning home
coming back home fills one with sadness.
Laus Ntsuag's father did not recognise his voice
Laus Ntsuag's mother did not remember his face
they did not permit him to approach the house.

Laus Ntsuag was so sad that his eyes turned black
with one kick he flung open the coffin
the cock showed me how to get to Oucai
and the cock showed me how to reach Ouniang
Oucai and I will make a pair
Ouniang and I will become a couple.

Laus Ntsuag has died of poisoning for three years
Oucai has died of anger for three years
Laus Ntsuag spends his nights with the cock and Laus
Ntsuag keeps company with the cock.

Heaven, Oh heaven!
Three years and several hundred years have passed
before Laus Ntsuag and OPucai could become husband and
wife
before Laus Ntsuag and Ouniang could live as man and
woman.
They have ascended to heaven
leaving the cock behind to tell the time
leaving the cock behind to crow in the morning.

Ouniang turned into the stars at night
watching over the people at night
Oucai became the moon in the sky
Laus Ntsuag turned into the sun into the sky

Laus Ntsuag travelling in the daytime
Oucai coming out only at night.

Oucai travels by herself at night
Laus Ntsuag asked her to change the day
but Oucai is too shy by day.
Laus Ntsuag gave her a needle to poke peoples' eyes
since then, Laus Ntsuag travels by night for the sake of the
moon
Oucai comes out by day for the sake of the sun.

Day changes (with) night, light changes (with) dark
the cock crows the time at set hours.
thanking the cock who sings at regular intervals
Oucai took 'sweet-and-bitter bamboo' to make a comb
and gave it to the cock to comb its hair.
but the cock knew not how to use it
wearing it on its head like a hairpin
with its spine facing the head and its teeth facing the sky
so the cock is said to wear a crown'.

Out came the sun. 'Kuku kuku kuku'. No more misty fog veiling the whole river. Nowhere could be seen the beautiful and fair-faced lady. A big black lacqueur wooden coffin stood by the bank of the river. At its head a cock was stretching out its neck to crow. On its head it indeed wore a comb, with its spine facing the head and its teeth facing the sky.

The uncle and aunt of Laus Ntsuag carried that big black lacqueur wooden coffin up the river bank, and arranged for a funeral for three days. They invited the specialists to conduct the funeral rituals. After this, they buried the coffin on a plain where chestnuts grew. And every morning, at fixed hours, the cock crowed, to tell people the time.
(Xiong Zonghua)[17]

We may wonder at Oucai apparently lamenting her lover's loss on such pragmatic grounds, but indeed a man's use is the measure of

---

[17] Also recorded in GMMG 1-8.

one's love for him. On the old man's coffin, coffins are commonly prepared in advance for one's own death. As in the previous two stories, the orphan is fed on bitter buckwheat; emphasising his poverty, while the references to 'clearing land' point us as in the first story towards an early stage of Hmong settlement, the transformation of shifting to settled cultivatuon.

The implied marriage to two sisters is not I think particularly significant; traditionally Hmong could have more than one 'wife', as indeed Chinese males could take 'concubines', and sometimes indeed these were sisters. 'Nuncle' (*laug laug*) is a familar term for FeB applied to older males, without I think any connection to the orphan's adoptive parents, who has more in common with the wicked old man of the first story whose daughters the hero wins. The references to three nights and days in clear or muddy (yellow) waters) have clearly some kind of spiritual significance, but I am unable to discover exactly what. Similarly, the description of the orphan ascending to a 'land above' to find a wife, where there was a wicked old man, is I am sure of enormous significance, since it seems to relate the orphan's mundane quest to a more heavenly one in which, as on earth, one is likely to be tricked, or poisoned.

This is an extremely odd tale, full of contradictions and ambiguous messages. While the orphan's death is lamented at length, and in this sense the story is truer to many accounts of the inauspicious ends of Hmong culture heroes than some of the more auspicious ones given here, at the same time there is an odd jubilation about it—the return of the orphan, suddenly gifted with parents, to his home—and his ultimate immortality as the sun (or is it the moon? an odd interchange is suggested by the verses here, since the Hmong sun is classically female, the moon masculine; while clearly here Hmongthink has again meshed with Chinese stories of the Moon-maiden and her undying love for the male Sun—and perhaps it is only eclipses which are referred to in this interchange?). It is hard to ignore the jubilance in the figure of the orphan kicking open his coffin, or the resentment in the final complaints about the orphan's rejection by his supposed parents, who fail to recognise him at all in his return home. . Yet at the start of the story these foster parents are expressly described as kind, and come out to see him from 'quite a long way'.

And at one level the story is quite clearly a tragic lament, for the orphan tricked and poisoned by his ogre-like father-in-law. Its tragic quality is emphasised by the sound of funeral reed-pipes when the ghostly maiden appears from the river, with her report to the still living of a crime which involves the dead, and which perhaps has to be restituted. And the tragic quality is also shown in the very clear references to Hmong funerals in the repetition of 'it was the cock which showed me the way', which one finds in the *Qhab Ki* song of death (above, Part Two)—and which is indeed associated with a tale (wordlessly told in one of the reed-pipe funeral laments) of the Divine Archer who shoots all but one of the original nine suns who then hides and must be enticed to return to earth with the aid of a cock's crow, on whose head the returning sun shines, lending him his crest for evermore. This tale also incidentally explains why it is that cocks crow every morning to summon the sun, and (by implication) why the cock should be seen as the harbinger who leads the soul of the dead on its journey to the village of ancestors (Lemoine 1972a). Here it is the cock's function as the regulator of time, in a somewhat Sinitic fashion, which is emphasised, but the mortuary implications of the whole story are clear enough.

The telling of the tale is in fact almost more remarkable than the narrative of the tale itself, with its odd admixture of joy and lamentation, the melodramatic way in which the old man's initial rudeness prepares the way for his eventual devilry, and the essentially naive way in which everyone seems to know the old man is trying to poison his prospective son-in-law—and the way the old man is not sure of the designs of this son-in-law! And indeed there is much of Hmong living here, from the arrival of the stranger at night to the sleeping of strangers under the eaves and the secretive pasing of rice-bowls, under cover of darkness, by the hearth...

The story could easily be read as one about time, the nature of time and the regulatuon of human events, the relations of men and women and the regularity rather than chaos of events, but these readings would result I think from the intersection of the Hmong orphan legend with those of the Chinese myths of unrequited loves being remade in heaven. In the light of the other Hmong stories we are considering here, it would be more appropriate to see this example as another story of the Orphan's original suffering, and his triumph through an eventual Mystic Marriage—even though this triumph is here mitigated by his death, and his eventual victory has to take place through a spiritual immortality.

(In terms of the association between the wife's sorrow and the coming of winds and rain, could it be that the orphan's stillness in other tales depicts a kind of death, a kind of surrender to the mystic forces of the female?)

The water images in the last tale are significant, since a whole series of orphan tales links him with water and sinitic legends of the dragon king, fertility and abundance, as in the following example:

THE ORPHAN AND THE TOAD (LEGEND 6)

Once upon a time there was an orphan named Ntsuag who was very poor. Every day, he went out fishing. One day, he caught a small fish. He took it home, but unfortunately he dropped it by the stove and the fish's tail got burnt. He took it to a pond and let it go, and then he went fishing again. This time he caught another fish. He took it back and put it in the water pot. Every day when he came back from work, he found that his house was tidy and clean. Wine, meat, and jellied beancurd were placed on the table ready for him to eat. The same thing happened every day. He was very surprised. Not knowing who it was that did all this for him, he went from door to door thanking all his neighbours. And all the neighbours shook their heads. They thought the orphan was off his head, for they had never come to cook food for him.

He had no alternative but to go and ask the Spirit of the Land (Tub Tiv). *The Spirit told him to go home and turn over an empty wooden tub and hide himself inside it. He should also take a broom with him. When someone swept the ground after cooking she would look for that broom, and then he might seize her and know who she was. So after the orphan had returned home, he did as the Spirit of Land had told him. One day, he hid himself inside the tub. At noon, a beautiful girl suddenly jumped out of the water pot. She cooked all the food and made all the jellied beancurd. After cooking, she went everywhere looking for the broom to sweep the floor, but she couldn't find it. At last she discovered the broom, half sticking out from under the grain tub. She stretched out her hand to take it. The orphan immediately jumped out and caught hold of her. Then he said, 'If you are mine, please don't leave me. We can set up a family together'. Eventually, the girl agreed to marry him, and they lived together happily. After they woke up from their wedding night, they found their simple hut had turned into a splendid mansion. They had herds of cattle and flocks of sheep, and became very wealthy.*

Some time later, another girl came who wanted to ruin their happy family. She turned out to be the fish whose tail had been burnt before. Her name was Nkaus Kom. It seemed that she had already been married to another man, but still she wanted to live with Ntsuag. Because now it was not very likely that she could do so, she was very jealous of that beautiful girl, and thought it was her who had seized her beloved young man. She said to Ntsuag, 'Your wife has a disease. You should desert her'. 'No, I've never found anything wrong with her', said Ntsuag, 'she is not sick'. 'When you go home, untie her leggings' insisted the girl, 'and surely you will find she is sick'.

Although Ntsuag didn't believe what she had said, when he went home he made his wife untie her leggings, and he found some scabs on her legs. Ntsuag thought his wife was really sick, so he decided to leave her. His wife begged him many times not to abandon her, but he wouldn't listen to her. She couldn't do anything about it, and rushed out of the house, and all the cattle and sheep followed her and ran away. When they arrived at the pond, in she jumped and went home to the Dragon's Palace, for she was no other than the daughter of the Dragon King himself. The cattle and the sheep also followed her into the pond. Ntsuag was very upset. He seized hold of one old sheep which was left, and dragged it along by its horns so hard that the horns became twisted. But when he had dragged the sheep all the way back, he saw that their splendid house was gone. Instead, his simple old hut stood there, with nothing left inside it. He was just as poor as he had been before.

Ntsuag knew that he had been tricked by that wicked girl. He was very sad and went back to the pond crying. While he was crying, a toad *leapt to his side. 'Why are you crying?' asked the toad. 'My wife has gone, and she has taken away all my wealth', replied Ntsuag. 'Don't cry' said the toad, 'wait until I drink up all the water in the pond. Then you will see your wife again'.*

The toad crawled over to the edge of the pond, and began to drink up all the water. It drank and it drank and it drank. When the pond was almost dry, his wife slowly appeared out of the water. Ntsuag was overjoyed, and began to laugh. The toad was amused too. It couldn't help laughing, it laughed so hard that eventually its stomach burst because it had drunk so much water. All the water flowed back into the pond, and soon it was full again. And his wife disappeared.

Ntsuag said to the toad, 'Do not fear, I'll mend your stomach. Then you can drink again'. Once the toad's stomach was mended, it began to drink again, and when the pond was nearly dry and his wife was halfway out of the water, Ntsuag jumped into the pond to hold her in his arms for fear she might escape again. He was so excited that he fainted right away. When he woke up, he found himself lying by the side of the pool. The dragon pond was full of water again. But his wife had a tender heart. After she had carried him up to the side of the pool, she had left him a hat. And this hat is the hair that people now grow.
(Ma Jixiang)

The 'dragon pool' referred to here is a common Chinese and Hmong term for well situated or large pools or lakes, classically associated with legends of the subterranean realms of the Dragon King. The narrator told me that the scabs on the mystic maiden's legs were commonly caused by the puttees which Hmong women still wear, but that the orphan did not realise this. It was the Chinese term for the local deity (*tub tiv* transcribed into Hmong) which was used here, although these local deities are not usually honoured by the the Hmong of Sichuan. One remarks that hostility to the orphan is here transferred from the figure of a paternal relative, such as a brother or paternal uncle, to a jealous sister-in-law, although indeed we have already met the hostility of the father-in-law or potential father-in-law.

The theme of the house being magically remade at night we have also met in Legends 3 and 4, while that of the magical helper's capture is virtually identical to the ending of Legend 2, the story of the wildcat who is transformed into a wife. In fact the first part of this story, up to his discovery of the magical helper who is presumably the fish in the water pot, really forms a tale in its own right, concluding as in Legend 2 with a happy marriage and a vision of prosperity and abundance.

This tale concludes, however, tragically with the loss of both the mystic spouse and of all fortune—and in this sense is more comparable to those which stress the orphan's ultimate *failure* to achieve success, as in the immediately preceding tale (where the orphan is poisoned by his prospective father-in-law). Yet this ultimately tragic ending is somewhat modified, both by the banal conclusion on the origin of peoples' hair and also by the images of fertility and plenitude which characterise the toad's drinking and expulsion of the waters of the lake. There seems to be a deliberate ambiguity here, a sort of dialectic between the orphan's success and his failure, achieved at a narrative level through the toad's first drinking up, then laughing out, then partly drinking up again, the waters, and figuratively through the irony that the fullness of waters should signify the *absence* of the marrying maiden.

This hesitance or ambivalence may have resulted from the *fusion* of well-known Chinese tales of the Dragon King who lives at the bottom of waters and whose daughter is often represented as an earthly maiden who comes to the help of a poor man, with some very antique Hmong myths and legends about the malevolent Toad associated with the Deluge, who was foolishly killed at the dawn of time and whose dying words curse the world to know, henceforth, sickness and death ('so from now on leaves will fall and forests grow thin', Lemoine 1972b). In the 1930s Graham collected a number of stories from the Hmong of Sichuan about the Toad whose tears drown the world and whose laughter brings drought (No.123), and an almost identical story (No.85) in which the toad drinks up the waters so the orphan can reclaim the Dragon King's daughter, but in which the orphan's head finally falls off (and without the two fish).

Here, then, despite a countertext or undercurrent of images of fertility and abundance, the downfall of the orphan is linked clearly with the origin and source of all evils and excess in the world, the origin of flood and drought, illness and death, surfeit and exhaustion. Probably a Freudian or Jungian analysis would make something of the final reference to hair as a symbol of virility, in its juxtaposition here with watery images of plenty and fertility, and while there are good arguments against such cross-cultural hermeneutics, it is at least tempting to relate this final image of regeneration (if that is what we agree it is) to the decapitation in Graham's comparable tale.

In some of Graham's other stories of the toad, the toad is born to a couple who try to kill him, and is himself in search of a wife, somewhat similarly to the orphan himself, and in one *succeeds in becoming the Emperor*. In the light of the historic tales in Gongxian about the Bo kings who could fly without their heads, the legendary inhabitants of the area who were suppressed by the imperial armies (Part Two), a historical context of armed uprising and suppression suggests itself, in which the orphan challenges, becomes, or is defeated by the Emperor. Here imperial birth itself becomes a symbol of supreme triumph, which eludes the orphan or which he succeeds in achieving. These imperial motifs are of course reflected in images of the dragon which abound in these stories as we shall see. In this sense these kind of tales form part of a continuing discourse about the nature of ultimate authority and challenges to it, and the realities of poverty and deprivation.

The basic skeleton of the fable is more clearly revealed in another tale which echoes the themes of many of the previous ones:

THE ORPHAN AND THE FISH GOD (LEGEND 7)

Once upon a time, there was an orphan. He was indeed very poor. He lived inside a stone cave. Every day he went fishing and he sold his catch for rice.

One day, the orphan caught a big white fish. The fish was so beautiful that he could not bear to sell it for rice. He took it home with him, placed it in the water tank and began to raise it. A few days later, when the orphan returned home from fishing, he found the table had been laid, with hot rice steaming and many dishes. The house had also been cleaned beautifully. But nobody could be seen doing all this work. The orphan was hungry. He told himself not to worry about who was doing all the work, but just to eat up the food.

Whenever the orphan came home after fishing, he always found his meal already prepared for him. He thought it might be some neighbour's wife, who was kindly and pitied him, who had cooked and cleaned his house for him. So he visited all his neighbours to thank them. But they took no notice of him. He was still wondering which of his neighbour's kind-hearted wives could be helping him. But his neighbours' wives just told him off, saying 'Can't you find any better way of starting a conversation? It will be your fault if my husband scolds me. Nobody here is free to make your meals and clean your house for you, over such a long time too. You probably just have nothing better to say!' After they had chided him, the orphan could not help but to go and ask the advice of Saub.

'It was not your neighbour who has been helping you cook and clean', said Old Saub, 'Do you want to know who it was?'

'Certainly I should like to know', replied the orphan, 'so that I may thank them for their kindness'.

'Then this is what you must do', said Saub, 'return home now. After breakfast you should pick up your net and say "Today I'll go fishing". Then pretend to go off fishing. But half way there, come back again, hide under the dustpan, and put the broom against the side of the dustpan. Remain very quiet and then you will be able to know who it is who is cooking and cleaning for you'.

So, after he had finished his breakfast on the next day, the orphan picked up his net and said aloud 'I'll go fishing today'. But half way there he turned around and came back again, and hid underneath the dustpan.

Soon he heard a noise coming out of the water tank. The orphan kept very quiet and watched everything that happened. In no time, a maiden jumped out of the water tank. She ran back and forth, cooking and tidying everything up. She made all the food and put it out on the table. Then she was busy with something else. The girl looked very beautiful indeed. She was a lovely looking girl. She looked up at the sky. Seeing that it was still early, she went about looking for the broom. She saw it lying against the side of the dustpan, and went to pick it up. At once the orphan undid the dustpan and caught hold of the girl. She could not escape, and in the end she married that orphan. And for the rest of their lives they remained together.
(Yang Guohua)

As I have said, the main outlines of the story, expressed in clear paratactic visual images, are particularly simply sketched here. As in the wildcat story (2), Saub advises the orphan to misplace the broom and to hide so he can catch the magical animal who is a wife in disguise and has been cleaning and cooking for him invisibly (in the previous story, the Spirit of the Land has been substituted for Saub, but otherwise the same themes appear, including that the supernatural helper is a fish. And as in the previous story, all the neighbours are asked about and deny all knowledge of these events.

The addition of the dustpan is, however, significant, since there is a repeated association between the orphan and the 'dustpan' or rice winnowing tray, with the help of which the decapitated Bo kings of Gongxian legend flew. In other stories, the imperial pretensions of the orphan are more clearly revealed:

LAUS NTSUAG BECOMES A DRAGON (LEGEND 8)

In a stockaded stone village lived a mother with her son. The son was named Laus Ntsuag. His mother was so old that she could not work any more. Laus Ntsuag had to look after the family all by himself, cutting grass and selling it.

One year, the place was hit by a drought. The grass all dried up on the mountain slopes. Laus Ntsuag could find no more grasses, and soon he would have to starve. Laus Ntsuag did not want his mother to worry about this, so he dared not tell her how short they were of rice. He always let his mother have a good bowl of rice at each meal. When his mother asked him whether he had eaten or not, he would say yes. In fact he had only gulped down some rice soup made from chaff and taken some wild herbs with it.

One day he put a pack on his back and left again looking for for some grassland. He walked and he walked, and yet he could find no grass on the mountain slopes. Then he sat down, beneath a tall crabapple tree, and began to sigh.

A small deer came out of the undergrowth and craned his neck out at Laus Ntsuag. It made some noises up into the sky. Then it moved away quietly. Laus Ntsuag thought this through; could it be that the deer wished to lead him to some grass? So he got up and followed it.

The small deer took Laus Ntsuag to a grassy plot. When it got there, it turned around to look at him. After again barking up at the sky, the deer disappeared.

Curious, Laus Ntsuag came right up to where the deer had been standing. And he was overjoyed to see that lush green grass covered the whole area. He set to cutting the grass and brought a big bundle home. He sold it for a good price. With the money, he bought half a sheng *(a half litre) of rice, took it home and poured all the grains into a rice container.*

The next morning Laus Ntsuag walked back in the direction of the grassplot. He wondered if he would be able to find any more grass that day. To his surprise, grass had already grown up where he had cut it down the previous day, and it was the same kind of lush green grass. He was filled with joy, and again took home a full bundle of grass.

Every day Laus Ntsuag went back to the same grassy plot, and every day he took home just one full bundle of grass. Curious, his mother asked him, 'My son, tell me, where do you find your grass every day when the weather is so dry?' Laus Ntsuag told his mother the whole story. But when she asked him where the grassplot was, he could not name the place. He could only say, 'It's the place where the deer made noises'. From that time on, they called the place 'Deernoise'.

One day, Laus Ntsuag said to his mother, 'Mother, I want to take some grass away from the grassplot and transplant it to the side of our house, so I don't have to go so far every day and can cut more grass. I can sell more grass and buy more rice so we can help our "brothers" in the stone stockaded village'. 'What a good idea', said his mother, 'tomorrow you go and take home some of that grass'.

The next morning after he had finished his morning meal, Laus Ntsuag left the house with the pack on his back. He tried to dig up the grass with a hoe. But the grass seemed to be rooted to the ground the first time he tried. The second time he tried, his hoe seemed to have hit a small hollow in the ground. His third attempt got the grass out of the ground, and out of it rolled a shining object on the ground. He picked it up, amd saw it was a shining pearl (precious stone).

And indeed it was a most beautiful pearl. Quickly Laus Ntsuag tucked it into his purse. Soon he was on his way home, bearing a load of grass together with its roots and stems and leaves. He planted the grass outside his house. But it did not grow well at all. Laus Ntsuag was sorry about this, and felt that he should not have taken the grass home. 'What if it all dies, then what shall I do?'

After tidying up the grass he had planted, he turned to his mother. 'Mother, this morning when I turned over the grass I found this pearl, rolling out of the ground. It was shining bright. But the grass does not seem to grow well here. I don't know if it will survive'.

'Go and water the grass', said his mother, 'and show me this pearl you were talking about'.

Laus Ntsuag took the pearl out and showed it to his mother. 'What a beautiful pearl!' she exclaimed, 'you must hide it in a very good place'.

Laus Ntsuag tried to find a good place to hide the pearl in, but no place seemed to be safe enough. In the end, he suggested to his mother that they should hide it in the rice container. 'That's a good idea', said she, 'there is still lots of rice left there'. 'No, only a few grains are left now', said Laus Ntsuag.

After putting the pearl carefully in the rice container, Laus Ntsuag picked up a bucket and fetched some water from the river to water the grass. Night fell. When the orphan returned home, he asked his mother, 'Did you light the lamp? It is so bright in here'. 'We have never lit a lamp in our life' replied his mother, 'it's that pearl of yours that is giving out all the light'.

Then Laus Ntsuag went to get some rice out of the rice container. 'Mother, mother, come and see. The rice bin is full of rice!' he exclaimed. They were both very happy and excited. Laus Ntsuag poured the rice out of the container, leaving just a few grains behind. He put the gleaming pearl into the rice container. In no time the rice had grown to fill the bin. The more he poured the rice out, the more the bin filled up again. From then on, he was able to help the poor people with their rice. Whenever he ran out of meat or salt, money or clothes, he would get the pearl to bring him more meat or salt, money or clothes. His family began to grow rich. None of the poor people in the stockaded stone village or in the area around the Deernoise grassplot had to worry about food or clothing any more.

A short time passed. The landlord heard about the pearl. He thought deeply about this. How was it that such a poor boy, who had to cut grass for a living, had acquired so much treasure that he could afford to eat and dress so well? I can hardly get anything special in this place, and wish I could rob him of his pearl. So he sent his servants to Lauis Ntsuag's house and searched the whole place. They searched high and low, turning over boxes and trunks, and yet they could not find the pearl. At last they came across the rice container, under the bed. The rice was still growing inside it. The servants grabbed at the container, and just as it was about to fall into their hands, it turned over and out rolled the pearl. Laus Ntsuag snatched it and ran off with it. The servants all went after him, running madly as well. When they had nearly caught up with him, Laus Ntsuag popped the pearl into his mouth. He was gasping so much the pearl went right down into his stomach. Soon the servants caught hold of him, they searched him all over, but could not discover the pearl. They had to let him go.

After swallowing the pearl, Laus Ntsuag grew thirsty. His mother handed him a bowl of water. But that was not enough. She changed to bigger bowls, but he emptied each bowl of water in no time at all. The more he drank, the thirstier he became. After he had drunk up their entire pot of water, his mother went to fetch more water from the river. Soon, she grew tired. But he had still not enough, and was desperate for more water. At last his mother said to him, 'Son, I cannot fetch any more water for you. You will have to go down to the river, and drink from there'. 'Very well' answered Laus Ntsuag. He went to the bank of the river, threw himself down there, and began to drink and drink and drink.

As soon as he dipped his head into the water, , the water rose up and carried him off to the middle of the river, turning him into a dragon. The tide swept Laus Ntsuag down the river. When his mother saw what was happening, she cried out 'My son! My son!' Hearing her cry, Laus Ntsuag turned his head to look over his shoulder. A big dragon pond sprang up where he looked. Twenty-four times his mother cried out to him, and twenty-four times Laus Ntsuag turned around to look, and whenever he looked another dragon pond appeared, until there were twenty-four dragon ponds there. 'My boy, will it be long before you come home again?' cried out his mother. 'Mother' called Laus Ntsuag, 'Mother, I shall only come home again when the flowers bloom from rocks and horns grow on horses', answered Laus Ntsuag.

Laus Ntsuag had gone. The people who remained in the stone stockaded village and Deernoise took care of his mother. The twenty-four dragon ponds remind people of those days long ago when Laus Ntsuag, the orphan, changed into a dragon.
(Yang Daihe)[18]

The place names refer to real places near Gongxian, and so this story is also partly a locality story, comparable to the legends of the Bo kings we considered in Part II. Again its tragic ending with the eventual death of the orphan, comparable with Legend 5 above where the body of Laus Ntsuag is also swept home along the river, is contradicted by the triumphant images of the orphan's transformation into a dragon, the symbol of imperial majesty. Again, therefore, this is an ambivalent conclusion in which the ultimate fate of the orphan remains uncertain, although it is clear that his return, if return there can be, must be accompanied by a complete *reversal* of the normal order of things, a reversal pictured in images like horns on horses very characteristic of messianic legends.

In fact the story is in three parts; in the first part, replicated as a whole in other tales which tell of a mystic marriage, the orphan's supernatural animal helper (here, the deer) aids him to a supreme success, a perpetual plenty and replenishment, first through the grass he cuts and then through the discovery of the magic pearl. But already the image of the precious stone, or 'pearl', reflects general Chinese ideas about imperial majesty and success, as in the many tales where the dragon guards the pearl of immortality which the hero must obtain.

The second part of the tale deals with the oppression of the orphan, and here oppression is transferred from the kinship relatives of other stories into the figure of a 'landlord'. In a more traditional context it is likely that the Hmong would have used 'official' for this 'landlord', referring to a pre-Qing time in which the separation of official and local powers had not yet fully occurred, or even specified this figure as a Chinese one. The use of 'landlord' here is a catch-all for figures of oppression, who might be officials or local despots, but would be understood by a Hmong audience as referring to a Chinese. Yet the use of 'landlord' places the story in a post-Maoist context in

---

[18] Also in GMMG 313-16.

which all folk heroes have become poor peasants and all villains feudal landlords, and this is of a piece with some of the language used to describe Laus Ntsuag's moral desire to help others and the poor.

The final part of the tale contains the ambiguous conclusion, with the defeat of the landlord but the apparent death of the orphan, and yet his transformation into the supreme figure of power, the Dragon. And here, as in (6) above (the story of the toad), it is images of inexhaustible capacity and desire (thirst) which characterise the hero; indeed, Laus Ntsuag's drinking up of the waters is identical to that of the toad's in Legend 6. Perhaps there is a hint here, a suggestion, that the drought from which the orphan originally suffers has returned with his removal, as he inexhaustibly drinks up all the waters from the river—and yet left behind are the twenty-four dragon pools, a memento inscribed in the very landscape, of a potential grandeur and triumph?

Rather than an object, to begin with, it is a place which assures the orphan of perpetual plenty and wealth, and here almost certainly, given the later theme of the dragon transformation, there are resonances in this reference to the power of place of geomantic tales which tell of the discovery of the ideal burial site which will assure the descendants of those buried there of supreme success, even Imperial status, which in other contexts are told by Hmong to describe how their orphan hero succeeded in becoming the Emperor of China (Tapp 1989).

The 'brothers' in the village whom the orphan wishes to help should be understood as lineage 'brothers' or clan relatives, while the mother's final exclamation, just before the fatal end, is also typical of other Hmong messianic tales (as in the Tswb Tchoj tale, Tapp 1989, or in the Bo king tales). The orphan here is transformed into an archetypically Hmong figure of the Toad, otherwise a symbol of violence and destruction.

An explicit relationship of enmity and opposition is posited between the poor hero and the current Emperor in another tale, which unites the pearl of plenty—cornucopia—images of the first part of the latter story, with the imperial pretensions of its final part:

THE POOR MAN AND THE EMPEROR (LEGEND 9)

Long, long ago, there was a couple who were very poor, because they had so many children. The husband had to go out and earn some money in order to support his family. One day he walked and walked, and when it got dark he came to a very big mountain cave (qhov). He stepped inside, and to his surprise found that there was stone bed, stone stools, stone knives and stone tables and so on inside. 'This is indeed a very good place to stay for the night', he said to himself and so he decided to sleep there.

No sooner had he lain down on the stone bed to sleep than a giant animal came in. Without any effort the monster picked up a huge stone slab and placed it at the mouth of the cave. Then he took out a pearl (precious stone, probably a pearl) and sat down at the stone table with it, calling 'Pearl, pearl, quickly bring me meat and wine'. Immediately there was wine and meat upon the table, and the giant animal began to enjoy its feast. The poor man hid himself and dared not make any sound. After a little while, the giant stopped eating and muttered, 'Why is there a smell of humans here?' He stood up and searched the cave, but did not find anything. He came back to the table and resumed his eating. Soon after this, the ogre still felt there was a smell of humans in the cave, and he this time searched everywhere, marking each place that he had searched. Finally he got to the bedside and found the poor man hiding by the corner of the bed. The giant animal wanted to punish him severely, but the poor man begged for mercy. The monster paid no attention to him. He went back to the table and continued to eat his food. After the meal, the giant animal lay down on the bed and fell asleep. The poor man began to think, 'How can I escape from the cave today?' He searched the cave and found a very sharp stone knife. Then he stole to the bedside and killed that giant animal. He took the pearl and got to the entrance. But the great stone slab was blocking the way. He cut the stone slab into pieces with his stone knife and left the cave.

Later, along the way, he met a person who carried two knives. 'Friend', he called, 'please come here, and have a drink with me'. The man agreed and came to sit beside him. The poor man took out his pearl and called 'Pearl, pearl, quickly bring me food and drink'. Food and drink immediately appeared before them. At the meal, the other man told him that his two knives were precious ones. He wanted to exchange his two precious knives for the poor man's pearl. 'What's the merit of your knives?' asked the poor man. 'They can cut anything I tell them to' he answered. In front of them, there were two apple trees. The strange man removed the two knives from his belt and called 'Precious knives, precious knives, quickly chop down those two apple trees for me'. The two knives flew off by themselves and cut down the trees in no time. The poor man thought that the two knives were really precious, so he exchanged his pearl for them.

Then they parted. Nobody knows how far they travelled. One day they came across each other again. The poor man said to the stranger, 'Last time I gave you dinner. This time maybe you should give me one'. But the stranger replied, 'since we've already exchanged our things, there is no point in me entertaining you this time'. The poor man took out his precious knives and called, 'Precious knives, precious knives, quickly kill that ungrateful wretch!' And the precious knives flew off, all by themselves, to kill the stranger, so that the poor man was able to recover his pearl.

He set off, and along the way he met a person blowing the horn. 'Friend, come here, let's have a drink!' The horn-blower agreed. The poor man took out his pearl and ordered it to bring them food and drink. At the meal, the horn-blower valued the pearl very much. 'This horn is also a special one, why do we not exchange them?' 'What's the merit of this horn?' asked the poor man. 'When I blow the horn, even if your mother and father were dead, they would come back to life', said the other. The poor man thought the horn was really precious, so he exchanged it for his pearl.

Then they parted. Nobody knows how long they travelled. One day, they met again once more. 'Friend', said the poor man, 'last time I gave you a meal, why don't you give me one this time?' 'Since we've already exchanged our things, why should I give you another meal?' The poor man was furious, he took out his knives and ordered, 'Precious knives, precious knives, go and kill that ungrateful wretch'. The knives flew off, all by themselves, to kill him, and the poor man was again able to retrieve his pearl. Then he took out the horn and blew it. The person who used to blow the horn was alive again. In this way, the poor man got another two precious objects.

Then he took them home. His wife and children were very happy to have him back home again, they thought he must have brought back a lot of food. 'You've been away for such a long time', they said, 'what have you brought back for us?' 'Nothing at all' he replied. His wife and children were sad to hear this news, for he had been away for such a long time, but had brought nothing back at all. They began to cry. 'Don't cry, set the tables and chairs'. After they did so, he took out the pearl and ordered, 'Pearl, pearl, bring us some food and drink'. Immediately, wine and meats appeared on the table. His wife and children had a very good meal,and all his family were happy. His wife felt they were rich now, so wherever she went, she boasted of the pearl to everyone. The news spread quickly enough.

*Soon the Emperor (*Huab Tais*) heard the news. He sent off some men to find the pearl. With them they took a false pearl which had been made before they left, and soon they came to the poor man's house. 'We have heard that your husband has a pearl, please let us have a look at it'. His wife wanted to show the pearl off, so she did show it to them. Those people secretly replaced it with the false one. Later the poor man came home. When he ordered the pearl to bring food and wine, he failed. His wife and children were very sad and began to cry. 'Don't cry. I'll go and find it', he said. He carried the precious knives and horn upon his back.*

Then he set out. When he arrived at the palace of the Emperor, he could see that there were many guards guarding the gates. He took out his precious knives and ordered, 'Precious knives, precious knives, go and kill all those soldiers!' And the knives flew off, all by themselves,and killed all the people in the court. Only the Empress remained unharmed. The poor man entered the palace and cried to the Empress, 'Give me back my pearl!' The Empress could see no way out. She went inside and brought out her precious box, opened it layer by layer, finally taking out a small box, she uncovered it and gave the pearl back to the poor man. After he had recovered his pearl, he left the gates of the palace. Then he started to blow the horn. The Emperor and his soldiers were alive again. The poor man returned to his home. Whenever they wanted something to eat, he called the pearl to bring them delicious food. And they lived happily after that.
(Ma Jixiang)

Without the conclusion, this would be a straightforward miracle story of how a poor man overcomes a monster or demon (who seems to echo the fearsome father-in-law figures of the first and fourth orphan tales) and takes his pearl of plenty, which together with the gift of taking away life and restoring it again, assure him of a happy married life. The magic implements the poor man discovers, and the ungrateful or cunning strangers he meets, are reminiscent of Brothers Grimm or Hans Anderson episodes (such as the Grimm Brothers story of the 'Wishing Table, the Gold-Ass, and the Cudgel in the Sack', in which two older brothers are cheated by strangers out of their magical objects, while it is the youngest brother with the help of his magic cudgel who retrieves the other two objects and returns home in triumph; while in 'The Knapsack, the Hat and the Horn', the youngest brother retrieves the magical tablecloth he has found first with the help of a magical knapsack he has exchanged for it, then with a magical hat and then a horn, which all have military power eventually enabling him to defeat the King and marry his daughter). And in a way we are coming to expect, it is the woman's indiscretion and gossip which lead to a final calamity.

But what is of interest here about this particular legend is that the Emperor is explicitly identified as the source of the oppression of the poor magically gifted hero, rather than a relative or 'landlord', the enmity and opposition of the hero to the Emperor is quite clear, as is the hero's eventual triumph over the Emperor.

This is comedy rather than tragedy; the poor hero wins and returns to a happy married life, rather than being further transformed, into for example a Dragon as in the previous story. The poor man in fact is given powers of life or death over the Emperor himself, who has cheated him out of his rightful property which must be returned to him. And that this should be accomplished through the slaughter of all the Imperial troops, albeit by supernatural means, makes the military allusions of the story even clearer.

The survival of the Empress is also significant, in that a direct relation is established between her and the Hmong hero; one remembers how commonly southern clan origin myths in China attempted to trace an imperial descent through a historic marriage to a daughter or sister of an Emperor, and also that many of these Hmong 'culture hero' tales identify the orphan's wife with the daughter of the Dragon King, who often serves as a symbolic substitute for the Emperor.[19] More is going on here than a simple visit of a poor man to the Emperor who succeeds in retrieving a magical cornucopia; a profound opposition between the Emperor and the Hmong hero is posited here, in which the affinal relatives of the Emperor play an ambivalent part. Cold the mystic marriage so often spoken of in these stories be implicitly signifying one with a *Chinese* woman?

What one is to make of the hero's restoration to life again of the Imperial troops, however, is something of a mystery, unless it can be seen to reflect the deep desire of the Sichuan Hmong for peace and friendship with people who have after all been their their historic enemies! (or again, the hero's goodness of character).

The next, Cinderella type of story, although of a different type to the others we have considered here, explicitly identifies a Hmong orphan with the Emperor of China:

THE ORPHAN WHO BECAME EMPEROR (LEGEND 10)

Once upon a time, there were three brothers who married three women. The eldest brother's wife was called Paag, the second brother's wife was called Ywv, and the youngest brother's wife was called Ntxhais. After the three brothers were married, they went out to work, and their three wives were left at home. One day, when they had no work to do, the eldest brother's wife said to the second brother's wife, 'Ywv, let's scoop some water and take a bath'. 'Fine', the second brother's wife agreed. So they scooped up some water to take a bath, but at that very moment, a star (hno qo) *fell into the basin. Paag and Ywv were frightened. They dared not take their bath, and called to the youngest brother's wife, 'Ntxhais, come here and take a bath'. 'Have you two already bathed?' she asked them, not knowing what had happened. 'Yes', the two women answered her.So then Ntxhais took her bath, but when she had finished bathing, she discovered that she was pregnant. Nobody knew what had caused her pregnancy except for Paag and Ywv, and they told nobody else about it.*

One year later, Ntxhais gave birth to a son who had a very big mouth and nine lumps on its head. Ntxhais was terribly frightened at the

---

[19]   See also Appendix IX, the story of how the orphan marries the Emperor's daughter, aided by three supernatural animal assistants.

sight of this strange creature. She called out for her elder sisters (veij) Paag and Ywv; 'I must have met a ghost tonight!' They hurried to her room, and were also horrified to see the appearance of her newly born son. They thought it must be a spirit (dlaa). 'Let's kill this spirit', suggested Paag. She went out and came back a moment later with a sharp knife, wanting to kill the son. 'If we are going to kill it, let's do it outside the house', said Ywv, 'I don't want to see it killed at home'. And taking the sharp knife with her, Ywv carried the child outside, as if to kill it there. But when she had taken the baby off to a cave behind their house, she could not bear to kill it, and besides, she was also afraid to perform such a bloody deed. So in the end she gave up the attempt to kill it. She left the child outside the cave, and threw away the knife. Then she went back, and told Paag and Ntxhais that she had already killed the spirit, and they believed her.

Not long after the boy had been abandoned, a bitch gave birth to a litter of puppies in their house. But instead of feeding its own puppies, it ran off secretly every day to feed the baby. Six or seven months later, the second brother's wife, Ywv, began to wonder what had happened to the child she had deserted in the cave. She didn't know whether it had been eaten up by tigers or leopards or some other animal, or whether it had starved to death, but when she went back to the cave she saw that the son had grown quite a lot, and later when she saw the bitch lying beside him, she realised what had happened. 'Oh', she exclaimed, 'I would never have believed you could have grown so much after I abandoned you, I thought you would have died!'

'Spark leopard!' spat the child (a curse), 'pigs are my fathers, and bitches are my mothers!' (which meant he wanted nothing to do with her or with the other two wives). After seeing the boy, Ywv returned home again.

When the boy was one year old, imperial envoys were sent by the court to every corner of the realm to seek out a successsor to the throne. And some of these envoys came to inquire of the three women, whether there was such a person in their family. Neither the eldest brother's wife nor the youngest brother's wife thought there was any such person in their family. But when the second brother's wife was asked, she told them there was a child there, but that he looked nothing like a human. 'No matter what you say about him, we *will go and take a look at him', said the imperial officials (*nom*). So the second brother's wife took them off to the cave. And as soon as they set eyes on the child, they all exclaimed 'That is exactly the child we are looking for!'*

*When the child had been born, he had been badly treated by the three women; the eldest brother's wife had wanted to kill him, the second brother's wife had thrown him away, and as for the youngest brother's wife, after she had given birth to the boy, she was so frightened by his appearance that she had covered him up with a basket. So after the boy had left with the imperial officials, on the way he said, 'Flowers bloom and flowers fall' (a reference to Paag, whose name means 'flower'). Then he told the imperial officials to go back and bring Ywv (meaning 'small') to be his maidservant in the imperial palace. And finally, he said that Ntxhais would have to carry a basket (*kaim*) on her back all the year round.*

*The officials thought that he must have meant that he wanted his mother to be his servant (*qhev*). But when they arrived back at the house, they found that the elder brother's wife, Paag, had fallen to the ground dead. Ntxhais, the youngest brother's wife, had a basket stuck on her back which she could not take off. Only the second brother's wife, Ywv, was unharmed. So they took Ywv with them back to the palace.*

*When they arrived back at the gates of the palace, a nine-gun salute was fired, showing that the successor had succeeded to the throne. Because the new Emperor had nine lumps on his head, they called him Bao Wenzheng ('bao' in Chinese meaning 'lumps'). The Emperor was in charge of worldly (*neeg*) affairs in the daytime, and ruled over spiritual (*dlaa*) affairs by night. The reason why he could also rule over the spiritual world was that, because the second brother's wife had saved his life, he had promised her that if she encountered spirits at night, the spirits too would help her. And we have a custom here that at Hmong funerals and weddings and other occasions, when a salute is fired, only three shots can be fired instead of nine. Only for someone with an official title may nine shots be fired, otherwise the rifles will be confiscated.*

(Tao Xiaoping)

The last remark was an imaginative addition, based on pre-Republican rules of etiquette, made for my benefit. Although the story lacks any sense of historical hostility towards the Chinese, here we find the abandoned Hmong orphan finally becoming Emperor of China. His virgin birth, out of water by a fallen star, while quite typical of legendary semi-divines in China, is also strongly reminiscent of the Southeast Asian Hmong stories about the orphan who became the Emperor and who has frequently been the inspiration of organised, messianic uprisings against the state (from colonial French Indochina to present day socialist Laos and Thailand). In the version of this story I collected the orphan is magically conceived after a boar breathes over a maiden, and later he grinds up the bones of his father the boar to make into a cake to tempt the ox which guards the geomantic site of imperial rebirth, and becomes Emperor (Tapp 1989). In another incarnation the orphan, who is constantly battling the Han Chinese for supremacy over the land, is born after a bubble has burst against the body of a bathing maiden. It is tempting to interpret this orphan's reference to pigs being his father, although clearly not literally intended here, in the light of these other Hmong stories of the orphan which do have him, quite literally, conceived from a pig.

This orphan is doubly an orphan, since not only has he no father, but he is also abandoned by his mother; and one should remember that the Hmong term for orphan (*ntsuag*) literally means bereaved or deserted, and may therefore refer either to children with no parents or to children with only a mother, as well as to widows and widowers. Given the strongly patrilineal features of the Hmong descent system, to be fatherless is effectively to be orphaned.

This orphan's inhuman characteristics, and the way in which its mother and other adults try to kill it, seem also to have borrowed something from the legends of the toad we have already referred to, who as we have seen in Graham's versions, sometimes does become the Emperor, and is often in search of a bride, or in search of a lucky place for a grave.For example, in (Graham's) 147, the daughter-in-law of a geomancer first gives birth to a son with nine faces, arms and feet, who she kills, and then to a warty toad who they do not kill, but who becomes a 'precious thing' who the Emperor captures (as the landlord covets the pearl in 8, or the Emperor steals it in 9) to protect the nation. In 605 the geomancer's son first gives birth to a son with big ears who she kills, but then to a warty toad who they raise. After a series of ordeals, the toad succeeds in marrying his mother's brother's daughter, who is then captured by the emperor. The toad then changes skins with the emperor, and becomes the emperor himself. In another story (85), as we have seen, the toad assists the orphan to retrieve his own, mystic wife. Several of these stories make the express point, after the killing of the first son, that children should never be killed however deformed they may be.

In this realm of endlessly creative transformations and substitutions, the abandoned and unnamed orphan who triumphs without parentage or kinship, with the blessing of heaven, and who is blessed with a heavenly marriage, becomes as much an image of the possibilities of identity transformation itself as a polysemic symbol of supreme success, as the orphan becomes Dragon, Sun, or Emperor. The naivety of the language, its insistence on a bare narration, is similarly reflected in the plain, honest nature of the orphan—his moral simplicity and straightforwardness, which finds its own reward. The fact of transformation itself is perhaps best expressed in the following story:

LAUS NTSUAG SEEKS SAUB's ADVICE (LEGEND 11)

Laus Ntsuag had been on a vegetarian diet for three years, but he still had not reaped any benefits from it. So he went off to ask Saub's advice.

Halfway along the road, a family asked Laus Ntsuag, 'Where are you going, young fellow?'
'I'm going to seek Saub's advice', said Laus Ntsuag.
'What is it that you want his advice on?' asked the family.
'Well, people I know who have been on a vegetarian diet were able to get something good out of it. I have been on such a diet for three years now, but still nothing good has come out of it. I'm going to ask Saub's advice about this', answered Laus Ntsuag.

'I see. Could you also seek Saub's advice for me? My daughter is already eighteen years old, but she still does not know how to talk. Could you ask Saub when she will be able to talk?'
'Alright, I'll do this for you'.

As Laus Ntsuag went further along his way, he met an old man guarding the land. He lived by the side of the road. No one offered

him any incense. So this old man asked, 'Where are you going, young fellow?'
'I'm going to seek Saub's advice', anserred the orphan.

'I see. Could you ask one thing for me. I have been living here for three years now, but no one has ever come to burn incense for me. Could you find out about this for me?'
'Alright. I'll help you about this'.

And again Laus Ntsuag continued on his way. This time he came across a phoenix. The phoenix asked, 'Where are you going, young fellow?'
'I'm going to seek Saub's advice', answered Laus Ntsuag.

'Could you ask one thing for me. I have been trying to hatch some eggs in my nest for three years, but nothing is ever hatched. Could you find about this for me?'
'Alright, I'll help you', said the orphan.

And he continued on his way. This time he encountered a crow, perched on a big nest.
The bird was hatching some eggs which were in the nest.
'Where are you going, young fellow?' asked the crow.
'I'm going to seek Saub's advice', answered Laus Ntsuag.

'I see. Could you ask one thing for me. I have been trying to hatch some eggs for three years, but nothing ever happens. Could you find out for me whether I am able to have baby birds or not?'
'Alright. I'll do that for you'.

And Laus Ntsuag continued on his way. He walked and he walked and he walked. He climbed up the mountain slopes. At last he found Old Saub, the Spirit, who was cutting wood. Thereupon, Laus Ntsuag cried out 'Saub! Saub!'

'Who's yelling from down there?' asked Old Saub.
'It's me'.
'And what can I do for you?'
'Well, I ran into a crow back there. It told me that it had been trying to hatch its eggs for three years, but that nothing much ever came of the hatching. It asked me to find out from you when it would be able to have some baby birds'.

'You go back and tell the crow to get someone to remove the three pots of silver and the three pots of gold which are buried under the tree. The crow will be able to hatch its eggs when this is done'.

'I came across a phoenix just then. It told me that it had been trying to hatch its eggs for three years, but that nothing much has ever come of its hatching. It wanted me to find out from you when it would be able to get baby birds?'

'Well, ask the phoenix to get someone to take away the three pots of silver, and the three pots of gold, which are buried under the tree. It will be able to have a baby phoenix when that is done'.

'I met an old man who was guarding the land on my way here. He has been living by the side of the road for three years, but no one has ever come to burn him incense He asked me to find out from you why this is so'.

'You go and tell him to have someone remove the three pots of gold, and the three pots of silver, from underneath his feet. People will burn incense for him after this has been done'.

'And I met a family', said Laus Ntsuag. 'The mother of that family told me her daughter was already eighteen years old, but was still not able to talk. When will her dumb daughter learn to talk?'

'Well, you go and tell that family that their daughter will talk again when an auspicious person visits their family'.

But before Laus Ntsuag had time to ask Saub about his own plight, Saub had vanished. He shouted at the top of his voice, but Saub was nowhere to be found. Laus Ntsuag started to cry. He cried and he cried and he cried, till the sun set and his eyes were all swollen. But still Saub did not hear him. Laus Ntsuag went on crying as he returned.

When he reached the crow, the bird asked him, 'Well, did you find out the answer for me, young man?'
'I've found everything out for all of you, but I haven't found out anything for myself. I feel very sad', said Laus Ntsuag, all in tears.
'Please don't cry. You said you had found it out for me. What did Saub say about it?'

Laus Ntsuag repeated the advice of Saub. When he had finished, the crow said to Laus Ntsuag, 'Would you mind, sir, helping to remove those pots of silver and gold from underneath my feet?'

'And where should I put all the treasure after I have removed it for you, all by myself?'

'Oh, don't worry about that. Just oblige me by helping me. And may good luck go with you'.

'That's a fine idea,' said Laus Ntsuag, 'I'll help you then'.

And Laus Ntsuag carried the three pots of silver and three pots of gold towards his home.

When he reached the phoenix, the phoenix asked him, 'Did you find anything out for me, young man?'

And Laus Ntsuag repeated Saub's advice.

'Would you help me, then, to remove those pots?'

And again Laus Ntsuag carried three pots of silver and three of gold towards his home.

But after some time, the six pots of silver and six pots of gold became too heavy for him to carry, and he paused for a rest. Two persons who burn the grass on the wasteland were coming his way. Laus Ntsuag asked them to help him. The three of them picked up the six pots of silver and the six pots of gold and continued their way home, heaving and panting as they went.

They walked and they walked and they walked, until they reached the old man who guarded the land. The old man asked, 'Well, did you find out the answer for me, young man?'

'I found everything out for all you people,' said Laus Ntsuag, 'but nothing for myself. I am still very unhappy'.

'Don't be unhappy', said the old man, 'What did Saub have to say about me?'

Laus Ntsuag repeated Saub's words. 'In that case', said the old man, 'I had better ask you to take those pots away for me',.

'But I've already taken away quite a number of pots. Where am I going to put them all?'

'Don't worry, don't worry', said the old man, 'you are sure to find some place after you have taken them away'.

Laus Ntsuag looked at the two persons who burnt the grass on the wasteland, and again asked them to help him.

When Laus Ntsuag finally reached the house of the dumb girl, she looked very happy to see him. She ran out to her mother and cried out, 'Mother, see who's over there. He looks like that person you asked to go and see Saub for us the other day'.
The mother was overjoyed that her daughter could speak. 'Hide yourself inside the house', she told her daughter, 'I'll ask him whether he found out the answer for us or not'.

Quickly the daughter hid herself inside a room. But she peeped out at them from the room. In no time, five or six people coulds be seen coming to the house, carrying nine pots of silver and nine pots of gold.

'Did you find out the answer for us, young man?' asked the woman.
In tears Laus Ntsuag told her, 'Yes, I found everything out for all you people, but I still have no answer to my own difficulties'.
'Don't get angry', said the woman, 'You found out the answer for us, what was it that Saub told you?'
'There is nothing wrong with your daughter', said Laus Ntsuag, 'she will talk the minute an auspicious person visits your family. And she will talk as soon as she meets the man she is to marry'.
'Wonderful, wonderful', exclaimed the mother.
'I shall have to leave all these things here', said Laus Ntsuag, 'living by myself, I have neither father nor mother, family nor house'.
'If you cannot find another place for your things, you can leave them here', offered the mother. And then she prepared some meat and beancurd cakes for the orphan.

Laus Ntsuag was about to leave after he had taken his dinner. But then, the dumb girl's mother said to him, 'Why don't you stay here? My home will be your home. You did the right thing for us. Before she was eighteen years old, my daughter could not speak a word. But as soon as you walked inside my house, she was able to speak again. I'll marry her to you as your wife'.
'Oh, I couldn't do that', said Laus Ntsuag.
'What do you mean, you could not do that? I'll marry you to my daughter and you can stay here. I don't want you to go anywhere else'.
'Very well', said Laus Ntsuag.

That evening, the dumb girl brought Laus Ntsuag hot water for his bath. And she found him some clothes and dresssed him up beautifully.
Laus Ntsuag married the girl and they started a family together. For the rest of their lives, they lived a fortunate and wealthy life.
(Yang Xiao Lian)[20]

In this final example, full of humour and humanity, the simplity of the narrative, and its almost musical repetition of episodes, emphasises the simple, honest nature of the orphan who is so selfless, so concerned with the welfare of others, that he forgets to plead on his own behalf, and is then more than amply rewarded. The transformations of the narrative reflect the transformations which the orphan himself undergoes, on his passage (or quest) from poverty and homelessness to wealth and the marital status.

While the poverty of the orphan is not foregrounded in this account (and imperial political pretensions are entirely absent), the concern with poverty is evident in the stores of silver and gold which he guilelessly receives, and in his final complaint about his *fatherless, motherless, homeless* status. What is privileged here are the various social problems which Saub, through the orphan, is capable of solving, and which the orphan takes it upon himself to help with—problems of the aged and of women, of respect for the aged and of unmarriageable children, and particularly of fertility—all problems which might in a traditional Chinese context be taken to a local deity for his (or her) blessing or advice. The dominating moral, religious concerns of the story are emphasised again in the incense burning expected for the old hermit, who must be a sage, and in the orphan's vegetarian, probably Buddhist, diet.

Again however the orphan's direct link with the sources of Hmong culture are posited in the way it is possible for him to communicate with Saub, while the images of his helpers burning grass on the wasteland and the old man who 'guards' the land reflect an early historic stage of settlement.

What is remarkable, though, is that the orphan forgets to ask the most important question when he finally meets the only Being capable of answering it, but this failure to speak, reflected in the

---

[20] Also recorded in GMMG 338-42.

maiden's dumbness, is finally cured and restored as Laus Ntsuag, who despite his own ignorance is the auspicious person who has been prophesied, visits her home. Here rhetoric itself is *initially* being dismissed as trivial and unimportant; what matters are the orphan's concern for others, an ultimately social concern, and it is in this that his salvation lies. The orphan does not need to be *primarily* defined in terms of a complex web of kinship and linguistic significations to achieve ultimate success; indeed, it is precisely the *original* absence of these kinship affiliations, and of the power of speech, which leads to supreme success.

And there is a historical agency which resides in the power to produce and transform identities, to enter into an elaborate and complex system of symbols in such a way as to effect a transformation of identity, and a transformation of the system itself. When through *marriage*, itself a complex image of the reaffirmation of differences despite unity and sameness, the orphan accomplishes a material transformation, his own identity has been transformed as he enters the realm of linguistic and social significances, the realm of metaphor, in a transformative way, and with this political weakness becomes strength and power, marginality centrality, the low high, the poor wealthy, the lacking abundant, the unfulfilled and isolated fulfilled and connected. Indeed this is Heaven, but it is a Heaven just around the corner if cultural meanings can be resignified. And of course it is the Hmong as a historical subject who the orphan is and who he represents—and what is spoken of is a *passage*; a prior, but gendered, formlessness, a *potency* which then precisely by willingly, wilfully, entering the symbolic realm of social/linguistic identifications and differentiations (where a disavowal of identification must take place for a specificity to be established), and which crucially depends on a *feminine* mediation (through marriage), succeeds in reversing everything.

The figure of the simple, dumb hero, the Simpleton or Dumbling, is not unknown in world mythology; indeed, Peredur in the Arthurian cycle may be its finest example, where the hero's failure to answer the riddle leads, finally, to the discovery of the Holy Grail—after the desolation of the wasteland. Here something more important even than imperial pretentions is being told; meaning is seen to reside initially in action itself, and action of a particularly humanitarian kind, rather than in the power of speech which may delude or mystify, but action alone is insufficient to determine meaning; the conscious adoption of speech implies the assumption of metaphor and rhetoric as the orphan then enters the realm of linguistic and kinship significations in a way which establishes a creative (that is, transformative) form of identity. We discover, then, in these tales, a specific theory of meaning, which dictates the very form of the tales themselves.

And it is appropriate that salvation should be achieved through the perfect marriage, for here too the potentiality of future generation is indicated, the survival of groups despite attempts to eradicate them (as in the flying beheaded Bo kings), the *issue* without which no marriage is complete. And so we see here in this story,an ultimate concern with reproduction, which springs from the birth of the orphan himself, is imaged in the birds who cannot hatch their eggs, and resolved through the orphan's eventual marriage; the power of speech is restored, as indeed flowers do bloom from rocks, and horses shall grow horns.

CONCLUSIONS

Identity

So what have we learnt from this strange endeavour to compare the Hmong of China with the Hmong of Southeast Asa ? One important conclusion may be that colonial and post-colonial ethnographers alike have collaborated with Hmong spokesmen from South East Asia in producing an image of their culture which is unnecessarily static and monolithic, and the production of which does seem to be connected with the artificial appearance of tribal solidarity assumed by the fragments of Hmong society dispersed into inaccessible mountainous locations across South East Asia. By comparison the situation in China, where state power has affected Hmong villages far more than in Thailand, reveals more clearly a fluid, dynamic situation of identity transformations and reassertions, the constant creation of local differentiations, a situation of cultural hybridity which contradicts the essentialising notions of cultural identity insisted on both by western ethnographers and by recent Chinese nationalities policy.

But we started with the definition of a Hmong identity, by Hmong themselves, in terms of a radical binary opposition and contrast to a Chinese identity, and the paradoxical revelation that a large part of what counts as the Hmong cultural inheritance is Chinese, or is at least shared with the Chinese, from whom they so strongly differentiate themselves. Assumptions of an originary, separable and distinctive Hmong cultural identity would lead to a consideration of the Chinese cultural influences upon them, which as we have seen might be understood in an evolutionist, a diffusionist, or in a radically diffusionist/subvertivist mode, according apparently to very arbitrary preferences of the researcher. We have also considered questions of structure and agency, and of discourse and agency, in terms of a powerful Chinese rhetoric structuring and informing Hmong subjectivity, and the problems of accounting for an agency which is not merely personal, but historical and inter-subjective, within the terms of such a dominating and determinative discursive rhetoric.

I think we can see here, something of the creative historical agency with which a marginalised minority population defined as 'Miao' by the dominating rhetoric, has sought to define themselves as 'Hmong' through establishing a series of contrasts and oppositions to an identity defined as *suav* (Han/other) *in despite* of a situation of de facto identity equivocality and doubt, transformation and disguise; a situation of cultural hybridity out of which meaningful identities have had to be formed.

In terms of current theory, it is possible to see this consistent assertion of identity and difference in the face of considerable resemblance and similarity, as a kind of *disavowal* (and the etymology of this term from notions of repression and prohibition is interesting) of identification with the Han Chinese who are in fact the objects of emulations and envious desire, the colonising majority who have historically marginalised the Hmong and other populations into the abject developmental positions they occupy today. And while yet remaining in the metaphorical realm, this does seem to be an *inverse* process (if Ricoeur's remarks on metaphor being the recognition of sameness despite differences can stand for metaphor in general) to that of metaphor, in that here it is the *differences* which are affirmed through cultural discourse, despite the *sameness* which, research which does not only listen to Hmong spokesmen reveals, is in fact characteristic of very large parts of Hmong culture.[21]

And we may well ask, what it means for the Hmong people to insist on such differentiations in the face of compelling resemblance, to establish a binary opposition and to disavow identifications with the people who are at the same time (seen as) the cause of that marginality and exclusion, their poverty and subjection?—the people who at the same time are the objects of a suppressed emulative envy, the apogee of the material/social success and prosperity to which Hmong may also aspire?

And yet it is here that historical agency must lie, in the power to resist total absorption by the dominating rhetoric whose very terms seem to define and represent them, in the pride-ful affirmation of a separate, and unique, identity which is the mark of self-confidence and self-reliance, and the very opposite of envy. Agency resides in that ability to undertake such rhetorical inversion of the metaphorical process, in this *disavowal* of an identification which is thereby productive of a distinctively creative form of (historical and cultural) identity.

This is figured above all in the image of the Orphan, who is precisely the figure of this bereavement and separation; the one who has not yet found his own Identity. As the disavowed identification with the 'mother' culture of the Chinese is itself a kind of inverted metaphor, through a series of transformations and substitutions the Orphan succeeds in reversing the terms of the distinction in which Hmong identity has been posited; the poverty and weakness associated with the Hmong side of the denied equation, becomes the wealth and power associated with its Chinese obverse. This is an

---

[21] Of course, sameness does not preclude difference. We may recognise an essential sameness with incidental differences we may respect; or we may recognise some sameness despite our apparent differences. The problem comes through introducing the notion of *essence* (as opposed to accidental) into this, and further assimilating this to an interior of depth (Sd) as opposed to an exterior of superficiality, the arbitrary (Sd); see Figure 1. Identity is of course a product of both sameness and difference (Figure 2). The Orphan is prior to both sameness and difference, in the sense that his Identity has not yet been established, and yet he is also their product, since he is *bereaved* and *derived*. The argument here is that a relation of Identity (sameness) with the Chinese must be rejected in order to establish a distinctive Hmong identity which is different from that of the Chinese; a kind of inversion of metaphor.

imaginative future which is spoken of, pointed to, through the fictive constitutive powers of language, the endless possibilities and potentialities of unravelling meanings and the escaped consequences of actions which unfold with a historical *inevitability* which is of an imaginative nature, towards a future Context which still has to be created, a Truth which remains to be revealed.

If there is fetishism here, it is the entirety of Hmong culture which has become fetishised in an affirmation of difference, as a sign of that humanity which is what it is that the Chinese origin *lacks*. But I would not wish to go so far as this in the attribution of psychic concepts to cultural forms. Rather let us say that if there is a fetishism here, it is an inter-subjective displacement from the present towards a future which, through imaginative means, invests the present with hope and therefore *meaning*; in the sense of an intentionality not limited to particular individuals, the tales we have considered indeed show the workings out a powerful historical *will* towards construction and creation, rather than its denial. And therefore, it is by the context of an as yet unrealised *future* that the symbol of the Orphan must be understood, and which it opens out onto even as it opens, with a limitless sense of inter-personal agency (which must be imagined before it is realised) the searching out new contexts, new 'worlds' in which to be fulfilled.

Context

And so, finally, we return to the problem of context. As Hobart (1986) put it, 'Part of the relevance of context in Southeast Asia is the weakness of correspondence theories of truth and meaning'. In a sense this work has been about, and has suffered from the problem of, attempting to locate an appropriate context for materials on the Hmong from Sichuan. In that it may have had much in common with the romanticism of the contextualist which is inevitably directed back towards a *lost* point of origin (Stewart 1993). But here, through the reconstruction of original events and texts, an emergent context has been aimed at, in which the Hmong would be allowed, as far as possible, to construct their own context, as in their daily lives they may be said to do, through a consideration of their wedding texts and funeral prayers, legends and the structure of their village lives. Yet clearly there are constraints on a peoples' construction of their own context, in particular those of politico-economic realities which may be said to supply a wider 'context' to the texture of everyday events and reflections of these in myth and legend, as indeed there also must be on our considerations of these events and their contexts, in terms of the anthropological baggage and philosophical traditions and modern concerns we bring with us to our consideration of 'other cultures'. It is time to consider, therefore, more narrowly, exactly what it is that we mean by 'context', which is surely more than a matter of scale or shifts between the local and the global (Strathern 1995).

To put things in perspective means to look at them in a certain way, so that things relative to them appear in a certain light (Diagram 55). Context is an essentially visual metaphor, rather than a philosophical concept.

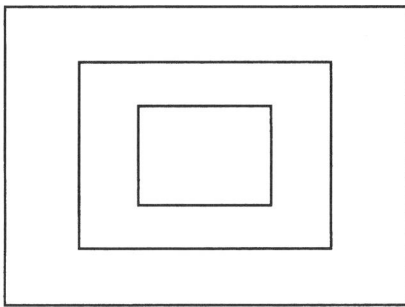

background, framework, perspective

Diagram 55: Visual context

Without such a perspective, no ORDER is apparent, only a primordial chaos.

By adopting a particular vantage point ('N'), a thing (X)—either an object or concept—can be seen in relation to other things (X1) in perspective, that is in a certain order (V). Perspective, or context, is therefore to be able to order things in a certain way (Diagram 56).

When we talk about the context of a 'text', we do not mean the original (or conscious) intention of its author, although that may be the context we tend to privilege, nor the circumstances of its production which we may see as its historical and social context, nor its various interpretations, effects or usages which supply a dynamic and constantly changing, context (Diagram 57).

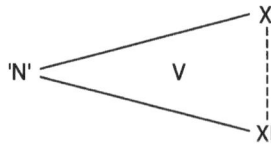

Diagram 56: Context as vantage and order

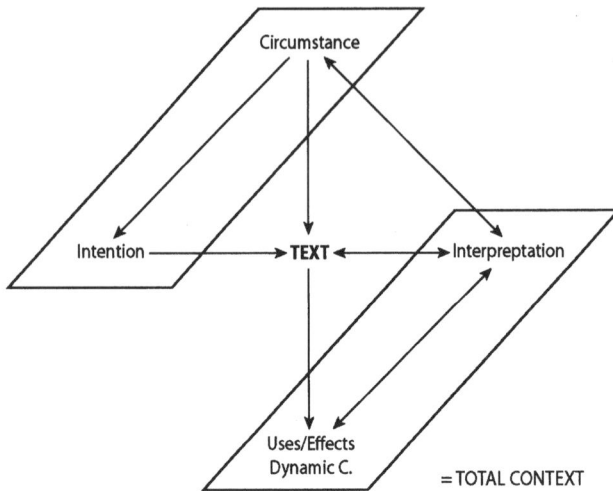

Diagram 57: Text and context

When we consider Hmong texts, which refer to and are produced in a given historical, political and social situation, besides 1) a specifically Hmong discourse on these phenomena we must also consider 2) the anthropological language, with its baggage of western philosophical leftovers which we bring with us to our consideration of these texts, and also 3) a dominating Chinese rhetoric which often informs them and to which they also refer (see Diagrams 58 and 59).

Should we examine these texts as texts alone, as in the old 'new' criticism, or in relation to other similar texts, variants and versions of which I have given? Should we consider them as texts within a purely Hmong tradition, comparing them to similar historical or present-day texts from Thailand, Laos and perhaps with some of those produced by Hmong refugees living overseas; or as part of a general body of southern Chinese folk tales which refer to emperors, burials, dragons and rebellion—or in wider terms, searching for their echoes and sources in Germanic or Celtic, Indo-Aryan or Japanese, folk traditions and universal myths of shamanism? In which of these general contexts—the comparativist universal, the merely Hmong, the wider Chinese, should we ground them? Or should we, ignoring these wider contexts of discourse, merely attempt to confine them to the realities of the social and economic, political or historical circumstances in which they were produced/are reproduced, and to which they often refer (Diagram 60)? How can we possibly 'circumscribe all possible contexts' (Hobart 1986)?

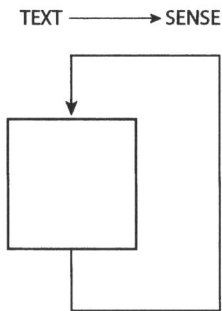

TEXT ⟶ SENSE

Diagram 58: Text to sense

TEXT ⟶ REFERENCE

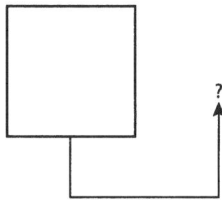

?

Diagram 59: Text to reference

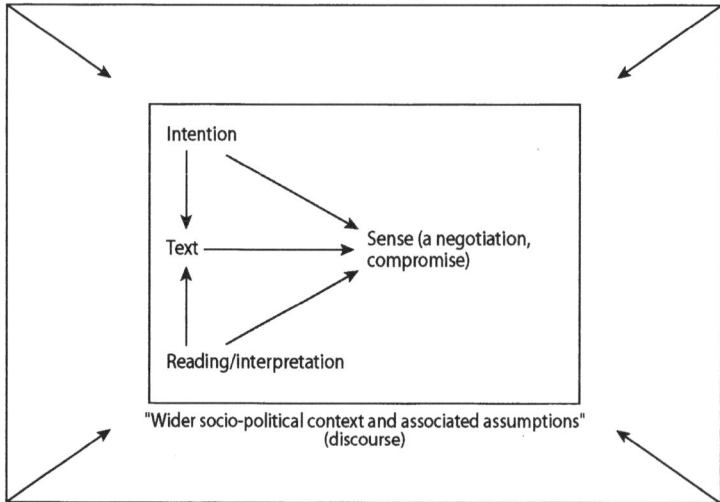

Diagram 60: The creation of sense

I have tried to do a little of all these things, painting the village context in which such tales are produced and told and retold as faithfully as possible, considering historical circumstances where these seemed relevant, drawing parallels with Hmong traditions elsewhere where these appeared significant, and considering general resemblances with other cultures if appropriate. The attempt has been, I suppose, to aim for an effect something like that which Merleau-Ponty attributed to Cézanne's apparent lack of 'perspective', as perspective was conventionally understood at the time; a multiplicity or plethora of perspectives, a plenitude which only appears chaotic because a number of different vantage points have been simultaneously taken on that which is represented (as we considered in the Conclusion to Part II).

And, as Hobart *nearly* says in his consideration of the problems of context (1985), there can be no final or closed context (quoting Donaghue on Ricoeur, 'The single, true interpretation is an autocrat's dream of power')—since context is *negotiable*.[22] That is, ultimately

---

[22] We are not alone in this perplexity. Culler (1997;67), for example, discussing the problems of whether to locate meaning in an authorial intention, the text itself, the 'context' it was produced in, or in the reader's experience, also remarks that,

it is the Hmong, through their interaction and refusal or disavowal of identification with others, who *create a context for themselves* (although this may be constrained by external factors which limit and define that context)—and they do this, at least partly, by telling the kind of tales we have considered here. And it is in this creation of a context that agency, and the extent of agency, lies. It is thus the *creation of a context* with which we have been concerned, and inasmuch as it has been possible I have attempted to allow the Hmong to do this for themselves through reproducing some of their texts here, in a way which I hope may have limited too much domination of the work by anthropological discourse and its western philosophical trappings. As others have remarked, a text is always marked by the history of its past encounters and yet open to a future interpretation.[23]

Problems of the 'Other' have been much discussed in recent reflexive anthropology and cultural theory, particularly of course in terms of problems of Voice in the texts we produce, of 'representation' in both its aesthetic and political senses, and generally of issues of cultural enablement and autonomy. The most, and the least, we can do, as cultural critics or anthropologists, is to address these issues squarely, in our texts or in our active engagements with the world, and make the attempt to voice the voiceless and speak the unsaid (although Taussig 1987 called this 'the ultimate anthropological conceit').

This may mean establishing new contexts as well as reflecting those which are already there, since as we have seen, context is a matter of negotiation; a 'total' context, although never finished, may be as it were temporarily supplied, through the combination of different perspectives and vantage points on a single issue, cultural situation, or 'text'. (New contexts are largely achieved through the surreal juxtaposition of never-before-thought-like elements. A 'better' context may be accomplished through a more inclusive consideration of various perspectives, and indeed this is what I see Hmong folk tales themselves as trying to achieve).

---

properly speaking, context covers the lot; 'Meaning is context-bound, but context is boundless'.

[23] Shepherd (1989).

The problem of context, then, is ultimately identical with the problem of interpretation, and good interpreters should be able to lose their voice and let others speak through them, as indeed the orphan does when he forgets to speak for himself, while his *wife* is enabled to speak for the first time. Let it be so!

End

We have, then, the answer to our paradox of the Hmong assertion of diametric differences from the Chinese despite the resemblances and crossing over of cultural forms, and to our question of how it is possible to interpret the borrowing from or miming of a dominant culture, as domination or subversion. For there is a genuine ambivalence here; in the case of the Hmong, there is a rage directed against the site of original identification, so closely associated as we saw in Part I with the loss of an original power and knowledge,[24] a contradictory desire to devour and engorge (to assimilate aspects of the dominant Chinese culture) and to become lost within it, *at the same time* as a fierce desire to differentiate from it, to establish differences (where we have located the sense of historical agency).[25] Indeed this sort of ambivalence may lie at the heart of processes of acculturation where assimilation does not occur. As we saw in the legends which directly speak of Hmong-Han differences and identities, we are constantly confronted by the statement 'we are *not* like the Han, though we are!'.

The clearest sign of this ambivalence towards the Han Chinese, perhaps, in historical terms, is the adoption by the Hmong—or the imposition on them—of the patrilineal system of Chinese kinship which, historians agree, replaced an earlier system of which we have very little evidence, but in which it is almost certain that women occupied a higher position than subsequently, and in which descent was probably not reckoned patrilineally; the submerging of the maternal.

---

[24] See for example the expressed desire of the Orphan in the story of Echo to trap his parents in the basket he is weaving, the mother's fatal exclamation in the story of the Orphan becoming a dragon.

[25] See for example the unquenchable thirst of the Orphan, like the Toad, in the story of the Orphan becoming a dragon.

The adoption of an entire kinship system, like the adoption of a language or writing system, would one might have thought have been sufficient to assure the re-submerging of the Hmong within the Chinese body, and to have eradicated any other traces of cultural and ethnic differences.

Yet this has not been so, since the kinship system shared with the Chinese paradoxically became the most powerful means of expressing differences of identity through the tracing of divergent lines, became indeed (like the practice of geomancy) the very idiom in which differences between the Hmong and Chinese could be expressed and articulated as if they were of an *intrinsic* (essential) kind.

Thus we see, in the story of the diverging descendants of two brothers who respectively became the Hmong and the Chinese, how the rivalry between siblings typical of the patrilineal kinship system becomes a powerful image of the differences between the Hmong and Han, *at the same time* as their claim to a common ancestor is asserted. In the tracing of paternal Hmong descent lines through an in-marrying Chinese male we find two cultural identities thought of as separate being brought temporarily together, only to be finally and irrevocably separated.

This is not a colonising discourse, which Bhabha (1994) argues recognises and disavows differences, but a subaltern idiom which recognises but disavows the sameness with the Other which leads to its own marginalisation; an idiomology necessarily referring to the contextualising past in terms of despair and bereavement, of loss and regret. Nor is it a refusal of dialogue with the other, since there must be an affirmation of self before dialogue can take place. This is why the figure of the Orphan, paradoxically prior to linguistic and social (kinship) differentiations and identifications, and yet already differentiated and identified as male since he is the product of the very cultural language in which difference and identity are *thought*, is so magically compelling; he is the sign of a signification which has been lost, but which nevertheless may be restored within a new 'context'.

The situation of cultural hybridity in which the Hmong of Sichuan find themselves today is nothing new for the Hmong; probably there has always been this intermingling and dialectic of cultural identities at the local level, and yet it is always and ever over, against this constant temptation of a return to unindividuality, that ethnic and cultural differences are insisted on and reaffirmed. Even in the remotest locations the long journeys of pioneer shifting cultivators will have meant encounters and exchanges with the members of other cultures and languages, while itinerant Chinese traders have since the earliest times made their homes among the Hmong.

And it must, surely, be in the power to affirm and maintain differences, those differentiations which result in a stable and secure identity, that the power of agency lies. It is then *not* in the reified or essentialised notions of an invariant 'Hmong culture' that we should look for the signs of historical agency, but in these constant reworkings and refashionings of it, its resignifications in the light of new contexts, that historical agency is best expressed. So that it is in the resignifications at work in the Yang clan's attempts to rewrite their genealogy and construct a clan ancestral hall, and in the resignifications of a transnational Hmong identity currently taking place though meetings with overseas Hmong refugees,[26] that Hmong agents best express their capacity to alter the text of a dominating rhetoric which otherwise defines them.

FIN

---

[26] See Schein (1998); Tapp (1999).

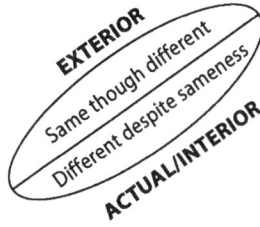

Figure 1: The essentialisation of difference

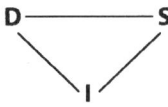

Figure 2: Identity as sameness and difference

WEIXIN WEDDING SONG (*Nkauj ua neej tshab*)

Yub!
pib ca cuaj ua lab tsi maj
nam pw cij plooj hab cib pwj tsev tub
nam nyob twm ncaaj mi txiv nyob tus rhoob maj
nam pwb cij cig yav nav
nam qav tub toos txuj kiv txuj neeb txheeb maj
txiv pwm cij caav maj
txiv qav tuj toos txuj kiv txoj neej tsaav maj
nam qawv ntxwv
txiv muaj nyog nqaij chawv tau nkuv thab
nam ua tsi txiv txoj qaab
nam ntim nkauj aib txiv ntim lub muag
nam ua tshais

txiv muaj nyog nqaij lus hau kuv maj
hu tub uj aam lab tuaj tsug maj
nam ua tshaws tom pes nav tau pib noj
txiv kw tlej tau pib haus maj
nam khaws tsseb tlub paam nraug tau pib qau maj
txiv khaws kauj txuj kauj vab tau pib thi cav
pib maaj ceej xyum qeb ku
nci toj xyoob looj tshaab taas maj
hmaab ku(v) qhab cij cheeb
nci toj xyoob looj nraa thee maj
tuav cuag ib lub zuj zos suav
tom cua il lub zuj zos ob mas
tsoom zos nyob tsi zoo nam mam maj
tsoob thau nyob tsi zoo suav
tuaj txug ntsib tau xyum lub ntsib tus ntsib zoo

   ntsib cuaj ntxhuv xyub
tsaj las nuam tau moos zeej xab xim yim nav
tsooj las nyob zoo na
tsooj thau nyob zaam zuag muaj

qaab vaas muaj lub zoo vaaj
ntshua vaaj ntshuav tsev ntshuab rauv paaj haab
qaum tsiv muaj tib poj teb tus
ntsho vaaj ntshob tsev muab tsiv
mas tau paaj ntshaab kub maj
pib cab mab. tub cwj tlaub tuj taug
tsheem cuam moos zeej xab xim looj meej saam maj
ch-j cum khuaj looj meej
haum cum tsim muav pwm cawb tsheej hab
haum cwm khuaj nyog looj meej khav
thim cum muab uj pa xeev hab

coj tuaj tuaj txug chauj cheej
xw tsi yi maj
yav caug paaj nyog phem txhim ti maj
txiv tim phem txiv nyauv
khaib huab tsheej twm
ci txiv tsheej suaab
tawg paaj nto nyog ntsis
txi txiv ruaj nyog txaag
coj moos weej keeb nqees txum txiv
yaas txi nqaws pom xeeb
coj moos civ lug xyaaj xyeeb, qaum taw
cev lag dlej kub dlej su nav

HOW RWG NTXAIS BECAME A TIGER

Once there was a man named Rwg Ntxais who fell sick and was going to become a tiger. But his wife knew all about this. So every day after she went out to work, she would come back secretly again to try to catch her husband turning into a tiger. And every day, Rwg Ntxais stayed at home (awaiting his opportunity).

One day, while his wife was working outside, he put one table on top of another in the central room, and seized all the chickens and put them in the central room. Then he jumped over the tables, caught a chicken and ate it (raw). And then he jumped back again, caught another chicken, and ate that one too. When his wife appeared and saw this, she shouted from outside the door, 'Eagles never came to take our chickens away in the past! Why have they come to take away our chickens today?'

When he heard this shout, Rwg Ntxais stopped jumping and quickly removed the tables. Then he rushed onto the bed, lay down and started groaning as if he were seriously ill (as usual). Things went on like this for three days, and then Rwg Ntxais died. His wife held a grand funeral for him. After the funeral, he was buried. Because his wife knew that he was turning into a tiger, she stayed by his grave and kept watch every night.

On the first night, she heard the growls of some tigresses in the diastance (when a man turns into a tiger, tigresses always come to lead him away). 'Rwg Ntxais, Rwg Ntxais' (they called), 'come here quickly if you wish. There's a big spotted dog sleeping beside your grave, and if you don't come soon...' Each night, the calls grew nearer and nearer. On the third night, the tigress approached the grave, and at daybreak, the grave suddenly cracked open. Out leapt Rwg Ntxais, trying to follow those tigresses. But seeing him jumping out, his wife quickly caught hold of his sleeve, saying 'Take me too if you want to go'. Rwg Ntxais was at his wits' end to know what to do.

'*Rwg Ntxais, Rwg Ntxais, who is this woman? We'll eat her all up*', *said the tigresses. 'No, you can't,' said Rwg Ntxais, 'she is my youngest sister. Please don't eat her'.*

So in the end the tigresses, along with Rwg Ntxais and his wife, all set off together. They walked and they walked, until they reached the Stone Tiger mountains, in Yunnan. On one side of the mountain there was a male stone tiger; on the other there was a stone tigress. They had to jump from the stone tiger on this side onto the one on the other side. Rwg Ntxais was asked to come too. 'You told us she was your youngest sister', said the tigresses, 'so carry her on your back and jump from this stone tiger to that one. If you don't sweat after jumping (e.g. showing he was used to carrying her), we won't eat her. Otherwise, we'll eat her up'.

But Rwg Ntxais was sweating all over after he had taken his wife on his back and jumped onto the stone tiger on the other side. However, his wife was very clever. She took a handkerchief from her bosom aand gave it to him so that he could wipe off all the sweat. And when the tigresses saw no sweat on him, they didn't eat her.

They kept on walking until they reached a huge cave, and there they stopped to stay the night. Rwg Ntxais had to sleep on one side of the cave and his wife on the other, together with all those tigresses. She slept outside and the tigresses just inside the cave. At midnight, when the others were sleeping, one of the tigresses stretched out its leg, trying to knock Rwg Ntxais's wife (Muas Ntxais) off the cliff and kill her. But just as the tigress was about to kick her, she woke up and cried out, 'This old woman is trying to kill me!' Hearing his wife's shriek, Rwg Ntxais woke up and pleaded, 'Oh no, please don't do that. She is my youngest sister. Don't do that'. So the tigress's plot was foiled again.

Setting out again the next morning, they walked a long way before finally reaching a crossing. There Rwg Ntxais' wife said to him, 'If you really mean to go further, kindly send me back home first'. 'But we've already passed through nine great forests', said Rwg Ntxais, 'how long will it take me to get back here again if I have to send you home?' 'But you must send me back', she said, and at last he agreed to her request and they started on the way home again.

When they reached the back of their home (uphill), Rwg Ntxais stopped and would go no further, since he had already turned into a tiger. So his wife said, 'Alright, if you won't come into the house with me, you just stay here for a bit and wait for me to come out again. I'll see you off later and then you can leave'. Rwg Ntxais agreed to this and stayed there, waiting for his wife to come back. When his wife went into the house, she called out, 'Mother, Father, your son is back home again, just behind the house. I'll go back there in a minute. Don't come out unless you hear me call; if I call, please come quickly'. And the old parents did just as she asked them to.

Then Rwg Ntxais' wife scooped some water up into one bottle, and poured some wine into another one, plucked a handful of green leaves (nplooj tais) and a bunch of tobacco. These she took out to Rwg Ntxais. She gave that bottle of wine to Rwg Ntxais to drink and she gave him the bunch of tobacco to smoke, while she herself just drank from the bottle of water and rolled up the leaves to smoke. Soon Rwg Ntxais became dead drunk and passed out. And his wife began to call, 'Father, Mother, come here quickly if you want to see your son!'

So his mother and father rushed out to see their son. Rwg Ntxais struggled to get up to greet them, but was too drunk to move. And then, all of a sudden, he turned into a cowpat! His wife, all of a fluster, said, 'here, quick, bring a dustpan here and take it into the house'. So they pushed the cowpat into the dustbin with a hoe and took it back inside the house and set it beside the hearth. After some time, a tiger's paw began to stretch out of the cowpat. Rwg Ntxais' wife, and his mother and father, cut it off at once. A moment later, out came a leg, and that was cut off too. Some time afterwards, a tiger's head appeared out of the cowpat, and they chopped that off too. And after a long time had gone by, finally the head, hands and feet of a person gradually came out of the cowpat, and at last Rwg Ntxais returned to his former shape again.

And he said to his wife and his mother and father, 'Since you do not wish me to leave, you must buy a big yellow cow to sacrifice for me, and then I will not go'. So his mother and father and wife went out, bought a big yellow cow, and sacrificed it to him. After that, he never became a tiger again.
(Ma Tianzi)

This death-defying story is told by some clans to their children to explain why cattle are sacrificed at the *ua nyuj dab* ritual. It incorporates some of the imagery of the *qhab ki* chant sung at death to guide the soul of the deceased on its passage home to the village of the ancestors, for example the nine stages of mountains, valleys and forests, and the stone-leaping dragon and tiger mountains of the journey through the Otherworld. And we find the themes of other legends also reflected here, like the wife falsely identified as younger sister to trick the tigresses.

APPENDIX III

THE ORPHAN AND THE EMPEROR'S DAUGHTER

Long ago, there lived (an orphan named) Laus Ntsuag. Both of his parents had died, and he lived all by himself. Every day he would take with him a spear to hunt in the mountains, and a net with which to catch fish.

One day, when he was walking through a great forest in the mountains, he saw a large eagle. And the eagle said to him, 'If you spare my life, I can help you when you have troubles'. So Laus Ntsuag let the eagle go.

Then he reached the side of a big pond where he cast his net. He caught a large female pig-fish. The pig-fish said to him, 'if you let me go free this time I'll come to your rescue in the future'. So he let the fish go. Soon, a 'furry dog' (a fox) came up behind him and said, 'please help me. People are hunting after me and they want to kill me'. Laus Ntsuag put a collar on it and started to lead it along.

The people running after the animal caught up with Laus Ntsuag and asked him, 'Have you seen a furry dog crossing your path?' 'No', said Laus Ntsuag. 'Why are you taking this animal for a walk?' they asked him. 'This is mine and I am looking after him', said Laus Ntsuag. So the people left him alone, and soon Laus Ntsuag released the furry dog. And the furry dog promised Laus Ntsuag that it would come to his help if needed in later trouble.

Laus Ntsuag went on with his own life as usual, passing each day hunting and fishing. One day, he passed the walls of the city, and saw many people standing there, reading a big notice on the wall. Laus Ntsuag could not read. So he asked an old man next to him to explain the notice to him. But before the old man could open his mouth, a sly rascal stepped out of the crowd and said, 'This notice is from the Emperor. He says that whoever tears down this notice from the wall may marry his daughter. I would have torn it down myself, if only I had not a wife at home already'.

Laus Ntsuag had heard how beautiful the Emperor's daughter was, and also how she loved hunting. So after hearing what the man had said, he tore the notice down off the wall. Then the sentry guarding the notice took him off to see the Emperor. The sovereign asked him, 'Did you tear that notice off the wall?'

'Indeed I did', replied Laus Ntsuag.

'And do you know what is written on that notice?' asked the Emperor.

'Everybody knows what is written on it,' said Laus Ntsuag. ' It says that the Emperor has a daughter, and that whoever tears down the notice can marry his daughter'.

'Yes I do have a daughter', said the Emperor, 'and it is true that whoever dares to tear down the notice from the wall may take my daughter as his wife. But on the notice it is also written that that person must be able to hide himself three times so well that my daughter can never find him. Only if my daughter fails to find him three times will I consent to the marriage. Ninety nine people to date have torn that notice off that wall, and ninety nine have been beheaded. Are you to be the hundredth?'

It was only then that Laus Ntsuag realised what trouble he was in. How could he escape execution, after so many people had already suffered the same fate? According to the Emperor's orders, he must find himself a really good hiding place. But where could such a place be? Walking into the great forest he sat down glumly by a field of millet, sick with worry. 'What is the matter?' inquired the eagle, flying up to him. Sighing, Laus Ntsuag told the eagle what had happened; 'I fear I shall not be able to get out of this', he said.

'Have no fear', replied the eagle, 'climb up on to my back, and I'll carry you to the middle heavens, flying high over the forest. And then how will the Emperor be able to find you?' So Laus Ntxuag got up onto the eagle's back, and the eagle bore him high up into the sky.

The Emperor's daughter came riding by, holding a mirror in one hand. She was searching high and low for Laus Ntxuag, using the mirror. In her mirror she saw the eagle flying high over the forest carrying Laus Ntxuag on its back, and shouted up to him 'Come down here. You are on the back of the eagle!'

The defeated Laus Ntxuag had to ask the eagle to bring him down. The princess took him to the Emperor's palace. 'Well', asked her father, 'did you find him?' 'I did find him', replied his daughter, 'but this man is no common one. He was flying in the skies'. 'Take him away and chop off his head', instructed the Emperor. 'Wait a minute', interrupted his daughter, 'he really is rather extraordinary. None of the other ninety nine could fly, and yet he was flying right over the forest. Give him one more chance'. 'Very well', agreed the Emperor.

Again Laus Ntxhuag had to find an excellent hiding place. But where should he go? Soon he found himself strolling beside the pond. And there he sat down, desperate with worry. Up came the big female pig-fish and asked him, 'What is the matter?'

Laus Ntxuag told the fish the whole story. 'Don't worry', said the fish, 'you just hide within my belly and I will swim inside a deep cave at the very bottom of the river. I doubt if she will ever find you there'. And Laus Ntxuag wriggled inside the pig-fish's stomach, and the fish quickly hid in a cave at the bottom of the river.

The princess rode by, flashing her mirror from side to side. At last she spied Laus Ntxuag hiding inside the fish's belly, and cried out 'Laus Ntxuag, come out here in the open. You are hiding inside that pig-fish's stomach'.

Once again Laus Ntxuag had lost. He came up to the surface of the water, and allowed himself to be led away by the princess. After they reached the palace, the Emperor asked his daughter, 'Well, where did you find him this time?' 'He was inside the belly of a fish, hiding at the bottom of a river', said his daughter, 'it was very difficult to find him'. So the Emperor gave orders for Laus Ntxuag to be taken away and have his head cut off. 'Not so fast, interrupted the princess, 'this is a wonderful man. Let him hide again one last time. Who knows where he will hide this time?' And so the Emperor agreed.

But this time Laus Ntxua was more anxious than ever. As he went walking through the deep forest, the furry dog came up to him and asked what the matter was. Laus Ntxua repeated the story again. After hearing the story, the furry dog asked, 'How can she do that, finding you each time?'

'Well,' said Laus Ntxua, 'she has a special mirror. She shines it everywhere and on everything. She can find you out wherever you hide'. The furry dog thought and thought and eventually said, 'Not to worry. I think I can help you'. Then the furry dog turned to face the sky and began to howl. And every furry dog in the forest came out of their holes and all together they dug a great tunnel leading all the way to a place directly beneath the bedroom of the princess. And there Laus Ntxuag hid himself for the last time, keeping very still, at the end of the tunnel underneath the princess' bedroom.

Again the daughter of the Emperor went riding off in search of Laus Ntxuag. She shone her mirror towards the ground, towards the sky, towards the mountain ranges. But Laus Ntsuag was nowhere to be seen. So at last she rode back to her own room. 'Laus Ntxuag, where are you hiding?' she called, 'I cannot possibly find you. Please come out of your hiding place quickly, so that we can be married'.

Laus Ntxuag heard her from his underground cave. Happily he agreed, saying 'Can you really not find me? I have been hiding directly under your feet!'

'Heavens', said the Emperor's daughter, 'you would have been in great trouble if I had shone my mirror in that direction!' And so Laus Ntxuag was able to marry the Emperor's daughter.
(*GMMG*, pp.328-331. Narrator: Wang Qiang (14 years old))

While there is no reason why children's inventions should not be more telling than those of adults, this Hans Anderson-like story was almost certainly one he had heard from an adult and was repeating. Apart from uniting the themes of the orphan, marriage, and imperial sovereignty, the tale is particularly apt for its unexpected twists and turns, as when the notice Laus Ntuag has read to him turns out to be at least partially correct, and when Laus Ntsuag is first discovered by the Emperor's daughter despite his magical help.

The three magical animals or 'supernatural helpers' in Aarne's classification (eagle, fish and fox) and the places they find for the hero to hide in (like the witches' magical mirror) are universal legendary and shamanic themes, from the Celtic story of Taliesin to the Germanic tales collected by the Brothers Grimm. For example, in the Grimm brothers tale of 'The White Snake' (17), the hero helps or saves fishes, ants and ravens in turn, who in turn help him to perform the three ordeals set by the King for whoever will marry his daughter, which he has also heard about through an announcement when visiting the city; an 'Animal Tale' VI in Joseph Campbell's formulation. The parallels in another tale, 'The Sea Hare' (191), classed by Campbell as a 17th. or 18th. century folk tale, are so close as almost certainly to suggest a direct borrowing; here a princess has executed 97 suitors who have tried unsuccessfully to hide from her, and two older brothers, until the younger brother is hidden first by a raven he has saved, then in the stomach of a fish he has saved, and finally by the help of a lame fox he has saved, who transforms him into a sea-hare bought by the princess who then hides beneath her hair. There is no princess' father, no visit to the city to read a poster or hear an announcement, he does not fly on the raven's back but hides in an egg, and so forth, but the general resemblance is indisputable.

The hero who cannot read and is cheated by those who can, however, may be a peculiarly Hmong motif.

APPENDIX IV

THE WOODEN FISH AND THE HANGING DRUM

In ancient times long ago, the ancestor of the Miao and the ancestor of the Chinese were brothers, the Chinese being the older brother and the Miao being the younger. One day the two brothers set out on their way to the palace of the Jade Emperor, in order to receive the holy scriptures from him. After undergoing numerous trials and ordeals, climbing 81 high mountains and crossing 81 muddy rivers, they finally arrived. A clever dog had showed them the way there. When they arrived, the Emperor gave each of them a text. Delirious with joy, the two brothers left for home. But just as they were approaching a bridge, they began to grow very tired. The older brother lay down on the eastern end of the bridge, while the younger brother stretched out on the western end of the bridge. Soon, they were both fast asleep.

When they woke up, the older brother found that half of his canon was missing, and the younger brother found that the whole of his was gone. They were desperate and felt very sorry for themselves. What could have happened?

Then the older brother discovered the scales and dribble of a fish on the remaining half of his book. He was sure that a fish had eaten up the other half. So he found some wood and carved out of it a wooden fish. Now whenever a Chinese dies, the Daoist priest will strike a wooden fish at the funeral mass conducted for him. Each knock on the wooden fish makes the fish pour out a single word. And the Chinese call this 'striking the fish to recover the canon'.

But the younger brother had come across the hoof prints of a cow. And he concluded that it must have been this animal which had eaten up his book. So he captured a wild cow and slaughtered it. He stripped off the cow hide and made it into a drum. And now whenever a Miao dies, they will hang up the drum of cow hide and people will beat on the drum. This is known as 'beating the drum to recover the canon'.

Since the Chinese still had half of his book left, so the Chinese came to have a written language. Since the Miao had lost the whole of his book, however, the Miao had no written language.
(*GMMG*, p.75. Narrator: Liu Guanqing)

This imaginative account, recorded in Gongxian, is an exemplary account of the kind of fusion and mixture of different tales, motifs and genres which is characteristic of the Hmong of Gongxian today, and may indeed stand as an excellent example of processes of 'bricolage' in general. Much more is going on here than the simple removal of the well-known story of how the Hmong lost their writing (books) owing to fleeing from the attacks of the Chinese from its normal context of historical opposition to the Chinese; first, the story has fused with another well-known Hmong tale of how the Hmong and Chinese were originally brothers, but grew apart after worshipping at different times of the year at the same ancestral grave, until in time their original affinity was forgotten; and second, the two Hmong stories have blended with the well-known Chinese account of the exploits of the legendary monk in his search for the Buddhist scriptures. Nor is this all, since the scriptures have become Daoist ones and their originator the Daoist Jade Emperor rather than the Buddha. And finally, another motif from a Hmong legend has been incorporated; the magical dog who leads them in their flight through a dark tunnel when they were escaping from the Chinese.

Yet this fusion and blending is not merely arbitrary; serious differences, of ancestry and origin, religious affiliation, belief and funeral practice, and social status, are being 'discussed' and 'thought' through this tale; very typically of Hmong and Chinese thought, the basic implication and sense of the story is that the origins of customary difference are to be sought in ancestral distinctions, and are in this sense ineradicable. Yet the gist and emphasis here is on the affinity and original unity of the Hmong with the Chinese; these striking differences of funeral practice for dead ancestors, typified in the contrast between Daoist and Hmong mortuary practice, are ultimately no more than differences of opinion, differences of interpretation, between brothers. Here the tale belongs more clearly with the account of burial differences than with stories of fighting and opposition to the Chinese, in the traditional Hmong 'canon'.

Despite this more overt intention, however, a shrewd analysis may prefer the gloss which would note the undercurrent of concern with the inferior status of the 'Miao', as seen in the loss of the whole book rather than half a book, and the conclusion on the lack of writing in comparison to the Chinese.

APPENDIX V

THE ORPHAN WHO CARRIED COAL

Once upon a time, there was an orphan named Laus Ntsuag (Louzhua). After his parents had died, his brother 'Duosou' and his brother's wife, threw him out of the house. His brother was extremely rich, while Laus Ntsuag himself was so poor that he did not even have a bowl for eating rice. Every day he heaved coal onto his back, and went around trying to sell it. And every day, he rested on the same huge boulder to get his breath back. And three years went by like this, life staying the same for him, and nothing getting any better.

One day, while Laus Ntsuag was resting on the boulder, the boulder began to speak to him. It said 'I know how poor you are. You just go home now and make a conically shaped pouch. When you get back I'll open my mouth, and you can get money by pulling some of my intestines, liver and heart out through my mouth'.

So Laus Ntsuag went home as the boulder had instructed, and made that conically shaped pouch. And then he came back with the pouch to the boulder. The boulder opned up its mouth, and Laus Ntsuag stretched in his hand to pluck out the intestines, liver and heart. Fearing that he might hurt the boulder, he picked the organs out very gently. He only took a tiny piece of each, to put inside his pouch. Then he thanked the boulder kindly, and returned home. When he looked inside his pouch to inspect the intestines, liver and heart again, he was surprised to find nothing but gold and pearls inside the pouch. He was still more surprised to find that while he had only taken a tiny piece of each organ, now the pouch was filled to the brim with precious stones and metals.

So Laus Ntsuag became rich. He had a big tiled house built. He bought herds and herds of cattle and horses to raise on his own land. His sheep grazed on the slopes, his swine guzzled in their sty, his geese swam on the ponds, and his ducks and chickens ran about outside. He also married a very beautiful wife. They lived together very happily.

Soon his brother and his brother's wife grew jealous of the orphan. His sister-in-law told his brother, 'Go and find out from him how he got so rich'.

'Oh no', said Laus Ntsuag's brother, 'I can't go now. When he was small we threw him out of the house. We never lifted a finger to help him when he was down and out. We were even afraid of him coming here asking for meals. Now that he has become rich, even though you have asked me time and time again, I still do not think I should go'. But his wife said, 'Where's the harm in just going to his house now? The next time he asks you, go to his house, and find out how he collected such a fortune'.

That very day, the brother pretended he had some affairs to deal with and rode past Laus Ntsuag's house. Laus Ntsuag invited him to come in. The brother got off his house and followed Laus Ntsuag inside the house. The house was a beautiful courtyard mansion with tiled roofs and many chambers. As soon as he entered, he spied gold cups and silver plates all over the place. He was seized with jealousy, and before long asked Laus Ntsuag, 'Only a few years back, you were still carrying coal on your back trying to sell it. You were so poor. How is it that you have become so wealthy so quickly?'

And Laus Ntsuag told his brother everything that had happened.

After hearing Laus Ntsuag's story, his brother thought and thought of how he could become rich like Laus Ntsuag. After they had eaten together, he said goodbye and went home. And he told his wife that he would do everything Laus Ntsuag had done. First he sold his horse. Then he sold his house and fields. And then he began to carry coal on his back every day, trying to sell it. And every day he took a rest on the big boulder, panting for breath. He told the boulder all his troubles. After six months, the boulder began to speak. It said, 'Don't press on my body so much when you pant. If you really want to be rich, go home and prepare a conically shaped pouch. When you come back, I'll open my mouth so you can scrape out some of my intestines, liver and heart, and become rich'.

Laus Ntsuab's brother was very excited. 'Ah,' he said, 'I've already brought along just such a pouch. Now open your mouth wide for me'.

So the big boulder opened its mouth. But he reached into the mouth and pulled hard at the intestines, trying to get them out altogether. Angry, the boulder suddenly shut its mouth. It clamped down on the brother's hand with its teeth and refused to let go.

His wife was waiting for her husband to come home. She waited for a very long time, but still he did not return home. So she wondered whether her husband, who had left home with coal on his back, could have collected so much intestines, liver and heart that it was too heavy for him to bring home. And she took up a shoulder pole with two paniers and set off for the big boulder herself. Heavens above! Her husband's hand had been caught by the boulder. He was shouting and screaming and lamenting, but there was nothing his wife could do to help him.

So she took his meals out to him there at the boulder every day for three years. Until one day his wife lost all patience and said, 'I can't keep on bringing your meals out here. You are of no use whatsoever! I'll let you have three mouthfuls of milk from my breasts, and then I'm going to leave you for good. Whether you live or die after that, it's all your own fault'.

When he heard his wife's words, 'Duosou' cried harder than ever. He was crying so hard that not only his mouth, but also his nose, began to take in the milk from his wife's breast. And seeing this, the huge boulder could not help but laugh. And when it laughed, it opened its mouth, so the brother's hand was freed. All his fingers were missing apart from one piece of bone.

And his wife ran off with somebody else after all that; Duosou lost his house and fields and lived out the rest of his life as a cripple.
(GMMG, pp.319-321. Narrator: Yang Xiaozhen)

This particularly nasty published story is a version of the story of the 'Orphan and the Wildcat' (Part III), and has at least the merit of making clear that the jealous rival is in fact a brother (who may be Chinese). The reference to drinking milk may be a reference to magic, since many Hmong believe that drinking milk is only practiced by supreme shamans and wizards. Again we see the triumph of the orphan and his journey from rags to riches, with the help of the natural and supernatural words, and the moral goodness of the orphaned brother (his concern for others' feelings—here the boulder) is contrasted with the greed and jealousy of his brother who meets a particularly horrible end. And as is all too often the case, it is the wife's brother, the woman, who provokes the fraternal jealousy, and all the troubles which ensue, besides finally deserting her wifely duties (feeding husband at the boulder).

HOW THE ORPHAN KILLED THE TIGER

A long time ago there lived an Orphan (Laus Ntsuag). His parents had both died, and he lived with his (paternal) uncle and aunt. His uncle was always away on business, sometimes for twelve to eighteen months. Laus Ntsuag's life with his aunt was miserable.

Every day he used to plough the fields. And every day, his aunt brought him out his lunch.

One day as usual his aunt had brought him his lunch, calling out 'Come and have your lunch'. Laus Ntsuag told his aunt to go home again; 'I'll finish my lunch after I have finished ploughing three times to the edge of the field and three times to the foot of the field'. And after his aunt had gone back again, Laus Ntsuag sang to the mountains; 'The cow is miserable, eating stalks of bitter grass, and Laus Ntsuag is desperately unhappy, eating crusts of bitter buckwheat, how bitter, bitter, bitter it is'.

And the maiden who lived in the stone cave opposite the fields heard Laus Ntsuag lamenting, and sang back to him; 'Run, Laus Ntsuag, flee, run home at dusk, find a sword and sharpen it, get hold of a knife and whet it, go to kill the striped tiger which guards the entrance to the cave. Together we'll walk, holding hands, to the place called Changning, and the town called Xufu, and together we'll eat "nine-nine rice" with chicken (glutinous rice eaten on festive occasions). There will be no more misery, an end to misery'. And Laus Ntsuag was uncommonly happy to hear these words.

The next morning Laus Ntsuag went off to the fields as usual, and as always his aunt brought him his lunch, calling out 'Come and have your lunch'. Laus Ntsuag told his aunt to leave his lunch there; 'I'll eat my lunch after I have done ploughing this field three time to the edge and three times to the corner'. After his aunt had left, Laus Ntsuag let the cow graze, and sang again up to the high mountain cliff. And the damsel who lived in the cave across the way heard him singing and replied again just as she had done the day before.

That night Laus Ntsuag returned home very late, to find his uncle had just returned from a business trip. Said Laus Ntsuag, 'you must help me find a big knife'. 'Whatever do you want a big knife for?' asked his uncle. 'I need to use it,' said Laus Ntsuag, 'you just help me to get one'. Soon his uncle found someone to make a big knife for Laus Ntsuag. Laus Ntsuag spent seven nights and seven days sharpening that knife, until it gleamed with sharpness.

When the knife was sharp enough, Laus Ntsuag said to his aunt, 'Now give me a skirt so that I can try my blade out on it'. 'However can you try your knife out on my skirt?' asked his aunt, 'my skirts are for wearing!' 'If you don't let me try it on your skirt, I shall leave you for ever', warned Laus Ntsuag. 'Well, if you really want my skirt, take it and try your knife on it', said the aunt.

Then Laus Ntsuag rolled the skirt up into a bundle, threw it into the air, and sliced it into two as it came down again. Then he turned to his uncle and said, 'Bring out that bull of yours. I want to try out my knife on it'. 'Whyever do you want to try out your knife on the animal?' asked his uncle, 'We need it for meat!' But Laus Ntsuag warned that he would leave them for good if they did not let him have the bull. 'Well, if you really want the bull, you can try your knife out on the animal', said his uncle. And he led out the big bull for Laus Ntsuag.

Laus Ntsuag picked up the whole animal and threw it into mid air. As it dropped to the ground again, he cut it into three pieces with the knife.

Then he said to his uncle and aunt, 'I am sorry for all the trouble I have caused you in the past. As soon as I leave this house, I am leaving for good'.

He picked up the big knife and walked away from the house. When he reached the foot of the cliff, he could not see the tiger the girl had told him about, so he sang up to the cliff instead. And the girl inside the cave heard him singing and answered him again.

Following the sound of her voice, Laus Ntsuag at last found his way to the entrance of the cave, crawling through the chasms. There he found a large striped tiger which was guarding the entrance to the cave. The animal was half asleep, but leapt at Laus Ntsuag as soon as it saw him.Laus Ntsuag sliced the tiger into three parts with no trouble at all, and the three chunks of the animal's body rolled down the cliff.

It was the girl who had made the tiger come into the cave. The tiger had left a heap of gold, silver and other treasures inside the cave. The girl took the treasure and ran off with Laus Ntsuag. They fled to Changning, to a town called Xufu. There they established their family and business, and there they lived happily ever afterwards. (*GMMG*, pp.325-27. Narrator: Wang Xiaojin.)

Changning county is in Xuyong. In this simple tale, the skeleton of the legend is particularly clear; the orphan's unhappiness with his father's brother and wife, the superhuman strength and magical talents of the hero, the ordeal of overcoming the tiger in order to obtain wealth and the fair maiden, and eventual happiness and prosperity linked with the idea of marriage. The story does not however stress the ill treatment of the orphan by his relatives, and indeed Laus Ntsuag threatens them with his departure although his final departure seems to be seen as a favour to them.

KINSHIP TERMS

Lemoine (1972a:173-81) has provided the fullest account of Hmong kinship terms, for the Green Hmong (Hmong Ntsuab) of Northern Laos. As he points out, three contrasting pairs of terms are used in ascendant generations: *puj/yawg*: *yawm/tais*: *nam/tswv*.

YAWG
yawg suab FFF+
yawg koob FFF
yawg FF
yawg laug FeB
yawg cuag S/D W/H F

PUJ
puj suab FFM+
puj koob FFM
puj FM
puj laug FeBW
puj nyaag FZ
puj cuag DHM
quas puj W (for a man)

YAWM
yawm MF
yawm laug MeZH
yawm hluas MyZH
yawm txwv WF
yawm dlaab WB
yawm yij ZH (for a man)
yawm vauv HZH (for a woman)

TAIS
tais MM
tais laug MeZ, WeZ, eZ (for a women)
tais hluas MyZ, WyZ, yZ (for a woman)
nam tais WM
tais dlaab WBW, BW (for a woman)

TXWV
txwv F
txwv ntxawm FyB
txwv dlaab MB
txwv kwj FZH
yawm txwv WF
txwv laug WeZH
txwv hluas WyZH

NAM
nam M
nam ntxawm FyBW, yBW
nam dlaab MBW
nam tais WM
nam tij eBW

Continuing Lemoine's description, in Ego's generation there are also three pairs of opposing terms: *nug/muam: kwv/tij: npawg (viv ncaug) npawg.*

NUG
nug B (for a woman)
nug npawg FZD, MBD, MZD (for a man)

TIJ
tij laug eB
tij nraab middle B
tij yau immediately eB
nam tij eBW

KWV
kwv yB
kwv nraab middle yB
kwv ntxawg youngest yB
kwv npawg FZS, MBS, MZS (for a man)

While below Ego's generation, there are only two pairs of terms: *tub ntxhais/vauv nyaab.*

tub S
ntxhais D
vauv DH
nyaab SW

Then there are general terms for grandsons and granddaughters, and their spouses (and separate terms for the children of BS and ZS).

As Lemoine points out, the White Hmong kin terms are very similar to Green Hmong, but in White Hmong *yawg laus* (FeB) replaces Green Hmong *txwv hlob*, while a single term (rather than a compound) is employed for FZ; *phauj*.

In White Hmong the MF becomes *yawm txiv*, while MM and WM are both known as *niam tais*, hence *niam tais laus* and *niam tais hluas* for MeZ and MyZ respectively.

(*Niam* is White Hmong pronunciation of Green Hmong *nam*; *txiv* is White Hmong for Green Hmong *txwv*.).

White Hmong has *tis nyab* for BW (for a woman), and *tis dab laug* for WBW, since the MB is called *dab laug*.

(Green Hmong *dlaab* is White Hmong *dab*; Green Hmong *nyaab* is White Hmong *nyab*.)

White Hmong is more precise than Green in distinguishing the wives of F's e/yB; *niam hlob* for FeBW, and *niam ntxawm* for FyBW, *niam laus* for WeZ, *niam hluas* for WyZ; and these are then also opposed to *niam tij* (eBW) and *niam ncaus* (yBW).

The Yachio or Magpie Hmong, or Han Miao, who referred to themselves as Hmong Ntsü (Hmong Ntsuab?), numbered some 10,000 and lived 'at the source of the Yungning River' in south Sichuan (28-29N/105-106E) when Ruey Yi-Fu studied them. They appear not to be the same group as the Hmong of Wutong since their kinship terms, reported by Ruey Yih Fu in the Bulletin of the Institute of History and Philology in 1958, were close to those of the Green Hmong reported on by Lemoine.

In a note on this Kroeber compared the Chinese and Miao kinship terms, arguing that their basic classificatory logic was fundamentally similar, although there were strong differences of detail. Ruey's (1960) argument however was that the Miao system had developed from a Hawaiian generational type, and that bilateral kindreds and neolocal residence had characterised the Hmong in the distant past.

(Thankfully we do not need to get involved in such arguments today, although on the face of it is difficult to know what Kroeber meant by the 'classificatory' logic of Chinese kinship terms, or to be convinced on the basis of Ruey's speculative history that Miao kin terms developed from any specific 'type'. Still the Miao is a partly classificatory system, in which generational differences are marked.)

One strong difference of detail between the Yochio system and that of the Hmong of Wutong today is in the term for Father, tsi in Yochio (as in White Hmong, and close to the *txwv* of Green Hmong), but *vaiv* in Wutong, similar to other groups in Yunnan, North Vietnam and Laos.

(Besides the Hmong Puas of Baccha in North Vietnam, who I found spoke essentially the same dialect as that of the Hmong of Wutong, with *vaiv* as the ceremonial term for F and *noj tsuas* as that for 'eating rice', and were locally known as 'Black Hmong' and even 'Hmoob Dub' because of the darkness of their costume (November 1996), in Sam Neua of Laos (December 1995) we interviewed a woman who the Hmoob Lees and Hmoob Si of that district called 'Hmong Dub' or 'Black Hmong' but who denied this, claiming to be a Hmong Dau (!) (which could not be mistaken for 'black' since in her dialect 'black' was *dua*) and who spoke similarly. There is a large and politically active group of these Hmoob Puas or 'Black Hmong' in Northern Laos who live in close association with the Hmoob Dawb (White Hmong) there, and the Wutong Hmong appear to be related to these—but not to be confused with the Chinese term for 'Black Miao' which refers to the Hmu of Guizhou who are not Hmong!)

While the Hmong of Thailand and Laos are still today very punctilious in their use of kinship terms, and very clear about their meanings, from North Vietnam through Yunnan up to Sichuan, while Hmong kinship terms continue to be used, there has been a Sinicisation and adaptation of the terms used by neighbouring Hmong groups and as a result some confusion. Slowly some fundamental features of the Hmong system such as special terms for nephews, distinctions between third and fourth ascending generations, and the use of an individual term for the WM, are being eroded by the influence of local dialect Chinese and replacement of Hmong by Chinese terms. Often informants produce the terms of neighbouring Hmong groups to demonstrate their own wide knowledge of Hmong kinship terms, and particular care is needed to separate terms used by men from terms used by women, and terms of reference from those of address.

As I received them in Wutong, *yiag laug* (FF) and *pos laug* (FM) were still terms used for the second ascendant generation, with *yiag* for the FF and *pos*, or *nas pos*, for the FM. The term usually used for

F was *vaiv*, and for M *nas*. Later in Yunnan I was to come across Hmong groups who used *vaiv* only as a formal term for the F, and also used the term commonly used for F by the White and Green Hmong, *txwv/txiv*, as a term of familiar address for the F; the term *vaiv* is unknown in Thailand. It appears that there may have once been two terms for F, a formal and a familiar term, of which the Hmong of Thailand have retained one for all uses, the Hmong of Wutong the other. Since the term *txiv* is used in ritual contexts by the Hmong of Wutong, in combination with *vaiv*, it appears this must have been the case.

FeB and FyB were known as *vaiv laug* and *vaiv yig* respectively, and their wives as *nas laug* and *nas ncius*. A special term was retained for the F's very youngest brother; *vaiv ntxawm*, while FeZ and FyZ had been collapsed into *muas nyaa*, and their husbands as *yiag yig*.

On the maternal side, the MF and MM were known as *yiav tais* and *pos taiv* respectively, very like the White and Green Hmong terms (here one must be careful; because of teknonymy, terms for M and W families are often collapsed, as the wife's father comes slowly to be referred to by the terms one's children use for him). The term *yiav* was retained for the WB, in combination with *dlaas*, the term for 'spirits', as in both Green and White Hmong, and *pos dlaas* for his wife (actually MBW as *pos laas*, and WBW as *muas daa*); an implication of respect for the WB by using the same term as for the ascending generation; while the MyZ and MeZ were known respectively as *nas hlua* and *nas laug*, and their husbands appropriately as *vaiv hlua* and *vaiv laug* (see Diagram 61).

The subtle tonal distinction which in Thailand differentiates the terms for 'husband' and 'wife' from those of FF and FM appeared to be absent, and also the differentiation between terms for FM and MM in pos.

However, although usually the terms for WF and WM were applied from those for MF and MM, the proper term for WF was *taiv yiav* and for WM just *taiv*, while her B was addressed as *yig* as well as referred to as *yiav dlaas* (and his W similarly as *hlua/pos dlaas*). W's sisters were referred to as *nas hlua* (y) and *nas laug* (e), their husbands as *vaiv hlua* and *vaiv laug*; exactly the same as for maternal aunts, in effect (see Diagram 62).

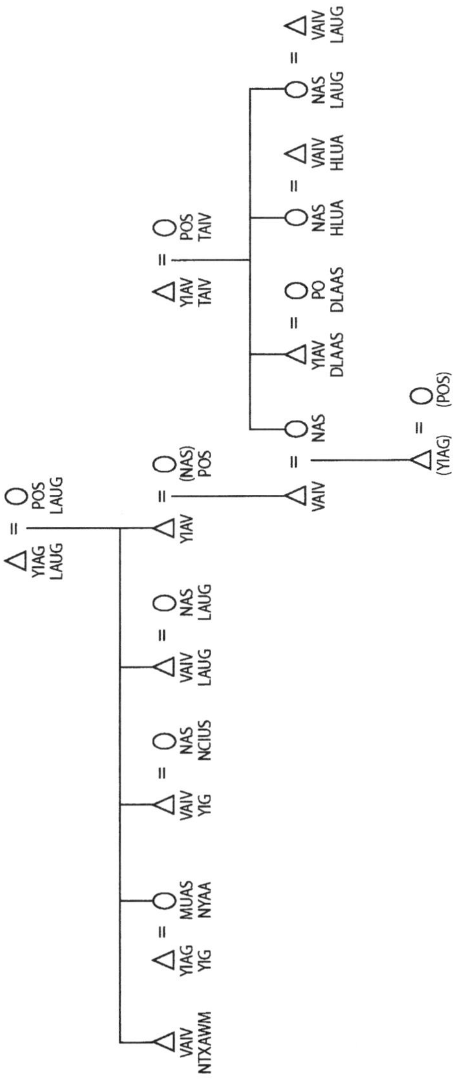

Diagram 61: Kin terms

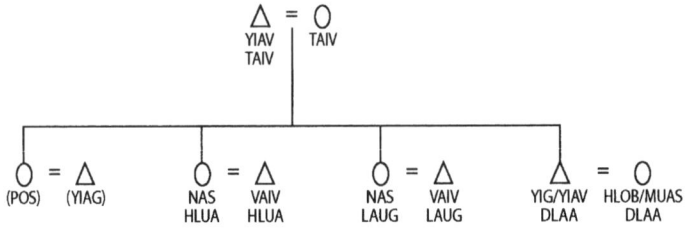

Diagram 62: Affinal terms

In Ego's own and descending generations terms were much the same as those used in White and Green Hmong in Thailand; that is, *tis* (or sometimes *tis laug*) for eB and *kwb* for yB, and *tus/ntxhai nthwv* for their male/female children; *muas* for the yZ and *veij* for the eZ, and *tus/ntxhai* cho for *their* male/female children (a more elaborate distinction than that in Thailand where distinctions are not commonly made between 'cross and parallel' nephews and nieces). The main differences are in the terms for siblings' spouses; *nyaas kwb/nyaas tis* for the wives of eB and yB respectively; and *muas vawj* forthe yZH and *veij vawj* for the eZH.

Tis and *Kwb* for eB and yB are the same terms in origin as the Chinese, but reversed in their reference to older and younger, as elsewhere for the Hmong.

As in Thailand, son is *tus* and D is *ntxhai*, and *vawj* the term for 'bridegroom' or DH (which we find here also in combination for the husbands of sisters), while *nyaas* is that for 'bride' or SW.

But there were also special terms for the F and M of children's spouses; *yiag cuag* (SWF/DHF) and *pos cuag* (SWM/DHM).

(*Ncius*, which we see here used in combination for FFBW, is normally a woman's term for her own yZ, which she will change to the term her husband uses after she marries.)

As elsewhere among the Hmong, *kwbtis* as patrilineal relations are contrasted to *neejtsa* as affinal ones (Diagram 63).

Apart from patrilateral parallell cousins, who are de facto unmarriageable, and are referred to by own-sibling terms, all other first cousins are included as *yiav npeig* or *nkaus muas* for female cousins (not patrilateral parallel cousins, since *npeig* functions identically to the Chinese kin term *wai* to indicate 'not of our house'). In these terms for first cousins Miao and Chinese kin terms

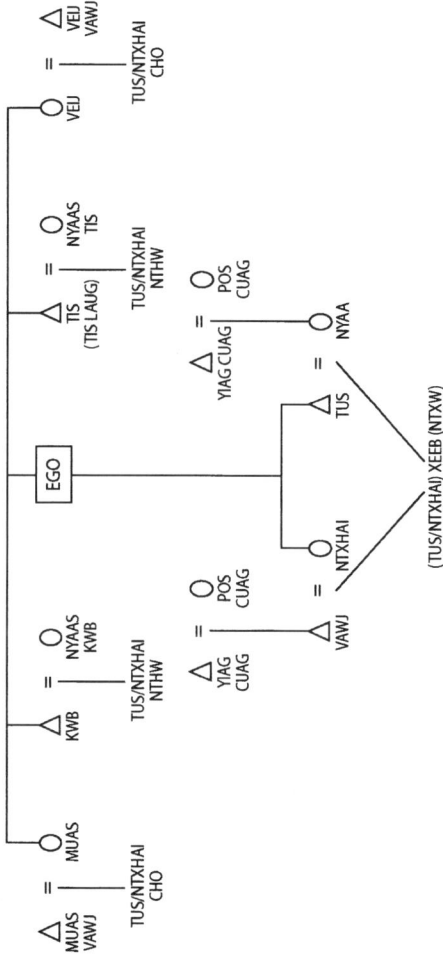

Diagram 63: Descending terms

are indeed identical, and in fact this may be the only trace of classificatory logic in the formal Chinese kin terms.

An alternative, or possibly older, term for the ZH, here rather lazily referred to as spouses of their wives, was *yiav yig*, or the same term used for FZH; teknonymy in action.

To give some idea of regional variation rather than intensely examining each case, since the basic system is identical, the Hmong Lees in Weixin had retained terms for paternal ascending generations (*yeuf zud/box zud*) similar to that recorded by Lemoine (as *suab*) for the Hmong in Laos, but lost by the Hmong of Wutong.

In Xinwei the Hmong all referred to their own FF as *yawg koob* and FM as *nai*, after the local Chinese practice.

The Hmong Lees also retained *yeuf hlob/hluak* for FFe/yB, and *box hlob/hluak* for their wives.

The terms *naf loud* and *daik loud* were used for WeZ by both the Hmong Lees and the Hmong of Xingyi in Guizhou, and *mik hluak/naf hluak* for WyZ, which were the same terms as those for MZ.

Mik nyangb was used for FZ by Hmong Leeg who referred to their H as *yeuf voud*, showing the quite frequent replacement of the Hmong term *muas* by the local Chinese mi or endearment for a sister.

In some cases, a combination of both the alternative terms for F, *vaiv* and *txiv/txwv*, are used to distinguish relatives; for the Hmong Leeg, F is *zid*, while MZH are called *zid hluak* for the younger one, and *vaif loud* for the older one, with *yeuf dlangb* as elsewhere used for MB; while similarly *zid yed* distinguished the FyB from the FeB who is called *vaif loud* (and their wives as *naf hluak* and *naf loud*), with the use of *yeuf* reserved for the FZH as *yeuf voud*.

However, the Xingyi Hmong in Guiozhou used *yeuf yed* to distinguish FZH (both elder and younger), and FFZH.

Incidentally, the sound I have transliterated as 'Dl' is a most peculiar and distinctive one, which I believe should be written in IPA as a L with a stroke across it; it is not a d nor an l nor a hard g, and is sometimes written 'dl' or 'gl' because no other sound like it seems to exist elsewhere, something like a semi-glottalised palatal, or a retroflexive d, perhaps, which has been described to me (personal communication, Tadahiko 25/3/92) as a 'lateral stop, pre-glottalised in WM'.

A STRUCTURAL ANALYSIS OF THE LEGENDS

If we wished to reduce the structures of these stories to their bare essentials, the main outline of a 'genotext' would appear clearly enough.An impoverished orphan is *deserted* by those who care for him or leaves home. He is *opposed by jealous rivals*, landlords or emperors, and fed on bitter buckwheat by his paternal relatives. He may have *unearthly origins*, signalled by an abnormal appearance, and has to *support himself* by hunting or fishing, cutting grass or selling coal. But he is gifted with marvellous *supernatural powers* (an inexhaustible capacity for rice, a capacity to carry enormous weights), and receives help from *heroic companions*, *magical objects* (scissors, knives, a boulder) and *animals* (the bitch who rears him, the wildcat or fish who becomes his wife). He may have to undergo various *ordeals* (hiding himself, the 88-strand rope, killing tigers or monsters) in order to discover *wealth*, or a magical object which brings wealth, or a *wife*. Because of his *kind, open nature* (saving wild animals, helping those in need), he receives *heavenly advice* (from Saub or the Spirit of the Land). His house is *magically cleansed*, his table wonderfully replenished, and he receives a mystic maiden in marriage. He is *transformed*, into the Sun, a Dragon, or the Emperor.

But the selection of stories considered here is an arbitrary, if one hopes intuitively sound, one. A closer examination of the tales and their structural combinations shows that it would be more appropriate to unpack this attempt to reveal a single, general sub-narrative, into three quite separate attempts, or sub-narratives, or themes, or tales,[1] which have been conjoined and blended in quite different ways. These, based on a structural consideration of the main elements in all the tales considered, would then be;

1) Hero kills monster in order to obtain 'pearl' (treasure, cornucopia)

2) Hero is in possession of valuable object (treasure, pearl) which others try to obtain from him

---

[1] Isotopies in Greimas' (1966) sense.

3) Transformations—of the wildcat, fish or star (dumb girl or Emperor's daughter), into a wife; of the hero into Sun, Dragon or Emperor

(where the hero is understood to be the deserted and poor orphan, who receives supernatural help, often from animals he has saved).

Tale 2 is then a version of theme 2 (the rival seeks to obtain the wildcat) followed by theme 3 (wildcat becomes wife). Tale 3 (star girl descends to marry orphan) is a simple transformation story; theme 3. Tale 6 entails a double transformation, both of wife from the saved fish and then into Dragon King's daughter, complicated by theme 2 in the form of the other, jealous fish whose tail was burnt and tries to ruin his marriage. Tale 7 is another transformation, of the saved white fish into the marrying maiden (theme 3). Tale 8 is also a perfect rendering of theme 2, as the landlord seeks to seize the pearl of plenty, ending with theme 3 as the hero becomes a dragon. Tale 9 combines theme 1 (the ordeal of killing the giant and taking his pearl) with theme 2, as the Emperor takes his pearl which has to be retrieved. Tale 10 is another simple transformation, as the orphan reared by a bitch becomes Emperor. Appendix V provides a perfect example of theme 2, with the jealous brother failing to obtain wealth from the boulder, while Appendix VI (in which the hero kills the tiger with the magic knife) is almost equally so of theme 1.

But we should note that, in Appendix VI, after killing the tiger, the hero receives not only treasure, but also the main ideal of most of the stories—the *wife*. Also in Tale 1, after the hero kills the tiger (and spares the life of his prospective father-in-law who is also a kind of monster, and eventually has to be tricked and defeated), the prize is also *marriage* to one of the seven daughters of the monstrous old man. Tale 4 again combines a simple ordeal (the plaiting of the rope ordered by the maiden in a cave) with the *marriage* to one of seven sisters, who build the hero a new home. The whole point of the orphan leaving home in Tale 5 is to find a *wife,* and here he is killed by the prospective father-in-law before his final vengeful transformation (theme 3) into the Sun. The objectives of the hero in both Tale 11 and Appendix III are to find a *wife* (combined with health and wealth in Tale 11); in Appendix III this is the daughter of the Emperor who sets various ordeals (the three concealments) for the hero to overcome, and in both tales it is because he has helped (respectively) the old man, dumb girl, phoenix and crow in Tale 11, and the eagle, pig-fish, and fox in Appendix III, that he is finally able to *win his bride*.

So we might wish to add a fourth theme to those above;

4) Hero overcomes ordeals (often connected with the figure of a father-in-law) to find wife

With very few exceptions, the orphan's marriage is an explicit concern of all these tales. Even in Appendix V the hero marries 'a very beautiful wife', although she is not evidently the main point of the story, and it is the orphan's new-found wealth which excites his brother's wife's jealousy. Apart from this, the only legends in which marriage is not a major explicit concern are 8, 9 and 10. In Tale 10 the hero is only one year old, while in Tale 9 the hero is happily married, and takes the pearl home to provide for his family, which they are then cheated out of by the imperial soldiers. It is, then, only in Tale 8 that there is a complete absence of references, where one might have thought them to be appropriate, to the importance of a wife, and we consider why this should be in more detail below.

It would be tedious to list all the legends in which the images of wealth and the happy marriage are combined.[2] We can easily see from the majority of these stories that the association of wealth with marriage is a constantly repeated one, as too are the images of fertility and plenty which accompany it. It seems to me that this is much more than a random or even merely syntagmatic association, and that by the image of the 'treasure', the pearl of plenty, or cornucopia, the precious object for which monsters and ogres must be slaughtered or deceived, and which jealous brothers or figures of political authority try to steal, we should understand that with which it is so frequently conjoined; *the wife*, as the supreme source of endless plenty and fertility.

Surely it is the incomprehensible magic of procreation and human regeneration of which, above all, these stories speak in their images of maidens descending from heaven and houses being magically cleaned, tables wonderfully replenished and jealous brothers and

---

[2] For the record, the only legends where they are *not* in some way combined are in Legend 8 which as we have seen is anomalous in that there is no marriage at all, in 10 where the hero is only one year old, in 5 where the hero becomes the Sun and could therefore hardly be described as wealthy, in Appendix III where the emperor's daughter is married and wealth is therefore assumed, and in Tale 1 where again the orphan's capacity to provide for himself has already been emphasised.

wicked fathers-in-law's designs being defeated? If by 'treasure' and 'the pearl' we are meant to understand a metaphor for the ideal wife who is the explicit point of so many of these stories, the helpmeet who transforms economic poverty into a productive life, bringing wealth and prosperity to the meanest household, then in the apparently anomalous Tale 8 we can see the wicked landlord pursuing the hero for his *wife*, whom he must 'swallow' (consume, protect) in order to achieve his own transformation into a dragon— itself the ultimate image of procreative potency. As we saw in the final Tale (11) about the marriage to the dumb girl who speaks, an overriding concern with reproduction and the issue which only marriage can rightfully bring is being expressed.

Ultimately, this shows a concern with the power of the kinship attachments which it is eventually necessary for the orphan (devoid of kinship affiliations) to *consciously* assume and adopt in order to achieve his supreme success and happiness. To extrapolate from a Hmong context to the wider context of Chinese folklore may be problematic, but it is at least conceivable that the image of the mystic Daoist pearl of immortality and longevity, secreted in the dragon's mouth, is often transmuted in the popular imagination, into a concern with physical reproduction and the bearing of children and heirs, symbolising the continuation and expansion of an ancestral lineage and thereby the gaining of power and wealth; the effective immortality of a founding ancestor. Or, if considered from the more mundane perspective in which these tales are generally told and to which they may be taken to refer, a good marriage is simply the only means possible to overcome poverty and achieve wealth; not only because your wife may be well connected and of a higher status to your own family, but because a wife will cook and clean the house for you, tend domestic animals and the crops, provide companionship and care, and above all with luck (or heavenly blessing in these stories) children—and thereby the succeeeding generations without whose help instituted poverty can never be unequivocally overcome.

At this point, then, we may return to our original three 'themes', combining the fourth theme with them, to obtain the only slightly modified oikotype;

1) Hero undergoes various ordeals (such as killing monster) in order to obtain 'pearl' (treasure, cornucopia)

2) Hero is in possession of treasure (such as 'pearl') which others try to obtain from him

3) Transformations—of a wife out of a wildcat, fish or star (dumb girl or Emperor's daughter); of the hero into Sun, Dragon or Emperor (powerful ancestral figure)

(where 'pearl' or 'treasure' is understood as referring to the abundance associated with a successful marriage).

And those legends (Appendix VI, Tales 1,4,5,11 and Appendix V) which at first seemed to lie beyond the boundaries defined by our original three themes and to be emphasising the importance of marriage in their stead, take on a new significance in the light both of these newly understood three themes and of the other tales, already considered, which represent more simple combinations of the three themes. In Appendix VI, we can now see more clearly why the hero should have to kill the tiger before he can obtain both wealth and wife. In the first tale above, we can see a doubling of the 'ordeal'; the hero not only has to kill a tiger to obtain freedom from his dependence on others, but also has to trap, save and trick his prospective (and monstrous) father-in-law in order to obtain his daughter in marriage. In Tale 4 we can see how appropriate it is that the ordeal (the plaiting of the rope) should lead directly to the perfect marriage. In Tale 5 it is again appropriate that the hero's ultimate transformation (into the Sun) should follow his battle of wits against the prospective father-in-law; here the hero is only temporarily defeated through being killed, but achieves final victory in the form of a mystic marriage with the Moon and Stars through his heavenly transformation. In Tale 11, the hero's long quest to ask Saub for his advice, the requests for help he receives along the way, and the laborious removal of the silver and gold, can all be seen as constituting the ordeals necessary before he can win both wealth and wife. And in Appendix III, as we have already seen, the orphan has to undergo the ordeal of concealing himself successfully, before he can marry the Emperor's daughter.

As we have seen, the remaining tales (2,3,6,7,8,9,10 and those in Appendices V and VI) already show clear combinations of the three themes we originally considered. Let us finally reconsider them to see what new light may be shed on some of them by the interpretation of the pearl or treasure as representing, as well as accompanying, an ideal marriage. In Tale 2, wife and wealth are

clearly united in the transformations of the wildcat. In Tale 3 the
orphan marries a star girl, who builds him a wonderful new house. In
Tale 6 we find the first magical transformation (theme 3) of the fish
into the orphan's wife who provides him with a clean house and
plenteous food complicated by the jealous fish (theme 2) but
resolved through the transformation of his wife into the daughter of
the Dragon King (theme 3 again). An ordeal (theme 1) is constituted
by his supernatural helper (the toad's) drinking of the water, and as
we have seen, although the ending remains ambiguous, the intent of
the tale is plain; to obtain or recover the hero's wife. Tale 7 provides
a particularly simple version, of the transformation (theme 3) of fish
into wife who cleans and provides endless meals (wealth).

We have also already considered how in Tale 8, the pearl of
plenty which the hero has to swallow in order to escape the rapacious
landlord must symbolise the wife whose consumption allows him to
transform into a (potent) dragon. In Tale 9 the pearl which the
Emperor steals can again be seen to stand for the hero's wife, which
is why its retrieval should lead to a happy family life. Tale 10 takes
up the dragonly theme of transformation alone, as the infant orphan
is shown becoming Emperor. And even in the otherwise gratuitiously
nasty Appendix V, we can see the brother's jealousy as more
understandably relating to a wife who is the source of the hero's
sudden wealth, and it is thus more than appropriate that in the end the
jealous, greedy brother, should be deserted by his own wife when she
finds his hand stuck fast in the very source of all this wealth and
plenty (the boulder's mouth!).[3]

---

[3] There is no confusion between sex and marriage here, as an old debate would
have had it; since the survival, let alone recognition, of children without a formal
kinship affiliation is unthinkable, only a social paternity is possible. Marriage and
procreation are thus identical here, in the Hmong creative imagination as much as in
bourgeois suppositions.

APPENDIX IX

A NOTE ON CONTEXT

John Thompson, favouring Bourdieu rather than Geertz, has argued that the meaning of the 'structural forms' (may we say 'texts'?) characteristic of 'culture' must be understood in terms of the 'social-historical contexts' of their production and reception (Thompson 1990). He does this by usefully distinguishing the 'intentional', 'conventional', 'structural', 'referential' and 'contextual' aspects of symbolic forms.[1] As he points out, to consider the meaning of a symbolic form purely in terms of its 'intention' would be inadequate; intentions may be vague, contradictory, or unconscious. The 'conventions' under which a given symbolic form is produced and received are those which allow it to be coded and decoded, but a text may be decoded according to different conventions (criteria?) from those used to encode it. By the 'structural' significance of a symbolic form he means its internal structural arrangement, such as that used in purely textual analysis, but also the structure of symbolic systems in which a symbolic form may be understood. The 'referential' aspect of a symbolic form indicates what it overtly represents. The 'contextual' characteristic of a symbolic form is seen as its embeddedness in given 'social-historical contexts and processes'; again, Thompson notes that the social-historical context in which a symbolic form is 'produced' may differ from that in which it is 'received'; and as features of the 'social context' he distinguishes social institutions, social structure, fields of interaction, and spatio-temporal settings, going on from this to discuss how social contexts are symbolically reproduced.

It seems to me that there are two problems here. The first is a matter of semantics; why should we reduce 'context' to the 'social-historical' context? Surely the 'total context' of a symbolic form, in the sense in which I have used the term, and the sense pioneered by Ogden and Richards (1923) in which a 'sign' works by evoking the context of which it is a part, should refer to all these five features of

---

[1]   As in hermeneutics, the intention and consistency of a text used to be distinguished from its social, historic and geographic environment.

symbolic forms; intentional and referential, structural and 'conventional', and what we should perhaps call 'situational' . The second problem is more structural; a transparency of the social context itself is assumed here, its ultimate unmediation by cultural factors and its openness to the analyst's gaze. But surely the social context in which a text, a work of art, or other symbolic form, is embedded in its production, in its conventional 'reception' (by which we should understand 'interpretation'), and in its critical or analytical 'reception' ('interpretation') by others, is in itself a matter of interpretation (and varied interpretation), both by immediate actors and social investigators; and these interpretations ('receptions'), analyses, and understandings, are themselves influenced if not determined by those more general cultural patternings or structured 'symbolic systems' which Thompson sees as typically expressed in symbolic forms.

In case I am thought to have confused them, let me distinguish the 'real life' of the Hmong in Wutong today from the Hmong tales and texts I have presented. Certainly the Hmong texts demonstrate authorial intentionality and certain conventions of composition, they refer to particular kinds of life experience and they may be analysed in terms of their internal structure as I have mostly done. Some of these texts may have been composed in quite different social circumstances to those in which they are now commonly told, and listeners may interpret them according to slightly different conventions than those according to which they were composed. But the social-historical context in which these tales are now told or in which they were originally composed, may itself be interpreted quite differently by Hmong actors of different social backgrounds, or by Chinese of varying social status, or by outside analysts of varying theoretical persuasions. And surely in seeking to explore the total context of these tales and texts, some sense of all these different features and characteristics of symbolic forms needs to be given and taken into account.

And when we consider the 'real life' of the Hmong in Wutong today, again a number of different interpretations could be made. In the interpretation I have provided, the importance of the production and transmission of symbolic forms figures quite prominently; I can imagine other accounts which would restrict themselves to purely economic or institutional analysis, seeing the ethnicity and historical memories of these agrarian peasants as of secondary importance; I know that the interpretations provided by the Hmong of their social-historical situations differ quite markedly from those of official party historians or even local cadres. But, given the possibility or likelihood of a variance of presentations and possible interpretations,[2] I think it is reasonable to privilege the accounts and interpretations of Hmong themselves inasmuch as this is possible, always of course in the light of the social historical circumstances which may constrain or sometimes partly explain those accounts and interpretations, and in the awareness of their potential error and the possibility of alternative accounts or interpretations.

Fentress and Wickham (1992) point out that narrative social memory can be importantly 'decontextualised' in the way that it adapts itself, through oral transmission, to new contexts and situations. Interestingly they distinguish between an 'external or social context' and the 'internal' context (which refers to a 'memory's' (read 'text') internal structure and relationship to a genre, arguing that narrative social memories tend to 'forget' (external) context-dependent information in order to be able to recontextualise, while it is the 'internal' context (such as the visual images of epic narrative, or the causal connections in fairy tales) which is retained. For an understanding of the *total* context, however, I would argue that we need to appreciate both the ways in which particular narratives have been recontextualised (which implies a knowledge of previous, 'external' contexts), as well as the ways its 'internal' context is constructed).

Reduced to its simplest essentials, the question is one of the extent to which 'real' social historical conditions condition, constrain or determine the production and reception of symbolic forms, and to what extent such symbolic forms may escape the bounds of such restraint altogether, to paint visions of otherwise unimaginable alternatives or futures, or to appeal to human passions and imagination across cultural frontiers. And the question is I think one of extent; Ricoeur has something when he talks of the 'distanciation' of the text from the conditions of its production and intentionality,

---

[2] See the Margaret Mead/Derek Freeman controversy, or publication of Malinowski diaries; what Clifford in 1988:22 called the 'bewildering variety of idioms' in which people interpret others and themselves.

but perhaps this is not true of all texts, or true of texts to varying degrees; again, it may be crucial to examine the social historical circumstances in which a given text is produced, but sometimes just as fruitful not to do so at all.[3]

---

[3] And if it does apear that distanciation, autonomy is a matter of degree, then it may be a useful enterprise to examine written texts from this point of view more closely; bracketing heuristically the historical and social reasons which might explain the popularity or wide distribution of certain forms of symbolic production, a history of the lengths of historical time under which given texts have enjoyed popularity and acclaim, and a study of the relative global distribution of works in translation; that is, a global history of publishing and printed circulation figures might yield some very interesting results in determining what kinds of text have successfully overcome the cultural and historical circumstances of their production.

LIST OF HOUSEHOLDS (GROUPS TWO AND THREE;
ANNOTATED VERSION OF LOCAL CENSUS)

1) Tao Minzeng, who had married Zeng Wanpei. Since Zeng Wanpei was separated from his wife and working in Gongxian, this was a female-headed household. Tao Minzeng was 48 and lived with her husband's 61-year old mother, two daughters aged 12 and 17, while a third aged 24 had married Yang Yuqing and had her own 1-year old daughter.

2) The household of another woman, Yang Daiyun (formerly known as Yang Dairong), whose husband, Zeng Wanlu, a *xiang* officer, was in prison for murder. She was 43 years old and also lived with three daughters aged respectively 15, 18 and 21. The eldest daughter had already married Wang Zhongping (in household number 13), but was still at home waiting for a new home to move into.

3) The house of Zeng Wanshou, aged 32 who had married a Yang girl aged 27 and also lived with three daughters aged 3,5 and 7.

4) The house of the Chinese teacher, Xie Peijiang, who lived with his old father of 82 and mother of 75. Xie Peijiang was 43 and his wife a year younger, and they had one son of 18 and three daughters aged 7,14 and 16.

5) Yang Wanke, born in 1928 with his Wang wife aged 57, an 18-year old daughter and three sons aged 13,16 and 20. The following three households were composed by his three older sons.

6) Yang Daikui, aged 35 and his 29-year old Liu wife with a son of 6 and a daughter of 8.

7) Yang Daizhong, aged 27 and his 24-year old Wang wife with two daughters of 1 and 4.

8) Yang Daiqing, aged 25 and his 23-year old Wang wife and their two-year old son.

9) The migrant household of Yang Daiquan who worked in the Furong coal mine although his wife (Wang Zhongyu), son and two daughters occupied the house.

10) The house of Yang Daijin aged 34, his widowed mother of 64, his bedridden elder sister of 39, his Xiong wife the same age as himself, his 7-year old son and two daughters of 9 and 10.

11) Yang Wangkun's house; he lived with an old father of 76, Yang Zhijun, the ritual expert, and his mother of 75; he was 44 and his wife 41,and the household included their 18-year old son who was away studying in Yibin and two daughters of 12 and 15.

12) The house of Yang Wanshun, his brother of 40 years old, with his Ma wife of 40 and three sons aged 12, 15 and 17.

13) The house of Wang Zhongping, aged 21, an unmarried older brother (Wang Zhongliang) of 33, and their mother of 53, as well Wang Zhongping's one year old son. The baby was being looked after by his mother, since his Zeng wife was still staying with her own family (in household no.2 above), and their new house was not yet ready.

14) Another brother of the above, Wang Zhongfu, aged 38 whose 34-year old wife was a Yang, and their 6-year old daughter.

15) Yang Wanzhong, aged 64 and his 58-year old wife with a young 19-year old son and a 15-year old daughter. The next three households were composed of his elder sons.

16) Yang Daifu, aged 32, who had married a Wang woman of 33 and had a 9-year old son and 7-year old daughter.

17) Yang Daihe (sometimes called Daike), aged 28 and just married, he was about to move out to join his wife's household in Luobiao.

18) Yang Daihua, aged 22 whose Han Chinese wife (surname Luo) had left him and remarried.

19) Yang Wanheng, brother of 15, aged 57 with his 54-year old wife and two sons of 16 and 20, besides two daughters aged 14 and 17.

20) Yang Daiming, who had left his Tao wife of 42 years old with his two unmarried sisters of 16 and 29. His father Yang Wanyu of 63 and Wang mother of 64 still lived with him, and in fact this was generally reckoned to be Yang Wanyu's house, as No.11's house was called Yang Zhijun's. Yang Daiming's own three children also formed household members; a son of 15 and two daughters of 7 and 12. The son was in Didong studying. The following three households were composed of other sons of Yang Wanyu.

21) Yang Dailu, younger brother of Yang Daiming, aged 33 and his Wang wife a year older, with their 6-year old son and 3-year old daughter. Yang Dailu was the party branch (village) secretary.

22) Another brother named Yang Daihe, aged 31 with his 24-year old Xiong wife and their one-year old daughter.

23) Yang Daijiang, born in 1965 and his Yu wife who was settled with him although her *hukou* remained in her natal home (Cheng Shen commune). In fact these four households still all inhabited the same large courtyard house of Yang Wanyu (first cousin to numbers 11 and 12).

24) The household of Yang Hong, aged 28 with his 27-year old Ma wife and his 3-year old son. Again Yang Hong lived with his 62-year old father, Yang Liping, whose house this was popularly reckoned to be, and his 59-year old Tao mother.

25) Yang Zhao, aged 25 and younger brother of the above, his 24-year old Ma wife and their 1-year old daughter.(Both these households still lived in Yang Liping's house).

26) Yang Wanli, a brother of Yang Liping, aged 42 and his 41-year old Li wife, with four sons aged 14,18,20 and 24. The eldest son's Wang wife also lived with them although her *hukou* was still in her original home (Chen Sheng) so officially she is not part of the village.

27) Yang Xianggao, aged 46 and his Zeng wife of the same age, with two sons of 13 and 15.

28) Yang Xiangchao, brother to the above, aged 43 whose Chinese (Liu) wife had left him taking with her one son and leaving him with a 17-year old son.

29) Wang Yingchen, aged 23, his 25-year old Ma wife and their 2-year old son. In fact he still lived in the house of his father, number 30 below.

30) Wang Zhailing, aged 53, whose second (Yang) wife of 37 still lived with him (his first wife had died) and his mentally ill 42-year old brother (who occupied a separate part of the house); and his two sons of 11 and 15 and two daughters of 13 and 17. His older son at household 29, above, was by his first wife.

31) Li surname (Han Chinese). This was the household of Li Peibing, aged 52, whose Xie wife (also Han) had died, leaving him with two sons of 16 and 17, and a daughter of 14.

32) The household of Li Guoqi, aged 22, a son of the above who lived in the same house, with his unregistered Luo (also Han) wife and daughter.

33) Li Peixin, aged 58 who had married a Xie of the same age (sister of household number 46), with a 22-year old son and 16-year old daughter.

34) This and the following two households were all headed by sons of Li Peixin at number 33 above. Li Guocheng, aged 36 and his Jiang wife of 27 with a son of 7 and a daughter aged 8.

35) Li Guoqian, aged 32 and his 30-year old Xie wife (the daughter of household number 51), with three sons aged 3, 8 and 10.

36) Li Guojin, aged 30, and his Liu wife of 25 together with her 47-year old mother as well as her three sisters, aged 13,15 and 18, and their 8-year old son.

37) Technically the household of a 78-year old Li man who actually lived in the household of number 41 below.He fell into one of the five categories of protected households (widowed, old and helpless) eligible for government (that is, local village committee) assistance (*wu baohu*).

38) Li Guohua,35, his wife of the same age and two sons aged 8 and 10.

39) The household of Li Peilong, whose son Li Guoping usually worked outside the village as a carpenter. Li Peilong was 59 and his Mu wife 58, Li Guoping was 38 and his Mu wife 32, and they had two sons of 7 and 13.

40) Yang Xiangying, aged 53 whose Xiong wife had died leaving him with a daughter of 35 who actually headed the household, with her own daughter of 7 and two sons of 3 and 5, and her Huang husband who lived with them but was not recorded.

41) Li Guoquan, aged 32, with a wife of 31 and a son of 7. Number 37 had moved in with them and they looked after him.

42) Li Peishu, aged 56, the father of number 41 above, whose Xie wife (Xie Peijia's older sister) was three years younger than himself, two sons aged 19 and 25, the oldest of whom had also married a Xie (daughter of Xie Peijia's first cousin) and had a one-year old son.

43) Li Guoliang, previously Li Guomin, another son of number 42, aged 35, with his Luo wife of 31 and their two sons of 7 and 10.

44) The household of Gu Yingshen, aged 45, and his Huang wife of 43 with their three sons aged 10,13 and 21, and their two daughters of 15 and 19.

Third Group:

45) The family of Huang Shuling, a Han Chinese who had moved in from Gongxian; he was 55 and his Yang (Hmong) wife 53 and they had three sons aged 14,18 and 21, and a daughter of 16.

46) Reckoned as a separate household, although living in the same house as him, was the family of number 45's oldest son of 27, Huang Xijun, with his Liu wife two years younger, and their one-year old son.

47) the household of Xie Shaoting, whose younger sister had married into the Li household number 33. Xie Shaoting was 67 and his Zhang wife 68, and they lived with their 28 year old son and his 25 year old Wen wife with their two daughters of 1 and 3.

(Xie surname also Han).

48) a much older son of the latter in number 47; Xie Yunshu, who had actually left his 41-year old wife, Liao Hefen, with three sons of 16, 19 and 21 and a daughter of 18, while he worked in the Didong Gongxiaoshe. The household was usually referred to as Liao Hefen's.

49) the household of another brother of the latter, Xie Yunhe, aged 32 and his Liu wife of 25 and their two sons of 3 and 5. But he lived still in his father's house at number 47.

50) The Hmong household of Yang Wanwen, aged 50, and his Tao wife of 49, their daughter of 15 and a son of 19 with his Xiong wife of 18 who was not officially recorded.

51) The household of a brother of Xie Shaoting at number 47; Xie Shaoju, born in 1930 and married to a Cheng of the same age. The Li wife of their 24-year old son had died leaving a 4-year old son, while another unmarried son of 34 lived with them who had been dumb from birth.

52) Another brother of household number 51 above; Xie Shaojun, born in 1932, whose Jiang wife was four years younger. They lived with a daughter of 16, a son of 11 and another son of 27 whose wife preferred her hometown to Wutong and was therefore not recorded. The family were expected to move with her shortly.

53) The Sun surname (also Han Chinese). This was the household of Sun Huaixiang, whose brother had been executed as a Guomindang supporter. He lived with his brother's Zeng widow, his own He wife three years younger than himself, and their two sons of 27 and 21 as well as two daughters of 15 and 18.

54) The household of another son of the above in number 53; Sun Xiyuan, aged 35, with his Chen wife of 32 and their two younger sons of 2 and 6.

55) The household of Hmong *paterfamilias* Yang Wanyi, aged 56 and his Wang wife of the same age. Three of their children were recorded as living with them; a son of 24 and another of 18, and another (with his own son aged 3) who had married the daughter of the brother of Zeng Minggao, the Gongxian party secretary. This son's entire family did not actually live in the house, but in Gongxian where the father was an agricultural cadre.

56) Yang Daiqing,another son of the latter, aged 36, with his Liu wife of 32, a son of 6 and a daughter of 9.

57) Another son of Yang Wanyi at number 55; Yang Daihong, aged 26, whose Yunnanese wife was not recorded (another unregistered marriage) with their one-year old son.

58) Yang Wanfang, a shaman, a man of 50 and his Liu wife of 53 who also practised shamanism. They had a son of 25 who was about to move out to join his Tao wife in Shangluo, a daughter of 22, and two other sons of 13 and 18.

59) A female-headed household; that of Tao Zhenyou aged 40 whose husband (Yang Wanlong, first cousin to number 58) had been killed by the avalanche. She had five daughters, aged 10,15,16,17 and 19.

60) This was a female-headed household; recorded under the name of Xiong Zhongying, a woman of 37 whose Yang husband worked as an iron worker in Chensheng. In fact she also lived there, so this was an absentee household.

61) The household of Yang Wanbing, an old man of 70 with his Xiong wife of 64 whose first husband had died. His daughter of 18 had actually already married and moved out, but was still recorded as a household member, and the rest of the household was composed of his 36-year old son with his Wang wife of the same age, and their two sons of 8 and 10.

62) The house of another Yang widow; Ma Chenglian, aged 60, the widow of Yang Wanhua, whose son Yang Daijin was 21 and daughter 18.

63) Yang Daiying was another son of the widow at number 62, aged 35 who like his father had married a Ma woman of 39 and had a daughter of 16 and two sons of 13 and 14.

64) The household of Wang Zhongqian, aged 56, and his Yang wife of 53 (the elder sister of number 27) and their four children; a boy of 13, two girls of 15 and 21, and a boy of 24,

65) The household of his older, 34-year old son, Wang Guoming, who had married the 36-year old elder daughter of Zeng Minggao, the Gongxian party secretary (see number 55), with their daughter of 9 and son of 12. In fact they all lived together with number 64 above.

66) Wang Guoyuan, aged 31, and younger brother to number 65, who also lived in the same house with his own family. This was composed of his 25-year old wife, a 2-year old son and a newly born daughter.

67) Yang Xiangfu, aged 56 whose Wang wife had died, with his old mother of 79 and his son aged 21.

68) His brother, Yang Xiangming, aged 34, with his 32-year old Xiong wife, a girl of 6 and a boy of 8.

69) Old Yang Wanjun, first cousin to number 62, who was a wedding expert, with his Wang wife a year older than him, and two sons aged 25 and 27. The 27-year old son had a one-year old son and a Wang wife whose records remained in her home village.

70) Yang Daiyun, aged 37, the second son of Yang Wanjun at number 69, with his Huang wife of 36, a girl of 12 and a boy of 8.

71) The fenale-headed household of 42-year old Liu Qizhen. Her husband, Yang Daifu, the oldest son of Yang Wanjun at number 69, had died of cancer. She lived with her daughter of 10 and a son of 13.

72) The household of Yang Daipei, aged 52, his Huang wife of 53, and their three children; two sons of 14 and 17 and a daughter of 20.

73) An older son of number 72; Yang Jianen, aged 22 whose 21-year old Wang wife and two-year old son were unregistered and so not recorded.

74) Yang Daihe, brother of number 72, aged 45, and his 39-year old Ma wife with three daughters and two sons. The eldest daughter

was 17 and the second 16 and both were a long way from home, studying in Chengdu, the provincial capital. Remaining were a son of 15 and one of 12, and a daughter of 9.

75) The Ma were incoming settlers in the village. Ma Jiankang, aged 37, lived with his widowed (surnamed Han) mother of 59 and his own Wang wife of 34 whose first husband, also a Ma, had died, leaving a young child as well as his own.

76) The family of the latter's brother Ma Jianqing, 32, his 29-year old Yang wife (from the 'O' lineage segment in Group One), and their two sons of 6 and 9.

77) The household of Yang Daisong, aged 52 and his Ma wife of 55. His father, now 86, lived with them, and the household also included a son of 14, a daughter of 17 who had in fact already married and moved out, and an older son of 24 with his own Xiong wife aged 25 and their two-year old daughter. Two of 77's other sons comprise the next two households:

78) Ma Jiaguan, or Jiayuan, 32, with his Zeng wife (Zhen Minggao's brother's daughter; see 65 & 55), a boy of 6 and girl of 8.

79) Ma Jiahua, aged 27 and his Wang wife of the same age with a son of 2 and a daughter of 5.

80) Another female-headed household; that of Huang Guoxiang, aged 64, whose husband, Yang Wanjin, had died.

81) the house of the latter's adopted son, Yang Daiyu, aged 43, his Li wife of 37, his son of 8 and daughter of 14. These two households were genuinely separated as they did not get on with each other.

82) the family of Wang Zhongyi, aged 48, and his Xiong wife of 39, still with five children; two daughters of 7 and 9, a son of 11, a daughter of 13 and a son of 15.

BIBLIOGRAPHY

Ahern, Emily 1981 *Chinese Ritual and Politics*. Cambridge: Cambridge University Press.

Aijmer, Goran 1968 'Being Caught by a Fishnet: On Fengshui in Southeastern China', *JHKBRAS* VIII.

Althusser, Louis 1965 *For Marx* (trans. Ben Brewster). London: Allen Lane.

Anagnost, Ann 1985 'The Beginning and End of an Emperor: A Counter-representation of the State', *Modern China* 11:2.

Antilla R 1972 *An Introduction to Historical and Comparative Linguistics*. London and New York: MacMillan.

Appadurai, Arjun 1990 'Disjunction and Difference in the Global World Economy', *Global Culture: Nationalism, Globalization and Modernity*, ed. Mike Featherstone. London: Sage Publications.

——1993 'The Production of Locality', *Counterworks*, ed. Richard Fardon. London and New York: Routledge.

Appiah, Anthony 1991 'Tolerable Falsehoods: Agency and the Interests of Theory', *Consequences of Theory*, ed. Jonathan Arac and Barbara Johnson. Baltimore, London: Johns Hopkins University Press.

Ardener, Edwin 1972 'Belief and the Problem of Woman', *Perceiving Women*, ed. Shirley Ardener. London: Dent.

Arnold, Mathew 1869;1971 *Culture and Anarchy* (ed. Dover Wilson). Cambridge: Cambridge University Press.

Auge, Marc (1979) 1982 *The Anthropological Circle: Symbol, Function, History*. Cambridge: EMSH and Cambridge University Press.

Bailey, F 1969;1980 *Stratagems and Spoils: A Social Anthropology of Politics*. Oxford: Basil Blackwell.

Baker, Hugh 1979 *Chinese Family and Kinship*. New York: Columbia University Press.

Bakhtin, M 1979 'Avtov i geroi vesteticheskoi deiatel'nosti' (Author and Hero in Aesthetic Activity', pp.7-180 of *M.M.Bakhtin: Estetika slovesnogo tvorchestva*. Moscow: Iskusstvo (in Gary Saul Morson and Caryl Emerson, *Mikhail Bakhtin: Creation of a Prosaics*. Stanford University Press, 1990).

Barth, Fredrick 1969 *Ethnic Groups and Boundaries*. Boston: Little, Brown.

Bartoli, M G 1925 *Introduzione alla Neolinguistica*. Geneva: Olschuki.

Baudrillard, Jean 1981 *Simulacra and Simulacrum* (trans. Sheila Glaser). Ann Arbor: University of Michigan Press.

Bell, Catharine 1989 'Religion and Chinese Culture: Towards an Assessment of 'Popular Religion', *History of Religions* 29:1.

Benedict, Paul K 1975 *Austro-Thai Language and Culture with a Glossary of Roots*. New Haven. Human Relations Area Files Press.

Bernstein, Basil 1975 *Class, Codes and Conduct*. London: Routledge Kegan Paul.

Bhabha, Homi K 1994 *The Location of Culture*. London and New York: Routledge.

Black, A 1986 'Gender and Cosmology in Chinese Correlative Thinking', *Gender and Religion*, ed. C Bynum, S. Harrell and P. Richman. Boston: Beacon Press.

Black, M 1962 *Models and Metaphors*. Ithaca: Cornell University Press.

Bloch, Ernst 1918 *Geist der Utopie*. Munich and Leipzig: Suhrkamp Verlag.

Bloch, Maurice 1977 'The Past and the Present in the Present', Malinowski Lecture, 7 December 1976, *Man* N.S. 12.

Bloch, Maurice 1985 'From Cognition to Ideology', *Power and Knowledge*: *Anthropological and Sociological Approaches*, ed. Richard Fardon. Edinburgh: Scottish Academic Press.

——1986 *From Blessing to Violence: History and Ideology in the Circumcision Ritual of the Merina of Madagascar*. Cambridge: Cambridge University Press.

——1987 'From Cognition to Ideology', *Power and Knowledge: Anthropological and Sociological Approaches*, ed. Richard Fardon. Edinburgh: Scottish Academic Press.

——1991 'Language, Anthropology, and Cognitive Science', *Man* N.S. 26:1.

——1992 *Prey into Hunter: The Politics of Religious Experience*. Cambridge: Cambridge University Press.

——1975 (ed.) *Political Language and Oratory in Traditional Society*. London and New York: The Academic Press.

Bourdieu, Pierre 1977 *Outline of a Theory of Practice* (trans. R. Nice). Cambridge: Cambridge University Press.

——1986 *Distinction: A Social Critique of the Judgement of Taste* (transl. Richard Nice). London & New York: Routledge & Kegan Paul.

Brummelhuis, Han, ten and Jeremey Kemp (eds) 1984 *Strategies and Structures in Thai Society*. Amsterdam: Anthropological-Sociological Centre, University of Amsterdam.

Butler, Judith 1990 *Gender Trouble: Feminism and the Subversion of Identity*. New York and London: Routledge.

——1993 *Bodies that Matter: On the Discursive Limits of 'Sex'*. New York, London: Routledge.

Chambers J and P Trudgill 1980 *Dialectology*. Cambridge: Cambridge University Press.

Cheung Siu-woo, Simon 1996 Subject and Representation: Identity Politics in Southeast Guizhou (Unpub. Ph.D. thesis), Seattle: University of Washington.

Chindasri, Nusit 1976 *The Religion of the Hmong Njua*. Bangkok: The Siam Society.

Chob Kacha-ananda 1972 'Le système de la famille Yao', *Journal of the Siam Society* 60:1.

Chodorow, Nancy 1974 'Family Structure and Feminine Personality', *Woman, Culture and Society*, ed. Michelle Rosaldo and Louise Lamphere. Stanford: Stanford University Press.

Chomsky, Noam 1957 *Reflections on Language*. Glasgow: Fontana.

——1966 *Cartesian Linguistics*. New York: Harper and Row.

——1971 *Selected Readings* (ed. J. Allen and Paul van Buren). London, New York, Toronto: Oxford University Press.

——1975 'On Innateness: A Reply to Cooper' *Philosophical Review* 84.

Christofferson, Gaye 1993 'Xinjiang and the Great Islamic Circle: The Impact of Transnational Forces on Chinese Regional Economic Planning', *China Quarterly* 133.

Clifford, James 1988 *The Predicament of Culture: Twentieth Century Ethnography, Literature and Art*. Harvard: Harvard University Press.

——1992 'Travelling Cultures', *Cultural Studies* I.

——and George Marcus (eds) 1986 *Writing Culture: The Poetics and Politics of Ethnography*. Berkeley, Los Angeles, London: University of California Press.

Cohen, Abner 1974 (ed.) *Urban Ethnicity* (ASA Mons.12). London, New York, Sydney, Toronto, Washington: Tavistock Press.

Cohen, Anthony 1982 (ed.) *Belonging: Identity and Social Organisation in British Rural Cultures*. Manchester: Manchester University Press.

Comaroff, John and Jean 1992 *Ethnography and the Historical Imagination*. Boulder, San Francisco, Oxford: Westview Press.

Cooper, Robert 1984 *Resource Scarcity and the Hmong Response: A Study of Settlement and Economy in Northern Thailand*. Singapore: Singapore University Press.

Croll, Elisabeth 1981 *The Politics of Marriage in Contemporary China*. Cambridge: Cambridge University Press.

Csordas, Thomas J 1994 *The Sacred Self: A Cultural Phenomenology of Charismatic Healing*. Berkeley, Los Angeles, London: University of California Press.

Culler, Jonathan 1988 *Framing the Sign: Criticism and its Institutions*. Oxford: Basil Blackwell.

——1997 *Literary Theory: A Very Short Introduction*. Oxford, New York: Oxford University Press.

Dang Nghiem Van 1993 'The Flood Myth and the Origin of Ethnic Groups in Southeast Asia', *Journal of American Folklore* 106(421):304-337.

De Certeau, Michel 1984 *The Practice of Everyday Life*. Berkeley, Los Angeles, London: University of California Press.

——1986 *Heterologies: Discourse on the Other* (trans. B. Massumi). Minneapolis: University of Minnesota Press.

Derrida, Jacques 1978 *Writing and Difference* (trans.A.Ross). Chicago: University of Chicago Press.

——1982 'White Mythology: Metaphor in the Text of Philosophy' in his *Margins of Philosophy*. Chicago and London: University of Chicago Press.

Dikotter, Frank 1992 *The Discourse of Race in Modern China*. London: C.Hurst & Co.

——1997 'Introduction', *The Construction of Racial Identities in China and Japan*, ed. Frank Dikotter. London: C. Hurst & Co.

Dodds, E R 1928 *The Greeks and the Irrational*. Oxford: Clarendon Press.

Doolittle, Justus 1895 *Social Life of the Chinese*. New York: Harper & Bros.

Downer, Gordon 1963 'Chinese, Thai, and Miao-Yao', *Linguistic Comparison in South East Asia*, ed. H. Shorto. London: School of Oriental and African Studies, University of London.

——1966 'Status of Loanwords in the Mien Dialect of Yao', *Asia Major* XVIII, Pt.1.

——1967 'Tone-change and Tone-shift in White Miao', *Bulletin of the School of Oriental and African Studies* XXX 3.

Dreyer, June 1968 'China's Minority Nationalities in the Cultural Revolution', *China Quarterly* 35.

——1976 *China's Forty Millions*. Cambridge: Harvard University Press.

Eagleton, Terry 1991 *Ideology: An Introduction*. London and New York: Verso Editions.

Eberhardt, Wolfram 1954 'Appendix' (Notes on the Connections of the Songs and Stories of the Ch'uan Miao with Chinese Folktales') to DC Graham, *Songs and Stories of the Ch'uan Miao* (Misc.Coll.123). Washington: The Smithsonian Institute.

Ebrey, Patricia 1996 'Surnames and Han Chinese Identity', *Negotiating Ethnicities in China and Taiwan*, ed. Melissa Brown. Berkeley. Institute of East Asian Studies, University of California.

Eco, Umberto 1992 *Interpretation and Overinterpretation*. Cambridge, New York and Melbourne: Cambridge University Press.

Elias, Norbert 1982 *The Civilizing Process: The History of Manners*. Oxford: Basil Blackwell.

Embree, John 1950 'Thailand—a Loosely Structured Social System', *American Anthropologist* 52.

Endicott, Stephen 1988 *Red Earth—Revolution in a Sichuan Village*. London. L.B.Tauris & Co.

Fan Wenlan 1958 Zi Han qi zhongguo cheng wei yige tongyi guojia de yuanyin. In *Han minzu xingcheng wenti taoluan*, by Fan Wenlan et.al. Beijing: sanlian shudian.(Lishi yanjiu 3 1953).

Fardon, Richard (ed.) 1990 *Localizing Strategies: Regional Traditions of Ethnographic Writing*. Edinburgh and Washington: Scottish Academic Press and Smithsonian Institute Press.

Faure, David 1988 (1990) 'The Man the Emperor Decapitated', *JHKBRAS* 28.

Faure, David and Helen Siu 1995 (ed.) *Down to Earth: The Territorial Bond in South China*. Stanford: Stanford University Press.

Fei, Xiaotong 1953 *China's Gentry: Essays in Rural-Urban Relations*. Chicago and London: University of Chicago Press.

——1981 *Towards a People's Anthropology*. Beijing: New World Press.

——1988 'Plurality and Configuration in the Configuration of the Chinese People', 15 November, Tanner Lecture, The Chinese University of Hong Kong.

——1991 'Zhonghua minzu yanjiu xintansuo', *Zhonghua minzu yanjiu xintansuo*, ed. Fei Xiaotong et.al. Beijing: Zhongguo shehui kexue chubanshe.

Fentress, James and Chris Wickham 1992 *Social Memory*. Oxford and Cambridge, MA: Basil Blackwell.

Feuchtwang, Stephan 1974 *An Anthropological Analysis of Chinese Geomancy*. Vientiane: Vithagna Press.

——1975 'Investigating Religion', *Marxist Analyses and Social Anthropology*, ed. Maurice Bloch (ASA Studies 3). London: Malaby Press.

——1991 'A Chinese Religion Exists', *An Old State in New Settings*, ed. Hugh Baker and Stephan Feuchtwang. Oxford: JASO.

——1992 *The Imperial Metaphor: Popular Religion in China*. Routledge: London and New York.

Firth, Raymond 1964 'Social Organization and Social Change' in his *Essays on Social Organization*. London: University of London Press.

Fitzgerald, C P 1935 *China: A Short Cultural History*. London: The Cresset Press.

——1941 *The Tower of Five Glories: A Study of the Min Chia of Ta Li, Yunnan*. London: The Cresset Press.

——1972 *The Southern Expansion of the Chinese Peoples*. London: Barrie & Jenkins.

Flower, John, and Pamela Leonard 1996 'Community Values and State Co-optation: Civil Society in the Sichuan Countryside', *Civil Society: Challenging Western Models*, ed. Chris Hann and Elizabeth Dunn. London and New York: Routledge.

Forbes, Andrew 1987 'The "Cin-Ho" (Yunnanese Chinese) Caravan Trade with North Thailand during the Late Nineteenth and Early Twentieth Centuries', *Journal of Asian History* 21: 1.

Foucault, Michel 1967 *Madness and Civilisation: A History of Insanity in the Age of Reason*. London: Tavistock.

Freedman, Maurice 1958 *Lineage Organisation in Southeastern China*. London: The Athlone Press.

——1966 *Chinese Lineage and Society*. London: The Athlone Press.

——1968 'Geomancy' (Presidential Address), *Journal of the Royal Anthropological Institute*, 1969.

Freeman, Derek 1983 *Margaret Mead and Samoa: The Making and Unmaking of an Anthropological Myth*. Middlesex: Penguin Books.

Friedman, Jonathan 1975 'Tribes, States and Transformations', *Marxist Analyses and Social Anthropology*, ed. Maurice Bloch (ASA Studies 3). London: Malaby Press.

——1990 'Being in the World: Globalization and Localization', *Global Culture: Nationalism, Globalization and Modernity*, ed. Mike Featherstone. London, California, New Delhi: Sage Publications.

——1992 'Narcissism, Roots and Postmodernity: The Constitution of Selfhood in the Global Crisis', *Modernity and Identity*, ed. Scott Lash and Jonathan Friedman. Oxford: Blackwell Books.

——1998 *System, Structure and Contradiction: The Evolution of Asiatic Social Formations*. Copenhagen: AltaMira Press, Sage Publications.

Gadamer, Hans-Georg 1984 'The Hermeneutics of Suspicion', *Hermeneutics: Questions and Answers*, ed. Gary Shapiro and Alan Sica. Amherst: University of Massachussetts Press.

Geddes, William R 1976 *Migrants of the Mountains: The Cultural Ecology of the Blue Miao (Hmong Njua) of Thailand*. Oxford: The Clarendon Press.

Geertz, Clifford 1983 *Local Knowledge: Further Essays in Interpretive Anthropology*. New York: Basic Books.

Giddens, Anthony 1971 *Capitalism and Modern Social Theory*. Cambridge: Cambridge University Press.

——1976 *New Rules of Sociological Method: A Positive Critique of Interpretative Sociologies*. London: Hutchinson.

——1984 'Hermeneutics and Social Theory', *Hermeneutics: Questions and Answers*, ed. Gary Shapiro and Alan Sica. Amherst: University of Massachussetts Press.

Gilligan C 1982 *In a Different Voice: Psychological Theory and Women's Development*. Cambridge MA: Harvard University Press.

Ginzburg Carlo 1980 *The Cheese and the Worms: The Cosmos of a Sixteenth Century Miller*. Baltimore: Johns Hopkins University Press.

Gladney, Dru 1991 *Muslim Chinese: Ethnic Nationalism in the Peoples' Republic*. Harvard: Council on East Asian Studies, Harvard University.

Godelier, Maurice 1986 *The Mental and the Material*. Bristol: Verso.

Gongxian Miaozu minjian gushiji, ed. Fan Zhongchen et al. (transl. Xiong Xiangmo). 1989. Gongxian: Gongxian minsu shiwu weiyuanhui.

Goody, Jack 1973 'Bridewealth and Dowry in Africa and Eurasia', *Bridewealth and Dowry*, ed. J. Goody and Stanley Tambiah. Cambridge: Cambridge University Press.

——1987 *The Interface between the Written and the Oral*. Cambridge: Cambridge University Press.

Graham, David Crockett 1937 'Ceremonies of the Ch'uan Miao', *Journal of the West China Border Research Society* 9.

——1954 *Songs and Stories of the Ch'uan Miao* (Misc.Coll.123). Washington: The Smithsonian Institute.

Gramsci A 1971 *Selections from Prison Notebooks*, ed. Quentin Hoare and Geoffrey Smith. London: Lawrence and Wishart.

Granet M 1930 *Chinese Civilization*. London: Kegan Paul.

Greimas 1966 *La semantique structurale*. Paris: Larousse.

Guha, R 1982 (ed.) *Subaltern Studies I*. Delhi: Oxford University Press.

Habermas, Jurgen 1988 *Legitimation Crisis*. Cambridge: Polity Press.

——1989 *The Structural Transformation of the Public Sphere*. Cambridge, MA: MIT Press.

Hall, Stuart 1997 (ed.) *Representation: Cultural Representations and Signifying Practices*. London, California, New Delhi: The Open University, Sage Publications.

——and Tony Jefferson (eds) 1976 *Resistance through Rituals: Youth Subcultures in Post-war Britain*. London, Melbourne, Sydney: Hutchinson.

Hann, Chris and Elizabeth Dunn 1996 (ed.) *Civil Society: Challenging Western Models*. London and New York: Routledge.

Harrell, Stevan 1989 'Ethnicity and Kin Terms among Two Kinds of Yi', *Ethnicity and Ethnic Groups in China*, ed. Chien Chiao and Nicholas Tapp. Hong Kong: New Asia College, The Chinese University of Hong Kong.

——(ed.) 1995 *Cultural Encounters on China's Ethnic Frontiers*. (Studies on Ethnic Groups in China). Seattle and London: University of Washington Press.

Harrell, Stevan and Sara Dickey 1985 'Dowry Systems in Complex Societies', *Ethnology* 105-120.

Hebdige, Dick 1979 *Subculture: The Meaning of Style*. London and New York: Methuen

Heberer, Thomas 1989 *China and its National Minorities: Autonomy or Assimilation?* New York and London: M.E. Sharpe & Co.

Heimbach, E 1979 *White Hmong-English Dictionary* (Data Paper 75). Ithaca: Southeast Asia Programme, Cornell University.

Hertz, Robert 1973 'The Pre-Eminence of the Right Hand: A Study in Religion and Polarity', *Right and Left: Essays on Dual Symbolic Classification* , trans. and ed. by Rodney Needham. Illinois: University of Chicago Press.

Hill, Anne 1982 Familiar Strangers: The Yunnanese Chinese in Northern Thailand (Unpub.Ph.D. thesis), University of Illinois at Urbana-Champage.

Hinton, Peter 1969 (ed.) *Tribesmen and Peasants in North Thailand*. Chiangmai: Tribal Research Centre.

Hobart, Mark 1982 'Meaning or Moaning? An Ethnographic Note on a Little Understood Tribe', *Semantic Anthropology*, ed. David Parkin. London, New York: Academic Press.

——1985 'Texte est un con', *Contexts and Levels: Anthropological Essays on Hierarchy*, ed. R.H. Barnes, Daniel de Coppet, R.J. Parkin. Oxford: JASO.

——1986 'Thinker, Thespian, Soldier, Slave? Assumptions about Human Nature in the Study of Balinese Society', *Context, Meaning and Power in Southeast Asia*, ed. Mark Hobart and Robert Taylor. Ithaca: Cornell Southeast Asia Project.

Hobsbawm, Eric 1990 *Nations and Nationalism since 1780: Programme, Myth, Reality*. Cambridge: Cambridge University Press.

Holy, Ladislav and Milan Stuchlik 1983 *Actions, Norms, Representations: Foundations of Anthropological Inquiry*. Cambridge: Cambridge University Press.

Hsieh Jiann 1986 'China's Nationalities Policy: Its Development and Problems'. *Anthropos* 81.

Hughes-Freeland, Felicia 1991 'Classification and Communication in Javanese Palace Performance'. *Visual Anthropology* 4.

Hutheesing, Othome 1990 *Emerging Sexual Inequality among the Lisu of Northern Thailand: The Waning of Dog and Elephant Repute.* Leiden, New York, Kobenhavn, Köln: E.J.Brill.

Jankowiak, William R. 1993 *Sex, Death and Hierarchy in a Chinese City: An Anthropological Account.* New York: Columbia University Press.

Jenks, Robert D 1994 *Insurgency and Social Disorder in Guizhou: The 'Miao' Rebellion, 1854-1875.* Honolulu: University of Hawaii Press.

Johnson, Charles 1985 (ed.) *Myths, Legends and Folk Tales from the Hmong of Laos.* St. Paul: Linguistics Department, Macalister College.

Johnson, David 1985 'Communication, Class and Consciousness in Late Imperial China', *Popular Culture in Late Imperial China*, ed. David Johnson, Andrew Nathan and Evelyn Rawski. Berkeley: University of California Presss.

Kandre, Peter 1967 'Autonomy and Integration of Social Systems: The Iu Mien ("Yao" or "Man") Mountain Population and their Neighbours', *Southeast Asian Tribes, Minorities and Nations*, ed. Peter Kunstadter. Princeton: Princeton University Press.

Kelly, Raymond 1974 *Etero Social Structure: A Study in Structural Contradiction.* Ann Arbor: University of Michigan Press.

Keyes, Charles F 1977 *The Golden Peninsula: Culture and Adaptation in Mainland Southeast Asia.* New York: MacMillan.

——1978 'Towards a New Formulation of the Concept of Ethnic Group', *Ethnicity* 3:202-12.

——1987 *Thailand: Buddhist Kingdom as Modern Nation-state.* Boulder and London: Westview Press.

Kroeber, A L 1958 'Miao and Chinese Kin Logic', *Bulletin of the Institute of History and Philology*, Academia Sinica XXIX.

Kunstadter, Peter 1983 'Highland Populations in Northern Thailand', *Highlanders of Thailand* (ed.) John McKinnon and Wanat Bhrukrasri. Kuala Lumpur, Oxford, New York, Melbourne: Oxford University Press.

Leach, Edmund 1954 *Political Systems of Highland Burma: A Study of Kachin Social Structures.* London: The Athlone Press.

——1960 *Rethinking Anthropology.* London: The Athlone Press.

——1982 *Social Anthropology.* Glasgow: Fontana Press.

Lehman, F K 1979 'Who are the Karen and If So, Why? Karen Ethnohistory and a Formal Theory of Ethnicity', *Ethnic Adaptation and Identity: The Karen on the Thai Frontier with Burma*, ed. Charles Keyes. Philadelphia: Institute for the Study of Human Issues.

Lemoine, Jacques 1972a *Un village Hmong vert du Haut Laos: milieu technique et organisation sociale.* Paris: CNRS.

——1972b 'L'Initiation du mort chez les Hmong', *L'Homme* XII 1-3.

——1972c 'Un curieux point d'histoire: l'aventure aventure des Mien', *Langues et techniques, nature et société* (II), ed. Jacqueline Thomas and Louis Bernot. Paris: Musée de l'Homme.

——1978 'Les ethnies non Han de la Chine', *Ethnologie Regionale II, Encyclopaedie des Pleiades*, ed.J. Poirier. Paris: Musée de l'Homme.

——1982 *Yao Ceremonial Paintings.* Bangkok: White Lotus.

——1983 'Yao Religion and Society', *Highlanders of Thailand*, ed. Wanat Bhrukrasri and John McKinnon. Kuala Lumpir: Oxford University Press.

Lemoine, Jacques 1986 'Shamanism in the Context of Hmong Resettlement', *The Hmong in Transition*, ed. Glenn Hendricks, Bruce Downing and Amos Deinard. New York: Center for Migration Studies.

——1987 *Entre la maladie et la mort: le chamane Hmong sur les Chemins de l'Au-dela*. Bangkok and Paris: Pandora.

——1989 Ethnologues en Chine, *Diogène* 133.

——1996 'The Constitution of a Hmong Shaman's Power of Healing and Folk Culture'. *Shaman* 4, 1-2.

——and Maurice Eisenbruch 1997 'L'exercice du pouvoir de guerison chez les chamanes Hmong et les maitres-guerisseurs khmers d'Indochine', *L'Homme* 144, 69-103.

Lévi-Strauss, Claude 1948:1969 *The Elementary Structures of Kinship*. Boston: Beacon Press.

——1976 'The Scope of Anthropology' in his *Structural Anthropology* II. Middlesex, New York: Penguin Books.

Levy-Bruhl, Lucien 1922 (1923) *La mentalité primitive (Primitive Mentality)* (trans. Peter Riviere (1975), Oxford: Blackwell). Paris: Alcan.

Liang Zuwu 1950 'Miao-Yi Minzu Fazhanshi': *Minzu Yanjiu Cankao Ziliao*, ed. Guizhousheng Minzu Yanjiusuo, vol.11. Guizhou.

Lin Yueh-hwa 1948 *The Golden Wing: A Sociological Study of Chinese Familism*. London: Institute of Pacific Relations.

Ling Shun-sheng and Ruey Yih-Fu 1947 *Xiangxi Miaozu Diaocha Baogao (A Report on an Investigation of the Miao of Western Hunan)* (trans. Human Relations Area Files 1963), (Monograph Series A, No.18), Shanghai: The Institute of History and Philology, Academia Sinica.

Liu Li 1998 The Influence of Fengshui on the Building of the City of Beijing in the Ming Dynasty (1368-1644), Unpub. Ph.D. thesis, Department of Architecture, University of Edinburgh.

Liu Tik-sang 1995 Becoming Marginal: A Fluid Community and Shamanism in the Pearl River Delta of South China. Unpublished Ph.D. thesis, University of Pittsburgh.

Liu Xin 1998 'Yao: The Practice of Everyday Space in Northern Rural Shaanxi', *Landscape, Culture and Power in Chinese Society*, ed. Wen-hsin Yeh. China Research Monographs No.49. Berkeley, California: Institute of East Asian Studies, University of California at Berkeley.

Lombard-Salmon, C 1972 *Un exemple d'acculturation Chinoise: la Province du Gui Zhou au XVIII siècle*. Paris: EFEO.

Lukes, Steven 1973 *Individualism*. Oxford: Basil Blackwell.

Lyman, Thomas 1970 *English-Meo Pocket Dictionary*. Bangkok: The Goethe Institute.

Lyotard, Jean-Francois 1979 *The Postmodern Condition: A Report on Knowledge*. Manchester: Manchester University Press.

McCoy, Alfred 1972 *The Politics of Heroin in Southeast Asia*. New York: Harper and Row.

Mackerras, Colin 1995 *China's Minority Cultures: Identities and Integration since 1912*. Sydney: Longmans.

Marcus, George and Michael Fisher 1986 *Anthropology as Cultural Critique: An Experimental Moment in the Human Sciences*. Chicago and London: University of Chicago Press.

Marriot, M 1955:1969 *Village India: Studies in the Little Community*. Chicago: University of Chicago Press.

Merleau-Ponty, Maurice 1962 *The Phenomenology of Perception*. London and New York: Routledge and Kegan Paul.
——1964 *Sense and Non-Sense* (trans.Hubert and Patricia Dreyfus). Illinois: Northwestern University Press.
Michaels, Walter Benn 1980 'The Interpreter's Self: Peirce on the Cartesian "Subject"', *Reader-Response Criticism*, ed. Jane Tompkins. Baltimore: Johns Hopkins University Press.
Miles, Douglas 1972 'Land, Labour and Kin Groups among Southeast Asian Shifting Cultivators', *Mankind* 8.
——1976 'Prophylactic Medicine and Kin Unit among Yao Ancestor Worshippers', *Ancestors*, ed. William Nevel. The Hague: Mouton.
——1989 'Capitalism and the Structure of Descent Units in China and Thailand: A Comparison of Youling (1938) and Pulangka (1968)', *The Hong Kong Anthropology Bulletin* III.
Moerman, Michael 1965 'Ethnic Identification in a Complex Civilization: Who are the Lue?' *American Anthropologist* 67.
——1968 'Being Lue: Uses and Abuses of Ethnic Unit Identification'. *Essays on the Problem of Tribe*, ed. J. Helm. Seattle: University of Washington.
Morechand, Guy 1968 'Le chamanisme des Hmong', *BEFEO* LXIV.
Moseley, G 1965 'China's Fresh Approach to the National Minorities Problem', *China Quarterly* 24.
——1973 *The Consolidation of the South China Frontier*. Berkeley: University of California Press.
Mottin, Jean 1980 *The History of the Hmong (Meo)*. Bangkok: Odeon Store Ltd.
——n.d. *Contes et Legendes Hmong Blanc*. Bangkok: Don Bosco Press.
Mueggler, Erik 1997 Specters of Power: Ritual and Politics in a Yi Community. Unpub. Ph.D. dissertation. Baltimore, Maryland: Johns Hopkins University.
Murdoch, Iris 1992 *Metaphysics as a Guide to Morals*. Harmondsworth: Chatto and Windus.
Murdock, George P 1964 'Genetic Classification of the Austronesian Language: A Key to Oceanic Culture History', *Ethnology* 3.
Nietzsche, Friedrich 1887:1956 *The Birth of Tragedy and the Genealogy of Morals*. New York: Doubleday and Co.
Obeyesekere, Gananath 1968 'Theodicy, Sin and Salvation in a Sociology of Buddhism', *Dialectic in Practical Religion*, ed. Edmund Leach. Cambridge: Cambridge University Press.
Ogden, C K and I A Richards 1923 *The Meaning of Meaning*. London: Routledge and Kegan Paul.
Parish, W and Martin Whyte 1978 *Village and Family in Contemporary China*. Chicago: University of Chicago Press.
Pease, Donald 1991 'Towards a Sociology of Literary Knowledge: Greenblatt, Colonialism and the New Historicism', *Consequences of Theory*, ed. Jonathan Arac and Barbara Johnson. Baltimore and London: Johns Hopkins University Press.
Petyt, K 1980 *The Study of Dialect: An Intoduction to Dialectology*. London: Andre Deutsch.
Pollard, Samuel 1919 *The Story of the Miao*. London: Henry Hooks.
Potter, J and S 1990 *China's Peasants: The Anthropology of a Revolution*. Cambridge: Cambridge University Press.
Pye, Lucien 1990 'China: Erratic State, Frustrated Society'. *Foreign Affairs* 69:4.

Pye, Lucien 1991 'The Challenge of Modernization to the Chinese National Identity', Wei Lun Lecture, 9 January, The Chinese University of Hong Kong.

Richards, I A. 1924 *Principles of Literary Criticism*. London: Routledge and Kegan Paul.

Ricoeur, Paul 1971 'The Model of the Text: Meaningful Action Considered as a Text', *Social Research* 38.

——1986 *Lectures on Ideology and Utopia*, ed. G. Taylor. New York: Columbia University Press.

Rorty, Richard 1991 *Objectivity, Relativism and Truth*.(Philosophical Papers Vol. I). Cambridge, New York, Melbourne: Cambridge University Press.

Roxborough, Ian 1979 *Theories of Underdevelopment*. London and Basingstoke. MacMillan.

Ruey Yih-Fu 1958 'Terminological Structure of the Miao Kinship System'. *Academia Sinica* XXIV.

——1960 'The Magpie Miao of Southern Szechuan', *Social Structure in Southeast Asia*, ed. George Murdock. Chicago: Quadrangle Books.

Sahlins, Marshall 1985 *Islands of History*. Chicago and London: University of Chicago Press.

Said, Edward 1978 *Orientalism*. London: Routledge Kegan Paul.

Sallnow, Michael 1989 'Cooperation and Contradiction: The Dialectcs of Everyday Practice', *Dialectical Anthropology* 14.

Sangren, Steven 1984 'Traditional Chinese Corporations: Beyond Kinship', *Journal of Asian Studies* 43 4.

Sapir, Edward 1913:1916 'Time Perspective in Aboriginal American Culture: A Study in Method', Memoirs of the Canadian Department of Mines, Geological Survey 90, in *Selected Writings of Edward Sapir in Language, Culture and Personality*, ed. D. Mandelbaum. California: University of California Press (1968).

Sautman, Barry 1990 Retreat from Revolution: Why Communist Systems Deradicalize. Unpub. Ph.D. thesis. Columbia University.

——1998 'Preferential Policies for Ethnic Minorities in China: The Case of Xinjiang', *Nationalism and Ethnoregional Identities in China*, ed. William Safran. London and Portland: Frank Cass.

Savina, F 1924:1930 *Histoire des Miao*. Hong Kong: Société des Missions Etrangères.

Schafer, E H 1969 *The Vermilion Bird: T'ang Images of the South*. Berkeley: University of California Press.

Schein, Louisa 1993 Popular Culture and the Production of Difference: The Miao and China. Unpub. Ph.D. thesis. Berkeley: University of California Press.

——1998 'Importing Hmong Brethren to Hmong America: A Not-So-Stateless Transnationalism', *Cosmopolitics: Thinking and Feeling beyond the Nation*, ed. Pheng Cheah, Bruce Robbins. Minneapolis and London: University of Minnesota Press.

Scott, James C 1985 *Weapons of the Weak: Everyday Forms of Peasant Resistance*. New Haven and London: Yale University Press.

Shepherd, David 1989 'Bakhtin and the Reader', *Bakhtin and Cultural Theory*, ed. Ken Hirschkop and David Shepherd. Manchester: Manchester University Press.

Shepherd, John 1993 *Statecraft and Poltical Economy on the Taiwan Frontier 1600-1800*. Stanford: Stanford University Press.

Shi Qigui 1986 *Xiangxi Miaozu Shidi Diaocha Baogao (Field Research Report on the Miao Nationality in West Hunan)*, Changsha: Hunan Renmin Chubanshe.

Shue, Vivienne 1988 *The Reach of the State: Sketches of the Chinese Body Politic*. California: Stanford University Press.

Siu, Helen 1989a *Agents and Victims in South China: Accomplices in Rural Revolution*. New Haven and London: Yale University Press.

——1989b 'Recycling Rituals: Politics and Popular Culture in Contemporary Rural China', *Unofficial China: Popular Culture and Thought in the People's Republic*, ed. Perry Link, Richard Madson, Paul Pickowicz. Boulder and London: Westview Press.

Skinner, George 1964-5 'Marketing and Social Structure in Rural China', *Journal of Asian Studies* (1-3).

Skorupski, John 1978 'The Meaning of Another Culture's Beliefs', *Action and Interpretation: Studies in the Philosophy of the Social Sciences*, ed. Christopher Hookway and Philip Pettit. London, Cambridge, New York, Melbourne: Cambridge University Press.

Smart, J J C and Bernard Williams 1973 *Utilitarianism For and Against*. Cambridge: Cambridge University Press.

Spence, Jonathan 1990 *The Search for Modern China*. New York and London: Norton and Co.

Spencer, Jonathan 1997 'Post-colonialism and the Political Imagination', *Journal of the Royal Anthropological Institute* 3:1.

Sperber, Dan 1975 *Rethinking Symbolism*. Cambridge: Cambridge University Press.

——1985 *On Anthropological Knowledge*. Cambridge: EMSH and Cambridge University Press.

Srinivas, M N 1952 *Religion and Society among the Coorgs of South India*. Oxford: Clarendon Press.

Stafford, Charles 1993 'The Discourse of Race in Modern China', *Man: The Journal of the Royal Anthropological Institute* 28:3.

Stalin, Joseph 1913 *Marxism and the National Question*. Moscow: Foreign Language Press.

——1929 'The National Question and Leninism' in his *Works*. Moscow: Foreign Languages Press.

Steiner, George 1975 *After Babel: Aspects of Language and Translation*. Oxford: Oxford University Press.

Stewart, Susan 1993 *On Longing: Narratives of the Miniature, the Gigantic, the Souvenir, the Collection*. Durham and London. Duke University Press.

Stocking, George 1987 *Victorian Anthropology*. New York: The Free Press, MacMillan Inc.

Strathern, Marilyn (ed.) 1995 *Shifting Contexts: Transformations in Anthropological Knowledge*. London: Routledge.

Tambiah, Stanley 1990 *Magic, Science, Religion and the Scope of Rationality*. Cambridge: Cambridge University Press.

Tanaka, Matsui 1991 *Patrons, Devotees and Goddesses: Ritual and Power among the Tamil Fishermen of Sri Lanka*. Kyoto: Institute for Research in Humanities, Kyoto University.

Tapp, Nicholas 1985 Categories of Change and Continuity among the White Hmong (Hmoob Dawb) of Northern Thailand. Unpub.Ph.D. thesis. London: University of London.

——1988 'The Minorities of Southern China: A General Overview', *Journal of the Hong Kong Branch of the Royal Asiatic Society*, Vol.26, 1986.

——1989 *Sovereignty and Rebellion: The White Hmong of Northern Thailand*. Singapore, Oxford, New York: Oxford University Press.

Tapp, Nicholas 1990 'Milieu and Context: The Disappearance of the White Hmong', *Proceedings of the 4th. International Conference on Thai Studies, 11-13 May 1990* (Vol.III). Kunming: Institute of Southeast Asian Studies.

——1995 'Minority Nationality in China: Policy and Practice', *Indigenous Peoples of Asia*, ed. R. H. Barnes, Andrew Gray and Benedict Kingsbury (Mon. and Occ.Pap.No.48). Ann Arbor: Association for Asian Studies Inc.

——1996 'The Kings who Could Fly without their Heads: "Local" Culture in China and the Case of the Hmong', *Unity and Diversity: Local Cultures and Identities in China*, ed. Tao Tao Liu and David Faure. Hong Kong: Hong Kong University Press.

——1999 'The Consuming or Consumed? Virtual Hmong in China', paper presented in the London China Seminar, School of Oriental and African Studies, London, 19 February.

Taussig, Michael 1980 *The Devil and Commodity Fetishism in South America*. Chapel Hill: University of North Carolina Press.

——1987 *Shamanism, Colonialism and the Wild Man: A Study in Terror and Healing*. Chicago and London: University of Chicago Press.

Taylor, Charles 1993 'To Follow a Rule...', *Bourdieu: Critical Perspectives*, ed. Craig Calhoun, Edward LiPuma, Moishe Postone. London: Polity Press in association with Basil Blackwell.

——1995 *Philosophical Arguments*. Cambridge, MA and London: Harvard University Press.

Thierry, F 1989 'Empire and Minority in China', *Minority People in the Age of Nation-States*, ed. Georges Chaliand. London: Pluto Press.

Thomas, Keith 1971 *Religion and the Decline of Magic*. New York: Scribners.

Thompson, John 1990 *Ideology and Modern Culture: Critical Social Theory in the Era of Mass Communications*. Cambridge: Polity Press in association with Blackwell Publications.

Thoraval, Joel 1990 'Le concept Chinois du Nation—est-il "obscur"? A propos du débat sur la notion de "Minzu" dans les années 1980', *Bulletin de Sinologie* 65 (mars 1990):24-41. Hong Kong: CEFC.

Tompkins, Jane 1980 *Reader-Response Criticism: From Formalism to Post-Structuralism*. Baltimore: Johns Hopkins University Press.

Turton, Andrew and Shigeharu Tanabe 1984 (ed.) *History and Peasant Consciousness in South East Asia* (Senri Ethnological Studies 13). Osaka: National Museum of Ethnology.

Wakeman, Frederick 1975 *The Fall of Imperial China*. New York: The Free Press.

——1977 'Rebellion and Revolution: The Study of Popular Movements in Chinese History', *Journal of Asian Studies*.XXXVI: 2.

Ward, Barbara 1965 'Varieties of the Conscious Model: The Fishermen of South China', *The Relevance of Models for Social Anthropology*, ed. Michael Banton. London: Tavistock.

Watson, James L. 1982 'Chinese Kinship Reconsidered: Anthropological Perspectives on Historical Research'. *China Quarterly* 92.

——1986 'Anthropological Overview of the Development of Chinese Descent Groups', *Kinship Organization in Late Imperial China*, ed. P. Ebrey and James L Watson. Berkeley: University of California Press.

——1991 'Waking the Dragon: Visions of the Chinese Imperial State in Local Myth', *An Old State in New Settings*, ed. Hugh Baker and Stephan Feuchtwang. Oxford: JASO.

Watson, Ruby 1985 *Inequality among Brothers*: *Class and Kinship in South China*. Cambridge: Cambridge University Press.

Wei Mingjing 1956 'Lun minzu de dingyi ji minzu de shizhi' in Fan Wenlan et.al (ed.). *Han minzu xingcheng wenti taoluan*. Beijing: sanlian shudian.

Wiens, H. 1954;1970 *China's March into the Tropics*: *Han Chinese Expansion in Southern China*. New York: Shoestring Press.

Wolf, Eric 1982 *Europe and the People without History*. Berkeley and Los Angeles: University of California Press.

Worsley, Peter 1968 *The Trumpet Shall Sound*. London: MacGibbon Kee.

Wu Bingan 1989 *Shenmi de Saman Shijie*. Shanghai. Shanghai Branch Press.

Yang C K 1954:1961 *Religion in Chinese Society*. Berkeley: University of California Press.

Yang Hanxian 1947 *Qianzi Miaozu Diaocha Baogao*.Guiyang: Guizhou Minzu Chubanshe.

Yang M 1994 *Gifts, Favours and Banquets*: *The Art of Social Relationships in China*. Ithaca, New York: Cornell University Press.

INDEX

acculturation, 20, 28, 33, 61
actor, rational, 51
affinal, 218, 220, 273, 276, 277, 313,
317
  connections, 221
  relations, 202, 218, 223
affinity, 32
agency, 37, 43, 45, 47, 48, 49, 52, 53,
55, 56, 57, 60, 61, 359, 360, 361, 383,
418, 420, 421, 422, 427, 428, 430.
See discourse
ancestor, 12, 15, 23, 34, 37, 45, 270,
271, 276, 284, 297, 302, 303, 304,
305, 314, 316
ancestral, 12, 114, 131, 149, 152, 187,
240, 284, 304, 311, 314
  altar, 77, 131, 161, 171, 194, 284,
305, 311, 312, 313
  descent, 149
  Father, 13
  grave, 164
  hall, 77, 241, 249, 259, 273, 313
  house-posts, 76
  Mother, 13
  rituals, 190, 196, 197
  spirits, 161, 162, 172, 191, 292, 297,
303, 313, 314
  worship, 187, 190, 190-200, 197, 273
archaic, 3, 40, 41, 45, 101, 108, 110,
114
army, 11, 232
Arnold, Mathew, 40, 358
assimilation, 20, 33. *See* acculturation
avalanche, 228

bamboo, 75-77, 93, 290
banquet, 270
Bartoli, 114
Baudrillard, Jean, 19
Beijing, 66, 231, 232, 234, 235, 243,
332
  massacre, 66
Bell, Catharine, 38, 39
Benedict, Paul K, 9
Bloch, 357, 359, 360, 361, 369
Bo, 68, 69, 144, 326-29, 331
Bourdieu, Pierre, 39, 40

bourgeoisie, 22, 40
bride, 270, 271, 272, 274, 278, 279,
280, 282-86, 288, 289, 290, 291, 292,
293, 295, 297, 298, 300-10, 312-25
  groom, 212, 271, 272, 274, 278, 280,
289, 292, 297, 298, 300, 301, 305,
310, 317, 318, 320, 321
  wealth, 274, 275, 282, 309, 310, 325
Buddhism, 8, 23, 43
Buddhist, 417
bureaucracy, 8, 14, 17, 19, 22, 25, 26,
94, 95, 96
Burma, 4, 7, 28, 43
Butler, Judith, 44, 47, 50

cadres, 26, 198
calendar, 82
capitalism, 28, 29, 30, 37, 38, 53
  accumulation, 44
  formations, 30
  forms of production, 19
  forms of social organisation, 29
  nations, 30
  societies, 29
Cartesian mentalism, 56
  model, 55
  opposition, 49
Cassirer, 352
central hall, 324
Cézanne, 59, 352, 426
chauvinism, 33, 34
Chengdu, 66, 70, 73, 81, 95, 96, 97, 101
Chenshi, 102, 105, 107
Cheung Siu-Woo, 198
Cheung, Simon, 32
Chiangmai, 14
China, 4, 10, 12, 13, 20, 24, 27, 65, 66,
67, 72, , 369, 378, 403, 407, 408, 411,
419
  south, 77
Chinese, 3, 8, 9, 10, 12, 13, 14, 15, 17,
18, 19, 20, 21, 22, 24, 25, 28-34, 36,
37, 39, 40, 41, 43, 45, 47, 52, 53, 55,
57, 59, 60, 67-71, 73, 75, 77, 81, 84,
95, 96, 98, 116, 117, 201-05, 210,
211, 218, 226, 230, 231, 232, 235,
237, 239, 240, 242, 246, 249, 250,

ABBREVIATIONS

CCP   Chinese Communist Party

CIA   Central Investigation Agency

KMT   Guomindang

PLA   People's Liberation Army

B   Brother

Z   Sister

H   Husband

W   Wife

F   Father

M   Mother

D   Daughter

S   Son

ILLUSTRATIONS

1: The village

2: A farmer's house

3: A poor man's house

4: Mixing flour outside the house

5: Spinning hemp

6: Raking sun-dried millet

7: Preparing the dry fields

8: Building the Party Vice-Secretary's house

9: A Chinese style altar

10: An ordinary altar

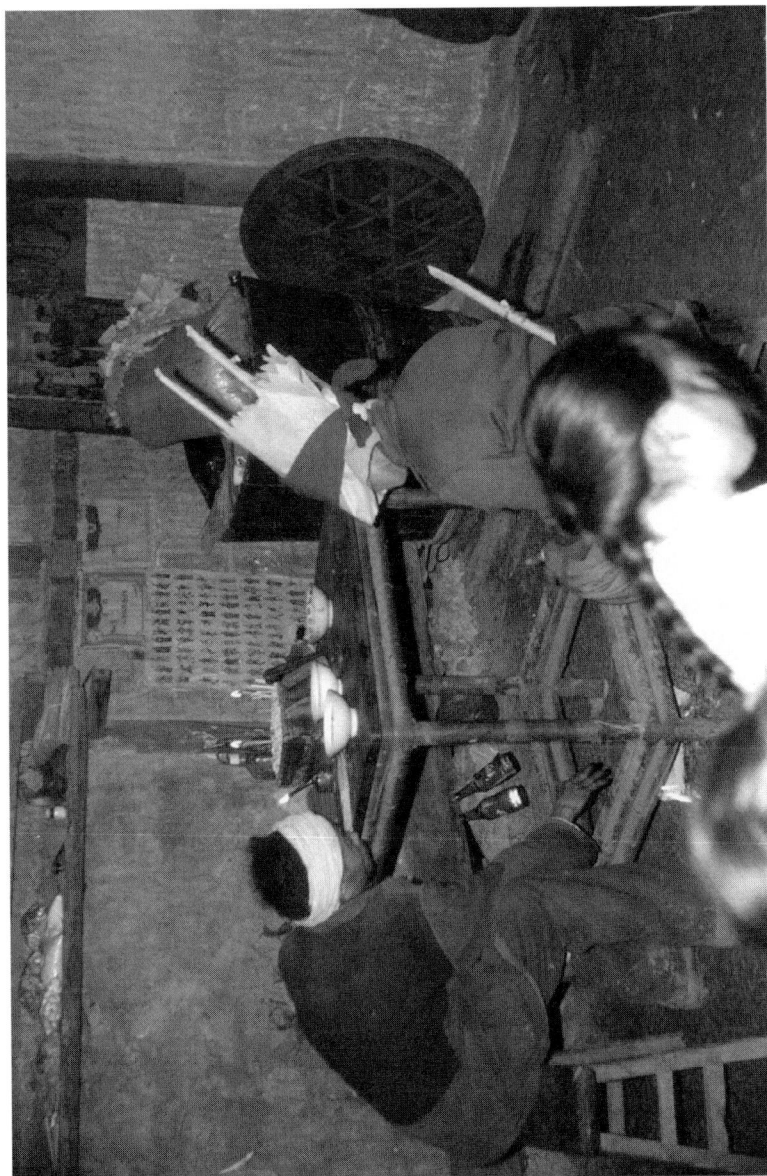

11: The shaman in trance

12: Yang Wanjun singing the 'song of the road' at a wedding

13: Plucking the bamboo sapling

14: The bridal procession

15: Bringing the dowry

16: The entry of the bride

17: The donning of the groom's costume

18: The bride and groom pay respects to the ancestors

19: The bridal feast

20: Onlookers from the loft at the bridal feast

21: Table set for the bride's reception

22: Paying the musicians

23: Onlookers at a wedding

24: White skirt Hmong style

25: Azure dress Hmong style

26: 'Jian Jian Miao', near Guiyang

27: A Hmu woman (Zenfong, Guizhou)

28: Funeral guests arriving with offerings

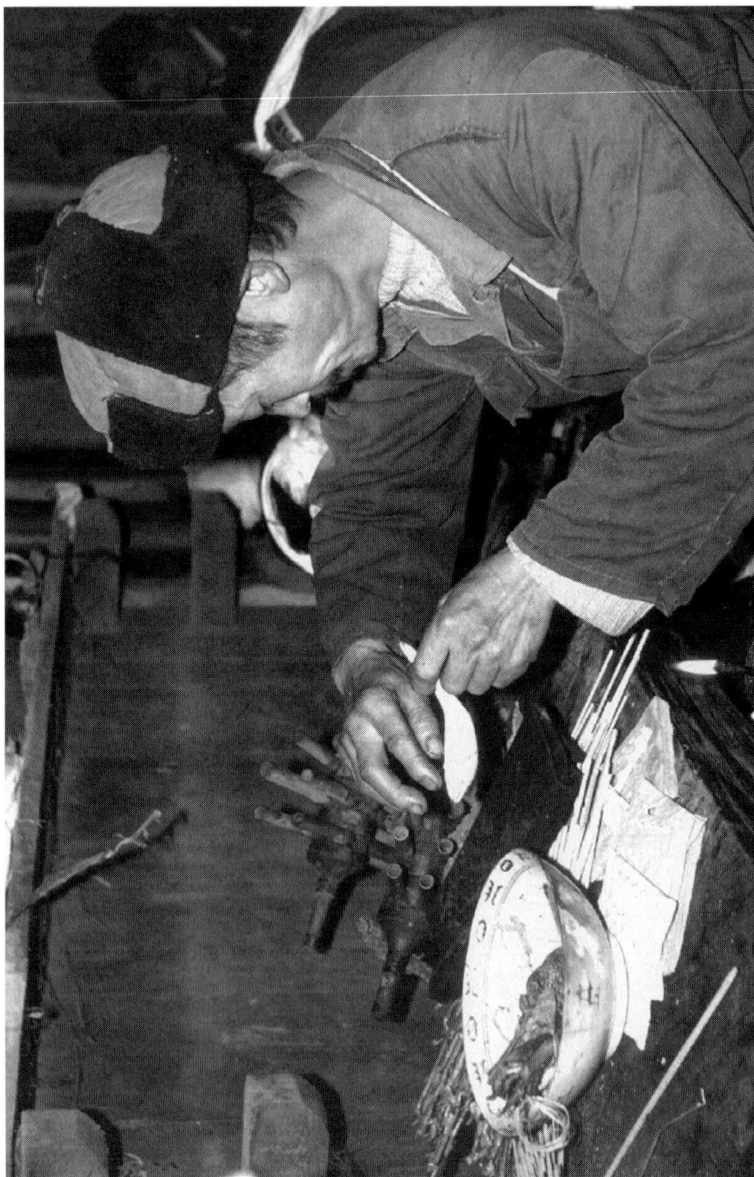

29: Ancestral offerings at the Hmong funeral

30: The funeral Drum

31: Playing the *Qeej* (Reed-Pipes)

32: The funeral company, about to prostrate

33: The funeral company, prostrating

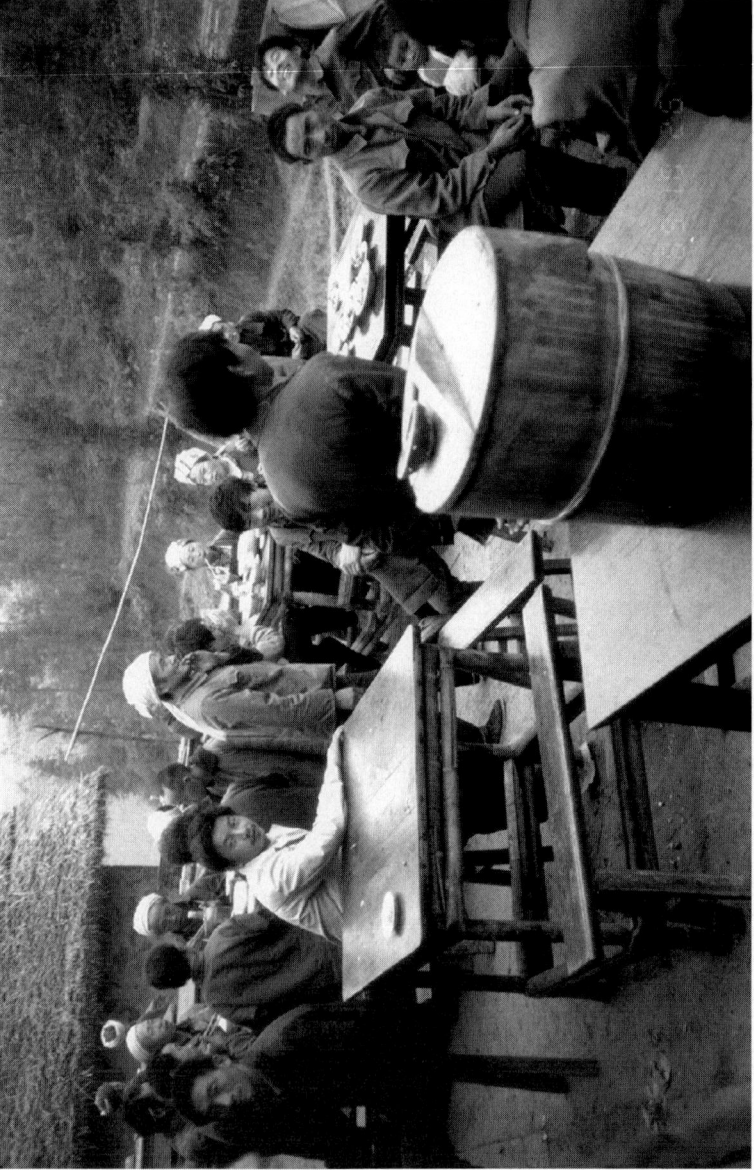

34: The funeral feast (outside)

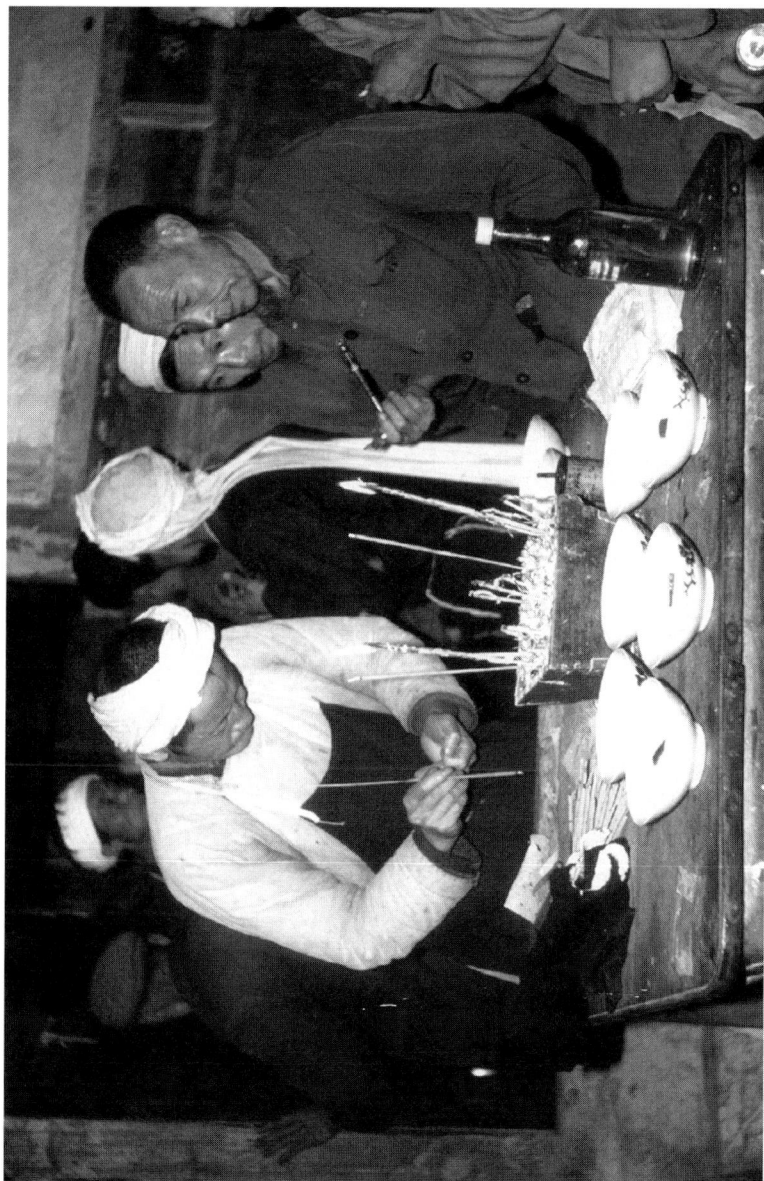

35: The Daoist Master performs a purification ritual at a Hmong funeral

36: Lowering the coffin for burial

37: A tombstone

38: Symbols of the dead at *a vang* (mortuary ritual)

39: Guan Yin shrine worshipped by Hmong in the mountains

40: Returning from visiting the neighbours

41: Inviting guests into the house

42: Visiting the market with the baby

43: A family portrait